THE UNIVERSITY OF MICHIGAN
CENTER FOR CHINESE STUDIES

RESEARCH GUIDE TO *PEOPLE'S DAILY* EDITORIALS, 1949-1975

by
Michel Oksenberg
and
Gail Henderson

Ann Arbor

Center for Chinese Studies
The University of Michigan

1982

Open access edition funded by the National Endowment for the Humanities/ Andrew W. Mellon Foundation Humanities Open Book Program.

Copyright © 1982

by

Center for Chinese Studies
The University of Michigan

Library of Congress Cataloging in Publication Data

Oksenberg, Michel, 1938-
   Research guide to People's daily editorials, 1949-1975.

   Includes bibliographical references.
   1. Jen min jih pao--Indexes. I. Henderson, Gail, 1949-   . II. University of Michigan. Center for Chinese Studies. III. Jen min jih pao. IV. Title.
AI21.J45   Suppl.   079'.51   82-4408
ISBN 0-89264-949-6   AACR2

Printed in the United States of America

ISBN 978-0-89264-949-5 (paper)
ISBN 978-0-472-12783-2 (ebook)
ISBN 978-0-472-90179-1 (open access)

The text of this book is licensed under a Creative Commons Attribution-NonCommercial-NoDerivatives 4.0 International License: https://creativecommons.org/licenses/by-nc-nd/4.0/

CONTENTS

Foreword	vii
Preface, by Michel Oksenberg and Gail Henderson	ix
I. Chronological Listing of the *People's Daily* Editorials	1
II. Outline of the Subjects in the Subject Index	85
Subject Index to the *People's Daily* Editorials	95

FOREWORD

A reference book of this kind is rarely the product of one person's labor. Work on the *Research Guide* began in 1974. Since that time, many people have been involved in the various stages of research. James Reardon-Anderson organized the initial team. Under his supervision, Sybil Aldridge, Tom Gottschang, Tony Kane, Ted Levine, and Tony Shaheen spent long hours looking through the volumes of *Survey of the China Mainland Press* for translated editorials. Dorothy Perng carefully created each editorial reference card. James Tong translated titles into English when they did not appear in the translation series. Mark Wolf did much of the actual subject indexing. Chan Wah-kong and Dan Benski laboriously checked columns of numbers during the final stage of manuscript preparation. Tim Christensen gallantly typed the entire manuscript with great patience, humor, and skill. India Bateman and Marla Camp provided administrative assistance. The project was funded by the Bureau of Intelligence and Research of the Department of State. We are thankful to the Department of State for its sponsorship, and we alone bear all responsibility for shortcomings in the project.

Michel Oksenberg
Gail Henderson

Ann Arbor, December 1981

PREFACE

Michel Oksenberg and Gail Henderson

In recent years, scholars have compiled a number of valuable English-language research aids to facilitate use of primary sources on contemporary China. Principal among these are Kenneth Lieberthal's *Research Guide to Central Meetings in China*, John Starr's *Post-Liberation Works of Mao Zedong*, John Emerson, et al., *The Provinces of the People's Republic of China: A Political and Economic Bibliography*, and T. T. Hsia's *Guide to Selected Legal Sources of Mainland China*.[1] These works provide quick access to the key, high-level decision meetings in China since 1949, all known post-1949 statements of Mao Zedong, available provincial budgets, economic development plans, political assessments, and major normative enactments.

The present guide to *People's Daily* editorials from 1949 to 1975 now joins this list. Its purpose is to provide researchers with an easy-to-use aid to this crucial series of policy statements. Arranged chronologically and with an extensive subject index, the *Research Guide* provides access to the only *continuous* source from China which illuminates high-level policy.

This preface provides information on how to use the *Research Guide*. At the outset, however, it seems wise to address four issues: the importance of *People's Daily* editorials in the Chinese system; the way *People's Daily* editorials are written; the research significance of the continuity of the editorials; and some suggestions as to specific research topics for which the *Research Guide* will prove particularly useful.

Significance of People's Daily *Editorials*

The *People's Daily (Renmin ribao)* is the daily organ of the Central Committee of the Chinese Communist Party. As such, it is the equivalent of *Pravda* in the Soviet Union, that is, the daily publication in the country which speaks for the government and the party. Franklin Houn correctly notes that unlike the Soviet government with its daily, *Izvestia*, the Chinese government apparatus does not publish its own daily paper, and thus the *People's Daily* in China plays a role analogous to both *Pravda* and *Izvestia* in the U.S.S.R.[2] The newspaper is China's national daily, printed on the same day in printing plants throughout China. Its circulation is enormous, totalling as of 1980 nearly eight million daily copies. Moreover, each copy has a high readership, circulating within the many production or residential units which receive copies and being displayed prominently on busy street corners and in entryways.

The general public is well aware that the *People's Daily* reflects the latest thinking of the top leadership. For much of Mao's era in particular, not only officials, but the attentive public avidly studied the *People's Daily* to acquire a sense of impending policy shifts that would require changes in personal conduct and utterances. And within this already authoritative publication, the editorial assumed special importance. In degree of authoritativeness, it ranks just below directives, Party resolutions, and, especially from 1965 to 1976, the statements of Chairman Mao himself.

These editorials often accompany directives to help explain their importance or are the overt manifestations of a secret Party directive. In either case, supplementary information is frequently disseminated through secret Party channels about the topic of the editorial. Moreover, the editorial often becomes the subject of discussion within the small units into which adult Chinese, especially in urban areas, are grouped.[3] *People's Daily* editorials are also often reprinted in other Beijing and provincial newspapers, and specialized editorials are reproduced in the relevant ministerial journals. Editorials are also disseminated through the Xinhua she (New China News Agency) wire service. They are frequently read over the radio, usually in abridged form but sometimes in their entirety. Particularly important ones are reprinted in such series as the annual *Renmin shouce* [People's handbook, 1949-1965], the monthly and semimonthly *Xinhua yuebao* [New China monthly] or *Xinhua banyuekan* [New China fortnightly], and the *Renmin ribao shelun xuanji* [Compilation of *People's Daily* editorials]. Finally, Chinese bibliographers have considered the editorials sufficiently important to have published a chronological listing of them to 1959.[4]

The conclusion is unmistakable: the editorials are a major means, at times *the* major means, by which the top leadership can communicate its policies directly to the population. Any effort to trace the evolution of a particular policy in China or to analyze a particular time span requires extensive familiarity with the pertinent *People's Daily* editorials.

The Writing of Editorials[5]

The *People's Daily* staff includes a section *(ke)* in charge of editorials. Given the significance of editorials, however, it should not be surprising that the editorials writers, in spite of their ideological or political astuteness, do not have the final word on topic selection or text approval. To be sure, some editorials originate within the section itself. The editorial writers have access to inner-Party directives and are aware of Politburo, Secretariat, and work-conference deliberations, and their experience frequently dictates what topics are worthy of editorial treatment. But inspiration for editorials can come from outside the editorial section as well. One important source is the editor-in-chief of the newspaper. Those who have held this post have never been members of either the Politburo or the Secretariat, but they have generally had significant access to the highest-level policy deliberations. Both the editor-in-chief and the head of the New China News Agency have been known to attend Politburo meetings and have been made well aware of the concerns of the top leaders. A second source of editorials is the top leadership itself. Mao Zedong, Liu Shaoqi, and Zhang Chunqiao, for example, are all known to have recommended and supervised the drafting of specific editorials at different times. A third source is inner-Party reports to the top leadership which the leaders recommend be turned into editorials. For example, Mao Zedong once thought particularly well of a summary by the Minister of Education concerning the proceedings of a national education conference and instructed that the report be prepared as a *People's Daily* editorial.

After an editorial has been drafted, it sometimes circulates among Politburo members for commentary before publication. A number of editorials are known to have been submitted to Mao, Zhou Enlai, Yao Wenyuan, and others for commentary and guidance. It seems that only editorials dealing with particularly sensitive issues require approval by the top levels, but it remains unclear who decides whether an editorial requires top clearance.

The Continuity of People's Daily *Editorials*

Another consideration enhances the research value of *People's Daily* editorials. The editorials are the only indicators of top-level policy available to the outside world continuously and in their entirety since the founding of the People's Republic. Because of severe disruptions in Chinese publishing during the Cultural Revolution, only two other national-level newspapers have appeared continuously since 1949:

Bright Daily (Guangming ribao [GMRB]) and *Liberation Army Daily (Jiefang junbao [JFJB])*. But *GMRB* is a voice of intellectuals and frequently floats trial balloons; it does not always authoritatively voice policy. Similarly, the voice of the People's Liberation Army (PLA) speaks for only a segment of the state structure, albeit a crucial one, and in any case, most issues of *JFJB* are not available in the West. To be sure, the theoretical journal *Red Flag (Hongqi)* is an equally authoritative publication of the CCP Central Committee and all of the issues published are available in the West. But *Red Flag* only began publication in 1958 and had no precisely equivalent predecessor. Further, it ceased publication for several months during the Cultural Revolution. Other important journals and newspapers, such as the journal of the Communist Youth League, *Chinese Youth (Zhongguo qingnian)*, the newspaper of the trade unions, *Worker's Daily (Gongren ribao)*, and the journal of the women's federation, *Chinese Women (Zhongguo funu)*, also ceased publication during the tumultuous 1966-76 decade.

Moreover, researchers lack direct total access to the major documentary series. The valuable *Compendium of Laws and Regulations of the People's Republic of China* covers only the period 1949 to 1963, and availability of major directives is a hit-and-miss affair after that date.[6] Holdings of the crucial Central Committee directive series *(zhong-fa)* are incomplete.[7] And the regime has been inconsistent in its reportage of the proceedings of National People's Congresses, National Party Congresses, Central Committee plenums, etc. Sometimes only a brief communiqué was released, while at other times the regime provided rather extensive coverage of major speeches and agenda items. The classified publications which circulate among high-level cadres, that is, the "internal documents" *(neibu wenjian)*, such as *Reference News (Cankao xiaoxi)*, are unavailable in the West. And statistical series exhibit discontinuities as well.[8]

So, we are left with the *People's Daily* as the only available continuous source on Chinese affairs. Any rigorous effort to chart trends requires constancy in primary sources, or else the researcher is uncertain whether apparent changes are the result of real change or of alteration in sources. In short, the *People's Daily* and its editorials provide a bedrock for analysis of Chinese politics.

As a result of having the entire universe of editorials, it becomes possible to measure change somewhat more rigorously and to draw a systematic sample of the whole. This is a rare opportunity in the China field: researchers on Chinese affairs are usually forced to draw "samples" from a clearly unrepresentative portion of the whole. Emigrés to Hong Kong who are interviewed on diverse topics are not "representative" of a whole; and, what is worse, since the profile of the whole remains largely unknown, the ways in which the Hong Kong pool of informants are unrepresentative can only be inferred.[9] The localities visited by foreigners in China are perforce distinctive. But without knowledge of the universe, and hence of what is "typical" or "average," we cannot precisely identify their unique characteristics.

Similar methodological problems, arising from paucity of information, confront analysts of the Chinese elite. Other than for members of the Central Committee of the CCP and a very few other organizational positions, the Chinese have not provided lists of all office-holders of particular positions, such as provincial Party secretaries and commanders and deputy commanders of PLA garrison and regional forces. The primary sources from which Western observers must laboriously assemble their data--largely from monitored radio broadcasts which sometimes refer to an individual holding a particular post--mean that researchers can never be sure they have identified the total universe. While they can attempt to compile biographical information about individual office-holders, such as age, education, or revolutionary background, there is no information available that covers a statistically significant proportion of the group. Thus, as Donald Klein has pointed out in his learned discussion of the subject, we tend to have more information about older, better-educated, KMT-associated Communists, thereby introducing biases into the aggregate data.[10]

We have gone into some detail on these points simply to demonstrate the uniqueness of the *People's Daily* editorial series, which lies in its continuity and its totality. Yet, in more subtle ways, even this series exhibits discontinuities.

The newspaper staff underwent major personnel changes, including replacement of the editor-in-chief, on several occasions, principally after the Hundred Flowers Campaign in 1957, at the start of the Cultural Revolution in 1966, during the curbing of the Cultural Revolution in 1968-69, upon the rehabilitation of many previously disgraced leaders in the journalism field in 1973-75, and then during the struggle over Mao's succession in 1976-78. These personnel changes at the newspaper, though related to shifts in policies and power alignments at the Politburo level, may have had their own dynamics and produced editorial changes that accentuated the political shifts. Hence, changes in the tone of editorials may reflect personnel changes at the paper as well as broader political trends.

The role of *RMRB* within the system has also changed over time. At times, as in the mid-fifties, the paper had no peer, while during the Cultural Revolution it was somewhat subordinate to and published key editorials in conjunction with *Red Flag* and *Liberation Army Daily*. In 1975-76 it appears to have been one of the power bases of the "radicals" in their struggle against Deng Xiaoping and his supporters, with the result that the paper did not fully expound Deng's policies of 1975 and did not accurately reflect the range of high-level thinking about the 1976 Tienanmen incident. Moreover, the frequency of editorials varied enormously over time. As a result of all these considerations, *People's Daily* editorials may mirror Central Committee policy somewhat imperfectly, with the degree of integration between Party policy and editorial policy possibly varying over time. These are important cautionary notes to bear in mind as the researcher seeks to use the editorials for rigorous analytical purposes.

Applications of the Research Guide

The *Research Guide* lends itself to a number of applications, some of which deserve mention here. Allowing for the hubris of the bibliographers, we believe that the *Guide* will encourage a degree of rigor in the study of Chinese politics and facilitate the testing of certain hypotheses which previously were not easily subject to scrutiny. Our claim requires some elaboration.

Following the Calendar. Chinese political life exhibits an annual rhythm, based on the agricultural, educational, and industrial calendars, annual holidays, and commemorations. The agricultural cycle, for instance, begins with the spring chores of plowing and planting, continuing through the summer tasks of harvesting and planting. Then come the fall activities of harvesting, collecting taxes, and storing grain, and the annual rhythm ends in winter with work on irrigation facilities, soil improvement, and repair of tools. The annual school calendar moves from summer examinations to enrollment, graduation, and placement of graduates. The industrial cycle revolves around preparation and implementation of the annual and quarterly plans and budgets. China's annual holidays are New Year's Day, the Spring Festival, May Day, Army Day (August 1), and National Day (October 1). Other annual occasions of national commemoration include International Women's Day, International Children's Day, the anniversary of China's entry into the Korean War, Soviet National Day, Sun Yatsen's birthday and the anniversary of his death, the anniversary of the 1911 revolution overthrowing the Qing dynasty, the anniversary of the May 4th and December 9th movements, the anniversary of Mao Zedong's speech on literature and art at the Yan'an forum, the anniversary of the suppression of intellectuals on Taiwan, and so on. *People's Daily* editorials frequently, but not always, mark these annual occasions. Built into the Chinese policy process, therefore, is the need to decide whether or not the annual event merits an editorial and, if so, what to say.

Curiously, students of Chinese politics have yet to analyze the annual rhythm of the Chinese political process in depth. This research guide facilitates such a study. In what years, in which contexts, and in what ways were each of these annual events deemed significant and noted in *RMRB* editorials? At a minimum, whenever an editorial related to the annual cycle appears, it must be compared to the previous annual editorials on the same subject before its true policy tenor can be discerned. For example, editorials on spring planting have tended to exhibit particular concern for peasant morale and signalled a reining in of whatever efforts had been underway during the winter to foster social or cultural change in the countryside. It was to be expected, in other words, that the month of April in the Chinese countryside during Mao's era was more "conservative" in terms of social or cultural policy than the preceding February. To assess accurately trends in rural policies, then, the analyst has to compare a period not so much with the immediately previous and subsequent months as with the same months of earlier years. The question the analyst should ask is, "Is this year's spring planting editorial similar to the ones in years of social change--1955, 1958, 1969--or is it similar to the years of calm--1954, 1956, 1963, 1972?" This guide facilitates such comparisons by providing ready bibliographic access to each annual editorial associated with an annual event.

Evolving Politburo Agenda. In the absence of direct access to Politburo proceedings, one of the best guides to the agenda of issues confronting the Politburo is the *RMRB* editorial. The chronological listing of the editorials records, month by month, many of the substantive problems with which the leaders were grappling. (Personal appointments and the structure of power are important exceptions; those major, highly divisive issues are not the subjects of editorials.[11]) The *Research Guide* facilitates a more rigorous treatment of the changing agenda. One hypothesizes, for example, that economic issues received great emphasis through the fifties, but as the Cultural Revolution approached, ideological concerns became paramount, only to fade somewhat in the 1971-74 era. A quantitative analysis of the frequency with which editorials have dwelt on various subjects would be one way to test the hypothesis, on the assumption that the editorials are an indicator of the shifting priorities of the leaders.

Another hypothesis is that, at any specific time, one or two regions of the country provide inspiration to Chinese leaders in their search for models worthy of national emulation that have successfully implemented their preferred policies: e.g., the Northeast in the early 1950s; Anhui and Shandong during the Great Leap; Shanghai during the Cultural Revolution. Reference to provinces, noted in the subject index, would help test this hypothesis.

Interrelationship of Issues. The *Guide* will not only help chart the relative importance of issues and localities over time; it also facilitates discovery of covariation of subjects. For example, it facilitates the testing of three notions about Chinese foreign policy. (1) Management of Chinese policy toward the United States was largely in the hands of Zhou Enlai, while Soviet policy fell more to Mao Zedong. The corollary would be that references to Zhou Enlai are more frequent in foreign policy editorials dealing with the United States, in contrast to editorials on the Soviet Union, which make more frequent references to Mao. (2) The Chinese perceive a conflict between pursuing constructive relations with the developed world and with the developing world. A corollary, based on study of *RMRB* editorials, would be that the number of favorable editorial references to Western Europe, Japan, and the United States on the one hand and to Third World countries on the other are inversely related. (3) Chinese crisis behavior exhibits recurring patterns of signalling to the adversary,[12] and the Chinese use external crises to mobilize the population for domestic purposes.[13] The editorials could be systematically studied through several crises to search both for the recurring themes (in contrast to noncrisis foreign policy editorial) and for correlations with domestic themes.

The *Guide* will also facilitate testing a portion of the interesting Skinner-Winckler theory concerning a "compliance cycle" in Mao's China.[14] Limited to the peasant sector, but applicable to other sectors as well, Skinner and Winckler have argued that the leaders followed a cycle in their application of power, primarily relying in succession upon remunerative power (material reward), normative power (ideology), coercive power (force and threat of force), remunerative power, and so on. The editorials cannot demonstrate a crucial aspect of the Skinner-Winckler theory, namely, that the nature of compliance with each type of power forces the leaders to adopt the successive type of power in the sequence. But one empirically verifiable assertion of Skinner and Winckler has never really been tested. Certain of the headings in the topical index deal with the utility of various policies (such as those concerning rural markets, wages, socialist education, and public security) in eliciting popular compliance with regime objectives. These policies are, of course, translatable into the Skinner-Winckler power typology: free markets involve remunerative power, socialist education involves normative power, and so on. One would only need to code these editorials according to whether they encourage or discourage the application of a particular type of power and then measure the variations in *RMRB* encouragement of the use of the three types of power to see whether the Skinner-Winckler assertion holds true. Whether the analysis verifies, modifies, or casts doubt on Skinner-Winckler, it would nonetheless permit a more refined understanding than we now have of fluctuations and trends in the regime's application of various types of power.

Relationship between Public and Internal Processes. We have thus far implied that *RMRB* editorials accurately represent the full array of leadership concerns and policies. This is not actually the case, however. At best, *RMRB* editorials form an imperfect mirror of the regime's use of power. They certainly do not expose with sufficient clarity, for example, the coercive dimension of Mao's system. Nor do they clearly reveal major upheavals among the leadership until sometime after the fact. *RMRB* editorials of the period referred only elliptically to the removal from office of Gao Gang in December 1953, the purge of Peng Dehuai in August 1959, and the fall of Lin Biao in September 1971. Only years later did *RMRB* editorials deal openly with these incidents. Similarly, *RMRB* editorials only hinted at the intensity of the Sino-Soviet dispute from 1959 to 1963 and referred in veiled form to the process of Sino-American rapprochement from 1969 to 1971. As a result, an accurate reading of *RMRB* editorials requires the ability to decode esoteric communications.[15]

With the completion of the *Research Guide*, we now have the opportunity to make major progress in honing our ability to "read between the lines." Using this guide in combination with Lieberthal's guides to central Party meetings and central documents and Starr's guide to known public and private statements of Mao will enable us to trace the relationship between public statements and inner-government processes and to assess the extent to which *RMRB* editorials mirror internal deliberations. To what extent are the issues known to have been discussed at secret CCP Central Work Conferences revealed in *RMRB* editorials? To the extent that they were reported, did the editorials illuminate these issues before, during, or after the conference in question? If before, did the editorials usually enunciate the policy which the conference subsequently adopted? An affirmative finding would suggest that the conferences merely ratified predetermined policies, which would cast doubt on the role Western analysts think they play. Did editorials in anticipation of a conference advocate policies that were being supported by a portion of the Politburo? If so, this would suggest that *RMRB* editorials can play an advocacy role. If the editorials illuminated the work conference agenda after its adjournment, did they always faithfully report what we now know were conference decisions? How long did it usually take before *RMRB* editorialized conference proceedings? Are there differences over time and among issues? The opportunity for rigorous, path-breaking research here is considerable. In fact, the Department of State sponsored this guide precisely on the grounds that it would facilitate research on the relationship between private, inner-Party processes and more open, public processes.

The *Research Guide*: An Introduction

The *Research Guide to* People's Daily *Editorials* is a chronological list of all editorials which appeared in the *People's Daily* from 1949 to 1975, with reference to translations in the *Survey of the China Mainland Press* when they appear and with a 571-item subject index of all the editorials, whether they appeared in the translation series or not. The subject index is based roughly on the original *SCMP* index, and because it refers researchers to the *SCMP* translations, the *Research Guide* uses the old *Peking Review* system of romanization which *SCMP* employed at that time (similar to the Wade-Giles system but omitting the apostrophe).

The *Research Guide* does not include other types of editorial commentaries often found in the *People's Daily*. We initially attempted to include *pinglun* ("commentaries") and *guancha* ("observations") as well as the editorials. However, time constraints and the fact that the editorials alone numbered over five thousand dictated the decision to select only the most important format of editorial expression. That was clearly the editorial. We also limited ourselves to using only one translation series. This was an easier decision since the vast majority of editorial translations are located in the *SCMP* series. Moreover, the two other major translation series—the Joint Publication Research Service and the Foreign Broadcast Information Service—are less readily available in libraries for the 1949-79 era.

Organization of the Research Guide

The *Research Guide* is divided into two sections. The first section includes the list of editorial titles and the reference to translations in the *SCMP* series. The format is as follows:

| Date Editorial Appears in the *People's Daily* | Editorial Title | Page Nos. in the *People's Daily* | *SCMP** Issue No. and Page Nos. (when the editorial was translated) |

For translated editorials, the title has been given exactly as it appeared in *SCMP*. This has perpetuated some awkward, and even inaccurate, translations, but it seemed more important to help the reader locate the text. Where there were no translations, we have provided our own. Many of the editorials also had subtitles; those which contained useful additional information have been summarized and placed in parentheses after the title.

The list of editorial titles provides a complete chronological overview of editorials. This is particularly valuable for the reader who cannot use Chinese-language sources and is forced to rely upon translations. Certainly, the percentage of editorials selected for translation varied remarkably from year to year, as table 1 illustrates.

The second section of the *Research Guide* is the subject index. Each subject heading is followed by a column of dates. These are the editorial publication dates and correspond to the dates by which the editorial titles are listed in the first section.

The subjects used to index the editorials fall under thirteen general categories: (1) Government, (2) Chinese Communist Party, (3) Democratic Parties, (4) Mass Organizations, (5) Campaigns (listed chronologically), (6) National Leaders, (7) Economy, (8) Education, Culture, and Health, (9) Demographic, Class, and Occupational Groups, (10) Regions of China, (11) Military, (12) International Relations, and (13) Countries of the World.

The index is organized in outline form, and that outline has been reproduced as a table of contents which precedes the index itself. This will serve both to acquaint the reader with the wide range of topics and to provide a more thorough definition of the abbreviated headings which are found in the index. Many of the topics in the index will be found relevant to a particular research project, and the reader should review the entire list of topics at the outset. For example, if one is tracing the evolution of agricultural policy in China, one would not only consult editorials indexed under "Agricultural Production," but also those listed for "Campaigns" with a rural focus and such "Economy" topics as "Rural Finance."

Each editorial has been indexed exhaustively. That is, each editorial was indexed for both its major and minor themes. An editorial generally contained about five or six themes. However, some touched on as many as fifteen, while others covered only one or two. To cope with this large number, the themes were divided into two

---

*In 1974, *Survey of the China Mainland Press* changed its name to *Survey of the People's Republic of China Press* and was thereafter known as *SPRCP*.

TABLE 1

Percentage of Editorials Translated in *SCMP*

Year	Total Number of Editorials in *RMRB*	Editorials Translated in *SCMP/SPRCP*	Percent Translated in *SCMP/SPRCP*
1949	49	0	0%
1950	137	25	18
1951	171	110	64
1952	140	113	81
1953	233	191	82
1954	282	234	83
1955	372	273	73
1956	369	291	79
1957	382	286	75
1958	442	290	66
1959	335	193	58
1960	459	206	45
1961	245	171	70
1962	147	129	88
1963	205	191	93
1964	223	211	95
1965	264	229	87
1966	192	162	84
1967	121	114	94
1968	42	39	93
1969	17	16	94
1970	41	37	90
1971	57	45	79
1972	58	42	72
1973	52	38	73
1974	56	47	84
1975	57	45	79

This is a revised version of a table which appears in Kenneth Lieberthal's *Research Guide to Central Party and Government Meetings in China, 1949-1975* (White Plains, N.Y.: International Arts and Sciences Press, Inc., 1976), p. xviii.

---

types: if more than one paragraph in an editorial was devoted to a subject, it was classified as a major theme; if a subject was contained in one paragraph or less, it was a minor theme. Briefly mentioned items were not indexed. The number of major themes in each editorial averaged two or three; depending on the length and depth of the editorial, however, it might range from one to five. In the index, an asterisk (*) after an editorial date indicates that the subject was a major theme in the editorial.

During the years when the greatest number of editorials were written, two and sometimes three editorials appeared in the *People's Daily* each day. Thus, one might occasionally find the same date repeated under one subject heading. Or, after consulting the subject index and referring to the list of titles, one might encounter several titles for the same date. The titles themselves will generally reveal enough about the content of the editorial to locate the correct one.

Finally, a technical note. The microfilm of the early years of the *People's Daily* is not complete, and twenty-five editorials could not be located at the University of Michigan. The following editorials, then, were included in the list of editorial titles but could not be indexed.

11-13-49	07-02-50	07-07-50	07-15-50	10-23-50
11-16-49	07-02-50	07-08-50	07-16-50	11-06-50
11-16-49	07-03-50	07-09-50	08-23-50	11-30-50
11-17-49	07-04-50	07-10-50	08-24-50	06-05-51
07-01-50	07-06-50	07-12-50	09-12-50	10-08-58

Using the Research Guide

     We have elaborated upon the significance of the *People's Daily* editorial in the Chinese political process and have suggested a number of ways in which the *Research Guide* could be applied to the study of modern China. The two sections of the *Research Guide* can function separately or as a unit. Readers interested in a particular time period will find the chronological list of editorial titles a useful summary of information. Those investigating one or several topics will turn to the second section.

     In all cases, however, extensive use of the *Research Guide* should not be made without referring to the editorials themselves. Editorial titles can only suggest the content and, in fact, often tell little about the range of issues covered. In addition, the nature and composition of the editorial itself changed radically over the years from 1949 to 1975. These changes must be read to be appreciated.

     It is probably most important to actually read the editorials when one is using the subject index. Particularly for those not well acquainted with the field, the interpretation of many of the index topics can be confusing. Even for those long involved in the study of China, accurate assessment of index subjects requires delving into the editorials themselves. Finally, the significance of major and minor themes varied with different index topics and can only be evaluated in context.

Notes

1. Kenneth Lieberthal, *A Research Guide to Central Party and Government Meetings in China, 1949-1975* (White Plains, N.Y.: International Arts and Sciences Press, Inc., 1976); John Starr and Nancy Dryer, *Post-Liberation Works of Mao Zedong* (Berkeley: Center for Chinese Studies, 1976); John Emerson, Robert Field, Michel Oksenberg, and Florence Yuan, *The Provinces of the People's Republic of China: A Political and Economic Bibliography* (Washington, D.C.: Department of Commerce, 1976); T. T. Hsia, *Guide to Selected Legal Sources of Mainland China* (Washington, D.C.: Library of Congress, 1967).

2. Franklin Houn, *To Change a Nation* (New York: The Free Press of Glencoe, 1961), pp. 103-7. See also Frederick T. C. Yu, *Mass Persuasion in Communist China* (New York: Praeger, 1964), pp. 96-101.

3. Kenneth Lieberthal, *Central Documents and Politburo Politics in China*, Michigan Papers in Chinese Studies no. 34 (Ann Arbor: The University of Michigan Center for Chinese Studies, 1978); Michel Oksenberg, "Methods of Communication within the Chinese Bureaucracy," *China Quarterly*, no. 57 (January-March 1974), pp. 1-39.

4. *Renmin ribao shelun soyin* [Index to *People's Daily* editorials] (Peking: Renmin ribao, 1959), 108 pp.

5. This section draws on conversations between Mr. Oksenberg and Chinese officials. See also Roger Garside, *Coming Alive: China After Mao* (New York: McGraw-Hill, 1981), p. 3.

6. State Council Bureau of Legislative Affairs, *Zhonghua renmin gongheguo fagui huibian* [Compendium of laws and regulations of the People's Republic of China] (Beijing: Falu chubanshe, 1956-). See also Carl Walter, "Facilities Offered for Research on Contemporary China by the National Library of Beijing," *China Quarterly*, no. 85 (March 1981), pp. 138-47.

7. Lieberthal, *Central Documents*, pp. 155-201.

8. The problems with statistical series are thoroughly covered in Alexander Eckstein, ed., *Quantitative Measures of China's Economic Output* (Ann Arbor: University of Michigan Press, 1980).

9. Through skilled analysis of the data, the problems with Hong Kong informants can be minimized. See, for example, William Parish and Martin Whyte, *Village and Family in Contemporary China* (Chicago: University of Chicago Press, 1978); and William Parish, "Egalitarianism in Chinese Society," *Problems of Communism* 30 (January-February 1981): 37-53.

10. Donald W. Klein, "Sources for Elite Studies and Biographical Materials on China," in Robert Scalapino, ed., *Elites in the People's Republic of China* (Seattle: University of Washington Press, 1972), esp. pp. 610-11.

11. Note, for example, the absence of editorials explicitly referring to the demise of Gao Gang, Peng Dehuai, or Lin Biao at the time of the purges or of editorials on the structure of the top-level decision-making apparatus (e.g., the issue of whether to have a "head of state," which has surfaced periodically since 1970).

12. Allen Whiting, *The Chinese Calculus of Deterrence* (Ann Arbor: University of Michigan Press, 1975), and *China Crosses the Yalu* (New York: The MacMillan Company, 1960).

13. For various formulations of this hypothesis, see Richard Solomon, *Mao's Revolution and the Chinese Political Culture* (Berkeley: University of California Press, 1971), p. 388; Richard Solomon, "America's Revolutionary Alliance with Communist China," *Asian Survey* 7, no. 12 (December 1967): 831-50; and Roger Brown, "Chinese Politics and American Policy," *Foreign Policy*, no. 23 (Summer 1976), pp. 3-23. The hypothesis has been examined in Kuang-sheng Liao, "Internal Mobilization and External Hostility in the People's Republic of China, 1960-62 and 1967-69" (Ph.D. diss., The University of Michigan, 1974).

14. G. William Skinner and Edwin Winckler, "Compliance Succession in Rural Communist China: A Cyclical Theory," in Amitai Etzioni, ed., *Complex Organization, A Sociological Reader*, 2d ed. (New York: Holt, Rinehart, and Winston, 1969), pp. 410-38.

15. Donald Zagoria, *The Sino-Soviet Conflict, 1956-1961* (Princeton: Princeton University Press, 1962), pp. 24-39. One of the finest examples of this kind of work is Roderick MacFarquhar's *The Origins of the Cultural Revolution* (New York: Columbia University Press, 1974), vol. 1.

I. Chronological Listing of the People's Daily Editorials

1949

- Jan 4 — Carry Out Thoroughly the New Agricultural Tax (North China region), 1.
- Feb 4 — Strive for the Establishment of New Democratic Peking (Inaugural issue of the Peiping edition of People's Daily), 1.
- Mar 17 — Change Cities of Consumption into Cities of Production, 1.
- Apr 9 — Struggle against Bureaucratic Elements, 1.
- Apr 28 — Our Government Policy Towards Private Banking Houses (Publication of the temporary control measures), 1.
- Jun 15 — Carry Out the Spirit of the North China Primary School Education Conference. Raise the Primary School Education a Step Further from Its Present Level, 2.
- Jun 23 — Lay a Victorious Foundation for Constructing an Industrial North China (The results of North China's first worker representatives conference), 1.
- Jul 3 — Struggle to Further Consolidate the Party in North China (Commemorating the 28th anniversary of the founding of the party), 1.
- Jul 29 — Severely Ban Speculative Activities. Keep Prices Stable, 1.
- Aug 2 — The Correct Way to Settle the Labor and Management Dispute (The collective contract of Chinese medicine professions in Peiping), 1.
- Aug 27 — The False Mask of the Tito Counter-Revolutionary Bloc Has Been Torn Off, 1.
- Sep 7 — Produce for Relief, Economize to Prepare for Famine, 1.
- Sep 8 — Continue Grappling with Disaster, Protect Autumn Harvest, 1.
- Sep 12 — A Lesson from the Sanhsing Incident (Export companies' fraud), 1.
- Sep 14 — Attach Importance to the Work of Planting for Others, 1.
- Sep 22 — Old China Is Dead, New China Is Born! (CPPCC opens), 1.
- Oct 1 — Long Live the People's Republic of China! (The CPPCC closes, the PRC is born), 2.
- Oct 2 — The Invincible People's Nation, 1.
- Oct 2 — Break Off Warmonger's Claws--Welcome "Struggle for International Peace Day," 2.
- Oct 6 — Long Live Sino-Soviet Friendship (Establishment of Sino-Soviet Friendship Association), 2.
- Oct 8 — New China Welcomes True, Friendly, and Equal Diplomatic Relations, 2.
- Oct 9 — The Proper Rights of Overseas Chinese Should Not Be Encroached Upon (Discrimination against overseas Chinese in Australia and Malaya), 1.
- Oct 11 — Welcome to Ambassador Roschin, 1.
- Oct 13 — Welcome the Delegation of World Trade Unions and the Representatives of International Democratic Women's Union, 1.
- Oct 13 — Congratulations to the German People (Founding of the provisional government), 1.
- Oct 14 — Seriously Implement the New Curriculum for Colleges of Liberal Arts and Colleges of Law, 1.
- Oct 16 — Celebrate the Liberation of Canton, 1.
- Oct 17 — The True Friendship between Chinese and Mongolians (Establishment of diplomatic relations), 1.
- Oct 17 — Protest the Persecution of American Communist Leaders by the American Imperialists, 1.

1949

- Oct 20 — The Institution of People's Democratic Dictatorship (Central government appoints officials), 1.
- Oct 21 — Achievements of Publisher's Conference, 1.
- Oct 21 — Bring the Chinese People's Friendship to the Soviet Union (Ambassador Wang Chia-hsiang leaves for Russia), 1.
- Oct 22 — Advocate New Democratic National Physical Education, 1.
- Oct 22 — Protest Australian Reactionary Government Persecuting Sharkey, 1.
- Oct 24 — American Reactionaries Will Definitely Court Self-Destruction (U.S. persecution of U.S. Communist leaders), 1.
- Oct 26 — Unite Chinese and German Peoples (Diplomatic relations established), 1.
- Oct 27 — Seriously Convene People's Congresses Everywhere (North China Bureau directive), 1.
- Oct 30 — Unfold the Struggle against Pestilence, 1.
- Nov 1 — Rescue Greek Patriots (Greek Communists sentenced to death), 1.
- Nov 13 — Punish Severely Incorrigible Counter-Revolutionaries, 1.
- Nov 16 — Uphold Foreign Minister Chou's Statement (On stripping Taiwan of rights in UN), 1.
- Nov 16 — Welcome the Leaders of World Trade Union, 1.
- Nov 17 — Unite the Whole World Working Class (World Trade Union and Austro-Asian Trade Union convenes in Peking), 1.
- Nov 21 — A Model for the Establishment of the Local People's Government (Second Peking People's Congress), 1.
- Nov 27 — Thanks to Our Ally's Act of Justice (Soviet Union supports Chou En-lai's statement), 1.
- Nov 27 — A Warning to Imperialist Gangsters (American sentenced for beating a Chinese worker), 1.
- Nov 30 — Chase and Liquidate the Escaping Bandits; They Should Not Be Concealed (Chou En-lai comments on the KMT's flight overseas), 1.
- Dec 18 — Chairman Mao Visits Soviet Union, 1.
- Dec 21 — A Tribute to the Great Stalin on His Birthday, 1.

1950

- Jan 5 — Oppose American Imperialist's Plot to Snatch Taiwan, 1.
- Jan 17 — Road to Japanese People's Liberation (Note the 1/6 issue on "Strive Towards Permanent Peace, Strive Toward People's Democracy"), 1.
- Jan 19 — New Victory of the Liberation Struggle of Oriental Peoples--Hail the Founding of Diplomatic Relations between China and Vietnam, 1.
- Feb 2 — Unfold the Spring Festival Support-Army Campaign, 1.
- Feb 6 — Learn Business Administration, 1.
- Feb 6 — War Criminals Must Be Brought to Trial and Punishment (Soviet Union demands trial of Japanese war criminals), 1.
- Feb 16 — Consolidate Sino-Soviet Fraternal Alliance (Signing of Sino-Soviet treaty), 1.
- Mar 3 — We Must Convene Well the Conference of People's Representatives of All Sectors, 1.
- Mar 7 — There Is Great Hope! (Economizing measure of Railway Ministry and Huolu County), 1.

1950

Mar 8	Correctly Settle the Problem of the Marriage System, 1.
Mar 9	Investigate Thoroughly the Case of Pu Yang Grain Transportation, 1.
Mar 10	Why Should National Financial and Economic Work Be Unified? (Government Affairs Council decision), 1.
Mar 18	American Lies and Asian Truth (On Dean Acheson's "America's Asia Policy"), 1.
Mar 18	Make a Good Job of This Year's Spring Cultivation and Production, 1.
Mar 22	The Function of Tax Collection in Our Nation's Work (Amended 3/23, p. 1), 1.
Mar 24	Unfold Criticism and Self-Criticism (The case of Pu Yang grain transportation), 1.
Apr 5	Hail to the Sino-Soviet Economic Cooperation which Is Beneficial to Chinese Economic Construction (China and Russia sign three industrial agreements), 1.
Apr 16	Implement the New Democratic Marriage System (Peking passes the "marriage law"), 1.
Apr 21	Hail to the Victory of Landing on Hainan, 1.
Apr 22	Commemorate Lenin, Study Internationalism (Lenin's eightieth birthday), 1.
Apr 23	Resolutely Unfold Criticism and Self-Criticism (Criticism campaign unfolds in media), 1.
Apr 23	Strengthen the Tie between Newspapers and the Masses, 1.
Apr 26	Hail the Founding of the China Changchun Railroad Company, 1.
May 3	Youth Should Be Good at Their Tasks, and Master Scientific Techniques--Greeting the May 4th Youth Day, 1.
May 10	Exert All-Out Efforts to Lead the Victims of Disaster in Spring Cultivation and Production, and Conquer Natural Disaster Eventually, 1.
May 15	Unfold Signature Drive for Peace, 1.
May 16	New Constructions in Democratic Regimes in the Big Cities (Peking People's Congress organizational regulations published), 1.
May 17	Attach Importance to Forests and Protect Forests, 1.
May 19	Celebrate Vietnamese Chairman Ho Chi Minh's Sixtieth Birthday, 1.
May 29	Live Through Spring Famine and Prevent Summer Famine, 1.
May 31	Hail "June First" International Children's Day; Develop Further Work for Children, 1.
Jun 1	Implement Correctly the Decision of the Government Affairs Council on Summer Levy, 1.
Jun 2	Exert All-Out Efforts in Leading Summer Harvest and Summer Sowing, 1.
Jun 2	Learn from the Experiences of the Regional Representatives' Congress in the Big Cities, 1.
Jun 3	Do a Good Job in Running Factory Management Committees. Seriously Implement Democratic Management (Amended 6/5, p. 1), 1.
Jun 4	Rebirth of the Machine Industry (National Machine Industry meeting), 1.
Jun 4	Unfold Staff and Worker's Spare Time Education, 3.
Jun 6	From the Fading False Purchasing Power to the Increase of Real Purchasing Power, 1.
Jun 6	Leading Institutions of All Levels Should Make Effective Use of Radio Broadcasting, 3.
Jun 8	How to Adjust the Relations of Public and Private Industrial and Commercial Enterprises (Amended 6/9, p. 1), 1.
Jun 9	Oppose MacArthur's Suppression of Japanese Patriotic People's Vanguard--The Japanese Communist Party, 1.
Jun 11	Strive for the Thorough Stabilization of Prices, 1.
Jun 17	The Private Industry and Trade Sectors Should Strive for Reforms, 1.
Jun 27	The Korean People Combat to Rebuff the Invaders (Korean War breaks out), 1.
Jun 29	Denounce Imperialist Robber Truman's Illegal Statement (U.S. will aid Korea and Taiwan) (Amended 6/30, p. 3), 1.
Jun 29	Implement Thoroughly the Trade Union Law (Promulgation of Trade Union Law), 2.
Jun 30	Struggle for the Realization of Land Reform in Whole China (Promulgation of Land Reform Law) (Amended 7/1, p. 3), 2.
Jul 1	Rectify the Party's Work Style; Improve the Conditions in the Party's Organization--Commemorating the 29th Anniversary of the Founding of Chinese Communist Party, 1.
Jul 2	Bid Farewell to Southwest Visiting Delegation, 1.
Jul 2	North China Party Struggles to Complete the New Great Task, 1.
Jul 3	Realize the Overall Reform of Coal Mining Methods, 1.
Jul 4	Strive for Greater Normalization of Labor-Management Relationships, 1.
Jul 6	The Victorious Future of the Korean People's War of Liberation, 1.
Jul 7	The Current Situation of the Struggle of the Japanese People (Amended 7/17, p. 1), 1.
Jul 8	Strengthen Flood Control and Overcome the Floods! 1.
Jul 9	Reinforce the Work of Economic Protection, 1.
Jul 10	Strive for the Better Life of Peasants in North China, 1.
Jul 12	Two Guiding Principles in Readjusting Taxation, 1.
Jul 15	Overcome Excessive Waste in Industrial Production (Amended 7/21, p. 1), 1.
Jul 16	Several Explanations of the General Organizational Principles of the Peasant Association (Amended 8/26, p. 1), 1.
Jul 21	Earnestly Prepare and Establish People's Courts (Amended 7/22, p. 1; 7/24, p.1), 1.
Jul 24	The Power for Peace Is On the Rise--On the Two Replies to Nehru's Proposals (Nehru's proposal for Korean question settlement) (Amended 7/25, p. 1), 1.
Jul 28	Diligently Overcome the Phenomenon of Some Teachers Losing Jobs and Students Missing School (Amended 8/2, p. 3), 1.
Jul 29	The Basic Link in Guiding the Rectification Campaign, 1.
Aug 3	Steadily Reform Higher Education and Rectify Learning Atmosphere, 1.
Aug 5	A Warning to MacArthur (MacArthur's Taiwan visit), 1.
Aug 7	Endorse the Proposal of Settling the Korean Question Peacefully (Soviet proposal in UN Security Council), 1.
Aug 8	Rectify the Working Style of Public Security Workers, 1.
Aug 14	Strive to Win Two Billion Signatures for Peace in the Whole Nation, 1.
Aug 15	Celebrate the Fifth Anniversary of Korea's Liberation, 1.
Aug 17	Reward Effectively the Inventions and Discoveries in Production Construction, 1.

1950

Aug 19 Hail the Fifth Anniversary of the Victory of the August Revolution of the Vietnamese People, 1.
Aug 22 Integrate the Rectification Campaign, Do a Good Job in Convening the Congresses of People's Representatives of All Levels, 1.
Aug 23 Intensify and Improve People's Supervisory Work in the Rectification Campaign (Amended 8/25, p. 1), 1.
Aug 24 A New Direction for the Banking Business (The national financial enterprise united meeting resolutions), 1.
Aug 26 Establish the People's Judiciary System Systematically, 1.
Aug 27 Unfold People's Scientific Work with Good Organization and Planning, 1.
Aug 28 Denounce the American Aggressor's Lies, 1.
Aug 28 A Protest of 475 Million People (U.S. airplanes invaded Chinese territorial air), 1.
Aug 30 Bidding Farewell to Northwest Visiting Delegation, 1.
Sep 1   Persist in the Struggle for Justice in UN Security Council, 1.
Sep 2   Greet the Fifth Anniversary of the Founding of the Democratic Republic of Vietnam, 1.
Sep 3   Now Is the Time for the Japanese People to Get Together and Fight against Their Enemies, 1.
Sep 4   State-Private Enterprises Cooperate to Unfold Foreign Trade, 2.
Sep 6   Struggle for Implementing Correctly the Agricultural Tax System in Newly Liberated Areas, 1.
Sep 7   How to Set Up the People's Police (Amended 9/11, p. 1), 1.
Sep 12 Current Main Tasks in Building the People's Regime, 1.
Sep 14 Oppose Commandism Resolutely, 1.
Sep 16 Guarantee This Year's Autumn Bumper Harvest; Strive for Next Year's Production Increase, 1.
Sep 18 Oppose Today's Aggressor in the Far East--American Imperialism--Commemorating the 19th Anniversary of September 18th.
Sep 19 The Fifth UN General Assembly and Its Future, 1.
Sep 20 Respect National Emblem and Cherish National Emblem (Promulgation of the national emblem), 1.
Sep 23 Uphold Soviet Union's Peace Proposal (In UN General Assembly), 1.
Sep 23 The Patriotic Campaign of the Christians, 1.
Sep 24 World's Youth Unite--Welcome the Delegation from the World Democratic Youth Union, 1.
Sep 25 Long Live the People's Heroes! (National conferences of military heroes and proletarian models open), 1.
Sep 25 Uphold the Korean People's Patriotism, 1.
Sep 27 UN Organ Should Not Be Transformed into America's Tool for Policy of Aggression--On Acheson's Speech at the Fifth UN General Assembly, 1.
Sep 30 Welcome the Representatives of Different Fraternal Nationalities to Peking to Attend the National Day Celebrations, 1.
Oct 9   Oppose Resolutely The Aggressor's Illegal "Resolutions" on the Korean Question (UN General Assembly proposal to invade Korea), 1.
Oct 10 Overcome the Pride and Complacency of Those People Who Claim Themselves as Heroes (Amended 10/11, p. 1), 1.
Oct 14 Eliminate the Bully's Working Style Resolutely, 1.
Oct 15 Struggle for the Permanent Control of the River Huai, 1.
Oct 18 Cadres of All Levels Have the Responsibility to Rectify Working Style, 1.
Oct 21 Punish Severely the Criminal Acts of Lawless Landowners in Undermining Land Reform, 1.
Oct 23 Correct Way to People's Sanitation Work, 1.
Nov 6   Why We Cannot Disregard America's Invasion of Korea, 1.
Nov 7   Soviet Union Is the Strongest Bulwark for World Peace and Democracy (33rd anniversary of the October Revolution), 1. SCMP 6, 6.
Nov 12 Smash Enemy's Slanders, Deceits, and Threats (Peking's response to speech of MacArthur and Austin), 1. SCMP 9, 5.
Nov 13 How to Lead the Rectification Campaign in Regional and Village Organs, 3.
Nov 14 Develop the Establishment of Political Power in Metropolitan Areas, 3. SCMP 10, 8.
Nov 17 The Power of Peace Is Invincible (Second World conference on protecting peace), 1. SCMP 12, 8.
Nov 17 Peking JMJP Comments on American Intrigues against Tibet (Amended 11/21, p. 2), 1. SCMP 15, 1.
Nov 20 Peking JMJP Editorial on Significance of Chinese People's Volunteers, 1. SCMP 14, 1.
Nov 25 Fight for Peace in Asia and the World (Second World Peace Conference), 1. SCMP 17, 9.
Nov 27 Oppose American Plots of Signing Separate Peace Treaty with Japan (Amended 11/28, p. 1), 1. SCMP 18, 3.
Nov 30 Check American Aggression in Taiwan (Chinese delegate's speech at UN Security Council), 1. SCMP 21, 1.
Dec 1   The Glorious Post of Our Patriotic Youths (Admission to military and cadre academies), 1. SCMP 21, 14.
Dec 2   Cut Off the Invading Long Lance of Imperialists (Comment on the Korean War), 1. SCMP 22, 1.
Dec 3   We Continue to Press Our Charge against American Imperialists for Their Criminal Acts (Amended 12/16, p. 1), 1. SCMP 22, 5.
Dec 6   Warmongers' Plot to Further Extend the War Is Doomed to Fail--On Truman's and Acheson's Statement (Amended 12/7, p. 1), 1.
Dec 7   "Pyongyang's Liberation" Leads All Other News in Press, 1. SCMP 26, 3.
Dec 13 On the Truman-Attlee Meeting Communique (Amended 12/16, p. 1), 1. SCMP 29, 1.
Dec 14 Develop Further the Anti-Imperialism and Patriotic Movement, 1.
Dec 14 Carry Through Earnestly the Policy of Taking Care of the Families of Martyrs and Servicemen, 2.
Dec 16 Do a Good Job in Running Cooperatives (Supply and marketing cooperatives), 1.
Dec 17 On the So-called "Proposal for Cease-fire in Korea," 1. SCMP 32, 3.
Dec 20 Ban the Yi-kuan Sect Resolutely, 1.
Dec 21 The American Imperialists' Fiasco in Asia (Amended 12/24, p. 1), 1. SCMP 36, 1.
Dec 22 Support the New Tax Laws, Assume the New Responsibility, 1. SCMP 36, 23.

1950

Dec 23 Only Peaceful Way to Settle the Korean Problem, 1. SCMP 36, 8.
Dec 26 Rectify Thoroughly the Deviation of Misinterpreting the "Policy of Magnanimity," 1. SCMP 39, 24.
Dec 27 Win Peace with Action (Supports proposal of Conference on World Peace), 1. SCMP 38, 14.
Dec 27 American Ruling Class Is Confused and Split, 1. SCMP 38, 2.
Dec 28 Keep Up the Effort to Extend the Scope and Range of the Resist-U.S., Aid-Korea, Protect Homes, and Defend Country Patriotic Movement, 1. SCMP 38, 7.
Dec 30 Clearing Away the Aggressive Economic and Cultural Influence of U.S. Imperialism in China, 1. SCMP 39, 10.
Dec 31 Making Good the Chu and Hsiang People's Representatives Conferences, 1. SCMP 61, 10.

1951

Jan 1   Consolidate Our Great Motherland under the Banner of Patriotism, 1. SCMP 40, 1.
Jan 3   An Important Link in Closely Uniting the Party with the Masses, 1. SCMP 50, 10.
Jan 4   Why Should the Purchase of Cotton Yarn Be Unified? (Committee on Finance and Economic Affairs decision), 1.
Jan 5   Peking JMJP Hails the Reliberation of Seoul, 1. SCMP 42, 2.
Jan 8   Welcoming the Patriotic Movement of the Chinese Catholics, 1. SCMP 44, 7.
Jan 11 Peking JMJP on 100th Anniversary of Taiping Revolutionary Movement (Amended 1/12, p. 1), 1. SCMP 47, 16.
Jan 11 Peking JMJP Commented on Matsukawa Case, 1. SCMP 47, 8.
Dec 12 Strengthening the People's Supervision Work, 1. SCMP 49, 8.
Jan 15 Peking JMJP on National Donation Campaign for Korean People, 1. SCMP 49, 1.
Jan 17 The Course for the Proper Development of Private-Operated Enterprises, 1. SCMP 52, 17.
Jan 24 Unite and Advance under the Great Banner of Patriotism--On the Achievements of the Central Committee Conferences of the Democratic Parties, 1. SCMP 56, 10.
Jan 26 America's Aggressive Imperialist Policy Is Foredoomed to Further Failure, 1. SCMP 59, 1.
Jan 28 Smash U.S. Plot to Rearm Japan; Fight for an Overall Just Peace Treaty with Japan (Amended 1/29, p. 1), 1. SCMP 58, 1.
Jan 29 Study Comrade Mao's Treatise "On Practice," 1.
Feb 3   U.S. Government Again Proves Itself Deadly Enemy of Peace (UN General Assembly illegally endorses the U.S. proposal), 1. SCMP 62, 4.
Feb 4   The New Methods of Electing People's Representatives in Peking City, 1.
Feb 8   Facts Are Clearer Than Quibbles (Commenting on Austin's Feb. 2 statement to the United Nations first committee), 1. SCMP 64, 7.
Feb 11 The Great Significance of Implementing the Control of Currency, 1.
Feb 13 Compulsory Insurance Must Be Enforced, 1.
Feb 14 Consolidate Sino-Soviet Alliance, Oppose Rearming of Japan by U.S. Imperialism, 1. SCMP 67, 4.
Feb 15 Struggle to Fulfill This Year's Tasks in Agriculture and Forestry, 1. SCMP 70, 11.

1951

Feb 16 "On Practice" Paves the Way for Our Thinking on Academic Revolution, 1.
Feb 17 Struggle to Fulfill This Year's Task for Water Conservancy, 1.
Feb 19 Stalin's Statement Points the Way to Halt the New War, 1. SCMP 70, 1.
Feb 21 Peking JMJP on Day of Struggle against Colonialism, 1. SCMP 71, 2.
Feb 22 Peking JMJP on Promulgated Regulations for Punishment of Counter-Revolutionaries, 1. SCMP 72, 8.
Feb 23 Soviet Armed Forces, Defenders of World Peace, 1. SCMP 72, 11.
Feb 28 In Commemoration of the Fourth Anniversary of the People's Uprising in Taiwan, 2. SCMP 74, 12.
Feb 28 Struggle to the End for Winning World Peace (Support resolution of World Peace Executive Council), 1. SCMP 75, 1.
Mar 2   Unfold the Campaign of Improving Agro-Techniques among the Masses; Work for a 1951 Agricultural Bumper Harvest, 1.
Mar 4   Strive for the Early Conclusion of a Peace Pact, 1. SCMP 77, 3 (extracts).
Mar 7   To Be Lenient to Counter-Revolutionaries Is to Be Cruel to the People (Amended 3/8, p. 1), 1. SCMP 79, 6.
Mar 10 To Improve Newspaper and Magazine Publication Work Is an Important Political Task, 1.
Mar 11 All Counter-Revolutionaries Shall Be Arrested and Brought to Justice, 1. SCMP 82, 3.
Mar 14 Experiences Gained in the Establishment of Propaganda in the Northeast, 1. SCMP 85, 27.
Mar 16 Make a Really Good Job of This Year's Spring Repairs to Conservancy Works, 1.
Mar 17 Eight Points of Attention during Spring Cultivation in North China, 1.
Mar 17 Everyone in China Must Be Given Patriotic Education on Resisting U.S. and Aiding Korea, 1. SCMP 85, 13.
Mar 21 Smash Sabotage Activities of American Imperialists (In Tientsin), 1. SCMP 87, 5.
Mar 22 Struggle for the Union and Development of the People of All Nationalities (Government Affairs Bureau decision), 1. SCMP 88, 20.
Mar 23 JMJP Expresses Warm Welcome to Visit of Peace Delegates, 1.
Mar 23 Book Reviews Constitute One Important Way to Lead the Work of Publications and Newspapers, 1.
Mar 24 To Do Spring Farming Well for Laying the Foundation of Bumper Crop This Year, 1. SCMP 87, 18.
Mar 26 Execute the Leading Counter-Revolutionaries, 1. SCMP 88, 12.
Mar 27 JMJP Hails the Founding of Vietnam Lao Dong Party, 1. SCMP 88, 1.
Mar 27 Do a Good Job in the Work of Protecting Forests and Preventing Fires, 1.
Mar 28 Pay Immediate Attention to the Work of the Safe Custody of Public Grain Stocks, 1.
Mar 29 Refute War Criminal MacArthur's Shameless Boast, 1. SCMP 89, 2.
Mar 30 Popularization of Patriotic Compact Movement, 1. SCMP 90, 8.
Apr 1   Unification of Currency and Greater Interflow of Supplies between Northeast and South of Great Wall (Government Affairs Council order), 1. SCMP 89, 27.
Apr 3   Suppression of Counter-Revolutionaries Must Be Done with Big Fanfare, 1. SCMP 90, 13.

1951

Apr 4	Draw Up Plans for Popularizing Resist U.S. and Aid Korea Campaign, 1. SCMP 91, 7.
Apr 5	We Should Attach Importance to and Make a Success of Secondary Education, 1. SCMP 92, 26.
Apr 5	Centralized Leadership and Divided Responsibility Is Correct Policy of Financial Work, 1. SCMP 91, 16.
Apr 6	American Imperialism Shall Not Be Allowed to Make Use of the Catholic Church for Aggression against China (Three Americans arrested in Tientsin), 1. SCMP 93, 11.
Apr 6	Further Regulation of Municipal Finance, 1. SCMP 91, 20.
Apr 9	Achievements of Catholic Reform Movement in Tientsin (Amended 4/12, p. 1), 1. SCMP 93, 12.
Apr 10	Exert All-Out Efforts for the Marketing of Native Produce, 1.
Apr 12	Protest against Criminal Action of French Government in Persecuting the World Peace Council, 1. SCMP 94, 13.
Apr 17	Sever Completely the Relations between Christian Churches and Imperialism (Conference on dealing with Christian organizations receiving U.S. subsidies), 1. SCMP 96, 9.
Apr 20	Intensify the Suppression of Counter-Revolutionaries in Cities, 1. SCMP 97, 21.
Apr 21	To Struggle for the Establishment of an Independent and Free New Customs Service (Temporary regulations promulgated), 1. SCMP 97, 16.
Apr 22	The Absurd and Preposterous American Draft Peace Treaty with Japan, 1. SCMP 98, 1.
Apr 23	Attach the Fullest Importance to Broadcasting, 1.
Apr 23	JMJP Hails Successful Completion of Soviet Post-War Five-Year Plan, 1. SCMP 98, 27.
Apr 24	Develop among Christians a Campaign of Accusations against American Imperialism, 1. SCMP 98, 14.
Apr 25	JMJP Greets International Union of Students Meeting, 4. SCMP 99, 4.
Apr 27	China Today Is No Longer China of the Old (Meeting of charitable organizations receiving U.S. subsidies), 1. SCMP 100, 29.
Apr 28	Second Discourse on the Necessity to Suppress Counter-Revolutionaries with Big Fanfare, 1. SCMP 100, 39.
Apr 29	Learn from the Experiences of Hsuchang Region and Do a Good Job in the Party's Propaganda Work, 1.
May 1	The Resist U.S., Aid Korea Movement Shall Be Brought to a New Stage of Development, 1. SCMP 101, 18.
May 4	Watch Over Counter-Revolutionaries' Retaliatory Sabotage Activities, 1. SCMP 103, 3.
May 6	Mobilize Immediately for the Timely Fulfillment of Cotton Sowing, 1.
May 7	Attach Importance to the Reform of Drama (Government Affairs Council directive), 1.
May 17	Popularize Tissue Therapy, 1.
May 20	Importance Should Be Attached to the Discussion of the Film "The Life of Wu Hsun," (Amended 5/21, p. 1), 1.
May 21	All-Out Mobilization of the Masses to Denounce and Bring to Justice All Counter-Revolutionaries, 1. SCMP 106, 1.
May 26	Division of Functions and Power between Central and Local Governments in Managing Financial and Economic Work, 1. SCMP 108, 22.
May 26	Two Proposals for Japanese Peace Treaty Lie Before World, 1. SCMP 108, 6.
May 27	Do a Good Job in Summer Levy, 1.
May 28	Support the Agreement on the Way to Peacefully Liberate Tibet, 1.
May 29	Consolidate and Develop Further the People's Democratic Dictatorship, 1.
May 30	Leading Papers in Peking Greet Returned Chinese People's Delegation from Korea, 1. SCMP 109, 11.
Jun 1	Answer the Nation's Call for the Unfolding of the Campaign to Sell and Save Cotton, 1.
Jun 1	JMJP Hails International Children's Day, 1. SCMP 110, 29.
Jun 2	Extensively Sign and Seriously Carry Out Patriotic Compacts, 1. SCMP 110, 10.
Jun 2	Two Important Aspects of the Work of Supporting the Front, 1. SCMP 110, 8.
Jun 3	Experiences Gained in the Exposure of the Tsunyi Counter-Revolutionary Case (Amended 6/13, p. 1), 1. SCMP 110, 41.
Jun 4	The Inventory of Assets and the Reappraisal of Capital Constitutes the First Step Toward the Enforcement of Economic Accounting (Promulgation of decision), 1.
Jun 5	Overcome Paralysis! Everybody Should Be on Guard and Stamp Out Counter-Revolutionary Activities, 1.
Jun 6	JMJP Calls for the Correct Use of Chinese Language (Amended 6/7, p. 1), 1. SCMP 111, 18.
Jun 7	Exert All-Out Efforts for the Development of Rural Finance, 1.
Jun 10	Do a Good Job in Organizing and Preparing to Struggle to Defeat This Year's Floods, 1.
Jun 11	Struggle for the Preservation of State Secrets (GAC promulgates temporary regulations), 1. SCMP 114, 7.
Jun 14	Exert Full Efforts for the Fostering of Cadres among Nationality Minorities, 1. SCMP 117, 10.
Jun 15	JMJP on Soviet Proposal about Japanese Peace Treaty, 1. SCMP 117, 1.
Jun 16	Without Engineering Design, No Work Should Be Undertaken, 1.
Jun 22	Papers in Peking Prominently Feature Arrival of Korean Delegation, 1. SCMP 122, 7.
Jun 22	U.S. Scheme Doomed to Failure, 1. SCMP 122, 10.
Jun 23	GAC Directive on Collection of Agricultural Tax in 1951, 1. SCMP 122, 25.
Jun 24	Smash the Fresh Plot of Imperialist Elements to Undermine Catholic Reform Movement, 1. SCMP 123, 11.
Jun 25	Patriotic Youths, Take Part in National Defense Construction Enthusiastically (GAC decision on military cadre schools admission), 1.
Jun 25	One Year of the Korean War (Amended 6/26, p. 1), 1. SCMP 124, 1.
Jul 3	Strive for a Peaceful Settlement of the Korean Question, 1. SCMP 127, 18.
Jul 5	Carry Out with Leadership and Planning the Work of Investigating Land Holdings to Determine Productivity (The Ministry of Finance promulgation) (Amended 7/6, p. 1), 1.
Jul 8	Strengthen the Cultural Work Corps; Develop the New People's Arts, 1.
Jul 11	Graduates Should Accept Unified Scheme for Assignment of Jobs and Participate in National Construction, 1.

1951

Jul 13	Regularize the Work of the Political Reporters, 1. SCMP 136, 7.
Jul 17	Destroy Pests, Strive for Bumper Harvests, 1.
Jul 20	The Advance of Chinese Students Under the Banner of Patriotism (15th convention of student delegates), 1. SCMP 141, 9.
Jul 21	Struggle for Greater Achievements in the Drive for the Purchase of Cotton and Acceptance of Cotton Deposits, 1.
Jul 22	Make a Good Job of Taking Care of Families of Martyrs and Servicemen, 1.
Jul 24	JMJP Hails Unity between Vietnam and China, 1. SCMP 142, 3.
Jul 25	The Great Significance of the Conference of Hsien Magistrates in North China, 1.
Jul 27	Uphold Laws and Discipline and Strive for Preserving State Properties and Purity of Government Agencies 1. SCMP 145, 17.
Jul 29	Strive for Timely Fulfillment of Plans for Production Increase and Plane Donations, 1. SCMP 146, 1.
Jul 30	Develop Ideological Struggle for the Successful Reevaluation of Capital in Enterprises, 1.
Aug 5	To Develop Potentialities Fully Is the Guiding Principle of Managing the People's Electric Power Industry, 1.
Aug 8	Strengthen the Leadership of the Party in the Work of Promoting the Implementation of Patriotic Compacts, 1.
Aug 10	Elections Must Oppose "Close-Doorism" and Formalism, 1.
Aug 10	Another Test of the Sincerity of the American Government's Desire for Peace, 1.
Aug 11	JMJP on Armistice Talks in Korea, 1. SCMP 152, 6.
Aug 14	Those Hsien People's Representative Conferences Which Have Not Done Well Should Make Amends (Amended 8/17, p. 1), 1. SCMP 158, 8.
Aug 16	Oppose U.S.-British Draft Peace Treaty with Japan, 1. SCMP 156, 23.
Aug 17	Stop the Wasteful Uses of the State's Lumber Resources, 1.
Aug 18	Lopping Off Aggressive Claws of Imperialism in China (Trial case of U.S. spies Li An-tung and co.), 1. SCMP 156, 20.
Aug 20	Make a Better Job of the Work of National Budgeting and Final Accounting, 1.
Aug 26	American Murderers Give the World a Lesson (The Korean peace talks stop), 1. SCMP 162, 3.
Aug 29	JMJP on Refusal of India and Burma to Sign U.S.-Japan Treaty, 1. SCMP 164, 7.
Aug 30	Rectify Several Ideological Deviations in the Work of the County People's Congress, 1.
Sep 5	JMJP on Deportation of Riberi from China, 1. SCMP 168, 5.
Sep 5	Strengthen and Consolidate People's Revolutionary Legal System, 1. SCMP 168, 7.
Sep 7	Strengthen Further the Work of Consultative Committees on All Levels, 1.
Sep 10	American Imperialist Plans to Enslave Asian People Can Be Defeated (San Francisco conference endorsement), 1. SCMP 171, 1.
Sep 12	JMJP Editorial on U.S. Provocations and Murders, 1. SCMP 173, 1.
Sep 13	Exert All-Out Efforts to Develop the Work of Broadcasting among the Workers, 1.
Sep 14	Develop Trade in the National Minority Areas, 1.
Sep 18	Smash American Aggressive Plans to Enslave the Asian Peoples (20th anniversary of the Sept. 18 incident), 1. SCMP 177, 3.
Sep 20	To Strengthen the Administrative Machinery Is the Center of National Reconstruction, 1. SCMP 181, 8.
Sep 23	JMJP Editorially Bidding Farewell to CPV (Chinese People's Volunteers) Delegates, 1. SCMP 180, 5.
Sep 29	Resolutely Carry Through Marriage Law, Protect Women's Rights, 1.
Sep 30	Strive for Fulfilling Patriotic Donation Plans (Amended 10/16, p. 1), 1.
Oct 3	Why Reform the School System? 1. SCMP 192, 18.
Oct 7	JMJP on Stalin's Replies on Questions on Atomic Weapon (Amended 10/8, p. 1), 1. SCMP 190, 1.
Oct 13	Stabilize and Develop Primary Education, Foster a Million People's Teachers, 1.
Oct 15	Develop Sino-Soviet Friendship Work Concretely and Penetratingly, 1. SCMP 195, 5.
Oct 19	Emulate Lu Hsun, Persist in Ideological Struggle, 1. SCMP 198, 13.
Oct 20	Forthright Stand of Soviet Union and Stalling Tactics of United States (Moscow on Korean question and Soviet-U.S. relations) (Amended 10/21, p. 1; 11/6, p. 1), 1. SCMP 199, 1.
Oct 25	Resisting American Aggression and Aiding Korea Is Central Task of Chinese People Today, 2. SCMP 203, 5.
Oct 31	Just Struggle of Iranian and Egyptian Peoples (Amended 11/6, p. 1), 1. SCMP 207, 6.
Nov 7	JMJP Editorially Greets Soviet October Revolution, 1. SCMP 212, 3.
Nov 9	Struggle for the Realization of the Decisions of the Third Session of the First National Committee of the People's Political Consultative Conference, 1. SCMP 213, 24.
Nov 10	Strive to Complete and Continue to Enlarge the Donation Campaign, 1. SCMP 214, 16.
Nov 11	Launch an Organized Campaign for Patriotic Delivery of Grain Levies, 1. SCMP 216, 8 (summary).
Nov 12	Continue Along the Road to Lasting World Peace, 1. SCMP 214, 1.
Nov 13	Make a Good Job of People's Tribunal Work, 1.
Nov 14	What Are Basic Reasons for Lack of Progress in Korean Armistice Negotiations? 1. SCMP 216, 4.
Nov 17	Introduce Experience of North China Magistrate's Conference, 1.
Nov 20	Launching Production Increase and Austerity Campaign Is State Central Task at Present, 1. SCMP 223, 7.
Nov 23	Relentless Struggle against Graft, 1. SCMP 224, 12.
Nov 25	Promote Physical Drill, Develop People's Physical Culture Work (Amended 11/26, p. 2), 1.
Nov 27	JMJP on Settlement of Second Item of Armistice Agenda, 1. SCMP 224, 2.
Nov 28	Achievements of City and Village Trade Exhibition in North China, 1.
Dec 6	Tsun Cadres Use Torture against Ten Women in Yungchun Hsien, Kwangsi, 1. SCMP 236, 17.
Dec 7	Launch Production Increase and Economy Campaign among State Trading Companies, 1.
Dec 13	JMJP on Exposure of Slansky Case, 1. SCMP 236, 7.

1951

Dec 13 Learn a Lesson from Case of Orders for Raincoats, Improve Management of Processing Orders, 1.
Dec 17 Raise Per Hectare Yield, Fight for Bumper Harvest in 1952, 1.
Dec 19 Further Consolidate and Develop Ranks of Propaganda Personnel, 1.
Dec 25 Why Are POW's of Both Sides Still Unable to Go Home Immediately? 1. SCMP 243, 2.
Dec 26 Why Are Americans Persisting to Interfere in Korea's Internal Affairs? 1. SCMP 243, 11.

1952

Jan 1   Greet 1952 with High Confidence and Determined Will, 1. SCMP 246, 1.
Jan 4   What Is the Determining Factor in Mobilizing the Masses for the Great Struggle against Corruption, Waste, and Bureaucracy? 1. SCMP 249, 12.
Jan 5   We Must Mobilize the Masses to Bring Corrupted Elements to Justice, 1.
Jan 6   Resolutely Eliminate Burglars Who Steal State Properties, 1.
Jan 7   JMJP Supports Vyshinsky's Proposal about Korea, 1. SCMP 250, 1.
Jan 11 Universally Carry Out Inspection of Work of Giving Care to Dependents of Servicemen during Spring Festival, 1.
Jan 12 How to Develop the Campaign against Corruption, Waste, and Bureaucracy in the Financial System, 1.
Jan 19 Greets Arrival of Delegations from Korean Front, 1. SCMP 259, 4.
Jan 21 On 28th Anniversary of Lenin's Death (Struggle against corruption, waste, and bureaucracy), 1. SCMP 260, 4.
Jan 22 To Purge State Economic Organs of Sabotage Activities of Bourgeois Class, 1. SCMP 263, 10.
Jan 23 American and Japanese Reactionaries Will Find Only Defeat in Taiwan, 1. SCMP 262, 2.
Jan 29 To Continue Our Chase of the Corrupt, 1. SCMP 271, 14.
Feb 1   To Strengthen Work in the Old Revolutionary Bases, 1. SCMP 269, 11.
Feb 4   Denounce the Slanderous U.S.-KMT Charge against Soviet Union, 1. SCMP 268, 2.
Feb 7   Repulse Bourgeois Attack, Consolidate Leadership Right of Working Class (29th anniversary of Feb. 7), 1. SCMP 272, 12.
Feb 13 Whole Country Should Take Urgent Precautions against Drought, 1. SCMP 275, 14.
Feb 14 Fraternal Alliance between China and the Soviet Union Is the Bulwark of Peace in the Far East and the World (Second anniversary of the Sino-Soviet treaty) (Amended 2/16, p. 1), 1. SCMP 276, 13.
Feb 16 Overcome Rightist Thought; Win Complete Victory of Anti-Corruption Campaign, 1. SCMP 281, 19.
Feb 17 Severely Punish Unscrupulous Merchants Who Do Injury to CPV, 1. SCMP 277, 12.
Feb 20 Exposes U.S. Atrocities against POW's, 1. SCMP 280, 7.
Feb 20 Denounces U.S. Objection to USSR as Neutral Nation (Korean armistice negotiations), 1. SCMP 280, 5.
Feb 21 Oppose the Criminal Act of Stealing State Economic Intelligence, 1. SCMP 284, 16.

1952

Feb 23 World People Urged to Stop American Inhuman Crimes (Bacteriological warfare in Korea), 1. SCMP 281, 2.
Feb 26 Eliminate the Bad Elements Hidden in the Revolutionary Troops, 1.
Feb 26 We Hold United States Responsible for Koje Island Massacre, 1. SCMP 282, 6.
Feb 27 Strive for Fulfilling 1952 Agricultural Production Tasks, 1. SCMP 284, 15.
Feb 29 On the "Thursday Dinner Club" (Capitalists of Chungking attack state economic interests), 1. SCMP 287, 8.
Mar 1   Stamp Out Effects of U.S. Germ Warfare, 1. SCMP 286, 9.
Mar 2   Economic Departments Should Strengthen Their Routine Operations during the Struggle against Corruption, Waste, and Bureaucracy, 1. SCMP 292, 11.
Mar 6   Resolutely Prevent and Quench Forest Fires, 1.
Mar 8   Work among Family Members Should Be Given Attention in Anti-Corruption and Anti-Theft Campaign, 2.
Mar 8   Punish American Butchers Who Are Bombing and Spreading Germs in Northeast China, 1. SCMP 291, 4.
Mar 12 Strive for the Complete Victory of the Struggle against Corruption and Stealing (GAC and Peking documents on Five-Anti campaign), 2.
Mar 13 Hand Over Productive Undertakings of Organs to the State, 1. SCMP 296, 13.
Mar 19 Smash Germ-Spreading American Aggressors, 1. SCMP 299, 4.
Mar 20 Strengthen Leadership over Spring Plowing, Fight for Timely Sowing, 1. SCMP 300, 17.
Mar 24 Solve Fertilizer Question, 1. SCMP 302, 7.
Apr 2   Develop Patriotic Production Increase Emulation and Win Greater Harvest This Year, 2. SCMP 308, 12.
Apr 2   Recover Stolen Goods and Pass Judgment According to Different Conditions (GAC regulations), 1. SCMP 309, 11.
Apr 3   Struggle for Accomplishing Water Conservancy Works and Tasks of 1952, 2. SCMP 312, 8.
Apr 5   Greet the Opening of the International Economic Conference, 1.
Apr 7   To Fight to the End in the Struggle against U.S. Germ Warfare, 1. SCMP 312, 2.
Apr 8   Reform and Develop Intermediate Technical Education, 1. SCMP 314, 29.
Apr 9   Boldly Promote Cadres, 1. SCMP 317, 8.
Apr 10 Promote the "Unified Contracts" of Mutual Aid Teams and Cooperatives, 1.
Apr 15 Momentous Significance of Lowering Official Prices of Merchandise, 1. SCMP 316, 12.
Apr 16 Positively Implement the Plans for the Reorganization of Colleges of Technology, 1. SCMP 317, 14.
Apr 26 Popularize Quick Methods for Learning Chinese Characters, 1.
Apr 29 Why POW Question Is Not Yet Settled, 1. SCMP 326, 9.
May 1   Strive for Lasting World Peace to Celebrate May 1st (Amended 5/3, p. 2), 1. SCMP 328, 2.
May 4   Peking Papers Pay High Tribute to Four Great Cultural Giants, 1. SCMP 329, 14.
May 6   Day of Judgment of U.S. Germ War Crime Is Fast Approaching, 1. SCMP 331, 4.

1952

May 7	Supports Chou En-lai's Recent Statement on Japan (Halt U.S. war schemes in the Far East), 1. SCMP 332, 2.
May 9	Resolute Opposition to Forcible Detention of POW's, 1. SCMP 332, 6.
May 12	Develop National Native Produce Exchange, 1.
May 14	Towards Successful Convening of a Peace Conference for Asia and Pacific Area, 1. SCMP 336, 4.
May 16	Smash U.S. Latest Scheme for Wrecking Truce Talks, 1. SCMP 337, 10.
May 23	Editorial on Anniversary of Chairman Mao's Talk at Yenan Literary Discussion Meeting, 1. SCMP 342, 15.
May 28	Purchase New Wheat Crops in Time, 1. SCMP 357, 9.
Jun 1	Protect Children and Develop the Work of Child Care and Child Education, 1.
Jun 4	Hails Preparatory Meeting of Peace Conference of Asia and the Pacific Regions, 1. SCMP 349, 10.
Jun 8	Make Penetrating and Widespread Purchase of Cotton in Advance, 1.
Jun 14	Assign Trained Technicians to Most Important Posts of Economic Construction, 1. SCMP 371, 9.
Jun 15	Conclude 5-Anti Campaign Victoriously (Directive on several questions in concluding the campaign), 1. SCMP 356, 12.
Jun 19	Strive for Completion of Collection of 1952 Agricultural Tax, 1. SCMP 359, 13.
Jun 22	Hails Malik's Proposal to Security Council (Prohibit use of bacterial warfare), 4. SCMP 360, 2.
Jun 25	We Will Continue Our Efforts for Peace in Korea, 1. SCMP 363, 6.
Jun 28	Condemns U.S. Inhuman Bombing of Yalu Power Station, 1. SCMP 365, 5.
Jun 29	Fight to the End for Banning the Use of Germ Weapons, 1. SCMP 365, 12.
Jul 1	Strengthen the Party's Militant Force to Usher in Great Task of National Construction (31st anniversary of founding of CCP), 1. SCMP 366, 3.
Jul 2	Unite All Industrialists and Merchants in the Country, Fight for Greater Prosperity of State Economy (National Federation founded), 1.
Jul 5	Develop Even Further the Patriotic Public Health Campaign, 1.
Jul 7	Chinese and Japanese People Unite to Struggle against U.S. Aggression, 1. SCMP 369, 2.
Jul 9	Peace Shall Conquer War; To Save Peace, Let All Peoples Craving for Peace Close Their Ranks and Continue to Advance Courageously (World Peace Council session concluded), 1. SCMP 371, 2.
Jul 11	Editorial on Twelve Months of Korean Truce Talks, 1. SCMP 372, 7.
Jul 15	Condemns U.S Indiscriminate Bombing of Pyongyang, 1. SCMP 375, 10.
Jul 15	Greets Japanese Communist Party Day, 1. SCMP 376, 2.
Jul 20	Increase Vigilance in Struggle against Flood This Year, 1. SCMP 379, 11.
Jul 27	Summarizes U.S. Disruptive Activities in Secret Talks, 1. SCMP 383, 6.
Jul 28	World Peace Is Seriously Menaced, 1. SCMP 384, 2.
Jul 31	Regular Education for Disabled Army Men Greatly Strengthened, 1. SCMP 388, 26.
Aug 4	To Effect Full Employment in a Planned and Systematic Manner (GAC decision), 1. SCMP 388, 57.
Aug 7	Glorious Task of College Graduates (Unified distribution) (Amended 8/8, p. 1), 1. SCMP 392, 11.
Aug 11	On Achievement of Balanced 1952 Budget, 1. SCMP 391, 6.
Aug 11	Fight to Uphold Humanitarian Principles and Traditional Spirit of International Red Cross Movement (18th IRC Conference), 4. SCMP 393, 6.
Aug 12	Resolutely Check American Aggressors' Crimes of Violating Geneva Conventions (Korean War POW's), 1. SCMP 394, 2.
Aug 13	General Program for Implementation of Nationality Regional Autonomy Comes into Effect, 1. SCMP 394, 9 (extracts).
Aug 15	Just Struggle of Korean People Will Certainly Win Final Victory, 1. SCMP 395, 3.
Aug 17	Judicial Work Must Be Thoroughly Reformed, 1. SCMP 401, 19.
Aug 25	Strengthen Work of People's Supervision and People's Denunciation Reception Rooms, 1.
Sep 1	People Throughout the World Will Gain Tremendous Strength from Struggle for Peace and Progress from 19th Congress of CPSU (B), 1. SCMP 406, 2.
Sep 3	Plot to Revive Japanese Militarism Is Doomed to Failure (Seventh anniversary of ending of Japanese war), 1. SCMP 408, 2.
Sep 4	Sum Up and Promote This Year's Bumper Harvest Experience, Strive for Bigger Crops Next Year (Ministry of Agriculture regulations on rewards to bumper harvests), 1.
Sep 15	On Report of International Scientific Commission, 1. SCMP 416, 6.
Sep 16	Develop Mighty Strength of Sino-Soviet Alliance (Sino-Soviet communique on Changchung Railway and use of Lu Hsun Naval Base), 1. SCMP 417, 3.
Sep 17	Production Safety Measures Must Be Fully Implemented, 1. SCMP 446, 21.
Sep 21	Flays Despicable Japanese Government Action against Peace (Refusal to grant visas to Asian-Pacific Peace Conference delegates), 1. SCMP 420, 6.
Sep 24	Make a Good Job of the Reorganization of Colleges and Departments of Institutions of Higher Learning and Cultivate Effectively Cadres for National Construction, 1.
Oct 1	Our Great Motherland Is Marching Forward to Peace Construction (National Day), 1. SCMP 428, 9.
Oct 2	Still Great Unity to Conquer the Menace of War and Defend Peace (Asian and Pacific Peace Conference), 1. SCMP 428, 25.
Oct 5	A New Development in Friendly Relations between China and Mongolia (Economic and cultural agreement), 1. SCMP 429, 5.
Oct 7	On 19th Congress of CPSU (B), 1. SCMP 430, 27.
Oct 9	Condemns Terrible U.S. Crime of Wrecking Korean Truce Talks, 1. SCMP 431, 17.
Oct 13	Editorial Endorses Resolutions Adopted by APPC, 1. SCMP 433, 23.
Oct 17	International Significance of 19th Congress of CPSU (B), 1. SCMP 436, 1.
Oct 18	Stresses Need for Vigilance in Face of U.S. Scheming (POW question), 1. SCMP 436, 6.
Oct 19	To Inherit the Revolutionary Patriotic Spirit of Lu Hsun (16th anniversary of his death), 1. SCMP 437, 15.

1952

Oct 25	On CPV Entry into Korean War (On second anniversary), 1. SCMP 440, 9.
Oct 30	Stalin's Great Work on the Economic Problems of Socialism Arms Us with a New Ideological Weapon, 1. SCMP 444, 1.
Nov 5	Learn and Expand the Experiences from China's Changchun Railway, 1.
Nov 6	Expressing Support for Soviet Proposal on Korea, 1. SCMP 448, 8.
Nov 7	Learn from Soviet Union and Thank for Its Help (October Revolution anniversary and Sino-Soviet Friendship Day), 2. SCMP 450, 2.
Nov 11	On Election of Dwight Eisenhower (Through deception of U.S. voters), 1. SCMP 451, 1.
Nov 15	Learn from the Soviet Artists (Four Soviet delegations), 1. SCMP 453, 1.
Nov 16	Proper Attitude Should Be Taken toward Dramatic Legacy of Fatherland, 1.
Nov 17	Strengthen the Centralized Nature of Our State Work to Meet Large-Scale Economic Construction (Central government decision), 1. SCMP 455, 3.
Nov 18	Put Capital Construction on the Forefront of All Talks, 1. SCMP 456, 9.
Nov 26	On the Necessity to Stress Theoretical Studying by Senior Cadres, 1. SCMP 465, 9.
Nov 29	Supports Foreign Minister Chou En-lai's Statement on Soviet Proposal on Korean Question, 1. SCMP 462, 3.
Nov 30	A Tremendous Victory of Czech People against Conspiracy, 1. SCMP 463, 12.
Dec 9	Eisenhower's Phony Pledge of "Ending the Korean War" Completely Exposed, 1. SCMP 469, 1.
Dec 14	Peace Must Triumph Throughout the Whole World (World People's Peace Conference), 1. SCMP 472, 8.
Dec 16	People's Just Demand Will Win Out in the End (POW question), 1. SCMP 474, 1.
Dec 17	Main Links Must Be Grasped in Large-Scale Construction Work, 1. SCMP 479, 6.
Dec 18	On Great Victory on Sangkumryung Front, 1. SCMP 476, 6.
Dec 19	Honorable Tasks of Chinese Geological Workers, 1. SCMP 479, 19.
Dec 23	Condemns Pongam Island Bloodshed (U.S. kills Chinese POW), 1. SCMP 479, 1.
Dec 23	Major Developments of International Tension (Five-Power peace pact), 1. SCMP 480, 5.
Dec 25	Chinese People Must Continue to Strengthen Work to Resist American Aggression and Aid Korea, 1. SCMP 480, 7.
Dec 26	Grasp Decisive Link, Tap Potentialities (Correct formulation of state construction plans), 1. SCMP 481, 21.
Dec 27	Stalin's Voice Inspires People Throughout the World (Interview with <u>New York Times</u>), 1. SCMP 481, 1.
Dec 27	Prevent and Resist Drought, Preserve Soil and Water, 1. SCMP 481, 39.
Dec 28	Key to Present Preparatory Work for Capital Construction Lies in Designing, 1. SCMP 481, 39.
Dec 28	Propagate the Experiences from Wusan Factory (Business administration), 1.
Dec 29	Establish a Unified National System for Statistical Work, 1. SCMP 525, 19.
Dec 30	Make a Good Job of Capital Construction Workers' Winter Training Work, 1.
Dec 30	Further Carry Out Planned Publication of and Subscription to Newspapers and Periodicals, 1.
Dec 31	Greet the Transfer of Chinese Changchun Railway to China, 1. SCMP 483, 18.
Dec 31	Enforce the Revised Tax System (Notice of GAC) (Amended 1/5/53), 1. SCMP 483, 24.

1953

Jan 1	The Year 1953 Confronts Chinese People with Three Great Tasks, 1. SCMP 483, 1.
Jan 1	Unfold Earnestly the Work of Supporting the Army and Caring for the Families of Servicemen and of Supporting the Government and Cherishing the People during the Spring Festival, 3.
Jan 4	National Health Conference Held in Peking, 1. SCMP 485, 4 (summary).
Jan 6	Supervisory Work Should Be Strengthened in Financial-Economic Agencies, 1. SCMP 495, 23.
Jan 6	The Tasks of Cooperative Workers in China (Commemorating Lenin's "On Cooperation"), 1. SCMP 501, 21.
Jan 7	Develop Great Potentialities of Agricultural Production (1952 bumper crop prize winners), 1. SCMP 492, 8.
Jan 10	Strive for Carrying Through Labor Insurance Regulations, 1.
Jan 15	To Practice the System of People's Congress Elected Through Universal Franchise, 1. SCMP 493, 5.
Jan 16	Important Achievements of Soviet State Security Work, 1. SCMP 494, 29 (summary).
Jan 17	Design Work Must Be Done Correctly, 1.
Jan 18	Intensify Forestry Construction; Cultivate and Expand Timber Resources, 1.
Jan 19	Editorially Calls Attention to Proper Handling of Public Complaints (Expose crimes of bureaucratism), 1. SCMP 498, 11.
Jan 22	The Importance of Measured Advance in Pedagogical Reform in Institutions of Higher Education, 1. SCMP 505, 14.
Jan 23	Anyone Who Suppresses Criticism Is the Deadly Enemy of the Party, 1. SCMP 502, 8.
Jan 24	A High Degree of Vigilance Should Be Maintained against American Imperialists' Plot to Extend the War, 1. SCMP 500, 2.
Jan 25	Oppose Conservative and Backward Thinking in Design Work, 1.
Jan 27	Cadres' Spare Time Theoretical Schools Should Be Promoted and Established, 1.
Jan 29	Results of Fulfillment of Soviet State Economic Plan in 1952, 1. SCMP 503, 1.
Jan 30	Conduct Well Labor Protection Work, Fully Implement the Safety Production Policy, 1. SCMP 506, 12.
Jan 31	Keep Up the Theoretical Studies of the Senior Cadres, 1. SCMP 518, 25.
Feb 1	Exert All-Out Efforts to Launch a Mass Movement in Preparing, Unfolding, and Carrying Out the Marriage Law, 1.
Feb 2	Faked American "Intelligence Report," 1. SCMP 505, 2.
Feb 3	Resolutely Rectify Coercive Work Style in Postal and Telecommunications Agencies, 1.
Feb 7	Uphold the Correct Policy of Labor Movement, Strive for National Industrialization (30th anniversary of the "February 7" incident), 1. SCMP 516, 15.
Feb 8	Pays Tribute to KPA and Korean People (Fifth anniversary of Korean Army Day), 1. SCMP 510, 2.

1953

Feb 10	Respond Fully to Chairman Mao's Great Call (Speech at fourth session of PPCC National Committee), 1. SCMP 511, 1.
Feb 11	Eliminate the Working Style of Commandism, 1. SCMP 512, 2.
Feb 12	Mobilize the Masses to Formulate and Discuss This Year's Industrial Production Plan, 1.
Feb 14	Hails Sino-Soviet Treaty Anniversary (Learn from the Soviet Union), 1. SCMP 513, 12.
Feb 18	Intensify the Leadership of Cadres' Spare Time Cultural Education, 1.
Feb 19	For Realization of 1953 State Budget, 1. SCMP 515, 1.
Feb 21	Day of Struggle against Colonialism, 1. SCMP 517, 24.
Feb 23	Greets Soviet Army Day, 1. SCMP 518, 6.
Feb 24	Comments on Signed Depositions on U.S. Germ Warfare, 1. SCMP 518, 9 (extracts).
Feb 25	Learn from the Lesson of the Work of Railway Transportation, 1.
Feb 27	False Peasant Models Must Not Be Tolerated, 1. SCMP 524, 5.
Feb 28	Strengthen the Leadership of the Party in Sanitation Work (Amended 3/1, p. 3; 3/31, p. 1), 1.
Mar 1	Comments on Stupidity of General Clark's Statement on Germ War, 1. SCMP 522, 6.
Mar 4	Support the Election Law and Unfold the Universal Suffrage Movement, 1. SCMP 524, 1.
Mar 6	Peoples of China and Russia Unite Yet More Intimately! (Stalin is sick), 1.
Mar 7	Mourning Our Teacher and Guide--The Great Comrade Stalin, 2. SCMP 526, 8.
Mar 11	Long Live the Triumphant Cause of the Party of Lenin and Stalin, 1. SCMP 529, 1.
Mar 11	Display Power of People's Supervision to Remove Obstacles from Path of National Construction, 3. SCMP 533, 16.
Mar 12	Resolutely Oppose the Illegal UN Resolution on Korean Question, 1. SCMP 530, 1.
Mar 13	Firmly Wage a Struggle against Bureaucratism While Linking Up with Present Work, 1. SCMP 532, 12.
Mar 14	Urges Increased Study of Marxism-Leninism (70th anniversary of Marx's death), 1. SCMP 531, 27.
Mar 16	On Death of Comrade Gottwald (Great Czechoslovak leader), 1. SCMP 532, 2.
Mar 17	Do Not Indiscriminately Get Teachers to Take Part in Social Activities, 3.
Mar 25	The Lesson We Get from Wang Chen-hai's Criminal Case, 1.
Mar 26	The Key to Leading Agricultural Production (Directive on mutual assistance in agriculture), 2.
Mar 28	A New Development in Sino-Soviet Economic Cooperative Relationship (Trade expansion and power stations), 1.
Apr 1	Rational Adjustment of Cotton-Grain Price Ratios and of Seasonal Price Differentials of Grain and Cloth, 1. SCMP 544, 26.
Apr 2	Strengthen the Organizational Leadership in Design Work, 1.
Apr 5	Endeavor to Bring about a Korean Armistice and Seek a Peaceful Settlement of the Korean Question (Amended 4/7, p. 1), 1. SCMP 545, 13.
Apr 7	Correctly Develop the Anti-Bureaucratism Struggle in Industrial Departments, 1. SCMP 548, 9.
Apr 8	Establish Planned Management on the Basis of Discussing the Plans, 1.
Apr 9	Anti-Illiteracy Work Must Be Readjusted, 1. SCMP 564, 15.
Apr 11	Grain Production Increase Is the Primary Task on Production Front, 1. SCMP 551, 14.
Apr 12	On UN Political Committee's Illegal Resolution (Investigation of bacteriological weapon), 1. SCMP 550, 1.
Apr 14	Chinese People Fully Endorse Polish Resolution at UN General Assembly, 1. SCMP 551, 1.
Apr 20	Peasants Blindly Flowing into Cities Should Return to the Countryside (GAC directive), 1. SCMP 555, 23.
Apr 23	Importance Must Be Attached to Handicraft Industry, 1. SCMP 566, 22.
Apr 25	To Learn Theories and Experience of Soviet Socialist Construction Is an Important Task of All Party Cadres (Directive on theoretical education for cadres, 1953-54), 1. SCMP 559, 23.
Apr 28	Do Not Bite Off More than You Can Chew (Problem of construction plans), 1. SCMP 565, 20.
Apr 29	Deeds Mean More than Words (Criticizing Eisenhower's speech), 1. SCMP 561, 1.
Apr 30	A Fundamental Method of Improving the Management of State Trade (Economic accounting system), 1. SCMP 564, 17.
May 1	Yet More Courage and Industry in Building Our Motherland (May 1st national labor holiday and the seventh Trade Unions Congress), 1. SCMP 562, 5 (extracts).
May 4	China's Youth Day, 1. SCMP 563, 1 (summary).
May 5	Use Marxist Theory to Guide China's Construction Work (135th anniversary of Marx's birth), 1. SCMP 564, 1.
May 6	To Carry Through the Marriage Law Is an Extremely Important, Continuing Task, 1.
May 13	Seventh All-China Congress of Trade Unions, 1. SCMP 571, 23.
May 14	Strengthen the People's Judiciary Work during National Construction, 1. SCMP 573, 19.
May 15	Strive to Advance the Work of Technological Reform of Present Enterprises, 1.
May 16	No Proposal Involving Forcible Detention of POW's Can Be Accepted, 1. SCMP 572, 6.
May 17	Produce More Grain and Strengthen Famine Relief Work, 1. SCMP 577, 16.
May 29	Continue to Speed Up Grain Shipment for Famine Relief, 1. SCMP 587, 17.
May 31	Hails *Pravda*'s May 24th Editorial (Only solution to current international problems), 1. SCMP 581, 1.
Jun 1	On Children's Day, 1. SCMP 582, 3.
Jun 2	The Rosenbergs Are Innocent, 1. SCMP 582, 7.
Jun 6	Create and Promote Experiences of Combining Election with Production, 1. SCMP 592, 14.
Jun 7	Unprecedented Growth in the World Women's Movement (World Women's Congress opens), 1. SCMP 584, 1.
Jun 9	Pave the Way for a Peaceful Settlement of the Korean Question (Signing of POW agreement) (Amended 6/10, p. 1), 1. SCMP 586, 1.
Jun 10	Purchase of Wheat, 1. SCMP 593, 6.
Jun 12	Speedily Raise the Quality of Coal Production, 1. SCMP 590, 8.
Jun 18	On All-China Youth Congress, 1. SCMP 593, 9.

1953

Jun 19 Learn the Use of Scientific Methods in Industrial Management, 1. SCMP 601, 14.
Jun 20 We Must Elevate the Quality of Check-up Work (Government work), 1. SCMP 602, 12.
Jun 21 American Side Must Take Responsibility for the Forced Detention of POW's, 1. SCMP 594, 10.
Jun 21 The Spirit of the Rosenbergs Will Never Die, 4. SCMP 594, 27.
Jun 23 On Campaign for International Negotiations (World Peace Council ends), 1. SCMP 596, 1.
Jun 23 Develop Fully the Important Function of the Machine Industry in Economic Construction, 1.
Jun 25 Persist in the Efforts for a Peaceful Settlement of the Korean Question (Third anniversary of Korean War), 1. SCMP 598, 1.
Jun 26 Eliminate the Phenomenon of "Five Too Many" in Rural Work (Tasks, meetings, documents and forms, organizations, and concurrent posts for cadres), 1. SCMP 602, 9.
Jun 27 Grasp the Important Link in Planned Management, 1.
Jul 3 Hail the Success of the Youth Congress, 1. SCMP 603, 18.
Jul 3 Great Victory of the German People (Berlin question), 4. SCMP 603, 8.
Jul 5 Rely on the Masses for Flood Control, 1.
Jul 8 The Strengthening of Labor Discipline Is an Imperative Task, 1. SCMP 608, 28.
Jul 10 Key Factor to Achievement of an Armistice (In Korea), 1. SCMP 608, 7.
Jul 12 On the Case of Criminal Activities of L.P. Beria, 1. SCMP 608, 1.
Jul 16 Stamp Out Imperialist Elements Hidden in the Catholic Church, 1. SCMP 617, 4.
Jul 18 Strengthen Seriously the Safety Devices in Factories and Mines, 1.
Jul 21 The United States Must Fulfill Its Assurances (Korean armistice), 1. SCMP 615, 1.
Jul 23 Propagate the Experience of the Work in Materials Supply in the Laiyang Special Region, 1.
Jul 26 Zealously and Steadily Lead the Struggle against Bureaucratism, 1.
Jul 28 The First Step Towards a Peaceful Settlement of the Korean Question (Signing of the armistice agreement), 1. SCMP 619, 13.
Jul 30 The Glorious Path of the Communist Party of the Soviet Union (50th anniversary), 1. SCMP 622, 16.
Aug 1 We Must Strengthen Leadership Immediately in the Work of Geology, 2.
Aug 12 Break the Plot of the Enemy of Peace to Undermine the Political Conference, 1. SCMP 630, 1.
Aug 14 The Correct Way to Ease International Tension, 1. SCMP 632, 1.
Aug 15 Greets Korea's Liberation Day, 1. SCMP 632, 7.
Aug 16 Measured Advance in the Promotion of Pedagogical Reform in Higher Engineering Schools, 3. SCMP 648, 19.
Aug 17 We Must Make a Success of the Unified Assignment of Work for University Graduates, 1. SCMP 636, 23.
Aug 18 Existing Factory and Mine Work Must Be Strengthened, 1. SCMP 639, 16.
Aug 19 Establish and Overhaul the Order of Trade Union Work in Factories and Mines, 1. SCMP 635, 11 (extracts).

Aug 25 Key to the Success of the Political Conference, 1. SCMP 639, 1.
Aug 27 Be Positive in Solving the Problem of Promoting Primary School Graduates to a Higher School, 1. SCMP 650, 19.
Aug 28 On Soviet Efforts to Find a Solution to the German Question, 1. SCMP 642, 25.
Aug 28 On the India-Pakistan Talks (Kashmir question), 1. SCMP 642, 23.
Aug 29 We Must Attach Importance to and Improve the Short-term Secondary Schools for the Workers and Peasants, 3.
Aug 31 Correctly Implement the Policy on Agricultural Tax, 1. SCMP 646, 24.
Sep 1 Effectively Improve Production Safety Work in Coal Mines, 1.
Sep 2 Greets the Independence Day of Vietnam, 1. SCMP 643, 6.
Sep 2 Make a Better Job of Farming Credit Work, 2. SCMP 645, 34.
Sep 3 Bright Future for the Asian People (Eighth anniversary of victory against Japan), 1. SCMP 644, 1.
Sep 6 Increase Production and Revenue, Practice Economy, Retrench Expenditures, and Overfulfill National Plans, 1. SCMP 646, 21.
Sep 7 Wipe Out the Confusion in Survey and Statistical Work, 1.
Sep 8 For Fulfillment of This Year's Capital Construction Plan, 1. SCMP 647, 1.
Sep 9 On Regional Autonomy Policy, 1. SCMP 648, 14.
Sep 10 Strive to Improve Postal and Telecommunications Work, 1.
Sep 11 Set Agricultural Tax on a Fair and Reasonable Basis, 1.
Sep 12 Concentrate Our Strength on Autumn Production, 2. SCMP 649, 36.
Sep 13 Task Facing World People Today (After Korean armistice), 1. SCMP 649, 20.
Sep 14 The Question of Enlarging the Composition of Political Conferences Must Be Discussed, 1. SCMP 650, 1.
Sep 16 Thanks to Soviet Union's Great Assistance (Peking telegram acknowledging Russian aid), 1.
Sep 20 Make a Good Job of Supply Work during Purchase of Grain, 1. SCMP 659, 5.
Sep 22 Improve and Strengthen Communications and Transportation, 1. SCMP 664, 15.
Sep 23 Exert Final Efforts to Raise Crop Yields, 1. SCMP 659, 7.
Sep 24 Oppose U.S. Scheme to Sabotage Explanation Work, 1. SCMP 657, 1.
Sep 25 Do a Good Job in Organizing the Work of New Students' Orientation in Institutions of Higher Learning Throughout the Nation, 3.
Sep 27 The Indestructible Great Friendship (Soviet-Korean negotiations), 1. SCMP 658, 30.
Sep 27 On Poland's Economic Exhibition, 4. SCMP 658, 27.
Sep 29 Make Preparations for Coming Year's Capital Construction, 1. SCMP 663, 3.
Oct 1 Work for the Great Perspective of Socialist Industrialization (National Day editorial), 1. SCMP 661, 15; SCMP 666, 32.
Oct 5 On American Sabotage of Explanation Work (POW's), 1. SCMP 662, 23.
Oct 5 On Departure of Chinese People's Delegation to Korea, 4. SCMP 662, 22.
Oct 6 Points to Be Noted in Production Increase and Economy Emulation, 1. SCMP 665, 29.

1953

Oct 7 Actively Unfold Production Increase and Economy Work in State-Operated Commercial Organs, 1. SCMP 665, 31.
Oct 8 Strive to Develop Literary and Art Creation, 1. SCMP 668, 15.
Oct 9 Hails Chou En-lai's Statement on Five-Power Conference, 1. SCMP 666, 16.
Oct 10 Implement Thoroughly the Nationalities Policy, Criticize the Ideology of Pan-Hanism (Amended 10/11, p. 1), 1. SCMP 666, 34.
Oct 13 Uphold the Impartial Work of the Neutral Nations Repatriation Commission, 1. SCMP 667, 1.
Oct 14 For Establishing Correct Concepts of Designing, 1. SCMP 669, 13.
Oct 15 Make a Good Job of the Marketing and Supply of Native Products, 1. SCMP 681, 10.
Oct 15 Struggle to Realize the Resolutions of the National Conference of Comprehensive Universities, 3. SCMP 673, 15.
Oct 17 Ideological Education for Designing Personnel Must Be Guided, 1. SCMP 683, 14.
Oct 18 Eliminate the Evil Practice of Concealing Mistakes and Falsely Reporting Achievements in State Factories and Mines, 1. SCMP 676, 31.
Oct 20 An Important Method of Guiding Agricultural Production (Cadres study agricultural production techniques), 1. SCMP 681, 12.
Oct 22 Geological Work Must Catch Up with Needs of National Construction, 1. SCMP 684, 19.
Oct 23 Significance of Higher Education for Teachers' Training Must Be Emphasized, 1. SCMP 705, 14.
Oct 24 Greets World Trade Union Congress (Strengthen the international unity of the working class), 4. SCMP 676, 27.
Oct 25 Three Glorious Years of the Fight for Peace (Third anniversary of CPV in Korean War), 4. SCMP 676, 3.
Oct 27 The U.S. Must Attend the Talks on Questions of Political Conference in Good Faith, 1. SCMP 677, 5.
Oct 29 Ensure Fulfillment of State Revenue Target by Strengthening Tax Collection during Brisk Business Season, 1. SCMP 692, 19.
Oct 30 For Building the Fatherland, Promote the Spirit of Hard Struggle and Subordination to Plans, 1. SCMP 686, 18.
Oct 30 On Sino-Japanese Relations, 1. SCMP 680, 1.
Oct 31 Useless U.S. Attempt to Cover Up Their Germ War, 1. SCMP 680, 19.
Nov 2 For Improvement of Disposal of Letters from the Public, 1. SCMP 691, 22.
Nov 3 Demands an End to Rule of Terror by Americans in the POW Camps, 1. SCMP 682, 22.
Nov 4 Raise Forestry Construction to a Higher Level, 1. SCMP 692, 21.
Nov 5 For the Correct Formulation of 1954 National Economic Plans, 1. SCMP 689, 17.
Nov 7 Greets October Revolution Anniversary, 1. SCMP 685, 7.
Nov 9 The General Line of the State during Transition Period Must Be Propagandized among Peasants with Fanfare, 1. SCMP 693, 27.
Nov 11 Proceed Further in Bringing Private Industry and Commerce to the Path of State Capitalism, 1. SCMP 688, 27.
Nov 11 To Strive to Foster the Younger Generation (Young Pioneers Conference closes), 3. SCMP 689, 24.
Nov 12 Condemns U.S. Germ War Denial, 1. SCMP 687, 19.
Nov 13 Hails Korean Government Delegation, 1. SCMP 688, 5.
Nov 14 The Bright Road for Private Industry and Commerce, 1. SCMP 687, 43.
Nov 15 Let's Help the Peasants to Make Up Three Accounts, 1. SCMP 689, 21.
Nov 15 Improve Railroad Transportation Work to Serve the Industrialization of Our Nation, 2.
Nov 16 Lead the Peasants to Take the Path of Prosperity for All, 1. SCMP 701, 22.
Nov 17 Lay the Groundwork for First Quarter's Industrial Production of 1954, 1. SCMP 696, 23.
Nov 18 Endorsing Molotov's Statement (Proposal for Five-Power conference), 1. SCMP 691, 18.
Nov 18 Take Advantage of the Opportunity to Do a Good Job in Winter Field Water Conservancy Work, 2.
Nov 19 Eliminate Grain Profiteering in Order to Ensure National Construction, 1. SCMP 701, 34.
Nov 19 State Commerce Must Keep Rural Markets Supplied with Industrial Goods, 2. SCMP 704, 21.
Nov 20 Peasants! Enthusiastically Sell Your Grain to the State to Help National Construction! 1. SCMP 701, 25.
Nov 21 Develop Emulation Drives to Ensure the Success of National Construction, 1. SCMP 704, 16.
Nov 22 Speedily Assign a Large Number of Elite Cadres to Strengthen the Industrial Front, 1. SCMP 699, 11.
Nov 22 Improve and Strengthen the Work of Urban Construction, 2. SCMP 704, 14.
Nov 23 Intensify Political Work during State Purchase of Grain, 1. SCMP 704, 18.
Nov 24 Hailing Sino-Korean Agreement (Economic and cultural cooperation), 4. SCMP 695, 1.
Nov 25 Consolidate the Workers' and Peasants' Alliance to Ensure the Realization of the General Line, 1. SCMP 701, 18.
Nov 26 Seriously Carry Out the Collective Leadership System, 1. SCMP 698, 17.
Nov 27 Actively Develop the Fuel Industry, 1. SCMP 699, 16.
Nov 28 The Explanation Work Cannot Be Carried Out if Secret Agents of American Side Are Not Completely Cleared, 1. SCMP 698, 8.
Nov 30 Intensify Economic Work for State Purchase of Grain, 1. SCMP 709, 28.
Dec 1 On Korean-Chinese Overall Proposal (U.S. should accept our proposal), 1. SCMP 699, 6.
Dec 1 Do a Good Job in This Year's Winter Training Work in Basic Construction Departments, 2.
Dec 1 Calls for Efforts to Ease International Tension (World Peace Council closes), 4. SCMP 699, 1.
Dec 2 We Must Not Only Do a Good Job in Purchasing Grain, But Also Achieve the Goal of Increasing Agricultural Production, 1.
Dec 3 Organize Primary School Graduates to Participate in Agricultural Labor, 1. SCMP 704, 23.
Dec 5 America Covers Up Its War Crimes with Lies, 1. SCMP 702, 6.
Dec 6 Party Leadership in Rural Economic Work Must Be Intensified, 1.
Dec 7 Condemns Illegal Resolution of UN General Assembly on Atrocity Charge, 1. SCMP 703, 9.
Dec 8 A Critical Situation in Korea (Amended 12/10, p. 1), 1. SCMP 704, 1.

1953

- Dec 9 On U.S.-Pakistan Military Alliance Talks (Threatens peace in Asia), 1. SCMP 705, 20.
- Dec 10 Greet the 1954 National Construction Bonds, 1. SCMP 705, 7.
- Dec 11 Teach Chu and Hsiang Cadres to Understand the General Line Thoroughly, 1. SCMP 741, 10.
- Dec 11 Do a Good Job in Running This Year's Winter Studies through Unified Propagation of the National General Line, 3.
- Dec 12 Propagandize the General Line to the Broad Working Masses, 1. SCMP 720, 14.
- Dec 13 Workers! Struggle for the Realization of Socialist Industrialization! 1. SCMP 709, 21.
- Dec 14 Promote Rural Savings Deposits for Accumulation of Production Funds for Coming Spring (Amended 12/17, p. 1), 1. SCMP 711, 18.
- Dec 14 Reorganize and Improve Primary School Education Step by Step, 3. SCMP 726, 24.
- Dec 15 Condemns American Side for Breaking Off Korean Peace Discussions, 1. SCMP 709, 7.
- Dec 16 Improvement of Living Must Be Conditioned on the Development of Production, 1. SCMP 720, 10.
- Dec 17 Supply and Marketing Cooperatives Should Go All-Out to Do a Good Job in Supplying Production Materials, 1.
- Dec 18 Make Determined Efforts to Win Greater Success in Production and Economy, 1. SCMP 714, 9.
- Dec 19 Hails Seventh Anniversary of Vietnamese War of Resistance, 4. SCMP 712, 6.
- Dec 20 Start and Develop Regular Education Work of Party Branches in Rural Villages, 1. SCMP 721, 11.
- Dec 21 A Good Way for Division of Labor between State-Operated Commerce and Cooperative Commerce, 1. SCMP 723, 16.
- Dec 22 Strengthen the Ideological Leadership of Institutions of Higher Education and Further Implement the Policy of the Party Toward Intellectual Elements, 1. SCMP 720, 24.
- Dec 23 Develop Textile Industry to Satisfy People's Needs, 2. SCMP 716, 4.
- Dec 24 Civil Affairs Work Must Serve General Line of State, 1. SCMP 717, 6.
- Dec 24 Denounces U.S.-Chiang Robbery on High Seas (Interception of Polish merchant vessel), 4. SCMP 715, 20.
- Dec 25 Pay Constant Attention to Increase Speed of Industrial Development of Our Country, 1. SCMP 715, 9.
- Dec 26 Explanation Work Must Be Continued (Ninety day explanation period), 1. SCMP 715, 36.
- Dec 26 Peking Press Voices Support for Recent Statement of Soviet Government on Prohibition of Atomic Weapons, 1. SCMP 715, 18 (summary).
- Dec 27 On Tremendous Success in China's Construction (Three steel mills begin production), 1. SCMP 715, 7.
- Dec 27 Hails Execution of Soviet Traitors (Beria group), 4. SCMP 715, 17.
- Dec 28 Direct the Peasants to Make a Good Job of Winter Production, 1. SCMP 725, 16.
- Dec 29 Review 1953 Experience in Industrial Construction, Greet New Victories, 1. SCMP 719, 10.
- Dec 30 Rouse the Peasants to Educate Themselves, 1. SCMP 727, 19.

1954

- Jan 1 Everything for the Implementation of the Nation's General Line, 1. SCMP 719, 2.
- Jan 4 The Fight to Ease International Tension, 1. SCMP 720, 1.
- Jan 5 We Must Persist in Persuasion and Education in Dealing with the Peasants (Work of purchasing grain), 1. SCMP 727, 23.
- Jan 6 Strengthen Production and Famine Relief Work along the General Line of the State, 1. SCMP 729, 19.
- Jan 7 Further Master the General Line of the Party during Transition Period, 1. SCMP 726, 11.
- Jan 8 Terms of Reference for NNRC (Neutral Nations Repatriation Commission) Should Be Fully Carried Out, 1. SCMP 724, 13.
- Jan 9 On Decision on Organized Farming, 2. SCMP 725, 23 (summary).
- Jan 10 Talks between the Two Sides Must Be Resumed at Once (Korean peace talks), 1. SCMP 724, 3.
- Jan 11 Propaganda on Workers' and Peasants' Alliance Must Be Intensified during Spring Festival, 1. SCMP 730, 13.
- Jan 12 On Development of Film Industry in China, 3. SCMP 727, 17 (summary).
- Jan 13 Strengthen Coordination and Cooperation between Various Branches of National Economy, 1. SCMP 732, 17.
- Jan 14 Draw a Lesson from the Case of Rubber Shoes for Army Use, 1. SCMP 737, 21.
- Jan 16 Give Active Leadership and Make Measured Advance to Strive to Realize Current Year's Plan of Developing Agricultural Producer Cooperatives, 1. SCMP 735, 11.
- Jan 17 Teach Rural Party and League Members to Love Farming Labor, 1. SCMP 735, 7.
- Jan 19 Mutual Aid Teams Constitute the Important Foundation of Agricultural Producer Cooperatives, 1. SCMP 735, 15.
- Jan 21 We Oppose the Handing Back of the POW's to the Former Detaining Sides, 1. SCMP 732, 2.
- Jan 21 Call for Study of Lenin's Teachings (30th anniversary of Lenin's death), 1. SCMP 733, 4.
- Jan 22 Strengthen the Cultural and Education Work for Worker and Peasant Cadres, 1. SCMP 740, 20.
- Jan 25 Surveying and Designing Plans Must Be Well Made to Meet Needs of National Construction, 1. SCMP 739, 18.
- Jan 26 Continue to Publicize the General Line of the State Penetratingly among the Peasants, 1. SCMP 741, 13.
- Jan 27 A Date for Resumption of Panmunjam Discussions Must Be Fixed at Once, 1. SCMP 737, 1.
- Jan 28 Industrial Production Targets for First Quarter of 1954 Must Be Fulfilled and Over-fulfilled, 1. SCMP 741, 18.
- Jan 29 Educate Rural Women in the Spirit of the General Line of the State, 1. SCMP 742, 15.
- Jan 30 Editorial on Foreign Minister Chou En-lai's Statement (On POW's), 4. SCMP 739, 5.
- Jan 31 Enthusiastic Purchase of National Construction Bonds, 1. SCMP 744, 5.
- Feb 1 Organize Martyrs' and Servicemens' Families to Take Part in National Construction, 1. SCMP 745, 9.
- Feb 2 Secondary School Education Work Should Take a Positive Step in Serving the General Line during the Transition Period, 1.

1954

Feb 6	Construction of the Yangtze River Bridge Has Great Significance, 1. SCMP 745, 7.
Feb 7	Foster "February 7" Revolutionary Spirit and Struggle to Implement the General Line of State for Transition Period, 1. SCMP 746, 5.
Feb 8	Give Play to Wang Chung-lun's Working Spirit to Fulfill National Plans ahead of Schedule, 1. SCMP 751, 11.
Feb 9	Positively Develop the Physical Culture Work of the Masses, 1. SCMP 748, 17.
Feb 10	Important Mission of Grain Work at Present, 1. SCMP 753, 15.
Feb 11	Strengthen the Normal Ties between Workers and Peasants, 1. SCMP 749, 8.
Feb 14	Friendship between China and Soviet Union Is Invincible (Fourth anniversary of Sino-Soviet treaty), 1. SCMP 747, 4.
Feb 17	Salute the People's Liberation Army (National people comforting PLA delegation), 1. SCMP 750, 12.
Feb 18	The Strengthening of Party Unity Is the Fundamental Guarantee for the Carrying Out of the General Line in the Transitional Period (Fourth plenum of Seventh Central Party Congress resolution), 1. SCMP 751, 5.
Feb 20	Complete Basic Level Elections Rapidly While Linking Up with Spring Production and Publicity on General Line, 1. SCMP 752, 25.
Feb 22	Editorial Supports Agreement on Geneva Conference (A step towards easing international tensions), 1. SCMP 752, 1.
Feb 23	Editorial Analyzes Berlin Conference, 1. SCMP 753, 1.
Feb 24	Simplify Administrative Machinery, Raise Work Efficiency, 1. SCMP 758, 15.
Feb 25	Reorganize Building Industry, Raise Construction Speed, 1. SCMP 764, 14.
Feb 28	Important Measures in China's History in the Solution of Nationality Problems, 1. SCMP 756, 4.
Mar 1	On Planned Purchase and Supply of Food (GAC order), 1. SCMP 759, 5.
Mar 3	Development of Heavy Industry Is the Central Link in Socialist Industrialization of the Country, 1. SCMP 762, 8.
Mar 4	Other Economic Enterprises Must Be Correspondingly Developed Simultaneously with Development of Heavy Industry, 1. SCMP 762, 12.
Mar 5	On Stalin Anniversary, 1. SCMP 761, 8.
Mar 8	Editorial Hails Molotov's Statement on Berlin Conference, 1. SCMP 762, 1.
Mar 10	Develop the Functions of Existing State-Operated Industrial Enterprises during Construction Period, 1. SCMP 773, 4.
Mar 11	Fully Develop the Functions of Local State-Operated Industries during Transition Period, 1. SCMP 777, 11.
Mar 12	Raise the Socialist Consciousness of the Working Class, 1. SCMP 769, 16.
Mar 13	U.S.-Japan Pact, New Yoke for Japanese People, 1. SCMP 766, 16.
Mar 15	Editorial Warmly Welcomes Korean Delegation, 1. SCMP 767, 2.
Mar 16	Strengthen Functions of Party Organizations in Enterprises to Ensure and Supervise Industrial Production, 1. SCMP 770, 15.
Mar 19	Fully Promote the Role of Technical Personnel in the Industrialization of the State, 1. SCMP 778, 8.
Mar 20	Make a Good Job of the Custody of Food to Consolidate the Achievements of the Grain Purchase Campaign, 1.
Mar 21	Learn from the Venus Medal Winners (Four winners of bumper harvest award), 1.
Mar 22	Study the Resolution of the Fourth Plenary Session and Properly Develop Criticism and Self-Criticism, 1. SCMP 779, 1.
Mar 23	Do Well People's Mediation Work to Strengthen People's Solidarity and Facilitate Production and Construction, 1. SCMP 784, 12.
Mar 24	Strengthen the Precautionary Work against Natural Calamities to Ensure the Security of Production Construction, 1. SCMP 780, 11.
Mar 25	Struggle for the Victorious Fulfillment of This Year's Plan for Cultural and Educational Enterprise, 1. SCMP 777, 17.
Mar 26	Develop Scientific Enterprise and Be of Better Service to Socialist Construction, 1.
Mar 27	Strive to Increase Cotton Production, 1. SCMP 782, 14.
Mar 28	Do Well the Advanced Purchase of Farm Products, 1. SCMP 788, 13.
Mar 29	Strive to Complete the Task of Spring Plowing and Sowing according to State Plan, 1. SCMP 785, 13.
Mar 30	Strengthen Further the Political and Legal Work during Period of Economic Construction, 1. SCMP 782, 10.
Mar 31	Further Strengthen Statistical Work during the Period of Economic Construction, 1. SCMP 784, 17.
Apr 1	Complete Preparations for Construction Work Immediately, 1. SCMP 805, 31.
Apr 3	U.S. Fears Talks, Fears Peace (Comment on U.S. position toward Geneva conference), 1. SCMP 781, 1.
Apr 4	Heighten Revolutionary Vigilance (Against sabotage of party unity), 1. SCMP 787, 1.
Apr 9	Success of Socialist Unity Party of Germany in Safeguarding the Unity of the Party (Suppression of anti-party clique), 1.
Apr 11	Enliven Primary Market, Intensify Interflow of Commodities between Cities and Counties, 1.
Apr 13	Preserve the Noble Qualities of Communist Party Members, Oppose the Base Individualism of the Bourgeois Class, 1. SCMP 793, 15.
Apr 14	Lead Handicraftsmen to the Path of Cooperativization, 1. SCMP 806, 29.
Apr 15	For Fulfillment of 1954 Capital Construction Plan, 1. SCMP 798, 22.
Apr 16	Summary of Editorial Hailing Anshan Exhibition, 1. SCMP 790, 42.
Apr 17	Propaganda on the Party's Task in Nationalities Question during the Period of Transition, 1. SCMP 795, 24.
Apr 18	Step Up the Production and Supply of Subsidiary Food, 1. SCMP 802, 25.
Apr 19	Get Well Prepared to Help 1954 Graduates of Middle and Primary Schools to Take Part in Production or Pursue Study in a Higher School, 1. SCMP 813, 22.
Apr 20	Party Committees Should Actively Lead Newspapers in the Current Development of Criticism and Self-Criticism, 1. SCMP 797, 26.
Apr 21	Mission of Chinese Delegation to Geneva, 1. SCMP 792, 4.
Apr 23	Observe Strictly the Principle of Collective Leadership, 1. SCMP 800, 27.
Apr 24	Nurture Qualified Higher Personnel for Financial and Economic Construction, 1. SCMP 807, 26.
Apr 26	Supply the Peasants Even More Capital Goods, 1.

1954

Apr 28	Consolidate Further Public Order in the Countryside, Safeguard Agricultural Production-Construction, 1. SCMP 805, 22.
Apr 30	Editorial on Sino-Indian Agreement on Tibet, 4. SCMP 799, 33 (summary).
May 1	Celebrate May Day, Strive for All-Round Fulfillment of State Plans, 1. SCMP 803, 13.
May 4	To Better Train the Younger Generation, 1. SCMP 802, 23.
May 6	Strengthen the Coordination of Production, Supply, and Sales to Fulfill the Production Plan of the Second Season, 1.
May 7	Maintain Modest Attitude, Oppose Conceit (Seventh plenum of fourth Central Party Congress plea), 1. SCMP 811, 21.
May 8	Strengthen People's Supervision Work, 1. SCMP 809, 45.
May 9	Editorial Hails Liberation of Dien Bien Phu, 1. SCMP 804, 37.
May 11	Strengthen City Traffic Control to Cope with Demand of National Construction, 1. SCMP 809, 50.
May 12	Peace Is the Desire of Millions (On Geneva conference), 1. SCMP 807, 1.
May 15	Take Active Steps to Cultivate Political and Judicial Construction Personnel, 1. SCMP 825, 26.
May 17	Correct the Business Policy of State Building Enterprises, 1. SCMP 825, 15.
May 18	Organize Seriously State-Led Primary Grain Markets in the Countryside, 1. SCMP 822, 17.
May 19	Consolidate the "Seek Instruction and Make Report" System, 1. SCMP 818, 25.
May 20	Establish and Operate Well the Circuit Courts, 1. SCMP 817, 26.
May 20	JMJP Condemns U.S.-Chiang's Piracy on High Seas, 1. SCMP 813, 14.
May 21	Strengthen Procurators' Work to Safeguard National Construction, 1. SCMP 821, 20.
May 23	Strengthen the Leadership of People's Professional Theatrical Troupes, 1.
May 25	Strive to Fulfill the Student Recruiting Task of the Institutions of Higher Education This Year, 1. SCMP 823, 44.
May 26	Concentrate Strength on Consolidation of the 95,000 Existing Agricultural Producer Cooperatives, 1. SCMP 822, 23.
May 27	Outstanding Example of Brotherly Love and Unity among Different Nationalities--Editorial on Ukraine Union with Russia Anniversary, 1. SCMP 821, 11.
Jun 1	Nurture the New Socialist Generation, 1.
Jun 2	New Steps Needed for World Peace (World Peace Council special session), 1. SCMP 821, 9.
Jun 4	Punish Sternly Persons Guilty of Corruption, 1. SCMP 828, 8.
Jun 5	For Improved Quality of Products, 1. SCMP 831, 12.
Jun 6	To Further Consolidate Labor Discipline, 1. SCMP 829, 12.
Jun 8	Develop Cultural Work in Factories and Mines, 1. SCMP 831, 27.
Jun 9	More on the Establishment of State-Led Rural Grain Markets, 1. SCMP 829, 9.
Jun 12	Actively Round Up and Severely Punish the Counter-Revolutionaries Still at Large, 1. SCMP 835, 9.
Jun 14	Find More Mineral Deposits for the Fatherland, 1. SCMP 834, 13.
Jun 16	Editorial on Draft Constitution, 1. SCMP 831, 6.
Jun 18	Exert Every Effort to Ensure Fulfillment of 1954 Budget, 1. SCMP 834, 1.
Jun 18	U.S. Cannot Change Korean Situation (Breakdown of Korean talks), 4. SCMP 832, 33 (extracts).
Jun 19	Strengthen Planned Purchase of New Wheat Crop, 1. SCMP 835, 13.
Jun 20	Greeting the Completion of Basic Level Elections throughout the Country, 1. SCMP 832, 5.
Jun 21	A Constitution Directed Toward the Building of Socialism, 1. SCMP 833, 5.
Jun 22	China's Constitution Is of the Socialist Type, 1. SCMP 835, 1.
Jun 24	Constitution Embued with Spirit of Equality, Fraternity, and Mutual Aid among Nationalities, 1. SCMP 836, 12.
Jun 25	Consolidate Peace in Korea (Fourth anniversary of Korean War), 1. SCMP 837, 35.
Jun 26	Sino-Indian Unity for Peace in the Far East and the Whole World (Chou En-lai's visit to India), 1. SCMP 837, 15.
Jun 27	JMJP and TKP Welcome Success of Stockholm Conference, 1. SCMP 837, 23 (summary).
Jun 29	Give Full Play to the Active Role of Young Workers in National Construction, 1. SCMP 843, 23.
Jun 30	Strive to Guarantee the Quality of Production Practice of Students of Institutes of Higher Learning and Secondary Technical Schools, 1. SCMP 848, 23.
Jul 1	Strengthen Party Discipline, 1. SCMP 847, 17.
Jul 2	The Correct Principle for Peaceful Coexistence among All Nations (Sino-Indian communique), 1. SCMP 841, 1.
Jul 3	The System of People's Congresses Is the State System of China, 1. SCMP 841, 28.
Jul 4	Strive for Comprehensive Fulfillment of Agricultural Production Plans, 1.
Jul 5	JMJP Hails Soviet Use of Atomic Energy for Peace, 1. SCMP 842, 7 (summary).
Jul 6	The Fundamental Rights and Duties of China's Citizens, 1. SCMP 843, 18.
Jul 7	Strengthen the Party's Guiding Policy of Rural Work (Amended 7/8, p. 3), 1. SCMP 848, 18.
Jul 8	To Further Educate Private Industrialists and Merchants To Be Patriotic and Law-Abiding, 1. SCMP 852, 29.
Jul 9	Oppose U.S. Military Intrigues in Asia, 1. SCMP 845, 28.
Jul 10	Nam Il Expresses Korean Will for Unification, 1. SCMP 845, 13.
Jul 11	Take Positive Steps in Teaching Students' Parents that To Labor Is Glorious, 1.
Jul 12	Persist in Efforts to Fulfill This Year's Plan to Step Up Production of Cotton, 1. SCMP 867, 14.
Jul 14	Exert Further Efforts for Early Peace in Indo-China, 1. SCMP 848, 5.
Jul 15	Raise the Level of Political and Artistic Cultivation of Art and Culture Cadres, 1.
Jul 16	U.S.-Chiang Aggression and Piracy Not To Be Tolerated, 1. SCMP 850, 1.
Jul 17	Universally Organize the Masses of the People to Discuss the Draft Constitution, 1. SCMP 865, 24.
Jul 18	Severely Sanction Criminals Who Disturb Social Order, 1. SCMP 856, 51.
Jul 20	Study More Profoundly the Resolution of Fourth Plenary Session, 1. SCMP 857, 41.

1954

Jul 21	Seriously Implement the Balancing of the Production and Marketing of Coal by Different Regions, and Reasonable Transportation Methods, 2.
Jul 22	Another Great Victory of Peaceful Negotiation (Geneva conference settles Indo-China question), 1. SCMP 854, 14.
Jul 22	Greet the Tenth Anniversary of the Polish Liberation, 3.
Jul 23	Chinese People Determined to Liberate Taiwan, 1. SCMP 855, 1 (summary and extracts).
Jul 24	The Honorable Mission of the PLA (Importance of modernization), 1. SCMP 856, 54.
Jul 26	Great Victory, Arduous Struggle (On Geneva conference), 1. SCMP 856, 2.
Jul 26	Supply and Marketing Cooperatives Must Carry Through the Policy of Serving Agriculture Production, 2.
Jul 27	JMJP Editorially Supports Soviet Proposal on Europe (Establishing European collective security), 1. SCMP 857, 32 (summary).
Jul 27	Korean Discussions Must Be Resumed (Anniversary of Korea armistice), 4. SCMP 857, 24 (summary).
Jul 28	Outrageous American Imperialist Aggression and Provocation (U.S. invasion of Chinese air and sea space), 1. SCMP 858, 1.
Jul 28	Chinese and German People Work for Peace (Chou En-lai's visit to East Germany), 4. SCMP 858, 15.
Jul 29	Strive for the Successful Distribution of Work among Graduates from Institutions of Higher Education, 1. SCMP 879, 28.
Jul 30	Draft Constitution Protects Women and Children, 1. SCMP 862, 24.
Jul 31	Bring into Full Play the Function of Rural Women in the Mutual Aid Campaign, 1.
Aug 1	Espionage Activities of U.S.-Chiang Brigands Must Be Smashed, 1. SCMP 860, 20.
Aug 2	Get Mobilized to Triumph Over Flood! (Amended 8/21, p. 2), 2. SCMP 861, 45.
Aug 3	Help Further All Agricultural Producer Cooperatives to Make a Good Job of Production Work, 2. SCMP 864, 55.
Aug 5	Economize Supplies, Overcome Wastes, 1. SCMP 887, 5.
Aug 7	Serious Waste and Confusions in Building Construction Must Be Overcome, 1. SCMP 887, 10.
Aug 8	JMJP Calls for Fulfillment of 1954 Farm Production Target, 1. SCMP 868, 13.
Aug 9	JMJP Greets Opening of WFDY (World Federation of Democratic Youth) Council Session, 1. SCMP 865, 12 (summary).
Aug 10	Soviet Proposal for Foreign Ministers' Conference Would Cement Peace, 1. SCMP 866, 1 (summary and extracts).
Aug 11	Thoroughly Implement Policy of Discriminate Construction for Cities, 1. SCMP 878, 23.
Aug 12	Seriously Do a Good Job in Managing Finance and Basic Construction in the Cultural and Educational Sectors, 1.
Aug 13	Strengthen the Building of New Industrial Areas, 1. SCMP 878, 26.
Aug 15	Work to Enhance China-Britain Relations (Welcoming the visit of the British Labor Party delegation to China), 1. SCMP 869, 13.
Aug 18	Make Good Use of Time to Speed Up Fulfillment of Plan to Study *History of CPSU(B)*, 1. SCMP 878, 20.
Aug 20	Justice Is Certain to Triumph (Chou En-lai's report on Taiwan liberation), 1. SCMP 874, 5.
Aug 21	Exert Great Efforts to Strengthen Economic Security Work, 1. SCMP 875, 48.
Aug 22	Make a Good Job of City Planning as Soon as Possible, 1. SCMP 916, 20.
Aug 23	Celebrating the Tenth Anniversary of the Liberation of Rumania, 3.
Aug 26	China Tolerates No U.S. Intervention in Taiwan's Liberation, Says JMJP (Democratic Partie's joint declaration), 1. SCMP 878, 1 (summary).
Aug 28	Reward Creative Work (GAC promulgation), 1.
Aug 29	Chiang's Crimes Must Be Ended, 1. SCMP 880, 1.
Aug 30	Editorial Condemns U.S. Act to Outlaw Communist Party, 1. SCMP 880, 22 (summary).
Aug 31	Importance Must Be Attached to the Question of Distribution of Profits of Agricultural Producer Cooperatives, 1. SCMP 890, 11.
Sep 1	Further Develop Peasants' Spare Time Cultural Education, 1.
Sep 4	Judicial Work Must Serve Economic Construction, 1. SCMP 885, 2.
Sep 5	JMJP Says Taiwan Compatriots Will Be Freed, 1. SCMP 883, 28.
Sep 6	Systematically Transform Capitalist Industry Beneficial to National Economy and People's Livelihood into Public-Private Jointly Operated Industry (GAC promulgation), 3. SCMP 884, 4.
Sep 7	Carry Through the Policy of Reforming Criminals Through Labor (GAC promulgates regulations), 1.
Sep 9	CPV Withdrawl Shows Good Faith for Korea Peace, 1. SCMP 885, 47.
Sep 9	Greet the Tenth Anniversary of the Liberation of Bulgaria, 1.
Sep 11	Firm Struggle Must Be Waged against Acts of Suppression of Criticism, 1. SCMP 911, 22.
Sep 12	Positively Develop Rural Credit Cooperatives, 1.
Sep 13	JMJP Editorial Condemns Southeast Asia Bloc, 1. SCMP 887, 28.
Sep 13	JMJP Editorial Calls for Vigilance against Spies (Shanghai sentences eight U.S. spies), 1. SCMP 887, 1.
Sep 14	Enforce Planned Purchase and Planned Supply of Cotton Cloth and Planned Purchase of Cotton (GAC orders), 1. SCMP 894, 8.
Sep 14	Forge Ahead on the Foundation of Victory in the First Year of Five-Year Plan (National Statistics Bureau report on 1953 economy), 2. SCMP 890, 8.
Sep 15	New Stage in the People's Democratic System in China (First session of first National People's Congress opens), 1. SCMP 889, 9.
Sep 15	Strengthen Financial Supervision of Capital Construction (GAC decision to establish Chinese People's Construction Bank), 2.
Sep 15	Make Efforts for Collective Peace in Europe, 4. SCMP 889, 16.
Sep 17	Carry Out Fully the Policy of Planned Purchase and Marketing of Cotton Cloth and Planned Purchase of Cotton, 1. SCMP 894, 13.
Sep 18	Correctly Develop the Improvement Campaign in Technology, 1.
Sep 20	Ensure Planned State Purchase of Cotton, 1. SCMP 894, 11.
Sep 21	The Constitution of the People's Republic of China--Powerful Weapon of the Chinese People for Building Up a Socialist Society, 1. SCMP 893, 2.

1954

Sep 22 Chinese People's Volunteers Divisions Return in Triumph, 1. SCMP 894, 30.
Sep 23 Exert Great Efforts in Increasing the Production of Oil-Bearing Crops and Improving the Supply of Cooking Oil, 1.
Sep 25 Cotton Merchants Should Follow the Policy of Unified Purchase and Distribution, 1.
Sep 29 A Milestone in the Historical Development of the People's Republic of China (First session of first National People's Congress closes), 4. SCMP 899, 1.
Oct 1 JMJP Reviews Five Years of Struggle (For peace, democracy, and socialism) (National Day editorial), 1. SCMP 900, 9.
Oct 2 JMJP Greets Opening of Soviet Exhibition (In Peking), 1. SCMP 900, 31 (summary).
Oct 4 Atom Weapons Must Be Banned, 1. SCMP 902, 30.
Oct 5 Strengthen the Preparation for Winter Work on Major Engineering Projects, 1.
Oct 6 Endeavor for Successful Planned Purchase of Grain This Year, 1. SCMP 919, 37.
Oct 7 JMJP Hails German People's National Day, 1. SCMP 904, 5.
Oct 8 The Initiative and Creativeness of Local State Organs Should Be Developed, 1. SCMP 907, 46.
Oct 9 Intensify Socialist Transformation of Capitalist Commerce, 1. SCMP 916, 17.
Oct 10 Germany Must Not Be Remilitarized (Comment on nine nation London conference), 1. SCMP 905, 13.
Oct 11 UN Must Stop U.S. Aggression against Taiwan (Chou En-lai's cable to UN), 1. SCMP 906, 10.
Oct 13 JMJP Editorial on Sino-Soviet Friendship (Sino-Soviet communique), 1. SCMP 907, 14.
Oct 15 Study Documents of First Session of first National People's Congress, 1. SCMP 913, 17.
Oct 16 Keep Up the Spirit of Production Increase and Economy, Fulfill 1954 National Economic Plans, 1. SCMP 917, 18.
Oct 17 New Soviet Aid to Our Construction Enterprise, 1. SCMP 915, 1.
Oct 18 Strive to Fulfill the Whole Year's Purchase and Distribution Plan for State Enterprises, 1.
Oct 19 Advance Sino-Indian Friendship and Consolidate Peace in Asia and the World (Nehru's visit to China), 1. SCMP 911, 7.
Oct 20 Implement the Correct Policy Toward Chinese Medicine, 1. SCMP 916, 22.
Oct 21 United Nations Must Condemn U.S. Aggression, 1. SCMP 913, 14 (summary).
Oct 22 Oppose Acts of Breach of Labor Discipline, 1. SCMP 922, 17.
Oct 23 Intensify Further Our Learning from Soviet Experts, 1. SCMP 919, 10.
Oct 24 JMJP Reviews China's Success in Fighting Flood, 1. SCMP 918, 12.
Oct 25 Speedy Peaceful Unification of Korea Urged (Fourth anniversary of CPV entering Korean War), 1. SCMP 915, 10 (summary).
Oct 27 New Development in Sino-Soviet Scientific and Technical Cooperation (Sino-Soviet agreement signed), 1. SCMP 917, 14.
Oct 28 Actively Fulfill the Autumn Sowing Duties According to State Plans, 1.
Oct 29 JMJP Urges Settlement of German Question, 1. SCMP 919, 18.
Oct 30 Consolidate and Develop Self-Instruction Organizations among Graduates of Urban Primary and Junior High Schools, 1.
Oct 31 JMJP Hails Sino-Indian Friendship, 1. SCMP 919, 1.
Nov 1 Introduce Compulsory Military Service to Increase Our Country's Defense Strength, 1. SCMP 921, 8.
Nov 2 Strengthen Control and Research in Medicinal Herbs, 1. SCMP 922, 30.
Nov 3 Inculcate on the People the Conscious Performance of Civil Duties, 1. SCMP 928, 9.
Nov 4 Current Pressing Tasks for State Enterprises, 1.
Nov 5 Cherish and Protect Public Property, 1.
Nov 6 Intensify Efforts to Fulfill 1954 Capital Construction Plan, 1. SCMP 928, 17.
Nov 7 Forever with Soviet Union (Anniversary of October Revolution), 1. SCMP 924, 14.
Nov 9 Industrial Products Should Be Sent Immediately to the Countryside, 1.
Nov 10 Resolutely Wipe Out the Activities of Rascals and Bandits, 1. SCMP 930, 10.
Nov 11 Draw Up 1955 National Economic Plan Seriously, 1. SCMP 934, 23.
Nov 12 Carry Through the Policy of Purchasing Even More Surplus Grain, and Strive for Overfilling the Task of Unified Grain Purchase, 1.
Nov 13 Strengthen Greatly the Spare Time Technical Education of Workers and Staff, 1.
Nov 14 Endeavor to Cultivate in the Younger Generation the Communist Virtues, 1. SCMP 930, 12.
Nov 15 Urgent Tasks of Capital Construction Workers, 1. SCMP 933, 23.
Nov 16 JMJP Editorial Hails Soviet Effort for European Peace, 1. SCMP 929, 1.
Nov 17 Benefits of Planned Purchase and Marketing of Grain to the Peasants, 1. SCMP 935, 24.
Nov 18 Intensify Education on Observance of Laws, 1. SCMP 937, 16.
Nov 19 Workers and Staff of the Light Industries Sector Should Strive to Economize the Use of Raw Materials, 1.
Nov 20 JMJP Editorial Refutes Dulles' Maniacal War Cry (Taiwan question), 1. SCMP 932, 1.
Nov 21 Socialist Ideological Education Must Be Conducted Penetratingly among the Peasants, 1. SCMP 942, 16.
Nov 23 To Actively Develop Credit Cooperatives, 1. SCMP 959, 17.
Nov 24 Further Strengthen the Association of State-Owned Commerce and Cooperative Commerce, 1. SCMP 945, 23.
Nov 25 Resolutely Smash the American Conspiracy to Subvert Our Nation through Spy Activities (Supreme People's Court sentences two U.S. spies), 1.
Nov 26 The Mongolian People's Thirty Glorious Years, 1.
Nov 27 JMJP Welcomes World Peace Council Call, 1. SCMP 936, 8 (summary).
Nov 28 Parents' Responsibility for Moral Education of Their Children, 1. SCMP 944, 17.
Nov 29 Albanian People Are Unconquerable (Tenth anniversary of Albanian liberation), 1. SCMP 937, 4.
Nov 30 The Chinese People Strongly Support the European Conference, 1. SCMP 938, 1.
Dec 2 Prime Minister U Nu's Visit Will Cement Peace, 1. SCMP 940, 8.
Dec 4 Moscow Joint Declaration Is Vital Step for European Peace, 1. SCMP 941, 26.
Dec 4 Make Timely Checkup and Improve the Work of Agricultural Producer Cooperatives, 2. SCMP 962, 15.

1954

Dec 5 Chinese People Determined to Liberate Taiwan (On U.S.-Taiwan common defense treaty), 1. SCMP 941, 2.
Dec 6 Machine Industry Should Intensify Planning and Raise the Standard of Production, 1.
Dec 7 Strive to Fulfill the Task of Unified Purchase of Cotton, 1.
Dec 8 Sincerely Carry Out the "Outline of Internal Labor Regulations for State-Operated Enterprises," 1.
Dec 10 The Mistakes of History Must Not Be Repeated (Chou En-lai's declaration on U.S.-Taiwan common defense treaty), 1. SCMP 946, 1.
Dec 12 Continue to Develop Further the Campaign of Technological Improvement, 1.
Dec 13 Combat Conceit among Leading Industrial Cadres, 1. SCMP 959, 10.
Dec 14 Chinese People Want Closer Friendship with Burma, 1. SCMP 948, 1.
Dec 15 Strengthen the Security Work in the Agricultural Mutual Aid and Cooperative Movement, 1. SCMP 960, 20.
Dec 16 Continue to Do a Good Job in Planned Supply of Cotton Cloth, 1.
Dec 19 Continue to Strive to Conquer Natural Disasters, 1.
Dec 20 Make Business Accounting the Work of the Masses, 1.
Dec 22 Wishing the Second CPPCC Satisfactory Accomplishment of Its Tasks, 1.
Dec 23 Greet the Flotation of 1955 National Economic Construction Bonds, 1. SCMP 956, 37.
Dec 24 The Dark Corners Must Not Be Allowed to Continue to Exist (Li Kwei-lin's suicide case), 1. SCMP 964, 24.
Dec 25 Create a Happy Life on the "Roof of the World"--Greet the Opening of Two Highways from Sikang and Tsinghai to Tibet, 1.
Dec 26 The Great Achievements of Three Months (Soviet economic and cultural construction exhibit closes), 1.
Dec 28 Chinese People Will Smash U.S.-Chiang Kai-shek Treaty, 1. SCMP 956, 4.
Dec 29 JMJP Editorial Urges Yet Closer Sino-Soviet Friendship (Sino-Soviet Friendship Association meeting), 1. SCMP 957, 5.
Dec 30 Normalization of Relations between Japan and China, 1. SCMP 958, 17.

1955

Jan 1 Meet the Tasks of 1955, 1. SCMP 959, 3.
Jan 1 JMJP Calls on Chiang Troops to Cross Over (Defense Ministry promulgates reward), 2. SCMP 959, 23.
Jan 2 Important Measures for Improving Basic Level Urban Political Power (Regulations promulgated), 1.
Jan 3 Prepare Production Personnel in New Enterprises, 1.
Jan 4 Conduct National Defense Education Regularly among the People, 1. SCMP 965, 13.
Jan 5 JMJP Editorial Welcomes Asian-African Conference, 1. SCMP 962, 3.
Jan 6 Propagate New Animal-Drawn Farm Tools, 1.
Jan 7 JMJP Editorial Urges Development of Silk Industry, 1. SCMP 964, 28.
Jan 8 For More Successful Suppression of the Enemy and Protection of the People (Arrest and detention regulations promulgated), 1. SCMP 966, 13.

1955

Jan 10 JMJP Editorial Supports Malenkov's New Year Statement, 1. SCMP 965, 5.
Jan 12 Do a Good Job in Ground Preparations Before Construction, 1.
Jan 15 Intensify Preparations for Spring Plowing, 1. SCMP 979, 19.
Jan 17 Every Accident Must Be Investigated and Dealt with Soberly, 1 SCMP 979, 22.
Jan 19 Two Different Courses on the Question of Atomic Energy, 1. SCMP 972, 1.
Jan 20 JMJP Editorial on Soviet Statement about Germany, 1. SCMP 973, 7.
Jan 21 PLA's Victories in Coastal Regions (Liberation of Yichangshan Island), 1. SCMP 973, 3.
Jan 22 Chinese Support World Peace Council's Call (Opposition to Paris agreement), 1. SCMP 974, 16.
Jan 23 Grasp the Winter and Spring Season to Develop Water Conservancy Work, 1.
Jan 24 The Glorious Task of Support for the Army and Care for Their Families, 1. SCMP 981, 18.
Jan 25 Properly Resettle Servicemen Demobilized for Construction and Transferred to Other Trades, 1. SCMP 990, 18.
Jan 27 The Key to Fulfillment of This Year's Capital Construction Plan, 1. SCMP 984, 23.
Jan 28 Don't Count On Subjective Wishes to Have Things Done (Hupei "collective housing" incident), 1. SCMP 983, 16.
Jan 29 Chinese People Resolutely Oppose U.S. War Provocations, 1. SCMP 977, 1.
Jan 30 Party's Basic Level Organizations in Rural Districts Should Strengthen Leadership over Agricultural Producer Cooperatives, 1. SCMP 983, 13.
Jan 31 "Ceasefire" Proposal Contravenes UN Charter, 1. SCMP 978, 1.
Feb 1 JMJP Supports Soviet Proposal (Taiwan straits problem), 1. SCMP 979, 1.
Feb 3 Have Regard for Indigent Laboring People, 1. SCMP 986, 15.
Feb 4 Reform Small Merchants and Peddlers in Rural Districts through Mutual Aid and Cooperation, 1. SCMP 999, 5.
Feb 5 JMJP Editorial Urges UN to Discuss Soviet Proposal (Taiwan straits problem), 1. SCMP 982, 1.
Feb 6 Supply and Marketing Cooperatives Should Adjust Retail Prices, 1.
Feb 7 Strengthen Financial Supervision over Capital Construction, 1. SCMP 1001, 16.
Feb 8 Help Transferred Cadres to Familiarize Themselves with Industries, 1.
Feb 9 JMJP Editorial on Tremendous Moral Support of Asian People for Chinese People's Struggle for Liberation of Taiwan, 1. SCMP 985, 6.
Feb 12 Strengthen Fight for Peace and Resolutely Oppose Menace of War, 1. SCMP 987, 17.
Feb 13 Signature Campaign Is Blow to Atomic War Schemes, 1. SCMP 987, 28.
Feb 14 JMJP Editorial Hails Alliance Anniversary (Sino-Soviet alliance) (Amended 2/15, p. 4), 2. SCMP 988, 5.
Feb 15 An Important Reform in Our Nation's Military System (Adoption of conscription), 1.
Feb 16 Redouble Efforts to Liberate Taiwan (Other offshore islands liberated), 1. SCMP 990, 1.
Feb 17 Conduct Well the Membership Meetings of the Party in Factories and Mines, 1. SCMP 997, 4.

1955

Feb 18 Support New Soviet Effort to Ease Tension in Far East (Soviet proposal to discuss Taiwan straits tension), 1. SCMP 992, 4.
Feb 19 Assist Agricultural Cooperatives to Cultivate Accounting Personnel, 1.
Feb 20 Intensify Agricultural Scientific Research Work, 1.
Feb 21 Support the Issue of New People's Currency, 1. SCMP 993, 16.
Feb 21 JMJP Urges Solidarity against Colonialism ("Anti-colonialism Day"), 4. SCMP 993, 40.
Feb 23 Strengthen Friendship between Chinese and Soviet Forces in Struggle for Defense of Peace (Soviet Union Army Day), 1. SCMP 994, 6.
Feb 25 JMJP on Immediate Tasks to Defend Peace (UN Disarmament Commission convenes in London), 1. SCMP 996, 42.
Feb 26 Japanese Have Choice of Two Different Paths, 1. SCMP 996, 37.
Feb 27 To Ensure that Scientific Workers Would Concentrate Their Efforts on Professional Activities, 1. SCMP 1003, 15.
Feb 28 Why Must Importance Be Given to Consolidation of Agricultural Producer Cooperatives? 1. SCMP 1002, 20.
Mar 1 Make a Good Job of Issuing New People's Currency, 1.
Mar 1 U.S. Schemes Behind Bangkok Conference, 1. SCMP 998, 1.
Mar 2 Planned Development of Local Industries Is Necessary, 1.
Mar 3 JMJP Editorial on Protection of Remittances from Overseas Chinese, 1. SCMP 999, 2.
Mar 3 U.S. Steps Up Sabotage of Geneva Agreements, 1. SCMP 1000, 1.
Mar 4 The Evil Results of Conceit (Taiyuan cadre abuse of power), 1. SCMP 1005, 12.
Mar 5 On Organizing Rural Spring Work, 1.
Mar 6 Fiction Not Fact in British Government POW Report, 1. SCMP 1001, 5.
Mar 6 U.S. Efforts to Abolish N.N.S.C. (Neutral Nations Supervisory Council in Korea) Exposed, 1. SCMP 1001, 2.
Mar 7 JMJP Analyzes Causes of Taiwan Tension, 1. SCMP 1002, 9.
Mar 8 Women of All China, Be Mobilized to Join the Gigantic Struggle for Socialist Construction of the Motherland, Liberation of Taiwan, and Safeguarding of Peace, 1. SCMP 1006, 15.
Mar 9 Publicize Fixed Production, Fixed Purchase, and Fixed Marketing of Grain Immediately among All Peasants, 1. SCMP 1010, 5.
Mar 10 Positively Utilize and Reform Rural Private Commerce, 1.
Mar 11 Strengthen the Role of Rural Party Branches as Bastions, 1. SCMP 1012, 6.
Mar 12 In Commemoration of Sun Yat-sen, the Great Democratic Revolutionist, 1. SCMP 1006, 2.
Mar 13 Geneva Agreements on Cambodia Must Be Observed, 1. SCMP 1006, 28.
Mar 13 New Stage Marked in Development of Tibet (Preparatory committees in autonomous region established), 1. SCMP 1006, 13.
Mar 14 Hong Kong British Government's Unjustifiable Act (Restrictions on Chinese emigration), 1.
Mar 14 Correctly Publicize Concrete Policy on Agricultural Cooperativization among the Peasants, 1. SCMP 1011, 1.
Mar 15 Do a Good Job in Supplying Capital Goods in Spring Farming, 1.
Mar 16 Let Publications Penetrate Villages to Promote the Mutual Aid Movement, 1.
Mar 17 JMJP Welcomes World Peace Council Decision Calling for Abolition of Nuclear Weapons, 1. SCMP 1010, 1.
Mar 18 Make Rational Use of College Graduates, 1. SCMP 1015, 13.
Mar 19 For the Conquest of Spring Famine, For a Bumper Harvest, 1. SCMP 1017, 4.
Mar 20 Endeavor to Develop Tea Production, 1.
Mar 21 Everybody Must Be Frugal in Grain Consumption, 1. SCMP 1018, 16.
Mar 22 What the State Industrial Enterprises Should Strive After, 1. SCMP 1022, 7.
Mar 24 Seriously Organize the Peasants' Year-Round Learning Program, 1.
Mar 25 Peasants! Let All Families Grow Oil-Bearing Crops, 1.
Mar 26 An Important Step for World Peace and European Security (JMJP editorial on eight nation consultations in Moscow), 1. SCMP 1016, 1.
Mar 27 Unprincipled Disputes Must Be Done Away With (Dairen industrial dispute), 1. SCMP 1026, 7.
Mar 28 Oppose Waste in Building Operations, 1. SCMP 1025, 6.
Mar 29 Build a Powerful People's Air Force (Conference of air force heroes opens), 1. SCMP 1018, 9.
Mar 30 Rectify the Capitalist Concept of Management in State-Operated Industries, 1. SCMP 1027, 9.
Mar 31 How to Implement This Year's Plan of Increasing Cotton Production, 1.
Apr 1 To Make a Greater Success of the State Mechanized Farms, 1. SCMP 1027, 12.
Apr 2 Exert Further Efforts to Develop Sino-Japanese Trade (Chinese trade delegation visits Japan), 1. SCMP 1021, 8.
Apr 3 Further Develop Cultural Activities of the Masses, 1.
Apr 4 Oppose Aggression, Coexist in Peace (JMJP editorial on Nehru's speech), 1. SCMP 1022, 13.
Apr 4 JMJP Honors Anniversary of Hungarian Liberation, 1. SCMP 1022, 17.
Apr 5 Struggle to Realize the Resolutions of the Party Congress, 1.
Apr 6 JMJP Welcomes Asian Countries Conference, 1. SCMP 1024, 2.
Apr 7 Basic Tasks of the First Five-Year Plan, 1. SCMP 1025, 1.
Apr 8 Peking and Tientsin Papers Denounce U.S. Atrocities, 1. SCMP 1025, 50.
Apr 8 Fight against Paris Agreements Will Go On, 1. SCMP 1025, 40.
Apr 9 New Developments in Sino-German Relations, 1.
Apr 10 Tremendous Victory of the Party in History (Purge of Kao Kang and Jao Shu-shih), 1. SCMP 1026, 3.
Apr 11 Subject Bourgeois Idealist Thought to Criticism, 1. SCMP 1034, 21.
Apr 12 Opportunely and Correctly Issue Agricultural Loans, 1.
Apr 12 JMJP Hails India-Vietnam Talks, 1. SCMP 1026, 21.
Apr 13 A Great Call in Defense of Asian Peace (Asian nations conference closed), 1. SCMP 1027, 16.

1955

- Apr 13 Plane Incident Is International Political Conspiracy (Sabotage of Chinese delegation to Afro-Asian conference), 1. SCMP 1027, 1.
- Apr 14 Mobilize the Whole Party and All People to Fight Bad Men and Bad Things (Party Central and Local Supervisory committees established), 1. SCMP 1034, 24.
- Apr 15 Peking Papers Hail Czechoslovak Exhibition, 1. SCMP 1030, 34.
- Apr 15 Adoption of Bureaucratic Attitude Toward Complaints Made by the Masses Must Not Be Allowed, 1. SCMP 1047, 18.
- Apr 16 Potentialities of Coal Mining Industry Should Be Actively Tapped, 1. SCMP 1039, 26.
- Apr 17 Carry Out Work to Retrench Personnel and to Simplify Organic Structure in Earnest, 1. SCMP 1042, 14.
- Apr 17 We Swear We Will Liberate Taiwan to Commemorate the Martyrs (Crash victims of Chinese delegates to Afro-Asian conference), 1. SCMP 1029, 24.
- Apr 18 JMJP Supports Talks on Austrian State Treaty (Soviet-Austrian talks), 1. SCMP 1030, 37.
- Apr 18 Greetings to the Triumphal Convening on the Asian-African Conference, 1. SCMP 1029, 3.
- Apr 19 Initial Results of Enforcement of Compulsory Military Service System, 1. SCMP 1031, 29.
- Apr 21 China To Increase High Yielding Crop Acreage, 1. SCMP 1035, 39.
- Apr 22 Study Lenin on Socialist Construction (Commemorating Lenin's birthday), 1. SCMP 1033, 51.
- Apr 22 Work for Success of Bandung Conference, 1. SCMP 1033, 22.
- Apr 23 Another Model of Peaceful Negotiations as Means for Solving International Problems (Sino-Indonesian agreement on dual nationality), 1. SCMP 1033, 29.
- Apr 24 Immediately Rely on the Masses to Reorganize Planned Marketing of Grain in Rural Districts, 1. SCMP 1043, 8.
- Apr 25 Glorious Tasks of Servicemen Demobilized for Transfer to Other Trades, 1. SCMP 1044, 29.
- Apr 26 Greet the Success of the Asian-African Conference, 1. SCMP 1034, 1.
- Apr 27 Reduce Building Cost, Raise Labor Productivity of Building Enterprises, 1. SCMP 1059, 29.
- Apr 28 JMJP Calls for More Young Pioneers, 1. SCMP 1037, 30.
- Apr 28 JMJP Welcomes Soviet, Polish Scientists, 1. SCMP 1037, 12.
- Apr 29 JMJP on Growing Sino-Indonesian Friendship (Sino-Indonesian communique), 1. SCMP 1038, 20.
- Apr 30 Civil Affairs Departments Should Take Tight Hold of Their Main Business, 1. SCMP 1044, 27.
- May 1 Work Like Heroes to Build Socialism, Urges JMJP, 1. SCMP 1038, 5.
- May 2 JMJP Welcomes Soviet Aid on Atomic Energy, 1. SCMP 1039, 1.
- May 3 Strive for the Prosperity and Improvement of Our Fine Arts, 1.
- May 4 Use Concrete and Practical Methods to Educate Youth, 1.
- May 5 Carry Out Keypoint Construction Policy, 1. SCMP 1047, 24.
- May 6 Carry Out the Policy of Overall Planning, Transform Capitalist Industry, 1. SCMP 1048, 32.
- May 7 The Leadership of Mutual Aid Teams Must Not Be Neglected, 1.
- May 8 Pay Attention to Commercial Work, 1. SCMP 1050, 15.
- May 9 The Tenth Anniversary of the Czechoslovakian Liberation, 1.
- May 9 Intensify Struggle for European Peace, 1. SCMP 1044, 1.
- May 10 Seize the Opportunity to Reorganize Planned Marketing of Grain in Rural Districts, 1. SCMP 1050, 9.
- May 11 Oppose the Corrosion of the Revolutionary Ranks by the Bourgeois Way of Life, 1. SCMP 1048, 26.
- May 12 Chinese People Support Warsaw Conference, Says JMJP, 1. SCMP 1047, 1.
- May 14 Launch an Overall Economy Drive, 1. SCMP 1054, 14.
- May 15 Establish Spare Time Higher Education, 1.
- May 15 British Seizure of Chinese Property Condemned (Chinese airline), 1. SCMP 1048, 49.
- May 16 JMJP Welcomes Signing of Austrian State Treaty, 1. SCMP 1049, 11.
- May 17 JMJP Hails Warsaw Achievements for Peace, 1. SCMP 1050, 1.
- May 18 Carry the Struggle against Criminals and Robbers to the End, 1.
- May 19 Attention Should Be Paid to Enrollment of New Party Members in Rural Districts, 1. SCMP 1056, 12.
- May 20 Further Mobilize Junior Middle School and Higher Primary School Graduates to Engage in Productive Labor, 1. SCMP 1059, 25.
- May 21 Stop Overstocking and Waste of Supplies, 1. SCMP 1061, 22.
- May 22 Wholesale Business with Private Merchants Must Be Strengthened, 1. SCMP 1070, 8.
- May 23 Educate and Observe Candidate Members Seriously, 1. SCMP 1057, 15.
- May 24 Endeavor to Raise the Level of Machine Building Industry, 1. SCMP 1061, 31.
- May 25 Public-Private Jointly Operated Enterprises Should Be Run Successfully, 1. SCMP 1065, 24.
- May 26 JMJP Welcomes Indonesian Prime Minister, 1. SCMP 1057, 4.
- May 27 Produce More and Better Fruit, 1.
- May 28 JMJP on Air Sabotage (Chinese delegation blown up by Nationalist agents), 1. SCMP 1058, 4.
- May 29 Make the Emulation Drive a Mass Movement of the Broad Workers and Staff Members, 1. SCMP 1063, 1.
- May 30 JMJP on Friendly Contact between Indonesia and China, 1. SCMP 1058, 30.
- May 31 Reform the Railway Rates System, 1. SCMP 1063, 14.
- Jun 1 Cultivate Children with Socialist Views and Methods, 1. SCMP 1064, 11.
- Jun 2 JMJP on Success of Sino-Egyptian Talks, 1. SCMP 1062, 18.
- Jun 2 JMJP on China-Indonesia Friendship Association, 1. SCMP 1061, 8.
- Jun 3 Important Steps to Strengthen Leadership Over Scientific Work (Chinese Academy of Sciences establishes departments), 1. SCMP 1064, 14.
- Jun 4 Grasp Time to Complete Anti-Flood Preparatory Work, 1. SCMP 1069, 1.

1955

Jun 5	Soviet-Yugoslav Declaration Vital Contribution to Peace, Says JMJP (Relations normalized), 1. SCMP 1062, 10.
Jun 6	Do a Good Job of Summer Planting in the Valleys of the River Huai and Yellow River, 1.
Jun 7	The New Tasks in the Wholesale Business of State-Owned Commerce, 1. SCMP 1068, 3.
Jun 8	JMJP Welcomes Statement on Vietnam General Elections, 1. SCMP 1065, 5.
Jun 9	Give Concrete Guidance to Worker's Economy Drive, 1. SCMP 1071, 13.
Jun 10	A Lesson Must Be Learned from the Hu Feng Incident, 1. SCMP 1070, 14.
Jun 11	JMJP on Soviet-West German Relations (Soviet proposal to establish relations), 1. SCMP 1067, 4.
Jun 12	Help Industrial Cadres Learn Their Trade, 1. SCMP 1074, 7.
Jun 13	Cotton Field Management Has to Be Strengthened, 1.
Jun 14	Advance the Promotion of Sino-Indian Cultural Exchange (Indian cultural delegation visits China), 1.
Jun 15	Strengthen Education of Middle and Primary School Students in Spontaneous Observance of Discipline, 1. SCMP 1074, 4.
Jun 17	Uphold the Dignity of Party Discipline, 1. SCMP 1076, 3.
Jun 18	Planned Marketing of Food in Cities Must Also Be Seriously Adjusted, 1. SCMP 1078, 16.
Jun 19	Resolutely Lower the Standards of Buildings of a Nonproductive Nature, 1. SCMP 1076, 5.
Jun 20	UN Should Return to Its Charter Says JMJP (Tenth anniversary of UN), 1. SCMP 1073, 24.
Jun 21	The Role of State Supervision Should Be Brought into Full Play in Combating Waste, 1. SCMP 1078, 20.
Jun 22	JMJP Welcomes World Peace Assembly, 1. SCMP 1075, 3.
Jun 23	The Guiding Principles and Policy of Present Cultural and Educational Work Should Be Correctly Implemented, 1. SCMP 1080, 7.
Jun 24	U.S.-Cambodia Military Pact Violates Geneva Accord Says JMJP, 1. SCMP 1077, 39.
Jun 25	JMJP Welcomes President Ho Chi Minh, 1. SCMP 1077, 6.
Jun 25	Soviet-Indian Friendship Contributes to Peace Says JMJP (Communique), 1. SCMP 1077, 33.
Jun 26	The Lessons from the Adjustment of Planned Marketing of Food in the Rural Areas, 1. SCMP 1083, 13.
Jun 27	Stamp Out Hidden Counter-Revolutionaries, and Safeguard the Mutual Aid Movement in Agreculture, 1.
Jun 28	Strive for the Road of Lasting Peace and International Safety, 1.
Jun 28	JMJP Discusses Spreading Influence of Five Principles (Anniversary of Sino-Indian communique), 1. SCMP 1079, 1.
Jun 29	Economy Must Also Be Practiced in Industrial Capital Construction, 1. SCMP 1087, 4.
Jun 30	A Good Job Must Be Made of Work to Enroll Students for Institutions of Higher Education This Year, 1. SCMP 1088, 13.
Jul 1	Oppose Empty Talk about Economy, 1. SCMP 1089, 10.
Jul 2	JMJP on Helsinki Achievements (World Peace Council), 1. SCMP 1081, 19.
Jul 3	Stamp Out All Hidden Counter-Revolutionaries, 1. SCMP 1087, 9.
Jul 4	Strive to Realize This Year's Oil-Bearing Crops Production Plan, 1.
Jul 5	JMJP on Tasks of National People's Congress, 1. SCMP 1082, 4.
Jul 6	Strictly Economize Investment in Temporary Engineering Works, 1.
Jul 7	Fulfill the Task of Summer Grain Unified Purchase on the Basis of the "Three Fixed" Policy (Fixed production, purchase, and marketing), 1.
Jul 8	Struggle for the Total Fulfillment of the First Five-Year Plan, 1.
Jul 9	JMJP Welcomes Sino-Vietnamese Talks (Communique), 1. SCMP 1085, 11.
Jul 10	Ensure Realization of the 1955 State Budget, 1. SCMP 1090, 12.
Jul 11	Vigorously Develop the Enterprise of Credit Cooperatives, 1.
Jul 12	Oppose Neglect of Politics, 1. SCMP 1091, 9.
Jul 13	Actively Improve Movie Projection Work, 1.
Jul 14	Mothers' Will for Peace Is Invincible, Says JMJP (World mothers' conference), 1. SCMP 1089, 28.
Jul 15	Cadres Must Learn Natural Science, 1.
Jul 16	Guard against Infiltration of Class Enemy into Party, 1. SCMP 1093, 7.
Jul 17	Strengthen Labor Distribution Work and Overcome Waste of Labor, 1.
Jul 18	JMJP Welcomes Big Four Conference (Geneva conference), 1. SCMP 1091, 26.
Jul 19	Strictly Economize the Bureaucracy's Administration Fees (Amended 7/23, p. 4), 1.
Jul 20	"Conquering Nature"; Says JMJP on Yellow River Plan, 1. SCMP 1093, 1.
Jul 21	Pham Van Dong's Note "An Important Step" Says JMJP, 1. SCMP 1094, 36.
Jul 22	The Guiding Policy of Solving Our Country's Food Problem (Speech of Chen Yun in the NPC), 1.
Jul 23	Strive to Fulfill the Task of Increasing Grease Production by One Hundred Thousand Tons, 1.
Jul 24	Verification of Food Supply Work in the Cities Must Be Well Done, 1.
Jul 25	The Masses Must Be Extensively Mobilized to Fight Hidden Counter-Revolutionaries, 1. SCMP 1101, 11.
Jul 26	The Positive Achievements of the Big Four Conference, 1.
Jul 27	Dispose of Reactionary, Obscene, and Bizarre Books with Resolution (State Council promulgates regulations), 1.
Jul 28	Distinguish Different Circumstances and Implement the Policy of Economizing Capital Construction, 1.
Jul 29	JMJP on Rational Distribution of Graduates from Institutions of Higher Education This Summer, 1. SCMP 1102, 8.
Jul 30	Endeavor to Cultivate Construction Cadres, 1.
Jul 31	Exert Double Efforts to Build Our Great Motherland (Second plenum of first NPC closed), 1.
Aug 1	JMJP Says Military Service Law Ensures National Defense, 1. SCMP 1100, 15.
Aug 3	Help Urban Grain Consumers Solve Three Problems, 1. SCMP 1106, 10.
Aug 4	Attach Importance to the Work of Economizing Food in Collective Food Units, 1.
Aug 5	Promote Small-Scale Daytime Nursery Schools and Kindergartens, 1.

1955

Aug 6	Continue to Struggle to Ban the Atomic and Hydrogen Bombs (Hiroshima conference), 1.
Aug 7	Continue Efforts to Put an End to the Cold War (Soviet report on Geneva conference), 1.
Aug 8	International Cooperation for the Peaceful Use of Atomic Energy Urged (Geneva conference), 1.
Aug 9	Project Budget an Important Link in Saving Funds, 1. SCMP 1113, 16.
Aug 10	Patriotism and Observance of Laws, the Condition and Hallmark of Accepting Transformation by Capitalist Industrialists and Merchants, 1. SCMP 1110, 14.
Aug 11	Make a Good Job of Mobilizing Middle School and Primary School Graduates to Engage in Productive Labor, 1.
Aug 12	Stop Rhee's Provocation, Says JMJP, 1. SCMP 1109, 1.
Aug 13	Carry Out General Checkup of Private Commerce and Food Trade, 1. SCMP 1110, 11.
Aug 14	Eliminate Waste in State-Owned Mechanized Farms, 1. SCMP 1119, 23.
Aug 15	JMJP Pays "Admiration and Respect" for Korean People (Amended 8/19, p. 4), 1. SCMP 1110, 4.
Aug 16	JMJP Urges Action to Ensure Geneva Accords (Condemns Diem's refusal to discuss general elections), 1. SCMP 1111, 1.
Aug 17	Seriously Review the Work of the Resettlement of Servicemen Demobilized for Construction, 1. SCMP 1124, 2.
Aug 18	Sincere Efforts to Settle Korean Question Urged by JMJP, 1. SCMP 1113, 8.
Aug 19	Make Determined Efforts to Fulfill This Year's Agricultural Production Increase Plan, 1. SCMP 1122, 4.
Aug 20	Greatly Economize Raw Materials in Industrial Production, 1. SCMP 1128, 14.
Aug 21	Cultivate the Communist Character of Youth in Actual Struggle, 1. SCMP 1136, 4.
Aug 22	Be Sincere and Honest (Amended 8/30, p. 3), 1. SCMP 1122, 1.
Aug 23	The Task of the Workers and Employees of the Machine Industry, 1. SCMP 1124, 8.
Aug 24	Indians Fight for Goa Certain of Victory, Says JMJP, 1. SCMP 1117, 20.
Aug 25	An Important Measure in Our Nation's Grain Work (Unified purchase and sale and rationing of grain announced), 1.
Aug 26	JMJP on Sino-Egyptian Trade Agreement, 1. SCMP 1119, 11.
Aug 27	Resolutely Implement the Method of Rationing Grain Supply, 1.
Aug 28	Mobilize the Masses More Extensively to Join the Struggle for Rounding Up Counter-Revolutionaries, 1. SCMP 1133, 25.
Aug 29	New Developments in the Work of Unified State Purchase and Supply of Grain, 1.
Aug 29	JMJP Welcomes Yugoslav Artists, 1. SCMP 1120, 37.
Aug 30	Illegal Decision of I.P.U. Protested by JMJP (Barring China's participation), 1. SCMP 1120, 3.
Aug 31	Utilize the Progressiveness and Creativity of Workers, Struggle for the Victorious Accomplishment of the Five-Year Plan, 1.
Sep 1	Stamp Out Counter-Revolutionary Elements in Every Nook and Corner, 1. SCMP 1133, 38.
Sep 2	JMJP Supports Vietnam's Struggle for Unification, 1. SCMP 1123, 6.
Sep 3	JMJP Reviews the Ten Years Since V.J. Day, 1. SCMP 1123, 1.
Sep 4	Inhabitants of Towns Should Support Measures for Fixed Supply of Grain, 1. SCMP 1131, 5.
Sep 5	Strengthen the Education of Juveniles and Children with Scientific Techniques, 1. SCMP 1138, 22.
Sep 6	Positively Cultivate the New Source of Strength in Scientific Research Work, 1. SCMP 1129, 31.
Sep 7	Expand the Economy Movement among State-Owned Commercial Departments (Amended 10/2, p. 2), 1. SCMP 1130, 9.
Sep 8	Peasants, Take Action to Implement the "Three Fixed" Policy, 1. SCMP 1131, 7.
Sep 9	Do a Good Job of the Supply of Industrial Goods during the Brisk Business Season, 1. SCMP 1134, 22.
Sep 10	Strengthen Party Leadership in Trade Union Work, 1.
Sep 11	The Tasks of the Workers and Employees of the Coal Industry, 1. SCMP 1139, 23.
Sep 12	JMJP on Sino-American Agreement, 1. SCMP 1128, 1.
Sep 13	Two Methods of Propagating Food Grain Work with Great Fanfare, 1.
Sep 14	JMJP on Truth about Chinese and Japanese Residents, 1. SCMP 1130, 20.
Sep 15	Momentous Reform of the System of Pay and Allowance for Government Employees, 1. SCMP 1134, 13.
Sep 16	JMJP Says Moscow Talks a Great Achievement (USSR and W. Germany talks), 1. SCMP 1132, 13.
Sep 17	Reorganize the Financial and Accounting Work in Agricultural Producer Cooperatives, 1. SCMP 1149, 8.
Sep 18	Geneva Agreements Must Be Fully Carried Out, 1. SCMP 1132, 19.
Sep 19	For All-Round and Greater Overfulfillment of This Year's Industrial Production Plan, 1. SCMP 1142, 8.
Sep 20	Let the Younger Generation Radiate Great Light and Heat (Conference of Young Socialist Builders opens), 1. SCMP 1140, 13.
Sep 21	JMJP Urges UN Efforts to Ease World Tension, 1. SCMP 1135, 1.
Sep 22	The Great Achievements of Soviet-Finnish Talks, 1.
Sep 23	Continue to March Forward in Victory, Create Better Conditions to Complete the Five-Year Plan (National Statistics Bureau publishes 1954 national economy report), 1.
Sep 23	Treaty on Relations between Soviet Union and Democratic Germany Welcomed, 1. SCMP 1137, 52.
Sep 24	JMJP Protests at UN Vote on China, 1. SCMP 1137, 27.
Sep 25	Make a Good Job of the Distribution of the Autumn Crop in Agricultural Producer Cooperatives, 1. SCMP 1149, 11.
Sep 25	Harvest and Thresh Meticulously to Ensure a Bumper Harvest, 1.
Sep 26	Strive for Fulfillment of This Year's Capital Construction Plan, 1. SCMP 1148, 3.
Sep 27	Make a Thorough Job of Carrying the "Three Fixed" Grain Policy Down to the Household Level, 1. SCMP 1147, 7.
Sep 28	Important Measure in the Modernization and Regularization of China's Army Forces (Ranks in PLA implemented), 1. SCMP 1147, 3.
Sep 29	Strive to Foster More Young Activists (Conference of Young Socialist Builders ends), 1. SCMP 1145, 11.

1955

Sep 30 JMJP on Sinkiang-Uighur Autonomous Region, 1. SCMP 1141, 60.
Oct 1 JMJP Greets National Day, 1. SCMP 1141, 16.
Oct 2 Develop Staff's and Worker's Physical Education Movement (First National Worker's Sports Meet opens), 1.
Oct 3 JMJP on Soviet Disarmament Proposals, 1. SCMP 1142, 26.
Oct 4 What Must Be Attended To in This Year's Cotton Unified Purchase, 1.
Oct 5 Good Harvests in USSR and People's Democracies, 1. SCMP 1144, 20.
Oct 6 Do a Good Job in Supplying Capital for the Purchase of Farm Produce, 1.
Oct 7 Make Efforts to Promote the Double-Wheel Double-Blade Plow, 1.
Oct 8 Improve the Non-Staple Food Supply Work in Cities and Mining Districts, 1.
Oct 9 Strictly Economize Metal Use, 1.
Oct 10 Exalt the Achievements of the National Workers' Sports Tournament, 1.
Oct 11 Reward the Creative Work of Scientists (Chinese Academy of Sciences establishes reward) (Amended 10/13, p. 3), 1. SCMP 1156, 18.
Oct 12 JMJP Urges Fresh Effort to Solve Korean Question (Another Chinese People's Volunteers troop withdrawl), 1. SCMP 1149, 34 (summary).
Oct 13 Store Well the Sweet Potato Crops Harvested This Year, 1. SCMP 1150, 1 (summary).
Oct 14 Dulles Prepares to Obstruct Geneva, Says JMJP, 1. SCMP 1151, 24 (summary).
Oct 15 Servicemen Demobilized for Construction Must Contribute Meritorious Service to Agricultural Cooperativization, 1. SCMP 1158, 15.
Oct 16 Deliver Means of Production and Means of Subsistence in Large Quantities into the Hands of Peasants, 1. SCMP 1156, 10.
Oct 18 Translate the Resolutions of the Sixth Plenary Session of the Seventh Central Committee Satisfactorily into Reality, 1. SCMP 1156, 8.
Oct 19 JMJP on Sino-Japanese Relations (Japan diet members visit China), 1. SCMP 1153, 15 (summary).
Oct 20 U.S. Should Renounce the Use of Force, Says JMJP, 1. SCMP 1154, 3.
Oct 22 There Must Be Active and Planned Leadership of the Movement for the Cooperativization of Agriculture, 1. SCMP 1158, 11.
Oct 23 Grain Supply Program Should Be Seriously Carried Out in Towns, 1. SCMP 1163, 5.
Oct 24 Annual Plan for 1956 Must Be Well Drawn Up, 1. SCMP 1160, 13.
Oct 25 Pay Attention to Quality in the Development of Agricultural Producer Cooperatives, 1. SCMP 1161, 10.
Oct 26 Strive to Promote the Reform of Chinese Characters, the Popularization of Mandarin, and the Standardization of the Chinese Spoken Language, 1. SCMP 1164, 11.
Oct 27 Welcome to Geneva Four-Power Conference of Foreign Ministers, 1.
Oct 28 Guard against Counter-Revolutionary Sabotage of Cooperativization Movement, 1. SCMP 1167, 6.
Oct 29 The Masses Must Be Mobilized for the Overall Planning of Agricultural Cooperativization, 1. SCMP 1162, 23.
Oct 30 Constantly Reorganize Party Rural Branches in Midst of Cooperative Building and Reorganization, 1. SCMP 1164, 3.
Oct 31 JMJP Supports Soviet Collective Security Proposal, 1. SCMP 1161, 2 (summary).
Nov 1 Solve Problems as Soon as They Are Encountered (Party committee leadership in Agricultural Producer Cooperatives movement), 1. SCMP 1167, 4.
Nov 2 Rely on Rural Party Branches for Running Agricultural Producer Cooperatives Successfully, 1. SCMP 1168, 11.
Nov 3 JMJP on East-West Contacts, 1. SCMP 1164, 33.
Nov 4 Speedily Complete Autumn and Winter Plowing on Schedule, 1.
Nov 5 Enthusiastically Mobilize Women to Participate in the Agricultural Producer Cooperative Movement, 1.
Nov 6 Soviet-Burmese Friendship Warmly Welcomed by JMJP, 1. SCMP 1165, 30.
Nov 7 JMJP Greets October Socialist Revolution Anniversary, 1. SCMP 1166, 27 (summary).
Nov 8 Promote the Positive Role of the Young People in Rural Areas in the Agricultural Cooperation Movement, 1. SCMP 1177, 13.
Nov 9 Cooperativization Should Be the Pivotal Task of Party Organs in Rural Areas, 1. SCMP 1173, 11.
Nov 10 Carry Out Well the Storing of Autumn Grain, 1.
Nov 11 Model Regulations for Agricultural Cooperatives (Regulations promulgated), 1. SCMP 1169, 14.
Nov 12 Don't Let the Rural Market Run Out of Consumer Goods, 1.
Nov 13 Local Industry Must Thoroughly Implement Policy of Serving Rural Economy, 1.
Nov 14 Question of Disarmament in Four-Power Foreign Ministers Conference, 1.
Nov 15 Manifest the Positive Quality of All Party Members, Strengthen the Work of Party Organizations in Enterprises, 1.
Nov 15 Writers and Artists, Go to the Rural Areas, 1.
Nov 16 Systematically Arrange Rural Work This Winter, 1.
Nov 17 Rectify the Phenomenon of Limiting Poor Peasants' Joining Cooperatives, 1.
Nov 18 JMJP Urges Conference on Korean Question, 1. SCMP 1174, 25.
Nov 19 JMJP on Four-Power Foreign Minister's Conference, 1. SCMP 1174, 21.
Nov 20 JMJP Welcomes Soviet Leader's Asian Visit (Khruschov's visit to India), 1. SCMP 1174, 35 (summary).
Nov 20 JMJP on Sino-Japanese Relations, 1. SCMP 1174, 30.
Nov 21 UN Membership Should Be Universal, 1.
Nov 22 Earnestly Carry Out the Transformation of Capitalist Industry and Commerce with Unified Understanding and Overall Planning, 1.
Nov 23 Strengthen City Planning Work, Reduce Building Costs in Municipal Construction, 1. SCMP 1181, 3.
Nov 24 Solve New Problems, Consolidate Cooperatives, 1. SCMP 1180, 6.
Nov 25 Promote Conversion of Industry into Public-Private Joint Ownership by Whole Trades with Preparation and Steadily, 1. SCMP 1182, 5.

1955

Nov 26   Educate the Peasants to Economize the Consumption of Grain, 1. SCMP 1183, 13.

Nov 27   Support the Japanese People in Struggle against the Maintenance of American Military Bases in Their Country, 1.

Nov 28   Recruit New Party Members while Overhauling and Building Agricultural Producer Cooperatives, 1. SCMP 1186, 10.

Nov 29   JMJP Greets Yugoslav Tenth Anniversary, 1. SCMP 1180, 33.

Nov 30   Eliminate Medical Accidents, 1.

Dec 1   Emulate Advanced Producers so as to Fulfill Annual Plans in a Better Way, 1. SCMP 1191, 11.

Dec 2   Strengthen Research Work in Antibiotics, 1.

Dec 2   Japanese Relations with China and USSR, 1. SCMP 1183, 37.

Dec 3   Equitably Appraise and Fix Output of Land Turned Over to Agricultural Cooperatives, 1. SCMP 1189, 16.

Dec 4   Lesson Learned through the Sinking of Dredge "Hsi Ho," 1.

Dec 5   Keep the Rural Market Continuously Supplied with Industrial Products during the Winter, 1.

Dec 6   Basically Eliminate Illiteracy among the Country's Youth within Seven Years, 1. SCMP 1188, 5.

Dec 7   The Management of Cooperative Members' Means of Production Should Have Adequate Prior Consultations, 1.

Dec 8   JMJP Welcomes German Government Delegation, 1. SCMP 1187, 16.

Dec 9   JMJP Welcomes Soviet-Burmese Joint Communique (Khruschov's visit), 1. SCMP 1188, 49 (summary).

Dec 10   Counter-Revolutionaries Will Never Be Allowed to Exploit Religion for Subversive Activities (Shanghai counter-revolutionary group), 1. SCMP 1207, 19.

Dec 11   Organize the Participation of Middle and Primary School Graduates in the Agricultural Cooperation Movement, 1.

Dec 13   Don't Be Conceited when Hearing of Victory (Development of agricultural cooperatives), 1. SCMP 1193, 10.

Dec 14   Expand the Socialist Transformation of Private Commerce in Cities, 1. SCMP 1196, 3.

Dec 15   Manufacture More, Better, and Cheaper New Farm Implements (Amended 12/17, p. 2), 1.

Dec 17   Strengthen the Leadership over Cultural Work in Factories and Mines, 1.

Dec 18   Stop the Falling Prices for Draft Animals, 1. SCMP 1200, 15.

Dec 19   Party Organizations in Industrial Enterprises Must Be Near the Masses, 1. SCMP 1199, 3.

Dec 20   Important Steps in Strengthening Research Work on Chinese Medicine (Research institute established), 1. SCMP 1200, 6.

Dec 21   JMJP Welcomes Soviet-Afgan Developments (Khruschov's visit), 1. SCMP 1196, 17.

Dec 22   Turn Out More and Better New Products, 1. SCMP 1205, 14.

Dec 23   Advance Purchase of Cotton Must Be Arranged on Time, 1. SCMP 1200, 11.

Dec 24   Chinese People Support Korean-German Joint Communique (Garaudy's visit to Korea), 1. SCMP 1199, 34.

Dec 25   The Valuable Initiative in Advance Fulfillment of Economic Targets, 1. SCMP 1199, 10.

Dec 26   JMJP Welcomes Growth of Sino-German Friendship (Treaty signed), 1. SCMP 1198, 41.

Dec 27   Mongolian-Indian Diplomatic Relations Welcomed by JMJP, 1. SCMP 1199, 42.

Dec 28   Continue to Rectify the Practice of Rejecting the Poor Peasants, 1. SCMP 1206, 13.

Dec 29   Strive to Purchase Cotton, Hemp, and Tobacco, 1.

Dec 30   JMJP on the Growth of Mongolian-German Friendship (Garaudy's visit to Mongolia), 1. SCMP 1201, 51.

Dec 30   Develop the Rural Broadcasting Network, 1. SCMP 1204, 8.

Dec 31   Expand Socialist Transformation of Handicrafts, 1. SCMP 1207, 4.

1956

Jan 1   Strive for the Overall Fulfillment and Overfulfillment of the Five-Year Plan ahead of Schedule, 1,2. SCMP 1201, 8.

Jan 2   Year of Advance for Peace and Anti-Colonialism, 1. SCMP 1202, 37.

Jan 3   Make a Better Job of the Transformation of Private Industry and Commerce, 1. SCMP 1210, 6.

Jan 4   JMJP Hails Friendship Railway, 1. SCMP 1203, 16.

Jan 5   JMJP Greets the Birth of the Republic of Sudan, 1. SCMP 1204, 36.

Jan 6   Speed Up Progress of Designing Supply Blueprints Early, 1. SCMP 1209, 6.

Jan 7   JMJP Greets Victory of French Communists, 1. SCMP 1205, 44.

Jan 8   Strive to Meet the Demand of Peasants for Popular Reading Matter, 1. SCMP 1213, 16.

Jan 9   Overfulfill the Task of Subscribing to National Economic Construction Bonds, 1. SCMP 1212, 4.

Jan 10   All Should Learn and Use the Vanguards' Experiences, 1.

Jan 11   Gigantic Victory in the Transformation of Private Industry and Commerce, 1. SCMP 1214, 17.

Jan 12   Get Rid of Four Pests, 1. SCMP 1215, 11.

Jan 13   The Great Victory in the Socialist Transformation of Handicrafts, 1. SCMP 1216, 3.

Jan 14   Award Prizes to Model Agricultural Laborers, 1. SCMP 1212, 12.

Jan 15   Overfulfill Agricultural Production Plan ahead of Schedule, 1. SCMP 1214, 13.

Jan 16   On the Forefront of the High Tide, 1. SCMP 1217, 17.

Jan 17   Intensify Ideological Education among Office Employees and Workers at High Tide of Socialist Transformation, 1. SCMP 1218, 8.

Jan 18   Recruit Party Members Actively and Carefully at High Tide of Joint Public-Private Operation, 1. SCMP 1221, 11.

Jan 19   Launch Emulation Drives between Factories of the Same Industry and between Operations of the Same Type, 1. SCMP 1221, 13.

Jan 20   U.S. Should Stop Dragging Out the Sino-American Talks, 1. SCMP 1220, 28.

Jan 21   Strengthen the Concrete Leadership of the Work of Eliminating Illiteracy, 1. SCMP 1221, 8.

Jan 22   The Great Victory in Socialist Transformation of Private Industry and Commerce of Shanghai (Amended 1/23, p. 3), 1. SCMP 1222, 9.

1956

Jan 23	Wipe Out Ten Major Insect Pests and Plant Diseases, 1. SCMP 1223, 12.
Jan 24	Look Forward and Not Backward, 1. SCMP 1223, 6.
Jan 25	Leave the Backward Out and Hurry the Advanced Along Is the Responsibility of Leaders, 1. SCMP 1224, 6.
Jan 26	JMJP Greets India's National Day Anniversary, 1. SCMP 1219, 36.
Jan 27	Eliminate Schistosomiasis with Determination, 1.
Jan 28	Publicize the Experiences of Bumper Cotton Harvest in Sinkiang and Chekiang, 1.
Jan 29	Make Overall Plans for Trial Manufacture and Production of New Products, 1. SCMP 1228, 6.
Jan 31	Unite As One to Build the Fatherland, 1. SCMP 1225, 6.
Feb 1	JMJP Welcomes New Peace Proposals, 1. SCMP 1223, 25.
Feb 2	Build Roads and Bridges, Dredge Rivers, 1. SCMP 1232, 8.
Feb 3	Speed Up the Creation of Written Languages for National Minorities, 1. SCMP 1232, 3.
Feb 4	JMJP Urges Efforts for Peaceful Liberation of Taiwan, 1. SCMP 1225, 30.
Feb 5	Seriously Prevent Forest Fires, 1.
Feb 6	Develop Regular Spare Time Education for Working People, 1.
Feb 7	Uproot the Counter-Revolutionaries while Overhauling Agricultural Producer Cooperatives, 1. SCMP 1235, 16.
Feb 8	Do a Good Job of Uniting with and Transforming Bourgeois Elements, 1. SCMP 1232, 18.
Feb 9	Exert All-Out Efforts to Develop Rural Clubs, 1.
Feb 10	Do a Better Job of Taking Care of the Families of Martyrs, 1.
Feb 11	Don't Change the Original Production and Management System Precipitously, 1. SCMP 1233, 12.
Feb 12	Fix Interest Payment and Take Inventory Properly, 1. SCMP 1236, 20.
Feb 12	Vigorously Promote the Vernacular Language, 1.
Feb 13	JMJP Welcomes Premier of Cambodia, 1. SCMP 1230, 37.
Feb 14	JMJP Lauds Sino-Soviet Alliance Anniversary, 1. SCMP 1231, 31.
Feb 15	Speed Up the Production of Double-Share Double-Wheel Plow, 1.
Feb 17	Afforest the Fatherland, 1. SCMP 1240, 17.
Feb 18	Telephones to Every Village, Postal Routes to Every Cooperative, 1. SCMP 1238, 8.
Feb 19	Khruschov's Report--A Historical Document, 1. SCMP 1237, 26.
Feb 20	New Sino-Cambodian Relations Says JMJP, 1. SCMP 1234, 26.
Feb 21	JMJP Editorially Urges Fight for Complete Abolition of Colonialism, 1. SCMP 1235, 27.
Feb 22	Statistical Work Must Satisfy the Needs of National Construction, 1. SCMP 1236, 3.
Feb 23	Promote the Positive Role of Young Businessmen in Socialist Construction, 1. SCMP 1240, 8.
Feb 24	Build Irrigation and Water Conservancy Projects to Stamp Out Flood and Drought, 1.
Feb 25	Raise More Hogs, 1. SCMP 1244, 10.
Feb 26	Strengthen Conception of Totality, Oppose Departmentalism, 1. SCMP 1245, 3.
Feb 27	Universalization of Obligatory Education, 1. SCMP 1246, 16.
Feb 28	World Significance of CPSU Congress, 1. SCMP 1239, 29.
Feb 29	Launch Socialist Emulation Drives to Fulfill Five-Year Plan ahead of Schedule, 1. SCMP 1246, 8.
Mar 1	Tighten Up the System of Personnel Organization, 1. SCMP 1248, 6.
Mar 1	JMJP Greets Mongolian Party Anniversary, 1. SCMP 1241, 16.
Mar 2	Young People, Afforest the Fatherland with All Your Efforts, 1. SCMP 1248, 17.
Mar 3	JMJP Greets Vietnam Party Anniversary, 1. SCMP 1242, 29.
Mar 3	Defend the Peace and Security of Middle and Near Eastern Countries, 1. SCMP 1249, 13.
Mar 4	Universally Overhaul Cooperatives, Develop Spring Tilling and Production, 1. SCMP 1246, 26.
Mar 5	Check Up the Preparatory Work for Spring Plowing, 1. SCMP 1247, 6.
Mar 6	Reclaim Wasteland, 1. SCMP 1248, 11.
Mar 7	Develop Mass Movement for Defense Training, 1. SCMP 1257, 5.
Mar 8	Fully Promote the Positive Role of Women in Socialist Construction, 1. SCMP 1258, 17.
Mar 9	Achieve Great Success in Planned Marketing of Grain in Rural Areas, 1. SCMP 1256, 11.
Mar 10	Protest against Unite States Dispatch of Military Reconnaissance Balloons, 1. SCMP 1251, 22.
Mar 11	Fully Support Workers' Enthusiasm in Production, 1.
Mar 12	Bring Peasants' Latent Power into Play, 1. SCMP 1255, 3.
Mar 13	Urgent Tasks of Enterprise Leaders, 1. SCMP 1266, 7.
Mar 15	Eternal Glory to Comrade Bierut, 1. SCMP 1251, 23.
Mar 16	Improve Quality, Increase Variety, 1. SCMP 1258, 7.
Mar 17	Strive to Complete This Year's Enrollment Plan for Institutions of Higher Education, 1. SCMP 1263, 11.
Mar 18	Work According to Circumstances, 1. SCMP 1259, 3.
Mar 19	Tasks for the Leaders of Capital Construction, 1.
Mar 20	Stop U.S. Nuclear Tests in Trust Territories, International Waters, 1. SCMP 1258, 39.
Mar 21	Make a Good Job of the Recruitment of Party Members among Intellectuals, 1. SCMP 1259, 21.
Mar 22	Develop the Work of Producing Standard Designs, 1. SCMP 1261, 9.
Mar 23	Inauguration of Pakistan Islamic Republic Greeted by JMJP, 1. SCMP 1257, 29.
Mar 24	JMJP Welcomes Nehru's Speech, 1. SCMP 1257, 33.
Mar 25	Writers, Meet the Expectations of the People! 1.
Mar 26	Don't Let Primary, Middle School Students Stop Their Studies Half Way, 1. SCMP 1264, 18.
Mar 28	Launch Agricultural Labor Emulations, 1. SCMP 1266, 10.
Mar 29	New International Cooperation in Atomic Energy Research, 1. SCMP 1263, 3.

1956

Mar 30	Develop the Movement for Advanced Producers, 1. SCMP 1274, 7.
Apr 1	Lead Positively the Movement for Eliminating Illiteracy, 1. SCMP 1269, 3.
Apr 2	Strengthen Concrete Guidance over Spring Sowing, 1. SCMP 1267, 3.
Apr 3	Endeavor to Develop Meteorological Enterprise, 3.
Apr 4	JMJP Supports WFSW Statement (Science for the welfare of mankind), 1. SCMP 1263, 25.
Apr 6	Forever Be Industrious and Thrifty (Amended 4/22, p. 2), 1. SCMP 1273, 6.
Apr 7	Support for Cambodia's Peaceful Neutrality, 1. SCMP 1270, 29.
Apr 7	For the Development and Popularization of Dramatic Art, 1.
Apr 8	Fully Promote the Positive Role of Business Women in Socialist Transformation, 1. SCMP 1276, 2.
Apr 9	New Development in Sino-Soviet Economic Cooperation, 1. SCMP 1268, 24.
Apr 10	Exercise Active Leadership over the Work Connected with Rationalization Proposals, 1. SCMP 1273, 3.
Apr 11	In Commemoration of the Martyrs Who Sacrificed Themselves for the Asian-African Conference, 1. SCMP 1271, 24.
Apr 11	Felicitations on the Inauguration of the Sino-Burma Air Service, 1. SCMP 1271, 31.
Apr 12	Support the Call of the World Peace Council, 1. SCMP 1274, 25.
Apr 13	Correctly Solve the Problem of Production Centralization and Decentralization in the Handicraft Industry, 1.
Apr 14	Penetratingly Transform Rural Private Merchants and Peddlers, 1. SCMP 1288, 12.
Apr 15	Sow Soya Beans According to Plan, 1. SCMP 1284, 12.
Apr 16	Study the Good Traits of the Models and Strengthen Security Work, 1. SCMP 1277, 4.
Apr 17	Help the Backward Catch Up with the Advanced, 1. SCMP 1277, 6.
Apr 18	JMJP Editorial on Bandung Conference Anniversary, 1. SCMP 1273, 27.
Apr 19	Improve the Quality of Heavy Industry Products, 1. SCMP 1284, 14.
Apr 20	For Gradual Industrialization of Building Construction, 1. SCMP 1286, 19.
Apr 21	Felicitations on Tenth Anniversary of Founding of Socialist Unity Party of Germany, 1. SCMP 1281, 26.
Apr 22	Gigantic Victory of the Nationalities Policy, 1. SCMP 1278, 12.
Apr 23	Strengthen the Archives Work of the State, 1. SCMP 1283, 14.
Apr 24	Greet the Opening of the Council Meeting of the International Union of Democratic Women, 1.
Apr 25	The Only Way Out for Counter-Revolutionaries Is to Give Themselves Up to the Authorities (Amended 4/26, p. 2), 1. SCMP 1284, 7.
Apr 26	Build Up the Circulation of Newspapers, 1. SCMP 1292, 14.
Apr 27	Have the Working Masses Individually Educated by Persuasion, 1. SCMP 1288, 7.
Apr 28	Carefully Transform Small Stores in Cities, 1. SCMP 1288, 14.
Apr 29	Momentous Event in International Relations, 1. SCMP 1287, 29.
Apr 30	Powerful Motive Force for Developing China's Economy, 1. SCMP 1286, 2.
May 1	In the Midst of the High Tide of Socialism, 1. SCMP 1285, 12.
May 3	Institute and Improve the Bonus System, 1. SCMP 1287, 9.
May 4	The Correct Way to Advance Towards Science, 1.
May 5	Intensify Party Control Work in Factories, Mines, Communications Transport Departments, 1. SCMP 1292, 4.
May 6	The Fulfillment of This Year's Task in Cured Tobacco Production Increase, 1. SCMP 1294, 8.
May 7	Ensure Safety of Workers during Production and Construction, 1. SCMP 1293, 13.
May 8	JMJP on Rumanian Communist Party Anniversary, 1. SCMP 1293, 26.
May 9	Produce More Oil-Bearing Crops, 1. SCMP 1294, 10.
May 10	Let the Rural Market Be Enlivened Further, 1. SCMP 1298, 2.
May 11	For a Lasting and Intensified Campaign of Outstanding Workers, 1. SCMP 1296, 13.
May 12	Mobilize Youth of the Standard of Junior Middle School Graduates to Sit for Entrance Examinations of Higher Institutes, 1. SCMP 1296, 10.
May 13	Heighten the Active Function of Party Members in Agricultural Cooperatives, 1. SCMP 1297, 5.
May 14	JMJP Greets Czechoslovak C.P. Anniversary, 1. SCMP 1291, 21.
May 15	Treat the Backward Workers Correctly, 1. SCMP 1304, 6.
May 16	Safeguard the Health of Women and Children in Rural Areas, 1. SCMP 1299, 5.
May 17	Take Proper Care of All the Draft Animals in the Cooperatives, 1. SCMP 1302, 14.
May 18	Further Talk on "A Play Which Saves a Kind of Play," 1.
May 19	Greeting the Friendly Decision of the Egyptian Government, 1. SCMP 1299, 26.
May 20	Develop Large Scale Geological Prospecting Work, 1.
May 21	New Development in Soviet-French Relations, 1. SCMP 1305, 32.
May 22	There Must Be Deserved Reward and Punishment, 1. SCMP 1306, 7.
May 23	Speed Up the Development of Petroleum Industry and Geological Prospecting of Petroleum, 1. SCMP 1307, 5.
May 24	Development of Sideline Production in Rural Areas, 1. SCMP 1302, 16.
May 25	Ensure Realization of This Year's State Plans, 1. SCMP 1304, 3.
May 26	Counter-Revolutionary Elements Should Have No Apprehensions But Be Frank and Give Themselves Up, 1. SCMP 1305, 10.
May 27	Foster Practitioners of Traditional Medicine to Swell the Ranks of Medical Workers, 1. SCMP 1311, 8.
May 28	Continue Efforts to Prevent and Cure Liver Fluke, 1. SCMP 1313, 7.
May 29	Make a Good Job of the Preliminary Distribution of Summer Harvests, 1. SCMP 1307, 3.
May 30	A New Stage of Economic Cooperation among the Socialist Countries, 1. SCMP 1305, 27.
May 31	Make a Good Job of the 1956 Elections, 1. SCMP 1305, 7.
Jun 1	Educating Children Is Society's Responsibility, 1.
Jun 1	Welcome to the Asian-African Students' Conference, 1. SCMP 1307, 17.

1956

Jun 2	Improve the Forward Purchase of Farm Produce, 1. SCMP 1308, 9.
Jun 3	Oppose U.S. Violation of Korea Armistice Agreement, 1. SCMP 1312, 28.
Jun 4	Develop Museum Enterprise to Do Scientific Research and to Serve the Masses, 1.
Jun 5	Take Better Care of the Livelihood of the Workers, 1. SCMP 1316, 6.
Jun 6	Do Not Neglect Financial and Accounting Work of Agricultural Cooperatives, 1.
Jun 7	Let the Cadres Attend Less Meetings and Spend More Time in the Field, 1. SCMP 1315, 12.
Jun 8	Foster the Progressive Backbone Elements of Industrial and Commercial Circles, 1. SCMP 1317, 10.
Jun 9	Asian and African Students Want Friendly Co-operation, 1.
Jun 10	Immediately Sow Summer Crops Well, 1.
Jun 11	Select and Promote Outstanding Cadres Boldly and Correctly, 1. SCMP 1320, 8.
Jun 12	Solve the Workers' Problem of Difficulties in Livelihood, 1. SCMP 1322, 10.
Jun 13	Immediately Check and Improve the Quality of Water Conservancy Projects, 1.
Jun 14	Peking Papers Welcome World Conference of Working Women, 1. SCMP 1312, 21.
Jun 15	Work Enthusiastically and Fulfill This Year's State Plans, 1.
Jun 16	Study 1956's State Budget Report, 1.
Jun 17	Glorious Model of Peaceful Use of Atomic Energy, 1.
Jun 18	JMJP Welcomes Egyptian People's Victory, 1. SCMP 1314, 23.
Jun 19	Further Implement Policies on Overseas Chinese Affairs, 1.
Jun 20	Oppose Both Conservatism and Hastiness, 1. SCMP 1321, 11.
Jun 21	Let Workers Have Better Working Conditions, 1. SCMP 1322, 8.
Jun 21	Peking Papers Welcome Soviet Fleet's Visit to China, 1. SCMP 1317, 29.
Jun 22	Soviet-Yugoslav Talks Achieve Big Results, 1. SCMP 1322, 28.
Jun 23	Sino-Combodian Economic Aid Agreement, 1. SCMP 1323, 32.
Jun 24	Grasp the Central Link in Summer Agricultural Operations, 1. SCMP 1326, 8.
Jun 25	The Picking, Processing, and Purchase of Tea, 1.
Jun 26	Solve the Housing Problem of Workers, 1. SCMP 1331, 7.
Jun 27	Cooperatives Cannot Be Properly Run with Methods of Compulsion and Commandism, 1. SCMP 1326, 5.
Jun 28	JMJP on Principles of Peaceful Coexistence, 1. SCMP 1323, 24.
Jun 30	Carry Out Carefully and Gradually the Economic Reorganization of Joint State-Private Industry, 1. SCMP 1329, 6.
Jul 1	Leniency Toward Japanese War Criminals, 1. SCMP 1329, 31.
Jul 1	Message to Readers, 1. SCMP 1328, 3.
Jul 2	Establish New Socialist Villages, 1.
Jul 3	Reckon the Major Issues, Breed More Hogs, 1. SCMP 1329, 14.
Jul 4	Economize Paper from Various Directions, 1. SCMP 1328, 6.
Jul 5	We Welcome Syria's Friendly Decision, 1. SCMP 1329, 33.
Jul 6	Carry Out Wage Reform, 1. SCMP 1331, 4.
Jul 7	May Sino-Vietnamese Friendship Be More Consolidated, 1.
Jul 8	Exploit the Potentiality of Coastal Industry, 1. SCMP 1335, 5.
Jul 9	Why Is the Proportion of Light Industry Investments Increased? 1. SCMP 1334, 7.
Jul 10	Can Rice Plants Be Widely Cultivated in the North? 1. SCMP 1337, 5.
Jul 11	Greetings to the Mongolian People, 1.
Jul 12	Beware of Imperialist Scheming and Counter-Revolutionary Activities at Home, 1. SCMP 1336, 5.
Jul 13	Do a Good Job in Convening Discussion Sessions in the Industrial and Commercial Sector, 1.
Jul 14	Raise Hog Purchasing Price Appropriately, 1. SCMP 1345, 3.
Jul 15	Fix Prices According to Quality, 1. SCMP 1342, 7.
Jul 16	About a Letter from a Party Member, 1. SCMP 1341, 6.
Jul 17	Do Not Force Goods on the Peasants, 1. SCMP 1343, 6.
Jul 18	Continue to Promote the "Geneva Spirit," 1. SCMP 1339, 27.
Jul 19	Deliver Goods to the Peasants, 1. SCMP 1343, 4.
Jul 20	Chinese Press on Soviet-German Talks, 1. SCMP 1336, 32.
Jul 21	Help Small Merchants and Pedlars Solve Difficulties, 1. SCMP 1343, 8.
Jul 22	Signing of the Technical Mutual Aid Pact, 1.
Jul 23	Break the Record, 1.
Jul 24	Geneva Agreements Must Be Respected and Carried Out, 1. SCMP 1343, 22.
Jul 25	A Lesson Not to Be Regarded with Indifference, 1. SCMP 1344, 14.
Jul 26	Aid the Prospecting Teams, 1. SCMP 1350, 7.
Jul 27	"Industry" and "Thrift" Must Go Together, 1. SCMP 1344, 3.
Jul 28	Extend Sino-Vietnam Economic Cooperation, 1. SCMP 1341, 30.
Jul 29	Organize the Rural Economic Life, 1. SCMP 1348, 4.
Jul 30	Support the Egyptian People's Struggle for Upholding Their Sovereignty and Independence, 1. SCMP 1348, 23.
Jul 31	Raise Designing Technology to a Higher Level, 1. SCMP 1350, 9.
Aug 1	Guarantee the Living Conditions of the Dependents of Martyrs and Servicemen, 1. SCMP 1351, 6.
Aug 2	Treasure the Trained Personnel, Give Them Proper Assignments, 1. SCMP 1356, 9.
Aug 3	Severely Punish Counter-Revolutionaries Who Carry on Subversive Activities, 1. SCMP 1353, 2.
Aug 4	Ensure the Quality of Building Work, 1. SCMP 1355, 8.
Aug 5	Get Rid of the Calamities Caused by Typhoon, 1. SCMP 1347, 4.
Aug 6	Don't Hinder Students from Vacationing, 1. SCMP 1356, 12.

1956

Aug 7	Hiroshima Tragedy Must Not Be Repeated, 1. SCMP 1355, 38.
Aug 8	Laos Taking the Path of Peace and Unification, 1. SCMP 1356, 41.
Aug 9	What to Do to Solve the Shortage of Building Materials, 1. SCMP 1355, 10.
Aug 10	JMJP on Nehru's Suez Statement, 1. SCMP 1350, 19.
Aug 11	JMJP on Soviet Suez Statement, 1. SCMP 1350, 22.
Aug 12	Bring Out with Thoroughness the Latent Strength of the Intelligentsia in China, 1. SCMP 1356, 2.
Aug 13	To Youth's Health, 1.
Aug 13	JMJP Nuclear Weapons Must Be Eliminated, 1. SCMP 1351, 35.
Aug 14	JMJP Welcomes Nasser's Statement in Editorial, 1. SCMP 1352, 30.
Aug 15	Use Your Own Money to Subscribe to Newspapers and Publications, 1.
Aug 16	Lead Well the Ranks 2 Million Strong, 1. SCMP 1360, 12.
Aug 17	China Supports Egypt, Says JMJP, 1. SCMP 1355, 27.
Aug 18	Demands for Physical Education Work, 1.
Aug 19	Do Everything to Prevent and Relieve Calamity and Increase Production of Late Crops, 1. SCMP 1360, 9.
Aug 20	Welcome to the Royal Laotian Government Delegation, 1. SCMP 1360, 35.
Aug 21	Leadership Over Outstanding Workers' Campaign Should Be Deepened, 1. SCMP 1363, 7.
Aug 22	JMJP Condemns Banning of German C.P., 1. SCMP 1358, 37.
Aug 23	What Does the Cheng Tien-chang Invalid Certificate Case Expose? 1. SCMP 1366, 14.
Aug 24	Yemen's Recognition of China Welcomed by JMJP, 1. SCMP 1360, 50.
Aug 25	JMJP on Failure of London Conference, 1. SCMP 1360, 52.
Aug 26	Foundation for the Development of Sino-Laotian Friendly Relations, 1.
Aug 27	Propagate the Tradition of Our People, Make Music and Art Prosper, 1.
Aug 28	Library Work Is Marching Towards Science, 1.
Aug 29	Defend the Frontier of Our Fatherland More Vigilantly, 1. SCMP 1369, 2.
Aug 30	JMJP on Sino-Mongolian Agreement, 1. SCMP 1363, 26.
Aug 31	Welcome the Heroes That Conquer the "Father of Tienshan," 1.
Sep 1	Don't Take Foolhardy Action, 1. SCMP 1371, 6.
Sep 2	To the Olympic Meet, 1. SCMP 1367, 10.
Sep 3	Is Afforestation Finished? 1. SCMP 1374, 6.
Sep 4	Personnel of Public Side Must Be Adept in Working with Personnel of Private Side, 1. SCMP 1371, 3.
Sep 5	Aid the Karami and Tsaidam Oil Areas, 1. SCMP 1377, 16.
Sep 6	Arranging and Reforming the Classic Book Trade, 1. SCMP 1379, 21.
Sep 7	Is Planning Still Needed for the Cooperatives? 1. SCMP 1382, 9.
Sep 8	Take a Correct View of the Relations between Our Nationalities, 1. SCMP 1388, 3.
Sep 9	How to Improve the Quality of Light Industry, 1.
Sep 10	Respect the Noble Work of Nurses, 1. SCMP 1391, 10.
Sep 11	Pressing Down Grade and Price Is Not Allowed, 1. SCMP 1379, 4.
Sep 12	JMJP on Failure of the Five-Nation Suez Mission, 1. SCMP 1371, 33.
Sep 13	A New Phase in Soviet-Indonesian Friendly Relations, 1.
Sep 13	Overall Solution of New Problems Arising after Agricultural Cooperativization, 1. SCMP 1382, 27.
Sep 14	The Most Important Way to Conquer Famine, 1.
Sep 15	Milestone for Our Great Socialist Enterprise, 1.
Sep 16	JMJP on Universal Disarmament, 3. SCMP 1373, 33.
Sep 17	New Phase in Sino-Ceylonese Relations, 1. SCMP 1380, 25.
Sep 21	JMJP Supports Egyptian Struggle, 1. SCMP 1376, 44.
Sep 23	Starting from the Model of Research, 1.
Sep 24	JMJP Editorial on Success of Sino-Nepalese Relations, 1. SCMP 1378, 24.
Sep 25	Important Problems in Food Production at Present, 1.
Sep 26	JMJP Welcomes Nepalese Prime Minister, 1. SCMP 1381, 21.
Sep 27	The New Party Constitution Inspires Us to Go Forward (Amended 9/28, p. 2), 1.
Sep 29	A Conference of Great Historic Significance, 1,2.
Sep 30	Jubilantly Welcome President Sukarno's Visit to Our Nation, 1.
Oct 1	Strive for National Construction, Protect World Peace, 1.
Oct 2	Pay Attention to Folk Artists, 1.
Oct 3	A Recent State Council Directive on Rapeseed Supply, 1. SCMP 1396, 11.
Oct 4	Training Students to Acquire the Faculty of Independent Thinking, 1. SCMP 1397, 8.
Oct 5	Discrimination against Primary School Teachers Cannot Be Allowed, 1. SCMP 1398, 3.
Oct 6	Welcome the Opening of the Japanese Commercial Exhibit in Peking, 1.
Oct 7	Create Even Higher New Records, 1.
Oct 8	Sino-Nepalese Joint Statement Greeted by Press, 1. SCMP 1388, 27 (extracts).
Oct 9	Don't Be Afraid of Opposing Views, 1. SCMP 1397, 5.
Oct 10	Give the Masses Intensified Leadership in Fishery, 1. SCMP 1398, 11.
Oct 11	Do Not Bend with the Wind, 1. SCMP 1400, 4.
Oct 12	Oppose Subjectivism in the Technological Renovation of Agriculture, 1.
Oct 13	Greeting the Formation of the National Federation of Overseas Chinese, 1.
Oct 14	Take a Correct View of the Improved Grain Situation in Our Country, 1. SCMP 1400, 12.
Oct 15	The Bridge of Friendship between China and Indonesia, 1.

1956

Oct 16 Learn the Merits of Personalities Outside the Party, 1. SCMP 1400, 7.
Oct 17 Reform the Wage System of New State-Private Enterprises, 1. SCMP 1403, 15.
Oct 18 JMJP Greets Suhrawardy, 1. SCMP 1395, 33 (extracts).
Oct 19 A Great Writer, a Great Fighter, 1.
Oct 20 The Great Victory in the Soviet Union's Development of Agriculture, 1.
Oct 21 Welcome the Reestablishment of Diplomatic Relations between the Soviet Union and Japan, 1.
Oct 22 Seriously Implement Elections at the Grass Roots Level, 1,4.
Oct 23 JMJP on Political Intrigue, 1. SCMP 1398, 29 (summary).
Oct 24 Peking Papers Welcome China-Pakistan Joint Statement, 1. SCMP 1399, 23 (extracts).
Oct 24 JMJP Protests against British Attitude (Hong Kong), 1,4. SCMP 1399, 19.
Oct 25 Make More Industrial Equipment with Our Own Hands, 1. SCMP 1413, 8.
Oct 26 For the Rapid Progress of Cotton Procurement Program, 1. SCMP 1410, 12.
Oct 27 Assist the Masses in Developing the Production of Chinese Herbs, 1.
Oct 28 Solve the New Problems in Universities, 1. SCMP 1414, 16.
Oct 29 Higher Scientific and Technical Knowledge for the Workers, 1. SCMP 1412, 14.
Oct 30 Develop the Art of Chinese Painting, 1.
Oct 31 Overtime Shifts and Overtime Hours Should Not Be Taken Lightly, 1. SCMP 1414, 24.
Nov 1   JMJP Attacks Anglo-French Aggression, 1. SCMP 1405, 24.
Nov 2   Halt British-French Aggression, Says JMJP, 1. SCMP 1406, 34.
Nov 3   JMJP on World Disgust over Aggression against Egypt, 1. SCMP 1406, 41.
Nov 3   JMJP Editorial on Unity of Socialist Countries, 1. SCMP 1406, 18.
Nov 4   JMJP on Hungarian Situation (Amended 11/5, p. 2), 1. SCMP 1406, 27.
Nov 5   Great Victory of Hungarian People, Says JMJP, 1. SCMP 1407, 16.
Nov 5   Aggression against Egypt Must Be Stopped, Says JMJP, 2. SCMP 1407, 32.
Nov 6   Teach the Workers Scientific and Technical Knowledge, 1. SCMP 1426, 18.
Nov 7   Britain and France Should Cease Fire Immediately, 1.
Nov 7   Long Live the Soviet Union, the Great Protector of Peace, 1,2.
Nov 8   Aggressive Forces, Get Out of Egypt, Says JMJP, 1. SCMP 1410, 30.
Nov 9   Support the Egyptian People to Drive Out the Invaders, 1.
Nov 10 Our Greetings on the Chinese Export Commodity Exhibition, 1. SCMP 1417, 8.
Nov 11 A New Effort in Strengthening the Friendly Relations between China and Burma, 1.
Nov 12 Sun Yat-sen Lives Forever, 1.
Nov 13 JMJP on Eleventh Session of UN General Assembly, 1. SCMP 1412, 22.
Nov 13 JMJP Warns Aggressors to Withdraw from Egypt, 1. SCMP 1412, 26.
Nov 14 JMJP on Hungary, 1. SCMP 1412, 35.
Nov 15 Centralize the Management of Rehabilitation Clinics, 1.
Nov 16 Give Support to Scientific Research Work, 1. SCMP 1426, 23.
Nov 17 The Invading Armies Must Withdraw Unconditionally from Egypt, 1.
Nov 18 Let There Be More Activists in Socialist Construction, 1. SCMP 1420, 14.
Nov 19 JMJP Welcomes New Soviet Disarmament Proposal, 1. SCMP 1416, 31.
Nov 20 Lay a Firm Hold on Leadership in Technical Schools for Workers, 1. SCMP 1426, 25.
Nov 21 JMJP Editorial on Soviet-Polish Talks, 1. SCMP 1418, 20.
Nov 22 Develop Healthily the Trading Activities of Peasants, 1. SCMP 1428, 18.
Nov 23 JMJP Greets Chinese-Vietnamese Communique, 1. SCMP 1419, 22.
Nov 24 Bring Grain Sales Rapidly Under Control, 1. SCMP 1421, 5.
Nov 25 Actively and Steadily Eliminate Illiteracy, 1. SCMP 1431, 20.
Nov 26 Bring the Hard and Thrifty Way of Work into Play, 1. SCMP 1429, 4.
Nov 27 Living Standards of the People Can Be Raised Only Gradually, 1. SCMP 1426, 2.
Nov 28 Overcome Obstacles to Democratic Management of APC's, 1. SCMP 1428, 14.
Nov 29 JMJP on Sino-Cambodian Statement, 1. SCMP 1423, 43.
Nov 30 Bring the Fighting Role of Trade Unions into Play in State-Private Enterprises, 1. SCMP 1433, 3.
Dec 1   Mass Line Should Be Pursued in Distributing Autumn Harvests, 1. SCMP 1431, 6.
Dec 2   JMJP on New Moves against Syria, 1. SCMP 1424, 42.
Dec 3   Have the Three Million Young Cadres Trained, 1. SCMP 1436, 5.
Dec 4   Master the Advanced Techniques as Fast as Possible, 1. SCMP 1438, 8.
Dec 5   Economize Timber Strictly, 1. SCMP 1433, 7.
Dec 6   JMJP Welcomes Soviet-Rumanian Statement, 1. SCMP 1428, 35.
Dec 6   JMJP on Anglo-French Withdrawl, 1,5. SCMP 1428, 37.
Dec 7   Designing of New Machines by Ourselves, 1. SCMP 1437, 8.
Dec 8   Continue to Make Positive Use of the Federation of Industrial and Commercial Enterprises, 1.
Dec 9   Inherit the "December 9" Youths Superior Tradition, 1. SCMP 1437, 3.
Dec 9   Aggressors Must Give Compensation to Egypt, JMJP Says, 1. SCMP 1429, 35.
Dec 10 Make Further Positive Use of the Industrial and Commercial Sector, 1.
Dec 11 Peking Papers on Premier Chou En-lai's India Visit, 1. SCMP 1431, 33.
Dec 12 Why Are Books in Short and Excessive Supply at the Same Time? 1. SCMP 1441, 25.
Dec 13 Push Gradually Forward Technical Reform of National Economy, 1. SCMP 1444, 8.
Dec 14 Resumption of Soviet-Japanese Diplomatic Relations Welcomed, 1. SCMP 1435, 30
Dec 15 The U.S. Must Stop Sabotaging the Eastern European Countries, Says JMJP, 1. SCMP 1435, 29.
Dec 16 Be Diligent and Frugal in Running Enterprises, 1. SCMP 1444, 10.

1956

- Dec 17 Have the Libraries in Institutions of Higher Education Well Run, 1. SCMP 1448, 10.
- Dec 19 Quality to Be Insured in Production Increase and Economy, 1,2. SCMP 1446, 14.
- Dec 20 How to Deal with Individual Handicraft Shops, 1. SCMP 1446, 17.
- Dec 21 The Peoples of China and Burma Are Fraternal Brothers, 1.
- Dec 22 Overall Plans for Construction in Mountainous Areas, 1. SCMP 1446, 19.
- Dec 23 Positively Lead the Young Students Forward, 1. SCMP 1444, 2.
- Dec 24 The Great Tasks of the Industrial and Commercial Sector from Now On, 1.
- Dec 25 Chinese Press Welcomes Recovery of Port Said, 1. SCMP 1440, 30.
- Dec 25 JMJP Greets Sino-German Treaty Anniversary, 1. SCMP 1440, 29.
- Dec 26 JMJP on Joint China-Pakistan Statement, 1. SCMP 1440, 21.
- Dec 27 On Japanese Commodity Exhibition, 1. SCMP 1441, 45.
- Dec 28 To the Cultural Workers, 1. SCMP 1449, 10.
- Dec 30 On Asian Writers' Conference, 1. SCMP 1442, 53.
- Dec 31 Subscribe Enthusiastically to Issue of State Economic Construction Bond of 1957, 1. SCMP 1452, 3.

1957

- Jan 1 Outlook on the New Year (Amended 1/2, p. 4), 1. SCMP 1446, 6.
- Jan 2 Greets Successful Talks in Laos, 1. SCMP 1444, 33.
- Jan 3 Undertake Capital Construction of Farmland with Strenuous Efforts, 1. SCMP 1457, 8.
- Jan 4 Utilize Waste and Substitutes, 1. SCMP 1453, 2.
- Jan 5 Key to Correctly Unfolding the Cultural Work of National Minorities, 1. SCMP 1457, 5.
- Jan 6 Give the Economic Results Full Consideration, 1. SCMP 1460, 3.
- Jan 7 The Traffic Problem during the Spring Festival, 1.
- Jan 8 On "Eisenhower Doctrine," 1. SCMP 1448, 27.
- Jan 9 On Unity among Socialist Countries, 1. SCMP 1449, 37.
- Jan 10 Condemns British Aggression in Yemen, 1. SCMP 1450, 37.
- Jan 11 Make State Supervisory Organs Exert Their Role in Fight against Bureaucratism, 1. SCMP 1455, 2.
- Jan 12 Eisenhower Doctrine Is Symbol of U.S. Colonialism, 1. SCMP 1451, 28.
- Jan 12 Promote the Spirit of Fortitude in Memory of Liu Hu-lan, 1. SCMP 1455, 6.
- Jan 13 Let All of Us Save Coal, 1. SCMP 1460, 6.
- Jan 14 Draw Up This Year's Agricultural Plans, 1. SCMP 1457, 10.
- Jan 15 Oppose U.S. Using UN to Interfere Illegally with Korea's Affairs, 1.
- Jan 15 Have We Enough Supplementary Food for the Spring Festival? 1. SCMP 1461, 10.
- Jan 16 Always Keep Safety in Mind, 1. SCMP 1466, 10.
- Jan 17 Support the Army and Honor the Dependents! Support the Government and Love the People! 1. SCMP 1459, 5.

1957

- Jan 18 Peking Papers Welcome Sino-Polish Statement, 1. SCMP 1456, 55.
- Jan 19 Peking Papers on Sino-Hungarian Joint Statement, 1. SCMP 1456, 57.
- Jan 20 On Sino-Soviet Talks, 1. SCMP 1456, 40.
- Jan 21 Consolidate Labor Discipline, 1. SCMP 1466, 2.
- Jan 22 Thorough Prevention and Cure of Schistosomiasis, 1. SCMP 1473, 14.
- Jan 23 Strive to Cultivate National Minority Cadres, 1. SCMP 1466, 7.
- Jan 24 Peking Press on Sino-Afghan Friendship, 1. SCMP 1460, 22.
- Jan 24 The Great Victory of the Polish People, 1,5.
- Jan 25 Our Nation's First Awards for Science, 1.
- Jan 26 One Example on How to Improve Leadership, 1. SCMP 1467, 6.
- Jan 27 The Glorious Task of Coal Workers, 1. SCMP 1464, 8.
- Jan 28 Wishes for This Year's Physical Education Work, 1.
- Jan 29 Deal Correctly with the Rural Free Market, 1. SCMP 1467, 4.
- Jan 30 On Chou En-lai's Tour of Nepal, 1. SCMP 1464, 34.
- Jan 31 Support for Basic-Level Cadres in the Rural Areas, 1.
- Feb 1 On Soviet-Czechoslovak Talks, 1. SCMP 1464, 49.
- Feb 2 Welcome the National People's Congress Delegation Home, 1. SCMP 1471, 5.
- Feb 3 Rush Spring Repair of Water Conservancy Works on Farmland, 1. SCMP 1468, 5.
- Feb 4 Strive for a Good Harvest This Year, 1. SCMP 1468, 3.
- Feb 5 Give the New Workers Political Education, 1. SCMP 1473, 8.
- Feb 6 Do Not Slack Off in Elimination of Illiteracy, 1. SCMP 1479, 9.
- Feb 7 Papers on Chinese-Ceylonese Joint Statement, 1. SCMP 1468, 31.
- Feb 7 The Contribution of the Working Staff in the Mines, 1.
- Feb 8 Workers in New Industrial Areas Cooperate to Overcome Difficulties, 1. SCMP 1473, 8.
- Feb 9 "Five Guarantee" System Must Be Correctly Enforced, 1. SCMP 1477, 16.
- Feb 10 Raise and Use Small Cattle, 1. SCMP 1478, 13.
- Feb 11 Why Supply of Certain Commodities Cannot Meet Demand, 1. SCMP 1477, 9.
- Feb 12 All Trades Need Experts, 1. SCMP 1476, 15.
- Feb 13 Make Proper Arrangements for Capital Construction Items, 1. SCMP 1477, 14.
- Feb 14 On Sino-Soviet Alliance, 1. SCMP 1473, 38.
- Feb 15 On Supreme Soviet Session, 1. SCMP 1474, 34.
- Feb 16 Do a Good Job in Supplying Agricultural Capital Goods, 1.
- Feb 17 Increase Production of Raw Materials and Exercise Economy on Use of Them, 1. SCMP 1481, 5.
- Feb 18 For a Bumper Harvest, 1. SCMP 1478, 12.
- Feb 19 Cotton Growers, Sell Your Surplus Cotton to the State, 1. SCMP 1486, 8.

1957

Feb 20 On Near and Middle East Situation, 1. SCMP 1477, 34.
Feb 21 A Grand Review on the Agricultural Front, 1. SCMP 1482, 5.
Feb 22 Inculcate Collectivism in the Peasants, 1. SCMP 1482, 7.
Feb 23 Soviet-Bulgarian Talks Strengthen Unity and Peace, 1. SCMP 1478, 31.
Feb 24 Spring Sowing Plans Must Be Made Advanced and Dependable, 1. SCMP 1486, 6.
Feb 25 Be Diligent and Thrifty with the Running of Schools, 1. SCMP 1484, 16.
Feb 27 Joint State-Private Workshops and Handicraft Cooperatives Increase Output while Practicing Economy, 1.
Feb 28 We Should Adequately Recover Waste Materials, 1.
Mar 1   Strenuously Develop the Pig-Raising Enterprise, 1.
Mar 2   Study Kuan Mu-sheng's Leadership Method, 1.
Mar 3   We Cannot Be Lax in the Work of Collecting Manure, 1.
Mar 4   Join Socialist Savings Enthusiastically, 1.
Mar 5   Exercise Appropriate Birth Control, 1. SCMP 1487, 6.
Mar 6   Greeting the Independence of Ghana, 1.
Mar 7   Strive to Overfulfill the Plan of Issuing Public Bonds This Year, 1.
Mar 8   More Fully Utilize Socialist Activism of Women, 1.
Mar 9   Peking Press on Czechoslovak Government Delegation Visit, 1. SCMP 1488, 22.
Mar 10 Persevere in the Development of Advanced Producer Movement, 1,5. SCMP 1493, 14.
Mar 11 Lower the Production Cost of State Farms, 1.
Mar 12 Build Up Powerful Naval Defense Force, 1. SCMP 1498, 5.
Mar 13 Tap the Potentiality of Stocks on Hand, 1. SCMP 1499, 2.
Mar 14 Strive to Improve the Transportation System (Amended 3/15, p. 6), 1.
Mar 15 Raise More Draft Animals, , 1.
Mar 16 Labor Education Must Be Regularized, 1.
Mar 17 Calamity-Stricken Areas Must Economize the More, 1. SCMP 1499, 5.
Mar 18 Carry Out a Penetrating Checkup of Preparations for Spring Plowing, 1. SCMP 1504, 3.
Mar 19 We Should Start Working on Spring Hygiene, 1.
Mar 20 Agricultural Cooperatives Must Regularly Publicize Their Accounts, 1.
Mar 21 Carry Through the Convention's New Democratic Spirit, 1.
Mar 22 Consult with the Masses about Business, 1.
Mar 23 Commune Cadres Should Participate in Productive Labor, 1.
Mar 24 Devise More Better Ways of Gathering a Bumper Harvest This Year, 1. SCMP 1505, 9.
Mar 25 Make Good Use of Large Farming Equipment Already Owned, 1.
Mar 26 Rationally Organize and Utilize Rural, Female Labor, 1.
Mar 27 Organize and Readjust This Year's Industrial Production, 1. SCMP 1507, 4.
Mar 28 On Sino-Czechoslovak Treaty, 1. SCMP 1502, 23.
Mar 29 Strengthen Ideological and Political Work in Schools, 1. SCMP 1513, 11.
Mar 30 Papers on Soviet-Hungarian Talks, 1. SCMP 1503, 29.
Mar 31 Economize the Use of Land in Capital Construction (Amended 4/6, p. 2), 1. SCMP 1510, 7.
Apr 1   Work Is a Matter of Honor for Both Workers and Peasants; the Living Standard of Both Workers and Peasants Has Been Bettered, 1. SCMP 1511, 1.
Apr 2   A Good Cotton Harvest This Year, 1. SCMP 1511, 5.
Apr 3   Cultivate Young Artists, 1.
Apr 4   Carry Through the Principles of Building Up the Metallurgical Industry, 1.
Apr 4   Overcome Difficulties, March Ahead Triumphantly (Hungarian liberation anniversary), 1.
Apr 5   Press Welcomes World Peace Council Appeal for Suspension of Nuclear Weapon Tests, 1. SCMP 1508, 24.
Apr 6   Educators Must Receive Education--On Reform of Intellectuals, 1. SCMP 1519, 1.
Apr 7   Welcomes Polish Delegation, 1. SCMP 1508, 16.
Apr 8   Problem of Primary and Middle School Graduates Taking Part in Agricultural Production, 1. SCMP 1513, 1.
Apr 9   Congratulations on Construction of Wuhan Steel and Iron Combine, 1. SCMP 1514, 9.
Apr 10 Continue Not to Interfere, Pursue the Principle of "Let a Hundred Flowers Bloom, Let a Hundred Schools of Thought Contend," 1.
Apr 11 More Things Can Be Done for Less Money--Preliminary Experience in Our Capital Construction, 1. SCMP 1518, 11.
Apr 12 Peking Papers Welcome Sino-Polish Statement, 1. SCMP 1512, 31.
Apr 13 How Shall We Deal with the Internal Contradictions of the People? 1. SCMP 1512, 1.
Apr 14 All Come to Aid the San Men Gorge, 1. SCMP 1514, 1.
Apr 15 Welcomes President Voroshilov (Presidium of Supreme Soviet of the USSR), 1. SCMP 1513, 39.
Apr 16 On Voroshilov's Visit and Sino-Soviet Friendship, 1. SCMP 1515, 30 (extracts).
Apr 17 Criticism Based on the Wish for Unity (Unity-criticism-unity method), 1. SCMP 1516, 1.
Apr 18 Marks Second Anniversary of Bandung Conference, 2. SCMP 1516, 52.
Apr 19 Improve the Feeding, Caring and Managing of Livestock, 2.
Apr 20 All Come to Economize Cotton Cloth (State Council decision), 1. SCMP 1518, 17.
Apr 20 Hails Increased Soviet-Albanian Friendship (Soviet-Albanian talks), 5. SCMP 1516, 29.
Apr 21 Congress of Agricultural Producers Cooperatives Members Must Be Well Held, 1. SCMP 1521, 9.
Apr 22 Industrialists and Merchants Must Continue to Transform Themselves and Work Hard, 1. SCMP 1524, 4.
Apr 23 Peking Press on Sino-Japanese Relations (Communique with Japanese socialist party mission to China), 5. SCMP 1517, 39.
Apr 23 Whole Party Must Seriously Study How to Solve Contradictions within the Ranks of the People Correctly, 1. SCMP 1518, 1.

1957

Apr 24	Peking Press Marks Anti-Colonialism Day, 1. SCMP 1518, 49.
Apr 25	Raise the Quality and Quantity of New Students in Higher Educational Institutes (Admissions work), 1.
Apr 26	"Long-Term Coexistence and Mutual Supervision" Discussed at Meetings of Democratic Parties, 1. SCMP 1524, 1.
Apr 27	Dare to Loosen the Reins, Don't Curtail Theatrical Repertoire, 1.
Apr 28	Turn Back Quickly the Trend of Decline in the Quality of Products, 1. SCMP 1534, 9.
Apr 29	Make an Adequate Estimate of the Labor Potential in Rural Cooperatives, 2.
Apr 30	Welcome the Emissaries of the Rumanian People (Rumanian National Assembly and Bucharest City Council delegation), 1.
Apr 30	A Good Example of Regional Autonomy of National Minorities of Our Country (Inner Mongolia), 2. SCMP 1528, 4.
May 1	Be Industrious and Thrifty in National Construction, 2. SCMP 1526, 1.
May 1	Soviet Statement on Jordan Is Timely Warning, 6. SCMP 1523, 34.
May 2	Why Must We "Rectify Working Style"? 1,2. SCMP 1525, 1.
May 3	On Soviet-British Relations (A timely move on part of Soviets toward improved relations), 5. SCMP 1525, 24.
May 3	Sharing Joys and Sorrows with the Masses, 1,2. SCMP 1528, 1.
May 4	Labor for Socialism--Editorial in Commemoration of "May 4" Youth Festival, 2. SCMP 1533, 7.
May 4	Explain Three Grain Purchase and Sale Principles to the Peasants, 4. SCMP 1531, 14.
May 6	Peking Papers Bid Farewell to Voroshilov, 1. SCMP 1526, 20.
May 7	Why Do We Have to Use Gentle Means in Rectification? 1,2.
May 8	More on the Economical Use of Land in Capital Construction, 1. SCMP 1534, 7.
May 9	Zealously Develop the Production of Supplementary Food Products in Cities and Vicinities of Industrial and Mining Areas, 1.
May 10	On U.S. Atomic Threats against China, 1. SCMP 1530, 12.
May 10	Welcomes Albanian Delegation, 1. SCMP 1530, 20.
May 12	Make Things Clear to Student's Parents, 1. SCMP 1534, 2.
May 13	On Labor Trouble, 1. SCMP 1536, 1.
May 14	Agricultural Cooperatives Should Volunteer to Publicize Accounts, 1.
May 15	Labor, Study, and Unite, Greeting the Opening of the Third Conference of National Delegates of the Youth League, 1.
May 15	Peking Press on Urgency to End Nuclear Armaments Race, 5. SCMP 1533, 25.
May 17	The Momentous Significance of Participation in Physical Labor by the Leadership Personnel, 1. SCMP 1538, 14.
May 18	Welcomes Soviet Mongolian Statements, 1. SCMP 1535, 20.
May 19	Continue to Contend, Aid the Rectification Campaign, 1. SCMP 1537, 3.
May 20	Fundamentally Solve the Problem of Vegetable Supply and Demand, 1.
May 21	Correctly Deal with the Question of Employing Apprentices as Workmen This Year, 1. SCMP 1545, 9.
May 21	Diem's Persecution of Overseas Chinese Protested, 5. SCMP 1537, 30.
May 22	In Construction We Should Pay Attention to Cooperation between Organizations and Enterprises, 1.
May 23	On Sino-Japanese Friendship, 1. SCMP 1539, 29.
May 24	Municipal Construction Must Conform to the Principle of Thrift, 1.
May 25	The People of Taiwan Will Not Submit, 1. SCMP 1542, 20.
May 26	Bids Farewell to Beloved President Voroshilov, 1. SCMP 1540, 24.
May 27	How to Ensure the Principles of Hindering neither the Rectification Campaign nor the Current Work, 1. SCMP 1547, 18.
May 28	On Anti-U.S. Demonstration in Taiwan, 1. SCMP 1542, 19.
May 29	Gradually Introduce the System of Worker's Congress in State-Owned Enterprises, 1. SCMP 1547, 10.
May 30	Early Precautions against Natural Disasters, 1. SCMP 1546, 12.
May 31	Problems that Can Be Solved Must Be Solved Right Away, 1. SCMP 1547, 16.
Jun 1	Take Comprehensive Care in Child Development, 1.
Jun 1	Stop the American Conspiracy in Korea, 6.
Jun 2	Strenuously Propagate the Experience of Feeding Draft Cattle, 1.
Jun 3	Strengthen the Work of Dealing with Letters and Visits from the People in Coordination with the Rectification Movement, 1. SCMP 1547, 3.
Jun 4	Rectification Movement Must Be Coordinated with Production Increase and Economy Movement, 1. SCMP 1551, 5.
Jun 5	Labor and Study Simultaneously, 1. SCMP 1555, 16.
Jun 6	On Khruschov's Televised Statement, 1. SCMP 1548, 33.
Jun 6	Make a Good Job of Agricultural Producer Cooperative's Distribution of Summer Harvest, 1. SCMP 1554, 5.
Jun 7	Agronomy Should Serve Agricultural Bumper Crop, 1. SCMP 1554, 7.
Jun 8	What Is This For? (Rectification campaign), 1. SCMP 1553, 2.
Jun 9	There Must Be Active Criticisms as Well as Correct Counter-Criticisms, 1. SCMP 1553, 4.
Jun 10	Workers Start to Speak Up, 1. SCMP 1553, 6.
Jun 10	Peking Papers Greet Colombo Peace Meeting, 3. SCMP 1550, 29.
Jun 11	Unite All People of Our Country on a Socialist Basis, 1. SCMP 1553, 8.
Jun 12	Rectification Movement Must Not Interfere with Production, 4. SCMP 1557, 10.
Jun 12	Correctly Handle the Well-Intentioned Criticisms, 1. SCMP 1553, 11.
Jun 13	Resolutely Deal Blows to Provocations, 1. SCMP 1552, 27.
Jun 13	Run Families Industriously and Thriftily to Serve Socialism, 1. SCMP 1557, 2.
Jun 14	Isn't It a Question of Stand? 1. SCMP 1556, 10.
Jun 16	Build More Small Enterprises, 1. SCMP 1559, 9.
Jun 17	Tense Struggle on Arrival of Rainy Season, 1. SCMP 1561, 6.

1957

Jun 18 Bureaucracy Disregarding Human Life Must Be Resolutely Combated, 2. SCMP 1562, 15.
Jun 18 Peking Papers Greet Egypt's National Day, 1. SCMP 1555, 20.
Jun 19 Colombo Meeting "A Great Step Forward," 1. SCMP 1556, 37.
Jun 22 The Unusual Spring, 1. SCMP 1559, 4.
Jun 23 Supports Korean-Chinese Protest, 1. SCMP 1558, 33.
Jun 24 An Important Problem in the Current Production of Handicraft Industries, 1.
Jun 25 Peking Papers on Korean War Anniversary (U.S. should remember the lesson learned as aggresdor), 1. SCMP 1560, 29.
Jun 26 Current Session of National People's Congress, 1. SCMP 1566, 8.
Jun 28 Do Not Allow the Accomplishment of the American Plot to Crush Peace, 1.
Jun 28 Peking Press on Principles of Peaceful Coexistence, 1. SCMP 1563, 18.
Jun 29 More on Question of Stand, 1. SCMP 1567, 4.
Jun 29 Further Strengthening the Establishment of the People's Police, 3.
Jul 1   Bourgeois Trend of Wen Hui Pao Should Be Subjected to Criticism (Amended 7/15, p. 1), 1. SCMP 1567, 18.
Jul 3   The Year 1956 as Seen from the Three Government Reports to the National People's Congress, 1. SCMP 1566, 10.
Jul 5   Emergency Work on Arrival of Flood Period, 2. SCMP 1573, 26.
Jul 8   The Struggle Is Being Intensified, 1. SCMP 1574, 7.
Jul 9   The Key to a Bumper Harvest, 1. SCMP 1573, 32.
Jul 10 Is the Party Supposed Not to Give Orders? 1. SCMP 1574, 8.
Jul 11 Make Proper Arrangements for Middle and Primary School Graduates to Go to the Countryside, 1. SCMP 1576, 6.
Jul 11 Propagate the Revolutionary Spirit of Nanniwan, Shensi (Self-sufficiency and integrated management), 1,2.
Jul 15 Unite Personal Desires with Needs of the Fatherland, 1. SCMP 1576, 10.
Jul 16 A Great Victory against the Rightists (NPC fourth session closed), 1. SCMP 1578, 1.
Jul 17 An Important Example of Peaceful Foreign Policy, 1.
Jul 18 Refute the Rightists over the Question of Rounding Up Counter-Revolutionaries, 1,2. SCMP 1597, 1.
Jul 19 Don't Miss the Golden Opportunity of Collecting Manure, 1.
Jul 20 On Obstruction of Vietnam Unification, 1. SCMP 1576, 42.
Jul 21 Go to the Locations and Posts That Our Nation Needs, 1.
Jul 22 Prevent Inundation and Work for a Bumper Crop, 1. SCMP 1586, 19.
Jul 23 Can Employees Be Taken on without Inquiring into Their Political Status? 1,2. SCMP 1583, 1.
Jul 24 A Four-Point Proposal for the Development of Agriculture, 1,2. SCMP 1584, 14.
Jul 25 Where There Are Poisonous Weeds, There Should Be Struggle, 1. SCMP 1584, 20.
Jul 26 Greet's Egyptian People's Day, 1. SCMP 1581, 34.
Jul 27 On Korean Armistice Anniversary, 1. SCMP 1581, 41.
Jul 28 Anti-Rightist Struggle Is a Crucial Test for Each Party Member, 1. SCMP 1590, 10.
Jul 29 The Problem of Direction in Handicraft Arts, 1.
Jul 30 On Kishi Cabinet's China Policy, 1. SCMP 1582, 24.
Jul 31 Why Have the Standards for Designs Been Raised? 5.
Aug 1   The Great and Glorious Thirty Years (Of the PLA), 1. SCMP 1588, 6.
Aug 2   Facts Have Crushed Lies (Results of implementation of the 1956 National Economic Plan published) (Amended 8/3, p. 4), 1.
Aug 3   On Vatican's Role in China (Patriotic movement of Chinese Catholics), 1. SCMP 1586, 6.
Aug 4   Why Must Labor Custody Be Enforced? 1. SCMP 1589, 3.
Aug 5   Food Grain Problem and Ideological Problem, 1. SCMP 1591, 4.
Aug 6   Greets Anti-Nuclear Weapons World Conference, 1. SCMP 1587, 40.
Aug 7   Agricultural Producer Cooperatives Ought Not to Speculate in Business, 1. SCMP 1592, 13.
Aug 8   What Should Be Done during Summer Vacation? 1. SCMP 1592, 22.
Aug 9   A Contradictory Problem That Must Be Solved in Industrial Development (Amended 8/24, p. 5), 1. SCMP 1595, 1.
Aug 10 Open Popular Debate in the Countryside, 1,4. SCMP 1592, 2.
Aug 11 Hails Success of World Youth Festival, 1. SCMP 1590, 45.
Aug 12 Sale of Food-Grains Can Be Reduced! 1. SCMP 1598, 26.
Aug 13 Another Important State Measure Concerning Overseas Chinese Affairs, 1. SCMP 1593, 34.
Aug 14 Oman Withdrawal Disadvantage for British, 7. SCMP 1593, 42.
Aug 14 A Lesson for Journalists, 1. SCMP 1600, 35.
Aug 15 Distinguish Right and Wrong over the Food-Grain Problem, 1,4. SCMP 1608, 3.
Aug 16 Carry Out the Struggle to a Further Greater Extent (Anti-rightist struggle), 1. SCMP 1604, 6.
Aug 16 Peking Press Welcomes Soviet-German Statement, 6. SCMP 1595, 35.
Aug 17 Editorial on Failure of U.S. Subversion in Syria, 7. SCMP 1595, 33.
Aug 17 On London Disarmament Talks, 1. SCMP 1595, 36.
Aug 18 Free Market Should Be Subjected to Strict Control, 1. SCMP 1599, 14.
Aug 18 The Hope and Guarantee of Peace, 6.
Aug 19 There Must Be Dictatorship for the Undesirable Characters, 1. SCMP 1598, 3.
Aug 20 Each and All Must Be Frugal with Cloth, 1. SCMP 1600, 5.
Aug 20 Everyone Should Save on Cotton Cloth, 1.
Aug 22 What the Students Who Fail to Gain Admittance into Institutions of Higher Education Should Do, 1. SCMP 1603, 17.
Aug 23 A Key Question in the Current Campaign of Increasing Production and Austerity, 1.
Aug 24 Further Strengthen the Solidarity of the Nationalities, 1,4. SCMP 1605, 11.

1957

Aug 25	A Great Deal of Wealth, 1.
Aug 26	We Should Continue to Exert Ourselves in Making Provisions for Students, 1. SCMP 1607, 37.
Aug 28	Consumption of Food Grains Should Be Planned, 1. SCMP 1608, 7.
Aug 29	The Serious Tasks of All Democratic Parties, 1,2. SCMP 1606, 1.
Aug 29	Peking Press Welcomes President Ho Chi Minh, 6. SCMP 1604, 43.
Aug 30	Purchase More Food Grains in Good Harvest Areas, 1. SCMP 1608, 9.
Aug 31	Peking Press Greets Malaya's Independence, 1. SCMP 1604, 32.
Aug 31	Papers Greet Asian Film Week, 1. SCMP 1605, 38.
Sep 1	Struggle for the Protection of the Socialist Line in Literature and Arts, 1,4. SCMP 1607, 1.
Sep 2	Food-Grain Consumption Must Be Reduced in Cities, 1. SCMP 1614, 15.
Sep 3	Advocate that the Masses Establish and Run Social Welfare Enterprises, 1.
Sep 4	Exposes U.S. Plans for Middle East Aggression (Syria), 1. SCMP 1606, 41.
Sep 4	Trade Unions Should Rely on Activists for Carrying Out the Mass Line, 1,4. SCMP 1611, 8.
Sep 5	Resolutely Keep Faith in the Majority of the Masses, 1,4. SCMP 1613, 5.
Sep 6	On U.S. "Hungarian Question" Intrigues, 1. SCMP 1608, 41.
Sep 7	Draw Up Well the Economic Plan for 1958, 1,4. SCMP 1612, 13.
Sep 8	An Important Task in the Transformation of Nature, 1.
Sep 9	Grasp Well the Work of Unified Purchase of Cotton, 1.
Sep 9	Mobilize the Whole Nation's Women to Build the Nation and Keep House through Diligence and Thrift (Third national women's convention opens), 1,3.
Sep 10	On the Middle East, 1,6. SCMP 1609, 49.
Sep 11	Handle Inner-Party Rightists Sternly, 1. SCMP 1616, 1.
Sep 12	Welcome the Honored Guests of Yugoslavia, 1.
Sep 13	Think of More Ways to Save on Coal, 1.
Sep 14	Peking Press Welcomes Bulgarian Delegation, 1. SCMP 1612, 39.
Sep 14	Time to Change Method of Disarmament Talks, 6. SCMP 1612, 33.
Sep 15	Why Do We Say Bourgeois Rightists Are Reactionaries? 1,2. SCMP 1615, 1.
Sep 15	Peking Press Supports Syrian People's Struggle, 6. SCMP 1612, 51.
Sep 16	Strong Press Exposure of UN Resolution on Hungary, 6. SCMP 1613, 40.
Sep 16	Welcomes Yugoslav Parliamentary Delegation, 1. SCMP 1613, 41.
Sep 17	Peking Press Welcomes Indian Vice-President, 1. SCMP 1614, 35.
Sep 18	Socialist Revolution on the Political and Ideological Fronts, 1. SCMP 1616, 10.
Sep 19	Peking Press Welcomes Indian Exhibition, 1. SCMP 1616, 33.
Sep 20	Autumn Levy of Agricultural Tax Must Be Completed, 1. SCMP 1624, 13.
Sep 21	An Important Reform in Farm Management, 1. SCMP 1624, 16.
Sep 22	Autumn Harvest Must Be Properly Led, 1. SCMP 1626, 11.
Sep 23	Air Views, Rectify Working Style, and Improve Work in Enterprises, 1. SCMP 1626, 13.
Sep 23	U.S.-British Protests on Vladivostok Belie Historical Facts, 6. SCMP 1618, 38.
Sep 24	Chinese People Support Hungarian Foreign Ministry's Statement, 6. SCMP 1619, 46.
Sep 24	Welcomes Soviet Peace Proposals, 1. SCMP 1619, 51.
Sep 25	Raise an Enthusiastic Wave of Water Conservancy Constructions for Agricultural Land, 1. SCMP 1626, 16.
Sep 26	The Glorious Task ahead of Cotton Growers, 1. SCMP 1627, 13.
Sep 27	Papers Welcome Czechoslovak National Assembly Delegation, 1. SCMP 1622, 43.
Sep 27	Sino-Hungarian Friendship Is Unbreakable, 1.
Sep 28	Streamline Administrative Structure of Enterprises in Revolutionary Spirit, 1,2. SCMP 1628, 7.
Sep 29	Peking Press Welcomes Soviet Delegation, 1. SCMP 1622, 19.
Sep 30	Make Up Our Mind to Rectify Our Working Style and Improve Our Work, 1. SCMP 1629, 1.
Oct 1	Cheers to the Eighth Anniversary of the Founding of Our Nation, 1,3.
Oct 3	Scientific and Technical Development Cannot Be Severed from Politics (Anti-rightist struggle in public health circle), 1. SCMP 1634, 14.
Oct 4	Papers Greet Opening of WFTU (World Federation of Trade Unions), 1. SCMP 1627, 21.
Oct 5	Peking Papers Welcome Joint Sino-Hungarian Communique, 1. SCMP 1627, 34.
Oct 6	To the Countryside! To the Labor Front! (Cadres transferred), 1. SCMP 1631, 1.
Oct 7	Peking Papers Welcome Soviet Scientific Achievement (Sputnik), 1. SCMP 1628, 40.
Oct 8	Overhaul the Backward Cooperative through Public Debates, 1. SCMP 1635, 2.
Oct 9	Grave Struggle Still Exists on Political and Legal Front, 1. SCMP 1636, 1.
Oct 10	How Should Statistical Work Be Improved? 1. SCMP 1639, 6.
Oct 11	Catch Up with and Surpass the Well-Off Middle Peasants in Production Level within Five Years (Amended 10/13, p. 3), 1. SCMP 1635, 5.
Oct 12	Papers Welcome Sino-Bulgarian Statement, 1. SCMP 1632, 24.
Oct 13	Khruschov Shows Road to Peaceful Coexistence (Khruschov's interview with New York Times reporter), 1. SCMP 1632, 31.
Oct 14	Overcome the Two Tendencies in Political and Legal Work (Negligence of dictatorship and party leadership), 1. SCMP 1638, 1.
Oct 15	On What Yangtze Bridge Signifies, 1. SCMP 1634, 5.
Oct 16	Stresses Urgency of Disarmament, 1. SCMP 1635, 47.
Oct 17	Emergency Mobilization for Fight against Drought, 1. SCMP 1639, 10.
Oct 18	Peking Press Supports Syria (Against U.S. aggression), 1. SCMP 1637, 21.
Oct 18	A New Victory of the International Unity of the Working Class (Fourth World Trade Union convention closed), 5.
Oct 20	Make Haste to Pick and Purchase Cotton, 1.

1957

Oct 21   Make Improvements in Work Resolutely, Boldly, and Thoroughly, 1. SCMP 1645, 1.
Oct 22   One Should Lead the Waterworks Construction and the Campaign to Collect Manure like Hopei, 1.
Oct 22   Warns U.S. and Turkey (About dangers of war against Syria), 6. SCMP 1638, 48.
Oct 23   Greets Afghan Prime Minister (On visit to China), 1. SCMP 1639, 37.
Oct 23   Keeping Order, a Glorious Duty of Every Citizen (Public security regulations promulgated), 4. SCMP 1646, 13.
Oct 24   Adopt Effective Measures to Prevent and Cure Endemic Diseases, 1.
Oct 25   We Will Build a Powerful Chemical Industry, 1. SCMP 1643, 3.
Oct 27   The Great Principles of Constructing Socialist Rural Areas (Revised draft of Principles of Agricultural Development) (Amended 10/28, p. 1), 1.
Oct 28   Two Important Sets of Regulations Having Bearing on the Livelihood of Every Individual (On pork supply and vegetable oil supply), 4. SCMP 1647, 4.
Oct 28   Peking Papers Welcome Joint China-Afghan Communique, 1. SCMP 1642, 50.
Oct 29   State Discipline Must Be Strengthened (State Council regulations on reward and punishment of state bureaucracy employees), 1. SCMP 1648, 5.
Oct 30   Help Youths in Their Self-Study by All Means, 1. SCMP 1653, 22.
Oct 31   Greets Soviet-Chinese Friendship Association, 1. SCMP 1645, 37.
Nov 1   The All-People Rectification Campaign Is an Important Development of the Socialist Democracy of Our Country, 1. SCMP 1654, 1.
Nov 2   U.S. Waging Cold War in Red Cross Conference, 1. SCMP 1646, 33.
Nov 2   Actively Increase the Output of Coal and Energetically Conserve Coal (State Council directive), 4. SCMP 1670, 21.
Nov 3   Our Hearts Are Turned to Moscow (Chairman Mao-led Chinese delegation arriving at Moscow), 1.
Nov 4   Another "Red Moon" (Launching of second USSR satellite), 1. SCMP 1647, 35.
Nov 6   Long Live the October Revolution! Long Live Socialism! 1.
Nov 9   Supports Supreme Soviet Appeal for Peace (October Revolution anniversary), 1. SCMP 1651, 49.
Nov 9   "Two Chinas" Notion Is Fantastic, 2. SCMP 1651, 35.
Nov 10   Provide Suitable and Good Conditions for Scientific Research Work (State Council on scientific work), 1. SCMP 1664, 21.
Nov 11   Settle Down and Establish One's Career in the Countryside (Rustication of middle and primary school graduates), 1. SCMP 1657, 1.
Nov 12   We Should Have a Powerful Column of Literature and Art of the Working Class, 1. SCMP 1664, 1.
Nov 13   Mobilize All the People to Discuss the Forty Articles of the Agricultural Program and to Stir Up a New High Tide in Agricultural Production, 1. SCMP 1661, 1.
Nov 14   How Much Money Do You Plan to Invest in National Bonds Next Year? 1. SCMP 1659, 1.
Nov 15   Mourns Demise of Zapotocky (Czech leader), 1. SCMP 1655, 32.

1957

Nov 15   Propagate Advanced Experiences, Mobilize the People to Develop Water Works on a Large Scale, 1.
Nov 16   Everyone Should Come to Support Agriculture, 1.
Nov 17   Resolutely Streamline Organs, Retrench Personnel, and Improve Work, 1. SCMP 1657, 12.
Nov 18   Improving Management in Industry, Commerce, and Finance (State Council regulations), 1. SCMP 1665, 10.
Nov 18   Pep Up Collection of Fertilizers (Emergency notice of Ministry of Agriculture), 1. SCMP 1664, 25.
Nov 19   Develop the Peasant's After-Work Cultural Education, 1.
Nov 21   Provide Further Solutions to Certain Questions of Wages, Insurance, and Welfare from the Viewpoint of Six Hundred Million People (Four drafts of State Council), 1. SCMP 1667, 1.
Nov 24   Strive for Next Year's Great Harvest of Wheat, 2.
Nov 25   On Moscow Declarations ("The great revolutionary declarations"), 1. SCMP 1660, 26.
Nov 26   Store Grain to Prepare for Famine, Make Up Losses by Full Harvest, 1.
Nov 27   Build the Road for the Self-Sufficiency of the Blind through Production, 4.
Nov 28   A Measure of Important Revolutionary Significance (Families of military officers to return to home towns), 1. SCMP 1668, 19.
Nov 29   Go Deeper in Propagating the Campaign of Increasing Production and Austerity, Create a New High Tide in Industrial Production, 1,3.
Nov 30   In Eliminating the Blood Fluke Disease, Policies Must Be Implemented and Integrated, 1.
Dec 2   Papers Greet Opening of Eighth Trade Union Congress, 1. SCMP 1665, 30.
Dec 4   Neither Production nor Overhaul of Cooperatives Should Be Hampered (Amended 12/5, p. 2), 1. SCMP 1673, 9.
Dec 4   Welcome the Honored Guests from Burma (Friendship and economic delegation), 5.
Dec 6   Appropriately Enlarge Common Reserve of Agricultural Cooperative, 1. SCMP 1673, 13.
Dec 7   Struggle of the Two Roads in the Countryside as Seen through an Exhibition, 4. SCMP 1690, 7.
Dec 8   Bright Future for Development of Mountain Economy, 1. SCMP 1683, 7.
Dec 9   March Forward on the Road of Integrating with the Workers and Peasants (December 9th movement anniversary), 1.
Dec 10   Emulate the Exemplars of High Yield in Cotton Production, 1.
Dec 11   The Current Tasks of Language Reform and the Principles of Pronunciation of the Chinese Language, 1.
Dec 12   We Must Stick to the Policy of Achieving "Quantity, Speed, Quality, and Economy" in Construction, 1. SCMP 1677, 5.
Dec 13   Create a New High Tide in Industrial Production (National Trade Unions convention closed), 1,3.
Dec 14   Hails the Soviet Union's Latest Peace Efforts (In UN General Assembly), 1. SCMP 1674, 33.
Dec 14   Run People's Hospitals Well through Diligence and Thrift, 7.
Dec 15   The Masses Must Be Relied On for the Massive Water Conservancy and Irrigation Projects, 1. SCMP 1684, 13.
Dec 16   Further Propagate the Principles of Housekeeping by Diligence and Thrift, 1.

1957

Dec 17   China's Firm Support for Indonesia (To recover West Irian), 1. SCMP 1676, 43.
Dec 18   A Good Method of Solving the Problem of Worker's Quarters (Hsiangchiang machine plant), 1.
Dec 19   Stop Blind Rural Exodus (Party Central and State Council directive), 1. SCMP 1682, 4.
Dec 19   Guaranteeing the 500 Thousand Horsepower Draining and Irrigating Machinery Will Go to the Rural Areas without a Hitch, 3.
Dec 20   Political and Law Departments Must Be Thoroughly Reorganized, 1. SCMP 1687, 2.
Dec 21   On NATO Summit Meeting, 1. SCMP 1679, 51.
Dec 22   Correctly Deal with Peasants Working on Their Own (State Council directive), 1. SCMP 1687, 14.
Dec 23   Launch with Vigor the Winter Patriotic Health Campaign, 1.
Dec 25   Raise a High Tide of Administrative Improvement in the Wake of High Tide of Contending and Blooming, 1. SCMP 1689, 1.
Dec 26   Hails Afro-Asian Solidarity Congress (Cairo congress), 1. SCMP 1681, 28.
Dec 27   What Are the Principal Tasks of the Handicraft Workers? (National handicraft cooperatives conference closes), 1.
Dec 28   Bumper Harvest Follows Bumper Harvest, Advancement Succeeds Advancement (Problem of agricultural rates of growth), 1.
Dec 29   A Provincial Party Congress which Reaps Tremendous Success (Purge of Chekiang anti-party clique), 1.
Dec 30   We Want Peaceful Coexistence, not Armament Race, 1. SCMP 1686, 1.
Dec 31   Press Editorials Greet Crown Prince of Yemen, 1. SCMP 1684, 51.

1958

Jan 1   JMJP New Year Greetings to Indonesia, 5. SCMP 1685, 38.
Jan 1   Full Steam Ahead, 1,4. SCMP 1685, 1.
Jan 2   Southwest and Northwest Linked with Nationwide Railway Network, 1. SCMP 1688, 14.
Jan 4   JMJP Evaluates Success of Cairo Conference, 1,5. SCMP 1686, 30.
Jan 6   Strive for Further Advance on the Basis of Tremendous Achievements Already Effected, 1. SCMP 1692, 6.
Jan 7   Attention Must Be Paid to Make Economic Use of Land in National Construction, 1. SCMP 1694, 10.
Jan 8   The Whole Country as Viewed from the Meilin Factory, 1. SCMP 1691, 6.
Jan 10   JMJP Commemorates Dr. Petru Groza, 1. SCMP 1691, 42.
Jan 10   Let Household Registration Work Render Greater Service to the People, 4. SCMP 1695, 10.
Jan 11   JMJP Supports Soviet Proposal for Summit Conference, 5. SCMP 1691, 28.
Jan 12   An Impressive Marxist Report, 1. SCMP 1698, 30.
Jan 13   JMJP on Sino-Yemeni Friendship, 1. SCMP 1692, 29.
Jan 14   Sideline Production in the Countryside Cannot Be Slackened, 1.

1958

Jan 15   Resolutely Oppose Rightist Ideology--A Serious Lesson from the Question of the Kuanchuang, 1. SCMP 1702, 10.
Jan 16   Soil Conservation Is Lifeline of Mountain Production, 1. SCMP 1704, 14.
Jan 17   Institutions of Higher Education Have Also to Oppose Waste, 1. SCMP 1705, 16.
Jan 19   Whither the United States? 1. SCMP 1696, 31.
Jan 20   Two Good Examples, 1.
Jan 21   Expand the Chemical Fertilizer Industry and Raise Agricultural Output, 1. SCMP 1706, 21.
Jan 23   Let Bare Mountains Be Afforested Quickly, 1.
Jan 24   General Mobilization of All People to Develop Patriotic Health Campaign, 1. SCMP 1722, 6.
Jan 27   Get Rid of the Bureaucratic Style, 1.
Jan 29   Let All Cities and Towns Fall in Line with Sungpu, 1. SCMP 1709, 9.
Jan 31   Fully Promote the Role of Youth as the Stimulating Force of the Revolution (Third Communist Youth League conference), 1. SCMP 1713, 18.
Feb 1   Give Heed to Field Management for Winter Crops, 1.
Feb 2   Our Action Slogan--Combat Waste, Build the Country through Diligence and Thrift, 1,2. SCMP 1721, 19.
Feb 3   Rouse Your Revolutionary Spirit, Climb Ever Onward, 1. SCMP 1714, 1.
Feb 4   High Productive Areas Can Make Another Leap, Low Productive Areas Can Also Make a Leap, 1.
Feb 6   JMJP Supports Korean Government's Unification Statement, 1. SCMP 1710, 40.
Feb 7   Mobilize the Masses to Break Old Rules, 1.
Feb 8   JMJP Supports China's Statement on Korea, 1. SCMP 1711, 31.
Feb 9   Break Away from Established Customs during Spring Festival, 1. SCMP 1715, 3.
Feb 10   Carry Out the Policy of Letting Masses Run Own Schools and Promotion of Education through Industry and Thrift, 1. SCMP 1730, 20.
Feb 11   A Great Event in Our Nation's Work on Labor Wages (State Council regulations), 3.
Feb 12   A Congress Which Fights for Big Advancement, 1,2.
Feb 13   Be Thorough with the Extermination of the "Four Evils" in China, 1.
Feb 13   Enjoy a Merry Spring Festival, 4. SCMP 1715, 1.
Feb 14   JMJP on Sino-Soviet Treaty (Alliance of eternity, alliance of peace), 1. SCMP 1716, 13.
Feb 14   Commercial Work Can Certainly Be Advanced by Leaps and Bounds, 1,4.
Feb 14   Emulate, Learn from, and Overtake the Advanced, 3.
Feb 15   Peking Press Welcomes Ho-Nehru Joint Statement, 5. SCMP 1716, 50.
Feb 15   Cultivation of Experimental Farming Plots--Road to Becoming "Both Red and Expert," 1. SCMP 1720, 12.
Feb 16   Let Trees Be Planted by Every Household, 1.
Feb 17   Energetically Develop Tea Production, 3. SCMP 1735, 2.
Feb 18   Combating Waste and Conservatism Is the Central Problem of the Present Rectification Campaign, 1. SCMP 1724, 1.

1958

Feb 19 Support the Government, Love the People, Help to Bring about a Great Leap in Production, 1.
Feb 20 JMJP Welcomes Sino-Korean Joint Statement, 1,3. SCMP 1718, 43.
Feb 21 JMJP Welcomes CPV Statement (For the sake of peace), 1,3. SCMP 1719, 14.
Feb 22 JMJP Endorses Soviet Statement on Korea, 1. SCMP 1719, 35.
Feb 23 Peking Press Greets Soviet Army Day, 1. SCMP 1719, 42.
Feb 24 JMJP Significance of U.A.R. (Solidarity under the anti-colonialist banner), 1. SCMP 1720, 53.
Feb 26 Take Advantage of the Victory to Forge Ahead and Operate on a Large Scale during Spring, 1.
Feb 27 Get More Zealous to Speed Up the Elimination of Schistosomiasis, 1.
Feb 28 Disturb the Old Balance and Establish a New One, 1. SCMP 1731, 1.
Mar 1 Examples of Anti-Conservatism and Great Leaps, 1.
Mar 2 To Hear about a Thing Many Times Is Not Equal to a Single Look at It, 1.
Mar 3 Great Leap in Water Conservancy Construction, 1.
Mar 5 Greeting the Birth of the Abundant and Beautiful Kwangsi-Chuang Nationality Autonomous Region, 1.
Mar 6 JMJP on Fourth Sino-Japanese Trade Agreement, 5. SCMP 1727, 60.
Mar 6 Bugle Call for Mobilization of All People Sounded, 1. SCMP 1734, 1.
Mar 7 Start Big Leap Forward in Massive Illiteracy Elimination Campaign, 1. SCMP 1735, 13.
Mar 8 Peking Papers Mark Women's Day, 1. SCMP 1729, 48.
Mar 8 Railway Workers to Save Large Sum for State, 3. SCMP 1731, 5.
Mar 9 JMJP on Democratic Vietnam's Peace Proposal, 3. SCMP 1729, 32.
Mar 10 Dictatorship Must Be Exercised against the Enemy to the End (Li Shih-nung's anti-Party group), 1,3. SCMP 1736, 21.
Mar 10 Shatter the Anti-Peace Provocations of the SEATO Manila Session, 1,5. SCMP 1729, 44.
Mar 10 There Are Advantages in Growing More Potatoes, 4.
Mar 11 Hsushui County Creates Good Experiences, 1.
Mar 11 JMJP Criticizes U.S. Obstruction to Summit Conference, 5. SCMP 1731, 37.
Mar 12 JMJP Denounces U.S. Interference in Indonesia, 1. SCMP 1731, 40.
Mar 13 JMJP Hails CPV Peace Initiative, 1. SCMP 1732, 39.
Mar 13 Ministry Calls for Greater Increase in Draft Animals, 2. SCMP 1735, 8.
Mar 14 Tientsin Factory Leaders Go to Workshops, 1. SCMP 1737, 19.
Mar 14 Defend Independence, Oppose Intervention (Indonesia), 1,5.
Mar 15 Peking Papers Comment on Manila Meeting (Dulles suffers another setback), 5. SCMP 1734, 37.
Mar 15 All for One, One for All, 1. SCMP 1755, 3.
Mar 16 Bigger Circulations, Faster Deliveries for Papers, 1. SCMP 1736, 9.
Mar 17 The Proper Road to Self-Reeducation, 1,2. SCMP 1737, 5.
Mar 18 Make a Clean Sweep of Conservative Thoughts in State-Owned Farms, 1. SCMP 1754, 5.
Mar 19 Enthusiastic Press Reaction to Sports Program, 5. SCMP 1739, 9.
Mar 19 Correctly Promote Big Leap Forward in Publishing Work, 1. SCMP 1743, 7.
Mar 20 Peking Press Welcomes Polish Government Delegation, 1. SCMP 1738, 27.
Mar 20 JMJP Hails Soviet Election Results, 1. SCMP 1738, 26.
Mar 21 The Main Thing Is for the Cooperatives to Build Small Conservancy Projects to Store Water, 1. SCMP 1744, 16.
Mar 22 Buds of Technical Revolution in Agriculture, 1. SCMP 1744, 7.
Mar 23 Onward to the Goal of "Thoroughly Red and Profoundly Expert," 1,2. SCMP 1747, 1.
Mar 24 New Experiences of "Experimental Farming" in Industry, 1. SCMP 1753, 17.
Mar 25 Store Up Water to Fight Drought, 1.
Mar 26 Take the Attitude of a Common Laborer, 1. SCMP 1755, 6.
Mar 27 Political Leadership Ensures the Running of Enterprises with Hard Work and Thrift, 1.
Mar 28 Cadres Dispatched Downward Should Bring Culture and Knowledge to the Peasants, 1. SCMP 1761, 6.
Mar 29 Burn Up Waste and Conservatism in Technical Designing, 1. SCMP 1755, 10.
Mar 30 Algeria's Independence Will Be Won, Says JMJP, 1. SCMP 1744, 44.
Mar 31 JMJP Cites Su Kuang-ming as Technical Innovator, 1. SCMP 1746, 12.
Apr 1 JMJP on Soviet Nuclear Tests Decision (Gospel of mankind), 1. SCMP 1746, 37.
Apr 2 JMJP Welcomes Rumanian Delegation, 1. SCMP 1746, 52.
Apr 2 JMJP Acclaims Success of Supreme Soviet (Amended 4/6, p. 6), 5. SCMP 1746, 44.
Apr 3 Kishi's Sabotage of Trade Agreement Not to Be Tolerated, 1. SCMP 1747, 32.
Apr 4 We Must Fight for the Bumper Harvest of Wheat Crops, 1.
Apr 5 Set the Index Figure at 100, Ways and Means at 120, and Hard Work at 240, 1.
Apr 6 JMJP on Care for Young Workers, 1,2. SCMP 1760, 6.
Apr 7 Pay Attention to the Tempo of Production Adjustment, 1.
Apr 7 Peking Papers Hail Soviet Proposal (Demands U.S. and Britain suspend nuclear tests), 5. SCMP 1749, 43.
Apr 8 JMJP Welcomes Sino-Polish Economic Cooperation, 1. SCMP 1749, 53.
Apr 8 Afforestation Needs Another New High Tide (Central Committee and State Council directive), 1.
Apr 9 Peking Press on Sino-Rumanian Joint Statement, 1. SCMP 1750, 47.
Apr 9 Let There Be More Advanced Units and Advanced Persons, 2.
Apr 10 JMJP Greets Youth Congress, 4. SCMP 1753, 4.
Apr 11 Develop Light Industry with Quantity, Speed, Quality, and Economy, 1. SCMP 1763, 14.
Apr 12 Much Use Can Be Made of Wild Plants, 1.
Apr 13 Make Bourgeois Individualism Stink, 1. SCMP 1757, 1.
Apr 14 China Collects Folk Songs, 1. SCMP 1754, 23.

1958

| Apr 14 | Contrive to Fulfill Production Increase Targets, 1. SCMP 1768, 39.
| Apr 15 | JMJP Denounces Kishi Government, 1. SCMP 1754, 44.
| Apr 16 | Enhance the Use of Double-Wheel Double-Blade Plows, 1.
| Apr 17 | Not a Moment of the Spring Sowing Time Can Be Wasted, 1.
| Apr 17 | Kishi Government Held Accountable for Liu Lien-jen Case, Says JMJP, 4. SCMP 1755, 51.
| Apr 19 | Linguistic Work among Minorities Needs Promoting, 1. SCMP 1762, 13.
| Apr 20 | Do Everything Possible to Tap the Latent Strength of the Existing Irrigation Equipment, 1.
| Apr 21 | Establish Large Numbers of Private Agricultural Middle Schools, 1. SCMP 1764, 14.
| Apr 22 | Four Hurdles to Be Negotiated on Way to Bumper Harvest, 1. SCMP 1763, 29.
| Apr 23 | Question of Grain Supply during Busy Season, 1. SCMP 1768, 28.
| Apr 24 | New Achievement of the Fraternal Mutual Assistance and Cooperation between China and Soviet Union, 1.
| Apr 24 | Peking Press Marks Anti-Colonialism Day, 1,4. SCMP 1760, 46.
| Apr 25 | Light of Freedom Rises in Africa (African independent nations conference closed), 1. SCMP 1760, 52.
| Apr 26 | More Short Literary and Art Works Must Be Composed, 1. SCMP 1767, 25.
| Apr 27 | Work Penetratingly and on a Business-Like Basis! 1. SCMP 1769, 2.
| Apr 28 | New Measures to Strengthen Economic Cooperation between China and Rumania, 1.
| Apr 29 | Two Ways of Doing the Statistical Work, 1,4. SCMP 1775, 4.
| Apr 30 | Make Maximum Use of All Men and Things, 1.
| May 1 | Strive for Greater Labor Day Achievements, 1. SCMP 1766, 14.
| May 3 | JMJP for Fair Supplementary Elections in Laos, 1. SCMP 1766, 38.
| May 4 | Let Them Be Both Red and Expert, and the Latecomers Take the Lead, 1,2. SCMP 1772, 1.
| May 5 | Modern Revisionism Must Be Criticized, Says JMJP, 1. SCMP 1767, 4.
| May 5 | JMJP Welcomes Korean People's Delegation, 2. SCMP 1767, 45.
| May 6 | Further Unfold the Movements for Renovating Farming Implements, 1. SCMP 1771, 6.
| May 7 | An Important Beginning for Reform of Industrial Management, 1. SCMP 1774, 1.
| May 8 | Have More and Better Work Done Faster and More Economically for the Development of Socialist Culture and Arts, 1,4. SCMP 1773, 12.
| May 9 | The Way to Be Both "Red" and "Expert", 1. SCMP 1774, 13.
| May 11 | JMJP Denounces Kishi's Hostility to China, 1. SCMP 1772, 47.
| May 12 | Develop Local Industry with Quantity, Speed, Quality, and Economy, 1,4. SCMP 1778, 12.
| May 13 | Do Everything Possible to Consummate Summer Harvest and Cultivation, 1. SCMP 1782, 20.
| May 14 | Firmly Protect Cotton Seedlings, 1.
| May 15 | The Hydro-Power Station--Incandescent Pearl in Rural Areas, 1. SCMP 1776, 14.
| May 16 | JMJP Refutes Nobusuke Kishi's Allegations, 1. SCMP 1777, 19.
| May 16 | Peking Press Hails New Soviet Satellite, 1. SCMP 1777, 27.
| May 17 | Peking Press Warns against U.S. Interference in Indonesia, 1. SCMP 1777, 43.
| May 17 | Peking Press Hails USSR-UAR Friendship, 5. SCMP 1777, 42.
| May 18 | A New Problem (Egg purchase in Anyang County), 1.
| May 19 | Rely on the Masses to Cultivate More Fine Strains, 1.
| May 20 | U.S. Provocation against Lebanon Commented by JMJP, 6. SCMP 1778, 56.
| May 20 | Eliminate Illiteracy with the Revolutionary Spirit, 1,4. SCMP 1787, 22.
| May 21 | Consummate Summer Grain Collection Work, 1. SCMP 1782, 33.
| May 22 | JMJP Says, Science Is No Mystery, 1. SCMP 1788, 18.
| May 23 | JMJP on Fascist Crisis in France, 1. SCMP 1780, 57.
| May 23 | Exterminate in Good Time the Insect Pests That Plague Agricultural Crops, 2.
| May 24 | Increase the Paddy Crop Acreage to Change the Low Production Situation in North China, 1. SCMP 1791, 17.
| May 26 | JMJP Welcomes Results of Moscow Economic Conference, 5. SCMP 1781, 49.
| May 28 | Peking Press Acclaims Warsaw Treaty States' Meeting, 5. SCMP 1782, 56 (summary).
| May 29 | What Do the Results of the General Election in Italy Indicate? 6.
| May 29 | Plant the Red Flag of the General Line All Over the Country, 1. SCMP 1785, 4.
| May 29 | JMJP Urges to Set Up Part-Time Schools for Workers, 7. SCMP 1787, 29.
| May 30 | Chinese People Support Lebanese People, Says JMJP, 5. SCMP 1784, 39.
| May 30 | JMJP on French People's Struggle, 1. SCMP 1784, 38.
| Jun 1 | Peking Papers Greet International Children's Day, 1. SCMP 1785, 18.
| Jun 2 | Open Wide the Door of Convenience, 1.
| Jun 3 | Carry Out the Technological Revolution (Amended 6/6, p. 3), 1. SCMP 1788, 2.
| Jun 4 | Modern Revisionism Must Be Fought to the End, Says JMJP, 1. SCMP 1787, 9.
| Jun 4 | Promote with Vigor the Mating of Draft Animals, 2.
| Jun 5 | Regulations That Will Press Forward Agricultural Production, 1. SCMP 1792, 14.
| Jun 6 | Why Regional Economic Construction Bonds Should Be Issued, 1. SCMP 1791, 2.
| Jun 6 | The Next Year as Seen through This Year, 1. SCMP 1797, 9.
| Jun 7 | People of Honan Set a Good Example, 1.
| Jun 8 | Raise High the Banner of Defense (International Democratic Women's Union conference), 3.
| Jun 9 | The Cultural Revolution Has Begun, 1. SCMP 1793, 21.
| Jun 10 | Industrial Departments Should Also "Look at the Next Year," 1. SCMP 1797, 11.
| Jun 10 | An Important Reform of the Taxation System, 3. SCMP 1793, 13.
| Jun 11 | Congratulations on Bumper Harvest of Rapeseeds, 2. SCMP 1804, 11.
| Jun 12 | Wheat Yield Broken Again, 1. SCMP 1794, 25.
| Jun 12 | Let the Whole Party and All the People Take Up Communication Work, 4.
| Jun 14 | Do Everything to Make a Success of Summer Planting, 2.

1958

Jun 14	Great Achievements in May (Amended 6/15, p. 2), 1. SCMP 1803, 8.
Jun 16	Fight Actively to Step Up the Yield of Early Rice, 2.
Jun 18	The Localities Can Also Develop Scientific Undertakings on a Large Scale, 1. SCMP 1804, 17.
Jun 19	A Great Year--JMJP Editorial on Anniversary of Mao's Article, 1. SCMP 1799, 5.
Jun 20	Rice Production Needs to Be Accelerated, 1.
Jun 20	Our Lessons from the Counter-Revolutionary Rebellion of the Nagy Clique, 1. SCMP 1801, 1.
Jun 21	Strive for Fast Tempo in Construction, 1. SCMP 1803, 10.
Jun 22	Khruschov's Letters "Timely and Reasonable," Says JMJP, 1. SCMP 1799, 38 (summary).
Jun 23	On-the-Spot Meetings--A Marxist-Leninist Method of Leadership, 1. SCMP 1802, 4.
Jun 24	The Masses Must Be Mobilized to Carry Out Technological Revolution, 1.
Jul 1	The Peasant Question Still Remains the Fundamental One, 1,2. SCMP 1815, 10.
Jul 1	Western Moves against Lebanon, Danger to Peace, 1. SCMP 1805, 60.
Jul 2	Landmark of Big Leap Forward for People in Peking, 1.
Jul 3	Strengthen the Leadership of the Party to Have Student Enrollment Work Better Carried Out for Institutions of Higher Learning, 1. SCMP 1810, 24.
Jul 3	JMJP Editorial Urges U.S. to Clarify Stand toward Ambassadorial Talks, 1,5. SCMP 1807, 1.
Jul 5	Strengthen the Management of Cotton Fields to Fight for Bumper Harvest, 1.
Jul 7	JMJP Welcomes Declaration of Fifteen Communist Workers' Parties, 1. SCMP 1807, 46.
Jul 7	The Chinese People Are Firmly Opposed to Japan's Latent Imperialism, 5. SCMP 1807, 53.
Jul 9	Let Us Start an "Anti-Drought" Campaign in Industry, 5. SCMP 1815, 23.
Jul 10	Let Us Arm Ourselves by Our Own Efforts, 1. SCMP 1815, 5.
Jul 11	Let Our Students Graduate in the Midst of Labor, 1. SCMP 1814, 38.
Jul 13	Cooperation Is Strength, 1.
Jul 14	Confidence of Experience of "Native" Experts and "Foreign" Experts, 1. SCMP 1820, 10.
Jul 15	Investment in Capital Construction Must Be Placed on a Contract System, 1. SCMP 1822, 2.
Jul 16	JMJP Hails Iraqi Revolution, 4. SCMP 1814, 51.
Jul 17	JMJP Denounces U.S. Aggression in Lebanon, 1. SCMP 1817, 23.
Jul 17	Speed Up Mechanization of Building Work, 4. SCMP 1826, 12.
Jul 18	JMJP Condemns U.S.-British Aggression, 1. SCMP 1817, 42.
Jul 20	JMJP Supports Chinese, Soviet Statements, 1. SCMP 1818, 19.
Jul 21	Eisenhower Hoists the Pirate's Skull and Crossbones (Amended 7/22, p. 5), 1. SCMP 1819, 30.
Jul 21	JMJP Greets UAR-Iraq Mutual Defense, 1. SCMP 1819, 36.
Jul 21	Where There Is a Work Site, There Will Be Vegetables to Eat, 6. SCMP 1826, 16.
Jul 22	JMJP Warns U.S., British Aggressors, 1. SCMP 1820, 25.
Jul 22	Can the Labor Force Be Expanded? 7.
Jul 23	The Lesson of This Year's Bumper Summer Harvest, 6. SCMP 1823, 15.
Jul 23	JMJP Says U.S.-British Forces Must Withdraw, 1. SCMP 1821, 26.
Jul 24	Peking Press Welcomes China-Cambodia Diplomatic Relations, 1. SCMP 1821, 38.
Jul 24	How to Spend Summer Vacation This Year, 7. SCMP 1825, 21.
Jul 25	Soviet Proposal a Major Step for Peace, 1. SCMP 1822, 13.
Jul 25	Chiang Kai-shek Clique Wants to Indulge in Vain Hopes, 1.
Jul 25	Peking Press Supports Stockholm Congress Call, 5. SCMP 1822, 50.
Jul 25	There Should Be a Big Leap Forward in the Production of Oil-Bearing Crops, 6.
Jul 26	Inextinguishable Flame of Rage in Middle East, 1. SCMP 1822, 24.
Jul 26	An Important Event in Renovation of Farm Implements, 5.
Jul 27	U.S. Intervention--A Paper Tiger (Korean War), 1. SCMP 1823, 40.
Jul 28	Workers Should Learn to Utilize More Kinds of Technology, 1.
Jul 28	A Rich Autumn Harvest Will Be Brought About This Year, 5. SCMP 1831, 23.
Jul 28	New State of Affairs on Theoretical Front, 7. SCMP 1825, 4.
Jul 29	Socialist Camp: Friend of All Nations Striving for Independence (Amended 7/30, p. 4), 1,4. SCMP 1825, 35.
Jul 30	JMJP Demands Immediate Summit Conference, 1. SCMP 1825, 47.
Jul 30	Ambition of People in Northern Anhwei Province--JMJP Editorial on Anhwei Conservancy Efforts, 5. SCMP 1833, 33.
Jul 30	Commercial Work in Hopei Is a Red Banner, 6.
Jul 31	The Baghdad Pact without Baghdad Is a Ghost That Cannot Be Recalled, 1. SCMP 1826, 47.
Aug 2	Be On the Alert! (JMJP editorial on Taiwan agents), 4. SCMP 1829, 43.
Aug 2	Strengthen Work on Folk Literature and Arts, 7.
Aug 3	JMJP Welcomes Korean Government Delegation, 1. SCMP 1828, 54.
Aug 3	JMJP Greets Iraqi Victory, 1. SCMP 1828, 40.
Aug 3	Year-End Account Reckoners Are Certain to Lose, 4. SCMP 1830, 21.
Aug 3	Organize the Sending of Cadres at Five Levels to the Fields, 5.
Aug 4	JMJP on Sino-Soviet Talks, 1. SCMP 1827, 32.
Aug 5	U.S. Imperialism, Deadly Enemy of Smaller Nations, 1. SCMP 1829, 47.
Aug 6	Mutual Assistance and Coordination (Communist working style), 1. SCMP 1831, 1.
Aug 7	JMJP Supports Latest Soviet Proposal on Middle East, 1. SCMP 1831, 56.
Aug 7	Dramatic Workers Should Strive to Portray Modern Life, 7.
Aug 8	Only through Resolute Struggle May Peace Be Defended, 1. SCMP 1832, 1.
Aug 8	Simultaneous Use of Native and Modern Methods Is Shortcut to Fully Developed Steel and Iron Industry, 6. SCMP 1836, 9.

1958

Aug 10	JMJP on UN Assembly's Urgent Task to Uphold Peace, 1,2. SCMP 1831, 62.
Aug 12	Trade Union Organizations Must Carry Out the Rectification Campaign to the End, 1. SCMP 1837, 6.
Aug 13	Congratualtions on the Shining "Satellites" of Rice and Peanuts, 1. SCMP 1837, 10.
Aug 13	All Party and People to Engage in Statistical Work, 3. SCMP 1839, 28.
Aug 14	Break the "Theory of Finality" to Fight for a Bigger Bumper Harvest, 1. SCMP 1840, 22.
Aug 15	Peking Press Welcomes Premier Sihanouk, 1. SCMP 1836, 19.
Aug 16	JMJP Editorial on U.S.-China Memorandum, 1,4. SCMP 1836, 1.
Aug 16	JMJP Mourns Joliot-Curie, 4. SCMP 1836, 45.
Aug 17	JMJP Criticizes Eisenhower's Middle East Plan, 1,3. SCMP 1837, 51.
Aug 18	Fight Hard for a Winter and a Spring for Basic Consummation of Water Conservancy Work (Amended 8/19, p. 2), 1,2. SCMP 1840, 35.
Aug 19	U.S. Tramples on UN Charter, 1. SCMP 1838, 49.
Aug 20	Peking Papers on U.S. Troops in Singapore, 1. SCMP 1839, 46.
Aug 20	Who Says Ants Cannot Gnaw at a Bone? 1. SCMP 1849, 13.
Aug 21	A Great Campaign for Improving Tools, 1. SCMP 1845, 21.
Aug 21	Peking Press Denounces IOC Scheme to Create "Two Chinas," 4. SCMP 1840, 39.
Aug 21	JMJP Says Seven-Nation Resolution, a U.S. Product, 4. SCMP 1840, 42.
Aug 22	Let Every Flower Bear a Fruit, 2.
Aug 22	Peking Papers Greet Successful World Conference (On disarmament), 5. SCMP 1842, 61.
Aug 23	UN Assembly Session a Serious Blow to Aggressors, Says JMJP, 1,4. SCMP 1842, 38.
Aug 24	U.S. Forces Must Get Out of Singapore, 1. SCMP 1841, 50.
Aug 25	A Brilliant Example of Peaceful Coexistence, 1,4. SCMP 1843, 38.
Aug 25	Why Hog Purchase Work Fails, 2.
Aug 26	JMJP Welcomes the Link between the Yangtze and the Tigris (China and Iraq establish relations), 1. SCMP 1843, 45.
Aug 27	Push Forward Steel Production by Every Means, 2. SCMP 1855, 4.
Aug 28	Large-Scale Cooperation Is an Effective Guarantee of Fulfillment of State Plans, 1,2. SCMP 1852, 15.
Aug 28	JMJP on Hongkong Provocation, 1. SCMP 1845, 36.
Aug 29	Full Use Must Be Made of Potatoes, 1. SCMP 1853, 30.
Aug 30	Academic Criticism Is a Profound Form of Self-Revolution, 1. SCMP 1856, 13.
Aug 31	Fight to Make the Late Rice Crop Yield More than the Early One, 1.
Aug 31	JMJP Refutes British Pretexts, 2. SCMP 1846, 20.
Sep 1	JMJP Supports Soviet Stand on Nuclear Tests, 5. SCMP 1847, 42.
Sep 1	Act Immediately to Fulfill the Great Mission of Doubling Steel Production (Amended 9/2, p. 3), 1. SCMP 1855, 6.
Sep 2	Let Land Be Turned Over on Large Scale (Deep ploughing), 4.
Sep 3	Raise High the Red Flag of the People's Commune and March Forward (Amended 9/4, p. 2), 1.
Sep 4	The Establishment of Communes Viewed from the Regulations of the "Satellite" Commune, 1.
Sep 4	JMJP Greets Opening of International Student's Congress, 4. SCMP 1848, 40.
Sep 5	Make Every Possible Effort to Ensure Smooth Steel and Iron Production, 1. SCMP 1855, 22.
Sep 7	600 Million People Mobilize to Crush the U.S. Aggressors' Military Threats and War Provocations (Taiwan question), 1. SCMP 1851, 3.
Sep 9	JMJP Warns U.S. to Stop Provocations, 1. SCMP 1852, 23.
Sep 10	First Put Up the Framework of the People's Commune, 2.
Sep 11	We Have Friends Everywhere, Says JMJP, 1. SCMP 1853, 42.
Sep 11	Celebrate National Day with Cleanliness (Central Committee decision on campaign to remove four pests), 2.
Sep 11	Miraculous Feats Must Also Be Performed in Physical Training (First national sports meet), 7.
Sep 12	Real Danger Lies in Continued U.S. Military Provocations, Says JMJP (Taiwan question), 1. SCMP 1854, 36.
Sep 12	Shortcut to Mechanization and Electrification of Farming (Successful run of rope-pulling machine), 6. SCMP 1867, 27.
Sep 13	For a Still Bigger Leap Forward in Agriculture Next Year (Five important Central directives on rural work and production), 1. SCMP 1857, 10.
Sep 13	Get More and Better Fertilizer Ready, 6.
Sep 14	JMJP Calls for Faster Iron, Steel Production, 1. SCMP 1855, 40.
Sep 14	Congratulating the Wuhan Iron and Steel Company, 2.
Sep 15	The Starting Point of a Still Greater Leap Forward (National industries and communications exhibit opens) (Amended 9/16, p. 5), 5. SCMP 1857, 28.
Sep 15	Trickery and Bluff of No Avail (JMJP refutes Eisenhower's speech), 1. SCMP 1856, 4.
Sep 16	Hold Tightly and with Vehemence (Steel production), 1.
Sep 16	JMJP Highlights Conclusion of IUS Congress, 4. SCMP 1858, 53.
Sep 16	Manifest with Thoroughness the Role of Folk Drama as the Vanguard of Literature and the Arts, 7.
Sep 17	Congratulating the Big Victory of Honan (Steel production), 1.
Sep 17	Autumn Harvesting and Autumn Planting Are Two Major Events in Current Agricultural Production, 6.
Sep 18	Start Immediately a Movement of All People Engaging in Transportation, 1. SCMP 1866, 39.
Sep 19	35 Thousand Carloads a Day Achieved After a Month of Struggle (Railroad), 1.
Sep 19	Scientific Enterprise Must Serve the Building of Socialism, 2.
Sep 19	Integrate with the Campaign to Eradicate the Four Pests, Buy Up Junk with Vigor, and Beautify Households, 7.
Sep 20	Put in Ten Days of Hard Work to Fight for the Fulfillment of the Steel and Iron Production Plan for September, 2.

1958

Sep 20	The Printing Enterprises Must Serve Politics Better (National newspaper printing conference), 7.
Sep 21	U.S. Pirates Get Out of Taiwan, 1. SCMP 1860, 48.
Sep 22	Peking Press Welcomes the Arrival of Bulgarian Delegations, 1. SCMP 1861, 34.
Sep 22	Eisenhower Can Find No Excuse, 1. SCMP 1861, 30.
Sep 22	Let the Technological Revolution Blossom and Bear Fruit in the Medical and Public Health Fields, 7.
Sep 23	Fight for High Yield over Large Areas, 2.
Sep 23	JMJP Welcomes Algerian Republic, 3. SCMP 1861, 44.
Sep 24	The Key Lies in the Launching of Mass Movements (Steel production), 1,2.
Sep 25	Whole People's Efforts Called For to Develop Copper Smelting, 1. SCMP 1866, 14.
Sep 25	Take Advantage of the Victory to Sweep Up a Surging Tide of Afforestation in Winter, 6.
Sep 25	Rally Under the Red Banner of the Workers (Education to combine with labor), 7. SCMP 1873, 11.
Sep 26	People's Communes Take Up Transportation Work, 2.
Sep 27	The Urgent Tasks in Commercial Work Today, 1. SCMP 1872, 2.
Sep 27	China Will Surpass the United States in This Year's Total Cotton Output, 3. SCMP 1866, 17.
Sep 28	Crush U.S. "Ceasefire" Plot, 1. SCMP 1865, 3.
Sep 28	Let Us All Play Our Part in Atomic Science (First nuclear reactor starts production), 2.
Sep 28	JMJP Greets New Stage in Sino-Korean Economic Cooperation, 3. SCMP 1865, 49.
Sep 29	Let Peasants All Spend a Happy National Day, 3. SCMP 1873, 4.
Sep 30	Counter-Blows to Provocations (Air battle over Taiwan Straits), 1. SCMP 1868, 35.
Sep 30	Peking Papers Greet New China-Iraq Friendship Association, 2. SCMP 1871, 83.
Sep 30	Play Your Part in Physical Labor--The Grand Melting Pot of Communism (A month of physical labor for all central cadres), 2.
Sep 30	Congratulating Fukien and Shanghai for Their Basic Extermination of Schistosomiasis, 7.
Sep 30	Strive to Make a Bigger Leap Forward in Literature and in Arts, 7.
Oct 1	Festival of the Whole Nation--Victory of the Whole Nation, 2. SCMP 1870, 33.
Oct 1	Let All "Satellites" Soar to the Sky, Let There Be Leap Forward After Leap Forward, 4.
Oct 1	JMJP Greets Formation of Friendship Associations, 7. SCMP 1871, 63.
Oct 1	Celebrating the Bumper Harvest, Leap Forward Once Again, 9.
Oct 4	Call for Mass Steel Smelting Movement, 1. SCMP 1872, 10.
Oct 4	Reform Teaching Matter According to the Party's Line of Education, 6.
Oct 4	Celebrating the First Anniversary of the Launching of the Red Moon, 5.
Oct 5	Fall Harvest and Planting Must Be Successful, 1.
Oct 7	We Must Have a Firm Grip on Leadership over the Literary and Art Work of the Masses, 6.
Oct 8	There Is a Far-Reaching Future for Schools Established by Factories, 6.
Oct 9	Rural Labor Power Urgently Needs Overall Arrangements, 1. SCMP 1875, 1.
Oct 9	JMJP Greets New African Republic, 5. SCMP 1873, 68.
Oct 10	Stop Talking About "Ceasefire", Withdrawal Is Best of All Choices, 1. SCMP 1875, 35.
Oct 10	We Must Choose and Promote the Good Furnaces, 2.
Oct 11	JMJP Editorial on Taiwan Straits Situation, 1. SCMP 1875, 38.
Oct 11	Guard against Frost to Ensure a Bumper Harvest, 3.
Oct 12	Use Native Iron to Refine Fine Steel, 1.
Oct 12	Reap the Full Fruit of the Bumper Crop, 1. SCMP 1886, 19.
Oct 13	Let All People Extensively Exploit Coal Pits, 1,2.
Oct 13	Organize the Participation of More Women in Fall Harvest and Fall Planting Work, 3.
Oct 14	JMJP Greets Success of Asian and African Writer's Conference, 5. SCMP 1876, 55.
Oct 14	To Raise a Still Greater High Tide in Water Conservancy Work on Farmland, 1,3. SCMP 1885, 15.
Oct 15	Supply the "Ants" with Enough "Bones" (Machine-making industry), 1,4.
Oct 17	Let Native Methods in Steel Refining Bloom Everywhere, 1,2.
Oct 17	Firmly Eliminate the Black Sheep from the Islamic Circle, 6.
Oct 18	Let the High Output "Satellite" Circle Forever in the Sky, 1.
Oct 18	Greeting the Great Victory of Kwangsi, 2.
Oct 18	Redouble Efforts to Bring About Renovation of Farm Implements, 3.
Oct 19	National Minorities March Forward at High Speed, 1,2. SCMP 1896, 46.
Oct 19	Press Ahead Consistently in the Production of Cast Steel, 2.
Oct 20	The Power of the Mass Movement Is Limitless--Renewed Greeting to Kwangsi (Steel refining), 1.
Oct 21	JMJP Editorial: "Fitting Punishment," 1. SCMP 1881, 35.
Oct 22	Adjustment of Worker's Housing, Revolution in Urban Social Life, 1. SCMP 1882, 5.
Oct 23	Large Enterprises Must Launch Mass Campaigns in a Big Way, 1,2.
Oct 23	Accomplish the Task of Buying Agricultural By-Products with Shock Tactics, 2.
Oct 24	A Revolutionary Measure in Agricultural Production, 2. SCMP 1898, 8.
Oct 24	Grip Firmly the Production of Large Machine Tools, 3.
Oct 25	JMJP Welcomes Triumphant Return of CPV, 1. SCMP 1884, 30.
Oct 25	The Vanguard Must Lead the Way, 3.
Oct 25	Run the Public Mess Halls Well, 4.
Oct 26	Peking Papers Greet Birth of Hui Autonomous Region, 1. SCMP 1885, 7.
Oct 26	After the Victory of the "Steel and Iron High Output Week," 2.
Oct 27	Let All People Take Up Training Under the System of Physical Training in Labor for National Defense, 6.
Oct 28	Forced Withdrawal, Shameful Exit, 4.

1958

Oct 30	Peking Press Opposes U.S. "Two Chinas" Plot (JMJP on Chiang-Dulles talks), 1. SCMP 1888, 32.
Nov 1	Peking Press Hails Success of Communist Party's Educational Policy (Integration of education with labor exhibit opens), 2. SCMP 1889, 7.
Nov 2	JMJP Welcomes Sino-Moroccan Diplomatic Relations, 3. SCMP 1889, 37.
Nov 3	Improvement of Quality Is an Urgent Task on the Iron and Steel Front, 1. SCMP 1895, 22.
Nov 4	The Method of "Making Small Equipment with Native Method by the Masses" Must Also Be Promoted in Railway Construction, 2.
Nov 4	Carry Out the Tool Renovation Campaign to the End, 3.
Nov 5	We Must Learn to Walk with Two Legs in Building Large Equipment, 1,2.
Nov 5	Let There Be a Big Leap Forward in Cotton Yield Next Year, 3.
Nov 6	Strive to Make a Complete Victory of the Autumn Harvest, 1.
Nov 6	Key to Expanding the Production of Chinese Drugs, 7.
Nov 7	Advance Jauntily and along the Glorious Road of the October Revolution (Amended 11/8, p. 2), 2. SCMP 1893, 17.
Nov 8	Mass Movement Blooms and Bears Fruit in the Coal Industry, 3.
Nov 9	See That Peasants Take Rest, 1. SCMP 1898, 12.
Nov 10	Good Meals Are Served (Public mess halls), 1,3.
Nov 12	Disperse Imperialism and All Reactionaries, 1,4. SCMP 1897, 6.
Nov 13	Launch a New High Tide in the Purchase and Distribution of Farm Produce, 1,2.
Nov 13	See That the Collection of Scientific and Technical Information Is Successfully Carried Out, 6.
Nov 14	How to Expedite the Building of New Enterprises for Production Purposes, 1,4.
Nov 16	Energetically Carry Out High Speed Construction, 1. SCMP 1912, 1.
Nov 16	Soviet Seven-Year Plan a Big Step Toward Communism, Says JMJP, 3. SCMP 1897, 42.
Nov 17	Steel Rolling Equipment--China's Second Major Industrial Battle, 1,2. SCMP 1898, 30.
Nov 19	A New Stage of the International Communist Movement (Anniversary of Moscow conference and manifesto), 1,4. SCMP 1900, 36.
Nov 20	JMJP on Japanese People's Future, 1,4. SCMP 1900, 50.
Nov 21	Young Activists' Conference Highlighted in Peking Press, 1. SCMP 1902, 3.
Nov 21	Exterminate Vermin in the Same Way the Four Pests Are Exterminated, 3.
Nov 22	JMJP Editorial on Korean Government Delegation's Visit, 1,4. SCMP 1902, 42.
Nov 22	Strengthen Wheat Field Management Work, 3.
Nov 24	Chemical Industry Must Also Launch the Campaign to Have Small Things Done with Native Method by the Masses, 3.
Nov 25	JMJP on Mass Campaign for Steel, 3. SCMP 1904, 19.
Nov 26	Let All People Learn Technology and Fight a Good Battle in the Water Conservancy Front, 1.
Nov 26	Enhance Further the Quality of Farm Produce Procurement Work, 2.
Nov 28	Conference Stresses Study of Traditional Medicine, 1. SCMP 1907, 20 (summary).
Nov 29	Love the Steel and Iron Army, Carry Out Labor Protection Work Well, 1,2.
Nov 29	Mourning Chairman Damyanov, 4.
Nov 30	Manifest the Wisdom of the Masses, and Produce Thousands of Native Machine Tools, 1.
Nov 30	Foreign Troops Must Withdraw from W. Berlin, 3. SCMP 1906, 51.
Nov 30	Unexpected Mineral Discoveries in China, 6. SCMP 1908, 13.
Dec 1	Peking Press Welcomes Algerian Government Delegation, 1. SCMP 1908, 32.
Dec 1	Peking Press Features Support for African Independence, 5. SCMP 1908, 42 (summary).
Dec 2	Peking Press Welcomes Opening of Sino-Sudanese Diplomatic Relations, 1. SCMP 1908, 40.
Dec 2	Let Power Be Generated by All People, 1,2.
Dec 3	JMJP Comments on French Political Situation, 1,6. SCMP 1909, 47.
Dec 4	JMJP on Women's New Position, 2. SCMP 1910, 11.
Dec 4	JMJP Welcomes Vietnam-Korea Talks, 5. SCMP 1910, 56.
Dec 5	A Red Flag Pertaining to the Launching of Mass Movement in Large Enterprises, 1,2.
Dec 6	Energetically Popularize the Achievements Made in Scientific and Technological Research, 1,2.
Dec 7	Establish Small Iron and Steel Combines Which Employ Both Native Technology and Foreign Technology, 1,2.
Dec 7	For the Service of Central Work, 6.
Dec 9	Peking Press Acclaims Sino-Korean Joint Statement, 1,2. SCMP 1913, 47.
Dec 10	Coordination of Hard and Skillful Work, 2.
Dec 12	JMJP Advises British Government against Its "Two Chinas" Clamors, 1. SCMP 1915, 37.
Dec 13	Get Enough Manure Ready to Bring About a Bumper Harvest Next Year, 1,3.
Dec 14	Traditional Chinese Medical Recipes Completed, 1. SCMP 1916, 13.
Dec 14	Berlin Must Be Returned to the German People, 3. SCMP 1916, 49.
Dec 15	Mobilize the Masses to Renovate Their Rock-Drilling Tools, 1.
Dec 15	JMJP Greets Achievements of Accra Conference, 4. SCMP 1916, 50.
Dec 20	Step Up the Production of Salt with Vigor and Make Comprehensive Use of the Resources of the Salt Industry, 2.
Dec 21	Combination of Exertion and Scientific Analysis, 1.
Dec 21	Peking Papers Feature Sino-Algerian Communique, 3. SCMP 1921, 41.
Dec 22	JMJP on Completion of Steel Target, 1. SCMP 1922, 12.
Dec 23	Important Improvement in the Rural Financial and Trade Administration, 1,2. SCMP 1929, 7.
Dec 24	JMJP Welcomes Mongolian Delegation, 1. SCMP 1924, 38.
Dec 24	Way to Turn Native Iron and Steel Swiftly into Products, 1,2.
Dec 24	Strive to Consolidate Achievement Pertaining to the Elimination of Illiteracy, 6.
Dec 25	Struggle for a Still Larger Crop Next Year, 1. SCMP 1933, 13.

1958

Dec 28 Step Up Production and Supply of Subsidiary Foodstuffs, 1. SCMP 1933, 10.
Dec 29 Factories Must Depend on the Masses When Establishing Schools, 7.

1959

Jan 1 Ready to Receive New and Bigger Victories (Amended 1/2, p. 2), 1,3. SCMP 1934, 1.
Jan 2 JMJP on Direction of Development of People's Communes, 1,2. SCMP 1937, 4.
Jan 4 The Socialist Song of Triumph Rings Throughout the Universe (Soviet missile), 1,2.
Jan 4 Native Railway--A New Means of Local Transportation, 3.
Jan 4 JMJP Comments on Defeat of U.S. Imperialism in Cuba, 4. SCMP 1930, 26.
Jan 5 Cheering China for Surpassing Britain in Coal Output, 1,4.
Jan 6 Power Industry Must Move Forward Quickly, 1.
Jan 7 Devise All Ways and Means to Produce More Steel Products, 1.
Jan 8 Fight for High Yield over Large Areas (National agricultural exhibit), 1.
Jan 9 There Must Be a Bigger Development in Light Industry, 1,2.
Jan 11 What We Hope of the Travellers Going Home during the Spring Festival, 1.
Jan 12 Strive to Complete the Task of Buying Subsidiary Farm Produce Before the Spring Festival, 1.
Jan 13 An Important Task before Us in the Machine-Building Industry Is to Build Complete Sets of Equipment, 1.
Jan 13 JMJP Important Step Towards Peaceful Settlement of German Question, 5. SCMP 1935, 40.
Jan 15 Keynote of Railway Construction Is Improvement of Existing Railways, 1. SCMP 1948, 14.
Jan 16 Strive to Make a Bigger Leap Forward in Science and Technology This Year, 1.
Jan 17 Make a Good Job of Health Work in Collective Life, 1.
Jan 17 JMJP on Sino-Albanian Economic Cooperation, 4. SCMP 1938, 32.
Jan 18 Paper-Making Industry Must Make a Greater Leap Forward, 1.
Jan 19 Make Sure that the Paotou Steel and Iron Combine Is Discriminately Supported, 1.
Jan 20 The Labor Force Must Be Disposed Rationally, 1,3. SCMP 1955, 1.
Jan 21 Speed Up the Improvement of Farm Tools, 1. SCMP 1951, 20.
Jan 21 Peking Papers Protest against Massacre in South Vietnam, 5. SCMP 1940, 38.
Jan 22 JMJP Welcomes GDR Government Delegation, 1,4. SCMP 1942, 18.
Jan 22 Implement Short-Distance Transportation Successfully, 2.
Jan 23 JMJP Supports Cuban People's Opposition to U.S. Interference, 1. SCMP 1942, 35.
Jan 23 A Peace Treaty Must Be Concluded with Germany, 5. SCMP 1943, 21 (summary).
Jan 24 Victory Belongs to Congolese, African People, 1. SCMP 1944, 18.
Jan 25 JMJP on Party's Policy Regarding Traditional Medicine, 1. SCMP 1944, 3.
Jan 27 Launch a Large-Scale Campaign for Accumulating Manure, 1. SCMP 1952, 15.
Jan 28 JMJP on Sino-German Friendship, 4. SCMP 1947, 44.
Jan 30 Exert Our Utmost Effort, Forge Ahead in the Flush of Victory, 1.
Jan 31 Strive to Redouble Iron Ore Production, 1. SCMP 1953, 13.
Feb 2 Beat the Drum Louder for Big Leap Forward, 1. SCMP 1954, 1.
Feb 4 Support the Army and Take Good Care of Army Dependents, Support the Government and Love the People, 1.
Feb 4 Carry On with the Launching of the Patriotic Health Campaign, 7.
Feb 5 JMJP Acclaims CPSU 21st Congress, 1. SCMP 1952, 36 (extracts).
Feb 6 Mass Efforts to Fulfill Coal Output Target, 1. SCMP 1955, 31.
Feb 8 JMJP: Victory Belongs to Peace and Socialism, 1. SCMP 1953, 35.
Feb 10 Greet Spring Sowing with Drive and Spirit, 1. SCMP 1963, 20.
Feb 10 JMJP Hails Cairo Youth Conference Resolutions, 3. SCMP 1954, 35.
Feb 11 Mass Efforts to Fulfill Coal Output Target, 1. SCMP 1955, 30.
Feb 12 JMJP on Battle for Eighteen Million Tons of Steel, 1. SCMP 1956, 16.
Feb 13 Take Good Care of the Revival of the Winter Wheat Crop, 1.
Feb 14 Unbreakable Everlasting Sino-Soviet Unity, 1. SCMP 1957, 33.
Feb 15 Build More Power Generating Equipment of Better Quality, 1,2.
Feb 17 People's Commune Must Establish Sound Responsibility System for Production, 1. SCMP 1969, 19.
Feb 19 Peking Papers Support Cameroon People's Struggle for Independence, 5. SCMP 1961, 32.
Feb 19 Scrapping of Geneva Agreement Not to Be Tolerated, 1. SCMP 1960, 41.
Feb 20 Make Communication a Vanguard of Economic Development, 1. SCMP 1964, 5.
Feb 20 JMJP on Sino-Vietnamese Economic Agreements, 4. SCMP 1964, 35.
Feb 21 Carry the Renovation of Tools into Fullest Effect, 1. SCMP 1964, 17.
Feb 22 Step Up the Production of Chemical Products on a Large Scale, 1,2.
Feb 23 Speed Up the Development of Animal Husbandry, 1,3. SCMP 1969, 10.
Feb 24 Take the Whole Country as a Coordinated Chess Game, 1,2. SCMP 1970, 1.
Feb 25 Fight for Giving the Crops Strong Ears of Corn, 1.
Feb 27 Make Sure That the Newly Built Power Stations Are Commissioned for Production as Soon as Possible, 1.
Feb 28 Capital Construction Must Implement in Totality the Line of Achieving Greater, Faster, Better, and More Economical Results, 1,2.
Mar 2 Organize Rational Transportation with Vigor, 1.
Mar 3 Concentrate Our Strength to Ensure the Fulfillment of Major Industrial Production Targets, 1. SCMP 1975, 18.
Mar 5 Time to Solve German Question, 4. SCMP 1969, 43.
Mar 6 Chinese, Japanese People's Common Cause, Says JMJP, 1. SCMP 1970, 40.
Mar 7 JMJP Welcomes Japanese Socialist Party Delegation, 1. SCMP 1971, 43.
Mar 7 A New Step Taken by the United States to Sabotage Peace in Asia, 5.

1959

Mar 8	Women of China, Put Up Skyrocketing Zeal and Make Greater Contributions, 1. SCMP 1971, 1.
Mar 9	Speed Up the Planting of Trees, Enhance the Quality of Afforestation Work, 1,3.
Mar 10	We Must Get 100 Million Tan of Ginned Cotton, 1,3. SCMP 1991, 13.
Mar 10	Machine Industry Must Make Economic Use of Raw Material, 2.
Mar 10	JMJP Welcomes Indonesia-Vietnam Communique, 4. SCMP 1973, 43.
Mar 11	Safeguard the Geneva Agreements, Defend Peace in Indo-China, 1. SCMP 1973, 44.
Mar 13	Fully Develop the Potentiality of Manpower within Our Enterprises, 1. SCMP 1982, 6.
Mar 13	Develop the Fishing Industry, 3.
Mar 14	The Production of Light Industrial Products for Daily Use Should Be Actively Expanded, 1. SCMP 1982, 22.
Mar 14	JMJP Urges Solution of German Question, 4. SCMP 1976, 41.
Mar 15	Where There Is Destruction, There Should Also Be Establishment, 1. SCMP 1979, 2.
Mar 16	Strive for a Great Harvest in Oil-Bearing Crops, 1.
Mar 17	Make Steel-Rolling Equipment in Sets by the Month, 1.
Mar 18	JMJP on Tito's Asian-African Tour, 1. SCMP 1978, 34.
Mar 19	JMJP Acclaims Chang Hsi-jo-Inejiro Asanuma Statement, 1. SCMP 1978, 40.
Mar 19	Implement the "Eight-Character Constitution" to Improve Crop Production, 3. SCMP 1991, 6.
Mar 20	JMJP Discusses National Interests of Arab People, 1. SCMP 1980, 30.
Mar 20	Peking Papers Support Soviet Proposal on German Issue, 4. SCMP 1980, 49.
Mar 20	Strive for Greater Victories in Eliminating Pestilence (Amended 3/21, p. 7), 6.
Mar 21	Do a Good Job in Planting Early Rice, Strive for Higher Yields, 1.
Mar 21	JMJP on Success of Polish Party Congress, 4. SCMP 1980, 51.
Mar 21	Promote the Scientific and Technical Activities of the Masses More Extensively, 7.
Mar 23	Devise All Ways and Means to Produce Pig Iron, 1.
Mar 23	Inclination of the French People, 5.
Mar 24	Create New Achievements, and Strive to Contend for Honor at the Heroes' Conference in Peking, 1.
Mar 25	Be More Industrious and Thrifty with the Running of Communes, 1,3.
Mar 26	Grasp Important Links in the Flow of Commodities--Transportation and Storage, 1,2.
Mar 26	Marching Ahead under the Anti-Imperialist Standard, 5.
Mar 27	Strive for a Greater Leap Forward in Hemp Production, 1. SCMP 1991, 19.
Mar 29	Speed Up the Production of Railroad Engines and Cars, 2.
Mar 30	Speed Up the Fostering of Teachers Who Are Both Red and Vocationally Proficient, 6.
Mar 31	Thoroughly Suppress the Tibetan Rebellion (Amended 4/1, p. 2), 1.
Apr 1	On Rational Close Planting, 1,4.
Apr 2	Peking Press on NATO Bloc, 1. SCMP 1986, 43.
Apr 3	Complete the Six Major Sets of Equipment and Installations according to Schedule, 1. SCMP 1994, 11.
Apr 3	Let Teaching-Learning, Productive Labor, and Scientific Research Be Combined, 6. SCMP 1992, 26.
Apr 4	Make Fierce and Skillful Attack on the Insect Pests, 1.
Apr 4	Converters Must Be Used to Produce More Steel of Fine Quality, 2.
Apr 5	Peking Press Observes "Algerian Week," 1. SCMP 1989, 36.
Apr 7	In Opposition to the Creation of a New Tense Situation by the United States in Asia, 1,5.
Apr 8	Strengthen Scientific Research Work in Campaign to Renovate Tools, 4.
Apr 9	The Decisive Quarter of the Year, 1. SCMP 1997, 8.
Apr 10	Modern Industries Must Continue Mass Campaign (Amended 4/17, p. 3), 1. SCMP 1997, 12.
Apr 12	Wellington Conference's Conspiracy against Peace, 1,4.
Apr 13	State Signs More Contracts with Communes, 1. SCMP 1995, 11.
Apr 15	A Great Milestone, 3.
Apr 15	Let the Light of Freedom Illumine the Whole Africa, 5. SCMP 1995, 45.
Apr 16	How to Raise the Communication Capacity for Post and Telecommunications, 3.
Apr 16	JMJP Supports Japanese Struggle against "Security Treaty," 6. SCMP 1996, 52.
Apr 17	What Should the Textile Industry Do in Production at the Moment? 3.
Apr 18	Conference of Solidarity, Conference of Leap Forward (Amended 4/19, p. 5), 1.
Apr 18	Uphold and Promote the "Bandung Spirit," 6.
Apr 20	Run Education for Workers in Industrial and Mining Enterprises Well, 2.
Apr 21	Produce and Supply Equipment by the Sets, 3.
Apr 25	Cheering the Momentous Victory Relating to the Suppression of the Rebels South of the Mountains in Tibet, 1.
Apr 28	Local Elections in Japan, 6.
Apr 29	Unite and Leap Forward to Greet the Tenth Anniversary of National Day--JMJP on National People's Congress, 2. SCMP 2006, 1.
Apr 29	Welcoming the Party and Government Delegation of Hungary, 3.
Apr 30	Peking Press Welcomes German Parliamentary Delegation, 3. SCMP 2006, 28.
May 1	Mobilize the Whole People to Launch a Campaign to Increase Production and Practice Economy, 2. SCMP 2009, 9.
May 4	Play Up the Glorious Traditions in the Reconstruction of the Great Fatherland (Anniversary of May fourth movement), 1,2.
May 5	Intensify Our Anti-Flood Precautions to Fight for the Conquest of Floods, 4.
May 7	New Stage of Sino-Hungarian Friendship and Cooperation, 2.
May 9	Put the Existing Irrigation Projects to Good Use under Proper Management, 3.
May 10	Good Prospect for Bumper Wheat Harvest in China, 1. SCMP 2015, 23 (summary).
May 11	Safely Generate and Supply Power, 2.

1959

May 13	Make Immediate Preparations for the Collection of Summer Grain and Oil Seed Crops, 2. SCMP 2020, 12.	
May 15	High Output Must Be Based on Good Quality, 1,2.	
May 16	World Peace Council Calls--Voice of Peoples, 4. SCMP 2018, 46.	
May 16	Unleash a Bigger Summer Production High Tide, 1. SCMP 2023, 9.	
May 17	Win the First Battle for Bumper Crop This Year, 1. SCMP 2023, 13.	
May 19	On the Raising of Labor Efficiency, 1,2. SCMP 2024, 6.	
May 20	Peking Papers Support Government Statement on Situation in Laos, 1. SCMP 2019, 31.	
May 20	Lay Equal Emphasis on Public and Private Rearing to Multiply Domestic Animals and Fowls, 3. SCMP 2023, 16.	
May 23	Make the Conference for Exchange of Products a Success, 2. SCMP 2024, 20.	
May 24	Protect Equipment by Conducting Inspection and Repair Periodically, 2. SCMP 2026, 14.	
May 25	Strive to Raise the Quality of Light Industrial Products, 1.	
May 28	Continue to Glorify the Revolutionary Traditions, 1.	
May 29	Fast Reaping, Threshing, Collection, and Transportation, 1. SCMP 2031, 5.	
May 30	Step Up the Production of Vegetables, 1. SCMP 2028, 23.	
May 31	Strengthen Field Control over Early Rice, 1.	
Jun 1	Take Another Step Forward in Work to Foster and Educate the New Generation, 1. SCMP 2028, 7.	
Jun 1	Fully Develop Waterway Transportation, 2. SCMP 2035, 16.	
Jun 2	To Render Positive Leadership over the Discussion on Close Planting, 1. SCMP 2043, 8.	
Jun 3	Tighten Our Grip on Seed-Selecting and Seed-Retaining Work, 1.	
Jun 3	Prepare Well for the Fight against Natural Calamities, 3. SCMP 2034, 23.	
Jun 3	Let the Balkans Become a Peace Zone (Soviet-Albanian communique), 5.	
Jun 4	Practice Saving with Enthusiasm, 1.	
Jun 5	Take Inventory of Stocks to Regulate Supply, 1.	
Jun 7	Energetically Raise the Quality of Products in the Machine-Building Industry, 1,2.	
Jun 9	Looking at the Production of More Consumer Goods from Soochow, 1.	
Jun 10	Hand Over and Sell Good Grain to the State, 1.	
Jun 11	Plant More Land and Gather More Crops, 1. SCMP 2040, 17.	
Jun 11	Make Sure of the Quality of the New Students to Be Enrolled by Institutions of Higher Education, 6. SCMP 2041, 23.	
Jun 14	Produce More Vegetables for the Benefit of City Dwellers, 1. SCMP 2038, 6.	
Jun 15	Traffic Inside the Factories Must Not Be Hampered, 1.	
Jun 16	Grasp the Key to Higher Cotton Yield, 1.	
Jun 17	There Must Be Safety in Production, 1. SCMP 2045, 10.	
Jun 22	The Way to Insure a Bumper Harvest in the Fall, 1.	
Jun 22	Important Efforts to Ease the Tense Situation in Europe, 4.	
Jun 23	It Is Imperative to Defeat the Flood, 1. SCMP 2047, 1.	
Jun 24	See That Large Numbers of Draft Animals Are Raised, 1.	
Jun 25	U.S. Troops Must Get Out of Korea, 1. SCMP 2049, 20.	
Jun 26	The Entire Coal Industry Must Leap Forward, 1.	
Jun 27	Increase Timber Production and Practice Economy in Timber Utilization, 1. SCMP 2048, 36.	
Jun 28	Fullest Utilization of Materials, 1. SCMP 2052, 4.	
Jun 29	Prompt Arrangement for Production of Autumn Vegetables (Amended 6/30, p. 2), 1. SCMP 2050, 12.	
Jun 30	Rapidly Restore and Develop the Production of Small Commodities by the Handicraft Industry, 1. SCMP 2051, 27.	
Jul 3	Soviet Union Adopts Gigantic Measures to Fulfill Seven Year Plan ahead of Schedule, 5.	
Jul 4	Big Chemical Works Built in Southwest China, 1. SCMP 2051, 25 (summary).	
Jul 5	Strive for a Great Bumper Harvest of Oil-Bearing Crops, 1. SCMP 2052, 11.	
Jul 5	Peking Papers Feature Support for Uganda, 4. SCMP 2052, 34.	
Jul 6	A Great Deal More Can Be Done in the Utilization of "Waste Materials," 1. SCMP 2057, 8.	
Jul 9	Produce More Cement of Good Quality, 1.	
Jul 9	JMJP Protests against Persecution of Greek Patriot, 5. SCMP 2054, 40.	
Jul 10	Economize Coal to Promote Production, 1. SCMP 2058, 16.	
Jul 11	Peking Papers Mark Mongolian Anniversary, 1. SCMP 2055, 32.	
Jul 11	A Good Deed (Government units, factories, and schools raising pigs and growing vegetables), 3.	
Jul 12	Salutation to the Large Area Bumper Wheat Harvest, 1. SCMP 2057, 13.	
Jul 13	Render Better Service to the Livelihood of the People, 1.	
Jul 14	Peking Papers Greet Anniversary of Iraqi Republic, 1. SCMP 2057, 46.	
Jul 15	Promote Multiple Undertakings, 1. SCMP 2060, 1.	
Jul 17	Strengthen Economic Accounting, Unceasingly Lower Costs, 1. SCMP 2062, 1.	
Jul 17	Brilliant Achievements of Korea in the Building of Socialism, 4.	
Jul 17	Important Action of the Democratic Republic of Vietnam, 5.	
Jul 18	People of Oman Will Triumph, 5. SCMP 2061, 38.	
Jul 18	Disaster-Stricken Areas Should Strive to Surmount Their Difficulties Caused by Natural Calamities by This Autumn or Winter, 1. SCMP 2063, 9.	
Jul 19	March Forward in the Flush of Victory, 1.	
Jul 20	Peking Press Marks Geneva Agreements Anniversary, 1. SCMP 2062, 50.	
Jul 22	JMJP Greets Polish National Day, 1. SCMP 2063, 29.	
Jul 23	Make Proper Preparations for a Bumper Summer Harvest Next Year, 1. SCMP 2066, 10.	
Jul 24	Potential Is Great for Increasing Output of Light Industries, 1. SCMP 2069, 13.	
Jul 24	Soviet-Polish Brotherhood Sees New Development, 4.	

1959

Jul 25	Work to Stamp Out Pests and Epidemics Must Be Carried Out Well in Summer and Autumn, 1.
Jul 26	People's Communes Must Take Inventory of Items Stored in Warehouses, 1. SCMP 2067, 18.
Jul 27	Strive to Reduce Per-Kilowatt Coal Consumption, 1. SCMP 2068, 6.
Jul 28	Make the Yield of Late Rice Equal to That of Early Rice, Follow One Bumper Harvest with Another, 1. SCMP 2070, 7.
Jul 29	Produce More Raw Material for Light Industry, 1.
Jul 30	Actively Organize Advance Transportation, 1. SCMP 2072, 9.
Aug 1	Raise Further the Quality of Pig Iron and Steel Put Out by Small Blast Furnaces and Converters, 1.
Aug 3	Fight Hard in August for a Bumper Harvest for Economic Crops, 1.
Aug 4	Tighten Our Grip on Coal Selection Process, 1.
Aug 5	Important Events in International Political Life before Us, 1.
Aug 5	New Upsurge of Opposition to U.S.-Japan Military Alliance and Nuclear Armament among Japanese People, 1,4.
Aug 6	Overcome Rightist-Inclined Sentiment and Endeavor to Increase Production and Practice Economy (Amended 8/7, p. 1), 1. SCMP 2074, 4.
Aug 6	Nothing Can Stand in the Way of Peace and Friendship, 4.
Aug 7	Defeat Calamities and Strive for a Bumper Harvest, 1. SCMP 2076, 21.
Aug 8	Seize Hold of the Good Opportunity to Produce and Accumulate Green Manure (Amended 8/9, p. 2), 1.
Aug 8	Economic Use Must Also Be Made of Coal for Civilian Consumption, 2.
Aug 9	Haul Out the Timber without Delay, 1. SCMP 2077, 10.
Aug 12	Correct Policy for Solving Problems of Supply of Subsidiary Food in Urban Areas, 1. SCMP 2078, 9.
Aug 13	Take Good Care of the Summer and Autumn Cotton Bolls to Fight for a Bumper Cotton Harvest, 1.
Aug 14	Pursue the Anti-Drought Struggle to the End, 1. SCMP 2080, 1.
Aug 14	Strive to Win a Bumper Paddy Harvest in the North, 3.
Aug 16	Conserve Working Capital, 1. SCMP 2081, 1.
Aug 17	Streamline Labor Organization and Raise Labor Productivity, 1. SCMP 2081, 5.
Aug 17	Train New Personnel to Continue the Trades from Generation to Generation, 2. SCMP 2082, 7.
Aug 18	Make the People's Communes Manifest Their Superiority to Beat Droughts, Floods, and Insect Pests, 1.
Aug 19	Strive to Reap a Bumper Harvest of Coarse Grain, 3. SCMP 2084, 27.
Aug 20	Cooperation between Agriculture and Commerce to Develop Diversified Productive Undertakings, 1. SCMP 2084, 11.
Aug 20	More Universally and Thoroughly Launch the Health Campaign, 4.
Aug 21	We Certainly Can Defeat the Insect Pests, 1.
Aug 22	Load and Unload Rapidly, 1. SCMP 2086, 8.
Aug 23	Celebrating the Great Liberation Day of Rumania, 1.
Aug 24	Actively Prepare for and Perfect the Purchase of Cotton, Hemp, and Tobacco, 1. SCMP 2087, 7.
Aug 27	Peking Press Acclaims Communist Party Resolution (Amended 8/28, p. 2), 2. SCMP 2089, 1 (summary).
Aug 28	Thoroughly Manifest the Nuclear Functions of Basic-Level Organizations of the CYL, 7.
Aug 29	Long Live People's Communes! (Amended 8/30, p. 2), 1,2. SCMP 2090, 11.
Sep 1	Let Us Put an End to the Theory: "What You Have Lost Is More than What You Have Gained," 1,2. SCMP 2091, 1.
Sep 1	The New School Year Has Begun, 4.
Sep 2	Produce More Coal, 1,4.
Sep 3	Fight for the Overfulfillment of the Production Plans for Grain and Cotton, 1,3.
Sep 5	Peking Press Welcomes Afghan Deputy Premier's Visit, 2. SCMP 2094, 40.
Sep 5	Fulfill the Task of Putting Out 12 Million Tons of Steel ahead of Schedule, 3.
Sep 6	Save Up the Money Which We Do Not Intend to Spend for the Time Being, 3.
Sep 7	It Is Very Good to Build Water Conservancy Projects on Extensive Scale, 1. SCMP 2094, 9.
Sep 8	Make Proper Preparations for Autumn Harvest to Insure High Yield and Bumper Harvest, 1. SCMP 2096, 11.
Sep 9	The Glorious and Victorious Road of the Bulgarian People, 1. SCMP 2096, 41 (summary).
Sep 11	Achieve a Forward Leap Both in Increasing Production and in Practicing Economy, 1. SCMP 2098, 1.
Sep 12	Truth of the Sino-Indian Border Question, 1,2.
Sep 13	Create the Finest Achievements for Dedication to National Day (The first national sports meet opens), 1.
Sep 15	Opening the Door to the Moon, 1.
Sep 15	A Visit of Great International Significance, 1. SCMP 2100, 47.
Sep 15	Carry Out Autumn Sowing Properly to Lay a Good Foundation for a Summer Bumper Harvest Next Year, 2. SCMP 2101, 24.
Sep 16	Our Expectations, 1. SCMP 2100, 31.
Sep 17	Over-All Arrangements for "Three Autumnal" Work, 1. SCMP 2104, 14.
Sep 17	Reconvene the Geneva Conference as Soon as Possible, 6.
Sep 18	Bright Future for Those Who Forsake Evil and Follow the Good, 1. SCMP 2103, 5.
Sep 19	Carry Out the Party's Educational Policy Thoroughly, 1. SCMP 2105, 28.
Sep 20	Review and Prospect of Market Conditions, 1. SCMP 2103, 8.
Sep 21	New Way to Solve the Disarmament Problem, 1.
Sep 21	Hail the Conference of Heroes with New Victories, 2. SCMP 2104, 2.
Sep 22	Community Dining Halls Have a Boundless Future, 1. SCMP 2105, 12.
Sep 23	Plan Your Living Carefully, 2.
Sep 23	All Flowers Vie in Splendor to Greet the National Day, 3.

1959

Sep 23	The Great Significance of the Talks between Premier Chou En-lai and Ishibashi Kanzan, 7.
Sep 25	Overall Fulfillment and Overfulfillment of Task of Purchase of Agricultural Products, 1. SCMP 2107, 18.
Sep 25	Product of the Great Leap Forward, 2. SCMP 2107, 24.
Sep 26	Carry Out Mass Short-Distance Transport Movement, 1. SCMP 2107, 30.
Sep 27	Greeting the First Output of Steel from Paotou Steel Plant, 2.
Sep 29	Comrade Khruschov's Achievements in His Visit to United States, 4. SCMP 2110, 42.
Oct 1	Fight for a Greater Victory in the Second Ten Years, 3.
Oct 3	Long Live the Solidarity of the Socialist Countries Headed by the Soviet Union, 1,2.
Oct 4	March Forward in Big Strides on the Strength of Victories (National sports meet) (Amended 10/5, p. 2), 2.
Oct 5	Greeting the Establishment of Diplomatic Relations between China and Guinea, 2.
Oct 7	Ten Years of Brilliant Victories for the German Democratic Republic, 1,2.
Oct 8	Strive to Fulfill Industrial Production Plan for This Year Ten to Fifteen Days ahead of Schedule, 1. SCMP 2116, 1.
Oct 9	Actively Promote Multiple Management and Strive for Continued Leap Forward in Agriculture, 1. SCMP 2117, 8.
Oct 10	Let the Key Projects Join Production at an Early Date (Amended 10/26, p. 3), 1. SCMP 2117, 3.
Oct 11	Plan and Economize Consumption of Food Grains, 1,2. SCMP 2118, 5.
Oct 12	Let Everyone Play His Part in the "Minor Fall Harvest," 1,2.
Oct 12	Ore Production Must Take the Lead, 3.
Oct 12	The Imperishable Meritorious Feat of the Inter-Planetary Station, 5.
Oct 13	Insist on Deep Plowing and Deep Furrowing, 2. SCMP 2120, 19.
Oct 14	Pigskin Tanning Worthy of Promotion, 3.
Oct 16	Overfulfill Target of Producing 12 Million Tons of Steel ahead of Schedule, 1,2. SCMP 2122, 6.
Oct 17	Make a Big Effort to Fulfill Agricultural Products Procurement Task, 1,2. SCMP 2124, 1.
Oct 19	Persevere in the "Eight-Word Charter" for Agriculture, 1,2. SCMP 2123, 4.
Oct 22	JMJP Editorial Welcomes Chinese, Japanese CP Statement, 1,2. SCMP 2125, 39.
Oct 23	Cultivate All the Wheat Crop Properly, 1. SCMP 2126, 13.
Oct 24	Against U.S. Aggravation of "Cold War," 1. SCMP 2126, 37.
Oct 25	Launch a Mass Campaign for Soil Improvement, 1,2.
Oct 26	Long Live the Mass Movement (Amended 10/27, p. 3), 1,2.
Oct 28	Welcome to a Bumper Autumn Vegetable Harvest, 1. SCMP 2131, 35.
Oct 29	U.S. Troops Must Pull Out of South Korea, 5. SCMP 2130, 32.
Nov 1	Loudly Beat the Battle Drum of Water Conservancy Construction! 1,4. SCMP 2135, 11.
Nov 2	Strive to Carry Out the Great Task of Technical Transformation of Agriculture, 1,2. SCMP 2134, 19.
Nov 4	Integrate the Production-Increase and Economy Campaign with Technical Innovation, 1,2. SCMP 2139, 1.
Nov 5	Make Ready More and Better Fertilizers for Agriculture Next Year, 1. SCMP 2137, 8.
Nov 7	Hold Aloft the Red Banner of the October Revolution and Advance Victoriously, 1. SCMP 2136, 50.
Nov 9	Let the Advanced Seeds Bloom and Bear Fruit Everywhere, 1.
Nov 10	Editorial Stressing the Development of Spare-time Education in Rural Areas to Keep Pace with the Economic Growth in the Countryside, 4. SCMP 2137, 21.
Nov 11	The Advantages of Hog-Raising Are Many, 1,2.
Nov 12	To Step Up Transportation Is an Urgent Task Now, 1,2. SCMP 2139, 9.
Nov 13	Launch the Winter Afforestation Campaign, 1,2.
Nov 15	Exterminate the Insects That Live Through the Winter to Insure Next Year of Bumper Harvest, 2.
Nov 16	An Example of Non-Staple Food Production for Cities, 1,3. SCMP 2144, 11.
Nov 19	Speed Up the Breeding of Large Domestic Animals, 1,3.
Nov 22	Great Vitality of the "Small, Modern, and Mass" Principle, 1. SCMP 2146, 1.
Nov 22	Strengthen Forest Protection and Fire Prevention in This Winter and Next Spring, 7. SCMP 2151, 25.
Nov 25	Peking Papers Mark "Congo Day," 1. SCMP 2147, 28 (summary).
Nov 26	Make Good Use of the Last Thirty Days of the Year in All Fields, 1. SCMP 2149, 5.
Nov 27	Japan Is Being Dragged onto the Road to a Revival of Militarism, 1. SCMP 2150, 42.
Nov 28	Plant the Red Flags of High Efficiency in All Water Conservancy Construction Sites, 1. SCMP 2151, 14.
Nov 29	A Heroic Nation Attains Brilliant Achievements, 1. SCMP 2149, 22.
Nov 30	Speed Up the Processing and Utilization of Wild Plants, 1. SCMP 2150, 2.
Dec 1	An Outstanding Store That Serves the Industrial and Mining Districts, 1.
Dec 2	Organize More "One Dragon" Transportation Lines, 1. SCMP 2151, 20.
Dec 3	In Commemoration of the 100th Anniversary of the Birth of Sen Katayama, 1. SCMP 2153, 45.
Dec 4	Next Year's Harvest Depends on This Winter's Work, 1. SCMP 2153, 6.
Dec 5	Perfect the Distribution, Economy, and Conservation of Food Grains, 1. SCMP 2154, 3.
Dec 6	The Key Lies in Intensifying Attention to Transport, 1. SCMP 2155, 4.
Dec 7	The Starting Point for Hungary to Accelarate the Building of Socialism, 1.
Dec 8	Simultaneously Promote Native and Foreign Methods to Speed Up Technical Transformation of Agriculture, 1. SCMP 2157, 4.
Dec 10	Policy of Concentrating Forces on Key Projects Must Be Firmly Pursued in Capital Construction, 1. SCMP 2158, 4.
Dec 12	Solve in Totality the Overseas Chinese Problem between China and Indonesia, 1,4.
Dec 15	Appearance of Hilly Areas Can Be Altered Rapidly, 1. SCMP 2161, 19.
Dec 16	Build Native-Type and Simplified Modern Railways on a Large Scale, 1. SCMP 2162, 6 (summary).

1959

- Dec 17 The Hog Is at the Head of the Six Domestic Animals, 1. SCMP 2163, 5.
- Dec 18 Is It Possible to Develop the Hog-Raising Business Rapidly? 4. SCMP 2164, 5.
- Dec 20 Further Raise the Average Work Efficiency in Water Conservancy Construction throughout the Country, 1. SCMP 2164, 7.
- Dec 21 Production Successes Should Begin from the Very Start of Next Year, 1. SCMP 2164, 1.
- Dec 21 Raise the Educational Quality of Secondary Schools in Totality, 4. SCMP 2174, 1.
- Dec 22 Present Urgent Tasks in Vegetable Work, 1. SCMP 2167, 5.
- Dec 23 Let All Communes and Brigades Establish Hog Farms, 1,3. SCMP 2168, 6.
- Dec 24 The Just Endeavors of the Korean People Will Certainly Triumph, 1.
- Dec 25 Establish Waterway Transportation Networks in Conjunction with the Water Conservancy Program, 1. SCMP 2167, 8.
- Dec 27 Be Concerned with the Livelihood of Laborers on Water Conservancy Construction Sites, 1. SCMP 2168, 10.
- Dec 28 Strive for Fulfillment of Procurement of Agricultural Products, 1. SCMP 2169, 1.
- Dec 28 The Elimination of Pestilence Must Involve Mass Movements, 6.
- Dec 30 Organize a Great Check-Up on Water Conservancy Engineering Projects, 1.

1960

- Jan 1 JMJP Editorial: Looking Forward to the Sixties, 1. SCMP 2171, 10.
- Jan 2 Overfulfill All Production Targets for the Coming Fiscal Year, 1.
- Jan 4 New Stage of Mass Campaign for Short-Distance Transportation, 1. SCMP 2173, 1.
- Jan 5 Technological Renewal Should Be Extended to the Raising of Pigs, 1.
- Jan 6 Strive to Innovate Utensils and Run Public Dining Halls Better, 1. SCMP 2175, 9.
- Jan 7 A Successful On-the-Spot Conference, 1. SCMP 2175, 4.
- Jan 7 Push to New Heights the Scientific Research Work of Institutes of Higher Education, 4.
- Jan 8 A Red Flag in the Financial Battle Front, 1.
- Jan 9 Increase the Number of Sows, Raise the Rate of Propagation, 1. SCMP 2176, 2.
- Jan 9 Welcome the Emissary of German Brothers, 5.
- Jan 11 Apply the Method of "Walking on Two Legs" to the Work of Training Technical Personnel, 1,4. SCMP 2179, 7.
- Jan 13 New Development of Tools Innovation in Rural Areas, 1. SCMP 2180, 6.
- Jan 14 Carry Out Work on Seed Strains Properly to Insure Continuing Bumper Harvests in Agriculture, 1. SCMP 2181, 4.
- Jan 15 Firmly Oppose Japan-U.S. Military Alliance, 1. SCMP 2181, 35.
- Jan 16 A Bright Path Is Opened for Universal Disarmament, 1. SCMP 2181, 42.
- Jan 17 An Important Way to Make Comprehensive Use of Timber, 1. SCMP 2183, 2.
- Jan 18 High Productivity and Standards in Construction Should Be Maintained, 1. SCMP 2184, 15.
- Jan 19 Vigorously Establish Medium and Small Petroleum Plants, 1. SCMP 2184, 11.
- Jan 20 New Achievements of Sino-German Cooperation Acclaimed by JMJP, 1. SCMP 2184, 42.

1960

- Jan 21 JMJP Editorial on U.S. Presidential Message, 1,4. SCMP 2185, 44.
- Jan 22 A New Step on the Road to Conquering the Universe, 5.
- Jan 23 New Stage in Socialist Construction--JMJP Editorial, 2. SCMP 2189, 5.
- Jan 24 Welcome Premier Ne Win, 1.
- Jan 24 Crushing the American-Japanese Reactionaries' New Conspiracy of War and Invasion, 1,4.
- Jan 26 Continue to Leap Forward on Road to Technical Innovation and Technological Revolution, 1. SCMP 2190, 4.
- Jan 27 Total Resolution of the Sino-Indonesian Problem of Overseas Chinese through Friendly Negotiations, 1.
- Jan 28 The Army and the People Jointly Celebrate Spring Festival, 1.
- Jan 29 A New Stage in Sino-Burmese Friendly Relations, 1.
- Feb 1 A New Model Example of Unity and Friendship among Asian Nations, 1,4.
- Feb 2 Strive to Prevent and Cure Hog Diseases, 3. SCMP 2192, 15.
- Feb 2 A Conference Directed Towards Independence and Unity, 5.
- Feb 3 Striding Towards the Mechanization of Loading and Unloading, 1.
- Feb 4 Modern Enterprises Should Also Innovate Techniques, 1. SCMP 2194, 4.
- Feb 5 Greet the Spring Sowing, 1. SCMP 2195, 5.
- Feb 6 A Decisive Force for Safeguarding Peace, 2. SCMP 2194, 47.
- Feb 7 Directing the Movement of Collecting Fertilizer to a New Climax, 1.
- Feb 8 Mass of Small Modern Enterprises Advances from Victory to Victory, 1. SCMP 2196, 1.
- Feb 9 The Key to This Year's Increase in Cotton Production, 1. SCMP 2198, 20.
- Feb 10 Take Early Measures against Drought, 1. SCMP 2199, 13.
- Feb 11 The Glorious Mission of Our Young Students, 1,4. SCMP 2199, 10.
- Feb 12 Make Sure That Wheat Will Survive the Early Days of Planting, 1.
- Feb 14 The Strong Fortress of World Peace--Long Live the Great Sino-Soviet Alliance (Amended 2/15, p. 4), 1,4.
- Feb 16 Destroy the "Blind Spot in Water Conservancy," 1.
- Feb 17 Strive to Manage Well the Two Million Pig Farms, 1. SCMP 2204, 5.
- Feb 18 Greatly Increase the Production of Spring Vegetables, 1. SCMP 2205, 6.
- Feb 20 This Is No Trivial Matter, 1.
- Feb 21 Make All-Round Arrangements for the Livelihood of Commune Members, 1. SCMP 2206, 2.
- Feb 22 Provide Information on Agricultural Production with Greater Speed and Quality, 1.
- Feb 23 Strive for a Bumper Harvest in Rape Vegetable, 1.
- Feb 24 Make Use of Scattered Plots of Land to Plant Oil-Producing Crops, 1.
- Feb 25 Launch an All-People Campaign for Mechanization and Semi-Mechanization of Manual Labor--JMJP Editorial, 1. SCMP 2212, 8.
- Feb 26 Assist in Repairing Farm Tools of the People's Commune, 1.
- Feb 27 Bring Iron and Steel Production to a New High Tide, 1. SCMP 2212, 4.

1960

Feb 28	Unite the Work of Surprise Purchase with That of Regular Purchase, 1,2.
Feb 29	There Should Be a Great Increase in the Production of Livestock, 1.
Mar 1	Industrialists and Businessmen Should Be Determined to "Pay Attention Only to One Side" and "Lean to One Side," 1. SCMP 2213, 13.
Mar 2	Strive for a Great Harvest in the Spring Fishing Season, 1.
Mar 2	Flames in Cuba Can Never Be Put Out, Says JMJP, 6. SCMP 2211, 43.
Mar 3	Readjusting Staff and Workers' Dormitories According to Production Units, 1. SCMP 2234, 16.
Mar 4	Strive for a Bumper Harvest in Early Rice, 1.
Mar 5	Inspection Aims at Promotion, 1. SCMP 2215, 13.
Mar 6	A Visit of Peace and Friendship (Amended 3/7, p. 6), 1.
Mar 6	Integrated Usage Is an Important Aspect of Technological Revolution, 3.
Mar 7	Technological Renewal and Technological Revolution Should Have Orderly Planning, 1.
Mar 7	Do a Good Job on the Prevention and Cure of Pig Diseases in the Spring Season, 3.
Mar 8	New Stage in the Women's Emancipation Movement in Our Country, 1. SCMP 2215, 5.
Mar 10	Quickly Assign the "Three Quotas" to the Production Teams, 1. SCMP 2219, 17.
Mar 10	The Inspiration We Get from the Coal Transporting Machine, 2.
Mar 11	Welcome Premier Koirala, 1. SCMP 2218, 42.
Mar 12	A Product of Communist Thought, 1.
Mar 12	Carry Out More Properly the Investment-by-Contract System, 2. SCMP 2220, 3.
Mar 12	DeGaulle's Plot Is Finally Exposed, 6.
Mar 13	A Good Experience in Directing Industry to Support Agriculture, 1. SCMP 2220, 7.
Mar 14	Fully Develop the Superiority of the People's Communes and Help the Poor Brigades to Catch Up Quickly with the Richer Brigades, 1. SCMP 2222, 4.
Mar 15	Local Railways Will Have a Great Future, 1. SCMP 2224, 6.
Mar 15	Grasp Together the Work of Production and Transportation, 2.
Mar 16	Learn to Grab with Two Hands, 1. SCMP 2225, 2.
Mar 16	Open More Agricultural Middle Schools and Run Them Well, 4. SCMP 2228, 15.
Mar 17	People's Communes Should Formulate Land Utilization Plans, 1,3. SCMP 2228, 2.
Mar 17	All Livestock Must Gain Weight, 3.
Mar 18	Sincere Cooperation Is the Key to Smooth Settlement of the Overseas Chinese Question, 1,4. SCMP 2223, 39.
Mar 19	Develop Extensively the Movement of "Little Spring Ploughing," 1.
Mar 20	The Struggle for Justice of the Latin American Peoples Will Triumph Eventually, 1.
Mar 21	Every Forestry Product Must Have a Base; Every Base Must Build a Logging Station; Every Logging Station Must Have Full Production, 1.
Mar 23	The Popular Movement for Spare-Time Education, 1. SCMP 2228, 21.
Mar 24	Strive to Fulfill Tasks Now without Delay and Overfulfill Transport Plans, 1. SCMP 2229, 8.
Mar 25	Peking Papers Hail Sino-Nepalese Friendship, 1. SCMP 2227, 44.
Mar 26	Everyone to Work on the Patriotic Hygiene Movement, 1,4.
Mar 27	Let the Production of Fiberboard Be Carried on Everywhere, 1. SCMP 2229, 5.
Mar 27	JMJP on China's Work on Cultural Relics and Museums, 3. SCMP 2231, 13.
Mar 28	Enlarge the Processing of Agricultural Bi-Products to Increase the Supply of Raw Materials for Light Industries, 1.
Mar 28	Increase the Production and Be Thrifty in the Consumption of Cotton for Industrial Use, 2.
Mar 29	Ways Whereby Financial and Banking Agencies May Promote Production, 1,2. SCMP 2232, 6.
Mar 31	We Must Continue to Leap Forward, We Will Continue to Leap Forward, 1,4.
Apr 1	Strive to Win an All-Round Great Bumper Harvest in the Summer, 1. SCMP 2235, 28.
Apr 2	Small Foreign Groups and High Speed, 1.
Apr 3	Organize Agricultural Production Rationally, 1.
Apr 4	A Glorious Victory of Socialism (Hungarian liberation anniversary), 1.
Apr 4	What Has Adenauer's Visit to Japan Indicated? 6.
Apr 5	Current Tasks of Art Education, 1. SCMP 2245, 22.
Apr 6	Build More Bases for Seedlings, 1.
Apr 7	A Lesson from the "Pinglu Incident," 4. SCMP 2239, 7.
Apr 8	Welcome the Guests of Honor from the Mongolian People's Republic, 1.
Apr 9	"Combination of the Three" Is Sharp Weapon for Technical Revolution, 4. SCMP 2243, 23.
Apr 11	Strive to Fulfill and Overfulfill the 1960 National Economic Plan, 2. SCMP 2242, 1.
Apr 11	Strengthen Unity, Insist on Anti-Imperialist Struggles (Second conference of Afro-Asian people's unity), 6.
Apr 12	Strive to Implement the National Agricultural Development Outline Two to Three Years ahead of Schedule, 1.
Apr 13	All Trades and Professions Must Render Support to Agriculture, 1. SCMP 2245, 17.
Apr 14	An Integrated Network (Transportation organization reform), 2.
Apr 15	General Services Work Must Continue to Take a Big Leap Forward, 4. SCMP 2254, 21.
Apr 16	A Great Achievement in the Agricultural Technological Revolution (Seedling sowing machine), 1.
Apr 17	Extensively Popularize and Greatly Elevate, 1,2.
Apr 17	In Developing Animal Husbandry, Propagate the Campaign of "A Hundred Offsprings to a Hundred Mothers," 2.
Apr 17	Long Live the Unity of Asian-African Peoples, 5.
Apr 18	The Future of Asian-African Peoples Is Boundless, 1,4.
Apr 19	For the Construction and Defense of Socialism, 1. SCMP 2247, 3.
Apr 20	Rural People's Communes Must Train Technical Personnel in Large Numbers, 6. SCMP 2248, 25.

1960

Apr 21	Strive to Overfulfill the Plan of Sowing Products for Industrial Materials, 1.
Apr 24	Continue to Uphold the Mass Nature of the Resist and Prevent Drought Movement, 1,3.
Apr 25	Spring Sowing Must Ensure Acreage, Quality, and Timeliness, 1.
Apr 25	The Angry Roar of the South Korean People, 5.
Apr 26	Animal Husbandry Must Develop with High Speed, 3.
Apr 27	JMJP's Editorial on Sino-Indian Premiers' Talks, 1. SCMP 2248, 33.
Apr 27	Cotton Must Be Planted Sufficiently, 3.
Apr 28	Greeting the Independence of Togo, 6.
Apr 29	Tribute to the Courageous South Korean People, 1,3. SCMP 2251, 29.
Apr 30	A New and Good Example of Peaceful Coexistence, 2. SCMP 2252, 45.
Apr 30	Welcome the Guests of Honor from Albania, 2.
May 1	Strive to Fulfill in the First Half of the Year Fifty Percent of the Plan for the Whole Year, 2. SCMP 2256, 1.
May 3	Greeting the First Steel Production of Paotow Steel Plant, 2.
May 4	U.S. Imperialism: Get Out of Turkey, 1. SCMP 2259, 36.
May 4	We Should Plant Some More Sweet Potatoes, 3.
May 5	Plant More, and Plant Even More, 3.
May 6	For Energetic Popularization and Improvement of Child Care Work, 1. SCMP 2263, 20.
May 7	Attention Should Be Paid to Vegetable Production in All Seasons of the Year, 3. SCMP 2256, 7.
May 7	Raise the Standards of All the "Large Numbers of Small Modern Enterprises" in the Iron Smelting Industry to Higher Levels, 1. SCMP 2266, 6.
May 8	The Machine Industry Should Continue to Revolutionize Its Products, 1.
May 9	A Provocation to the USSR Is a Provocation to the Whole Socialist Camp, 1,2.
May 9	The Process of Taking Care of Wheat Ends Only When the Wheat Is in the Silo, 3.
May 9	Fifteen Years of Glorious Victory in Czechoslovakia, 4.
May 10	Plant on Waste Lands as Soon as They Are Reclaimed, Strive for a Full Harvest This Year, 7.
May 10	Strengthen Visits of Friendship and Unity, 2.
May 10	Chinese and Japanese Peoples Unite, Down with American Imperialism (Amended 5/11, p. 6), 2.
May 11	Vigorously Popularize the Chinese Phonetic Alphabet for Learning Chinese Characters, and Strive to Eradicate Illiteracy as Soon as Possible, 1. SCMP 2264, 8.
May 11	Spring Sowing Should Start Well and End Well, 3.
May 12	Stop the American Japanese Reactionary's Activities, 1.
May 13	A Red Flag for Rural Food Grain Work, 6. SCMP 2263, 15.
May 13	JMJP Editorial: Eisenhower's Self-Exposure, 1,4. SCMP 2261, 33.
May 14	Make a Good Harvest of Rapeseed, 7.
May 14	There Is No "Misunderstanding" Whatsoever, 1,4.
May 14	Develop the Production of Silk Worm Cocoons with Great Speed, 7.
May 15	An Example of Technical Revolution in Building Construction, 1. SCMP 2265, 13.
May 15	Strengthen Sino-Vietnamese Friendship, Support World Peace, 1,4.
May 15	Theatrical Music Needs Constant Renewal, 7.
May 16	Mutual Unity and Mutual Support for the Common Struggle, 2.
May 16	JMJP Welcomes Four-Nation Summit Conference, 4. SCMP 2262, 37.
May 16	Push into New High Tide the Technical Revolution Movement in Financial and Trade Departments, 6. SCMP 2265, 7.
May 17	Vigorously Reform and Create Teaching Materials, 4.
May 18	Fight for a Sweeping Bumper Harvest of Summer Crops, 6. SCMP 2266, 10.
May 19	New Task for Commercial Departments, 6. SCMP 2269, 1.
May 20	U.S. Torpedoes Summit Meeting (Of four powers), 1. SCMP 2265, 21.
May 20	Hold High the Flag of Anti-Imperialism and Advance Together, 5.
May 20	Fight for Complete Output Increase on All Farm Land, 7. SCMP 2266, 12.
May 21	Manufacture Fiberboards by Revolutionary Methods, 7.
May 22	Continue the Struggle till the End, 1,2.
May 22	Insure that All Newborn Pigs Will Survive and Grow Well, 6. SCMP 2268, 23.
May 23	Technological Revolution and the Saving of Labor, 6.
May 24	Start Taking Care of the Early Rice Soon, 6.
May 25	Summer Harvest Has Begun, 5.
May 26	Plant Right After Harvest, Plant Fully and Well, 1.
May 26	Keep Up with the Case of Wang Tien-hsiang, 5.
May 27	JMJP on China's 100th Warning, 1. SCMP 2270, 37.
May 28	Teacher by Negative Example, 1. SCMP 2271, 48.
May 28	Greeting the Successful Climbing of the World's Highest Summit, 2.
May 28	March Towards Modern Scientific Culture (Conference of progressive elements in culture and education of the PLA), 7.
May 29	The Prospects of the Current Political Situation in Japan, 1,4.
May 29	Closely Plant Full Cotton Seedlings, 5.
May 30	Increase the Production of High Quality Paper, 5.
Jun 1	Welcome the High Tide of a New and Greater Cultural Revolution, 1,2.
Jun 1	A New Development in the Relationship of Friendship and Mutual Assistance between China and Mongolia, 3.
Jun 1	Foster Communist Heirs with Better Care, 2. SCMP 2277, 2.
Jun 2	Welcome the Heroic People's Emissary, 2.
Jun 3	The Heroic Japanese People Firmly Grasp Struggle, 5.

1960

Jun 4   Strive for the Overfulfillment of the Quota for the Enrollment of Students in Institutions of Higher Education, 4. SCMP 2285, 16.
Jun 4   Make June a Month of Large Increase in Output, 1. SCMP 2286, 1.
Jun 5   Enlighten U.S.-Japanese Reactionaries with a Sharp Knock on the Head, 1.
Jun 5   Crush the American New War Scheme in Asia, 4.
Jun 5   Concentrate Efforts on Summer Harvest and Summer Planting, 6.
Jun 7   JMJP Editorial Supports Soviet Disarmament Proposals, 2. SCMP 2277, 30.
Jun 8   Insist on Using the New Technologies in Production, 1.
Jun 9   Establish Porter-Transportation on a Large Scale, 1.
Jun 10 The Working Class of the Whole World Is Marching Ahead in Unity and Struggle against Americanism, 1.
Jun 12 Forever Be Advocates of the Cultural Revolution, 4.
Jun 13 Penetrate into the First Line of Production, 1. SCMP 2297, 7.
Jun 13 Carry Out Preparations for Flood Prevention as Soon as Possible, 3. SCMP 2285, 19.
Jun 13 A New Development in the Spare-Time Cultural and Art Activities of Workers, 4.
Jun 13 JMJP on Eisenhower's Tour of Far East, 5. SCMP 2279, 39.
Jun 15 Go Deep into the Forefront of Production, Grasp Tightly the Production of Raw Materials (Amended 6/16, p. 2), 1.
Jun 15 Stick to the Good Habit of Eating, Living, and Laboring Together with the Masses, 1,4. SCMP 2285, 27.
Jun 15 The Farther We Go, the Broader the Road, 2. SCMP 2293, 5.
Jun 16 The "Two-Five System" Evolved by Wuchia Hsien Party Committee Deserves Study, 1. SCMP 2286, 19.
Jun 16 Work Hard in the Last Fifteen Days of June, 2. SCMP 2293, 7.
Jun 17 The Key to Increased Cotton Production Is to Increase and Protect the Buds, 3.
Jun 17 JMJP Hails Initial Victory of Japanese People's Struggle, 4. SCMP 2282, 28.
Jun 19 Emulate the Example of the Huanghua Salt Field, 2.
Jun 20 Greetings to the Independence of the Mali Federation, 4.
Jun 20 The Japanese People Will Never Acquiesce, 1.
Jun 20 Promote Intercropping, 7.
Jun 21 Make Necessary Arrangements for Livelihood as We Do for Production, 4. SCMP 2297, 11.
Jun 21 JMJP Editorial on Eisenhower's Far Eastern Tour, 1. SCMP 2285, 34.
Jun 22 Make Extensive Integrated Use of Agricultural Bi-Products, 3.
Jun 23 We Need to Grasp Relentlessly, as Well as to Grasp Meticulously and Realistically, 2.
Jun 24 A New Victory of the Japanese People, 1.
Jun 24 Paving the Way for New Products (Promote sowing machines), 3.
Jun 25 Drive U.S. Imperialism Out of Asia, 1,4. SCMP 2288, 46.
Jun 25 Grasp the Opportunity, Make Good Preparations, 2.
Jun 26 There Is No Height That Cannot Be Reached, 4.
Jun 26 Go Forward, Malagasy! 6.
Jun 26 Greetings to the Birth of Somalia, 6.
Jun 27 Learn from the Creative Spirit of Popai County in Realizing Three Harvests in One Year, 3.
Jun 29 Hold High the Flag of the Marxism-Leninism Revolution of the Moscow Manifesto, 1.
Jun 29 A Successful Experience in Propagating New Technologies, 4.
Jun 30 Be a Thorough and Realistic Progressive, 1.
Jun 30 Jubilantly Celebrating the Birth of the Republic of Congo, 5.
Jul 1   Struggle against Natural Disasters till the End, 1,4.
Jul 1   Wishing the Republic of Ghana to Become More Prosperous Every Day, 6.
Jul 1   Greetings to the People of Somalia, 6.
Jul 2   Raise the Management of Paddy Fields to a Higher Level, 1.
Jul 3   Concentrate Forces in Key Projects for Faster Progress, 1. SCMP 2298, 1.
Jul 4   Turn Out More and Better Small Commodities, 1.
Jul 5   Build More Power Stations in Villages, 1,4.
Jul 6   Mass Production of Chlorella in China, 1. SCMP 2295, 17.
Jul 6   A New Stage in Sino-Canadian Friendly Relations, 1.
Jul 7   JMJP Denounces U.S. Empty Talk about Disarmament, 1. SCMP 2295, 34.
Jul 8   Transporting Coal Should Be the Main Task of Railroad Transportation, 1.
Jul 9   Grasp the Golden Opportunity of Planting after Rain, 1.
Jul 9   Plant More Melons and Vegetables, 1.
Jul 11 Give Priority to the Mining Industry, 1.
Jul 12 We Oppose the Military Intervention in Congo, 1,5.
Jul 13 Help the Backward Catch Up with the Advanced, 1,4. SCMP 2303, 11.
Jul 13 Wholehearted Support of the Reasonable Demands of the Democratic Republic of Vietnam, 5.
Jul 14 Uphold the Friendly Relations between China and Indonesia, 1.
Jul 16 Unite and Struggle to Win World Peace, 6.
Jul 16 Grasp the Golden Opportunity of Developing the Hog-Raising Enterprise, 1.
Jul 17 The Heroic Cuban People Will Not Be Conquered, 1.
Jul 17 Industrial Enterprises Should Adopt the Idea of Taking Agriculture as the Foundation, 2. SCMP 2304, 6.
Jul 17 March Forward, Brotherly Vietnamese People! 5.
Jul 18 Thoroughly Solve Specific Problems One after Another, 1. SCMP 2308, 10.
Jul 19 Fertilizer Is the Key to Achievement of Continued Forward Leaps in Agricultural Production, 1. SCMP 2310, 17.
Jul 20 Peking Press Supports Congolese Struggle, 1,4. SCMP 2304, 13.

1960

Jul 20	Resolutely Struggle to Protect the Peace in Indo-China, 1,4.	
Jul 20	Strive to Increase the Production of Autumn Vegetables, 2. SCMP 2309, 6.	
Jul 21	Raise the Standard of Products to Higher and Higher Levels and Produce Large Quantities of Products of Excellent Quality, 1. SCMP 2313, 21.	
Jul 21	Strengthen Leadership, Work Harder and Raise More Pigs, 3. SCMP 2313, 29.	
Jul 21	Strive to Improve the Hygiene Knowledge of Cooks and Nursery Personnel, 4.	
Jul 22	Further Improve the Rural People's Communes, 1. SCMP 2313, 6.	
Jul 23	The Commercial Sector Should Wholeheartedly Support the Technological Transformation of Agriculture, 3.	
Jul 24	Grasp Tightly the Work of Producing, Assembling, Using, and Repairing of Irrigation and Drainage Equipment, 3.	
Jul 25	Add Effort to Ambition, Strive to Become First Rate, 1. SCMP 2315, 4.	
Jul 25	Grasp the Critical Period in Managing Cotton Fields, 2.	
Jul 26	Continue to Develop the "Link-Up of Factories and Communes," 1.	
Jul 27	Use the Main Labor Force in the Fields, 1. SCMP 2314, 9.	
Jul 28	Perfect the Purchase and Supply of Vegetables, 1. SCMP 2315, 10.	
Jul 28	Chinese People Support Polish Government's Stand on Its Western Frontiers, 5. SCMP 2310, 35.	
Jul 29	The Situation of Production Must Be Thoroughly Known and Understood, 1. SCMP 2316, 14.	
Jul 29	Move a Proportion of Technician-Workers to Support Agriculture, 1.	
Jul 29	The American Plan to Incorporate the Congo Is Being Speedily Implemented, 5.	
Jul 30	Peking Papers Mark "Congo Day," 5. SCMP 2311, 33.	
Jul 30	New Development in Participation by Cadres in Production and Supervision of Production, 1,4. SCMP 2317, 9.	
Jul 31	Lay a Solid Foundation for Next Year's Bumper Summer Harvest, 1,2. SCMP 2320, 5.	
Jul 31	To Grasp the Work of Pig-Raising We Have to Grasp the Work of Fodder, 4.	
Aug 1	We Must Score Total Victories in Harvesting and Sowing Hastily, 1.	
Aug 3	JMJP Welcomes Success in Sino-Burmese Talks on Boundary Question, 1. SCMP 2313, 44.	
Aug 3	The Current Important Task of Spare-Time Education, 4. SCMP 2318, 6.	
Aug 4	Intercropping of Trees and Grain Has Three Advantages, 1. SCMP 2321, 6.	
Aug 5	Persist in Industry and Economy in Running Rural Communes and Strengthen Financial Management, 1. SCMP 2321, 13.	
Aug 6	Let All Sectors Support the Technological Reform of the Mines, 1,2.	
Aug 6	Extending Hog-Raising Should Follow the Principles of Collective Raising as the Leading Factor, Uphold Both Collective and Private Raising, 3.	
Aug 7	Turn Out More Chemical Fertilizers, 1. SCMP 2323, 13.	
Aug 7	JMJP Greets Independence of Four West African Countries, 1. SCMP 2316, 37.	
Aug 8	The Middle Crop and Late Crop Should Surpass the Early Crop of Rice, 3.	
Aug 9	Take the Initiative in the Campaign to Resist Natural Calamities, 1. SCMP 2325, 14.	
Aug 10	Use More Wild Plants in Building Socialism, 1. SCMP 2329, 23.	
Aug 11	Peking Papers Acclaim Success of Anti-A-H Bomb Conference, 1. SCMP 2319, 36.	
Aug 12	Learn from the Experience of Fuhsin in Doing Transportation Work Realistically, 1,3.	
Aug 13	JMJP Refutes U.S. State Department Statement, 1. SCMP 2320, 39.	
Aug 13	Upgrading of Third Grade Rice Sprouts, 3. SCMP 2329, 25.	
Aug 14	Cultivate Another Autumn Crop, 1. SCMP 2329, 26.	
Aug 15	Celebrate the Fifteenth Anniversary of the Liberation of Korea, 1,5.	
Aug 15	Display the Revolutionary Role of Socialist Literature and Art to a Great Extent, 1. SCMP 2327, 7.	
Aug 16	Pay Close Attention to Workers' Teams, 1. SCMP 2331, 20.	
Aug 16	Greeting the Independence of Cyprus, 6.	
Aug 17	Zealously Develop the Coal Industry of the South, 1.	
Aug 17	JMJP Greets Independence of Four Equatorial African Countries, 6. SCMP 2323, 28.	
Aug 18	Develop Immediately a Campaign for Higher Output and Economy, with Emphasis on Grain and Steel, 1. SCMP 2331, 14.	
Aug 20	Make the Comprehensive Modernization of Farm Tools a Reality, 1,3.	
Aug 21	Take Early Action and Make Early Preparations, 1. SCMP 2330, 7.	
Aug 22	What Has the UN Brought to the Congo? 6.	
Aug 23	Increase the Production of Pesticide to Ensure a Bumper Autumn Harvest, 2.	
Aug 24	Manufacture Mining Equipment with Haste, 1.	
Aug 25	Vigorous Promotion of Agriculture and Food Output by the Whole Party and the Whole People, 1. SCMP 2333, 14.	
Aug 26	Strive for a Greater Autumn Grain Harvest, 1.	
Aug 27	An Important Way to Raise the Theoretical Standards of Hsien and Commune-Level Functionaries, 1. SCMP 2339, 1.	
Aug 28	JMJP Editorial: Another Example of Peaceful Coexistence, 1. SCMP 2330, 29.	
Aug 28	Continue to Weed with Greater Effort, 3.	
Aug 29	Strive for a Better Quality and Higher Yield in the Production of Pig Iron from Small Blast Furnaces, 1.	
Aug 30	Raise More Hogs, Plant More Grain, Collect More Manure, Manufacture More Tools, 1,3.	
Aug 31	Coordinating Efforts Increase the Efficiency of Transportation, 1.	
Aug 31	Purchase Castor Oil Seeds and Sunflower Seeds in Time, 1.	
Sep 1	All Should Prepare for the Autumn Harvest Like This, 1.	
Sep 1	How Can One Tolerate the Lawlessness of U.S. Imperialism? 5.	
Sep 2	The Fifteenth Anniversary of the Glorious Victory of the Vietnamese People, 1.	
Sep 2	Strengthen Unity, Assist Each Other and Struggle Together, 6.	
Sep 3	Eliminate the Damage to Crops Caused by Pests in Autumn, 1.	

1960

Sep 4	Increase Autumn Sowing Acreage by All Means, 1. SCMP 2344, 4.
Sep 5	The Cleaning of Coal Is an Important Step in Increasing Steel Production, 1.
Sep 6	Strive for Greater Production and Higher Yields in the Late Rice, 1.
Sep 7	Fulfill and Overfulfill Daily, Ten-Day Period and Monthly Production Plans, 1. SCMP 2344, 1.
Sep 8	JMJP on 100 Meetings of Sino-American Talks, 1. SCMP 2337, 32.
Sep 8	Give Fuller Scope to the Role of Associations of Science and Technology, 4. SCMP 2340, 8.
Sep 9	Eternal Glory to Wilhelm Pieck, 1. SCMP 2338, 28.
Sep 9	Seriously Examine the Arrangement of the Agricultural Labor Force, 2.
Sep 10	JMJP Welcomes President Sekow Toure of Guinea, 1. SCMP 2338, 38.
Sep 10	Grasp the Opportunity to Store Adequate Feed for Livestock, 3.
Sep 11	The Two Tasks of the Communication and Transportation Sector in Supporting Agriculture, 6.
Sep 12	A Magnificent Battle in Overcoming Disasters, 1.
Sep 12	Defeat the Early Frost and Strive for a Full Harvest, 2.
Sep 12	JMJP Greets Success of Vietnam Party Congress, 5. SCMP 2340, 28.
Sep 13	Ideological Political Work Should Go First, 2.
Sep 14	JMJP Hails Friendly Cooperation between China and Guinea, 2. SCMP 2342, 34.
Sep 15	Aggression and Interference in Congo Must Be Stopped Immediately, 1. SCMP 2342, 21.
Sep 15	Carry Out the Autumn Harvest and Wheat Sowing Well, 2.
Sep 16	Work on the Weak Points in a Progressive Area, Work on the Leading Factors in a Backward Area, 1,4.
Sep 17	Use Conserved Labor Forces where They Are Urgently Needed, 1. SCMP 2348, 3.
Sep 18	Select Good Seeds in the Autumn Harvest, Use Good Seeds in the Autumn Sowing, 1.
Sep 19	Propagate the Good Experiences of Transforming Railway Stations, 1,4.
Sep 19	Spread the Movement of "Small Autumn Harvest" on a Big Scale, 2.
Sep 20	Sow Late Wheat as Early as Possible, 1. SCMP 2351, 10.
Sep 21	Purchase of Agricultural Produce in the Prosperous Season, 1. SCMP 2351, 3.
Sep 22	Speed Up the Mechanization of Agriculture, 1. SCMP 2355, 3.
Sep 23	Organize Community Living Meticulously, 1,2.
Sep 24	Saving on Coal and Coke Is an Important Measure in Increasing the Production of Iron and Steel, 1.
Sep 25	The Path for the Democratic Parties to March Forward, 1,3.
Sep 26	Gather More, and Much More! 1. SCMP 2355, 7.
Sep 26	Strive for Completing the Production Tasks of Chemical Fertilizer Plants ahead of Schedule, 3.
Sep 27	Take Advantage of the Autumn Harvest to Collect Raw Materials to Increase the Production of Light Industrial Commodities, 2.
Sep 27	Extracting the Latent Labor within the Communes, 3.

1960

Sep 28	Store Up Water to Prevent Drought, 2. SCMP 2362, 3.
Sep 28	All Chinese People Enthusiastically Welcome Premier U Nu, Says JMJP, 1. SCMP 2351, 30.
Sep 29	To Have a Friend Overseas Makes Distant Shores Closer, 2.
Sep 29	JMJP Welcomes Algerian Premier, 2. SCMP 2352, 28 (extracts).
Sep 29	Purchase New Cotton Zealously, 5.
Sep 29	One Should Collect More Manure while Raising Pigs, 6.
Sep 30	JMJP on Fourth Volume of Chairman Mao's Works, 4. SCMP 2353, 2.
Oct 1	Celebrating Our Great National Day, 2.
Oct 1	Greeting the New Birth of the Federation of Nigeria, 7.
Oct 2	Jubilantly Celebrate the Signing of the Sino-Burmese Border Treaty, 3.
Oct 5	Inspect and Promote Autumn Harvesting and Autumn Sowing, 5.
Oct 5	May the Sino-Burmese Friendship Building Be Even Brighter, 2.
Oct 6	Transport More Coal, Produce More Iron; Transport More Iron, Produce More Steel, 4. SCMP 2363, 10.
Oct 6	JMJP Hails Comradeship-in-Arms between Chinese, Algerian People, 2. SCMP 2357, 15.
Oct 7	Intensively Develop Labor Emulation Campaign at Level of Work Squads and Groups, 1. SCMP 2363, 12.
Oct 9	Harvest, Store and Process Sweet Potatoes in Organized Manner, 1. SCMP 2366, 11.
Oct 10	Promote the Smelting of Iron Ore, and Build Rich Mines on a Large Scale, 1.
Oct 11	Lower the Level of Waste in Smelting Iron, and Produce Better Steel, 1.
Oct 11	Greatly Increase the Production of Coke, Raise the Quality of Coke, 1.
Oct 12	JMJP Editorial on UN Debate, Voting on China's Representation, 1. SCMP 2361, 44.
Oct 13	Plant More Early Ripening Crops, 1.
Oct 14	Continue to Deepen the Technological Revolution, 1.
Oct 15	Higher Education Institutions Should Do a Better Job in Accelerating the Process of Rusticating the Intelligentsia, 1,4.
Oct 16	Guarantee All-Round Victory in Procurement of Farm Products, 1. SCMP 2366, 9.
Oct 17	Make a Success of the Workers' Hostel Work, 1. SCMP 2384, 10.
Oct 17	Grow More Oil-Bearing Trees, 2. SCMP 2366, 13.
Oct 18	Full Speed Ahead, 1.
Oct 18	Zealously Purchase Tobacco, Hemp, and Autumn Tea, 2.
Oct 18	JMJP Greets New Development of Sino-Mali Friendship, 1. SCMP 2364, 34.
Oct 19	JMJP on Fifteenth Session of UN General Assembly, 1. SCMP 2364, 37.
Oct 19	Let Everyone Work to Harvest and Preserve Autumn Vegetables Well, 2. SCMP 2368, 15.
Oct 20	Asanuma Will Not Have Shed His Blood in Vain, 1. SCMP 2365, 30.
Oct 21	Improve Furnaces, Economize Fuel, 1.
Oct 22	Attach High Priority to the Production of Mechanical Parts, 1.

53

1960

Oct 22	Promote Extensively the Scientific Technological Activities of Youths, 4.
Oct 23	Love Farm Work, Strengthen Agricultural Production, and Build Five Happy Rural People's Communes, 1. SCMP 2373, 3.
Oct 24	Improve Directing Methods by Industrial Control Authorities, 1. SCMP 2378, 19.
Oct 25	JMJP Editorial on Guard for Asian and World Peace, 1. SCMP 2368, 35.
Oct 25	Organize the Higher Production and Greater Distribution of Coal, 2.
Oct 27	Accelerate the Development of Suburban Agriculture, 3. SCMP 2378, 23.
Oct 27	Accelerate the Technological Transformation of Means of Transportation among the People, 1.
Oct 28	Diligently Harvest in Autumn, Plant Well to Have a Full Harvest Next Year, 1.
Oct 28	Greeting the Establishment of Relations between China and Mali, 1.
Oct 28	Strenuously Develop Research Work on the Scientific Technology of Agricultural Machinery, 4.
Oct 29	Take Another Step Towards Developing the Integrated Use of Agricultural By-Products, 1.
Oct 29	Strenuously Develop the Processing of Agricultural By-Products, 1.
Oct 30	The Key to Insist on Using New Technology, 1.
Nov 1	Persistence in Struggle Means Victory, 1. SCMP 2373, 30.
Nov 2	Zealously Build a Network of Repairing Agricultural Machinery, 1.
Nov 3	Universally Enforce the System of Stationing Rural Financial and Trade Personnel in Production Brigades, 1. SCMP 2386, 9.
Nov 4	A Very Important Task in the Movement to Collect Night Soil, 1.
Nov 6	Make a Good Preparation for Extensive Production of Chlorella for Next Year, 3.
Nov 7	JMJP Hails October Revolution Anniversary, 1. SCMP 2377, 16.
Nov 9	Make Overall Arrangements and Promote Energetically the Production of Small Commodities, 1. SCMP 2382, 5.
Nov 10	With Reliance upon the Masses, Push the Campaign for Purchase of Farm Products to an Upsurge, 1. SCMP 2386, 1.
Nov 11	The Many Benefits of Technicians Making Farm Calls, 1.
Nov 12	JMJP: Korean Question Must Be Settled by Koreans, 5. SCMP 2381, 23.
Nov 12	Make Another Step in the Movement of Mechanization and Semi-Mechanization of Loading and Unloading, 1.
Nov 13	The Commodity Revolution in the Machine Industry Must Be Deeply Promoted, 1.
Nov 14	Take Advantage of the Slack Farm Season to Develop Subsidiary Production, 1. SCMP 2386, 4.
Nov 15	Tightly Grasp the Repairing and Manufacturing of Agricultural Machinery and Tools, 1.
Nov 17	JMJP Editorially Welcomes Cuban Government Delegation, 1. SCMP 2384, 27.
Nov 18	Acquire the "Piano-Playing" Working Method (Experience of Luchou Harbor in tapping latent resources in transportation), 1.
Nov 19	U.S.A. Deliberately Intensifies International Tension, 1,4.
Nov 20	Sum Up the Experiences of Communes and Strengthen the Development of Communes, 1. SCMP 2388, 1.
Nov 21	Give Full Play to Revolutionary Spirit of 1957 Moscow Declarations, 1. SCMP 2385, 46.
Nov 21	Peking Papers Welcome Expression of Friendship by Laotian Government, 4. SCMP 2385, 43.
Nov 22	Extend Winter Irrigation, Prevent Spring Drought, 1.
Nov 23	Make a Breakthrough in the Weak Link of Winter Crops, 1.
Nov 24	Develop Even More Repair and Service Stations, 1.
Nov 25	JMJP: Dark Clouds over Congo Will Dissipate Eventually, 5. SCMP 2388, 20.
Nov 25	Fully Develop the Fighting Role of Production Teams, 1. SCMP 2394, 8.
Nov 26	What Can We Learn from the Yimen Mess Hall? 1.
Nov 28	Out with All Colonialists from Africa, 1. SCMP 2390, 27.
Nov 30	Develop a Realistic Style of Work--Perfecting the Weighing and Storage of Food Grains, 1. SCMP 2400, 8.
Dec 1	JMJP Hails Further Development of Sino-Cuban Friendship, 1. SCMP 2391, 34.
Dec 3	Increase Digging Speed to Ensure Increased Production of Coal, 1.
Dec 3	Pay Great Attention to the Packaging of Commercial Commodities, 3.
Dec 4	How Strength Should Be Concentrated to Master the Major Links, 2. SCMP 2400, 1.
Dec 7	JMJP Editorial: The Banner of Victory, the Banner of Unity, 1,2. SCMP 2396, 19.
Dec 9	Inspect Safe Growth at Every Stage of Work, 3.
Dec 9	Resolutely Support the Struggle of the Congo People, 6.
Dec 10	JMJP Acclaims Sino-Soviet Friendship, 1. SCMP 2398, 38.
Dec 10	Organize the Work of Moving, Loading, and Unloading Better, 2.
Dec 11	Speaking about Mining Lamps, 3.
Dec 11	JMJP Supports New Program for Peaceful Unification of Korea, 2. SCMP 2399, 33.
Dec 12	Establish a United Front to Oppose the Imperialist Policies of Aggression and War, Prevent a World War, and Strive for Lasting Peace, 1. SCMP 2399, 1.
Dec 13	Strengthen and Improve the Achievements of Irrigation and Water Conservancy Construction, 3.
Dec 13	Sino-Afghan Friendship Enters New Stage, 1. SCMP 2400, 30.
Dec 14	Turning Bad Lands into Good Lands through Planting, 1.
Dec 14	JMJP Protests at French Atrocities in Algeria, 5. SCMP 2400, 32.
Dec 14	Make Preparations to Prevent the Outbreak of Disasters, 4.
Dec 15	JMJP Editorial Welcomes Prince Sihanouk's Visit to China, 1. SCMP 2402, 28.
Dec 15	Everything Has to Pass through Experimentation (Small nitrogenous fertilizer plant management), 2.
Dec 16	JMJP Supports Laotian People's Struggle against U.S. Aggression, 6. SCMP 2403, 32.
Dec 17	The Closest Possible Cooperation, 2. SCMP 2409, 11.
Dec 17	JMJP Greets Establishment of Sino-Somali Diplomatic Relations, 1. SCMP 2403, 37.
Dec 18	Use Manpower Reasonably, Increase Labor Efficiency Continuously, 1.

1960

Dec 20 JMJP Says: Colonialism Must Be Abolished, 6. SCMP 2405, 26.
Dec 20 Inspect, Calculate and Plan Winter Irrigation, 2.
Dec 21 The Three-Level Ownership System with the Production Brigade as the Basic Level Is the Basic System for People's Commune at the Present Stage, 1. SCMP 2408, 10.
Dec 22 A New Page in Sino-Cambodian Relations, 1. SCMP 2407, 29.
Dec 23 Help Draft Animals through the Winter Safely, 1.
Dec 24 JMJP Welcomes Settlement of Overseas Chinese Dual Nationality Question, 1. SCMP 2408, 36.
Dec 25 The Only Way to Solve the Current Crisis of Laos, 5.
Dec 25 Celebrate the Fifth Anniversary of the Signing of the Sino-German Treaty of Friendship and Cooperation, 1. SCMP 2408, 31 (summary).
Dec 26 Victory Will Certainly Belong to the Latin American Peoples Who Are Rich in the Tradition of Revolutionary Struggles, 1. SCMP 2409, 43 (summary).
Dec 28 Practice of Economy on Coal Consumption Is a Long-Term Task of the Iron and Steel Industry, 1. SCMP 2420, 2.
Dec 29 Resolutely Carry Out and Continually Perfect the "Three Guarantees and One Reward" System, 1. SCMP 2420, 10.
Dec 30 For the Miners, 1.
Dec 31 Concentrate Efforts on Perfecting Coal Transportation, 1. SCMP 2420, 4.

1961

Jan 1   Unite Completely, Depend on the Masses: New Victories in the Struggle for World Peace and Domestic Socialist Construction, 1. SCMP 2414, 1 (extracts).
Jan 1   Cuba Will Triumph, 5.
Jan 3   Destiny of Africa Must Be Decided by African Peoples, 5. SCMP 2413, 22 (summary).
Jan 4   An Important Task of Industries and Enterprise in January, 1.
Jan 5   New Milestone in Sino-Burmese Friendly Relations, 1. SCMP 2414, 25.
Jan 6   Collecting Manure Is an Important Task in Winter Production, 1.
Jan 8   Develop Hunting in Winter, 1.
Jan 9   JMJP Highlights Anshan Workers' Emulation Drive, 1. SCMP 2416, 14 (summary).
Jan 10 The Peoples of China and Burma Will Live in Friendship for Thousands and Thousands of Years, 1,4.
Jan 11 JMJP Welcomes Albanian Economic Delegation, 1. SCMP 2418, 25 (summary).
Jan 12 People's Communes in Rural Areas Should Do a Good Job in Management Work, 1.
Jan 14 Maintenance and Servicing Takes Precedence over Manufacture, 1. SCMP 2425, 7.
Jan 15 JMJP Supports Prince Sihanouk's Proposal, 1. SCMP 2421, 23 (summary).
Jan 15 JMJP Supports Soviet New Effort for Settling Congolese Question, 4. SCMP 2421, 18 (summary).
Jan 16 Make Sure to Increase the Production of Light Industrial Commodities for Daily Use before the Spring Festival, 1.

1961

Jan 17 Be Prepared with an Ample Supply of Seeds for Spring Sowing, 1. SCMP 2426, 10.
Jan 18 All Cities Should Make an Effort to Produce More Vegetables, 1. SCMP 2429, 16.
Jan 19 Further Promote Diversified Undertakings and Multiple Utilization, 1. SCMP 2434, 9.
Jan 20 Proper Management of Finance Work Is the Important Link in Strengthening the Building of Communes, 1. SCMP 2431, 11.
Jan 22 Struggle to Realize the Common Task in the Moscow Declaration, 1.
Jan 22 Protest the New Crime of Persecuting Premier Lumumba, 4.
Jan 23 Production Plans of People's Communes Must Be Rooted among the Masses, 1. SCMP 2430, 4.
Jan 26 Grasp the Key for the Management of Wheat Fields, 1.
Jan 26 JMJP Hails Success of Afro-Asian Solidarity Council Meeting, 5. SCMP 2429, 24 (summary).
Jan 27 Democratic Centralism Is the Organizational Principle for People's Communes, 1. SCMP 2434, 11.
Jan 28 A Glorious Example of Developing the Friendly Relations of Asian and African Nations, 1.
Jan 28 To Pass a Happy and Meaningful Winter Vacation, 4. SCMP 2432, 9.
Jan 29 Greatly Promote Investigation and Study, 1. SCMP 2435, 5.
Jan 30 Understanding the Actual Condition Is the Prerequisite for Proper Accomplishment of Tasks, 1. SCMP 2436, 8.
Jan 31 Prepare Well the Small Agricultural Tools for Spring Sowing in Winter, 1.
Feb 1   JMJP Editorial Hails Extended Economic Cooperation between China and Vietnam, 1. SCMP 2432, 28 (summary).
Feb 2   Using Reality as the Starting Point, 1.
Feb 3   Chinese, Albanian Peoples Will Forever Advance Together, Says JMJP, 1. SCMP 2434, 26 (summary).
Feb 4   Dig First, Process Later, 1.
Feb 4   Produce More Native Chemical Fertilizer, 2.
Feb 5   Correctly Implement Party Policies, 1. SCMP 2442, 9.
Feb 6   Don't Let Go of Opportunities, 1.
Feb 7   Make Use of the Opportunity to Collect and Transport Timber, 1.
Feb 8   Make a Good Job of the Management of Wheat Fields, 1. SCMP 2444, 11.
Feb 9   A Good Way to Repair and Assemble Agricultural Machinery and Tools, 1.
Feb 10 JMJP Editorial Supports Struggle of Laotian People, 1. SCMP 2440, 27 (summary).
Feb 11 The Manufacturing of Parts Should Receive a Higher Priority than the Main Unit, 1.
Feb 12 Disease Prevention during the Spring Season, 1. SCMP 2444, 14.
Feb 13 Always Consider the Interests of the Masses, 1.
Feb 14 A Great Unity, an Eternal Friendship, 1,4.
Feb 15 Exhaust All Measures to Strive for a Bumper Harvest This Year, 1. SCMP 2447, 10.
Feb 15 Support the PLA, Give Preferential Treatment to Service Dependents, Support the Government, Love the People, 4. SCMP 2447, 7.

1961

Feb 16	JMJP Condemns Imperialist Murder of Lumumba, 1. SCMP 2442, 35 (summary).
Feb 17	Properly Manage and Increase the Production of Green Fertilizer, 1. SCMP 2447, 13.
Feb 18	New and Old Colonialists Get Out of Congo! 1,2.
Feb 20	Why Has the Chinghsi Coal Mine Scored All Victories? 1.
Feb 21	Endeavor to Extend the Irrigated Area as Much as Possible in the Spring, 1. SCMP 2451, 11.
Feb 22	The Chinese People Will Stand Closely by the Congolese People, 1.
Feb 22	All Enterprises Should Establish and Strengthen Responsibility Systems, 1,4.
Feb 22	A Milestone Marching along the Great Road of Socialism (Albanian party congress), 6. SCMP 2446, 22 (summary).
Feb 23	Apply Fertilizer Reasonably and Control Wheat Growing Well, 1.
Feb 23	Actively Develop the Production of Chinese Medicinal Herbs, 1. SCMP 2452, 14.
Feb 24	What Kanglieh Production Brigade Reveals, 1. SCMP 2450, 16.
Feb 25	Oppose New U.S. Interventionist Plot against Laos, 1. SCMP 2447, 23.
Feb 26	Manage Rapeseed Well, 1.
Feb 28	Speedily Train Cadres for Agricultural Mechanization, 1. SCMP 2452, 6.
Feb 28	The Great Achievements of the Work of Resettling Repatriated Overseas Chinese, 4. SCMP 2449, 16 (summary).
Mar 1	Planting Plans Must Be Realistic and Practical, 1. SCMP 2458, 3.
Mar 2	Good Preparation Is a Prerequisite for Increasing the Production of Coal (Kuancheng coal mine), 1.
Mar 3	JMJP Editorial on the Way to Solve Congo Question, 1. SCMP 2452, 22.
Mar 4	A Good Example of Overcoming Difficulties and Developing Production in a Disaster Area, 1.
Mar 5	Learn from the Spirit of Conscientiousness of the Comrades in Sui County, 1.
Mar 7	Need for More "Five-Good" Cadres, 1. SCMP 2462, 8.
Mar 8	Women, Contribute More to the Effort to Win a Bumper Harvest of Crops This Year, 1. SCMP 2463, 13.
Mar 9	Propagate the Excellent Style of Combining Revolutionary Fervor with Scientific Spirit, 1.
Mar 9	JMJP Supports Korean Government's Plan for Peaceful Unification, 5. SCMP 2456, 24 (summary).
Mar 11	Coordination of Points with Surfaces, 1. SCMP 2462, 12.
Mar 12	JMJP Exposes Malaya's "Neutrality," 1. SCMP 2458, 28 (summary).
Mar 13	Every Train Must Be Safe and Punctual, 1.
Mar 13	The Voice of 200 Million Latin American Peoples, 3.
Mar 14	Make Agricultural Machinery Serve Agricultural Production Better, 1.
Mar 16	Oppose Imperialist Scheme to Carve Up Congo, Says JMJP, 1. SCMP 2461, 24 (summary).
Mar 17	Advance in Raising the Efficiency of Labor in Industrial Enterprises (Steel works), 1. SCMP 2462, 10 (summary).
Mar 18	The Great Pioneering Act that Was the Paris Commune, 1. SCMP 2471, 3.
Mar 19	Ask Old Peasants for Advice, 1. SCMP 2468, 11.
Mar 21	Do Better Work in Providing Information on Agricultural Production, 1.
Mar 22	Zealously and Realistically Raise the Quality and Quantity of Commodities, 1.
Mar 24	The Time Factor Is of Great Importance in Agricultural Production, 1. SCMP 2472, 9.
Mar 25	Carry Out Disease Prevention and Medical Treatment at the First Line, 1. SCMP 2472, 11.
Mar 26	Strive for a Full Harvest in Spring Fishing, 1.
Mar 28	Solving Concrete Problems Should Begin with Investigation and Research, 1.
Mar 29	Thoroughly Perfect Maintenance and Repair of Metallurgical Equipment, 1. SCMP 2476, 20.
Mar 31	What Should Be Noted in This Year's Afforestation Work, 1. SCMP 2475, 15.
Apr 1	Grain and Cotton Should Be Given Equal Consideration, 1. SCMP 2475, 13.
Apr 2	Conscientiously Implement Policies of Rural People's Communes, 1. SCMP 2476, 24.
Apr 2	Peking Papers Acclaim Resolutions of Third All-African People's Conference, 4. SCMP 2472, 22 (summary).
Apr 3	All Things Must Go through Trials, 1. SCMP 2479, 1.
Apr 4	Greeting the Opening of the Twenty-sixth World Table Tennis Championship Games, 1.
Apr 4	New Stage in Sino-Indonesian Friendly Relations, 1. SCMP 2473, 23.
Apr 6	Discover Sources for New Materials, Increase the Production of Industrial Commodities for Daily Use, 1.
Apr 7	Advanced Units Should Make Continuous Efforts to Develop Fine Points and Overcome Shortcomings, 1. SCMP 2480, 15.
Apr 8	Firmly Grasp Spring Salt-Making to Increase the Production of Salt, 1.
Apr 10	The Locomotive Operation Contract System Is an Effective System of Responsibility, 1. SCMP 2484, 10.
Apr 11	The Key to Solving the Problem of Fertilizers, 1.
Apr 12	U.S. Must Stop Intervention in South Vietnam, 1. SCMP 2478, 33 (summary).
Apr 13	JMJP Hails First Successful Manned Flight into Space, 4. SCMP 2479, 37 (summary).
Apr 14	Produce More Famous Brand Goods, 1. SCMP 2485, 7.
Apr 15	The Great Success of the Twenty-sixth World Table Tennis Championship Games, 1.
Apr 15	JMJP Marks "African Freedom Day," 7. SCMP 2480, 26 (summary).
Apr 16	The Bugle Call against U.S. Neo-Colonialism (Afro-Asian people's solidarity council meeting), 4. SCMP 2481, 24 (extracts).
Apr 17	Peking Press Supports Cuban People's Struggle against U.S. Aggression, 1. SCMP 2481, 35 (summary).
Apr 18	Bandung Spirit in Full Radiance, 1. SCMP 2482, 32.
Apr 19	The Whole World's People Mobilize to Check U.S. Aggression against Cuba, 1. SCMP 2483, 18 (summary).
Apr 20	The Weak Sectors that Need to Be Grasped for Increasing the Production of Acid and Alkali, 6.
Apr 21	Saluting the Heroic Cuban Peoples, 1.

1961

Apr 22	Peking Press Welcomes Prince Phouma's Visit to China, 1. SCMP 2485, 40 (summary).
Apr 22	The Plan for Sowing and Planting Should Be Founded on Realistic and Feasible Grounds, 6.
Apr 26	Peking Press Hails Chou En-lai-Souvanna Phouma Joint Statement, 1. SCMP 2487, 28 (summary).
Apr 27	JMJP Urges Efforts for Peaceful Settlement of Laotian Question, 1. SCMP 2488, 36 (summary).
Apr 27	JMJP Greets Independence of Sierra Leone, 5. SCMP 2488, 40 (summary).
Apr 28	Strive to Fulfill the Sowing Plans for Economic Crops, 1. SCMP 2495, 20.
Apr 29	Further Improve Management over Repair Service, 1. SCMP 2498, 6.
May 1	JMJP Marks May Day, 1. SCMP 2490, 10.
May 3	JMJP Acclaims Exchange of Instruments of Ratification of Sino-Cambodian Treaty, 1. SCMP 2492, 29 (summary).
May 4	Enhance the Spirit of Revolution and Science, 1. SCMP 2498, 1.
May 5	Constantly Clean Up Material Supplies, 1.
May 7	Regular and All-Round Arrangements Should Be Made for Producing Small Commodities for Everyday Use, 1. SCMP 2500, 3.
May 8	True Face of Kennedy Administration, 1. SCMP 2496, 38.
May 9	Peking Papers Hail Angola People's Struggle, 4. SCMP 2496, 27 (summary).
May 16	Save on Coal, 1.
May 18	Struggle for Success of Enlarged Geneva Conference, 1. SCMP 2502, 28.
May 18	JMJP Editorial on "Lyndon Johnson's Dirty Mission," 5. SCMP 2503, 38.
May 19	Path of Neutrality in Laos, 1. SCMP 2503, 36 (extracts).
May 20	An Important Task in the Work on Food Supplies, 3.
May 21	JMJP on the Military Coup in South Korea, 4. SCMP 2505, 37 (summary).
May 24	JMJP Reviews First Week of Enlarged Geneva Convention, 1. SCMP 2507, 39 (summary).
May 26	Check New U.S. Military Provocations in Laos, 1. SCMP 2508, 41 (summary).
May 28	Clarify the Situation before Jumping to a Conclusion, 1. SCMP 2517, 2.
Jun 1	Educate Children according to Their Particular Qualities, 1.
Jun 1	John Kennedy's Facing a Severe Test, 1. SCMP 2511, 46.
Jun 2	Peking Papers Congratulate All-African Trade Union Congress on Its Success, 6. SCMP 2512, 34 (summary).
Jun 4	Earnestly Assist Shift and Group Leaders, 1. SCMP 2517, 18.
Jun 8	Carry Out Inspection and Repairs in a Planned Manner, 1. SCMP 2521, 17.
Jun 9	JMJP Editorial Hails Japanese People's Struggle against Fascist Bill, 1,5. SCMP 2517, 38 (extracts).
Jun 10	JMJP Welcomed DRV Government Delegation, 1. SCMP 2517, 44 (extracts).
Jun 11	Properly Manage and Make Better Use of Farm Machinery, 1. SCMP 2526, 11.
Jun 13	JMJP Welcomes President Sukarno, 1. SCMP 2519, 39 (summary).
Jun 14	No Encroachment on Laos' Sovereignty Will Be Tolerated, 5. SCMP 2520, 22.
Jun 16	JMJP Editorial Hails Success of President Sukarno's China Visit, 3. SCMP 2522, 32 (summary).
Jun 16	JMJP Welcomes Japanese Communist Party Diet Members Delegation, 3. SCMP 2522, 35 (extracts).
Jun 17	JMJP Hails Success of Premier Pham Van Dong's Visit, 2. SCMP 2523, 43 (summary).
Jun 21	Respect the Authority of Production Teams, 1. SCMP 2531, 18.
Jun 23	Strengthen Sino-Japanese People's Common Struggle against U.S. Imperialism, 1,4. SCMP 2527, 35 (summary).
Jun 23	JMJP Editorial on U.S. Plan for International Control over Laos, 6. SCMP 2527, 29.
Jun 24	Angolan People Will Surely Win Victory, Says JMJP, 1. SCMP 2528, 26 (summary).
Jun 25	JMJP Editorial on Korea's Peaceful Unification, 1. SCMP 2529, 40 (extracts).
Jun 26	Seriously Carry Out Summer Sanitation Work, 2. SCMP 2535, 20.
Jun 27	Foliage Can Be Abundant Only When the Root Is Deep (Development of science and training of researchers), 4. SCMP 2534, 14.
Jun 28	Time to Conclude Peace Treaty with Germany, 1. SCMP 2530, 35 (summary).
Jun 30	JMJP: Fight on to End under Banner of Lumumba, 1. SCMP 2532, 34.
Jun 30	Stevenson's South America Visit a Dirty Mission and Failure, Says JMJP, 6. SCMP 2532, 42 (summary).
Jul 1	The Great Glorious Forty Years, 4.
Jul 4	Stop British Armed Intervention against Kuwait! Says JMJP, 1. SCMP 2534, 30 (summary).
Jul 5	The Way to Have More Young Hogs, 1. SCMP 2545, 19.
Jul 10	JMJP Welcomes Korean Party and Government Delegation, 1. SCMP 2537, 32 (summary).
Jul 11	British Troops Must Withdraw Immediately from Kuwait, 7. SCMP 2539, 30 (extracts).
Jul 11	Peking Papers Hail Anniversary of Mongolian Revolution, 1. SCMP 2539, 33 (summary).
Jul 12	Peking Papers Welcome Sino-Korean Treaty, 1,5. SCMP 2540, 27 (summary).
Jul 14	There Is Only One China, No Two Chinas, 1,4. SCMP 2541, 47.
Jul 16	JMJP Hails Further Consolidation of Sino-Korean Friendship, 1. SCMP 2542, 31 (summary).
Jul 20	JMJP Editorial Supports Vietnamese People's Just Struggle, 1. SCMP 2545, 36 (summary).
Jul 22	Strengthen Labor Protection, 1. SCMP 2552, 18.
Jul 26	Cuban Revolution Will Certainly Continue to Advance Victoriously, Says JMJP Editorial, 1. SCMP 2549, 19 (summary).
Aug 4	Solve Problems One by One in a Systematic Manner, 1. SCMP 2560, 8.
Aug 8	Produce More and Better Light Industrial Goods, 1. SCMP 2561, 14.
Aug 9	JMJP Editorial Marks Anniversary of Patriotic Laotian Coup d'Etat, 1. SCMP 2558, 33 (extracts).
Aug 10	Further Delay in Concluding German Peace Treaty, JMJP Editorial Demands, 1. SCMP 2559, 30 (summary).
Aug 12	Don't Miss the Opportunity to Collect and Make Green Fertilizer, 1.
Aug 13	Peking Papers Welcome Distinguished Guest from Brazil, 1. SCMP 2561, 26 (summary).

1961

Aug 14   JMJP Editorial Welcomes President Nkrumah, 1. SCMP 2561, 40 (summary).
Aug 17   JMJP Editorial Hails Success of Tokyo World Conference against Atomic Bomb, 1. SCMP 2564, 44 (summary).
Aug 19   JMJP Editorial Hails Sino-Ghanian Joint Communique, 3. SCMP 2566, 38 (summary).
Aug 22   JMJP Acclaims Sino-Ghanian Friendship Treaty, 1. SCMP 2568, 22 (summary).
Aug 23   Take Early Action to Store Up Fodder Grass for Livestock, 1. SCMP 2570, 11.
Aug 25   Strive Vigorously for a Good Autumn Harvest, 1. SCMP 2574, 19.
Aug 29   Let Each Shoulder His Responsibility and Develop His Ability, 1. SCMP 2574, 16.
Sep 1   Peking Papers Support Soviet Government Statement on Conducting Nuclear Tests, 1. SCMP 2574, 45 (summary).
Sep 5   JMJP Editorial Mourns Death of Comrade Foster, 1. SCMP 2576, 37 (summary).
Sep 6   Tighten the System of Inspection, 1.
Sep 8   Sow Well This Fall, Harvest More Next Summer, 1.
Sep 9   Further Strengthen United Front against Imperialism and Colonialism, Urges JMJP, 1. SCMP 2578, 28.
Sep 13   JMJP Marks Anniversary of Sino-Guinean Friendship Treaty, 1. SCMP 2581, 23 (summary).
Sep 15   Develop Aquatic Production by Fully Utilizing Water Resources, 1. SCMP 2593, 22.
Sep 18   JMJP Editorial Calls for Vigilence against Japanese Militarism, 1. SCMP 2584, 32 (summary).
Sep 20   JMJP Greets Successful Conclusion of Korean Workers' Party Congress, 1. SCMP 2586, 36 (summary).
Sep 21   Organize Firewood Burning in Rural Areas as Soon as Possible, 1.
Sep 22   Peking Papers Welcome Cuban President, 1. SCMP 2588, 35 (summary).
Sep 22   Firmly Oppose New U.S. Scheme, 1. SCMP 2588, 46.
Sep 25   Grasp the "Small Autumn Harvest" Well, 1.
Sep 26   Hold High the Banner of Unity and Anti-Imperialism, Advance Towards New Victories (Games of the new emerging forces), 3.
Sep 28   Grasp Autumn Fishing Well, 1.
Sep 28   Greeting the Opening of the Polish Industrial Exhibition Fair, 4.
Sep 29   Peking Papers Welcome the Distinguished Guests from Nepal, 1. SCMP 2592, 36 (summary).
Oct 1   Hold High the Great Banner of the General Line to Win New Victories, 2.
Oct 3   JMJP Hails Comradeship-in-Arms between Chinese and Cuban Peoples, 2. SCMP 2594, 37.
Oct 10   A Great Democratic Revolution (1911 revolution anniversary), 2.
Oct 11   Examining the Ways of Developing Large Livestock from the Viewpoint of Wan Jung, 1,4.
Oct 13   JMJP Acclaims Birth of Sino-Nepalese Boundary of Peace, Friendship, 1. SCMP 2602, 39.
Oct 14   Peking Papers Hail Signing of Sino-Burmese Boundary Protocol, 1. SCMP 2602, 24 (summary).
Oct 15   Expeditiously Procure Farm Products while Properly Arranging the Livelihood of the Rural Populace, 1. SCMP 2605, 10 (summary).
Oct 19   JMJP Calls for Immediate Stop to U.S. Military Provocations in South Vietnam, 1. SCMP 2605, 43 (summary).
Oct 25   A Good Example of Sowing and Planting According to Field Conditions, 1.
Nov 1   The Algerian People Are Marching Forward Triumphantly, 1.
Nov 3   Fully Develop the Role of Labor Models, 1. SCMP 2623, 18.
Nov 5   Develop Household Sideline Occupations of Commune Members while Giving Priority to the Development of Collective Economy, 1. SCMP 2622, 9.
Nov 7   JMJP Editorial on October Revolution Anniversary, 1. SCMP 2617, 33.
Nov 8   JMJP Greets Twentieth Anniversary of Albanian Labor Party, 1. SCMP 2619, 28.
Nov 10   Seriously Carry Through the Policy of Simultaneously Protecting, Raising, and Hunting Wild Animals, 1. SCMP 2626, 22.
Nov 14   Distribute and Utilize Raw Materials in an Appropriate Manner, 1. SCMP 2629, 9.
Nov 16   There Is Much Room for Development in Mountainous Regions, 1. SCMP 2635, 19.
Nov 17   Further Develop the Role of Technical Personnel in Industrial Enterprises, 1. SCMP 2635, 4.
Nov 21   Expeditiously Procure Economic Crops, 1. SCMP 2638, 1.
Nov 22   The Experience of Two Thermo Flask Factories, 1.
Nov 23   Irrigation Systems Being Built in Various Parts of China, 1. SCMP 2628, 22 (summary).
Nov 25   Technical Innovations Must Be Repeatedly Tested, 1. SCMP 2641, 16.
Nov 26   Raise More Sheep, 1.
Nov 30   U.S. Must Immediately Stop Its Adventure in South Vietnam, Says JMJP, 1. SCMP 2632, 32 (summary).
Dec 1   JMJP Editorial: Holding High the Marxist-Leninist Revolutionary Banner of the "Moscow Statement," 1,3. SCMP 2633, 1.
Dec 2   China's Rural Situation Inspiring, JMJP Says, 1. SCMP 2634, 17 (summary).
Dec 2   No Force Can Arrest African National Liberation Movement, Says JMJP, 3. SCMP 2634, 28 (summary).
Dec 3   The Secret of Success Lies in Inflating the Will, 1. SCMP 2638, 24.
Dec 5   Enhance Revolutionary Enthusiasm and Do a Good Job in Preparing for Next Year's Industrial Production, 1. SCMP 2645, 11.
Dec 7   The True Story of Nehru's Instigating the Indian Anti-Chinese Movement, 1.
Dec 9   Rationally Organize the Planning of Agricultural Commodities, 1.
Dec 9   Peking Paper Salutes Tanganyika's Independence, 4. SCMP 2639, 35 (summary).
Dec 12   Develop Patriotic Spirit, Victoriously Fulfill Task of Requisitioning of Agricultural Products, 1. SCMP 2645, 7.
Dec 12   Peking Papers Greet Establishment of Sino-Tanganyikan Diplomatic Relations, 1. SCMP 2641, 38 (summary).
Dec 12   U.S. Must Stop Interference on Korea's Peaceful Unification, Says JMJP, 3. SCMP 2641, 35 (summary).
Dec 13   Make Good Use of Non-Agricultural Raw Materials, Increase the Production of Light Industrial Commodities, 1.

1961

Dec 15 Strengthen Economic Cooperation, 1.
Dec 17 Establish and Perfect the Responsibility System among the Masses, 1. SCMP 2654, 3.
Dec 19 An Example of Peaceful Coexistence among Nations with Different Social Systems, 1.
Dec 20 Support India in Taking Back Goa, 1.
Dec 21 JMJP Supports Indonesian People's Struggle for Liberation of West Irian, 1. SCMP 2647, 21 (summary).
Dec 21 Continue to Struggle for a Peaceful Solution to the Problem of Laos, 1,4.
Dec 22 America Insists on Being an Enemy of the Chinese People, 1,3.
Dec 23 Make Full Use of Leading Role of Old Workers in Production, 1. SCMP 2658, 21.
Dec 24 Each and Every Enterprise Must Strengthen Economic Accounting, 1. SCMP 2660, 1.
Dec 27 Grasp the Important Link in Increasing Wheat Production, 1. SCMP 2658, 24.
Dec 30 Grand Exposure of Ikeda Government's True Face, 1. SCMP 2652, 39.

1962

Jan 1 New Year Editorial, 1. SCMP 2653, 1.
Jan 2 Cuba's Revolutionary Cause Will Certainly Win, 1. SCMP 2654, 32.
Jan 3 JMJP Condemns U.S. Sabotage of Laotian Princes' Talks (Amended 1/4, p. 3), 1. SCMP 2655, 39.
Jan 4 The Glory of Collectivism, 1. SCMP 2662, 17.
Jan 12 Make Overall Arrangements for Light Industrial Production, 1. SCMP 2668, 7.
Jan 15 Expresses Support for Just Struggle of CPUSA, 1. SCMP 2662, 36.
Jan 17 Marks Anniversary of Lumumba's Murder, 1. SCMP 2664, 17.
Jan 18 A Typical Case Relating to the Conservation of Water and Soil by the Masses Themselves, 1. SCMP 2674, 13.
Jan 19 Kennedy's Insolent Challenge (Amended 1/20, p. 3), 1,4. SCMP 2666, 27.
Jan 20 The New Contribution of Chelimumeng, 1.
Jan 22 Opposition to U.S. Imperialism, World People's Common Task, 1,3. SCMP 2668, 29.
Jan 22 Make Good Use of Grassy Hills and Grassy Beaches to Propagate Draft Animals, 2.
Jan 24 Experiences and Lessons from Two Irrigation Areas, 1. SCMP 2678, 8.
Feb 10 Acclaims Second Havana Declaration, 1. SCMP 2679, 35.
Feb 14 On Anniversary of Sino-Soviet Treaty, 1. SCMP 2681, 37.
Feb 16 Maintain the Fine Traditions, Strive for a Good Harvest, 1. SCMP 2688, 20.
Feb 25 Check U.S. Armed Intervention in South Vietnam, 1. SCMP 2688, 33.
Feb 26 Develop the Mountain Areas, 1.
Mar 2 Execute Party Policy Correctly, Zealously Develop the Production of Handicraft Industries, 1.
Mar 10 Reinforce the Agricultural Front from All Aspects, 1. SCMP 2703, 14.
Mar 15 Thoroughly Inventory the Warehouses and Handle Material Supplies in a Unified Manner, 1. SCMP 2707, 5.

1962

Mar 20 Algerian People's Great Victory, 1. SCMP 2705, 23.
Mar 27 Marks Sino-Czechoslovak Treaty Anniversary, 1. SCMP 2709, 32.
Mar 29 Play for Safety and Advance Step by Step, 1. SCMP 2716, 10.
Apr 1 Greeting the First Anniversary of the Signing of the Sino-Indonesian Friendship Treaty, 1. SCMP 2719, 26.
Apr 3 Censures U.S. Stand at Geneva Disarmament Conference, 1. SCMP 2715, 23.
Apr 6 Carry Out Timely and Appropriate Spring Irrigation, 1. SCMP 2722, 19.
Apr 8 Raise Efficiency and Conserve Manpower, 1. SCMP 2722, 7.
Apr 10 Major Keys to Increasing the Efficiency and Benefit of Water Conservancy Projects, 1. SCMP 2726, 16.
Apr 15 Marks African Freedom Day, 1. SCMP 2723, 27.
Apr 17 Unite to Strive for New Victory, 1,2.
Apr 18 Greets Anniversary of Bandung Conference, 1,3. SCMP 2725, 27.
Apr 22 Let's Begin with "Supposing I Were a Customer," 1.
Apr 27 Serious Warning to the U.S. Aggressors, 1,2. SCMP 2733, 27.
Apr 28 Marks Sino-Nepalese Treaty Anniversary, 1. SCMP 2731, 29.
Apr 28 Man Will Destroy Nuclear Weapons, 4. SCMP 2731, 33.
Apr 29 A Way to Solve the Problem of Agricultural Production Funds, 1. SCMP 2741, 10.
May 1 On International Labor Day, 1. SCMP 2732, 8.
May 3 Diversified Undertakings Centered on One Single Enterprise, 1. SCMP 2743, 9.
May 4 Eternal Friendship between Chinese, Korean Peoples, 1. SCMP 2735, 40.
May 10 Correctly Develop the Supervisory Role of Banks, 1. SCMP 2745, 11.
May 12 Attach Importance to the Work of Constructing Mountain Communities, 1.
May 16 Improve the Financial Work of Production Brigades, 1.
May 19 Drive U.S. Aggressors Out of Southeast Asia! 1. SCMP 2745, 35.
May 20 Attach Importance to the Maintenance, Repairs, and Manufacture of Medium-Sized Agricultural Tools, 1.
May 22 Work in Strict Accordance with Established Systems, 1. SCMP 2755, 7.
May 23 To Serve the Greatest Number of the Masses (Anniversary of publication of Comrade Mao's "Talk at the Yenan Forum on Literature and Art"), 1.
May 29 Conscientiously Protect the Forests, 1. SCMP 2763, 11.
Jun 1 The Responsibility of Parents, 1. SCMP 2762, 6.
Jun 2 How to Raise Hogs, 1. SCMP 2763, 5.
Jun 3 Radiance of Peaceful Coexistence Principles Can Never Be Obscured, 1. SCMP 2755, 26.
Jun 5 The Sino-Pakistan Border Talks Are a Good Thing, 1.
Jun 6 A Problem Which Should Be Speedily Solved, 1. SCMP 2764, 5.
Jun 7 Service for U.S. Aggressors, 7. SCMP 2758, 30.

1962

Jun 8 Better Fulfill the Task of Selecting and Retaining Fine Seed Strains during Summer Harvest, 1. SCMP 2764, 15.
Jun 10 We Must Do a Good Job in Water and Soil Conservation (Amended 7/6, p. 2), 1. SCMP 2764, 16.
Jun 14 Hails Major Victory of Laotian People, 1. SCMP 2762, 25.
Jun 15 The Honorable Duties of Accountants, 1. SCMP 2769, 4.
Jun 16 Welcomes Envoys of Heroic Korean People, 1. SCMP 2763, 27.
Jun 19 The Success of Growing Sinkiang Walnuts, 1. SCMP 2775, 13.
Jun 21 Peking Papers Denounce U.S. High-Altitude Nuclear Test, 1. SCMP 2767, 24.
Jun 22 Peking Papers Support Vietnamese People's Patriotic, Anti-U.S. Struggle, 1. SCMP 2768, 36.
Jun 23 Peking Papers Support Korean Supreme People's Assembly Documents, 1. SCMP 2768, 29.
Jun 25 What History Tells U.S. Aggressors, 1. SCMP 2769, 29.
Jun 25 Greets Formation of Laotian Union Government, 1. SCMP 2770, 25 (extracts).
Jun 27 A Living Lesson, 1. SCMP 2790, 15.
Jul 2 Greets Independence of Rwanda, Burundi, 3. SCMP 2774, 25.
Jul 2 Peking Papers Bid Farewell to Korean Supreme People's Assembly Delegation, 1. SCMP 2774, 31.
Jul 5 Hails Algerian Independence, 1. SCMP 2775, 24.
Jul 7 Marks Anniversary of Anti-Japanese War, 1,2. SCMP 2776, 1.
Jul 9 Warns India "To Rein In on the Brink of the Precipice," 1. SCMP 2778, 24.
Jul 11 Peking Papers Greet Anniversary of Sino-Korean Treaty, 2. SCMP 2779, 23.
Jul 12 National Aspiration of Laotian People Will Certainly Be Realized, 1. SCMP 2780, 27.
Jul 13 Strengthen Cotton Field Management in Good Time, 1. SCMP 2788, 16.
Jul 19 Peking Papers Call for Defense of 1954 Geneva Agreements, 1. SCMP 2785, 31.
Jul 24 Hails Success of Geneva Conference on Laos, 1. SCMP 2789, 24.
Jul 26 Marks Cuban Revolutionary Uprising Anniversary, 1. SCMP 2790, 29.
Aug 1 Marks China's Army Day, 7. SCMP 2794, 3.
Aug 9 Hails Successes of Tokyo Conference against Atomic and Hydrogen Bombs, 1. SCMP 2799, 20.
Aug 16 Hails New Soviet Achievements in Conquest of Space, 1. SCMP 2804, 35.
Aug 18 Marks Sino-Ghanian Friendship Treaty Anniversary, 1. SCMP 2805, 27.
Aug 19 Greets Indonesian People's Important Success in Struggle to Recover West Irian, 1. SCMP 2806, 23.
Aug 20 Denounces U.S. Move to Create "Two Chinas," 1. SCMP 2806, 27.
Sep 6 Hails Successful Close of Fourth Asian Games, 1. SCMP 2817, 25.
Sep 7 India Lacks Sincerity in "Peaceful Settlement" of Sino-Indian Boundary Question, 1. SCMP 2818, 29.
Sep 8 Selection of Fine Seeds Must Be Carried Out on a Yearly Basis, 1. SCMP 2826, 1.
Sep 15 An Indictment of U.S. Aggressors, 1. SCMP 2822, 9.
Sep 17 Degradation of Modern Revisionists, 1. SCMP 2823, 23.
Sep 20 Carry Out Autumn Harvesting, Autumn Plowing, and Autumn Sowing Well so as to Lay the Foundation for a Universal Increase of Production Next Year, 1. SCMP 2830, 12.
Sep 22 Chinese People Indignant at Indian Provocations, 1. SCMP 2827, 24.
Sep 30 Greets Birth of Algerian Democratic People's Republic, 2. SCMP 2834, 21.
Oct 1 Struggle to Win New Victories in Our Nation's Socialist Enterprise, 2.
Oct 4 Hails New Growth of Sino-Ceylonese Friendship, 1. SCMP 2835, 25.
Oct 5 Marks Sino-Nepalese Boundary Treaty Anniversary, 1. SCMP 2836, 34.
Oct 6 Hails South Vietnamese Struggle against U.S. Aggression, 1. SCMP 2836, 37.
Oct 9 Hails Uganda's Independence, 1. SCMP 2838, 27.
Oct 10 Challenges Indian Authorities, 1. SCMP 2839, 28.
Oct 12 Intensify Scientific and Technological Research in Agriculture, 1. SCMP 2852, 8.
Oct 13 Hails Militant Sino-Vietnamese Friendship, 1. SCMP 2841, 37.
Oct 14 Warns Nehru to Pull Back from Brink of Precipice, 1. SCMP 2842, 25.
Oct 20 Hails the Establishment of Sino-Uganda Diplomatic Relations, 4. SCMP 2845, 34.
Oct 22 Concentrate the Strength of the Whole Party and Whole Nation in Support of Agriculture, 1. SCMP 2856, 3.
Oct 23 Do a Good Job in Procuring Farm and Subsidiary Products, 1. SCMP 2856, 1.
Oct 24 Stop the New Adventure of American Imperialism, 1.
Oct 24 The Glorious Victory of the Korean People, 4.
Oct 27 Fair and Reasonable Proposals, 1. SCMP 2850, 23.
Oct 28 JMJP Editorial Supports Cuba, 1. SCMP 2851, 24.
Oct 31 Defend Cuban Revolution! 1. SCMP 2852, 21.
Nov 1 Hails Algeria's First National Day, 3. SCMP 2854, 19.
Nov 2 Go All-Out in the Struggle for a Bumper Harvest Next Year, 2. SCMP 2861, 14.
Nov 3 Vigorously Develop the Production of Cotton and Other Economic Crops, 2. SCMP 2860, 14.
Nov 5 Fearless Cuban People Are Most Powerful Strategic Weapon, 1. SCMP 2856, 31.
Nov 7 The Red Banner of the October Revolution Will Fly All Over the World, 3. SCMP 2858, 30.
Nov 8 Please Stop to Think Again, Mr. Nehru, 2. SCMP 2860, 36.
Nov 9 Actively Realize Technical Transformation of Our Country's Agriculture Step by Step, 1. SCMP 2864, 15.
Nov 12 Strive to Overfulfill the Industrial Production Plan of This Year, 1.
Nov 13 To Adjust and Maintain Water Conservancy Projects Is the Most Important Task in Irrigation Areas in This Winter and in the Ensuing Spring, 1. SCMP 2872, 12.
Nov 15 On Developing the Revolutionary Spirit of the Moscow Declaration and the Moscow Statement, 1. SCMP 2862, 26.

1962

Nov 16 Step Up Winter Repair of Farm Machinery, 1. SCMP 2870, 8.
Nov 18 Peking Papers Support Premier Castro's Stand in Defense of Cuban Sovereignty, 1. SCMP 2865, 22.
Nov 20 Urges Indian Government to Return to Conference Table, 1. SCMP 2865, 25.
Nov 22 Hopes India Will Respond Positively to China's Decisions, 1. SCMP 2867, 26.
Nov 26 Next Year Depends on This Winter, 1. SCMP 2875, 13.
Nov 27 Work Hard and Practice Thrift, Store Up Grain for Future Urgent Needs, 2. SCMP 2880, 2.
Nov 28 Marks Albanian People's Festivals, 1. SCMP 2870, 28.
Nov 29 Hails Revolutionary Cuba, 1. SCMP 2871, 27.
Nov 30 Make Preparations for Industrial Production Next Year in a Positive Manner, 2. SCMP 2881, 1.
Dec 2 Make Unified and Overall Arrangements; Fulfill the Procurement Plan for Farm Produce Promptly, 1. SCMP 2881, 3.
Dec 5 Handicraft Industry Should Better Serve the Needs of Agriculture, 1. SCMP 2885, 12.
Dec 7 Energetically Engage in the Work of Propagating Farming Techniques, 1. SCMP 2884, 12.
Dec 9 Hails Founding of Tanganyikan Republic, 5. SCMP 2879, 38.
Dec 10 Greets Opening of Six-Nation Colombo Conference, 1. SCMP 2879, 22.
Dec 14 Actively Carry Out Plant Protection Work in Agriculture (Amended 12/17, p. 2), 1. SCMP 2890, 14.
Dec 15 The Whole World's Proletariat Unites to Oppose Our Common Enemy, 1,2.
Dec 16 Intensify Standard Control Work in Production and Construction, 1. SCMP 2893, 5.
Dec 19 Employ Every Means to Achieve a Production Increase in Cotton, 1. SCMP 2889, 16.
Dec 20 Mark Anniversary of South Vietnam National Liberation Front, 1. SCMP 2886, 29.
Dec 22 Go to the Rural Areas, 1. SCMP 2894, 1.
Dec 23 Gives Factual Analysis of Indian Claim of "Non-Alignment," 1. SCMP 2888, 25.
Dec 24 JMJP Editorial Denounces U.S. Intervention in "Korean Question" through UN, 1. SCMP 2889, 25 (summary).
Dec 25 Peking Press Welcomes Chairman Tsedenbal, 1. SCMP 2888, 38.
Dec 27 JMJP Editorial Hails Signing of Sino-Mongolian Boundary Treaty, 1. SCMP 2889, 38.
Dec 28 Oppose the "Korean-Japanese Talks" Instigated by U.S., 1.
Dec 29 JMJP Hails Sino-Pakistan Agreement on Boundary Question, 1. SCMP 2890, 44.
Dec 30 Celebrate the Important Victory of Complete Destruction of Armed U.S.-Chiang Agents, 1. SCMP 2895, 1.
Dec 31 The Difference between Comrade Togliatti and Us, 1,2,3.
Dec 31 Peking Press Welcomes Ceylonese Premier, 4. SCMP 2892, 33 (summary).

1963

Jan 1 Strengthen the Great Achievement, Win New Victories, 1.
Jan 2 JMJP Welcomes Dr. Subandrio, 1. SCMP 2893, 27 (summary).
Jan 2 JMJP Marks Cuban Revolution Anniversary, 1. SCMP 2892, 37 (summary).
Jan 8 Sustained Efforts for Asian Peace, Afro-Asian Solidarity, 1. SCMP 2909, 24.
Jan 9 Accounting Work Is Important Work for Economic Management, 1. SCMP 2909, 8.
Jan 11 Strengthen the Leadership Hardcore of the Production Teams, 1. SCMP 2905, 11.
Jan 15 Actively and Practically Promote the Patriotic Health Campaign, 1. SCMP 2910, 16.
Jan 19 JMJP Welcomes Nepalese Guests, 3. SCMP 2904, 32 (summary).
Jan 21 Peking Papers Hail Signing of Sino-Nepalese Boundary Protocol, 1. SCMP 2906, 27 (summary).
Jan 24 JMJP Greets New Development of China-Ghana Friendship, 1. SCMP 2908, 24 (summary).
Jan 25 Further Strengthen the Worker-Peasant Alliance, 1. SCMP 2913, 1.
Jan 27 Let Us Unite on the Basis of the Moscow Declaration and Moscow Statement, 1. SCMP 2908, 29.
Jan 28 JMJP Editorial Welcomes Effort of Colombo Conference to Promote Sino-Indian Talks, 1. SCMP 2909, 21.
Jan 30 Actively Develop Sideline Production in the Countryside, 1. SCMP 2915, 5.
Feb 4 JMJP Greets Afro-Asian Solidarity Conference, 1. SCMP 2914, 22 (summary).
Feb 7 Exert Vigorous Effort to Increase Production and Practice Economy (Anniversary of "February 7" strike), 1. SCMP 2927, 16.
Feb 8 JMJP Greets Korean Army Day, 1. SCMP 2918, 31 (summary).
Feb 11 Apply the "Triple-Combination" Method of Leadership More Properly, 1. SCMP 2926, 1.
Feb 12 Peking Press Welcomes Prince Sihanouk, 12. SCMP 2919, 21 (summary).
Feb 12 Unfold Mass Spring Afforestation Campaign! 2. SCMP 2932, 9.
Feb 13 JMJP Editorial Hails Success of Moshi Conference, 1. SCMP 2921, 23 (extracts).
Feb 17 Improve Management of Veterinary Centers, 1. SCMP 2935, 17.
Feb 20 Strengthen Short-Distance Transportation in Hsien and Hsiang in Service of Agriculture, 1. SCMP 2934, 13.
Feb 25 Actively Organize and Develop Diversified Agricultural Operations, 1. SCMP 2933, 16.
Feb 27 Whence the Difference? 1. SCMP 2929, 25.
Feb 28 JMJP Hails New Development of Sino-Cambodian Relations, 1. SCMP 2930, 24 (summary).
Mar 1 JMJP Editorial Welcomes Pakistani External Affairs Minister, 4. SCMP 2932, 28.
Mar 4 JMJP Greets New Era in Friendly Sino-Pakistani Relations, 5. SCMP 2934, 33 (summary).
Mar 5 JMJP on China's Stand for Peaceful Settlement of Sino-Indian Border Question, 3. SCMP 2934, 25.
Mar 6 JMJP Welcomes Laotian Guests, 1. SCMP 2934, 30 (summary).
Mar 7 Mobilize the Masses to Prevent and Resist Drought, 1. SCMP 2941, 1.
Mar 8 A Comment on the Statement of the CPUSA, 1. SCMP 2936, 27.
Mar 8 Women, Struggle and Strive for New Victories, 2. SCMP 2942, 1.
Mar 9 A Mirror for Revisionists (Amended 3/10, p. 1), 1. SCMP 2937, 40.

1963

Mar 10 Chemical Industry Should Render Better Service in Providing Food, Clothing, and Daily Commodities, 1. SCMP 2943, 4.

Mar 11 Peking Papers Hail New Development of Sino-Laotian Friendship, 1. SCMP 2939, 22 (summary).

Mar 15 Make Further Strides in Raising Quality and Increasing the Variety of Industrial Products, 1. SCMP 2947, 16.

Mar 17 Looking at Spring Farming from an Overall Point of View, 1. SCMP 2947, 9.

Mar 20 Do Accounting Work Well, Promote Increased Output and Economy, 1. SCMP 2956, 6.

Mar 23 Realistically Improve the Management and Operation of Commercial Enterprises, 1. SCMP 2952, 14.

Mar 24 A Big Account--Speaking from the Spirit of "A Single Penny," 1. SCMP 2953, 2.

Mar 25 Cultural and Artistic Work Must Serve Rural Areas Better, 1. SCMP 2958, 2.

Mar 27 Endeavor to Raise the Educational Quality of Middle and Primary Schools, 1. SCMP 2959, 5.

Mar 29 Exert Greater Efforts to Develop Aquatic Production, 1. SCMP 2959, 12.

Mar 31 Grasp Well the Work of Planting Trees and Afforestation in the Yellow River Valley, 1.

Apr 2 Strengthen Economic Cooperation, 1. SCMP 2966, 4.

Apr 3 JMJP Editorial Hails Chinese Decision to Release All Captured Indian Military Personnel, 1. SCMP 2955, 21.

Apr 4 JMJP Editorial Greets Success of Niteroi Congress, 1. SCMP 2956, 23.

Apr 5 Peking Papers Condemn U.S. Imperialism for Murdering Qunim Pholsena, 1. SCMP 2957, 26 (summary).

Apr 6 Raise Agricultural Science to a New Level, 1.

Apr 8 Strengthen the Technical Management of Industrial Enterprises, 1. SCMP 2967, 12.

Apr 10 Increase the Production of and Save on Timber, 1.

Apr 12 JMJP Editorial Hails Liu Shao-chi's Visit to Indonesia, Burma, 1. SCMP 2961, 39.

Apr 13 Do a Good Job in Electoral Work, 1. SCMP 2968, 1.

Apr 15 A Great Victory of Our Nation's Table Tennis Players, 1.

Apr 15 JMJP Editorial Marks "African Freedom Day," 3. SCMP 2962, 21.

Apr 17 Stay U.S. Imperialist Hand in Laos, Urges JMJP, 1. SCMP 2963, 25.

Apr 17 Peking Press Expresses Support for Cuban and Other Latin American Peoples, 4. SCMP 2964, 37.

Apr 18 JMJP Editorial Marks Eighth Anniversary of Bandung Conference, 4. SCMP 2964, 21.

Apr 20 JMJP Looks Forward to New Advance in Sino-Burmese Kinship, 1. SCMP 2966, 27.

Apr 21 Peking Press Welcomes Aly Sabry, 2. SCMP 2966, 39 (summary).

Apr 21 JMJP Acclaims Everlasting Militant Friendship between Chinese and Indonesian People, 2. SCMP 2966, 30.

Apr 23 Extend and Use Agricultural Loans in an Effective Manner, 2. SCMP 2970, 9.

Apr 25 Plant Bamboo Extensively and Make Economical Use of Bamboo, 2. SCMP 2976, 13.

Apr 26 JMJP Hails Sino-U.A.R. Friendship, 1. SCMP 2969, 40.

Apr 27 JMJP Acclaims Sino-Burmese Friendship, 2. SCMP 2970, 24 (summary).

Apr 28 JMJP Editorial Welcomes Chinese Nationals Home from India, 1. SCMP 2970, 37 (extracts).

May 1 Carry Out the Campaign for Production Increase and Economy in a More Extensive and More Intensive Manner, 2. SCMP 2975, 1.

May 1 JMJP Hails Sino-Cambodian Friendship, 1. SCMP 2972, 28.

May 2 JMJP Congratulates Indonesia on Restoration of Administration of West Irian, 3. SCMP 2973, 29 (summary).

May 3 Peking Papers Greet Success of Asian and African Journalist Conference, 1. SCMP 2974, 24 (summary).

May 3 Prevent Diseases and Inspect Pests Injurious to Agricultural Crops, 2. SCMP 2980, 16.

May 4 Inherit and Develop the Party's Revolutionary Tradition from Generation to Generation, 1. SCMP 2979, 1.

May 7 Peking Press Hails Sino-Cambodian Joint Statement, 2. SCMP 2976, 23.

May 8 Forever Maintain the Revolutionary Spirit of Fighting amid Hardship, 1. SCMP 2981, 4.

May 9 Carefulness in Everything, 1. SCMP 2987, 6.

May 10 JMJP Hails Sino-Vietnamese Friendship, 1. SCMP 2979, 40.

May 11 Take a Firm Hold on the Task of Inspecting and Protecting Cotton Sprouts without Delay, 2. SCMP 2985, 2.

May 14 Manage and Use Agricultural Machines Well, 1. SCMP 2989, 3.

May 16 JMJP Calls for Action to Check U.S. Aggressive Moves in Laos, 1. SCMP 2983, 30 (summary).

May 18 JMJP Hails New Growth in Sino-Vietnam Friendship, 1. SCMP 2984, 38.

May 19 Strive to Propagate Big Livestock, 1. SCMP 2994, 16.

May 23 JMJP Welcomes Chairman Liu Shao-chi Back to Capital, 1. SCMP 2988, 34 (summary).

May 27 JMJP on Complete Repatriation of Captured Indian Military Personnel, 1. SCMP 2991, 28.

May 28 Peking Papers Mark Success of African Heads of State Conference, 1. SCMP 2992, 24 (summary).

May 29 Love the Collective but Love the State More, 1. SCMP 3001, 14.

May 30 Do Summer Harvest Work Well, Strive for Full Production and Full Harvest, 1.

Jun 1 Strive to Bring Up Staunch Successors to the Revolutionary Cause with All-Round Development, 1. SCMP 2997, 1.

Jun 2 The Great Revolutionary Significance of Participation in Labor by Cadres, 2. SCMP 3006, 14.

Jun 4 JMJP Calls for Immediate Cessation of U.S. Intervention in Laos, 1. SCMP 2995, 31 (summary).

Jun 5 Insist on Vigilantly Organizing Students to Participate in Productive Labor, 1.

Jun 6 JMJP Editorial Welcomes Korean President Choi Yong Kun's Visit to China, 1. SCMP 2997, 28.

Jun 8 India Must Stop Persecution of Chinese Nationals, Says JMJP, 1. SCMP 2998, 25 (summary).

Jun 10 Momentous Juncture in the Raising of the Cotton Output, 1. SCMP 3003, 9.

Jun 16 U.S. Aggression and Intervention in Laos Must be Checked, 1. SCMP 3003, 46.

1963

Jun 19	Educate the Young Workers in the History of Class Struggles, 1. SCMP 3012, 10.
Jun 22	A Bright Way Out for Military and Civil Personnel in Taiwan (Amended 6/23, p. 2), 1. SCMP 3013, 14.
Jun 23	It Is Everybody's Responsibility to Protect Forests, 1. SCMP 3014, 12.
Jun 24	JMJP Hails New Height of Friendship and Unity between Chinese and Korean Peoples, 1. SCMP 3009, 27.
Jun 25	Vigorously Purchase, Promote the Production, and Increase the Supply of Agricultural and Rural Sideline, 1. SCMP 3015, 3.
Jun 26	Step Up Scientific and Technical Publication Work (Amended 6/28, p. 2), 1. SCMP 3016, 13.
Jun 27	A Discussion of Great Significance in Education, 1. SCMP 3016, 11.
Jun 27	Chinese Press Acclaims China's Efforts to Make Games of New Emerging Forces a Success, 2. SCMP 3011, 23 (summary).
Jun 30	Greet the Victory of Armymen and Civilians in Southwest Coastal Areas in Smashing Landing by Enemy Special Agents, 1. SCMP 3015, 2.
Jul 4	An Important Way of Establishing Close Relations between Cadres and the Masses, 1. SCMP 3025, 1.
Jul 5	JMJP Marks Algerian Independence Anniversary, 4. SCMP 3015, 21 (summary).
Jul 7	Develop the Revolutionary Spirit of Running Enterprises with Industry and Thrift and Carry Out a Strict System of Business Accounting, 1. SCMP 3031, 1.
Jul 10	JMJP Editorial Marks Albanian People's Army Day, 4. SCMP 3018, 26.
Jul 11	A Friendly Festival of the Chinese and Korean People, 1.
Jul 13	We Want Unity, Not Schism, 1.
Jul 13	Continue Intensified Efforts at Managing Cotton Fields Properly, 2. SCMP 3026, 16.
Jul 17	Rural Party Branch Secretaries Must Be Both Red and Expert, 1. SCMP 3026, 1.
Jul 18	Strenuously Develop Livestock Production in Pasture Areas, 1.
Jul 19	Expose U.S. Nuclear Fraud, 1. SCMP 3025, 29.
Jul 19	Peking Papers Hail South Vietnamese People's Struggle against U.S. Aggression, 3. SCMP 3025, 34 (summary).
Jul 21	Create Favorable Conditions for Rural Party Branch Secretaries to Take Part in Labor, 1. SCMP 3035, 4.
Jul 23	Correct Way of Conducting Agricultural Scientific Experiments, 1. SCMP 3037, 7.
Jul 25	Earnestly Study the Marxist Theory of Knowledge, 1. SCMP 3036, 9.
Jul 26	Peking Papers Greet Cuban Revolutionary Festival, 1. SCMP 3030, 24.
Jul 27	JMJP Supports Korea's Patriotic Anti-U.S. Struggle, 1. SCMP 3030, 37 (summary).
Jul 28	A Grave Step Taken by India to Menace Asian Peace, 1. SCMP 3031, 23.
Jul 29	Teaching by Word and by Deed, 1. SCMP 3039, 1.
Jul 30	Good in Labor, Good in Work, Good in Thinking, 1. SCMP 3039, 4.
Aug 2	The Whole World's People Unite to Win a Total Ban On and Complete Eradication of Nuclear Weapons, 1.
Aug 3	This Is Betrayal of Soviet People, 1. SCMP 3035, 35.
Aug 4	Peking Papers Welcome Distinguished Guests from "Horn of Africa," 1. SCMP 3036, 27 (summary).
Aug 6	Why Grafting Severed Hand Can Be Successful, 1. SCMP 3044, 12.
Aug 8	March Toward Agricultural Production in Depth and Width, 1. SCMP 3046, 11.
Aug 10	JMJP Editorial Hails Success of Hiroshima Conference, 3. SCMP 3039, 40.
Aug 11	Peking Papers Greet Success of Somali Prime Minister's Visit to China, 1. SCMP 3040, 20 (summary).
Aug 12	JMJP Editorial Supports Just Struggle of American Negroes, 1. SCMP 3040, 42 (extracts).
Aug 13	Be Diligent and Thrifty, Run Supply and Marketing Cooperatives Well, 2.
Aug 17	Carry Out Ideological Education Penetratively and Scrupulously and Unremittingly Raise the Voluntary Consciousness of Cadres in Taking Part in Labor, 1. SCMP 3049, 1.
Aug 22	No One Can Save Indian Reactionaries from Political Bankruptcy, 1. SCMP 3047, 17.
Aug 23	Go into Prompt Action and Arrange All Aspects of Rural Work for the Coming Half Year, 1. SCMP 3050, 8.
Aug 26	Strengthen Late-Stage Cotton Field Management to Strive for a Richer and Better Harvest, 1. SCMP 3058, 14.
Aug 27	Grasp the Opportunity and Make Continuing Efforts to Strive for a Bumper Autumn Harvest, 1. SCMP 3057, 15.
Aug 28	Peking Paper Supports Government Decision to Bring Back More Victimized Chinese Nationals from India, 1. SCMP 3052, 27 (summary).
Aug 29	The Great Economic Significance of Cadres' Participation in Labor, 1. SCMP 3059, 1.
Aug 29	Another Fresh Blossom of Sino-Korean Friendship, 2. SCMP 3052, 34 (summary).
Aug 30	JMJP on Further Exposure of Soviet Leaders' Betrayal, 2. SCMP 3053, 32.
Sep 2	Uphold Firmly the Political Orientation of Running Enterprises with Industry and Thrift, 1. SCMP 3064, 11.
Sep 9	JMJP Greets Korean Anniversary, 1. SCMP 3059, 32 (summary).
Sep 12	JMJP Supports Vietnamese People's Struggle, 1. SCMP 3061, 26 (summary).
Sep 15	JMJP Hails Chairman Liu Shao-chi's Visit to Korea, 1. SCMP 3063, 35.
Sep 20	Typical Experimenting Is a Scientific Method, 1. SCMP 3076, 1.
Sep 23	The Most Concrete Support for the Games of the New Emerging Forces, 1.
Sep 25	Strengthen Class Education and Improve the Army of Commercial Workers, 1. SCMP 3077, 1.
Sep 27	Peking Paper Greets Founding of World Federation of Scientific Workers' Peking Center, 4. SCMP 3072, 45 (summary).
Sep 27	Peking Papers Welcome Envoys of Friendship from Indonesia, 1. SCMP 3072, 30 (summary).
Sep 29	JMJP Hails Success of Chairman Liu Shao-chi's Visit to Korea, 1. SCMP 3073, 40 (summary).
Sep 29	JMJP Welcomes Envoys of Friendship from Algeria, 2. SCMP 3074, 29 (summary).
Sep 29	Peking Papers Back Korean Government Statements, 5. SCMP 3073, 39 (summary).
Oct 1	Strive to Be Great, Build Our Nation through Diligence and Thrift (National Day editorial), 3.

1963

Oct 5	Peking Papers Greet Inauguration of China-Japan Friendship Association, 2. SCMP 3076, 36 (summary).
Oct 6	JMJP Editorially Greets Opening of Japanese Industrial Exhibition, 1. SCMP 3077, 32 (summary).
Oct 8	An Important Method for Increasing the Class Consciousness of Cadres and the Masses (learning from Lei Feng), 1. SCMP 3086, 1.
Oct 13	Full Text of JMJP Editorial on India's Lack of Sincerity, 1. SCMP 3082, 26.
Oct 14	Effectively Carry Out Procurement of New Cotton Crop Well, 1. SCMP 3089, 10.
Oct 16	Strive to Produce More Cotton and Other Economic Crops Next Year, 1. SCMP 3089, 13.
Oct 19	The Voice of Peace and Justice from Phnom Penh, 1. SCMP 3086, 32.
Oct 20	Bring Socialist Activism of the Masses into Full Play (Story of worker), 1. SCMP 3091, 1.
Oct 21	No Hurricane Can Overpower Cuban People, 1. SCMP 3087, 28.
Oct 23	Peking Press Welcomes Nepalese National Panchayat's Visit to China, 1. SCMP 3089, 28 (summary).
Oct 24	Actively Expand the Interflow of Goods and Stimulate the Market during the Brisk Session, 1. SCMP 3095, 15.
Oct 25	JMJP Editorial Denounces U.S. Manipulation of UN to Oppose China, 1. SCMP 3090, 42 (extracts).
Oct 27	Consolidate and Improve Handicraft Cooperatives, Actively Develop Handicrafts Production, 1. SCMP 3098, 9.
Nov 4	U.S. Imperialism, Get Out of South Vietnam! 1. SCMP 3097, 42 (summary).
Nov 5	JMJP Hails Victory in Smashing Armed U.S.-Chiang Agents, 1. SCMP 3097, 10 (summary).
Nov 7	Long Live Great October Revolution, 1. SCMP 3099, 28.
Nov 8	Shihkochieh Coal Mine Work Style of Fighting amid Hardship, 1. SCMP 3105, 9.
Nov 9	JMJP Hails Tenth Anniversary of Cambodia's Complete Independence, 3. SCMP 3100, 37 (summary).
Nov 10	JMJP Hails Opening of First GANEFO, 1. SCMP 3101, 29 (summary).
Nov 11	JMJP on New Victory over U.S. Imperialism, 1. SCMP 3101, 41 (summary).
Nov 14	Development of Rural Collective Sideline Production Is of Great Importance to the Consolidation of the Collective Economy, 1. SCMP 3109, 7.
Nov 15	U.S. Imperialism Cannot Save Itself in South Vietnam, Says JMJP, 1. SCMP 3104, 31 (summary).
Nov 16	Work Energetically to Fulfill the Task of Procuring Farm Products in All Respects, 1. SCMP 3116, 13.
Nov 20	JMJP Hails Afghanistan Envoys, 1. SCMP 3107, 23 (summary).
Nov 21	JMJP Marks Anniversary of China's November 21 Statement on Sino-Indian Border Conflict, 1. SCMP 3108, 22 (summary).
Nov 22	JMJP Voices Support for Cambodian Peoples, 1. SCMP 3109, 32.
Nov 23	A New Stage in the Friendly Relations of China and Afghanistan, 2.
Nov 23	JMJP Hails Sino-Korean Solidarity, 3. SCMP 3109, 45 (summary).
Nov 23	JMJP Acclaims Success of First GANEFO, 4. SCMP 3109, 34 (summary).

1963

Nov 26	Run Tractor Stations Truly Well, 1. SCMP 3115, 9.
Nov 29	A Firm Grip Should Be Kept on Class Education Regularly, 1. SCMP 3119, 3.
Nov 30	Actively Make a Good Job of Water Conservancy Construction Work for This Winter and Next Spring, 1. SCMP 3118, 8.
Dec 1	JMJP Marks Imperialism Quit Africa Day, 1. SCMP 3113, 19 (summary).
Dec 2	Encourage Inventions and Technical Improvements by Rewards in Order to Promote Development of Our Production and Construction, 1. SCMP 3117, 14.
Dec 4	Continue to Strive to Build an Independent, Complete, Modern National Economic System, 2. SCMP 3117, 2.
Dec 7	Twenty Years of Tenacious Fighting along Road of Organization (Collectivization of Wukung village, Hopei), 1. SCMP 3120, 15.
Dec 10	JMJP Greets Zanzibar Independence, 1. SCMP 3119, 29 (summary).
Dec 11	To Press Ahead Together by Comparing, Learning from, Catching Up with, and Helping One Another, 1. SCMP 3126, 1.
Dec 12	JMJP Greets Kenya's Independence, 4. SCMP 3121, 25 (summary).
Dec 13	JMJP Welcomes Establishment of Sino-Zanzibar Diplomatic Relations, 1. SCMP 3122, 30 (summary).
Dec 13	Strengthen the Management of Irrigated Areas and Irrigation and Pumping Stations, 2. SCMP 3130, 13.
Dec 14	JMJP Hails Chinese Leaders' Visit to African Countries, 1. SCMP 3122, 31 (summary).
Dec 15	JMJP Acclaims China-Kenya Diplomatic Relations, 1. SCMP 3123, 23 (summary).
Dec 18	JMJP Supports Afro-Asian Demand for Broader Representation in UN Bodies, 1. SCMP 3124, 27.
Dec 18	Peking Papers Condemn UN Resolution on Korean Question, 4. SCMP 3125, 25 (summary).
Dec 20	JMJP Marks Third Anniversary of South Vietnam Liberation Front, 1. SCMP 3127, 47 (summary).
Dec 23	Milestone in Sino-U.A.R. Friendship, Solidarity, 4. SCMP 3128, 38.
Dec 24	JMJP Hails Establishment of China-Burundi Diplomatic Relations, 1. SCMP 3129, 28 (summary).
Dec 26	A Great Achievement in the Higher Production and Economy Campaign, 2. SCMP 3134, 9.
Dec 30	JMJP Acclaims Sino-Algerian Friendship Cooperation, 1. SCMP 3132, 32.
Dec 31	Common Ideology and Common Cause Have Bound Us Closely Together, 1. SCMP 3132, 30.

1964

Jan 1	JMJP Celebrates Fifth Anniversary of Cuban Liberation, 3. SCMP 3133, 37.
Jan 1	Advance from Victory to New Victory, 1. SCMP 3132, 1.
Jan 1	JMJP Editorial Hails Success of Premier Chou En-lai's Moroccan Visit, 2. SCMP 3132, 49.
Jan 3	It Is the Revolutionary Responsibility of Parents to Give Their Children Class Education, 2. SCMP 3141, 1.
Jan 6	Do a Good Job in Developing Rural Spare-Time Education, 2. SCMP 3146, 1.
Jan 11	JMJP Hails Success of Premier Chou's Visit to Albania, 2. SCMP 3139, 24.

1964

Jan 12	The Panamanian People Cannot Be Insulted, 1. SCMP 3140, 15 (summary).
Jan 13	JMJP Hails Sino-Tunisian Joint Communique, 3. SCMP 3140, 34.
Jan 18	JMJP Acclaims Success of Premier Chou's Visit to Ghana, 4. SCMP 3144, 25.
Jan 19	Scientific and Technical Research in Agriculture Must Be Closely United with Its Extension Work, 1. SCMP 3153, 1.
Jan 20	Final Victory Will Certainly Belong to the Panamanian People Who Persevere in Struggle, 1.
Jan 21	JMJP Urges Unity of World Forces against U.S. Imperialism, 1. SCMP 3146, 35.
Jan 23	JMJP Greets New Milestone in Sino-Mali Friendship, Cooperation, 3. SCMP 3148, 39.
Jan 23	Rapidly Organizing Supply of Industrial Products to the Rural Areas, 2. SCMP 3158, 1.
Jan 24	Strive to Eradicate Schistosomiasis on the Basis of Achievements Already Made, 2. SCMP 3160, 4.
Jan 26	Make a Good Job of Spare-Time Education for Workers in a Revolutionary Spirit, 1. SCMP 3161, 1.
Jan 28	Proper Management and Utilization of State Funds for Agriculture, 2. SCMP 3162, 1.
Jan 29	New Chapter in the Relations of Friendship and Cooperation between China and Guinea, 3. SCMP 3152, 24.
Jan 29	JMJP Greets Establishment of Sino-French Diplomatic Relations, 1. SCMP 3151, 23.
Jan 30	Sum Up Experience in Agricultural Production in Order to Strive for a Steady and Higher Production, 1. SCMP 3163, 1.
Feb 1	The Whole Country Must Learn from the PLA, 1,2. SCMP 3164, 1.
Feb 1	JMJP Hails New Development of China-Sudan Friendship, 3. SCMP 3154, 50.
Feb 2	Intensify Activities to Compare with, Learn from, and Catch Up with the Advanced, and Help the Backward, and Strive to Become "Five-Good" Enterprises and "Five-Good" Workers, 1. SCMP 3164, 10.
Feb 3	JMJP on Sino-Ethiopian Relations, 3. SCMP 3155, 25.
Feb 4	JMJP Supports Angolan People's Struggle, 5. SCMP 3156, 17.
Feb 5	JMJP Greets Development of Sino-Somali Friendship, Cooperation, 3. SCMP 3157, 40.
Feb 5	Actively Develop New Socialist Chu-i (Theater arts), 1. SCMP 3165, 1.
Feb 6	JMJP Reviews Premier Chou En-lai's Africa Tour, 2. SCMP 3158, 26.
Feb 7	Display Achievements, Progress, and Experience, 1. SCMP 3168, 1.
Feb 8	Education Outside the School Is an Important Aspect of Socialist Education, 1. SCMP 3169, 1.
Feb 9	Catch Up with the Advanced Production Level by Developing the Revolutionary Spirit, 1. SCMP 3170, 1.
Feb 10	A Good Example of Building the Hilly Regions in a Revolutionary Spirit, 1. SCMP 3171, 1.
Feb 16	Continue to Mobilize and Organize Young Intellectuals in Urban Areas to Take Part in the Construction of the New Socialist Countryside, 1. SCMP 3174, 1.
Feb 18	Inspiration from Kuo Hsing-fu's Teaching Method, 1,2. SCMP 3175, 1.
Feb 20	Commercial Departments Should Also Learn from the Liberation Army, 1,2. SCMP 3177, 1.
Feb 20	JMJP Cheers Sino-Burmese Friendship, 3. SCMP 3165, 23.
Feb 23	Propagate Three-Eight Work Style, 1. SCMP 3178, 1.
Feb 24	JMJP Greets Establishment of China-Congo Diplomatic Relations, 3. SCMP 3167, 24.
Feb 24	A Year of Great Comparison, a Year of Great Learning, 1. SCMP 3179, 1.
Feb 26	JMJP Acclaims New Development of Sino-Pakistan Amity, 3. SCMP 3169, 24.
Feb 28	Show Deep Concern for Intellectual Youths Who Return to Their Native Villages or to the Countryside, 1,2. SCMP 3182, 1.
Mar 2	The Friendship between the People of China and Ceylon Will Last for Generations to Come, 3.
Mar 3	JMJP Hails Success of Chinese Leaders' Visits Abroad, 1. SCMP 3173, 16.
Mar 4	JMJP Greets Japanese People's Struggle against U.S. Imperialism, 5. SCMP 3174, 24.
Mar 4	U.S. Heading Toward Complete Collapse, Says JMJP, 1. SCMP 3174, 26.
Mar 6	Carry Out the Spring Patriotic Sanitation Campaign in a Penetrating Manner, 1. SCMP 3187, 1.
Mar 7	Energetically Launch the Mass Movement for Scientific Experiments in Farming, 1. SCMP 3189, 1.
Mar 8	Women, Promote the Revolutionary Spirit and Fight for New Victories, 1. SCMP 3191, 1.
Mar 10	Learning the Revolutionary Tough-Bone Spirit of the Liberation Army, 1. SCMP 3192, 1.
Mar 11	Establish Stable and High-Yield Farmland by Relying on the Strength of the Masses, 1. SCMP 3193, 1.
Mar 17	JMJP Editorial Supports Palestine and Arab People, 1. SCMP 3183, 21.
Mar 18	To Create a Five-Good Workshop, Efforts Must First Be Made to Establish a Firm and Efficient Party Branch, 1. SCMP 3195, 7.
Mar 19	Carry Out the Movement to Compare with, Learn from, and Catch Up with the Advanced and Help the Less Advanced More Intensively and Realistically in the Countryside, 1. SCMP 3195, 9.
Mar 20	The Migration of Young Intellectuals to Rural and Mountainous Areas Is a Revolutionary Move to Eliminate Outmoded Habits and Customs, 1. SCMP 3195, 12.
Mar 23	State Farms Should Vigorously Establish Stable and High-Yielding Farmland (Amended 2/27, p. 3), 1. SCMP 3200, 11.
Mar 24	Maintain a Grip on Dynamic Thinking, 1. SCMP 3196, 1.
Mar 26	Strive to Learn the Thought of Mao Tse-tung Well, 1. SCMP 3196, 5.
Mar 27	JMJP Supports South Korean People's Patriotic Struggle, 5. SCMP 3189, 46.
Mar 27	JMJP Supports North Kalimantan People's Struggle against "Malaysia," 1. SCMP 3189, 43.
Apr 1	Create More and Better Dramas for the Masses, 1. SCMP 3205, 10.
Apr 2	Maintain a Firm Grip on Both Upper and Lower Levels (Working style of industrial departments), 1. SCMP 3201, 1.
Apr 4	Industrial and Communications Departments Must Master the Good Experiences of the PLA, 2. SCMP 3200, 4.
Apr 4	JMJP Welcomes Honored Guests from Laos, 1. SCMP 3194, 32.
Apr 5	Manage Socialist Hospitals Successfully with Revolutionary Spirit, 1. SCMP 3204, 6.

1964

Apr 6	Compare Self-Reliance, Compare Contributions to the State, 1. SCMP 3210, 8.
Apr 9	JMJP Calls for Promotion of Sino-Laotian Friendly Relations, 1. SCMP 3198, 32.
Apr 10	Greets Preparatory Meeting of Second Asian-African Conference, 1. SCMP 3199, 15.
Apr 11	JMJP Demands Release of Arrested Chinese by Brazil, 4. SCMP 3199, 19.
Apr 11	Cultivate a Lively, Active Climate of Study on One's Own Initiative, 1. SCMP 3207, 11.
Apr 14	Learn by Helping Others, Help Others while Learning, 1. SCMP 3210, 11.
Apr 15	Long Live Independent, Free, New Africa, 1. SCMP 3202, 19.
Apr 16	JMJP Condemns Brazilian Authorities' Atrocity against Chinese, 1. SCMP 3203, 21.
Apr 17	Peking Rally Supports Cuban, Latin American People's Struggle, 1. SCMP 3204, 45.
Apr 18	Greets Success of Preparatory Meeting for Asian-African Conference, 1. SCMP 3204, 28.
Apr 19	Handle Properly in a Planned Way the Task of Popularizing Hydraulic Turbine Pumps, 1. SCMP 3212, 14.
Apr 22	U.S.-Engineered Coup in Laos Threatens Peace in Indo-China, 1. SCMP 3206, 34.
Apr 24	Rural Hospitals Must Serve Peasants Wholeheartedly, 2. SCMP 3218, 2.
Apr 28	New Plot in the Making, Says JMJP on SEATO Meeting, 2. SCMP 3210, 36.
Apr 28	JMJP Greets Guests from Burundi, 1. SCMP 3210, 21.
Apr 29	An Airline of Friendship, an Airline of Peace, 3. SCMP 3211, 30.
Apr 30	What Are Lessons from Brazilian Coup? 1. SCMP 3212, 26.
May 1	JMJP Condemns Phoumi Nosavan's "Eight-Point Program," 4. SCMP 3212, 36.
May 1	Carry Out in a More Practical Manner the Production-Increase and Economy Movement of "Comparing, Learning, Catching Up, and Helping," 1. SCMP 3217, 10.
May 4	Educated Youth Should Become One with the Worker and Peasant Masses, 1. SCMP 3219, 1.
May 5	U.S. Imperialism, Hands Off Cuba! 1. SCMP 3215, 20.
May 6	JMJP Hails Congolese (Leopoldville) People's Armed Struggle, 1. SCMP 3216, 17.
May 7	JMJP on Historic Significance of Victory of Dien Bien Phu, 1. SCMP 3217, 25.
May 8	Practice What One Has Learned, 1. SCMP 3224, 1.
May 10	We Must Win a Victory in Prevention and Control of Paddy Rice Borers This Year, 1. SCMP 3229, 14.
May 12	China's Sovereignty over Taiwan Brooks No Interference, 1. SCMP 3220, 15.
May 12	Make Great Efforts to Strengthen the Publication of Rural Reading Matter, 2. SCMP 3224, 4.
May 13	JMJP Editorial: Dangerous Developments in Laos Must Be Checked, 1. SCMP 3221, 22.
May 15	Promote Advanced Experiences in a More Concrete and Thoroughgoing Manner (By Sung Cheng and Yen Ling), 1. SCMP 3229, 7.
May 16	Warmly Welcoming the Distinguished Guest from Sudan, 1. SCMP 3223, 19 (summary).
May 18	Stop New U.S. Adventure in South Vietnam, 1. SCMP 3224, 44.
May 19	JMJP Hails Opening of Air Service between China and Cambodia, 3. SCMP 3225, 20.
May 20	JMJP Hails Growth of Sino-Sudanese Friendship, 3. SCMP 3225, 30.
May 21	Steadily Develop Mass Scientific Experiment Activities in the Countryside, 1. SCMP 3231, 5.
May 23	Correctly Handle Relationships among Hilly Areas, Rivers, and Farmlands, 1. SCMP 3232, 1.
May 26	Carry Out Grain Procurement Work Well by Helping Production, 1. SCMP 3234, 11.
May 27	Enthusiastically Cultivate the Young Shoots of New Things, 1. SCMP 3242, 18.
May 28	Anti-"Malaysia" Struggle Will Win, 1. SCMP 3230, 32.
May 29	JMJP Calls for Immediate International Conference on Laos, 1. SCMP 3230, 28.
May 29	Build a Powerful Force of Scientific and Technical Workers, 2. SCMP 3236, 4.
May 30	From a Few but Good to Both Many and Good, 1. SCMP 3235, 12.
Jun 1	JMJP Welcomes Yemeni President, 1. SCMP 3232, 40.
Jun 1	Revolutionary Parents Should Act as Revolutionary Guides to Their Children, 2. SCMP 3235, 16.
Jun 2	In Extending Primary School Education, Yangyvan Hsien Is a Red Banner on the Educational Front, 1. SCMP 3240, 8.
Jun 4	Carry Out More Work with Less Money, 1.
Jun 5	Anti-U.S. Storm in South Korea Cannot Be Quelled, 1. SCMP 3235, 35.
Jun 6	A New Stage of Development of the Art of Peking Opera, 1. SCMP 3242, 9.
Jun 9	Lead Agricultural Production with a Strict Scientific Attitude, 1. SCMP 3245, 3.
Jun 11	JMJP Welcomes Guests of Honor from Tanganyika and Zanzibar, 1. SCMP 3239, 31.
Jun 11	JMJP Hails New Chapter in Sino-Yemeni Friendship, 3. SCMP 3239, 34.
Jun 14	Carefully Find Differences, Consciously Narrow Gaps, 2. SCMP 3246, 16.
Jun 15	JMJP on Major U.S. Provocation in Laos, 1. SCMP 3242, 28.
Jun 15	Sino-Yemeni Treaty, Communique Hailed by JMJP, 3. SCMP 3241, 39.
Jun 16	Sample Plots Are Good Means for Popularizing Advanced Experiences, 1. SCMP 3247, 15.
Jun 19	Peking Papers Hail New Development of Friendship between China and United Republic of Tanganyika and Zanzibar, 3. SCMP 3245, 41.
Jun 19	Courageously Forge Ahead along the Road of Self-Reliance, 1,2.
Jun 23	The Correct Direction for Farm Machine Plants, 1. SCMP 3252, 13.
Jun 24	JMJP Hails Revolutionary Developments in Congo (Leopoldville), 1. SCMP 3248, 22.
Jun 25	JMJP Hails Success of Second Asian Economic Seminar, 4. SCMP 3249, 23.
Jun 25	JMJP Marks Fourteenth Anniversary of Korean War, 1. SCMP 3249, 28.
Jun 27	JMJP Supports DRV Statement on Laos, 3. SCMP 3250, 39.
Jul 1	Resolutely Shatter U.S. Imperialism's War Threats and Provocations, 3.
Jul 4	Properly Manage All Farmland so as to Build Stable and High Yield Farmland, 1. SCMP 3264, 17.
Jul 5	Build Stable and High Yield Farmland according to Local Conditions, 2. SCMP 3263, 13.
Jul 5	Peking Papers Condemn Vientiane "Consultations," 1. SCMP 3254, 31.

1964

Jul 6   Rely on the Masses' Own Effort in Building Stable and High-Yield Farmland, 1. SCMP 3263, 11.
Jul 6   JMJP Greets Malawi's Independence, 4. SCMP 3254, 36.
Jul 8   Educate the Younger Generation to Be Revolutionaries Forever (Conference of Communist Youth League), 1,2.
Jul 9   Another Punishment on U.S.-Chiang Kai-shek Gang, 1. SCMP 3257, 20.
Jul 9   Chinese Papers Denounce U.S. Attempt to Extend Aggressive War in South Vietnam, 3. SCMP 3257, 29.
Jul 12 Quality of Farm Work Depends upon Ideological Political Work, 1. SCMP 3271, 11.
Jul 15 Ever Ready to Smash U.S. War Schemes, 2. SCMP 3261, 24.
Jul 16 Never Be Self-Complacent, Forever March Forward (Railway), 2.
Jul 17 A Good Method Brings About Manifold Advantages (Improvement of organization of labor in Lingli sugar refinery of Kwangsi), 1. SCMP 3269, 7.
Jul 20 Combat U.S. Aggression, Defend Peace in Indo-China, 3. SCMP 3264, 38.
Jul 23 JMJP Greets Success of African Summit Conference, 4. SCMP 3267, 22.
Jul 26 JMJP Greets Anniversary of Cuban Uprising, 1. SCMP 3269, 23.
Jul 27 It Is of Great Advantage for Workers' Dependents to Return to Countryside to Engage in Production, 1. SCMP 3274, 8.
Jul 29 JMJP Hails Santiago Declaration, 1. SCMP 3271, 19.
Aug 1   Carry to the End the Socialist Revolution on the Literary and Art Front (Peking opera festival ends), 2. SCMP 3275, 8.
Aug 2   JMJP Protests against U.S. Kidnapping of Chinese Embassy Official, 1. SCMP 3274, 30.
Aug 3   Cultivate and Train Millions of Successors Who Will Carry On the Cause of Proletarian Revolution, 1. SCMP 3277, 2.
Aug 5   Water Conservancy and Stable, High-Yield Farmland, 1. SCMP 3284, 7.
Aug 6   High and Stable Production in Agriculture Is Inseparably Linked with the Development of Forestry, 2. SCMP 3284, 11.
Aug 6   U.S. Must End Its Armed Aggression against DRV, 1. SCMP 3276, 27.
Aug 6   JMJP Greets Great Victory of World Peace, 4. SCMP 3276, 33.
Aug 7   JMJP Editorial: U.S. Aggressors Cannot Conceal Their Ugly Countenance, 1. SCMP 3277, 35.
Aug 8   JMJP Marks Anniversary of Chairman Mao's Statement Supporting American Negroes' Struggle, 5. SCMP 3277, 33.
Aug 8   JMJP Warns against U.S. Intrigue at United Nations, 1. SCMP 3277, 45.
Aug 9   JMJP Supports Vietnamese People's Struggle against U.S. Aggressors, 1. SCMP 3278, 34.
Aug 14 Create Fertile Soil to Extend Farmland with Stable and High Yields, 2. SCMP 3289, 13.
Aug 15 U.S., Hands Off Congo (Leopoldville)! 1. SCMP 3282, 26.
Aug 15 JMJP Greets Revolution Anniversary of Congo (Brazzaville), 4. SCMP 3282, 25.
Aug 21 A Boundless Prospect for Scientific Development in the Four Continents (Peking science seminar), 1,2. SCMP 3287, 16 (summary).
Aug 23 JMJP Greets Rumanian Liberation Anniversary, 4. SCMP 3288, 31.
Aug 27 JMJP Hails Anti-U.S.-Khanh Storm in South Vietnam, 1. SCMP 3291, 32.
Aug 28 Only by Persevering in Labor Will Cadres Be Able to Persevere in Revolution, 1. SCMP 3298, 12.
Aug 29 U.S. Cannot Ward Off Its Doom in South Vietnam (Anniversary of Mao's statement), 1. SCMP 3292, 40.
Aug 30 Only by Regularly Taking Part in Labor Will Cadres Be Able to Maintain Close Ties with the Masses, 1. SCMP 3297, 13.
Sep 1   Contribute Strength Toward Scientific Development and Social Progress (Peking science seminar), 2.
Sep 3   Strive for Higher Standards in Autumn Sowing, 1. SCMP 3300, 16.
Sep 5   Look Farther Ahead, 1. SCMP 3304, 13.
Sep 9   Victory Belongs to Indonesian People, 1. SCMP 3298, 32.
Sep 9   JMJP Warns U.S. against New Venture in Vietnam, 4. SCMP 3298, 42.
Sep 10 Undergo Steeling in Strong Winds and High Waves, Conquer Rivers, Lakes, and Seas, 2. SCMP 3309, 3.
Sep 11 Rely upon Poor and Lower Middle Peasants for Proper Operation of Credit Cooperatives, 1. SCMP 3305, 10.
Sep 14 JMJP Hails Success of Arab Summit Conference, 4. SCMP 3301, 16.
Sep 20 Halt New Adventure of U.S. Imperialism, 1. SCMP 3304, 34.
Sep 21 Fully Recognize the Current Favorable Situation, Take a Firm Grip on the Task of Procurement of Farm Products in the Fall, 1. SCMP 3308, 8.
Sep 21 JMJP Welcomes Ceylonese Guests, 1. SCMP 3305, 26.
Sep 22 Genuinely Take Part in Labor Like an Ordinary Laborer, 1. SCMP 3313, 16.
Sep 24 Hold High the Revolutionary Banner of Marxism-Leninism, 1. SCMP 3307, 23.
Sep 24 U.S. Must Be Forbidden to Concoct Lies, 5. SCMP 3307, 36.
Sep 27 Peking Papers Bid Welcome to Prince Sihanouk, 1. SCMP 3309, 29.
Sep 28 Peking Press Hails Brazzaville Congo President, 2. SCMP 3310, 25.
Sep 29 The Chinese People Warmly Welcome President Keita, 2. SCMP 3311, 30.
Oct 1   Long Live the General Line of Going All-Out, Aiming High, and Achieving More, Faster, Better, and More Economical Results in Building Socialism, 5.
Oct 3   JMJP Hails Establishment of Diplomatic Relations between China, Central African Republic, 3. SCMP 3314, 18.
Oct 4   Peking Press Hails New Phase in Friendship, Cooperation between China, Congo (Brazzaville), 3. SCMP 3314, 23.
Oct 6   A New Chapter in Sino-Cambodian Friendship, 2. SCMP 3316, 21.
Oct 7   JMJP Hails Fifteenth Anniversary of the Founding of the GDR, 4. SCMP 3316, 26.
Oct 11 A Stern Stand, 2.
Oct 14 JMJP Pays Tribute to Non-Aligned Conference, 1. SCMP 3320, 29.
Oct 15 The Spirit of Self-Reliance Must Be Upheld in Farm Implement Innovation Movement, 1. SCMP 3329, 14.

1964

Oct 22	Break Nuclear Monopoly, Destroy Nuclear Weapons, 1. SCMP 3325, 21.
Oct 24	Agricultural Scientists, Go Down to the Countryside, 1. SCMP 3329, 4.
Oct 24	JMJP Greets Republic of Zambia, 4. SCMP 3326, 32.
Oct 25	"Demonstration Farms" Are Main Centers through Which Agricultural Science May Serve Production, 1. SCMP 3338, 14.
Oct 27	Do Not Forget to Practice Economy while Achieving a Bumper Harvest, 1. SCMP 3336, 6.
Oct 28	Develop a Mass Movement for Water and Soil Conservation in the Middle Reaches of the Yellow River, 1. SCMP 3336, 11.
Oct 30	JMJP Editorial Welcomes Afghan Royal Guests, 1. SCMP 3330, 28.
Nov 1	Armed Struggle Is the Path That Leads to National Liberation (Algerian revolution anniversary), 2. SCMP 3332, 22.
Nov 3	Peking Papers Support Cambodian People, 3. SCMP 3333, 21.
Nov 5	Peking Press Hails New Milestone in China-Mali Friendship, Cooperation, 2. SCMP 3335, 21.
Nov 6	JMJP Acclaims Establishment of Diplomatic Relations between China, Zambia, 4. SCMP 3335, 45
Nov 7	JMJP Editorial Marks October Revolution Anniversary, 1. SCMP 3335, 39.
Nov 13	JMJP Hails Sino-Afghan Friendship, 1. SCMP 3339, 24.
Nov 15	JMJP Greets Diplomatic Relations between China and Dahomey, 3. SCMP 3340, 28.
Nov 16	Scientifically Sum Up Bumper Harvest Experience, 1.
Nov 17	Strengthen the Building of the Militia in the Socialist Education Movement, 1. SCMP 3344, 1.
Nov 19	Build Water Conservancy Projects by Relying on the Masses, 1. SCMP 3347, 18.
Nov 22	New Starting Point for Strivings for Complete Ban on Nuclear Weapons, 1. SCMP 3345, 20.
Nov 24	Grasp the Opportunity and Strengthen Leadership to Speed Up Fulfillment of Procurement Plans for Farm Produce, 1. SCMP 3349, 13.
Nov 25	JMJP Pays Tribute to People of Vietnam, 1. SCMP 3347, 40.
Nov 28	JMJP Condemns Johnson Administration as Chief Culprit of Aggression against Congo (Leopoldville), 1. SCMP 3348, 29.
Nov 29	JMJP Celebrates Anniversary of Albania's Liberation, 4. SCMP 3349, 22.
Dec 1	JMJP Marks "Imperialism Quit Africa Day," 3. SCMP 3350, 23.
Dec 3	JMJP Hails Success of Japanese Communist Party Congress, 1. SCMP 3352, 31.
Dec 4	U.S. Will Fail in Anti-China Manoeuvres in UN, 4. SCMP 3353, 28.
Dec 5	JMJP Salutes Embattled Congo (Leopoldville), 1. SCMP 3353, 23.
Dec 6	Looking Downward, 1. SCMP 3363, 7.
Dec 15	Make an Early Preparation for Developing the Afforestation Movement, 1. SCMP 3392, 15.
Dec 16	Forestry Construction Should Be Based on Cultivation of Forests, 1. SCMP 3392, 17.
Dec 18	Lumbering and Forest Renewal Must Be Carried Out Side by Side, 1.
Dec 20	JMJP Greets Anniversary of South Vietnam National Liberation Front, 1. SCMP 3364, 30.
Dec 22	JMJP Marks Anniversary of Vietnam People's Army, 2. SCMP 3365, 23.
Dec 25	Brazilian Authorities Must Repeal Their Unlawful Sentence, 1. SCMP 3366, 32.
Dec 30	Develop the Revolutionary Spirit of Being Capable of Both Labor and Literary and Art Work, 2. SCMP 3396, 14.
Dec 31	Nuclear Blackmail Cannot Cow Revolutionary People, 4. SCMP 3371, 34.

1965

Jan 1	On New Year's Day, 1965, 2. SCMP 3371, 3.
Jan 1	Greets Anniversary of Cuban Liberation, 4. SCMP 3371, 27.
Jan 2	Condemns U.S. Maneuvers to Extend War in South Vietnam to Laos, 1. SCMP 3372, 33.
Jan 5	Acclaims Successful NPC Session (First session of third NPC), 2. SCMP 3373, 6.
Jan 6	Greets Binh Gia Victory, 1. SCMP 3374, 30.
Jan 6	JMJP Hails Opening of Direct Sino-Indonesian Air Service, 3. SCMP 3374, 27.
Jan 6	Supports Indonesian Decision to Quit UN, 4. SCMP 3374, 24.
Jan 10	Hails Indonesia's Withdrawal from UN, 1. SCMP 3377, 28.
Jan 14	Dispatch of South Korean Troops to South Vietnam--A Grave U.S. Step to Expand War in Indo-China, 1. SCMP 3380, 35.
Jan 15	Advance from Victory to Greater Victory, 1. SCMP 3395, 18.
Jan 17	The Spirit of Lumumba Is Motivating the People of Congo (Anniversary of the assassination of Lumumba), 5.
Jan 18	A Model Example of Reforming Regulations and Systems, 1. SCMP 3399, 12.
Jan 23	Welcomes Indonesian Envoys, 1. SCMP 3386, 27.
Jan 23	Apply the Mass of Achievements of Scientific Research to Production with Greater, Faster, Better, and More Economical Results, 1. SCMP 3397, 4.
Jan 28	Marks Anniversary of Sino-Burmese Friendship Treaty, 4. SCMP 3390, 18.
Jan 30	Hails Success of Visit of Indonesian Delegation, 1. SCMP 3391, 24.
Feb 1	Accept What They Have Sent without Rejecting Any and Wipe Them Out Lock, Stock, and Barrel, 1. SCMP 3392, 23.
Feb 2	U.S. and Belgian Imperialist Scheme Is Doomed to Bankruptcy, 3. SCMP 3392, 34.
Feb 9	U.S. Aggressors Must Be Punished, 2. SCMP 3396, 31.
Feb 10	Lyndon Johnson's Gangster Language, 2. SCMP 3397, 33.
Feb 12	Salutes Heroic People of South Vietnam, 2. SCMP 3399, 32.
Feb 14	JMJP Marks Fifteenth Anniversary of Sino-Soviet Treaty of Friendship, Alliance, and Mutual Assistance, 2. SCMP 3400, 36.
Feb 15	Hails Preparatory Meeting of Indo-Chinese People's Conference, 4. SCMP 3401, 24.
Feb 15	Dare to Struggle and Be Good at Struggle, 1. SCMP 3410, 14.
Feb 16	Make Use of the Revolutionary Spirit to Do a Good Work in Commerce in 1965, 1,2.
Feb 17	Promote Production Democracy, Put Production Plans on a Practical Basis, 1. SCMP 3411, 13.

1965

Feb 17 Welcomes President Nyerere (Tanzania Republic) in China, 1. SCMP 3402, 38.
Feb 18 Greeting the Independence of Gambia, 4.
Feb 19 The Johnson Administration Is Caught in a Dilemma (Amended 2/20, p. 3), 1.
Feb 20 We Must Take the Initiative in Struggling with Nature, 1. SCMP 3412, 3.
Feb 22 Shift the Center of Gravity in Rural Work to Spring Plowing, 1. SCMP 3412, 1.
Feb 23 Production High Tide and the Art of Leadership (Amended 2/24, p. 2), 1. SCMP 3417, 22.
Feb 23 On Initialling of Japan-South Korea "Basic Treaty," 4. SCMP 3407, 28.
Feb 24 Arrange Rural Manpower according to Farm Seasons, 1. SCMP 3412, 6.
Feb 25 Indo-Chinese People's Anti-U.S. Struggle Will Triumph, 3. SCMP 3407, 26.
Feb 25 Look What Has Become of UN, 1. SCMP 3407, 32.
Feb 25 Greets New Phase of Sino-Tanzanian Friendship, 4. SCMP 3407, 30.
Feb 26 A Revolutionary Measure for Health Work, 1. SCMP 3418, 14.
Feb 27 We Have to Raise Still More Hogs Even When Hogs Have Multiplied, 1. SCMP 3418, 23.
Feb 28 Supports Korean Government's Stand against ROK-Japan Basic Treaty (Amended 3/1, p. 2), 1. SCMP 3409, 34.
Mar 1   Lashes at U.S. Government's War Blackmail, 1. SCMP 3409, 37.
Mar 1   Learn from the Revolutionary School Discipline of Changsha Political School, 1. SCMP 3417, 12.
Mar 2   Welcomes President Ayub Khan, 1. SCMP 3410, 29.
Mar 4   Calls for Defeat of U.S. Gangsterism, 1. SCMP 3411, 35.
Mar 4   Guideline for Cotton Production in 1965, 2. SCMP 3426, 15.
Mar 8   Salutes International Women's Day, 1. SCMP 3415, 20.
Mar 9   Welcomes New Development of Sino-Pakistan Relations, 3. SCMP 3415, 33.
Mar 11 Learn from Tienpai, Make the Hometown and the Motherland Green, 1. SCMP 3428, 19.
Mar 12 Strive to Achieve a Double Bumper Harvest in Grain and Cotton in Cotton Producing Areas, 1. SCMP 3426, 18.
Mar 12 Hails Success of Indo-Chinese People's Conference, 4. SCMP 3418, 35.
Mar 14 The New Yu Kung of the Socialist Era (Transforming nature), 1. SCMP 3429, 4.
Mar 17 Resolutely Smash War Blackmail, 1. SCMP 3421, 36.
Mar 21 Pays Last Tribute to Comrade Gheorghiu-Dej, 2. SCMP 3424, 33.
Mar 21 Supports Just Struggle of Palestine, Arab Peoples, 6. SCMP 3424, 24.
Mar 22 U.S. Aggressors Must Get Out of South Vietnam, 1. SCMP 3424, 38.
Mar 25 Calls for Worldwide Assistance to South Vietnamese People to Beat U.S. Aggressors, 2. SCMP 3426, 40.
Mar 25 Condemns U.S. Gas Warfare in South Vietnam, 2. SCMP 3427, 40.
Mar 25 Nazi War Criminals Must Be Brought to Justice, 5. SCMP 3427, 32.
Mar 26 Hails Major Development of Sino-Afghan Friendship, 2. SCMP 3428, 29.
Mar 28 Operate "Three Combination" Demonstration Farms Well, Promote the Movement for Conducting Experiments in Agronomy, 2. SCMP 3440, 1.
Mar 28 Acclaims New Development in Sino-Pakistan Friendship, 5. SCMP 3429, 39.
Mar 29 Strive to Aid Vietnamese People in Resisting U.S. Aggression, 1. SCMP 3429, 44.
Apr 1   Militant Friendship, Great Solidarity, 3.
Apr 2   Actively Develop the Work on Scientific and Educational Films, 2. SCMP 3441, 15.
Apr 4   What to Do When Most People Say It Is Impossible (Houying brigade, Hopei leads in terrace field construction), 3.
Apr 5   Hails Great Victory of Vietnamese People, 1. SCMP 3434, 41.
Apr 5   Hails Success of Vice-Premier Chen I's Visit to Afghanistan, Pakistan, and Nepal, 2. SCMP 3434, 27.
Apr 6   Adhere to Materialistic Dialectics in Scientific Experiments, 2. SCMP 3444, 13.
Apr 7   Hails Success of Premier Chou En-lai's Tour, 1. SCMP 3436, 27.
Apr 7   Smash "ROK-Japan Talks," 1. SCMP 3436, 32.
Apr 9   A Highly Favorable Situation on the Drama Stage, 1. SCMP 3444, 18.
Apr 9   Resolutely Oppose Rabid Provocations of West German Militarism, 5. SCMP 3428, 30.
Apr 10 Struggle for Revolutionizing Designing Work, 2. SCMP 3448, 7.
Apr 11 The Spirit of Self-Reliance Forever Wins (Pishihhang water conservation project in Anhwei), 2. SCMP 3451, 6.
Apr 12 The Solemn Oath of Thirty Million Vietnamese People, 1.
Apr 12 China's Territorial Air Space Is Not to Be Violated, 1. SCMP 3439, 42.
Apr 12 U Thant Knocking at Wrong Door (Vietnam peace settlement), 3. SCMP 3439, 37.
Apr 13 Johnson's "Peace" Address Is Short-Lived Hoax, 1. SCMP 3440, 39.
Apr 15 Vietnamese People's Struggle against U.S. Imperialism Will Surely Win, 1. SCMP 3441, 36.
Apr 16 Urges Worldwide Action to Force U.S. to Quit Vietnam, 1. SCMP 3442, 40.
Apr 17 Hog Raising and Policy, 3. SCMP 3450, 25.
Apr 17 Acclaims New Upsurge of Anti-U.S. Struggle in South Korea, 5. SCMP 3442, 33.
Apr 18 Marks Bandung Conference Anniversary, 2. SCMP 3443, 24.
Apr 18 There Are Great Possibilities for Raising More Hogs, 3. SCMP 3452, 9.
Apr 20 Salutes South Korean People's Anti-U.S. Struggle, 1. SCMP 3444, 41.
Apr 20 Congratulates Chinese Table Tennis Players, 2. SCMP 3444, 25.
Apr 20 Marks Anniversary of Giron Beach Victory (Cuba), 5. SCMP 3444, 38.
Apr 21 The Johnson Administration's War Blackmail Will Never Succeed, 2. SCMP 3444, 46.
Apr 21 Anti-China Plot of U.S. and Brazilian Reactionaries Goes Bankrupt, 4. SCMP 3444, 36.
Apr 22 On the Seventeen Nation Appeal, 1. SCMP 3445, 36.
Apr 22 Correct Design Should Come from Practice, 3.
Apr 23 An Urgent Task on the Agricultural Front, 2. SCMP 3456, 16.
Apr 24 War "Escalation" Leads to Gates of Hell, 2. SCMP 3447, 45.
Apr 24 Fight Doggedly to the End for a Bumper Summer Harvest, 3. SCMP 3458, 12.

1965

Apr 26	Hails Outstanding Achievements of Chinese Table Tennis Players, 1. SCMP 3447, 20.
Apr 28	Johnson Administration--Real Enemy of American People, 1. SCMP 3448, 47.
Apr 28	How Should We Deal with Those Who Have Lagged Behind? 3. SCMP 3460, 8.
Apr 28	Greets Sino-Nepalese Peace and Friendship Treaty Anniversary, 5. SCMP 3448, 42.
Apr 29	Be a Revolutionary Optimist (Yunnan experience in production and popularization of phosphate fertilizer), 2. SCMP 3457, 10.
Apr 30	We Must Understand Agriculture Before Supporting It (Yunnan experience in producing and popularizing phosphate fertilizer), 2. SCMP 3463, 9.
May 1	Greets International Labor Day (Build socialism and assist Vietnam), 1. SCMP 3450, 1.
May 3	Supports Cambodia's Just Stand on International Conference, 3. SCMP 3451, 27.
May 3	Peking Papers Support Dominican People's Resistance to U.S. Armed Aggression, 5. SCMP 3451, 29.
May 4	Hails Cambodian Step to Deflate U.S. Arrogance, 1. SCMP 3452, 20.
May 4	Fully Arouse Young People's Enthusiasm for Building Socialism, 3. SCMP 3462, 1.
May 5	Show Earnest Concern for Young Intellectuals Working in Rural and Hilly Areas, 2. SCMP 3476, 12.
May 7	Marks Eleventh Anniversary of Dien Bien Phu Battle, 1. SCMP 3455, 39.
May 11	U.S. Imperialism Challenges Whole of Latin America, 4. SCMP 3457, 30.
May 12	Promote Specialization and Cooperation in Processing Industries with the Revolutionary Spirit, 5. SCMP 3473, 4.
May 14	"Johnson Doctrine" Is Neo-Hitlerism, 2. SCMP 3460, 36.
May 16	Supports Arab Countries' Severance of Diplomatic Relations with West Germany, 4. SCMP 3461, 28.
May 18	UN Plays Disgraceful Role on Question of Dominican Republic, 1. SCMP 3462, 28.
May 19	Organize Circulation of Commodities according to Economic Regions, 2. SCMP 3477, 6.
May 20	Royal Kingdom of Cambodia Is Not to Be Bullied, 1. SCMP 3464, 26.
May 20	Farce of Suspending Bombing Raids, 2. SCMP 3464, 30.
May 20	Hails Success of Winneba Conference (Afro-Asian solidarity conference), 4. SCMP 3464, 22.
May 21	How to Treat the Advanced, 1. SCMP 3484, 1.
May 25	Chinese People Support Struggle of Korean Residents in Japan for Their Rights, 3. SCMP 3467, 27.
May 26	Study the Labor Skills of the Common Laborer, 1.
May 30	Strive to Run Half-Farming, Half-Study Schools Well, 2.
Jun 1	In Commemoration of "June 1" International Children's Day, 2. SCMP 3483, 5.
Jun 2	Put Excellence in the Lead (Organize an upsurge of industrial production and construction), 1. SCMP 3487, 3.
Jun 3	Make as Many Preparations for as Many Eventualities (Struggling against nature), 1.
Jun 3	Acclaims Premier Chou En-lai's Visit to Pakistan, Tanzania, 1. SCMP 3473, 27.
Jun 4	Commercial Work Should Take Another Step to Face the Rural Areas (Rural markets), 1,2.
Jun 5	We Need More Commercial Personnel in Rural Areas, 1.
Jun 5	On War Situation in South Vietnam, 3. SCMP 3475, 36.
Jun 8	Learn from and Carry Forward the Democratic Tradition of the Chinese People's Liberation Army, 1. SCMP 3482, 1.
Jun 10	On Premier Chou's Visit to Tanzania, 1. SCMP 3477, 29.
Jun 11	On Johnson's Order for Direct Combat Action by U.S. Troops in South Vietnam, 1. SCMP 3478, 29.
Jun 16	Turn Out and Supply More Industrial Products Required at the Countryside, 1. SCMP 3516, 15.
Jun 19	China Resolutely Supports Korean Effort to Defeat "Japan-ROK Talks," 5. SCMP 3483, 26.
Jun 20	South Vietnam National Front for Liberation Is Sole Representative of South Vietnamese People, 1. SCMP 3484, 19.
Jun 21	Coordination between Labor and Leisure (Organize upsurge in industrial production and construction), 1. SCMP 3494, 1.
Jun 23	Develop the Revolutionary Spirit to Fulfill the Task of Requisitioning Summer Grain, 2. SCMP 3498, 6.
Jun 25	Marks Fifteenth Anniversary of Korean People's Liberation, 1. SCMP 3488, 27.
Jun 25	Calls for Efforts to Scrap Japan-South Korea "Treaty," 4. SCMP 3488, 22.
Jun 26	UN Must Be Thoroughly Reorganized, 5. SCMP 3489, 36.
Jun 27	The Chinese People Will Surely Liberate Taiwan, 1. SCMP 3489, 19.
Jun 29	Make Continued Efforts for Success of Afro-Asian Conference, 1. SCMP 3490, 25.
Jul 2	Advanced Experiences Must Be Popularized and Spread, 1. SCMP 3502, 6.
Jul 3	Transform a Progressive "Point" to a Progressive "Plane" (Steady production and high yield over a great area in Tsunhua county, Hopei), 1.
Jul 4	Provide the Masses with Good Leadership over Swimming, 1. SCMP 3505, 9.
Jul 5	On U.S. Bombing of Nam Dinh, 1. SCMP 3493, 28.
Jul 6	Skillful Work Develops Potentials (Organize upsurge in industrial production and construction), 1. SCMP 3504, 6.
Jul 10	Develop Agriculture and Animal Husbandry Simultaneously, Use Animal Husbandry to Promote Agriculture, 1. SCMP 3507, 16.
Jul 11	Marks Fourth Anniversary of Sino-Korean Treaty, 1. SCMP 3497, 22.
Jul 12	Welcome the Emissary of the Heroic Vietnamese People, 3.
Jul 12	Welcomes Distinguished Guest from Uganda, 3. SCMP 3498, 20.
Jul 13	Serves Warning to U.S. Aggressor, 1. SCMP 3498, 21.
Jul 16	Supply Is Necessary, Procurement Even More So, 2. SCMP 3501, 12.
Jul 18	Acclaim Sino-Uganda Friendship, 4. SCMP 3502, 20.
Jul 19	Not Just "For Pocket Money," 1. SCMP 3520, 6.
Jul 19	Supports Pakistan's Defense of Sovereignty against U.S. Pressure, 4. SCMP 3503, 17.
Jul 20	Grasp Accurately, Relentlessly, and to the End, 1.
Jul 20	Marks Eleventh Anniversary of Geneva Agreement (U.S. troops must quit South Vietnam), 3. SCMP 3503, 14.

1965

Jul 21	Welcomes Somali President, 2. SCMP 3504, 22.
Jul 22	The Key Lies in the Cadre's Thinking, 2. SCMP 3524, 10.
Jul 23	In Praise of "Fans of Mountain Communities," 2.
Jul 24	Welcomes Chairman Ne Win (Burma), 1. SCMP 3506, 21.
Jul 27	Greets China-Mauritania Diplomatic Relations, 1. SCMP 3509, 22.
Jul 29	New Chapter in Sino-Somali Relations Opens, 4. SCMP 3510, 32.
Jul 29	Coordination between Long-Range and Short-Range Interests Is Necessary in Development of Diversified Operations, 2.
Jul 30	Take Good Care of Machinery and Equipment as Fighters Do Their Weapons (Organize upsurge in industrial production and construction), 1. SCMP 3526, 2.
Jul 30	Smash New U.S. Military Venture in Laos, 3. SCMP 3511, 40.
Aug 2	Hails Full Blossoming of Sino-Burmese Friendship, 4. SCMP 3512, 32.
Aug 3	Smash the U.S. Adventurous Plan for War in the Course of Its "Creeping Escalation," 1. SCMP 3513, 30.
Aug 5	Zealously Develop the Integrated Use of Construction in Water Conservancy, 1.
Aug 5	Greets Opening of Rumanian Economic Exhibition, 4. SCMP 3514, 30.
Aug 7	Smash New U.S. "Peace Talks" Swindle through UN, 1. SCMP 3515, 33.
Aug 7	Resolutely, Completely, Thoroughly, and Entirely Wipe Out the Enemy Who Dares to Invade Us! 1. SCMP 3519, 17.
Aug 11	Hails Victory of Eleventh Anti-A and H Bomb Conference, 4. SCMP 3518, 18.
Aug 12	Major Reforms in Grain Work, 1. SCMP 3550, 8.
Aug 14	Develop Multiple Undertakings to Strive for an All-Round Upsurge in Agriculture and Sideline Production, 1. SCMP 3530, 8.
Aug 18	Send Ideas, Labor, Commodities, and Technologies All Down to the Village, 2.
Aug 19	Hails Latest Revolutionary Storm of American Negroes, 3. SCMP 3524, 38.
Aug 21	Extend the Struggle to Improve Low-Yield Fields to Large Areas (Chu county), 1.
Aug 24	Hails China-Japan Youth Friendship Festival, 4. SCMP 3527, 27.
Aug 26	Marks Anniversary of Sino-Afghan Friendship, Non-Aggression Treaty, 5. SCMP 3529, 26.
Aug 31	Management of Agricultural Machinery Should Better Serve Agricultural Production, 2. SCMP 3543, 9.
Sep 1	Direct the Focus of Medical and Health Work to Rural Areas in a Practical Way, 1. SCMP 3540, 17.
Sep 2	In Celebration of the Chinese People's War of Resistance to Japanese Aggression, 1. SCMP 3541, 7.
Sep 2	Greets Twentieth Anniversary of Founding of Democratic Republic of Vietnam, 4. SCMP 3533, 28.
Sep 6	The Principle of "Less but Finer" Must Be Applied to Teaching Work--Greeting the 1965 New School Year, 1. SCMP 3543, 21.
Sep 7	The Fine Practice of Operating the Electricity Service in Rural Areas on a Part-Work and Part-Farming Basis, 1. SCMP 3544, 12.
Sep 8	We Must Go Deep into Reality and Serve Production and Construction when Carrying Out the Work of Regulating Material Supplies, 3. SCMP 3545, 5.
Sep 8	South Koreans Will Win Their Anti-U.S. Struggle, 5. SCMP 3536, 37.
Sep 10	Strive to Construct a Socialist New Tibet (Establishment of Tibet autonomous region), 2.
Sep 11	On the Second National Games, 1. SCMP 3538, 18.
Sep 11	Indian Reactionaries Are Plain Aggressors, 1. SCMP 3538, 31.
Sep 13	Greeting the Fifth Anniversary of the Signing of the Sino-Guinean Friendship Treaty, 5.
Sep 14	UN Is Sanctuary for Indian Aggressor, 1. SCMP 3539, 31.
Sep 15	A Good Method of Learning Advanced Experiences, 1. SCMP 3548, 21.
Sep 18	Who Are Backing Indian Aggressor? 1. SCMP 3542, 26.
Sep 19	Think on Behalf of Commune Members in a More Comprehensive Manner, 1. SCMP 3553, 7.
Sep 21	An Important Strategic Task in Building National Defense, 2. SCMP 3553, 14.
Sep 24	Turning to Work Shifts and Groups, Turning to the Worker Masses for the Purpose of Serving Production (Whip up upsurge of serving production), 1. SCMP 3555, 2.
Sep 25	Turn Minor Autumn Harvest into a Big Bumper Harvest, 2. SCMP 3554, 16.
Sep 26	Link Up Daily Work with Lofty Goals of the Revolution (Business and financial and trade work), 1. SCMP 3558, 2.
Sep 26	Hold High the Banner of Unity and Anti-Imperialism, March Towards New Victories (GANEFO Asian Committee established), 3.
Sep 27	Welcomes Distinguished Guests from Indonesia, 1. SCMP 3549, 37.
Sep 28	Welcomes Cambodian State Guests (Sihanouk), 3. SCMP 3549, 31.
Sep 29	Hails China's Second National Games, 2. SCMP 3550, 21.
Sep 30	A Great Victory of the Party Policy on Racial Unity (Anniversary of founding of Sinkiang Uighur autonomous region), 2.
Sep 30	UN, Hands Off China's Internal Affairs! 4. SCMP 3551, 42.
Oct 1	Hold High the Great Red Flag of Mao Tse-tung Thought and March Forward Bravely (National Day editorial), 3.
Oct 5	Praises Sino-Cambodian Friendship, 3. SCMP 3554, 22.
Oct 9	Develop Mountains and Till Land for Revolution's Sake (Emulate Nankunlungkou Valley people), 1. SCMP 3563, 4.
Oct 10	The Importance of Developing Rural Sideline Production as Viewed from the Example Provided by Hsihsia, 1. SCMP 3565, 13.
Oct 11	All Work Is for the Revolution, 1. SCMP 3564, 6.
Oct 16	Water Conservation by Depending on the 500 Million Peasants, 1. SCMP 3571, 7.
Oct 18	Pays Tribute to Awakened American People (About war in Vietnam), 1. SCMP 3563, 34.
Oct 23	Postponement of Second Afro-Asian Conference, 1. SCMP 3566, 26.
Oct 24	To Organize Rural Sideline Production Is a Glorious Task for Commercial Departments, 1. SCMP 3573, 10.
Oct 25	Marks Fifteenth Anniversary of Chinese People's Volunteer's Entry into Korean War, 1. SCMP 3568, 33.

1965

Oct 28	Positively and Methodically Reform the Production Team's Accounting System, 2. SCMP 3581, 6.
Oct 29	Uphold Afro-Asian Solidarity, Oppose Afro-Asian Split, 1. SCMP 3571, 22.
Nov 1	Agriculture Depends on the Tachai Spirit (National exhibition of Tachai-type farming units opens), 1. SCMP 3576, 13.
Nov 4	Carry Forward Cause of Afro-Asian Solidarity against Imperialism, 1. SCMP 3575, 21.
Nov 5	It Is an Important Matter to Supervise Water Supply and Nightsoil Disposal in Countryside, 1. SCMP 3586, 17.
Nov 5	The Good Management of Sewage in the Rural Areas Is Important Business, 1,3.
Nov 5	Hails Victories in Plei Me, Chu Lai, Da Nang, 3. SCMP 3576, 44.
Nov 7	Forge Ahead along Path of October Revolution, 1. SCMP 3577, 35.
Nov 8	Fear neither Hardship nor Death (Emulate Wang Chieh), 1,2.
Nov 8	Vietnamese People Will Win, 4. SCMP 3577, 37.
Nov 8	What the Japanese People Will Absolutely Prohibit, 5.
Nov 9	Hails Success of Laotian Political Consultative Conference, 4. SCMP 3578, 27.
Nov 9	Zimbabwe People Want Real Independence, 5. SCMP 3578, 28.
Nov 12	Hospitals in Socialist Rural Areas Need to Standardize This Way, 1.
Nov 13	Break the Cult of Foreign Technology, Develop Creativeness, 1. SCMP 3588, 3.
Nov 14	Just Struggle of Zimbabwe People Will Surely Win, 4. SCMP 3580, 31.
Nov 15	A Serious Measure in the American and Japanese Reactionaries' Plan to Instigate War, 1.
Nov 16	Peking Papers Welcome Young Japanese Friends, 4. SCMP 3581, 32.
Nov 18	Korean People Oppose Scheme of U.S.-Japanese Reactionaries, 1. SCMP 3583, 32.
Nov 18	Comments on Remarkable Tass Corrections (Exposes double-faced tactics employed by Khruschov's successors), 3. SCMP 3583, 35.
Nov 19	Urges Breaking of U.S. Domination over UN, 1. SCMP 3584, 32.
Nov 19	South Vietnamese People's War Shines Forth in All Its Radiance, 3. SCMP 3584, 37.
Nov 22	Welcomes Tanzanian Second Vice-President, 1. SCMP 3585, 34.
Nov 28	Learn and Apply Materialistic Dialectics in the Midst of Struggle, 1. SCMP 3595, 15.
Nov 29	Hails American People's March on Washington, 4. SCMP 3590, 30.
Nov 30	For Further Revolutionization of Capital Construction, 1. SCMP 3593, 9.
Dec 1	UN Has No Right to Discuss Korean Question, 3. SCMP 3591, 26.
Dec 2	Promote Revolutionary Spirit of the People of Wushenchao, 1.
Dec 4	The Family Sideline Is an Assistant to the Socialist Economy, 1. SCMP 3599, 11.
Dec 9	Historic Road for Young Intellectuals (Anniversary of December 9 patriotic students movement), 1. SCMP 3597, 5.
Dec 9	The American Invading Army Cannot Stand the Beating, 3.
Dec 11	Carry Out Well Part-Work, Part-Study Education by Upholding the Guideline of "Accomplishing Experimentation in Five Years and Popularization in Ten Years," 1. SCMP 3601, 8.
Dec 13	How Should We Understand and Organize Mass Movement for Comparing, Learning, Catching Up, Assisting, and Surpassing? (Whip up upsurge in industrial production and construction), 1. SCMP 3606, 1.
Dec 14	JMJP on U.S. Administration's New "Peace Gesture," 3. SCMP 3600, 28.
Dec 16	Link the Livelihood of the Masses with the Revolutionary Task, 1. SCMP 3614, 11.
Dec 18	Create More Tachai-Type Advanced Counties, 1.
Dec 18	Hails New Chapter in African People's Anti-Imperialist Struggle, 4. SCMP 3603, 20.
Dec 19	Salutes Embattled South Vietnamese People, 1. SCMP 3604, 36.
Dec 19	Hails Sublime Sino-Cambodian Friendship, 4. SCMP 3604, 21.
Dec 21	Anti-China Farce in UN Denounced by Peking Papers, 5. SCMP 3605, 26.
Dec 22	Penetratingly Develop Revolution in Product Designing, Rapidly Raise the Technical Level of China's Industrial Production, 1. SCMP 3611, 8.
Dec 23	Rural Youths Should Take an Active Part in Scientific Experiment, 5. SCMP 3612, 10.
Dec 24	Cambodian Territory Inviolable, 4. SCMP 3607, 24.
Dec 24	"ROK-Japan Treaty" Is a Scrap of Paper (Support declaration of North Korean government), 4. SCMP 3607, 33.
Dec 25	UN Is Instrument for U.S. Aggression against Korea, 3. SCMP 3607, 36.
Dec 26	The Potentials Are Great, and Much Can Be Done in Tapping Them (Improve swampy and saline areas in North China), 1. SCMP 3615, 5.
Dec 27	A Highly Important Question, 1.
Dec 27	UN Is American-Soviet Political Marketplace, 4. SCMP 3608, 34.
Dec 29	Carry Out Finance and Trade Work as if It Were Political Work, 1. SCMP 3621, 7.

1966

Jan 1	Usher in 1966, the First Year of China's Third Five-Year Plan (New Year's Day statement), 1. SCMP 3610, 10.
Jan 1	Marks Seventh Anniversary of Victory of Cuban Revolution, 3. SCMP 3610, 37.
Jan 2	The Correct Path of China's Industrialization, 1. SCMP 3621, 20.
Jan 3	Forever Keep Revolution Young, 1. SCMP 3613, 44 (summary).
Jan 4	For the People, 1. SCMP 3613, 44 (summary).
Jan 4	Voices Full Support for Cambodian People, 3. SCMP 3612, 27.
Jan 5	Only When We Have a Revolutionary Team, Would We Have Revolutionary Enterprises, 1.
Jan 6	The Thought of Mao Tse-tung Controls Everything, 1. SCMP 3620, 12.
Jan 8	Be a Conscious Revolutionary (On "All Work Is for the Revolution"), 1. SCMP 3624, 14.
Jan 11	There Can Be Tachings Everywhere in the Country, 1. SCMP 3618, 27 (summary).
Jan 13	Bear the Heavy Burden of Revolution, 1.
Jan 14	Johnson Administration Cannot Escape Justice, 1. SCMP 3619, 30.
Jan 16	Workers in Philosophy, Pack Up and Go among the Worker, Peasant, and Soldier Masses, 1. SCMP 3622, 4.

1966

Jan 16	Conference Studies Ways of Raising China's Rice Output, 2. SCMP 3621, 28.
Jan 17	A Mirror, 1.
Jan 18	The Revolutionary Tough-Bone Spirit Is Invincible, 1. SCMP 3632, 13.
Jan 18	No One Can Stem Tide of Anti-Imperialist Revolutionary Struggle of Asian, African, and Latin American Peoples, 4. SCMP 3622, 22.
Jan 19	Comments on Johnson's State of Union Message, 3. SCMP 3623, 36.
Jan 20	The Road for Fostering Scientists and Technicians in China, 1. SCMP 3632, 14.
Jan 21	Happy to See the Growth of Revolutionary Successors, 1. SCMP 3631, 15.
Jan 24	Develop Science and Technology by Following Our Own Road, 1. SCMP 3632, 16.
Jan 24	Johnson Administration's Self-Exposure, 3. SCMP 3625, 31.
Jan 25	Guide the Broad Masses of Peasants to Study Chairman Mao's Works in a Big Way, 1. SCMP 3631, 5.
Jan 26	Learn from the Revolutionary Taching Spirit, Launch the Movement for Increased Production and Economy, 1. SCMP 3632, 6.
Jan 27	Enthusiasm for Work Must Be Great, the Pace Must Be Steady, 1. SCMP 3636, 1.
Jan 28	A Victory of the Unity of Revolutionary Spirit and Scientific Attitude, 1.
Jan 29	Direct Production in Pastoral Areas with the Revolutionary Viewpoint of Development, 1. SCMP 3639, 22.
Jan 30	Revolutionary Spirit Must Be Grounded on Scientific Attitude, 1.
Jan 30	Forceful Reply from Firm Stand, 1. SCMP 3630, 28.
Jan 30	Soviet Government Has Again Exposed Itself, 3. SCMP 3630, 24.
Feb 1	On U.S. Resumption of Bombing of North Vietnam, 1. SCMP 3631, 35.
Feb 2	UN Has No Right to Discuss Vietnam Question, 1. SCMP 3632, 28.
Feb 2	Be Clear-Headed Promoters, 2. SCMP 3638, 8.
Feb 5	Production Upsurge and the Mass Line, 1. SCMP 3642, 6.
Feb 6	The Party Hsien Committee Must Include Tree Planting and Management as an Important Item on the Order of the Day, 3. SCMP 3644, 11.
Feb 7	Learn from Comrade Chiao Yu-lu, 1. SCMP 3639, 1.
Feb 8	Latent Resources That Can Never Be Exhaustively Tapped, 1.
Feb 9	Greater Numbers of Good Cadres of This Kind Are Needed, 1. SCMP 3645, 8.
Feb 9	Strive for Still Higher Yields of Cotton and a Bumper Harvest of Both Grain and Cotton, 2. SCMP 3645, 15.
Feb 10	Follow Our Own Road by Starting from Reality, 2. SCMP 3645, 18.
Feb 11	The Most Precious Class Feelings, 3. SCMP 3645, 9.
Feb 12	Honolulu Conference Is Prelude to New U.S. Military Venture, 1. SCMP 3639, 41.
Feb 13	Make Special Effort with Regard to "Application," 1. SCMP 3647, 5.
Feb 14	Carry On the Study in the Spirit of Rectification, 1. SCMP 3645, 10.
Feb 15	Celebrates South Vietnamese Liberation Forces' Anniversary, 1. SCMP 3641, 30.
Feb 16	Be Realistic, 1. SCMP 3647, 15.
Feb 20	Marks Anniversary of China-Tanzania Treaty of Friendship, 4. SCMP 3645, 32.
Feb 20	Refutes William Bundy's Anti-China Speech, 4. SCMP 3645, 34.
Feb 20	Investigation Is a Way to Solve Problems, 1. SCMP 3650, 15.
Feb 22	Literary and Art Workers, Go to the Countryside to Temper Yourselves! 1. SCMP 3649, 1.
Feb 23	Welcomes President Kwame Nkruma, 1. SCMP 3646, 42.
Feb 23	The Most Effective Leadership, 2. SCMP 3650, 27 (summary).
Feb 23	Promote the Spirit of Uninterrupted Revolution, Round Out Water Conservation Projects with Auxiliary Works in the Fields, 3. SCMP 3654, 18.
Feb 26	Grasp the Truth and We Will Win Everywhere, 1.
Feb 27	Let Us Be Armed with the Thought of Mao Tse-tung and Become Proletarian, Revolutionary Fighters in Literature and Art, 1. SCMP 3654, 1.
Feb 28	Use the Thought of Mao Tse-tung, Sum Up Experiences Incessantly, 1.
Mar 1	Establish the Revolutionary Viewpoint of Long-Term Construction of Grasslands, 2. SCMP 3658, 18.
Mar 3	Thought Reform Never Has a Limit, 1.
Mar 4	The Greatest Fighting Power, 1. SCMP 3659, 1.
Mar 6	Promote the Style of Fighting amid Hardship, 1. SCMP 3654, 47 (summary).
Mar 8	Be Outstanding in Politics, Make Another Step to Release the Great Resources in Women, 1.
Mar 10	Why It Is Necessary to Fix the Right to Use Pastureland, 2. SCMP 3665, 16.
Mar 11	Heroic People in Calamity-Stricken Area Are Not Alarmed by Difficulties, 2. SCMP 3658, 3.
Mar 12	Planting of Trees Must Be Preceded by Nurturing of People, 2. SCMP 3660, 16.
Mar 16	Political Leadership Is Primary (Shanghai stable and high yields), 1. SCMP 3665, 13.
Mar 17	Marks Anniversary of Vietnam's Anti-U.S. Struggle, 3. SCMP 3662, 30.
Mar 20	Old Cadres Should Assume a Greater Leading Role, 1.
Mar 25	We Must Be Able to Stand Two Tests, 1. SCMP 3673, 12.
Mar 25	Stay the U.S. Aggressor's Hand, 4. SCMP 3669, 50.
Mar 27	Hails Chairman Liu Shao-chi's Tour Abroad, 3. SCMP 3669, 33.
Mar 27	Pays Tribute to American People's Struggle against Vietnam War, 4. SCMP 3669, 48.
Mar 29	Advocate a Living Philosophy Derived from Practice and Applied to Practice, 2.
Mar 29	Warns Sato Government, 5. SCMP 3670, 32.
Mar 30	Voice of Truth Can Never Be "Shut Down," 1. SCMP 3671, 27.
Mar 31	Struggle with the Bourgeoisie to Win over the Next Generation, 1. SCMP 3676, 16.
Apr 1	Where Lies the Key to the Proper Operation of State Farms? 2. SCMP 3678, 10.
Apr 3	Run Enterprises in Line with the Thought of Mao Tse-tung, 1. SCMP 3679, 1.

1966

Apr 6	Placing Politics in a Prominent Position Is the Root of All Work (On placing politics in command), 1. SCMP 3680, 1.
Apr 6	Analyzes the Threat of U.S. War against China, 2. SCMP 3675, 39.
Apr 7	Dare to Compete with the Strongest, 3.
Apr 8	An Example to Be Emulated, a Goal to Be Strived For, 1.
Apr 9	Hails New Growth of Sino-Afghan Friendship, 3. SCMP 3677, 36.
Apr 10	Learn the Dialectical Method in Struggle, 1.
Apr 11	To Know Objective Laws We Should Be Outstanding in Politics, 1.
Apr 12	While Importance Is Attached to Farming, Stockbreeding Must Not Be Slighted, 2. SCMP 3685, 7.
Apr 14	Politics Commands Functional Work (On placing politics in command), 1. SCMP 3682, 3.
Apr 15	Marks "African Freedom Day," 1. SCMP 3681, 19.
Apr 15	Be Outstanding in Politics, Take the Lead in Spring Ploughing, 1.
Apr 16	On "Full-Scale Fascist Outrage" in Djakarta, 1. SCMP 3681, 31.
Apr 18	Sino-Pakistan Friendship Can Stand Tests, 3. SCMP 3682, 33.
Apr 19	Supports South Korean People's Anti-U.S. Struggle, 4. SCMP 3683, 30.
Apr 20	Chinese, Burmese Will Live in Friendship Forever, 3. SCMP 3683, 28.
Apr 21	Welcomes Chairman Liu Shao-chi Home from Successful Visit, 1. SCMP 3684, 37.
Apr 21	The Unlimited Power of the Great Masses of People, 2. SCMP 3686, 10.
Apr 22	To Put Politics in Forefront, It Is Necessary to Put the Thought of Mao Tse-tung Firmly in Command (On placing politics in command), 1. SCMP 3688, 1.
Apr 22	Develop Democracy in Production, 2. SCMP 3689, 8.
Apr 24	The Dominican People Are Advancing in Struggle, 3.
Apr 26	Create a Great and Lasting Enterprise, 1.
Apr 26	Hails Unity of Progressive Afro-Asian Journalists, 3. SCMP 3687, 19.
Apr 27	The Head May Be Cut Off, Blood May Be Shed, but the Dignity of the Mother Country Cannot Be Disgraced, 2.
Apr 28	Welcomes Arrival of Albanian Party and Government Delegation, 1. SCMP 3689, 29.
May 1	U.S. "Air Superiority" Myth Punctured, 6. SCMP 3691, 41.
May 1	Steadfastly Put Politics in the Forefront, Promote the New Upsurge in Industrial Production and Construction (International Labor Day), 5. SCMP 3693, 1.
May 4	Passing the Torch of Revolution on from One Generation to Another ("May 4" Youth Day), 4. SCMP 3696, 2.
May 8	The Era for Peasants to Master Agricultural Science and Philosophy Consciously Has Begun, 4. SCMP 3704, 9.
May 13	Strongly Condemns U.S. War Provocation, 1. SCMP 3699, 31.
May 15	A Document of Great Historical Significance, 2.
May 15	Supports Palestinian Arabs' Struggle, 6. SCMP 3701, 21.
May 26	Greeting the Victorious Ending of the Weight-Lifting Invitational Games of the Newly Emerging Forces, 4.
May 26	Greets Independence of Guyana, 4. SCMP 3709, 47.
Jun 1	Sweep Away All Monsters, 1. SCMP 3712, 1.
Jun 1	Nurturing the Revolutionary Younger Generation with the Thought of Mao Tse-tung (International Children's Day), 2. SCMP 3716, 8.
Jun 2	A Great Revolution That Touches the People to Their Very Souls, 1. SCMP 3713, 1.
Jun 2	The Bright Spring of the Great Proletarian Cultural Revolution ("Spring in Shanghai"), 3.
Jun 3	Calls for Capture of Bourgeois Positions in Historical Studies, 1. SCMP 3714, 8.
Jun 4	Tear Aside the Bourgeois Mask of "Liberty, Equality, and Fraternity," 1. SCMP 3714, 1.
Jun 4	New Victory for Mao Tse-tung's Thought, 1. SCMP 3714, 12.
Jun 8	Calls for Criticism of the Old World, 1. SCMP 3717, 1.
Jun 8	On Growth of Heroic Chinese Armyman, 1. SCMP 3717, 21.
Jun 16	Mobilize the Masses Freely, Knock Down the Counter-Revolutionary Black Gang Completely, 1. SCMP 3726, 5.
Jun 17	Hails Chou En-lai's Visit to Rumania, 1. SCMP 3723, 35.
Jun 18	On Importance of Transforming Chinese Educational System, 1. SCMP 3724, 13.
Jun 20	On Use of Posters in Current Cultural Revolution, 1. SCMP 3725, 1.
Jun 24	The Sunlight of the Party Illuminates the Road of the Great Cultural Revolution, 1. SCMP 3728, 1.
Jun 25	On Sino-Albanian Friendship, Premier Chou's Visit, 1. SCMP 3728, 22.
Jun 25	On Korean War Anniversary, 5. SCMP 3728, 26.
Jun 27	Unite and Join in the Heated Combat (Emergency meeting of the Afro-Asian writers opens), 1.
Jun 27	The Five-Star Red Flag Must Be Planted on Taiwan Province, 2. SCMP 3730, 17.
Jun 29	Hails Sino-Albanian Militant Friendship, 1. SCMP 3731, 30.
Jun 30	Indonesian Authorities Must Immediately Stop Persecution of Chinese Nationals, 5. SCMP 3732, 30.
Jul 1	Long Live the Thought of Mao Tse-tung, 1. SCMP 3733, 1.
Jul 5	The U.S. Is Setting No Bounds to Its Aggression, and Our Counter-Aggression Also Knows No Bounds, 1. SCMP 3735, 30.
Jul 10	Hails Success of Afro-Asian Writers' Emergency Meeting, 2. SCMP 3738, 20.
Jul 11	Marks Fifth Anniversary of Sino-Korean Treaty, 5. SCMP 3738, 28.
Jul 17	A New Stage of the Socialist Revolution in China (Amended 7/18, p. 2), 1. SCMP 3743, 1.
Jul 18	Chinese People Determined to Back Vietnamese People, 2. SCMP 3743, 29.
Jul 21	From the Masses, to the Masses, 1. SCMP 3748, 5.
Jul 23	Developing a Scientific Culture of Our People in the Revolutionary Struggle of Anti-Imperialism (Peking summer physics forum opens), 4.
Jul 24	Voices Stout Backing for Vietnamese People, 1. SCMP 3748, 39.

1966

Jul 26 Follow Chairman Mao and Advance in the Teeth of the Great Storms and Waves, 1. SCMP 3749, 1.
Jul 28 A Good Son of the People, 1. SCMP 3751, 22.
Jul 29 Be a Pupil of the Masses before Becoming Their Teacher, 1. SCMP 3757, 1.
Aug 1 The Whole Country Should Become a Great School in Mao Tse-tung's Thought (Anniversary of founding of PLA), 1. SCMP 3754, 6.
Aug 1 Struggle against Imperialism and Colonialism, and Develop a Scientific Culture of Our People (Peking summer physics forum ends), 3.
Aug 7 Welcomes Pakistan Parliamentary Delegation, 2. SCMP 3758, 15.
Aug 8 A Big Joyful Event for the People of the Whole Country, 1. SCMP 3759, 14.
Aug 8 Marks Third Anniversary of Chairman Mao's Statement in Support of American Negroes, 4. SCMP 3758, 17.
Aug 11 Take Hold of the Ideological Weapon for the Great Cultural Revolution, 1. SCMP 3763, 25.
Aug 13 Study, Get Familiar with, and Apply the Sixteen Articles, 1. SCMP 3766, 21.
Aug 15 Sailing the Seas Relies on the Helmsman, 1. SCMP 3763, 1.
Aug 17 On Vital Role of Practice, 1. SCMP 3765, 15.
Aug 19 Welcomes Distinguished Guests from Zambia, 4. SCMP 3767, 41.
Aug 20 Chairman Mao Is with the Masses, 1. SCMP 3767, 6.
Aug 23 It Is Fine! 1. SCMP 3769, 1.
Aug 23 Workers, Peasants, and Soldiers Must Firmly Support Revolutionary Students, 1. SCMP 3769, 3.
Aug 24 Hails Birth of Peking University's New Journal, 1. SCMP 3770, 16.
Aug 25 Great Strategic Concept (Twentieth anniversary of Mao's publication on imperialism), 1. SCMP 3771, 17.
Aug 26 Wash Away Old Culture and Create New, 4. SCMP 3771, 16.
Aug 28 Revolutionary Youth Should Learn from the Chinese PLA, 1. SCMP 3772, 4.
Aug 29 Salutes Red Guards, 1. SCMP 3773, 9.
Aug 29 Welcomes Brazzaville Congolese National Assembly Delegation, 4. SCMP 3773, 29.
Sep 5 Struggle by Reasoning, Not by Coercion or Force, 1. SCMP 3777, 1.
Sep 5 Marching Forward Hand-in-Hand Is the Enterprise of Uniting to Oppose Imperialism, 2.
Sep 7 Take Firm Hold of the Revolution in Order to Stimulate Production, 1. SCMP 3779, 1.
Sep 8 Chinese Press Expresses Warm Welcome to Somali Guests, 4. SCMP 3779, 33.
Sep 11 Masses of Workers and Peasants Should Unite with Revolutionary Students under the Banner of the Thought of Mao Tse-tung, 1. SCMP 3785, 5.
Sep 15 Salute and Learn from Workers, Peasants, and Soldiers, 1. SCMP 3784, 5.
Sep 19 Take Firm Hold of the Autumn Harvest, 1. SCMP 3791, 31.
Sep 24 Disseminate the Thought of Mao Tse-tung, 1. SCMP 3801, 1.
Sep 24 U.N.O. Has No Right to Poke Its Nose into Vietnam Question, 4. SCMP 3790, 42.
Sep 26 The Thought of Mao Tse-tung Is the Very Soul of the Revolutionary People, 1. SCMP 3801, 4.

1966

Oct 1 Arm 700 Million People with Mao Tse-tung's Thought (National Day editorial), 3.
Oct 8 Welcomes Victimized Chinese Nationals Home from Indonesia, 1. SCMP 3799, 26.
Oct 10 Exposes Big Conspiracy of "Inducement to Peace Talks by a Suspension of Bombings," 4. SCMP 3800, 47.
Oct 12 Mao Tse-tung's Thought Must Be Studied with All Earnestness and Diligence, 1. SCMP 3802, 1.
Oct 19 Learn from Lu Hsun's Revolutionary Spirit of Unyielding Integrity, 2. SCMP 3806, 7.
Oct 22 Red Guards Do Not Fear the Trials of a Long March, 1. SCMP 3810, 10.
Oct 22 Make Revolution at the Very Center of One's Being (Learn from worker Yu Feng-hing), 2. SCMP 3810, 25.
Oct 28 Take the "Three Much-Read Articles" as a Compulsory Subject for Bringing Up Communist New Men, 1. SCMP 3815, 1.
Nov 8 Learn to Grasp Living Ideas Well, 1. SCMP 3822, 16.
Nov 10 More on the Question of Grasping the Revolution Firmly and Stimulating Production, 1. SCMP 3825, 1.
Nov 10 Great Beacon of Socialism in Europe, 3. SCMP 3821, 28.
Nov 18 Peking Papers Call for Nationwide Emulation of Good Fighter of Chairman Mao (Tsai Yunghsiang), 1. SCMP 3826, 17.
Nov 25 Acclaims Opening of First Asian GANEFO, 4. SCMP 3830, 32.
Nov 29 Warmly Hails 22nd Anniversary of Albania's Liberation, 3. SCMP 3832, 24.
Dec 2 China Asks No Favor of United Nations, 4. SCMP 3835, 29.
Dec 7 Asian GANEFO Opens New Era in Asian Sports History, 4. SCMP 3838, 19.
Dec 9 Praises Heroism of Young Chinese from Indonesia, 1. SCMP 3840, 24.
Dec 15 The Great Vietnamese People Cannot Be Intimidated, 2.
Dec 20 Victory Certainly Belongs to Great Vietnamese People, 2. SCMP 3847, 24.
Dec 24 Hails New Major Scientific Achievement, 1. SCMP 3849, 28.
Dec 26 Welcome the Upsurge of the Great Cultural Revolution in Industrial and Mining Enterprises, 1. SCMP 3852, 1.

1967

Jan 5 JMJP Hails Heroic Exploits of Crew of Chinese Cargo Vessel, 1. SCMP 3856, 24.
Jan 19 Let Mao Tse-tung's Thought Occupy All Positions in the Press, 1. SCMP 3866, 1.
Jan 22 JMJP Editorial on Great Alliance of Proletarian Revolutionaries and Their Seizure of Power, 1. SCMP 3868, 1.
Jan 25 Great Victory in the Great Proletarian Cultural Revolution in Shansi Province, 2. SCMP 3873, 4.
Jan 26 JMJP Editorial on Practicing Economy in Carrying Out Revolution, 1. SCMP 3871, 1.
Jan 27 JMJP Says: Hit Back Hard at the Violent Provocations of the Filthy Soviet Revisionist Swine! 1. SCMP 3872, 45.
Jan 30 The Great Alliance Is the Key, 1. SCMP 3874, 1.
Feb 1 JMJP Editorial Welcomes Triumphant Return of Glorious Anti-Revisionist Fighters, 3. SCMP 3876, 37.

1967

Feb 1	A Thunder in Southwest China, 1. SCMP 3876, 1.
Feb 2	JMJP Acclaims Seizure of Power by Revolutionary Rebels in Northeast China Province, 1. SCMP 3877, 11.
Feb 6	Outrage of a Savagery Seldom Seen in the History of World Diplomacy, 1. SCMP 3879, 28.
Feb 10	Good Example in Struggle by Proletarian Revolutionaries to Seize Power, 1. SCMP 3880, 5.
Feb 11	Start Spring Plowing Well by Grasping Revolution and Stimulating Production, 1. SCMP 3884, 23.
Feb 17	JMJP Editorial on Policy of "Three-Way Alliance," 1. SCMP 3884, 1.
Mar 1	JMJP Commends New Form of Proletarian Revolutionaries' Alliance, 1. SCMP 3892, 1.
Mar 2	JMJP Editorial Acclaims Revolutionary "Three-Way Alliance" in Struggle to Seize Power in Shantung, 2. SCMP 3893, 24.
Mar 7	Middle and Primary Schools Re-Open Classes and Make Revolution, 1. SCMP 3900, 17.
Mar 12	On the Setting Up of a Frontline Command for Grasping Revolution and Stimulating Production, 1. SCMP 3902, 21.
Mar 13	There Will Be No Seizure of Power in Production Brigades and Production Teams during the Spring Farming Period, 1. SCMP 3904, 10.
Mar 18	JMJP Editorial Extols a Dauntless Proletarian Heir (Learn from Kuo Chia-hung), 1. SCMP 3904, 22.
Mar 19	JMJP Salutes Heroic Vietnamese People, 2. SCMP 3904, 44.
Apr 2	JMJP on Correct Treatment of Young Revolutionary Fighters, 1. SCMP 3912, 1.
Apr 8	Raise High the Proletarian Revolutionary Banner of Criticism and Repudiation, 1. SCMP 3917, 13.
Apr 15	JMJP Editorial on Revolutionary Criticism and Alliance, 1. SCMP 3922, 1.
Apr 21	JMJP Editorial Hails Establishment of Peking Municipal Revolutionary Committee, 4. SCMP 3925, 20.
Apr 24	JMJP Editorial Emphasizes Repudiation of Bourgeois Reactionary Line on Cadre Question, 1. SCMP 3927, 1.
Apr 26	Down with Anarchism, 1. SCMP 3928, 19.
Apr 27	JMJP Condemns Indonesian Reactionaries' Anti-China Outrages, 2. SCMP 3929, 33.
Apr 30	JMJP Editorial Honors May Day, 1. SCMP 3931, 10.
May 4	JMJP Editorial on Youth Movement, 1. SCMP 3934, 1.
May 7	JMJP Editorial on Turning China into Great School of Mao Tse-tung's Thought, 1. SCMP 3936, 4.
May 12	Further Strengthen Unity between the Army and the People, 1. SCMP 3945, 1.
May 14	JMJP Marks Anniversary of Sino-Albanian Joint Statement, 2. SCMP 3940, 23.
May 15	Another JMJP Editorial on Practicing Economy in Carrying Out Revolution, 1. SCMP 3941, 17 (extracts).
May 16	JMJP Commends Military-Political Training, 1. SCMP 3944, 10.
May 22	Immediately Curb Struggle by Force, 1. SCMP 3950, 4.
May 23	Beacon Light for the Great Proletarian Cultural Revolution (Anniversary of publication of Mao's "Talks at the Yenan Forum"), 4. SCMP 3946, 16.
May 23	JMJP Condemns U.S. Invasion of Demilitarized Zone in Vietnam, 5. SCMP 3946, 38.
May 28	JMJP Editorial Hails Publication of Chairman Mao's Militant Documents on Literature and Art, 2. SCMP 3950, 2.
May 29	JMJP Editorial on Importance of Army Literature and Art Forum Summary, 4. SCMP 3951, 18.
May 29	JMJP Backs Arab People against U.S.-Led Aggression, 5. SCMP 3951, 31.
May 31	Fine Models of Revolutionary Literature and Art, 1. SCMP 3952, 22.
May 31	Tightly Grasp the Summer Harvest, 1. SCMP 3955, 28.
Jun 1	A Great Strategic Measure, 1. SCMP 3952, 14.
Jun 3	Resolutely Repel British Imperialist Provocations, 1. SCMP 3954, 30.
Jun 6	JMJP Supports Arab People's War against Aggression, 1. SCMP 3955, 40.
Jun 8	Hold Fast to General Direction of Struggle; Strengthen Dictatorship of Proletariat, 1. SCMP 3957, 5.
Jun 8	JMJP Acclaims Vietnamese People's Victory, 4. SCMP 3957, 33.
Jun 11	JMJP Calls on Arab People to Unite and Fight Imperialism to the End, 1. SCMP 3959, 35.
Jun 14	Third Discourse on Practice of Economy in Making Revolution, 1. SCMP 3965, 3.
Jun 15	JMJP Hails Arab People's Anti-U.S. Upsurge, 5. SCMP 3962, 38.
Jun 18	JMJP Editorial on Distinguishing Correctly between Two Types of Social Contradictions, 2. SCMP 3964, 18.
Jun 18	JMJP Editorial Acclaims Success of AAJA Secretariat Meeting (Afro-Asian journalists), 5. SCMP 3964, 31.
Jun 21	Unity, Criticism, Unity, 1. SCMP 3966, 11.
Jun 21	Warm Welcome to Distinguished Zambian Guests, 1. SCMP 3966, 27.
Jun 22	JMJP on Intensified U.S.-Soviet Collusion, 5. SCMP 3967, 33.
Jun 28	JMJP Welcomes Red Diplomatic Fighters of Chairman Mao, 2. SCMP 3971, 32.
Jun 30	JMJP Editorial Commemorates Anniversary of Birth of Chinese Communist Party, 1. SCMP 3974, 1.
Jun 30	Burmese Government Must Stop All Anti-Chinese Atrocities at Once, Says JMJP, 2. SCMP 3973, 31.
Jul 5	JMJP Calls for Fiercer Struggle against British Violence in Hong Kong, 4. SCMP 3975, 27.
Jul 5	JMJP Hails Indian Peasants' Armed Uprising in Darjeeling Area, 5. SCMP 3976, 37.
Jul 7	People's War Is Invincible (Anniversary of Sino-Japanese war), 1. SCMP 3981, 1.
Jul 9	Insist on the Correct Orientation of Going to Rural Areas for Educated Youths, 2. SCMP 3983, 14.
Jul 10	JMJP Serves Severe Warning to Ne Win Reactionary Government, 1. SCMP 3979, 21.
Jul 16	JMJP Editorial Commemorates Anniversary of Chairman Mao's Swim in the Yangtze, 1. SCMP 3983, 11.
Jul 21	JMJP Editorial Says Great Vietnamese War against U.S. Aggression Will Be Crowned with Victory, 1. SCMP 3987, 29.
Jul 24	Carry Revolution Mass Criticism and Repudiation through to the End, 1. SCMP 3989, 10.
Jul 26	Peking Supports You, 1. SCMP 3993, 1.

1967

- Jul 26 Lifting a Rock to Drop It on One's Own Foot, 2. SCMP 3993, 2.
- Jul 28 Salute the Broad Revolutionary Masses of Wuhan, 1. SCMP 3999, 1.
- Jul 29 March Forward in Triumph along Chairman Mao's Proletarian Revolutionary Line, 1. SCMP 3999, 5.
- Jul 30 Rats Are Running across the Street with Everyone Yelling "Kill Them, Kill Them!" 1. SCMP 3999, 9.
- Jul 30 Long Live the Great Unity of the Proletarian Revolutionaries of Wuhan, 1. SCMP 3999, 11.
- Jul 31 Strongest Pillar of Dictatorship of the Proletariat (Anniversary of founding of PLA), 1. SCMP 3994, 1.
- Aug 2 JMJP Editorial: Chairman Mao Backs Us Up, We Must Win for Chairman Mao, 1. SCMP 3998, 8.
- Aug 4 Hold High the Great Banner of "Support the Army and Cherish the People," 1. SCMP 4000, 27.
- Aug 5 JMJP Editorial on First Anniversary of Chairman Mao's Big-Character Poster, 1. SCMP 3997, 13.
- Aug 8 A Great Milestone, 1. SCMP 3998, 17.
- Aug 8 JMJP on Fourth Anniversary of Chairman Mao's Statement of Support for Afro-Americans, 2. SCMP 3999, 43.
- Aug 10 Proletarian Revolutionaries Should Be Models of Grasping Revolution and Promoting Production, 1.
- Aug 11 Strive to Win Fresh Merit in Serving the People, 2. SCMP 4001, 16.
- Aug 13 Song of Triumph on Tsinghai Plateau, 1. SCMP 4005, 13.
- Aug 16 Peng Te-huai and His Behind-the-Scenes Boss Cannot Shirk Responsibility for Their Crimes, 2. SCMP 4004, 4.
- Aug 17 Be Models of the Revolutionary Grand Alliance, 1. SCMP 4012, 9.
- Aug 19 The Core of Revolutionary Great Alliance Is Formed during Mass Struggle, 1. SCMP 4013, 1.
- Aug 22 We Will Resolutely, Thoroughly, and Exhaustively Destroy the Invaders, 1.
- Aug 25 A Very Important Problem of Policy, 1. SCMP 4018, 8.
- Aug 26 Take Another Step in Practicing Thrift to Make Revolution, 1.
- Aug 28 Launch a Vigorous Campaign on a Larger Scale to Support the Army and Cherish the People, 1. SCMP 4021, 3.
- Aug 29 JMJP Marks Anniversary of Chairman Mao's Statement (Opposing aggression against South Vietnam), 2. SCMP 4013, 34.
- Sep 2 Proletarian Revolutionaries Pledge to Be Models in Supporting the Army, 1. SCMP 4017, 14.
- Sep 9 Grasp the Great Goal of Revolutionary Struggle, Deepen and Broaden Great Revolutionary Criticisms, 1.
- Sep 9 If the Enemy Dares to Stir Up Trouble, We Will Destroy Them Completely, 4.
- Sep 10 Sato Government Treads Tojo's Beaten Path, 5. SCMP 4020, 31.
- Sep 14 Promote Revolutionary Alliance through Revolutionary Criticism, 1. SCMP 4024, 28.
- Sep 16 Get Mobilized and Do a Good Job of "Three Autumn" Farm Work, 1. SCMP 4030, 23.
- Sep 18 A Brilliant Victory for Chairman Mao's Latest Instructions (Shanghai revolutionary great alliance), 1. SCMP 4031, 10.
- Sep 21 JMJP Editorial Hails South Vietnam National Liberation Front's Political Program, 4. SCMP 4027, 33.
- Sep 22 A Great Historical Current, 1. SCMP 4033, 7.
- Sep 24 Do Six Things Well in Agriculture during the Great Proletarian Cultural Revolution, 1. SCMP 4033, 15.
- Sep 26 JMJP Welcomes Distinguished Albanian Guests, 1. SCMP 4031, 25.
- Sep 27 JMJP Welcomes Comrades-in-Arms from Anti-U.S. Front, 1. SCMP 4033, 37.
- Sep 27 JMJP Editorial Warmly Welcomes Distinguished Congolese (Brazzaville) Guests, 2. SCMP 4031, 31.
- Sep 27 JMJP Denounces U.S., Soviet Intervention in Vietnam through UN, 6. SCMP 4031, 37.
- Oct 6 JMJP Editorial on Combating Self-Interest and Repudiating Revisionism, 2. SCMP 4038, 17.
- Oct 12 Organize Classes for the Study of Mao Tse-tung's Thought throughout the Country, 1. SCMP 4045, 1.
- Oct 19 Obey Chairman Mao's Instructions, Bring About Revolutionary Great Alliances in Individual Systems, 1. SCMP 4049, 8.
- Oct 20 JMJP Editorial Warmly Welcomes President of Mauritania, 2. SCMP 4046, 38.
- Oct 21 Correctly Carry Out Chairman Mao's Cadre Policy, 1. SCMP 4048, 1.
- Oct 25 Universities and Middle and Primary Schools Must Resume Classes while Making Revolution, 1. SCMP 4049, 1.
- Oct 29 JMJP Condemns Indonesian Reactionaries for Disrupting Sino-Indonesian Relations, 1. SCMP 4052, 34.
- Nov 2 Red Sun Shines on Grasslands of Inner Mongolia, 3. SCMP 4056, 31.
- Nov 19 JMJP Editorial on Significance of Cadres Going among Masses, 1. SCMP 4065, 1.
- Nov 26 Another Editorial Calling on Universities, High Schools, and Primary Schools to Return to the Schools to Make Revolution, 1.
- Nov 28 JMJP Marks Anniversary of Chairman Mao's Statement Supporting Congolese (Kinshasa) People, 2. SCMP 4070, 27.
- Nov 29 The Albanian People Are Advancing Triumphantly on the Revolutionary Road, 1,2.
- Dec 1 JMJP Hails Southern Yemen's Independence, 6. SCMP 4073, 30.
- Dec 4 Combine the Study of Mao Tse-tung's Thought with Application so as to Get Quick Results, 2. SCMP 4076, 19.
- Dec 7 JMJP, Chieh-fang Chun-pao (CFCP) Hail Establishment of Tientsin Municipal Revolutionary Committee, 1. SCMP 4077, 20.
- Dec 19 JMJP Greets Anniversary of South Vietnam National Front for Liberation, 1. SCMP 4085, 38.
- Dec 22 JMJP Editorial on Nationwide Movement to Run Study Courses in Mao Tse-tung's Thought, 1. SCMP 4088, 26.

1968

- Jan 1 Ushering in the All-Round Victory of the Great Proletarian Cultural Revolution (New Year's Day editorial), 2. SCMP 4092, 3.
- Jan 7 JMJP and CFCP Welcome Kiangsi Provincial Revolutionary Committee, 1. SCMP 4096, 26 (extracts).
- Jan 26 Kansu Provincial Revolutionary Committee Hailed by JMJP and CFCP, 1. SCMP 4110, 10 (extracts).

1968

Jan 30　JMJP and CFCP Hail Honan Provincial Revolutionary Committee, 1. SCMP 4111, 16 (summary).

Feb 2　JMJP Cheers South Vietnam Victory, 1. SCMP 4112, 32.

Feb 3　JMJP Acclaims Establishment of Diplomatic Relations between China, Southern Yemen, 6. SCMP 4113, 30.

Feb 5　Editorial Hails Founding of Hopei Provincial Revolutionary Committee, 1. SCMP 4114, 22.

Feb 7　Peking Papers Greet Hupeh Provincial Revolutionary Committee, 1. SCMP 4115, 23.

Feb 15　JMJP Greets Anniversary of Unification of South Vietnam PLAF, 2. SCMP 4121, 30.

Feb 23　JMJP Editorial Greets Kwangtung Provincial Revolutionary Committee, 1. SCMP 4126, 22.

Mar 10　JMJP and CFCP Joint Editorial Hails Establishment of Kirin Provincial Revolutionary Committee, 1. SCMP 4138, 16.

Mar 19　JMJP, CFCP Pay Glowing Tribute to Vietnamese People, 1. SCMP 4144, 28.

Mar 25　Editorial Hails Kiangsu Revolutionary Committee, 1. SCMP 4148, 18.

Mar 30　Revolutionary Committees Are Fine, 1. SCMP 4151, 16.

Apr 10　Peking Papers Acclaim Hunan Revolutionary Committee, 1. SCMP 4158, 19.

Apr 12　Founding of New Regional Revolutionary Committee in Northwest China Hailed by Peking Papers, 1. SCMP 4159, 28.

Apr 20　Victory for the Proletarian Revolutionaries, 1. SCMP 4168, 19.

May 1　May Day Editorial: Advance from Victory to Victory, 1. SCMP 4170, 1.

May 3　The Yenan Spirit Shines Forever (Foundation of Shensi provincial revolutionary committee), 1. SCMP 4179, 12.

May 12　JMJP and CFCP Editorial Hails Founding of Liaoning Provincial Revolutionary Committee, 1. SCMP 4180, 13.

May 17　An Epoch-Marking Document (Second anniversary of the publication of the "Directive"), 1,2.

May 27　JMJP Greets Revolutionary Mass Movement in France, Europe, North America, 1. SCMP 4190, 31.

Jun 2　The 70 Million People of Szechwan March Forward (Szechwan revolutionary committee established), 1. SCMP 4198, 5.

Jun 18　JMJP Warmly Welcomes President Nyerere of Tanzania, 1. SCMP 4204, 37.

Jul 1　Propagate the Party Style of Work of Closely Uniting with the Masses (Anniversary of the birth of CCP), 2.

Aug 1　Firm Pillar of the Dictatorship of the Proletariat (PLA anniversary), 2. SCMP 4233, 14.

Aug 5　Unite under the Leadership of the Proletarian Headquarters Headed by Chairman Mao (Anniversary of Mao's "Bombard the Headquarters--My Big Character Poster"), 1. SCMP 4236, 13.

Aug 15　Warmly Acclaim Establishment of Yunnan Provincial Revolutionary Committee, 1. SCMP 4242, 25.

Aug 18　JMJP Editorial Marks Second Anniversary of Chairman Mao's First Review of Red Guards, 1. SCMP 4244, 13.

Aug 21　JMJP and CFCP Editorial Acclaims Fukien Provincial Revolutionary Committee, 1. SCMP 4246, 23.

Aug 28　Kwangsi Revolutionary Committee Acclaimed in Editorial, 1. SCMP 4250, 19.

Sep 1　Carry the Great Revolution on the Front of Journalism through to the End, 1. SCMP 4253, 17.

Sep 7　JMJP, CFCP Joint Editorial: Long Live All-Round Victory of the Great Proletarian Cultural Revolution, 1. SCMP 4255, 13.

Sep 12　JMJP and Hung-chi Commentators' Article: On the Question of Re-educating Intellectuals, 1. SCMP 4259, 19.

Sep 18　JMJP Editorial: The Course Toward Victory for Revolutionary People of All Countries, 2. SCMP 4264, 26.

Sep 20　JMJP Hails Revolutionary Action of Albania, 1. SCMP 4265, 23.

Sep 25　Joint Editorial by JMJP and CFCP on First Anniversary of Chairman Mao's Inspection Tour, 1. SCMP 4269, 23.

Sep 29　Editorial: A Great Fighting Friendship, 1. SCMP 4271, 34.

Oct 1　March Forward Bravely on the Road of Victory (National Day joint editorial), 2.

Nov 25　Study History of Struggle between Two Lines Conscientiously, 3. SCMP 4309, 25.

Nov 29　JMJP Editorial: Glorious and Militant Road, 2. SCMP 4312, 36.

Dec 14　Persevere in the Great Principle of Practicing Frugality in Carrying Out Revolution, 1. SCMP 4324, 6.

1969

Jan 1　Place Mao Tse-tung's Thought in Command of Everything, 2. SCMP 4332, 9.

Feb 17　JMJP Editorial: Be Good at Translating the Party's Policy into Action of the Masses, 1. SCMP 4364, 10.

Feb 21　JMJP Editorial: Grasp Revolution, Promote Production and Win New Victories on the Industrial Front, 1. SCMP 4365, 12.

Mar 4　JMJP and CFCP Editorial: Down with the New Tsars! 1. SCMP 4373, 17.

Mar 22　Grasp Revolution and Promote Spring Farming to Win a New Bumper Harvest, 1. SCMP 4385, 10.

Apr 17　JMJP Marks Anniversary of Chairman Mao's Statement in Support of Afro-American Struggle, 4. SCMP 4401, 22.

May 4　Jubilee of the May Fourth Movement (Joint editorial by JMJP, Hung-chi, and CFCP), 3. SCMP 4412, 8.

Jun 9　Hold Aloft the Banner of Unity of the Party's Ninth Congress and Win Still Greater Victories, 1. SCMP 4437, 12.

Jul 1　Long Live the Communist Party of China! (Joint editorial), 2. SCMP 4450, 14.

Aug 1　The People's Army Is Invincible (Joint editorial), 2. SCMP 4470, 13.

Aug 25　Firmly Grasp Revolutionary Mass Criticism (Joint editorial), 1. SCMP 4485, 14.

Oct 1　Struggle to Continue to Consolidate the Dictatorship of the Proletariat (National Day joint editorial), 2.

Nov 5　JMJP Editorial: Pay Attention to Methods of Work, 1. SCMP 4536, 12.

Nov 20　JMJP Editorial: Cadres Should Persist in Taking Part in Collective Productive Labor, 1. SCMP 4545, 14.

Nov 23　JMJP Editorial: Long Live Fighting Friendship between Chinese and Albanian Peoples, 5. SCMP 4547, 22.

Nov 28　JMJP Editorial Condemns Criminal Schemes of U.S.-Japanese Reactionaries, 1. SCMP 4550, 40.

1969

Nov 29 JMJP Editorial Greets 25th Anniversary of Liberation of Albania, 2. SCMP 4551, 24.

1970

Jan 1   Usher in Great 1970's, 2. SCMP 4572, 135.
Feb 3   JMJP Warmly Greets 40th Anniversary of Vietnam Worker's Party, 1. SCMP 4595, 101.
Mar 7   Consult the Masses and Wrest Another Good Harvest, 1. SCMP 4615, 129.
Mar 29 Implement Principle of Self-Reliance and Hard Struggle in Every Basic Unit, 1. SCMP 4630, 14.
Apr 1   Advance from Victory to Still Greater Victory along the Course Charted by Ninth National Congress of Communist Party of China, 1. SCMP 4632, 119.
Apr 30 Signal Victory of Militant Unity of Three Indo-Chinese Peoples, 1. SCMP 4652, 233.
May 1   A Great People, Brave, Industrious, and Intelligent (Labor Day editorial), 2. SCMP 4652, 202.
May 5   New War Adventure of Nixon Administration, 1. SCMP 4656, 171.
May 23 Reform the World View (Anniversary of publication of Mao's "Talks at the Yenan Forum"), 1,2.
Jun 9   JMJP Editorial Welcomes Rumanian People's Envoy of Friendship, 1. SCMP 4678, 105.
Jun 23 Resolutely Smash Aggressive U.S.-Japan Military Alliance, 1. SCMP 4688, 85.
Jun 24 JMJP Envoy Warmly Welcomes Envoys of Heroic Korean People, 1. SCMP 4689, 114.
Jun 25 People of Asia, Unite and Drive U.S. Aggressors Out of Asia (Joint editorial), 1. SCMP 4688, 99.
Jul 1   Communist Party Members Should Be Progressive Elements of the Proletariat (Joint editorial on CCP anniversary), 2.
Jul 9   Grasp Well the Work on Intellectual Youths Who Settle in the Country, 1. SCMP 4702, 126.
Jul 21 New Development in Friendly Relations and Cooperation between China and Congo, 1. SCMP 4707, 130.
Jul 27 U.S. Imperialism Has Not Laid Down Its Butchers' Knife, 1. SCMP 4711, 77.
Aug 1   Heighten Vigilance, Defend the Motherland (PLA anniversary), 2. SCMP 4714, 13.
Aug 2   Warm Welcome to Distinguished Southern Yemeni Guests, 2. SCMP 4715, 77.
Aug 6   Warm Welcome to Distinguished Sudanese Guests, 2. SCMP 4719, 29.
Sep 2   JMJP Editorial Salutes Heroic Vietnamese People Standing in Forefront of Anti-U.S. Struggle, 1. SCMP 4737, 130.
Sep 3   Down with Revived Japanese Militarism, 1. SCMP 4738, 14.
Sep 14 JMJP Editorial Greets Triumphant Close of Third Summit Conference of Non-Aligned Countries, 1. SCMP 4744, 193.
Sep 23 In Agriculture, Learn from Tachai, 1. SCMP 4750, 172.
Oct 1   Continue the Revolution and March Ahead in Victory (Joint editorial on National Day), 1,2.
Oct 12 Laotian People's War against U.S. Aggression and for National Salvation Is Bound to Win, 1. SCMP 4763, 199.
Oct 15 Welcome the Establishment of Diplomatic Relations between China, Canada, 1. SCMP 4765, 25.

1970

Oct 22 Greet Establishment of Diplomatic Relations between China and Equatorial Guinea, 1. SCMP 4768, 165.
Oct 25 A Great Friendship Sealed in Blood (Anniversary of CPV entry into Korean War), 1. SCMP 4771, 73.
Oct 30 Study Chairman Mao's Philosophic Works Conscientiously, 1. SCMP 4775, 16.
Nov 8   Welcome the Establishment of Diplomatic Relations between China and Italy, 1. SCMP 4781, 109.
Nov 9   JMJP Editorial Greets National Day of Kingdom of Cambodia, 1. SCMP 4781, 103.
Nov 10 JMJP Editorial: Warmly Welcome Distinguished Pakistan Guests, 1. SCMP 4782, 149.
Nov 20 JMJP Expresses Support for Latin American Countries' Struggle in Defense of Ocean Rights, 1. SCMP 4789, 70.
Nov 21 JMJP Refutes Laird's Arrogant Ravings, 1. SCMP 4789, 81.
Nov 22 The Vietnamese People Are Fighting Well! 1.
Nov 29 JMJP Editorial Marks 26th Anniversary of Liberation of Albania and Victory of Albanian People's Revolution, 1. SCMP 4793, 29.
Dec 3   JMJP Greets Establishment of Diplomatic Relations between China and Ethiopia, 1. SCMP 4795, 111.
Dec 13 Resolutely Support Vietnamese People in Carrying War against U.S. Aggression and for National Salvation to Complete Victory, 1. SCMP 4802, 163.
Dec 18 Long Live Militant Friendship between Chinese and Cambodian Peoples, 1. SCMP 4806, 140.
Dec 20 Ten Years of Brilliant Victories (NLF anniversary), 1. SCMP 4808, 76.

1971

Jan 1   JMJP Editorial: Advance Victoriously along Chairman Mao's Revolutionary Line, 1,2. SCMP 4814, 146.
Jan 6   JMJP Editorial Greets Fifteenth Anniversary of Founding of Laotian Patriotic Front, 1. SCMP 4818, 78.
Jan 7   JMJP Editorial: New Chapter in Relations between China and Chile, 1. SCMP 4819, 105.
Jan 11 JMJP Marks Anniversary of People's Republic of Albania, 1. SCMP 4822, 65.
Jan 23 JMJP: Down with Doctrine of Big-Nation Hegemony, 1. SCMP 4830, 110.
Jan 31 JMJP: Victory for Chairman Mao's Line on Party Building, 1. SCMP 4834, 75.
Feb 12 JMJP: Hail Establishment of Diplomatic Relations between China and Nigeria, 2. SCMP 4843, 87.
Feb 14 JMJP Editorial: All-Out Support to Peoples of Three Countries in Indochina in War against U.S. Aggression and for National Salvation, 1. SCMP 4844, 130.
Feb 18 JMJP: Advance along Chairman Mao's Revolutionary Line to Achieve Another Good Harvest, 1. SCMP 4847, 25.
Mar 11 JMJP: Long Live Great Friendship and Militant Unity between Chinese and Vietnamese Peoples! 2. SCMP 4862, 43.
Mar 23 JMJP: A Year of Battle, a Year of Victory, 1. SCMP 4870, 188.
Mar 28 JMJP: Warm Congratulations on Spectacular Victory on Highway Nine, 1. SCMP 4873, 93.

1971

Apr 4   JMJP Editorial Greets Establishment of Diplomatic Relations between China and Cameroon, 1. SCMP 4877, 126.

Apr 15   JMJP: Korean People's Struggle for Unification of Fatherland Is Bound to Win, 1. SCMP 4884, 38.

Apr 25   JMJP: Fifty Million Indochinese People Are Invincible, 1. SCMP 4891, 115.

Apr 27   JMJP Editorial: Salute to American People Who Are Fighting Valiantly, 2. SCMP 4893, 234.

May 1   Long Live the Great Unity of the People of the World (Labor Day joint editorial), 1,2.

May 3   JMJP: Salute Heroic Palestinian People, 1. SCMP 4897, 214.

May 5   JMJP: Warm Congratulations and Resolute Support, 1. SCMP 4899, 33.

May 7   The Inevitable Road in the Revolutionary Process ("May 7 Directive" anniversary), 1.

May 9   JMJP Editorial Hails Establishment of Official Relations with San Marino, 1. SCMP 4901, 145.

May 20   The Principle of Anti-Imperialist Struggle (Joint editorial), 1.

May 29   JMJP: Welcome Establishment of Diplomatic Relations between China and Austria, 1. SCMP 4914, 134.

Jun 1   JMJP: Warmly Welcome the Distinguished Rumanian Guests, 1. SCMP 4915, 182.

Jun 6   JMJP: Salute Heroic People of South Vietnam, 2. SCMP 4919, 143.

Jun 20   JMJP: In Industry, Learn from Taching, 1. SCMP 4925, 87.

Jun 25   The Asian People's Struggle in Opposing U.S. Imperialist's Invasion Will Triumph, 1.

Jul 4   JMJP: A Just Stand, a Reasonable Proposal, 1. SCMP 4936, 165.

Jul 11   The Strong Alliance Opposing Imperialist Invasion (Joint editorial on Sino-Korean treaty anniversary), 1,2.

Jul 20   The Vietnamese People's Nationalistic Hopes Will Be Fulfilled, 1.

Jul 27   JMJP: Heroic Korean People Are Invincible, 1. SCMP 4951, 163.

Aug 1   JMJP Editorial: New Chapter in Sino-Sierra Leone Friendship, 1,3. SCMP 4954, 142.

Aug 7   JMJP Editorial: Greeting the Establishment of Diplomatic Relations between China and Turkey, 1. SCMP 4958, 92.

Aug 19   JMJP Editorial: Greeting Establishment of Diplomatic Relations between China and Iran, 1. SCMP 4966, 60.

Aug 27   JMJP Editorial: Our Party Is Advancing Vigorously, 1. SCMP 4970, 86.

Aug 31   Crush the U.S. Imperialist Military Adventure in Invading Laos, 1.

Sep 2   JMJP Editorial: U.S. Imperialism Doomed to Defeat, Vietnamese People Bound to Win, 1. SCMP 4974, 87.

Sep 9   JMJP Editorial Marks 23rd Anniversary of Founding of Democratic People's Republic of Korea, 1. SCMP 4978, 41.

Sep 18   JMJP Editorial: On Embarkation of Japanese Militarism on Old Road of Aggression, 1. SCMP 4984, 91.

Oct 6   JMJP Editorial: Warm Welcome to Distinguished Ethiopian Guests, 1. SCMP 4996, 45.

Oct 12   JMJP Editorial Extends Warm Greeting on Lao Independence Day, 1. SCMP 4999, 219.

Oct 28   JMJP Editorial Greets Establishment of Diplomatic Relations between China and Belgium, 2. SCMP 5008, 217.

Oct 28   The Historical Trend Is Inevitable, 1.

Nov 2   JMJP Editorial: Promote Friendship, Improve Skill Together, 1. SCMP 5012, 197.

Nov 4   JMJP Editorial Hails Establishment of Diplomatic Relations between China and Peru, 1. SCMP 5013, 256.

Nov 8   JMJP Editorial: Glorious Course, Great Victory, 1,2. SCMP 5017, 161.

Nov 9   JMJP Editorial: Heroic Cambodian People Are Bound to Triumph, 1. SCMP 5017, 166.

Nov 12   JMJP Editorial Welcomes Establishment of Diplomatic Relations between China and Lebanon, 1. SCMP 5020, 79.

Nov 15   JMJP Editorial: A Grand Meeting of Friendship, a Tremendous Success, 1. SCMP 5022, 142.

Nov 16   JMJP Hails Establishment of Diplomatic Relations between China and Rwanda, 1. SCMP 5022, 150.

Nov 20   JMJP Editorial: Warm Welcome to Glorious Envoys of Vietnamese People, 1. SCMP 5025, 177.

Nov 28   The Unbreakable Militant Bond of the Chinese and Vietnamese Peoples, 2.

Nov 29   Heroic People, Glorious Festival (Albanian liberation anniversary), 1,4.

Dec 1   JMJP, Hung-chi, and CFCP Editorial: Sum Up Experience in Strengthening Party Leadership, 1. SCMP 5032, 22.

Dec 12   Welcome the Establishment of Diplomatic Relations between the Senegal Republic and Our Nation, 1.

Dec 16   Welcome the Establishment of Diplomatic Relations between the Republic of Iceland and Our Nation, 1.

Dec 27   JMJP Editorial Comments on 26th Session of UN General Assembly, 1. SCMP 5054, 205.

1972

Jan 1   Unite to Win Greater Victories (New Year's Day joint editorial), 1,2.

Jan 14   JMJP Editorial Hails Establishment of Diplomatic Relations between China and Cyprus, 1. SCMP 5060, 76.

Jan 29   A Great Proposal in Hastening the Peaceful Unification of Korea, 1.

Jan 31   The Indian Invasion of East Pakistan Must Not Be Legalized, 1.

Feb 3   JMJP Editorial: Resolute Support for Pakistan People's Just Struggle, 2. SCMP 5076, 102.

Feb 4   JMJP Editorial: U.S. Imperialism Must Stop War of Aggression against Vietnam at Once, 1. SCMP 5076, 90.

Feb 17   JMJP Editorial Greets Establishment of Diplomatic Relations between China and Mexico, 1. SCMP 5081, 65.

Feb 20   JMJP Editorial Greets Establishment of Diplomatic Relations between China and Argentina, 1. SCMP 5084, 204.

Feb 27   JMJP Editorial Hails Establishment of Diplomatic Relations between China and Malta, 1. SCMP 5089, 183.

Mar 9   JMJP Editorial: Grasp Education in Line and Promote Spring Farming, 1. SCMP 5097, 62.

Mar 23   The Cambodian People's War to Resist the U.S. and Save Their Nation Will Triumph, 1.

Apr 2   JMJP Editorial Welcomes Distinguished Guests from Malta, 1. SCMP 5113, 250.

1972

Apr 16 JMJP Editorial: Take Grain as Key Link and Insure All-Round Development, 1. SCMP 5122, 223.
Apr 17 JMJP Editorial: New Development in China-Mauritius Friendly Relations, 2. SCMP 5123, 34.
Apr 18 JMJP Editorial Says Vietnamese People Will Surely Win, U.S. Aggressors Are Bound to Fail, 1. SCMP 5123, 41.
Apr 24 Banner of Struggle, Path of Victory (Anniversary of establishment of Korean people's revolutionary army), 1.
Apr 24 JMJP Editorial: Learn from Past Mistakes to Avoid Future Ones, Cure the Sickness to Save the Patient, 2. SCMP 5133, 1.
Apr 25 JMJP Editorial: The People of the Three Indochinese Countries Are Fighting in Unity and Advancing in Victory, 1,3. SCMP 5128, 27.
May 9 JMJP Editorial Hails Founding of Asian Table Tennis Union, 1. SCMP 5137, 215.
May 14 JMJP Editorial: Warmly Welcome Distinguished Somali Guests, 1. SCMP 5140, 136.
May 23 To Persist in the Revolutionary Line of Chairman Mao Is Victory (Anniversary of Mao's talks at the Yenan Forum), 1.
May 25 JMJP Editorial Warmly Greets Ninth Anniversary of African Liberation Day, 1. SCMP 5148, 66.
Jun 5 The Righteous Struggle of the Arab People Will Triumph, 1.
Jun 6 JMJP Editorial: Heroic Vietnamese People Stride Forward in Triumph, 1. SCMP 5155, 153.
Jun 7 JMJP Editorial: Welcome Establishment of Diplomatic Relations between PRC and Greece, 1. SCMP 5156, 31.
Jun 10 JMJP Editorial: Promote Physical Culture and Build Up People's Health, 1. SCMP 5158, 97.
Jun 25 The Righteous Endeavor of Resisting Invasion Is Invincible (Korean liberation war anniversary), 1,2.
Jun 25 JMJP Welcomes Distinguished Guests from Sri Lanka, 1. SCMP 5168, 117.
Jun 30 JMJP Greets Establishment of Diplomatic Relations between China and Guyana, 1. SCMP 5172, 112.
Jul 6 JMJP: Editorial on Study of Marxist Theory, 1. SCMP 5176, 61.
Jul 9 JMJP Editorial: A Good Beginning, 1. SCMP 5177, 117.
Jul 20 JMJP Editorial: A Just Cause Is Invincible, 1. SCMP 5185, 35.
Jul 28 JMJP Warmly Congratulates Samdech Norodom Sihanouk on Complete Success in Five-Nation Visit, 1. SCMP 5190, 74.
Aug 1 Develop Our Glorious Tradition (Joint editorial on anniversary of founding of PLA), 1,3.
Aug 2 A Just Position, a Reasonable Proposal, 1.
Aug 4 JMJP Hails Vietnamese People's Fresh Victory, 1. SCMP 5196, 142.
Aug 13 JMJP Editorial Says Iron Will of Vietnamese People Is Unshakable, 1. SCMP 5202, 169.
Aug 28 JMJP Editorial: Principle and Justice Upheld, 1. SCMP 5212, 43.
Sep 1 Victory Will Go to the Heroic Vietnamese People (North Vietnam national day), 1.
Sep 2 JMJP Editorial: Promote Friendship, Strengthen Unity, 1. SCMP 5215, 175.
Sep 9 JMJP Editorial Greets 24th Anniversary of Founding of Democratic People's Republic of Korea, 1. SCMP 5219, 119.

1972

Sep 14 JMJP Editorial: Monumental Gathering of Friendship and Unity, 1. SCMP 5223, 72.
Sep 28 JMJP Editorial Warmly Greets Establishment of Diplomatic Relations between China and Togo, 1. SCMP 5232, 50.
Sep 30 JMJP Editorial: New Page in Annals of Sino-Japanese Relations, 2. SCMP 5233, 96.
Oct 1 To Win New Victories (National Day joint editorial), 1.
Oct 13 JMJP Greets Establishment of Diplomatic Relations between China and Federal Republic of Germany, 1. SCMP 5242, 161.
Oct 16 JMJP Editorial Hails Establishment of Diplomatic Relations between China and Maldives, 1. SCMP 5243, 205.
Nov 1 JMJP Editorial Says U.S. Government Faces Test, 1. SCMP 5253, 251.
Nov 8 JMJP Warmly Greets Establishment of Diplomatic Relations between China and Malagasy, 1. SCMP 5258, 233.
Nov 9 JMJP Editorial Warmly Greets Cambodian People's Glorious Festival, 1. SCMP 5259, 31.
Nov 15 JMJP Warmly Welcomes Distinguished Nepalese Guests, 1. SCMP 5263, 41.
Nov 18 JMJP Welcomes Establishment of Diplomatic Relations between China and Luxembourg, 1. SCMP 5264, 86.
Nov 25 Welcome the Establishment of Diplomatic Relations with Jamaica, 1.
Nov 28 The Heroic Albanian People Are Invincible, 1.
Nov 30 Welcome the Establishment of Relations with the Republic of Chad, 1.
Dec 9 Welcome Honored Guests from Guinea, 1.
Dec 24 JMJP Hails China's Establishment of Diplomatic Relations with Australia and New Zealand, 1. SCMP 5289, 127.
Dec 27 JMJP Editorial: Warm Welcome to Honored Envoy of South Vietnamese People, 1. SCMP 5291, 87.

1973

Jan 1 New Year's Joint Editorial, 1.
Jan 10 JMJP Editorial Welcomes Distinguished Guests from Zaire, 1. SCMP 5300, 41.
Jan 26 JMJP Editorial Strongly Condemns New Crime of Portuguese Colonialism, 5. SCMP 5311, 130.
Jan 28 JMJP Editorial Hails Signing of Vietnam Agreement, 1. SCMP 5312, 40.
Feb 22 JMJP on Work of Communist Youth League, 1. SCMP 5326, 6.
Feb 28 JMJP Editorial Hails Signing of Laos Agreement, 1. SCMP 5328, 116.
Mar 1 JMJP Editorial: Paris Agreement Must Be Strictly Implemented, 1. SCMP 5332, 69.
Mar 2 JMJP Editorial: Go All Out to Do Spring Farming Well, 1. SCMP 5333, 90.
Mar 3 JMJP Editorial: Congratulate Paris International Conference on Its Successful Conclusion, 1. SCMP 5333, 111.
Mar 8 JMJP Editorial: Working Women Are Great Revolutionary Force, 1. SCMP 5337, 59.
Mar 12 JMJP Welcomes Establishment of Diplomatic Relations between China and Spain, 1. SCMP 5339, 157.
Mar 23 JMJP Editorial: Cambodian People Are Bound to Win, 1. SCMP 5347, 72.

1973

Mar 25   JMJP Editorial: Warm Welcome to Distinguished Guest from Cameroon, 1. SCMP 5348, 113.
Apr 3   JMJP Editorial: Continue to Strive for Complete Implementation of Paris Agreement, 1. SCMP 5354, 184.
Apr 11   Warmly Greets the Great Success of Prince Sihanouk's Inspection of the Cambodian Liberated Areas, 1.
Apr 11   The Korean People's Wish to Unify Their Nation Will Be Realized, 4.
Apr 19   Welcome to President Eche Verria, 1.
Apr 24   Make Better Use of the Main Forces in the Working Class, 1.
Apr 25   Three Years of Unity, Struggle, and Victory, 1.
May 25   JMJP Editorial: African People's Festival of Militant Unity, 1. SCMP 5388, 74.
Jun 4   JMJP Editorial: Warmly Welcome Vietnamese Comrades-in-Arms to China, 1. SCMP 5394, 172.
Jun 6   JMJP Editorial: Salute to Heroic South Vietnamese People, 2. SCMP 5396, 48.
Jun 17   JMJP Editorial: Work Persistently for Full Implementation of Paris Agreement, 1. SCMP 5403, 150.
Jun 20   JMJP Editorial Welcomes Distinguished Malian Guests, 1. SCMP 5405, 234.
Jun 25   JMJP Marks 23rd Anniversary of Fatherland Liberation War of Korea, 1. SCMP 5408, 152.
Jul 5   JMJP Greets Samdech Sihanouk's Triumphant Tour of Africa and Europe, 1. SCMP 5415, 29.
Jul 11   JMJP Editorial: "May 7" Cadre Schools Must Be Run Well, 1. SCMP 5420, 59.
Jul 27   JMJP Editorial Welcomes Congolese President, 1. SCMP 5430, 66.
Jul 27   JMJP Editorial Says Korea Must Be Reunified, 1. SCMP 5429, 30.
Aug 7   Do a Better Job in Sending Educated Youth to the Countryside, 1.
Aug 25   A Meeting of Unity, a Meeting of Friendship (Asian-African-Latin American ping-pong games), 1.
Sep 2   JMJP Greets 28th Anniversary of Democratic Republic of Vietnam, 4. SCMP 5454, 144.
Sep 7   JMJP Hails Conclusion of Tri-Continental Table Tennis Tournament, 1. SCMP 5458, 202.
Sep 9   A Glorious History of Struggle (North Korean national day), 2.
Sep 11   JMJP Editorial: A Warm Welcome to President Pompidou, 1. SCMP 5460, 322.
Sep 13   JMJP Editorial Greets Successful Conclusion of Fourth Summit Conference of Non-Aligned Countries, 2. SCMP 5462, 90.
Sep 16   A Great Step in Achieving Racial Harmony in Laos, 1.
Sep 16   JMJP Greets Establishment of Diplomatic Relations between China and Upper Volta, 1. SCMP 5463, 174.
Sep 29   Do a Good Job in Managing the Militia, 1.
Oct 1   Study Seriously, and Continue to March Ahead (National Day joint editorial), 1.
Oct 1   JMJP Editorial Greets Founding of Republic of Guinea-Bissau, 3. SCMP 5473, 178.
Oct 10   JMJP Editorial Warmly Welcomes Canadian Prime Minister Trudeau to Visit China, 1. SCMP 5480, 75.
Oct 12   JMJP Editorial: Warm Greeting to Glorious Day of Laos People, 1. SCMP 5481, 139.
Oct 15   JMJP Editorial: Arab People's Cause against Aggression Invincible, 1. SCMP 5483, 27.
Oct 26   JMJP Editorial: Naked Display of Power Politics, 1. SCMP 5489, 79.
Oct 31   JMJP Editorial Warmly Welcomes Distinguished Guests from South Pacific, 1. SCMP 5493, 25.
Nov 6   JMJP Editorial Warmly Welcomes Sierra Leone President Stevens' Visit to China, 1. SCMP 5496, 173.
Nov 9   Warm Greetings to the Glorious Festival of the Cambodian People, 1.
Nov 18   JMJP Editorial Warmly Welcomes Close Comrades-in-Arms from South Vietnam, 1. SCMP 5503, 83.
Nov 24   JMJP Editorial: Korean People's Struggle for Reunification Will Be Victorious, 2. SCMP 5508, 95.
Nov 29   The Glorious Festival of the Heroic Albanian People (Anniversary of Albanian liberation), 1.
Dec 8   JMJP Editorial Warmly Welcomes Distinguished Nepalese Guests, 1. SCMP 5517, 37.

1974

Jan 1   New Year Message--1974 New Year's Day Editorial, 1. SPRCP 5532, 162.
Jan 27   JMJP Editorial: Paris Agreement Should Be Thoroughly Implemented, 1. SPRCP 5547, 116.
Feb 2   JMJP Editorial: Carry the Struggle to Criticize Lin Piao and Confucius through to End, 1. SPRCP 5550, 36.
Feb 20   JMJP Editorial Criticizes Lin Piao's Reactionary Program, 1. SPRCP 5563, 154.
Feb 21   JMJP Editorial: Warm Welcome to President K.D. Kaunda, 1. SPRCP 5563, 176.
Feb 25   JMJP Editorial: Warm Welcome to President Houari Boumediene, 1. SPRCP 5567, 156.
Mar 3   JMJP Editorial: Criticize Lin Piao and Confucius, Do Spring Farming Well, 1. SPRCP 5571, 101.
Mar 8   JMJP Editorial: Let All Women Rise Up, 1. SPRCP 5575, 51.
Mar 15   JMJP Editorial: Further Criticism of "Restrain Oneself and Return to the Rites," 1. SPRCP 5580, 47.
Mar 22   Welcome the Establishment of Relations with Guinea (Bissau), 1.
Mar 23   JMJP Editorial: Heroic Cambodian People Advancing Triumphantly, 1. SPRCP 5584, 33.
Mar 24   JMJP Editorial: Warm Welcome to President Nyerere, 1. SPRCP 5585, 66.
Apr 1   JMJP Editorial Welcomes Comrades-in-Arms from Heroic Land of Cambodia, 1. SPRCP 5591, 150.
Apr 7   JMJP Warmly Greets Laos People's New Victory, 1. SPRCP 5595, 124.
Apr 9   Resolutely Support the Just Demands of the Third World, 1.
Apr 10   JMJP Editorial: Grasp Criticism of Lin Piao, Confucius and Promote Industrial Production, 1. SPRCP 5598, 15.
Apr 24   JMJP Editorial Hails Anniversary of Indochinese People's Summit Conference, 1. SPRCP 5607, 36.
Apr 30   Welcome the Establishment of Diplomatic Relations with Gabon Republic, 1.
May 4   JMJP Editorial: Commemorate 55th Anniversary of May Fourth Movement, 1. SPRCP 5613, 59.
May 5   JMJP Acclaims Victory of Third World's United Struggle against Hegemonism, 1. SPRCP 5614, 129.

1974

May 6	JMJP Editorial: A Warm Welcome to President Leopold Sedar Senghor, 1. SPRCP 5615, 186.
May 11	JMJP Editorial: Warm Welcome to Friendly Envoy from Pakistan, 1. SPRCP 5618, 84.
May 17	JMJP Editorial Welcomes President Makarios, 1. SPRCP 5622, 34.
May 28	JMJP Editorial: New Development of Friendly Relations between China and Malaysia, 1. SPRCP 5630, 243.
Jun 6	JMJP Warmly Greets Anniversary of Provisional Revolutionary Government of Republic of South Vietnam, 1. SPRCP 5636, 43.
Jun 18	JMJP Editorial: Train a Contingent of Theoretical Workers in Struggle, 1. SPRCP 5644, 134.
Jun 20	JMJP Editorial: African People Go Forward in Triumph, 1. SPRCP 5645, 26.
Jun 23	JMJP Acclaims Establishment of Diplomatic Relations between China and Trinidad and Tobago, 1. SPRCP 5646, 79.
Jun 25	JMJP Editorial Marks 24th Anniversary of Korean Fatherland Liberation War, 1. SPRCP 5648, 40.
Jun 30	Welcome the Establishment of Relations with Venezuela, 1.
Jul 1	JMJP Editorial: The Party Exercises Leadership in Everything, 1. SPRCP 5652, 217.
Jul 3	It Makes a Big Difference in Strengthening Leadership (Commerce work), 1.
Jul 4	JMJP Editorial on Korea's Reunification, 1. SPRCP 5654, 82.
Jul 22	JMJP Editorial: Warmly Greet Establishment of Diplomatic Relations between China and Republic of Niger, 1. SPRCP 5666, 148.
Aug 8	Do a Good Job in the Patriotic Hygiene Campaign, 1.
Aug 7	JMJP Editorial Greets New Development in Relations between China and Brazil, 1. SPRCP 5683, 23.
Aug 23	Warm Greetings to the Glorious Festival of the Rumanian People, 1.
Sep 2	JMJP Warmly Greets DRVN National Day, 1. SPRCP 5695, 234.
Sep 2	JMJP Editorial: Warm Welcome to Distinguished Togolese Guests, 1. SPRCP 5695, 212.
Sep 6	The Great Victory of the Guinean (Bissau) People, 1.
Sep 8	Welcome to Honored Guests from Nigeria, 1.
Sep 9	JMJP Editorial: Greets Korean People's Glorious Festival, 1. SPRCP 5700, 222.
Sep 14	JMJP Editorial: Important Achievements of Mozambican People, 1. SPRCP 5703, 153.
Sep 17	JMJP Editorial: Warm Welcome to Mauritanian President Daddah, 1. SPRCP 5705, 251.
Sep 17	JMJP Warmly Hails Successful Conclusion of Seventh Asian Games, 1. SPRCP 5705, 273.
Sep 29	JMJP Greets Opening of China-Japan Regular Air Service, 1. SPRCP 5713, 215.
Oct 1	JMJP Editorial: Forward along Great Road of Socialism, 1. SPRCP 5715, 16.
Oct 4	JMJP Editorial Warmly Welcomes Distinguished Gabonese Guests, 1. SPRCP 5718, 284.
Oct 12	JMJP Warmly Greets Independence Day of Laos, 1. SPRCP 5724, 153.
Oct 18	JMJP: Warm Welcome to Distinguished Visitors from Denmark, 1. SPRCP 5727, 163.
Nov 5	JMJP Editorial: Warm Welcome to Prime Minister Williams, 1. SPRCP 5736, 100.
Nov 10	JMJP Editorial: Warmly Welcome Chairman Salem Robaya Ali to China, 1. SPRCP 5739, 248.

1974

Nov 28	JMJP Editorial: Push Ahead with the Movement in Criticism of Lin Piao and Confucius and Do It Well, 1. SPRCP 5751, 126.
Nov 29	JMJP Greets Albania's Liberation Anniversary, 1. SPRCP 5751, 137.
Dec 16	JMJP Editorial Welcomes Distinguished Guests from Zaire, 1. SPRCP 5761, 125.
Dec 19	JMJP Greets Establishment of Diplomatic Relations between China and Gambia, 1. SPRCP 5763, 80.

1975

Jan 1	New Year's Day Joint Editorial, 1.
Jan 7	JMJP Editorial: Warm Welcome to Distinguished Maltese Guests, 1. SPRCP 5775, 181.
Jan 9	JMJP Greets Establishment of Diplomatic Relations between China and Botswana, 1. SPRCP 5776, 36.
Jan 22	JMJP Editorial: Important Victory of Angolan People, 1. SPRCP 5785, 182.
Feb 3	JMJP Editorial Greets 45th Founding Anniversary of Vietnam Worker's Party, 1. SPRCP 5793, 39.
Feb 9	JMJP Editorial: Study Well Theory of Dictatorship of Proletariat, 1. SPRCP 5796, 132.
Feb 20	JMJP Editorial Welcomes Mozambique Comrades-in-Arms, 1. SPRCP 5803, 68.
Feb 27	JMJP Editorial Welcomes Congolese Prime Minister Henri Lopes, 1. SPRCP 5807, 37.
Feb 28	JMJP Editorial: Study Theory, Grasp Line, Promote Spring Farming, 1. SPRCP 5808, 61.
Mar 11	JMJP Editorial: Grasp Theoretical Study, Promote Industrial Production, 1. SPRCP 5816, 174.
Mar 12	JMJP Editorial Warmly Welcomes Distinguished Guests from Guyana, 1. SPRCP 5816, 184.
Mar 21	JMJP Editorial: Leading Cadres Should Take the Lead and Study Well, 1. SPRCP 5823, 90.
Mar 23	Five Years of Victorious Advance of the Cambodian People, 1.
Apr 1	JMJP Editorial Welcomes Tunisian Prime Minister, 1. SPRCP 5829, 167.
Apr 18	JMJP Editorial Warmly Welcomes President Kim Il Sung, 1. SPRCP 5841, 81.
Apr 18	JMJP Editorial: Great Historic Victory, 2. SPRCP 5841, 69.
Apr 19	JMJP Editorial Warmly Welcomes Distinguished Belgian Guests, 2. SPRCP 5842, 117.
Apr 25	Get Mobilized and Take Care of Hygiene, 1.
Apr 25	JMJP Editorial: Indochina Belongs to Indochinese Peoples, 2. SPRCP 5847, 123.
May 1	JMJP Warmly Greets Liberation of Saigon as Great Victory of World Significance, 2. SPRCP 5851, 111.
May 9	JMJP Editorial Commemorates Thirtieth Anniversary of Victory over German Fascism, 1. SPRCP 5856, 84.
May 20	JMJP Editorial: Illustrious Historic Document--in Celebration of the Fifth Anniversary of the Publication of Chairman Mao's "May 20" Statement, 1. SPRCP 5864, 20.
Jun 6	JMJP Editorial: Heroic People, Glorious Festival, 1. SPRCP 5876, 128.
Jun 7	JMJP Editorial Welcomes President and Mme. Marcos of Philippines, 1. SPRCP 5876, 113.
Jun 11	JMJP Editorial Warmly Welcomes Gambian President Dawda Kairaba Jawara, 1. SPRCP 5879, 26.

1975

Jun 25   JMJP Editorial: Great Victory of Korean People's Anti-Imperialist Revolutionary Struggle, 1. SPRCP 5888, 27.

Jun 25   JMJP Editorial: Warm Congratulations on the Rebirth of Mozambique, 1. SPRCP 5888, 34.

Jun 26   JMJP Editorial Marks Anniversary of Chairman Mao's Directive on Medical and Health Work, 1. SPRCP 5890, 108.

Jun 27   JMJP Editorial Warmly Welcomes President El Hadj Omar Bongo, 1. SPRCP 5889, 82.

Jun 30   JMJP Editorial Warmly Welcomes Distinguished Thai Guests, 1. SPRCP 5891, 183.

Jul 18   JMJP Greets Establishment of Diplomatic Relations between China and Sao Tome and Principe, 1. SPRCP 5903, 31.

Aug 3   JMJP Editorial: Fighting in Unity, Advance in Big Strides, 1. SPRCP 5914, 118.

Aug 15   JMJP Editorial: Warm Welcome to Glorious Envoys of Cambodian People, 1. SPRCP 5921, 195.

Sep 2   JMJP Editorial: Warm Greetings on Vietnamese People's Glorious Day, 1. SPRCP 5933, 154.

Sep 3   JMJP Editorial: In Commemoration of Thirtieth Anniversary of Victory in War of Resistance against Japan, 1. SPRCP 5934, 173.

Sep 4   JMJP Editorial: Unfold Criticism of "Water Margin," 1. SPRCP 5935, 16.

Sep 9   A Socialist New Tibet Is Marching Forward (Anniversary of founding of Tibet autonomous region), 1.

Sep 9   Wishing the Korean People Greater Victories, 2.

Sep 12   JMJP Editorial Hails Opening of Third National Games, 1. SPRCP 5941, 68.

Sep 22   JMJP Editorial Warmly Welcomes Vietnam Party and Government Delegation, 1. SPRCP 5948, 234.

Oct 1   JMJP Editorial: Sinkiang Is Advancing in Struggle to Combat and Prevent Revisionism, 2. SPRCP 5954, 40.

Oct 6   JMJP Editorial Warmly Welcomes Distinguished Yugoslav Guests, 1. SPRCP 5958, 124.

Oct 8   JMJP Greets Establishment of Diplomatic Relations between China and the People's Republic of Bangladesh, 1. SPRCP 5960, 220.

Oct 10   A Glorious History of Struggle, 1.

Oct 12   JMJP Warmly Greets Laos Independence Day, 1. SPRCP 5962, 34.

Oct 19   Commemorating the Fortieth Anniversary of the Victory of the Long March, 2.

Oct 21   JMJP Editorial: Build Up Tachai-Type Counties throughout Country, 1. SPRCP 5967, 73.

Oct 25   The Chinese and Korean Peoples Will Forever Unite and Struggle Together (Anniversary of CPV entering Korean War), 1.

Oct 29   JMJP Editorial: Warm Welcome to Chancellor Helmut Schmidt, 1. SPRCP 5971, 52.

Nov 7   JMJP Greets Establishment of Diplomatic Relations Between China and Fiji, 1. SPRCP 5977, 66.

Nov 11   JMJP Editorial Warmly Welcomes Distinguished Burmese Guests, 1. SPRCP 5979, 146.

Nov 14   JMJP Greets Angolan People's Victory, 5. SPRCP 5982, 79.

Nov 16   JMJP Greets Establishment of Diplomatic Relations between China and Western Samoa, 1. SPRCP 5983, 151.

Nov 20   Welcome the Establishment of Diplomatic Relations with Comoro Islands, 1.

Nov 29   March Forward in Great Strides on the Road of Victory, 1.

Dec 6   The Great Historical Victory of the Laotian People, 1.

Dec 21   Welcome to President da Costa, 1.

II. Outline of Subjects in the Subject Index
- A. Government
    1. Chinese People's Political Consultative Conference
    2. Establishment of Political Power (Includes establishment of revolutionary committees)
    3. National People's Congress
    4. Government Structure
        a. Local Government
        b. Elections and Local Congresses
        c. Urban Communes
        d. Local-National Balance of Power
        e. National Government
    5. Judicial System
    6. Public Security System
    7. Supervision Work
    8. General Bureaucratic Problems (See "Campaigns" for the Three-Anti and Five-Anti Campaigns)
    9. Government Institutions (Includes Academy of Agricultural Science, Academy of Science, Language Research Institute, and National Economic Commission)

- B. Chinese Communist Party
    1. Organization
        a. Central Party Meetings (Includes national conferences, congresses, and plenums)
        b. Local Party Structure
        c. Party Membership and Party Building
            1. Young Pioneers
            2. Communist Youth League
        d. Party Cadres
            1. Basic Level Cadres
            2. Middle Level Cadres
            3. National Level Cadres
        e. May Seventh Cadre Schools
        f. Revolutionary Three-Way Alliance
    2. Ideology
        a. Party Activities in Society (Includes mass line, propaganda, and general ideological work)
        b. Party Struggle Method (Criticism, self-criticism)
        c. Study Training Movements (See also "Campaigns")
        d. Marxism, Leninism, and Stalinism
        e. Red versus Expert

- C. Democratic Parties

- D. Mass Organizations
    1. All-China Athletic Federation
    2. All-China Federation of Industry and Commerce
    3. All-China Federation of Literary and Art Circles (Includes Union of Chinese Writers)
    4. All-China Federation of Supply and Marketing Cooperatives
    5. All-China Federation of Trade Unions
    6. All-China Students' Federation
    7. All-China Youth Federation
    8. China Committee for the Promotion of International Trade
    9. China Scientific and Technical Association
    10. Chinese People's Committee for World Peace
    11. Friendship Associations
        a. Sino-Albanian
        b. Sino-Algerian
        c. Sino-Cambodian
        d. Sino-Cuban
        e. Sino-Czechoslovakian
        f. Sino-Indonesian
        g. Sino-Japanese
        h. Sino-Mongolian
        i. Sino-Nepalese
        j. Sino-Soviet
    12. Red Cross Society of China
    13. Women's Federation

E. Campaigns
   1. Land Reform
   2. Marriage Law Reform
   3. Peace Signature Campaign
   4. Suppression of Counter-Revolutionaries
   5. Christian Reform Movement (Three-Self Renovation)
   6. Patriotic Compact Movement
   7. Resist-U.S. Aid-Korea
   8. National Patriotic Donation Campaign (For the Korean people)
   9. Production Increase and Austerity Campaign (For the Korean War)
   10. Three-Anti Campaign (Against corruption, waste, and bureaucracy)
   11. Five-Anti Campaign (Against bribery, tax evasion, stealing state properties, cheating on government contracts, and theft of state economic intelligence)
   12. Patriotic Public Health Campaigns
   13. Learn from the Advanced Experience of the U.S.S.R.
   14. Struggle against Bureaucratism, Commandism, and Unlawful Acts (Includes the Five Too Many: Tasks, meetings, documents, organizations, and concurrent cadre posts)
   15. Campaign to Increase Production and Economize (Includes all general production increase campaigns for the entire period)
   16. Technical Renovation Movement
   17. Campaign to Create Agricultural Producers' Cooperatives
   18. Study the General Line of the Party in the Period of Transition
   19. Oppose Bourgeois Individualism, Liberalism, Sectarianism, Dispersionism, Conceit, and Parochialism in the Party
   20. Worker Emulation, Advanced Producers, and Model Units
   21. Illiteracy Campaign
   22. Anti-Pest Campaign
   23. Anti-Hu Feng and Su-ching Anti-Counter-Revolutionary Campaign
   24. Party Rectification
   25. One Hundred Flowers
   26. Anti-Rightist Campaign of 1957
   27. Cadre Hsia-fang and Rectification (Includes 1957 Socialist Education Campaign)
   28. Great Leap Forward and Technical Renovation Movement (See earlier campaign for Production Increase)
   29. Anti-Rightist Campaign of 1959
   30. Socialist Education Movement of 1963-65 (Includes cadre hsia-fang; called Four-Clean-Ups after 1/65)
   31. Campaign to Learn from the PLA
   32. Study the Thought of Mao Tse-tung
   33. Campaign to Compare, Learn from, Catch up with, and Help
       a. Campaign to Learn from Tachai
       b. Campaign to Learn from Taching
   34. Great Proletarian Cultural Revolution
   35. Campaign to Criticize Revisionism and Rectify Work Style
   36. Campaign to Criticize Lin Piao and Rectify Work Style
   37. Campaign to Criticize Lin Piao and Confucius
   38. Study the Theory of the Dictatorship of the Proletariat
   39. Campaign to Criticize Water Margin

F. National Leaders
   1. Chen Tu-hsiu
   2. Chen Yi
   3. Chen Yun
   4. Chiang Ching
   5. Chi Pen-yu
   6. Chou En-lai
   7. Chou Yang
   8. Chu Chiu-pai
   9. Chu Te
   10. Ho Lung
   11. Hsia Yen
   12. Kang Sheng
   13. Kao Kang
   14. Kuo Mo-jo
   15. Li Fu-chun
   16. Li Hsien-nien
   17. Li Li-san
   18. Li Te-sheng
   19. Liao Mo-sha
   20. Lin Piao
   21. Liu Shao-chi

22. Lo Jui-ching
23. Lu Hsun
24. Lu Ting-yi
25. Mao Tse-tung (Includes works of Mao)
26. Peng Chen
27. Peng Te-huai
28. Po Yi-po
29. Soong Ching-ling
30. Sun Yat-sen
31. Tan Chen-lin
32. Tao Chu
33. Teng Hsiao-ping
34. Teng Ying-chao
35. Teng To
36. Tung Pi-wu
37. Wang Jen-chung
38. Wang Ming
39. Wu Han
40. Wu Lung-hsi
41. Yang Hsien-chien
42. Yao Wen-yuan

G. Economy
1. General Economic Background
2. Economic Construction in the Early Years
3. Economic Planning and the Five-Year Plans
    a. General Economic Planning
    b. Balanced Economic Planning
    c. First Five-Year Plan
    d. Second Five-Year Plan
    e. Third Five-Year Plan
    f. Fourth Five-Year Plan
4. Socialist Transformation of the Economy
    a. Private Enterprise
    b. Part-State, Part-Private Enterprise
    c. Socialist Transformation of Industry and Agriculture
5. Industry
    a. General Industrial Production
    b. Industrial Technology and Quality Control
    c. Heavy Industry
    d. Building Construction
    e. Light Industry
    f. Fuel and Power (Oil, gas, coal, and electricity)
    g. Mining and Metallurgy
    h. Local Industries
    i. Handicraft Industries (Includes socialist transformation of handicrafts)
6. Agriculture
    a. Agricultural Plans and Policies
    b. Agricultural Production
    c. Agricultural Sideline Production, Draft Animals, and Husbandry
    d. Seasonal Planting and Harvest
        1. Spring Planting
        2. Summer Harvest and Planting
        3. Autumn Harvest and Winter Sowing
    e. Agricultural Techniques, Machinery, and Mechanization (Includes fertilizers)
    f. Agricultural Organization (See "Campaigns" for Land Reform)
        1. Mutual Aid Teams
        2. Lower and Higher Agricultural Cooperatives
        3. Communes
        4. State Farms and PLA-Run Farms
    g. Rural Financial Relationships (Includes three-tiered ownership of communes and income distribution)
    h. Water and Soil Conservation (Includes land reclamation)
    i. Fishing
    j. Forestry
7. Capital Construction (Includes both industry and agriculture)
8. Commerce
    a. General Domestic Commerce
        1. State-Controlled Commerce (Includes Socialist transformation of commerce and supply and marketing cooperatives)

           2. Rural Free Markets
           3. Primary Grain Markets
        b. Foreign Trade
    9. Finance
        a. General Finance
        b. Tax
           1. General Tax
           2. Agricultural Tax
        c. Prices
        d. Budget
        e. Banking and Currency
        f. Credit Cooperatives and Loans
        g. Bonds
        h. Savings
        i. Insurance
        j. Statistical Work
           1. Accounting System
           2. Contract System
           3. Work Reports
    10. Management
        a. General Management
        b. Soviet Responsibility System
        c. Labor Discipline
        d. Triple Combination (Cadre, technician, and worker)
    11. Employment
    12. Working Conditions
    13. Wages (Includes material incentives)
        a. Workers' Wages
        b. Peasants' Wages
    14. Transportation and Communication
        a. General Transportation and Communication
        b. General Transportation (Includes grain and short-distance transport)
           1. Railroads
           2. Water Transportation
           3. Air Transportation
        c. Postal and Telecommunications
    15. Cities

H. Education, Culture, and Health
    1. General Education, Culture, and Health Concerns (Includes general reforms)
    2. Education
        a. Primary School
        b. Middle School
        c. Higher Education
        d. Technical Education
        e. Education of Workers and Peasants (Includes literacy work)
        f. Spare-Time Educational Activities for Workers, Peasants, and Cadres
        g. Combination of Labor and Education (Includes hsia-fang youth and cultural revolution reforms)
        h. Education Mobility
        i. Teachers and Teacher Training
    3. Culture
        a. Cultural Bureaucracy
        b. Mass Media
        c. Language
        d. Literature and Art
        e. History
        f. Science
        g. Religion (See "Campaigns" for Christian Reform Movement)
        h. Holidays
           1. New Year's
           2. Spring Festival
           3. February Seventh Incident
           4. International Women's Day
           5. International Labor Day
           6. Youth Day (May Fourth)
           7. International Children's Day
           8. Founding of the CCP
           9. Army Day
           10. Victory in War of Resistance against Japan

11. Founding of the PRC (National Day)
12. October Revolution
 4. Health and Environment
   a. Public Health (Includes barefoot doctors)
   b. Sports and Physical Fitness (Includes international sports)
   c. Social Welfare
   d. Population
   e. Weather, Natural Disasters, and Relief Work

I. Demographic, Class, and Occupational Groups
  1. Women
  2. Marriage and Family
  3. Children and Youth
  4. Students (Includes Red Guards)
  5. National Minorities
  6. Overseas Chinese
  7. Workers
  8. Peasants
  9. Worker-Peasant Alliance
 10. Scientists and Technicians
 11. Intellectuals
 12. Merchants, Commercial Workers, and Peddlers
 13. Industrialists
 14. Bourgeois Capitalists and Petty Bourgeoisie
 15. KMT Remnants and Reactionary Elements
 16. Bad Classes (Includes landlords, rich peasants, counter-revolutionaries, bad elements, rightists, and other defeated exploiting classes)
 17. Counter-Revolutionary Revisionists

J. Regions of China
  1. General Geography (Includes administrative demarcations and boundary disputes)
  2. North China
     a. General North China
     b. Hopei
     c. Inner Mongolia
     d. Peking
     e. Shansi (See "Campaigns" for Tachai)
     f. Tientsin
  3. Northeast China
     a. General Northeast China
     b. Heilungkiang (See "Campaigns" for Taching)
     c. Kirin
     d. Liaoning
  4. Northwest China
     a. General Northwest China
     b. Kansu
     c. Ninghsia
     d. Shensi
     e. Sinkiang
     f. Tsinghai
  5. East China
     a. General Coastal China
     b. Anhwei
     c. Chekiang
     d. Fukien
     e. Kiangsi
     f. Kiangsu
     g. Shanghai
     h. Shantung
  6. Central-South China
     a. General Central-South China
     b. Canton
     c. Honan
     d. Hunan
     e. Hupei
     f. Kwangsi
     g. Kwangtung (Includes Hainan)
  7. Southwest China
     a. General Southwest China
     b. Kweichow
     c. Szechuan

        d. Tibet
        e. Yunnan

K. Military
   1. General Defense
   2. Nuclear Weapons
   3. People's Liberation Army
      a. Air Force
      b. Army
      c. Navy
   4. Conscription
   5. Military Training
   6. Korean War (Note: Not cross-listed with Korea)
   7. Chinese People's Volunteers (In Korean War)
   8. Militia
   9. Army Propaganda Activities
   10. Civil-Military Relations (Includes Veterans Administration)

L. International Relations
   1. General International Relations
   2. International Law
   3. Struggle against Imperialism and Colonialism
   4. International Conferences and Organizations
      a. International Conferences
         1. Second World Peace Conference
         2. Five-Power Peace Conference (Asian and Pacific area)
         3. International Economic Conference
         4. Congress of Peoples for Peace
         5. Stockholm Conferences
         6. Geneva Conferences
         7. Soviet-European Conference
         8. London Nine-Power Conference
         9. Asian-African Conferences (Includes Bandung, Cairo, Havana, and Moshi)
         10. Bangkok Conference
         11. Moscow Congresses of Communists and Workers
         12. Warsaw Pact Conferences
         13. Helsinki Conference
         14. World Congress of Mothers
         15. Inter-Parliamentary Union Conference
         16. Asian Countries Conference
         17. Colombo Conferences
         18. London Disarmament Conferences
         19. Japan Disarmament Conferences
         20. World Youth Festivals
         21. Conferences of Independent African States and African Heads of State
         22. Baghdad Pact Conference
         23. Accra (Ghana) Conference
         24. Wellington (New Zealand) Conference
         25. East-West Ministers Conference
         26. Bucharest Conference
         27. OAS Conferences
         28. Latin America-Mexico Conference
         29. All-African People's Conference
         30. Conferences of Non-Aligned Nations
         31. Niteroi (Brazil) Congress
         32. Addis Ababa (Ethiopia) Conferences
         33. Japan Peace Conference
         34. Pyongyang (North Korea) Economic Conference
         35. African Summit Conferences
         36. Peking Science Conferences
         37. Arab Summit Conference
         38. Indochina People's Conference
         39. Honolulu Conference
         40. Geneva Indochina Conferences
         41. Paris Vietnam Peace Talks
         42. Asian Ping-Pong Founding Conference
      b. International Red Cross
      c. International Federation of Democratic Youth
      d. International Scientific Commission Investigating Germ Warfare
      e. International Union of Students
      f. International Women's Organizations

g. NATO
h. SEATO
i. United Nations
j. World Federation of Scientific Workers
k. World Federation of Trade Unions
l. World Peace Council

M. Africa
1. North Africa
   a. General North Africa
   b. Algeria
   c. Mali
   d. Mauritania
   e. Morocco
   f. Niger
   g. Sudan
   h. Tunisia
   i. United Arab Republic (Includes Egypt, 1949-75; Syria, 1958-61)
2. Sub-Saharan Africa
   a. General Sub-Saharan Africa
   b. Central Africa
      1. Angola
      2. Cameroon
      3. Chad
      4. Central African Republic
      5. Gabon
      6. People's Republic of the Congo (Brazzaville)
      7. Sao Tome and Principe
      8. Zaire (Republic of the Congo until 1971)
      9. Zambia
   c. East Africa
      1. Burundi
      2. Comoro Islands
      3. Ethiopia
      4. Kenya
      5. Malagasy Republic
      6. Malawi
      7. Mauritius
      8. Mozambique
      9. Rwanda
      10. Somalia
      11. Tanganyika
      12. Tanzania (Includes Tanganyika and Zanzibar after 1965)
      13. Uganda
      14. Zanzibar
   d. South Africa
      1. Botswana
      2. Rhodesia (Zimbabwe)
      3. South Africa
   e. West Africa
      1. Dahomey
      2. Gambia
      3. Ghana
      4. Guinea
      5. Ivory Coast
      6. Liberia
      7. Nigeria
      8. Senegal
      9. Sierra Leone
      10. Togo
      11. Upper Volta

N. North America
1. Canada
2. The Caribbean
   a. General Caribbean
   b. Cuba
   c. Dominica
   d. Dominican Republic
   e. Haiti
   f. Jamaica
3. Central America
   a. General Central America

               b.   Guatemala
               c.   Mexico
               d.   Nicaragua
               e.   Panama
         4.   United States
               a.   Domestic U.S.
               b.   General International U.S. (Includes general imperialism,
                    colonialism, alliances, and atomic energy and weapons)
               c.   U.S. and Asia
                    1.   General U.S. and Asia
                    2.   U.S. and Japan
                    3.   U.S. and Korea (Includes Korean War)
                    4.   U.S. and P.R.C.
                    5.   U.S. and Taiwan (China)
                    6.   U.S. and South Asia
                    7.   U.S. and Southeast Asia (Includes Vietnam War)
               d.   U.S. and Australia and New Zealand
               e.   U.S. and Europe
               f.   U.S. and Latin America
               g.   U.S. and Middle East and North Africa
               h.   U.S. and Sub-Saharan Africa
               i.   U.S. and U.S.S.R.

O.   Asia
     1.   General Asia
     2.   Central Asia--People's Republic of Mongolia
     3.   East Asia
          a.   Democratic People's Republic of Korea
          b.   Hong Kong
          c.   Japan
          d.   Taiwan (China)
          e.   Republic of Korea
     4.   South Asia
          a.   Afghanistan
          b.   Bangladesh
          c.   India
          d.   Nepal
          e.   Pakistan
          f.   Republic of Maldives
          g.   Sri Lanka (Ceylon)
     5.   Southeast Asia
          a.   General Southeast Asia
          b.   Burma
          c.   Cambodia
          d.   Democratic People's Republic of Vietnam
          e.   Indonesia
          f.   Laos
          g.   Malaya
          h.   Malaysia
          i.   Philippines
          j.   Republic of Vietnam
          k.   Singapore
          l.   Thailand

P.   Australia and New Zealand

Q.   Europe
     1.   Eastern Europe
          a.   General Eastern Europe
          b.   Albania
          c.   Bulgaria
          d.   Czechoslovakia
          e.   German Democratic Republic
          f.   Hungary
          g.   Poland
          h.   Rumania
          i.   Yugoslavia
     2.   Scandinavia
          a.   Denmark
          b.   Finland
          c.   Iceland
          d.   Norway
          e.   Sweden

3. Southern Europe
   a. Cyprus
   b. Greece
   c. Italy
   d. Malta
   e. Portugal
   f. San Marino
   g. Spain
4. Western Europe
   a. General Western Europe
   b. Austria
   c. Belgium
   d. Federal Republic of Germany
   e. France
   f. Ireland
   g. Luxembourg
   h. The Netherlands
   i. United Kingdom

R. South America
   1. General South America
   2. Argentina
   3. Brazil
   4. Chile
   5. Guyana
   6. Peru
   7. Trinidad and Tobago
   8. Venezuela

S. The Middle East
   1. General Middle East
   2. Iran
   3. Iraq
   4. Israel
   5. Jordan
   6. Kuwait
   7. Lebanon
   8. Oman
   9. Palestine
   10. People's Democratic Republic of Yemen
   11. Saudi Arabia
   12. Syria (See also "North Africa")
   13. Turkey
   14. Yemen Arabic Republic

T. U.S.S.R.
   1. Domestic U.S.S.R.
   2. U.S.S.R. Leaders
      a. Stalin
      b. Khruschov
      c. Brezhnev and Kosygin
   3. General International U.S.S.R. (Includes general social imperialism, alliances, treaties, and atomic energy and weapons)
   4. U.S.S.R. and Asia
      a. U.S.S.R. and Japan
      b. U.S.S.R. and Korea
      c. U.S.S.R. and P.R.C.
         1. U.S.S.R. and P.R.C.: Culture
         2. U.S.S.R. and P.R.C.: Economics
         3. U.S.S.R. and P.R.C.: Politics
         4. U.S.S.R. and P.R.C.: Soviet Advisors
      d. U.S.S.R. and Taiwan (China)
      e. U.S.S.R. and South Asia
      f. U.S.S.R. and Southeast Asia
   5. U.S.S.R. and Europe
      a. U.S.S.R. and General Europe
      b. U.S.S.R. and Albania
      c. U.S.S.R. and Austria
      d. U.S.S.R. and Belgium
      e. U.S.S.R. and Bulgaria

            f. U.S.S.R. and Czechoslovakia
            g. U.S.S.R. and Federal Republic of Germany and German Democratic Republic
            h. U.S.S.R. and France
            i. U.S.S.R. and Greece
            j. U.S.S.R. and Hungary
            k. U.S.S.R. and Poland
            l. U.S.S.R. and Rumania
            m. U.S.S.R. and United Kingdom
            n. U.S.S.R. and Yugoslavia
      6. U.S.S.R. and Latin America and the Caribbean
      7. U.S.S.R. and the Middle East and North Africa
      8. U.S.S.R. and Sub-Saharan Africa
      9. U.S.S.R. and U.S.

U. International Communist Parties
   1. Communist Bloc
   2. Communist Parties out of Power
      a. General Communist Parties out of Power
      b. French Communist Party
      c. Indian Communist Party
      d. Italian Communist Party
      e. Japanese Communist Party
      f. Mongolian Communist Party
      g. United States Communist Party
      h. Vietnamese Communist Party

Subject Index to the *People's Daily* Editorials

Using the Subject Index

1. Under each subject heading is a column of dates. These are the editorial publication dates and correspond to the dates by which the editorial titles are listed in the first section of the *Research Guide*.

2. Preceding the subject index is the entire outline of index topics. The entire organization of the index is presented in this way in order to acquaint the reader with the wide range of topics in the index and to provide a more thorough definition of the abbreviated headings found in the index itself. Often many of the topics will be relevant to a research topic, and the reader should review the entire list of topics at the outset.

3. In the index, an asterisk (*) after an editorial date indicates that the subject was a major theme in the editorial. Each editorial was indexed exhaustively. That is, each editorial was indexed for both its major and minor themes. An editorial generally contained about five or six themes. However, some touched on as many as fifteen, while others only covered one or two. To cope with this large number, the themes were divided into two types: if more than one paragraph in an editorial was devoted to a subject, it was classified as a major theme; if a subject was contained in one paragraph or less, it was a minor theme. Briefly mentioned items were not indexed. The number of major themes in each editorial averaged two or three; depending upon the length and depth of the editorial, however, it could range from one to five.

4. During the years when the greatest number of editorials were written, two and sometimes three editorials appeared in the *People's Daily* each day. The titles themselves will generally reveal enough about the content of the editorial for the reader to locate the desired one.

5. Finally, because the microfilm of the early years of the *People's Daily* is incomplete, twenty-five editorials are missing. A list of those missing editorials can be found in the Preface to the *Research Guide* (see p. xvi).

A. Government

1. Chinese People's Political Consultative Conference
    09-22-49*
    10-01-49*
    10-02-49*
    09-07-51
    10-25-51
    11-09-51*
    11-10-51
    11-20-51
    01-01-53
    01-15-53
    02-10-53*
    03-04-53
    03-13-53
    07-16-53
    06-16-54
    06-24-54
    09-21-54
    12-22-54*
    12-28-54
    01-31-56*
    03-21-57*
    04-26-57
    04-18-59*
    04-11-60
    12-04-63

2. Establishment of Political Power
    02-04-49*
    03-03-50*
    05-16-50*
    06-02-50*
    07-21-50
    08-26-50
    08-30-50
    09-20-50*
    11-14-50*
    12-31-50*
    01-02-55*
    04-22-56*
    10-22-56*
    06-29-57*
    03-05-58*
    09-04-58
    10-26-58*
    03-31-59*
    04-25-59

    09-10-65*
    09-30-65*
    01-25-67*
    01-30-67*
    02-01-67*
    02-02-67*
    02-10-67*
    02-17-67*
    03-01-67*
    03-02-67*
    04-15-67
    04-21-67*
    06-08-67*
    10-21-67
    11-02-67*
    12-07-67*
    01-07-68*
    01-26-68*
    01-30-68*
    02-05-68*
    02-07-68*
    02-23-68*
    03-10-68*
    03-25-68*
    03-30-68*
    04-10-68*

    04-12-68*
    04-20-68*
    05-01-68
    05-03-68*
    05-12-68*
    05-17-68
    06-02-68*
    07-01-68*
    08-01-68*
    08-05-68
    08-15-68*
    08-21-68*
    08-28-68*
    09-07-68*
    10-01-68
    01-01-69
    06-09-69
    07-01-69
    10-01-69

3. National People's Congress
    01-15-53
    02-10-53
    06-16-54
    06-22-54

95

07-03-54
09-15-54*
09-21-54*
09-29-54*
10-15-54*
02-15-55
04-07-55
06-17-55
07-05-55*
07-31-55*
10-18-55*
06-16-56
10-09-56
02-02-57*
04-26-57
06-26-57*
07-03-57*
07-16-57*
08-04-57
11-18-57
11-21-57
02-12-58
05-29-58
06-05-58
06-06-58
06-10-58
04-18-59*
04-29-59*
09-16-59
09-18-59
03-31-60
04-11-60*
04-12-60*
04-17-62*
05-04-62
04-13-63
12-04-63
01-05-65*
06-09-69*
07-01-69
01-01-70
04-01-70*

4. Government Structure

 a. Local Government
10-01-49*
10-02-49*
10-27-49*
11-21-49*
03-03-50*
05-16-50*
06-02-50*
08-22-50*
12-31-50*
07-25-51*
08-14-51*
08-30-51*
09-05-51
09-20-51*
11-17-51*
11-20-51
08-13-52
12-24-53*
07-03-54
10-08-54*
03-11-55
05-31-56*
11-15-56*
10-06-57
10-29-57
10-09-58
11-26-63

 b. Elections and Local
     Congresses
10-27-49*
11-21-49*
03-03-50*
05-16-50*
08-22-50*
12-31-50*
02-04-51*
08-10-51
01-01-53
01-15-53*
02-10-53
03-04-53*
05-14-53
06-06-53*
12-24-53*
12-28-53
01-01-54
02-20-54*
03-30-54
06-16-54
06-20-54*
07-03-54*
10-08-54
05-31-56*
04-13-63*

 c. Urban Communes
03-31-60
04-11-60*
04-15-60
05-06-60
05-19-60*
06-01-60
10-27-60
11-09-60*
11-24-60

 d. Local-National Balance
    of Power
01-12-51*
05-26-51*
06-20-53*
12-28-53*
06-16-54
07-03-54
10-08-54
08-24-57
11-18-57*
06-05-58
06-10-58*
12-23-58
02-24-59*
01-01-62

 e. National Government
10-01-49*
10-02-49*
10-20-49*
11-17-52*
06-16-54
07-03-54
06-21-55
10-06-57
10-29-57
06-01-66*
06-04-66
07-01-66
01-19-67
01-22-67
07-26-67
07-31-67

5. Judicial System
11-27-49*
03-08-50*
04-16-50*
06-29-50*
06-30-50*
07-21-50*
08-26-50*
10-21-50*
11-14-50
12-26-50*
12-31-50
05-29-51*
09-05-51*
09-29-51
11-13-51*
04-02-52
06-15-52
08-17-52*
08-25-52*
01-01-53
01-15-53
02-01-53
03-04-53
05-06-53*
05-14-53*
11-14-53
11-19-53*
03-23-54*
03-30-54*
04-28-54
05-15-54*
05-20-54*
05-21-54*
06-04-54*
06-16-54*
06-20-54
06-21-54*
06-22-54*
06-24-54*
07-03-54*
07-06-54*
07-17-54*
07-18-54
07-30-54*
08-01-54
08-21-54
09-04-54*
09-07-54*
09-21-54*
09-29-54*
10-08-54
10-22-54
11-01-54
11-03-54*
11-05-54
11-18-54*
11-25-54*
12-24-54
01-02-55
01-08-55*
01-17-55
02-15-55*
05-18-55*
06-27-55*
07-05-55
07-27-55
08-10-55
12-04-55*
12-10-55
02-05-56
05-31-56
07-01-56*

08-03-56*
08-23-56
06-29-57
08-19-57*
10-09-57
10-14-57
10-23-57*
10-29-57*
11-18-57
12-20-57*
01-10-58*
10-17-58
03-31-59
04-13-63
08-13-66

6. Public Security System
07-21-50
08-08-50*
09-07-50*
11-14-50
12-20-50*
12-26-50
12-30-50*
03-21-51
04-06-51
06-11-51*
07-27-51*
08-18-51
02-17-52
02-21-52
08-25-52*
07-16-53
03-30-54
04-28-54*
05-11-54
05-15-54
05-21-54*
06-12-54
07-18-54*
08-01-54
08-21-54*
09-04-54*
09-07-54*
11-03-54
11-05-54
11-10-54*
11-18-54
11-25-54*
12-15-54*
12-24-54*
01-02-55*
01-08-55*
04-01-55
04-14-55*
05-18-55*
06-27-55*
07-25-55*
07-27-55
12-10-55*
02-07-56
03-01-56*
04-16-56*
08-03-56
06-29-57*
07-18-57
08-04-57
08-19-57
10-09-57
10-14-57*
10-23-57*
10-29-57*
01-10-58*

  97

    01-15-58   06-06-50   04-14-55*   09-23-57
    03-10-58   06-08-50   04-15-55*   10-06-57
    10-17-58*   07-28-50   04-17-55*   10-10-57
    03-31-59   08-08-50*   04-30-55*   10-21-57*
    12-30-62*   08-14-50   05-07-55*   10-29-57
    05-22-67*   08-17-50   05-15-55   11-01-57*
                       08-26-50   05-18-55   11-15-57*
7. Supervision Work   09-04-50   06-21-55   12-18-57
    04-23-50*   09-06-50   06-27-55   12-20-57
    04-23-50*   09-14-50*   07-11-55   12-23-57
    05-16-50   10-10-50   07-13-55   12-25-57*
    06-02-50   10-14-50*   07-19-55*   01-24-58
    08-08-50   10-18-50*   07-24-55   01-27-58*
    08-22-50*   10-21-50   08-04-55*   04-29-58
    09-07-50   11-13-50   08-17-55   05-09-58
    01-12-51*   12-14-50   08-25-55*   08-06-59*
    05-26-51*   12-26-50*   08-27-55   08-07-59*
    03-11-53*   12-31-50   08-29-55*   06-13-60
    03-13-53   07-27-51   11-10-55   06-15-60
    06-20-53*   11-20-51   11-13-55   07-22-60
    10-18-53   11-23-51*   11-17-55   10-01-61
    05-08-54*   01-01-53   11-22-55   10-01-62
    05-21-54   01-18-53   11-30-55   06-02-63*
    06-04-54*   01-19-53*   12-19-55   06-19-63
    06-05-54   01-23-53   01-27-56   11-08-63
    06-20-54   02-01-53   03-30-56   04-02-64
    06-21-54   02-03-53*   04-06-56   08-03-64
    06-22-54   02-10-53   05-05-56*   08-28-64*
    09-29-54   02-11-53*   05-18-56*   08-30-64*
    10-08-54   02-28-53*   05-22-56*   10-01-65
    11-06-54   03-11-53   06-05-56*   01-01-66
    01-02-55   03-13-53   06-07-56*   04-03-66
    04-10-55   03-17-53*   06-11-56*   01-22-67
    04-14-55   03-26-53   06-16-56
    04-15-55   04-07-53*   06-19-56*   9. Government Institutions
    06-21-55*   04-30-53   07-16-56*   02-03-56
    09-10-55   06-06-53   07-25-56*   06-07-57
    03-05-56   06-20-53*   08-02-56   07-23-63
    03-09-56   06-26-53*   08-23-56*   05-29-64
    07-25-56   07-05-53   08-27-56   12-22-65
    07-27-56   07-23-53   08-28-56
    08-04-56   07-26-53*   09-15-56   B. <u>Chinese Communist</u>
    01-11-57*   08-18-53   09-23-56   <u>Party</u>
    03-13-57   08-29-53*   10-02-56*
    03-18-57*   09-02-53   10-12-56   1. Organization
    03-21-57*   09-07-53*   10-16-56
    04-26-57   09-10-53*   10-22-56*   a. Central Party Meetings
    05-29-57   09-11-53   10-30-56*   02-18-54*
    06-03-57   10-18-53   11-15-56*   04-05-55*
    09-30-57   11-02-53   12-08-56   04-07-55
    10-29-57   11-04-53   01-11-57   04-10-55*
    12-20-57*   11-09-53   01-26-57   10-18-55*
    03-10-58*   12-24-53   01-31-57   09-15-56*
    04-27-58   12-28-53   03-13-57   09-23-56
    08-24-59   12-29-53   04-13-57*   09-25-56
    01-18-60   01-05-54   04-17-57   09-27-56*
    03-05-60*   02-02-54   04-23-57*   09-29-56*
    01-09-63   02-24-54   05-03-57*   10-09-56
                       03-26-54   05-17-57   12-16-56
8. General Bureaucratic   03-31-54   05-19-57*   11-01-57
   Problems   04-11-54   05-27-57*   12-29-57
    04-09-49*   05-23-54   05-31-57*   05-29-58*
    03-03-50*   07-11-54   06-03-57*   12-21-58*
    03-07-50*   07-15-54   06-04-57   01-01-59*
    03-09-50*   11-05-54*   06-08-57   01-02-59
    03-18-50   11-06-54   06-14-57   01-29-59
    03-22-50   01-02-55   06-17-57   08-27-59*
    03-24-50   01-28-55*   06-18-57*   09-18-59
    04-23-50   02-19-55   06-22-57   10-10-59
    05-16-50   03-24-55   06-29-57   04-11-60
    05-17-50   03-27-55   08-02-57   01-22-61
    05-29-50   04-03-55   09-04-57   01-27-61
    06-03-50   04-12-55*   09-21-57*   03-08-61

04-13-63
08-11-66*
08-13-66*
08-15-66
08-17-66
11-25-68
06-09-69*
07-01-69
01-01-70
04-01-70*
01-31-71
08-27-71
10-01-73

b. Local Party Structure
07-03-49*
07-29-50
10-14-50
10-18-50
11-13-50*
04-29-51
04-09-52
12-28-52
03-25-53
11-25-53
12-06-53
07-26-54
01-30-55*
02-17-55*
03-11-55*
03-27-55
04-05-55*
04-14-55
04-17-55
05-07-55
05-19-55*
06-27-55
09-10-55*
10-30-55*
11-02-55*
11-17-55*
12-07-55
12-28-55
01-18-56
03-18-56*
04-27-56
05-13-56
07-29-56*
09-27-56*
09-29-56*
01-26-57
04-08-57
05-07-57
07-10-57*
08-28-59*
03-17-60*
03-19-60*
11-26-60
12-17-60*
01-08-61
12-17-61
06-27-62
01-11-63
06-02-63
01-01-68*
07-01-68
07-01-69*
07-01-70
07-09-70
01-31-71*
08-27-71
10-21-75

c. Party Membership and
   Party Building
07-30-49*
07-29-50*
08-22-50
09-14-50*
10-10-50*
10-14-50*
10-18-50*
11-13-50*
07-01-52
03-25-53*
12-01-53
10-24-54
03-11-55
04-05-55*
05-11-55
05-19-55*
05-23-55*
07-16-55*
08-22-55*
10-30-55*
11-17-55
11-28-55*
01-18-56*
03-01-56*
03-21-56*
04-27-56
05-13-56
03-20-57
03-23-57
05-07-57
07-28-57*
12-29-57
11-17-61
01-22-67
01-25-67
01-30-67
02-01-67
02-02-67
02-10-67
02-17-67
03-01-67
03-02-67
04-15-67
04-21-67
06-08-67
07-28-67
07-29-67
07-30-67
07-30-67
11-02-67*
12-07-67*
01-01-68*
01-26-68*
01-30-68*
02-05-68
02-07-68
02-23-68
03-10-68
03-25-68
03-30-68
04-10-68
04-12-68
04-20-68
05-03-68
05-12-68
06-02-68
07-01-68
08-01-68
08-15-68
08-18-68
08-21-68

08-28-68
09-07-68
10-01-68*
01-01-69*
02-17-69*
02-21-69
06-09-69*
07-01-69*
08-25-69*
10-01-69*
01-01-70
04-01-70
07-01-70*
10-01-70
01-01-71
01-31-71*
08-27-71*
12-01-71
01-01-72
04-24-72*

1. Young Pioneers
11-11-53*
04-28-55*
06-01-55
06-15-55
02-17-56
08-06-56
06-01-58
06-01-59
02-08-64
06-01-65
06-01-66

2. Communist Youth League
05-03-50*
09-24-50*
06-18-53*
07-03-53*
09-25-53
01-17-54
02-09-54
05-04-54*
06-29-54*
10-24-54
11-14-54
03-08-55
05-04-55*
06-01-55
06-15-55
08-21-55
08-22-55
11-08-55
12-06-55
03-02-56
03-30-56
08-06-56
11-20-56
12-23-56
05-04-57
05-15-57*
10-08-57
01-31-58*
05-20-58
08-28-59*
10-23-60
09-30-62
06-19-63
02-08-64
02-28-64
05-04-64
07-08-64*
05-04-65*

06-01-65
05-04-66*
01-01-68
08-27-71
02-22-73*
08-07-73

d. Party Cadres
1. Basic Level Cadres
04-09-49
03-28-51
04-05-51
05-06-51
05-29-51
06-14-51
07-21-51
07-27-51
08-10-51
08-30-51
10-03-51
11-13-51
11-23-51
12-06-51
12-07-51
01-01-52
02-01-52
03-02-52
03-20-52
03-24-52
04-09-52*
06-14-52
01-19-53
02-01-53*
02-18-53*
02-27-53
03-13-53
03-17-53*
05-06-53
06-06-53
06-12-53
06-20-53
06-26-53
09-12-53
09-20-53
09-23-53
10-07-53
11-23-53
12-01-53*
12-02-53
12-11-53*
12-20-53
12-24-53
01-07-54
01-16-54
01-17-54
01-19-54
01-22-54*
02-20-54
03-16-54
03-21-54
03-23-54
03-25-54
03-27-54
03-31-54
04-28-54
06-20-54
08-08-54
10-28-54
11-12-54
11-21-54
12-04-54
12-07-54

12-13-54*	04-08-57	08-27-60*	03-19-64
12-16-54	04-13-57	09-09-60	03-23-64
12-19-54	04-21-57	09-10-60	03-26-64
01-02-55	04-23-57	09-16-60	04-06-64
01-28-55*	05-01-57	09-23-60	05-12-64
01-30-55	05-03-57	10-24-60*	05-21-64
02-03-55*	05-14-57*	11-03-60	05-29-64
02-17-55*	05-17-57	11-20-60	06-16-64
03-04-55*	06-17-57	11-26-60*	07-05-64
03-11-55*	06-18-57	11-30-60	07-12-64
03-24-55	07-19-57*	12-04-60	08-28-64*
04-17-55	07-23-57*	12-21-60	08-30-64*
04-24-55*	08-05-57	01-23-61	09-03-64
05-10-55	08-10-57	01-30-61	09-21-64
05-19-55	08-24-57	02-02-61*	09-22-64*
05-22-55	09-20-57	02-05-61	10-25-64
08-21-55	09-23-57*	02-08-61*	12-06-64
09-15-55	09-25-57	02-13-61	02-16-65
09-25-55	09-28-57	02-15-61	02-17-65
10-07-55	09-30-57	02-28-61	02-23-65*
10-29-55	10-06-57*	03-04-61*	03-04-65
11-01-55	10-08-57	03-07-61*	03-11-65
11-09-55	10-14-57	03-24-61	03-12-65
11-12-55*	10-21-57	03-25-61	03-28-65
11-17-55	10-29-57	04-03-61	04-04-65*
11-24-55	11-13-57	04-22-61*	04-10-65
12-06-55	11-16-57	06-04-61	04-11-65
12-07-55*	11-17-57	06-21-61	04-23-65
12-13-55*	11-30-57	06-27-61	05-05-65
12-29-55	12-04-57	10-25-61	05-21-65*
12-31-55	12-08-57	11-16-61	05-26-65
01-17-56	12-15-57	11-21-61	06-08-65*
01-21-56	02-15-58	12-03-61	06-21-65
02-05-56*	03-07-58	02-16-62*	07-22-65
02-07-56	03-26-58	03-10-62	07-29-65
03-05-56*	03-28-58*	04-29-62	09-07-65
03-08-56	04-14-58	06-27-62*	09-15-65
03-17-56	05-09-58*	07-13-62	09-19-65*
03-18-56	05-20-58	09-20-62	01-03-66*
04-02-56	06-23-58	10-22-62	01-21-66
04-06-56	08-03-58*	11-13-62	02-05-66
04-15-56	08-13-58*	12-02-62	02-07-66*
05-06-56	08-28-58	12-19-62	02-09-66*
05-09-56	12-23-58	12-22-62*	02-11-66*
05-29-56	12-25-58	01-11-63*	02-13-66*
05-29-56	01-12-59	01-25-63	02-14-66
06-06-56	04-10-59	02-11-63	02-20-66*
06-07-56	05-16-59	03-17-63	02-23-66
06-11-56*	05-20-59	04-13-63	02-23-66*
06-25-56	06-17-59	05-14-63	03-03-66*
06-27-56*	06-30-59	05-29-63	03-12-66
08-01-56	08-06-59*	05-30-63	03-20-66*
09-08-56	08-07-59	06-02-63*	04-02-66
10-05-56	08-17-59	06-10-63	04-06-66
10-11-56	10-17-59	07-04-63*	04-27-66*
10-12-56	12-15-59	07-13-63	10-12-66
10-16-56	12-18-59	07-17-63*	01-22-67
10-22-56*	12-21-59	07-21-63*	02-11-67
10-26-56	12-28-59	07-23-63	03-13-67
11-28-56*	01-07-60	07-29-63*	04-02-67
12-01-56*	03-03-60	07-30-63*	04-08-67
12-03-56	03-23-60	08-08-63	04-24-67*
12-22-56	04-15-60	08-13-63*	05-31-67
01-05-57	05-20-60	08-17-63*	07-09-67
01-15-57	06-13-60	08-26-63	08-25-67*
01-16-57	06-15-60	08-29-63*	09-24-67
01-23-57	06-16-60*	10-08-63	10-06-67
01-26-57*	06-21-60	10-27-63	10-12-67
01-31-57*	07-21-60	12-11-63	10-21-67*
03-02-57*	07-30-60*	12-13-63	11-19-67*
03-17-57	08-05-60	01-06-64	12-22-67
03-18-57	08-16-60	02-18-64	03-30-68
03-23-57*	08-18-60	02-20-64	05-12-68

01-01-69
02-17-69
02-21-69
06-09-69
07-01-69
11-20-69*
03-07-70
07-09-70
02-18-71

2. Middle Level Cadres
10-18-50
11-13-50
03-27-55*
06-12-55*
06-17-55
06-23-55
09-15-55
11-01-55
11-09-55*
11-24-55
01-24-56
01-25-56
01-29-56
02-26-56
03-13-56*
03-18-56
04-02-56
04-10-56
05-01-56
05-07-56
05-12-56
05-15-56
06-05-56
06-07-56
06-11-56*
06-27-56*
07-16-56
08-21-56
08-23-56
10-09-56
10-31-56
11-16-56
11-18-56
11-30-56*
12-04-56
12-28-56
01-14-57
01-21-57
01-22-57
01-23-57
01-26-57
04-13-57
04-23-57
05-03-57
05-13-57
05-17-57*
05-31-57
06-06-57
07-23-57*
08-16-57
09-11-57
09-21-57
09-23-57*
09-28-57
09-30-57
10-06-57
10-08-57
10-14-57
10-17-57
10-21-57*
10-29-57

11-17-57
01-15-58
01-24-58
02-15-58*
03-14-58*
03-24-58*
03-26-58*
03-28-58*
04-14-58
05-07-58*
05-09-58*
11-16-58
04-10-59
05-16-59
06-11-59
07-27-59
08-60-59*
08-07-59
08-17-59
10-08-59
12-18-59
01-07-60
03-14-60
04-09-60*
04-15-60
06-13-60*
06-15-60*
06-16-60*
07-03-60
07-13-60
07-29-60
07-30-60*
08-18-60
08-27-60*
09-07-60
10-24-60*
12-04-60
01-30-61
02-05-61
02-28-61*
03-07-61*
04-03-61
06-04-61*
11-16-61
03-15-62
05-22-62
12-02-62
12-22-62
02-11-63
02-17-63
02-25-63
05-29-63
07-29-63*
07-30-63
08-29-63*
09-20-63
10-08-63
02-07-64
03-26-64
04-02-64*
04-04-64
05-29-64
05-30-64
06-16-64
08-06-64
08-28-64*
08-30-64*
09-22-64*
10-25-64
02-17-65
02-23-65*
04-10-65

04-23-65
05-04-65
06-08-65*
06-21-65
07-06-65
07-22-65
07-30-65
09-15-65
09-19-65
09-24-65*
12-13-65
12-22-65
01-21-66
02-05-66
02-20-66
03-10-66
04-03-66
04-06-66
07-29-66
09-07-66
10-12-66
12-26-66*
02-10-67*
02-11-67
03-02-67
03-13-67
04-02-67
04-08-67
04-24-67*
06-01-67
08-13-67
08-25-67*
09-24-67
10-06-67
10-12-67
10-21-67*
11-19-67*
12-22-67
03-30-68
05-12-68
01-01-69
02-17-69
02-21-69
06-09-69
07-01-69
11-20-69*
03-07-70
12-01-71
07-06-72*
01-01-73
07-11-73
02-02-74*
02-20-74*
03-03-74
04-10-74
06-18-74
02-09-75
03-11-75

3. National Level Cadres
03-09-50
03-24-50*
07-29-50
01-31-52
08-25-52
11-26-52*
03-11-53
03-13-53
03-25-53*
11-26-53
03-21-54*
03-25-54

11-28-54
02-08-55*
04-05-55
04-15-55
04-17-55
06-17-55
06-23-55
07-15-55*
07-25-55
09-06-55
09-15-55
11-02-55
04-23-56
05-22-56
06-05-56
06-11-56*
07-16-56
10-12-56*
01-11-57
03-16-57
04-13-57
04-23-57
05-13-57
05-17-57*
09-11-57
09-23-57
09-30-57
10-06-57
10-14-57
10-21-57*
10-29-57
11-29-57
12-20-57
12-25-57
12-28-57
01-24-58
01-27-58*
02-15-58*
08-03-58*
10-23-58
01-07-60
08-16-60
08-18-60
04-03-61
08-06-66
06-01-67
01-01-69
02-17-69
02-21-69
06-09-69
07-01-69
11-20-69*
05-01-71*
07-06-62*

e. May Seventh Cadre
   Schools
   11-20-69*
   07-11-73*

f. Revolutionary Three-
   Way Alliance
   01-22-67
   01-25-67*
   01-30-67*
   02-01-67*
   02-02-67*
   02-10-67*
   02-17-67*
   03-01-67*
   03-02-67*

04-15-67*
04-21-67*
06-08-67*
07-28-67
07-29-67
07-30-67
07-30-67
09-22-67*
10-06-67
10-19-67*
10-21-67
10-24-67
11-02-67
12-04-67
12-07-67
12-22-67
01-01-68
01-07-68*
01-26-68*
01-30-68*
02-05-68*
02-07-68*
02-23-68
03-10-68*
03-25-68
03-30-68*
04-10-68
04-12-68
04-20-68
05-01-68
05-03-68
05-12-68*
06-02-68
08-01-68*
08-05-68
08-15-68
08-28-68
09-07-68
03-22-69
06-09-69*
07-01-69*
08-01-69
01-01-70

2. Ideology

a. Party Activities in
   Society
   07-03-49
   10-21-49*
   03-03-50
   03-18-50*
   03-22-50
   04-16-50
   04-23-50*
   06-02-50*
   06-06-50*
   06-30-50
   07-29-50*
   08-08-50
   08-14-50
   08-22-50*
   08-26-50
   09-07-50
   09-14-50
   09-16-50*
   09-23-50*
   09-25-50
   09-30-50
   10-10-50*
   11-13-50
   11-14-50*
   12-22-50

12-28-50*
12-31-50*
01-03-51*
02-04-51
02-16-51
03-10-51
03-14-51*
03-17-51
03-23-51
04-04-51
04-05-51
04-23-51
04-29-51*
05-01-51
05-29-51
06-02-51
07-08-51
07-13-51
07-29-51
08-08-51
08-30-51
09-13-51
09-30-51
10-15-51
11-09-51
11-11-51
11-23-51
12-19-51*
01-01-52
01-05-52
02-01-52*
03-02-52
04-09-52
05-28-52
07-01-52
08-17-52
12-28-52
12-30-52
01-01-53*
01-22-53
01-23-53
01-27-53*
02-01-53
02-11-53
02-18-53
02-28-53
03-06-53
03-11-53
03-13-53
03-25-53*
03-26-53*
04-20-53
05-06-53*
06-20-53
06-23-53
06-26-53
07-05-53
07-18-53
07-23-53
08-19-53
08-29-53
08-31-53
09-25-53*
10-06-53
10-08-53
10-10-53
10-17-53*
10-18-53
10-23-53
11-04-53
11-09-53*
11-11-53
11-15-53

11-16-53
11-18-53
11-22-53
11-23-53*
11-25-53
11-26-53*
12-02-53
12-06-53*
12-11-53*
12-11-53
12-11-53
12-12-53*
12-13-53
12-20-53*
12-22-53*
12-24-53
12-25-53
12-29-53
12-30-53*
01-01-54
01-05-54*
01-07-54*
01-11-54*
01-12-54
01-14-54
01-16-54
01-17-54*
01-19-54
01-26-54*
01-29-54*
01-31-54
02-02-54
02-08-54
02-09-54
02-11-54
02-18-54
02-20-54
03-04-54
03-12-54*
03-16-54*
03-22-54
03-25-54
03-26-54
03-28-54
03-30-54*
04-11-54
04-17-54*
04-19-54
04-20-54*
04-23-54*
04-28-54
05-04-54
05-07-54*
05-15-54*
05-19-54*
05-23-54
05-25-54
05-26-54
06-04-54
07-01-54*
07-04-54
07-07-54*
07-08-54
07-11-54*
07-17-54*
07-20-54*
07-21-54
07-31-54
08-03-54
08-07-54
08-13-54
08-31-54
09-01-54

09-04-54
09-11-54
09-12-54
09-15-54
09-18-54
09-21-54
10-06-54
10-09-54
10-22-54
10-23-54
10-28-54
11-01-54
11-03-54*
11-05-54*
11-09-54
11-12-54
11-13-54
11-14-54*
11-18-54*
11-21-54*
11-23-54
11-28-54
12-04-54*
12-07-54
12-12-54
12-16-54*
12-19-54
12-22-54
12-23-54
12-24-54
01-01-55
01-04-55*
01-06-55*
01-15-55
01-17-55*
01-23-55
01-28-55*
01-30-55
02-03-55*
02-06-55*
02-15-55
02-17-55*
02-28-55*
03-01-55*
03-04-55*
03-08-55*
03-11-55
03-14-55
03-16-55*
03-25-55
03-27-55*
04-03-55*
04-05-55
04-10-55
04-11-55*
04-14-55
04-15-55*
04-17-55
04-19-55
05-07-55
05-08-55
05-11-55*
05-18-55
05-20-55
05-23-55
05-25-55
05-29-55*
06-03-55
06-17-55*
06-26-55
06-30-55
07-03-55
07-07-55*

101

07-11-55	06-13-56*	08-05-57*	02-27-58*
07-12-55*	06-19-56	08-07-57*	03-02-58*
07-13-55*	07-01-56	08-10-57*	03-03-58*
07-24-55*	07-16-56	08-15-57	03-06-58*
07-25-55	07-22-56	08-16-57	03-11-58*
07-27-55*	07-23-56*	08-19-57*	03-15-58
08-03-55	07-25-56	08-20-57	03-17-58*
08-04-55*	08-15-56*	08-23-57*	03-23-58
08-11-55*	09-11-56	08-25-57*	03-27-58*
08-14-55	09-15-56*	08-29-57	04-04-58*
08-21-55	09-23-56	09-04-57*	04-05-58*
08-25-55	10-09-56	09-05-57*	04-06-58
08-27-55	10-14-56	09-08-57	04-07-58*
08-28-55*	10-28-56	09-09-57*	04-08-58*
08-29-55*	11-20-56	09-09-57*	04-09-58*
08-31-55	11-22-56	09-11-57	04-12-58*
09-01-55	12-01-56*	09-15-57	04-14-58*
09-10-55*	12-08-56	09-18-57	04-16-58*
09-13-55*	12-10-56	09-22-57*	04-20-58
09-23-55	12-23-56	09-23-57	04-27-58
10-02-55	12-24-56	09-25-57	04-29-58
10-04-55	01-12-57	09-30-57*	04-30-58
10-06-55	01-22-57	10-01-57*	05-07-58
10-08-55	01-26-57*	10-09-57	05-08-58
10-09-55*	01-31-57*	10-20-57*	05-09-58
10-22-55	02-05-57	10-21-57*	05-14-58*
10-25-55	02-09-57	10-22-57	05-18-58*
10-29-55	02-22-57*	10-24-57*	05-19-58
10-30-55	02-24-57	10-27-57	05-23-58*
11-01-55*	02-27-57	11-02-57	06-02-58*
11-09-55*	03-01-57	11-02-57	06-03-58
11-10-55*	03-07-57*	11-11-57	06-04-58
11-17-55	03-08-57*	11-15-57*	06-06-58*
11-22-55	03-10-57	11-16-57*	06-07-58*
11-24-55	03-14-57	11-19-57	06-09-58
11-30-55*	03-16-57*	11-21-57	06-12-58*
12-07-55*	03-19-57*	11-24-57*	06-19-58
12-11-55	03-20-57*	11-27-57*	06-20-58*
12-14-55	03-21-57	11-30-57*	06-23-58*
12-15-55	03-22-57*	12-10-57*	06-24-58*
12-17-55	03-25-57	12-11-57*	07-02-58*
12-19-55*	03-26-57	12-13-57	07-03-58*
12-28-55	03-29-57*	12-14-57*	07-09-58*
12-30-55	04-06-57	12-16-57*	07-13-58
01-10-56*	04-08-57*	12-18-57*	07-22-58
01-17-56*	04-10-57*	12-19-57	07-25-58*
01-21-56	04-13-57*	12-22-57*	07-26-58*
01-25-56	04-17-57*	12-23-57*	07-28-58
01-27-56*	04-21-57*	12-25-57*	07-30-58*
02-05-56*	04-22-57	12-27-57*	07-30-58*
02-06-56	04-23-57*	12-28-57*	08-02-58*
02-08-56*	04-25-57*	12-29-57*	08-03-58*
02-09-56*	04-27-57*	01-01-58	08-06-58*
02-12-56*	05-01-57	01-07-58	08-07-58*
02-17-56	05-02-57*	01-12-58	08-22-58*
02-23-56	05-03-57	01-14-58*	08-25-58*
02-24-56*	05-04-57	01-15-58*	08-31-58*
02-26-56	05-07-57*	01-17-58	09-02-58*
03-08-56	05-15-57*	01-23-58*	09-03-58*
03-11-56*	05-17-57*	01-24-58	09-10-58*
03-18-56	05-20-57	01-31-58*	09-11-58*
03-25-56*	05-22-57*	02-01-58*	09-11-58*
03-28-56	05-27-57	02-03-58*	09-13-58*
04-13-56	06-03-57*	02-04-58*	09-13-58*
04-26-56	06-04-57	02-11-58	09-14-58
04-27-56*	06-08-57	02-12-58*	09-14-58*
05-04-56	06-24-57	02-13-58	09-16-58*
05-05-56*	06-29-57*	02-13-58*	09-16-58*
05-13-56*	07-05-57	02-14-58*	09-17-58*
05-15-56	07-10-57*	02-14-58*	09-17-58*
05-20-56	07-15-57	02-18-58*	09-18-58*
06-04-56	07-21-57	02-19-58*	09-19-58*
06-08-56	07-25-57	02-26-58*	09-19-58*

103

09-19-58*	01-17-59*	10-12-59*	06-05-60*
09-20-58	01-18-59*	10-17-59	06-12-60*
09-20-58*	01-19-59*	10-23-59	06-13-60*
09-22-58*	01-22-59	10-25-59*	06-13-60*
09-23-58*	01-30-59*	10-26-59*	06-16-60*
09-24-58*	02-04-59*	11-09-59*	06-19-60
09-25-58*	02-13-59*	11-10-59	06-23-60
09-28-58*	02-15-59*	11-11-59*	06-24-60*
09-30-58*	02-22-59*	11-13-59	06-25-60
09-30-58*	02-25-59	11-15-59*	06-26-60*
10-01-58*	02-27-59*	11-19-59	06-27-60
10-01-58*	02-28-59*	11-22-59	06-29-60*
10-01-58*	03-02-59*	12-01-59*	06-30-60*
10-04-58*	03-03-59	12-04-59	07-01-60*
10-05-58*	03-09-59*	12-18-59	07-02-60*
10-07-58	03-13-59*	12-21-59	07-04-60*
10-11-58*	03-16-59*	12-21-59*	07-09-60*
10-12-58	03-17-59*	12-27-59	07-09-60
10-13-58	03-20-59*	12-28-59	07-11-60*
10-13-58	03-21-59*	12-28-59*	07-13-60*
10-15-58*	03-21-59*	12-30-59*	07-21-60
10-17-58*	03-23-59	01-02-60*	07-21-60*
10-18-58	03-24-59*	01-05-60	07-22-60
10-18-58*	03-26-59*	01-07-60*	07-23-60
10-19-58*	03-29-59	01-08-60*	07-24-60
10-20-58*	03-30-59*	01-23-60	07-25-60*
10-23-58*	04-01-59*	01-26-60	07-31-60*
10-23-58*	04-03-59	01-28-60*	08-06-60*
10-24-58*	04-04-59*	02-03-60	08-12-60*
10-25-58*	04-04-59	02-05-60	08-16-60*
10-25-58*	04-08-59*	02-07-60	08-17-60*
10-26-58*	04-10-59*	02-09-60	08-20-60*
10-27-58*	04-15-59*	02-11-60	08-24-60*
11-04-58*	04-16-59	02-12-60	08-27-60
11-04-58	04-20-59*	02-16-60*	08-30-60*
11-05-58*	05-05-59	02-22-60	09-01-60*
11-05-58	05-15-59	02-24-60*	09-03-60*
11-06-58*	05-25-59*	02-28-60*	09-09-60*
11-08-58*	05-28-59*	02-29-60*	09-12-60*
11-10-58*	05-31-59*	03-01-60*	09-12-60*
11-13-58*	06-03-59	03-04-60	09-13-60*
11-13-58*	06-04-59*	03-07-60*	09-15-60*
11-14-58*	06-05-59*	03-07-60	09-16-60*
11-21-58*	06-07-59	03-10-60	09-23-60*
11-22-58*	06-09-59	03-12-60*	09-24-60
11-24-58*	06-15-59	03-15-60*	09-25-60*
11-26-58*	06-22-59	03-16-60	09-26-60
11-26-58*	06-26-59	03-21-60*	09-27-60*
11-29-58*	07-09-59*	03-26-60*	09-29-60*
11-30-58*	07-11-59	03-27-60	09-29-60
12-02-58*	07-13-59*	03-28-60	10-01-60*
12-05-58*	07-19-59*	04-02-60*	10-05-60*
12-06-58*	07-25-59*	04-03-60	10-10-60
12-07-58*	07-27-59	04-05-60*	10-11-60*
12-07-58*	07-29-59*	04-16-60*	10-11-60
12-10-58*	08-01-59	04-17-60*	10-14-60*
12-13-58	08-06-59	04-19-60	10-16-60*
12-15-58*	08-08-59	04-21-60*	10-17-60
12-20-58*	08-08-59*	04-24-60*	10-22-60
12-23-58	08-14-59	05-03-60*	10-27-60
12-24-58*	08-17-59	05-07-60	10-28-60*
12-24-58*	08-18-59	05-08-60	10-29-60*
12-29-58*	08-21-59	05-14-60*	10-30-60*
01-04-59*	08-28-59	05-15-60	11-10-60*
01-05-59*	08-29-59	05-17-60*	11-11-60*
01-06-59*	09-13-59*	05-21-60	11-12-60*
01-07-59*	09-18-59*	05-25-60	11-18-60*
01-08-59*	09-23-59*	05-26-60*	11-20-60
01-09-59*	09-23-59*	05-28-60*	11-22-60*
01-11-59*	09-27-59	05-28-60*	11-25-60
01-12-59*	10-01-59*	06-01-60*	12-04-60*
01-13-59*	10-04-59*	06-04-60	12-10-60
01-16-59*	10-11-59*	06-04-60*	12-14-60

12-15-60*	04-13-63*	08-01-64*	01-25-66
12-17-60*	04-15-63*	08-03-64*	01-30-66*
12-29-60	05-01-63	08-05-64	02-05-66*
12-30-60*	05-04-63*	08-21-64*	02-06-66
01-06-61*	05-08-63*	08-30-64*	02-08-66
01-12-61*	05-11-63	09-05-64	02-16-66
01-16-61*	05-29-63	09-10-64	02-23-66*
01-22-61	05-30-63*	09-22-64*	03-03-66*
02-04-61*	06-01-63	09-24-64	03-08-66*
02-05-61*	06-02-63*	10-01-64*	03-10-66
02-07-61*	06-19-63*	10-24-64	03-12-66*
02-13-61*	06-27-63	10-27-64	03-16-66*
02-20-61*	07-04-63*	10-28-64	03-29-66
03-04-61	07-07-63	11-17-64	04-01-66
03-05-61*	07-17-63*	11-24-64	04-03-66
03-07-61*	07-18-63*	12-15-64	04-06-66*
03-08-61	07-21-63*	12-18-64*	04-11-66*
03-09-61*	07-29-63*	12-30-64	04-14-66*
03-11-61*	07-30-63	01-15-65*	04-15-66*
03-14-61*	08-17-63*	02-16-65*	04-22-66
03-22-61	09-02-63*	02-17-65	05-01-66
03-28-61*	09-25-63*	02-23-65	05-04-66
04-02-61	10-01-63*	02-27-65	06-01-66
04-03-61*	10-08-63*	03-14-65	06-02-66
04-08-61*	10-20-63*	03-28-65	06-08-66*
04-15-61	10-27-63	04-04-65*	06-24-66
04-20-61	11-16-63	04-10-65	07-17-66
05-04-61	11-26-63	04-17-65	07-21-66
05-05-61*	11-29-63*	04-22-65	08-08-66
05-16-61	11-30-63	04-28-65*	08-23-66
05-20-61*	12-04-63	04-30-65*	09-05-66*
05-28-61*	12-07-63	05-05-65*	09-26-66
07-01-61*	12-11-63	05-12-65	10-22-66
09-08-61*	01-01-64*	05-19-65	11-08-66*
09-28-61*	01-03-64*	05-21-65*	12-26-66*
10-01-61*	01-24-64	05-30-65*	01-19-67
10-10-61*	01-26-64	06-01-65	02-10-67
10-11-61*	01-30-64	06-21-65*	03-13-67
11-03-61	02-02-64	07-02-65	04-08-67*
11-17-61	02-07-64*	07-03-65*	04-15-67
11-25-61	02-08-64	07-06-65	04-21-67*
12-03-61*	02-09-64	07-11-65	04-24-67*
12-15-61*	02-20-64	07-19-65	04-26-67*
12-17-61	02-23-64	07-20-65*	05-04-67
12-23-61	02-24-64	07-22-65*	05-07-67*
12-24-61*	02-28-64	07-23-65*	05-12-67
01-01-62	03-06-64	07-30-65	05-16-67
01-20-62	03-07-64	08-05-65	05-22-67*
01-22-62	03-08-64	08-12-65	05-23-67
02-16-62	03-18-64*	08-21-65	05-28-67*
03-02-62*	03-19-64	08-31-65	05-29-67*
04-17-62*	03-24-64*	09-01-65*	06-01-67*
04-22-62*	04-02-64*	09-06-65	06-08-67
05-12-62*	04-04-64*	09-07-65	06-18-67*
05-23-62*	04-05-64*	09-08-65	06-21-67*
06-27-62*	04-06-64*	09-10-65*	06-30-67*
10-01-62*	04-14-64	09-19-65	07-07-67
11-03-62	04-24-64	09-24-65	07-16-67*
12-02-62	05-01-64	09-26-65*	07-24-67*
12-05-62	05-08-64*	09-30-65*	07-30-67
12-14-62	05-15-64	10-01-65*	07-30-67
12-19-62	05-21-64	10-10-65	08-04-67
01-11-63*	05-26-64	11-05-65	08-05-67
01-15-63	05-30-64	11-08-65	08-08-67*
01-25-63	06-01-64*	12-02-65*	08-13-67*
02-11-63*	06-02-64*	12-13-65	08-17-67*
02-17-63	06-06-64	12-16-65	08-19-67*
03-17-63	06-14-64*	12-18-65	08-25-67
03-25-63*	06-19-64*	12-27-65*	09-14-67*
03-27-63	07-05-64	12-29-65	09-16-67*
03-31-63	07-06-64*	01-01-66	09-22-67
04-06-63	07-08-64*	01-08-66	10-06-67*
04-08-63	07-12-64*	01-17-66*	10-12-67*

10-19-67*	03-11-75	04-17-57*	06-05-65*
10-21-67*	03-21-75	04-23-57*	11-12-65*
10-25-67*	04-25-75*	04-26-57	01-03-66*
11-19-67	06-26-75	05-02-57	01-11-66
12-14-67	09-09-75	05-07-57*	01-30-66*
12-22-67	09-12-75	05-15-57*	02-14-66
01-01-68*	10-01-75	05-29-57	06-08-66*
01-07-68*	10-19-75	05-31-57	06-24-66
01-30-68	10-21-75	06-09-57	08-01-66
02-07-68		06-10-57	09-05-66
03-10-68	b. Party Struggle Method	06-11-57*	06-21-67*
03-25-68	03-03-50	06-12-57*	06-30-67
03-30-68	03-09-50*	06-14-57*	08-04-67
05-01-68	03-22-50	06-22-57	08-17-67*
05-03-68	03-24-50*	06-26-57	10-21-67
05-12-68	04-23-50*	06-29-57*	11-19-67
08-01-68	04-23-50*	07-01-57*	12-22-67*
08-05-68	08-08-50	07-08-57*	01-01-69
08-15-68	08-22-50*	07-16-57	06-09-69
08-21-68	08-26-50	08-16-57	08-25-69
08-28-68*	09-07-50	09-04-57*	05-23-70*
09-07-68*	09-14-50	09-05-57*	01-01-71*
09-12-68*	10-14-50	09-18-57*	01-31-71
09-25-68*	12-31-50*	09-30-57*	04-24-72*
11-25-68	01-19-53	10-08-57*	03-08-73
01-01-69	01-23-53	10-21-57*	07-01-74
02-17-69*	01-25-53	11-01-57	03-21-75*
02-21-69*	02-01-53	11-17-57	
03-22-69*	02-11-53	12-04-57	c. Study Training Movements
05-04-69	02-28-53	12-25-57*	07-03-49
06-09-69*	03-11-53	12-29-57*	03-08-50
07-01-69*	03-13-53	01-01-58	04-23-50
08-25-69*	03-25-53*	01-27-58*	06-04-50
11-05-69*	06-06-53	02-02-58	06-04-50*
11-20-69	10-08-53	03-06-58*	07-29-50
01-01-70	11-02-53*	03-19-58	08-08-50
03-29-70*	11-26-53	03-23-58	09-07-50
04-01-70*	12-28-53	03-26-58*	09-25-50
05-23-70*	12-29-53	04-13-58	10-18-50
07-01-70*	02-18-54*	05-01-58	12-22-50
07-09-70*	03-05-54	05-07-58	11-26-52*
08-01-70	03-22-54*	05-08-58	12-14-52
09-23-70*	03-23-54	08-30-58*	01-23-53
10-01-70*	03-25-54	09-30-58	01-27-53*
01-01-71*	04-20-54*	10-23-58	01-31-53*
02-18-71*	05-07-54*	11-21-58*	02-18-53*
08-01-71*	05-08-54	12-05-58*	04-25-53
04-16-72*	06-04-54	12-07-58*	06-26-53
05-23-72	07-01-54	12-07-58*	11-23-53
06-10-72*	07-20-54*	12-21-58*	12-01-53*
07-06-72	08-13-54	01-04-59*	12-11-53*
08-01-72*	09-11-54*	06-07-59	12-11-53*
01-01-73*	11-03-54	09-03-59*	12-20-53
03-02-73*	12-13-54	10-26-59*	12-30-53*
04-24-73*	02-17-55	11-19-59	01-07-54*
07-11-73*	05-18-55	12-28-59*	01-16-54
08-07-73*	08-04-55*	04-17-60*	01-17-54
09-29-73*	08-25-55	08-16-60	01-21-54
10-01-73*	11-17-55	02-02-61*	01-22-54*
01-01-74	11-30-55*	04-22-62*	01-26-54*
02-20-74	12-17-55	05-23-62*	02-18-54
03-03-74*	02-05-56*	10-01-62*	03-12-54*
03-08-74*	02-08-56	04-13-63	03-21-54
04-10-74*	02-09-56*	07-17-63	03-25-54
06-18-74*	04-30-56	09-20-63*	03-30-54
07-01-74*	05-15-56	09-25-63	07-15-54*
07-03-74*	05-22-56	12-04-63	07-20-54
08-08-74*	01-31-57*	06-04-64*	08-18-54*
10-01-74*	02-05-57	08-03-64*	10-15-54*
11-28-74	03-20-57*	08-01-64	01-23-55*
01-01-75	03-21-57	12-18-64*	02-08-55*
02-09-75	03-22-57*	01-05-65*	02-19-55*
02-28-75*	03-25-57	04-22-65	

105

04-11-55
05-04-55
05-15-55*
05-23-55
07-15-55*
07-16-55
07-23-55
07-31-55
10-22-55
11-30-55
12-11-55
04-07-56
05-13-56
07-22-56
08-13-56
08-15-56
08-28-56
10-16-56
12-08-56
12-10-56*
01-23-57*
02-16-57
03-25-56
05-03-57*
05-15-57*
07-21-57
12-19-57
03-02-58*
04-20-58
07-28-58*
08-22-58
11-24-58
08-27-60
05-16-62*
05-17-68
07-01-70
10-01-70*
07-06-72*
07-11-73*
10-01-73*
01-01-74*
02-20-74
04-10-74
05-04-74
06-18-74*
07-03-74
10-01-74
11-28-74*
01-01-75*
02-09-75*
03-21-75*
10-21-75

  d. Marxism, Leninism, and
     Stalinism
    12-21-49
    02-16-50
    04-05-50*
    04-22-50*
    05-03-50
    09-14-50
    11-07-50
    02-16-51
    10-15-51
    10-19-51
    11-09-51
    01-21-52
    05-01-52
    10-07-52
    10-19-52
    10-30-52
    01-06-53*
    01-27-53

02-10-53
03-07-53
03-11-53
03-14-53*
04-25-53
05-05-53*
05-06-53
05-14-53
07-30-53
09-09-53
10-08-53
10-17-53
11-07-53
11-19-53
11-25-53
12-12-53
12-22-53
01-05-54
01-07-54
01-11-54
01-13-54
01-16-54
01-21-54*
01-22-54
02-18-54
02-24-54
02-28-54
03-05-54
03-12-54*
03-30-54
04-23-54
05-27-54
06-22-54*
07-01-54
07-03-54
07-06-54
07-20-54
09-21-54
10-08-54
10-15-54
10-22-54
11-10-54
11-14-54
11-21-54
11-26-54
12-22-54
04-10-55
04-11-55
04-22-55*
05-03-55
05-11-55
06-19-55
07-12-55
09-11-55
11-22-55
12-26-55
01-01-56
01-22-56
02-14-56
02-19-56
02-26-56
02-28-56
03-25-56
04-07-56*
04-21-56
07-11-56
09-15-56*
09-29-56
10-19-56
11-03-56
11-07-56
11-12-56*
12-03-56

03-30-57
04-06-57*
04-10-57*
04-13-57*
04-30-57
05-02-57
05-07-57*
05-15-57
05-17-57*
05-19-57
06-09-57
06-22-57
07-23-57
09-04-57
09-12-57*
09-27-57*
10-28-57
11-01-57
11-03-57
11-06-57*
11-15-57
11-25-57
01-15-58
01-31-58
02-02-58
02-03-58
02-20-58
02-23-58
02-28-58
05-04-58
05-05-58*
05-08-58
05-15-58
05-18-58
05-20-58
05-29-58
06-03-58
06-04-58*
06-09-58
06-10-58
06-14-58
06-19-58
06-20-58
06-24-58
07-02-58
07-24-58
07-26-58
07-28-58*
08-04-58
08-28-58
09-19-58
09-30-58
11-12-58
11-19-58
12-21-58
12-23-58
01-16-59
03-15-59
04-29-59
05-04-59
05-19-59
07-11-59
08-29-59*
09-01-59*
09-19-59
09-22-59
09-25-59
10-01-59
10-03-59*
10-26-59
11-07-59
12-03-59
01-01-60

03-01-60
03-08-60*
03-13-60
03-14-60
03-16-60
03-23-60
04-04-60
04-05-60
05-06-60
05-28-60
06-02-60*
06-12-60
06-25-60
06-29-60*
07-18-60
08-15-60
08-27-60
09-02-60
09-25-60
09-30-60*
11-07-60
11-20-60
11-21-60*
12-07-60*
12-12-60*
01-22-61*
01-29-61*
02-02-61
02-14-61*
03-11-61*
03-18-61*
05-01-61
05-04-61
05-28-61*
06-16-61
07-01-61*
09-20-61
09-28-61
10-01-61
10-10-61
11-07-61
11-08-61
12-01-61*
12-15-61
12-24-61
01-04-62*
04-08-62
05-23-62
06-15-62
06-27-62
09-17-62*
10-01-62
11-07-62
11-09-62
11-15-62*
11-28-62
12-15-62*
12-22-62
12-31-62*
01-25-63*
01-27-63*
02-27-63
03-08-63
03-09-63
05-01-63
05-04-63
05-18-63
06-01-63
06-02-63
06-05-63
06-19-63
06-23-63
06-24-63*

06-27-63	04-22-66*	06-20-71*	08-12-56
07-04-63	04-28-66	08-01-71	10-28-56
07-11-63*	05-15-66*	08-27-71	11-06-56
07-13-63*	06-01-66	11-08-71	12-23-56
07-17-63	06-02-66	11-20-71	02-05-57*
07-25-63*	06-03-66	11-28-71	07-23-57*
08-22-63	06-04-66	11-29-71*	10-03-57*
08-29-63	06-08-66	12-01-71*	01-15-58*
09-20-63*	06-24-66	01-01-72*	01-31-58*
10-01-63	06-25-66	04-24-72	02-15-58*
10-20-63	06-29-66	04-24-72	03-06-58
11-07-63*	07-01-66	05-23-72	03-14-58
11-29-63*	07-26-66	07-06-72	03-19-58
01-01-64	08-08-66	08-01-72	03-22-58
01-03-64	08-11-66	09-01-72	03-23-58*
01-06-64	08-15-66	10-01-72	03-24-58*
01-11-64	08-17-66	11-28-72*	04-13-58*
01-28-64	10-12-66	01-01-73	04-19-58
02-01-64	12-24-66*	02-22-73	04-21-58
02-05-64	01-22-67	03-08-73	04-29-58
02-08-64	01-27-67	04-24-73	05-04-58*
02-09-64	04-21-67	06-04-73	05-09-58*
02-23-64	04-26-67	06-25-73	05-21-58
03-07-64	04-30-67	09-09-73	06-03-58
03-24-64*	05-14-67	10-01-73	06-09-58
03-26-64*	05-28-67	11-29-73	07-03-58*
04-01-64	06-01-67	01-01-74	07-11-58
04-02-64	06-18-67	02-02-74*	07-14-58*
04-05-64	06-21-67	02-20-74	09-25-58
05-04-64	06-30-67	03-03-74	11-01-58
05-27-64	07-07-67	03-08-74	03-08-59
05-29-64	07-24-67	04-10-74	03-30-59*
07-12-64*	07-31-67	05-04-74*	04-03-59
08-03-64*	08-05-67	06-18-74	06-11-59
08-14-64	08-08-67	06-25-74	09-19-59
08-21-64	09-26-67*	08-23-74*	09-21-59
09-24-64*	10-06-67	09-02-74	12-21-59
10-01-64	11-26-67	09-09-74	01-11-60
10-24-64*	11-29-67*	10-01-74	02-11-60*
11-07-64*	12-04-67	11-28-74	03-16-60
01-01-65	12-22-67	11-29-74	04-05-60*
01-05-65	04-20-68	01-01-75	04-09-60
01-23-65	05-27-68	02-03-75	05-06-60
02-14-65	07-01-68	02-09-75*	06-01-60
02-23-65	08-01-68	03-11-75*	06-04-60
03-12-65*	08-05-68	03-21-75	05-04-61
03-14-65*	08-18-68	04-18-75*	11-17-61*
04-01-65*	09-01-68*	05-09-75	03-27-63
04-02-65	09-07-68	09-04-75	07-17-63*
04-06-65*	09-18-68*	09-09-75	07-29-63
04-09-65*	09-29-68	09-12-75	08-06-63
04-10-65	10-01-68	10-01-75	09-25-63*
04-28-65	11-25-68*	10-10-75*	12-04-63
04-29-65*	11-29-68	10-19-75	02-05-64
04-30-65	01-01-69	10-25-75	02-18-64
05-01-65*	03-04-69	11-29-75*	03-10-64
05-04-65	04-17-69		04-04-64
06-21-65*	05-04-69	e. Red versus Expert	04-24-64
07-30-65	06-09-69	04-09-52	05-29-64*
09-02-65*	07-01-69	06-14-52	09-05-64
11-07-65*	08-25-69	11-22-53*	09-10-64
11-19-65	11-23-69	11-26-53	12-30-64
11-28-65	11-29-69	12-22-53	03-28-65*
12-11-65	01-01-70	03-19-54*	04-10-65*
12-13-65	04-01-70	04-23-54	04-26-65
12-16-65	05-01-70	04-24-54	05-05-65
01-01-66	05-23-70	12-13-54	07-02-65*
01-06-66	07-01-70	01-17-55	09-24-65
01-16-66*	09-03-70	02-27-55*	11-30-65
01-25-66	01-11-71*	03-18-55*	12-23-65
02-13-66	01-31-71	03-21-56	01-02-66
03-16-66	05-01-71*	05-15-56	01-20-66
04-06-66*	06-01-71*	06-11-56	01-21-66

04-06-66
04-14-66*
08-07-73
09-12-75*

C. Democratic Parties
01-24-51*
08-26-54
09-15-54
07-13-56
09-15-56
09-27-56
04-26-57*
06-08-57
07-01-57
08-29-57*
09-18-57
03-17-58*
09-25-60*

D. Mass Organizations

1. All-China Athletic Federation
08-18-56
08-31-56
10-07-56*
08-21-58

2. All-China Federation of Industry and Commerce
11-14-53
06-09-55
08-10-55
11-22-55
01-01-56
01-03-56
02-29-56
07-13-56
12-08-56*
12-10-56*
12-24-56*
03-01-60*

3. All-China Federation of Literary and Art Circles
10-08-53
04-03-57
09-01-57
11-12-57
08-15-60*

4. All-China Federation of Supply and Marketing Cooperatives
12-18-55

5. All-China Federation of Trade Unions
06-23-49*
02-06-50
06-17-50
06-29-50*
01-10-53*
02-07-53
05-01-53*
05-13-53*
07-08-53*
08-19-53*
10-24-53*
11-21-53
06-08-54

03-08-55
05-06-55
05-29-55
06-01-55
08-23-55
08-31-55*
09-10-55*
09-11-55
10-02-55*
12-17-55
01-17-56
01-19-56
03-30-56
06-05-56
06-12-56
06-14-56
08-16-56*
10-11-56
11-30-56*
02-07-57
05-29-57*
09-04-57*
10-04-57*
10-18-57*
12-02-57*
12-13-57*
07-17-58
08-12-58*
09-30-62
02-07-63
02-05-64
08-02-67
04-24-73*

6. All-China Students' Federation
08-11-55
02-11-60*

7. All-China Youth Federation
06-18-53*
07-03-53*
09-20-55
09-29-55*
04-10-58
11-21-58*

8. China Committee for the Promotion of International Trade
11-10-56

9. China Scientific and Technical Association
08-27-50*
09-18-54*
12-08-54
12-12-54*
07-14-58
09-19-58*
03-21-59
09-08-60
04-06-63
05-21-64
05-08-66

10. Chinese People's Committee for World Peace
10-02-49
05-15-50

08-14-50*

11. Friendship Associations

a. Sino-Albania
11-29-59

b. Sino-Algeria
09-30-62

c. Sino-Cambodia
12-18-70

d. Sino-Cuba
04-17-64

e. Sino-Czechoslovakia
03-28-57

f. Sino-Indonesia
06-02-55*

g. Sino-Japan
09-03-53
09-14-55
07-01-56
05-23-57
10-05-63*
10-06-63

h. Sino-Mongolia
03-01-56

i. Sino-Nepal
03-25-60

j. Sino-Soviet
10-06-49*
02-14-51*
02-14-52*
02-14-53*
11-07-53
02-14-54*
10-13-54*
12-29-54*
02-14-55*
02-23-55
02-14-56*
06-21-56
02-14-57
04-15-57
04-16-57
10-31-57*

12. Red Cross Society of China
07-01-56
04-03-63

13. Women's Federation
07-31-54*
03-08-55
03-08-57
09-09-57
12-16-57
03-08-61
09-30-62
03-08-63
03-08-64
03-08-65
08-07-73

E. Campaigns

1. Land Reform
03-18-50
06-30-50*
10-21-50
06-23-51
07-05-51*
09-20-51
11-11-51
11-13-51
12-17-51
01-01-52
04-02-52
09-04-52

2. Marriage Law Reform
03-08-50*
04-16-50*
09-29-51*
02-01-53*
05-06-53*

3. Peace Signature Campaign
05-15-50*
08-14-50*

4. Suppression of Counter-Revolutionaries
07-21-50*
12-26-50*
02-22-51*
03-07-51*
03-11-51*
03-26-51*
04-30-51*
04-20-51*
04-28-51*
05-04-51
05-21-51*
05-29-51
06-03-51*
06-10-51
06-11-51*
06-24-51
08-14-51
09-05-51
09-20-51

5. Christian Reform Movement
09-23-50*
12-14-50
12-28-50
01-08-51*
04-06-51
04-09-51*
04-17-51*
04-24-51*
06-24-51*
09-05-51*
07-16-53*
12-10-55*
08-03-57*

6. Patriotic Compact Movement
12-28-50
03-30-51*
06-02-51*
08-08-51*

7. Resist-U.S. Aid-Korea
   12-14-50*
   12-28-50*
   01-24-51
   01-26-51
   02-03-51
   03-17-51*
   04-04-51*
   04-06-51
   04-17-51*
   05-01-51*
   05-30-51
   06-02-51*
   06-25-51
   07-20-51
   07-29-51
   08-08-51
   09-20-51
   09-23-51
   09-30-51*
   10-15-51
   10-25-51*
   11-09-51
   11-10-51*
   11-14-51
   01-01-52
   01-11-52
   07-01-52
   07-28-52
   10-25-52
   12-25-52*
   01-01-53
   01-24-53
   02-10-53
   07-16-53
   09-27-53
   10-25-53
   11-24-53

8. National Patriotic Donation Campaign
   01-15-51*
   07-29-51*
   09-30-51*
   11-10-51*

9. Production Increase and Austerity Campaign
   06-02-51
   07-29-51*
   11-09-51
   11-20-51*
   11-23-51
   12-07-51*
   12-19-51
   01-21-52
   04-02-52*
   07-01-52

10. Three-Anti Campaign
    11-23-51
    12-19-51
    01-01-52
    01-04-52*
    01-12-52*
    01-21-52*
    01-22-52*
    01-29-52*
    02-07-52
    02-16-52*
    02-21-52*
    03-02-52*
    03-08-52*

03-12-52
03-13-52
04-02-52*
04-08-52
04-09-52
04-15-52
04-16-52
05-12-52
05-28-52
06-14-52
06-15-52
07-01-52
07-02-52
08-17-52
08-25-52
01-23-53
03-04-53
03-13-53
07-26-53*
04-13-54
06-04-54
12-24-54
05-08-55

11. Five-Anti Campaign
    01-05-52*
    01-06-52*
    02-21-52*
    03-08-52*
    03-12-52*
    04-09-52
    04-15-52
    05-12-52
    05-28-52
    06-15-52*
    07-01-52
    07-02-52
    08-17-52
    08-25-52
    11-14-53
    04-13-54
    07-08-54
    05-08-55

12. Patriotic Public Health Campaigns
    07-05-52*
    01-04-53
    01-27-56
    03-19-57*
    10-24-57
    12-23-57*
    02-13-58*
    02-27-58*
    01-17-59
    02-04-59*
    07-25-59*
    08-20-59*
    03-26-60*
    04-15-60
    01-15-63*
    03-06-64*
    11-05-65
    08-08-74*
    04-25-75

13. Learn from the Advanced Experience of the U.S.S.R.
    11-07-52*
    11-15-52*
    01-22-53
    01-23-53

01-29-53*
01-31-53
02-10-53
02-14-53
04-23-53
04-25-53*
04-28-53
05-04-53
05-05-53
05-14-53
06-19-53*
08-16-53
09-16-53*
09-29-53
10-15-53
10-30-53
11-07-53
11-16-53
11-22-53
12-25-53
12-27-53
12-29-53
02-07-54
02-14-54
09-18-54
10-02-54*
10-23-54*
11-13-54
12-12-54
12-20-54*
12-26-54*
12-29-54
01-03-55
02-20-55
04-16-55
05-15-55
06-12-55
07-19-55
09-10-55
10-02-55
10-10-55
11-07-55
11-30-55
01-10-56*
01-28-56
03-11-56
09-15-56
11-06-57
12-14-57

14. Struggle against Bureaucratism, Commandism, and Unlawful Acts
    01-19-53*
    01-23-53
    02-10-53
    02-11-53*
    03-11-53*
    03-13-53*
    04-07-53*
    04-30-53
    06-06-53
    06-20-53*
    06-26-53*
    08-18-53
    09-02-53
    10-18-53
    11-02-53
    11-04-53
    11-09-53
    12-24-53
    12-28-53
    12-29-53

01-05-54
02-24-54
03-31-54
01-28-55
04-17-55*

15. Campaign to Increase Production and Economize
    04-11-53*
    05-01-53
    09-06-53*
    10-01-53
    10-06-53*
    10-07-53*
    11-17-53*
    11-21-53*
    12-12-53
    12-18-53*
    12-29-53
    01-01-54
    01-28-54
    02-07-54
    02-10-54
    08-05-54*
    08-07-54
    08-08-54
    10-16-54*
    11-11-54
    03-21-55
    03-22-55*
    03-28-55*
    04-16-55
    04-27-55
    05-01-55
    05-11-55
    05-14-55*
    05-21-55*
    06-09-55*
    06-18-55
    06-19-55*
    06-21-55*
    06-29-55*
    07-01-55*
    07-10-55
    07-17-55
    07-19-55*
    07-23-55
    07-24-55
    07-28-55
    07-31-55
    08-03-55*
    08-04-55*
    08-09-55
    08-14-55*
    08-20-55*
    08-23-55*
    09-07-55*
    09-19-55
    09-26-55
    10-09-55*
    10-23-55
    10-24-55
    11-23-55
    11-26-55*
    12-01-55
    01-19-56*
    01-25-56
    02-29-56*
    03-28-56*
    03-30-56*
    04-01-56
    04-06-56

109

04-10-56*	07-24-59*	04-13-63*	01-01-55*
05-01-56	07-27-59*	05-01-63*	01-07-55
05-03-56	08-06-59*	05-08-63	02-28-55*
05-05-56	08-16-59	07-07-63*	03-14-55*
11-26-56*	08-17-59*	09-02-63*	09-25-55
12-16-56*	08-20-59	10-20-63	10-15-55*
12-28-56	08-28-59	10-27-63*	10-18-55*
01-01-57	09-02-59*	11-08-63*	10-22-55*
01-04-57*	09-03-59*	11-16-63	10-25-55*
01-12-57*	09-05-59*	11-26-63	10-28-55*
01-13-57	09-06-59*	12-04-63	10-29-55*
01-16-57	09-11-59*	12-11-63	10-30-55
01-27-57	09-17-59	12-26-63*	11-01-55*
02-07-57	09-21-59*	01-01-64	11-02-55*
02-17-57*	09-23-59*	02-02-64	11-08-55*
02-25-57*	09-25-59*	02-09-64*	11-09-55*
02-27-57*	09-26-59*	05-01-64*	11-11-55*
03-04-57*	10-01-59	05-08-64*	11-24-55*
03-08-57	10-08-59	05-15-64*	11-28-55*
03-13-57*	10-10-59*	05-26-64	12-03-55
03-17-57*	10-11-59*	06-14-64*	12-06-55
03-21-57*	10-12-59*	10-27-64*	12-13-55
03-27-57	10-13-59*	11-19-64	12-18-55
03-31-57*	10-16-59*	01-05-65	12-23-55
04-11-57*	10-28-59	05-01-65	12-28-55
04-20-57*	11-04-59*	06-02-65*	12-30-55
04-28-57	11-12-59	06-21-65*	01-01-56
05-08-57*	11-26-59	07-30-65*	01-14-56
05-21-57*	12-20-59	08-14-65	01-15-56
05-30-57	01-02-60	09-08-65*	01-16-56
06-04-57*	03-12-60	09-24-65*	01-24-56*
06-13-57*	03-24-60*	12-22-65	02-18-56
06-24-57	03-29-60	01-06-66	02-22-56
07-05-57	03-31-60*	01-26-66*	03-04-56*
08-12-57	04-17-60*	02-02-66*	05-01-56
08-20-57*	08-05-60	02-08-66	05-16-56
08-23-57	08-17-60	02-16-66*	09-13-56
08-28-57*	08-18-60*	01-26-67*	07-03-57
09-02-57*	08-21-60	05-15-67*	
09-07-57*	08-23-60*	06-14-67*	18. Study the General Line of the Party in the Period of Transition
09-09-57	08-26-60*	08-26-67	
11-02-57*	08-29-60	12-14-68*	
11-10-57	08-31-60*	02-21-69	11-07-53
11-14-57	09-07-60*	03-29-70	11-09-53*
11-17-57	09-13-60		11-11-53
11-28-57	09-17-60	16. Technical Renovation Movement	11-16-53
11-29-57	09-21-60		11-23-53
12-12-57*	09-24-60	05-15-53	11-25-53*
12-14-57	10-01-60*	05-01-54*	12-01-53
12-27-57	10-05-60	05-04-54	12-11-53
01-07-58*	10-06-60*	06-29-54	12-11-53*
01-08-58*	10-07-60	09-14-54	12-12-53*
01-17-58*	10-10-60	05-29-55	12-20-53
02-02-58*	10-11-60		12-24-53*
02-10-58	10-14-60	17. Campaign to Create Agricultural Producers' Cooperatives	12-30-53*
02-14-58	10-16-60		01-01-54
02-18-58*	10-30-60		01-06-54
03-01-58*	12-28-60	03-26-53	01-07-54*
04-06-58	01-20-61	01-05-54	01-11-54
04-11-58	05-16-61*	01-06-54	01-16-54
05-01-59*	11-14-61	01-09-54*	01-17-54
05-04-59	04-29-62*	01-16-54*	01-22-54
05-13-59	05-22-62*	01-17-54	01-26-54*
05-15-59*	11-12-62*	01-19-54	01-29-54*
05-19-59*	11-13-62	01-26-54*	02-02-54
05-28-59	11-27-62*	05-26-54	02-07-54*
06-04-59*	11-30-62*	07-07-54*	02-18-54*
06-05-59*	02-07-63*	07-31-54	02-20-54*
06-17-59*	03-15-63	08-03-54*	03-11-54
06-27-59	03-20-63*	09-14-54	03-12-54
07-06-59*	03-23-63	11-21-54	04-05-55
07-10-59*	03-24-63*	12-04-54*	
07-17-59*	04-10-63*	12-15-54*	

19. Oppose Bourgeois Individualism, Liberalism, Sectarianism, Dispersionism, Conceit, and Parochialism in the Party
    02-18-54*
    03-22-54*
    04-04-54*
    04-13-54*
    04-19-54
    04-23-54*
    05-07-54*
    05-08-54
    05-19-54
    05-26-54
    06-04-54
    06-05-54
    07-20-54*
    12-13-54*
    03-04-55
    03-29-55
    04-10-55
    04-11-55
    04-15-55

20. Worker Emulation, Advanced Producers, and Model Units
    08-31-55*
    09-10-55
    01-28-56
    03-11-56
    03-19-56*
    04-17-56*
    04-19-56
    04-27-56
    04-30-56*
    05-11-56*
    05-25-56
    06-08-56
    06-15-56
    06-24-56
    07-06-56
    07-22-56*
    07-27-56*
    08-21-56*
    09-23-56*
    12-10-56
    12-19-56*
    02-18-57
    03-10-57*
    05-17-57
    12-13-57
    02-14-58*
    03-01-58*
    03-02-58*
    03-03-58
    03-11-58
    03-27-58*
    04-05-58*
    04-09-58*
    04-20-58
    04-30-58
    05-18-58*
    06-07-58
    06-24-58*
    07-30-58*
    03-24-59*
    05-01-59
    10-26-59*
    11-28-59
    01-07-60*

    01-13-60
    01-18-60
    02-09-60*
    02-27-60
    03-13-60
    03-17-60
    04-13-60
    05-20-60
    06-01-60
    06-12-60*
    07-31-60*
    08-16-60
    08-18-60
    08-21-60
    09-26-60
    10-07-60*
    01-09-61*
    02-24-61*
    03-01-60
    03-07-61*
    03-19-61
    04-07-61*
    11-03-61
    01-18-62*
    01-15-63
    02-07-63
    03-17-63
    05-01-63
    07-29-63
    08-17-63*
    09-02-63
    12-07-63*
    12-11-63
    01-23-64
    01-30-64
    02-07-64
    03-07-64
    03-19-64*
    03-23-64
    04-02-64
    04-14-64*
    05-15-64*
    05-21-64
    06-14-64
    07-12-64
    07-16-64*
    10-25-64*
    01-15-65
    03-11-65*
    03-12-65
    03-14-65*
    03-28-65*
    04-28-65*
    05-04-65*
    05-19-65*
    07-02-65*
    07-03-65*
    08-12-65
    10-10-65
    11-05-65
    12-23-65
    03-06-66*
    09-25-68*
    11-05-69
    03-07-70

21. Illiteracy Campaign
    11-08-55
    12-06-55*
    12-30-55
    01-08-56
    01-21-56*
    02-03-56

    02-27-56
    04-01-56*
    04-26-56
    06-20-56
    11-25-56*
    12-12-56
    02-06-57*
    03-07-58*
    03-28-58*
    05-20-58*
    06-09-58
    03-14-59
    03-23-60*
    05-11-60*

22. Anti-Pest Campaign
    07-12-54
    01-12-56*
    01-23-56*
    01-24-58*
    05-01-58
    09-11-58*
    09-19-58

23. Anti-Hu Feng and Su-ching Anti-Counter-Revolutionary Campaign
    06-10-55*
    07-03-55*
    07-12-55*
    07-16-55*
    07-25-55*
    07-31-55
    08-22-55*
    08-28-55*
    09-01-55*
    10-28-55*
    11-28-55
    12-10-55*
    02-07-56*
    03-01-56*
    04-16-56*
    04-25-56*
    05-05-56
    05-26-56*
    07-12-56*
    08-03-56*
    10-24-56

24. Party Rectification
    12-13-55*
    12-19-55
    02-07-56
    02-26-56*
    05-13-56*
    06-20-56*
    06-27-56*
    07-16-56*
    07-25-56*
    08-16-56
    08-23-56
    10-05-56*
    10-09-56*
    10-11-56*
    11-25-56
    11-28-56*
    01-07-57
    01-11-57*
    01-26-57
    04-13-57*
    04-17-57*
    04-23-57*
    05-07-57*

    01-01-58

25. One Hundred Flowers
    04-26-57
    05-01-57*
    05-02-57*
    05-03-57*
    05-04-57
    05-08-57
    05-12-57
    05-13-57*
    05-17-57*
    05-19-57*
    05-27-57*
    05-31-57*
    06-03-57
    06-04-57*
    06-08-57*
    06-09-57*
    06-10-57*
    06-11-57
    06-12-57*
    06-12-57*
    06-14-57*
    06-22-57*
    06-26-57*
    06-29-57*
    07-01-57
    07-03-57
    07-08-57
    07-10-57
    07-23-57*
    07-25-57
    08-05-57
    08-10-57
    09-01-57
    09-04-57
    09-05-57
    09-23-57*
    09-30-57*
    10-08-57*
    10-21-57*
    11-01-57*
    11-18-57
    12-04-57
    01-01-58
    02-02-58
    02-18-58*
    04-26-58
    05-01-58
    05-08-58
    08-12-58
    08-30-58*
    03-13-59

26. Anti-Rightist Campaign of 1957
    07-08-57*
    07-16-57*
    07-21-57
    07-28-57*
    08-08-57
    08-14-57*
    08-16-57*
    08-29-57*
    09-01-57
    09-04-57
    09-05-57*
    09-11-57*
    09-15-57*
    09-18-57*
    09-30-57*
    10-01-57

111

    10-03-57*
    10-09-57*
    10-10-57
    10-14-57*
    10-21-57*
    10-23-57
    11-01-57*
    11-10-57
    11-12-57*
    12-20-57*
    01-01-58
    04-26-58
    05-01-58
    07-28-58
    08-12-58

27. Cadre Hsia-fang and Rectification
    08-23-57
    09-09-57
    09-28-57*
    09-30-57*
    10-06-57*
    10-20-57
    10-21-57*
    10-27-57
    11-13-57
    11-15-57
    11-17-57*
    11-18-57
    11-28-57*
    12-04-57*
    12-08-57*
    12-25-57*
    12-27-57*
    12-29-57*
    01-01-58
    01-06-58
    01-08-58
    01-14-58
    01-15-58*
    02-12-58
    02-14-58
    03-05-58
    03-14-58*
    03-28-58*
    04-10-58*
    05-07-58*
    05-09-58*
    06-13-60*
    06-15-60*
    06-16-60*
    07-22-60
    07-29-60*
    07-30-60*
    08-16-60*
    08-18-60
    08-25-60
    08-27-60*
    09-25-60
    10-24-60
    11-03-60
    01-12-61*
    02-15-61
    02-21-61
    03-08-61
    03-11-61*
    04-02-61
    03-10-62
    12-22-62*
    01-25-63

28. Great Leap Forward and Technical Renovation Movement
    01-29-58
    02-13-58
    02-28-58*
    03-01-58*
    03-06-58*
    03-07-58*
    03-08-58*
    03-13-58
    03-14-58
    03-15-58*
    03-17-58*
    03-18-58*
    03-19-58*
    03-22-58*
    03-23-58*
    03-24-58*
    03-26-58
    03-29-58*
    03-31-58
    04-11-58*
    04-14-58*
    04-19-58
    04-21-58
    04-22-58
    04-23-58*
    04-26-58
    04-27-58*
    04-29-58
    05-04-58*
    05-06-58
    05-07-58
    05-08-58
    05-09-58
    05-12-58*
    05-13-58
    05-15-58
    05-20-58
    05-21-58
    05-24-58
    05-29-58*
    06-03-58*
    06-06-58
    06-09-58*
    06-10-58*
    06-10-58
    06-11-58
    06-18-58
    06-23-58
    07-01-58*
    07-09-58*
    07-10-58*
    07-11-58*
    07-14-58
    07-17-58
    07-21-58
    07-24-58
    07-28-58
    08-03-58*
    08-06-58*
    08-08-58
    08-13-58
    08-20-58*
    08-21-58*
    08-27-58
    08-28-58*
    09-01-58*
    09-03-58*
    09-05-58*
    09-13-58*
    09-14-58

09-15-58*
09-18-58
09-25-58*
09-27-58
09-27-58
09-29-58
10-01-58*
10-04-58*
10-19-58
11-03-58
11-19-58
11-25-58
12-04-58
12-07-58
12-10-58*
12-15-58*
12-21-58
12-22-58
12-25-58*
12-28-58
01-01-59
01-02-59
01-20-59*
01-21-59*
01-27-59
01-31-59*
02-02-59*
02-12-59
02-14-59*
02-20-59
02-21-59*
02-23-59*
02-24-59
03-03-59*
03-08-59
03-10-59
03-13-59
03-14-59*
03-15-59
03-21-59*
03-27-59
04-03-59*
04-09-59*
04-10-59*
04-16-59
04-17-59
04-29-59*
05-01-59*
05-13-59
05-16-59
05-19-59*
06-03-59
05-17-59
07-10-59
07-12-59
07-24-59
07-30-59
08-06-59*
08-12-59
08-22-59
08-27-59*
08-29-59*
09-01-59*
09-08-59
09-11-59*
09-19-59
09-20-59*
09-21-59
09-25-59
09-25-59*
10-08-59
10-10-59
10-13-59

10-19-59
10-23-59
10-26-59*
10-28-59
11-04-59*
11-05-59
11-09-59*
11-22-59
11-26-59
11-28-59
12-02-59
12-08-59
12-16-59
12-21-59*
12-21-59
12-25-59
01-01-60
01-04-60
01-06-60*
01-07-60
01-09-60
01-11-60
01-13-60*
01-14-60
01-17-60
01-19-60
01-23-60*
01-26-60*
02-04-60*
02-05-60
02-08-60*
02-09-60*
02-11-60
02-18-60
02-21-60
02-25-60*
02-27-60*
03-01-60
03-03-60
03-05-60
03-06-60*
03-07-60*
03-08-60
03-10-60
03-10-60
03-12-60
03-14-60
03-15-60
03-15-60
03-16-60*
03-16-60
03-17-60
03-24-60*
03-27-60
03-29-60
04-05-60
04-11-60
04-13-60
04-15-60*
04-19-60
04-20-60
05-01-60
05-03-60
05-07-60
05-08-60*
05-15-60*
05-16-60*
05-17-60*
05-18-60
05-23-60*
05-30-60
06-01-60
06-04-60

06-08-60*
06-13-60
06-15-60
06-16-60
06-16-60
06-29-60*
06-30-60*
07-05-60
07-13-60
07-17-60
07-18-60
07-19-60
07-21-60
07-22-60
07-25-60
07-29-60
07-31-60
08-18-60
08-25-60
09-07-60
09-08-60*
09-17-60
09-20-60
09-21-60
09-22-60
09-26-60
09-28-60
10-06-60
10-07-60
10-21-60*
10-23-60
10-24-60
11-09-60
11-13-60*
11-20-60
12-03-60*
12-04-60
01-01-61
03-17-61*
03-29-61*
07-01-61
11-17-61
11-25-61
12-23-61
01-01-62*
01-12-62
10-01-64
07-01-66

29. Anti-Rightist Campaign of 1959
08-28-59
09-05-59
09-21-59
09-22-59
10-08-59
10-10-59
10-16-59
10-17-59
11-28-59
09-25-60

30. Socialist Education Movement of 1963-65
05-01-63
06-01-63
06-02-63*
06-19-63*
06-27-63*
07-04-63*
07-17-63*
07-21-63
07-25-63*

07-29-63*
07-30-63*
08-08-63
08-17-63*
08-29-63*
09-25-63*
10-08-63
10-16-63
10-20-63
10-27-63*
11-08-63*
11-14-63
11-16-63*
11-29-63*
12-04-63
12-11-63*
01-01-64*
01-03-64*
01-06-64
02-01-64*
02-02-64
02-07-64*
02-08-64
02-20-64
02-24-64*
03-20-64
04-02-64
05-01-64
05-12-64
06-01-64
06-16-64
07-08-64
07-12-64*
08-05-64
08-06-64
08-28-64*
08-30-64*
09-03-64
09-11-64
09-22-64*
10-01-64*
10-24-64*
11-17-64*
11-19-64
11-24-64
12-06-64
01-01-65*
01-05-65
01-15-65
02-16-65*
02-17-65
02-22-65
02-23-65*
02-26-65
04-24-65
04-28-65
05-01-65
05-05-65*
06-01-65
07-22-65*
09-06-65
09-15-65*
09-21-65
09-24-65
10-01-65*
10-09-65
10-10-65
10-11-65
11-01-65
12-23-65
01-01-66*
01-16-66
01-27-66

01-29-66
02-02-66
02-09-66
02-22-66*
02-27-66
03-16-66
04-03-66
04-06-66
04-14-66
04-22-66
05-08-66
06-02-66*
07-01-66
07-17-66
08-01-66*
08-15-66
09-07-66
09-15-66*
09-19-66
03-13-67
04-08-67
07-09-67

31. Campaign to Learn from the PLA
01-01-64
02-01-64*
02-02-64*
02-18-64*
02-20-64*
02-23-64*
02-24-64
03-06-64
03-07-64
03-08-64
03-10-64*
03-18-64
03-24-64
04-02-64
04-04-64*
04-05-64*
05-01-64
09-10-64*
10-01-64
01-01-65
02-16-65
03-01-65*
04-26-65
05-04-65
06-08-65*
07-04-65
07-30-65
09-11-65
09-21-65
09-24-65
09-26-65
11-08-65*
11-30-65
01-01-66
01-08-66
01-25-66
02-02-66
02-09-66
02-22-66
04-22-66
05-01-66
08-28-66*
10-12-66
05-04-67
05-12-67
05-16-67*
01-01-71*
05-07-71*

06-20-71
01-01-75

32. Study the Thought of Mao Tse-tung
02-18-64
02-23-64
03-06-64
03-08-64
03-10-64
03-20-64
03-24-64*
03-26-64*
04-01-64
04-02-64*
04-04-64*
04-05-64*
04-14-64
05-04-64
05-27-64
05-30-64
07-08-64
07-12-64
08-01-64
08-03-64
08-08-64*
08-28-64
08-30-64
09-10-64*
10-24-64
11-17-64
12-30-64
02-15-65
02-20-65
02-23-65
03-01-65*
03-04-65
03-08-65
03-11-65
03-14-65
03-28-65*
04-02-65
04-06-65
04-09-65*
04-10-65
04-26-65
04-28-65
05-01-65
05-04-65*
05-05-65
06-01-65
06-02-65
06-08-65*
07-02-65
07-06-65
07-19-65
07-22-65
07-30-65
08-31-65
09-06-65
09-11-65
09-19-65
09-21-65
09-24-65*
09-26-65*
09-29-65
10-11-65*
10-16-65
10-28-65
11-01-65
11-05-65
11-13-65
11-28-65*

113

114

11-30-65	10-01-66*	05-01-71*	12-13-65
12-09-65	10-12-66*	05-07-71*	01-01-66
12-11-65*	11-18-66	06-20-71*	01-02-66*
12-13-65*	12-09-66*		01-05-66*
12-16-65*	12-24-66*	33. Campaign to Compare,	01-11-66*
12-22-65	01-05-67*	Learn from, Catch up	01-13-66*
12-23-65*	01-19-67	with, and Help	01-17-66*
01-02-66*	01-22-67	02-02-64*	01-26-66*
01-03-66*	01-25-67*	02-09-64	01-28-66*
01-04-66*	01-27-67*	04-06-64*	01-30-66*
01-05-66*	01-30-67*	04-14-64*	02-02-66*
01-06-66*	02-01-67*	05-08-64*	04-03-66
01-08-66*	02-17-67	05-15-64*	04-07-66*
01-11-66*	03-01-67	06-04-64	06-20-71*
01-13-66*	03-07-67	06-14-64*	01-01-75
01-16-66*	03-13-67	06-16-64	
01-17-66*	04-21-67	06-19-64	34. Great Proletarian
01-21-66*	04-24-67	07-16-64*	Cultural Revolution
01-24-66*	04-30-67*	09-05-64	05-08-66*
01-25-66*	05-07-67*	11-17-64	06-01-66*
01-26-66	05-15-67	02-16-65	06-01-66*
01-28-66*	05-16-67*	03-14-65*	06-02-66*
01-29-66	06-30-67*	04-28-65*	06-02-66*
01-30-66*	08-11-67	05-21-65*	06-03-66
02-02-66	09-14-67*	10-01-65	06-04-66
02-05-66*	10-12-67*	10-11-65	06-04-66
02-07-66*	10-19-67*	12-11-65*	06-16-66*
02-08-66*	11-19-67*	01-16-66	06-18-66*
02-09-66*	12-04-67*	02-09-66	06-24-66*
02-10-66	12-07-67	05-01-66	06-27-66
02-11-66*	12-22-67*	09-25-68*	07-01-66
02-13-66*	01-01-68*		07-17-66*
02-14-66*	01-07-68*	a. Campaign to Learn	07-21-66*
02-16-66	02-05-68*	from Tachai	07-23-66
02-20-66*	02-07-68*	02-10-64*	07-26-66*
02-22-66	03-10-68*	04-06-64*	07-28-66
02-23-66	03-30-68*	07-04-64	07-29-66*
02-26-66*	04-10-68*	07-06-64	08-01-66
02-27-66*	04-12-68*	08-14-64	08-08-66*
02-28-66*	04-20-68*	10-01-64	08-11-66*
03-03-66*	05-01-68*	12-06-64	08-13-66*
03-04-66*	05-03-68*	01-05-65	08-15-66
03-06-66*	05-12-68*	02-15-65	08-17-66
03-08-66*	06-02-68*	02-24-65	08-20-66
03-12-66	08-01-68*	03-04-65	08-23-66*
03-16-66	08-05-68*	05-21-65	08-28-66
03-20-66*	08-15-68*	07-10-65	08-29-66*
03-29-66*	08-18-68	07-19-65	09-05-66*
03-31-66	08-21-68	10-09-65*	09-07-66*
04-01-66*	08-28-68	10-16-65*	09-11-66*
04-03-66*	09-01-68	11-01-65*	09-15-66*
04-06-66*	09-12-68	12-18-65*	09-19-66
04-08-66	01-01-69	12-26-65*	09-26-66
04-10-66*	02-17-69	01-01-66	10-01-66*
04-11-66	02-21-69	01-04-66*	10-12-66*
04-14-66	05-04-69	01-27-66*	10-19-66*
04-15-66*	06-09-69*	02-09-66	10-22-66
04-21-66	07-01-69	02-23-66	10-28-66*
04-22-66*	08-01-69	04-03-66	11-10-66*
04-26-66*	10-01-69*	05-01-66	11-18-66
04-27-66*	11-05-69*	03-22-69	12-26-66*
05-01-66*	01-01-70*	03-07-70	01-19-67
05-04-66*	03-07-70	09-23-70*	01-22-67*
05-08-66*	04-01-70*	02-18-71*	01-24-67*
06-01-66*	05-01-70*	01-01-75	01-26-67*
06-02-66*	07-01-70*	10-21-75*	01-27-67
06-04-66*	07-09-70		01-30-67*
06-08-66	07-23-70*	b. Campaign to Learn	02-10-67*
06-08-66*	10-01-70*	from Taching	02-11-67*
06-16-66*	10-30-70*	10-01-64	02-17-67*
08-01-66*	01-01-71*	01-05-65	03-01-67*
08-08-66*	01-31-71	07-30-65*	03-02-67*
09-05-66*	02-18-71*	09-24-65	03-07-67*

03-12-67	05-01-68*	05-04-74*	10-15-54
03-13-67*	05-03-68	06-18-74	07-21-56
03-18-67	05-12-68	07-01-74*	
04-02-67*	05-17-68*	07-03-74	4. Chiang Ching
04-08-67	06-02-68	08-08-74*	05-29-67
04-15-67	06-18-68	10-01-74*	05-31-67
04-21-67	07-01-68*	11-28-74*	
04-24-67	08-01-68*	01-01-75*	5. Chi Pen-yu
04-26-67	08-05-68*	02-28-75	04-08-67
04-30-67*	08-15-68	03-11-75	
05-04-67	08-18-68*	04-25-75*	6. Chou En-lai
05-07-67	08-21-68		11-27-49
05-12-67	08-28-68	38. Study the Theory of the	11-30-49
05-14-67	09-01-68*	Dictatorship of the	12-23-50*
05-15-67*	09-07-68*	Proletariat	08-16-51
05-22-67*	09-12-68	02-09-75*	11-17-51
05-23-67	09-25-68*	02-28-75*	03-08-52
05-28-67	10-01-68*	03-21-75*	05-07-52
05-29-67	11-25-68*	10-01-75	05-14-52
05-31-67*	12-14-68*		11-29-52*
06-01-67*	01-01-69*	39. Campaign to Criticize	12-16-52
06-03-67	02-17-69*	Water Margin	12-23-52
06-14-67*	02-21-69	09-04-75*	01-24-53
06-18-67*	03-22-69	10-19-75	02-08-53
06-21-67*	05-04-69		04-05-53
06-30-67	06-09-69	F. National Leaders	08-25-53
07-09-67	07-01-69		09-14-53
07-16-67*	08-01-69	1. Chen Tu-hsiu	10-08-53
07-24-67	08-25-69*	11-25-68	10-09-53*
07-26-67	10-01-69*	07-01-69	10-27-53
07-26-67*	11-20-69*		10-30-53
07-28-67	01-01-70	2. Chen Yi	12-07-53
07-29-67*	05-01-70	04-03-58	01-10-54*
07-31-67	05-23-70	09-21-58	01-30-54*
08-02-67*	10-01-70*	03-18-60	04-17-54
08-04-67*	01-01-71*	07-28-60	04-30-54
08-05-67	05-07-71*	08-28-60	05-12-54
08-08-67*	08-27-71*	02-25-61	06-02-54
08-10-67*	12-01-71	04-04-61	06-18-54
08-11-67		05-18-61	06-26-54
08-13-67*	35. Campaign to Criticize	05-19-61	07-02-54
08-16-67	Revisionism and Rec-	06-14-62	07-16-54
08-22-67	tify Work Style	12-30-62	07-22-54
08-25-67	12-01-71	04-12-63	07-28-54
08-26-67*	01-01-72*	04-20-63	08-15-54
08-28-67	03-09-72*	12-14-63	08-20-54
09-02-67	05-23-72*	12-18-63	09-29-54
09-09-67*	07-06-72	12-23-63	10-11-54
09-14-67	08-01-72	12-30-63	10-15-54
09-16-67	10-01-72*	12-31-63	10-19-54
09-18-67	01-01-73*	01-01-64	10-25-54
09-22-67	02-22-73*	01-11-64	10-31-54
09-26-67	03-02-73*	01-13-64	11-16-54
09-27-67	03-08-73*	01-18-64	12-10-54
10-06-67*	04-24-73	01-23-64	12-28-54
10-12-67*	07-11-73	01-29-64	01-29-55
10-19-67	08-07-73	02-01-64	04-22-55
10-21-67*		02-03-64	04-26-55
10-24-67	36. Campaign to Criticize	02-05-64	05-15-55
11-02-67	Lin Piao and Rec-	02-06-64	05-30-55
11-19-67*	tify Work Style	02-20-64	08-01-55
11-26-67*	09-29-73	02-26-64	08-26-55
12-22-67*	10-01-73	03-03-64	12-26-55
01-01-68*	01-01-74*	07-09-64	02-04-56
01-07-68*		01-30-65	07-01-56
02-05-68	37. Campaign to Criticize	04-05-65*	08-12-56
02-07-68	Lin Piao and Confucius	07-30-65	08-20-56
02-23-68	02-02-74*	03-27-66	09-21-56
03-10-68	02-20-74*	04-21-66	10-24-56
03-25-68	03-03-74*		11-23-56
03-30-68	03-08-74*	3. Chen Yun	12-11-56
04-12-68	03-15-74*	12-19-52	12-21-56
04-20-68*	04-10-74*	09-29-54	01-24-57

115

01-24-57
01-30-57*
03-05-57
07-10-57
07-16-57
01-13-58
02-20-58
02-22-58
03-09-58
04-07-58
04-19-58
08-21-58
09-07-58
10-01-58
10-11-58
01-23-59
02-14-59
04-29-59*
05-04-59
06-03-59
06-04-59
09-05-59
09-12-59
09-16-59
09-23-59*
01-29-60
03-11-60
04-11-60
04-27-60*
04-30-60
05-10-60
08-03-60
08-11-60
08-13-60
09-08-60
10-06-60
12-14-60
12-22-60
12-24-60
01-05-61
01-10-61
01-15-61
02-16-61
04-02-61
04-19-61
04-26-61
05-18-61
06-30-61
10-14-61
01-02-62
04-17-62
10-27-62
11-08-62
11-20-62
11-22-62
01-28-63
02-11-63
02-12-63
04-04-63
05-07-63
12-14-63
12-23-63
12-30-63
12-31-63
01-01-64*
01-11-64*
01-13-64*
01-18-64*
01-23-64*
01-29-64
02-01-64
02-03-64
02-05-64

02-06-64
02-20-64
02-24-64
02-26-64
03-03-64
04-09-64
06-19-64
01-30-65
03-02-65
04-01-65
04-07-65*
04-30-65
06-03-65*
06-10-65*
07-21-65
02-20-66
05-13-66
06-17-66*
06-25-66
06-29-66
07-01-66
07-05-66

7. Chou Yang
    08-26-66
    10-19-66
    05-23-67
    05-28-67
    05-29-67
    05-31-67
    09-01-68

8. Chu Chiu-pai
    11-25-68

9. Chu Te
    07-24-54
    09-29-54
    12-27-57
    04-29-59

10. Ho Lung
    12-11-56

11. Hsia Yen
    05-28-67
    05-29-67

12. Kang Sheng
    04-21-56
    10-22-58
    02-06-60

13. Kao Kang
    03-27-55
    07-01-66
    05-03-68

14. Kuo Mo-jo
    04-17-64

15. Li Fu-chun
    06-29-55
    07-08-56
    04-29-59
    04-09-60
    04-16-60

16. Li Hsien-nien
    04-29-59
    11-29-69

17. Li Li-san
    11-25-68

18. Li Te-sheng
    11-29-69

19. Liao Mo-sha
    09-01-68

20. Lin Piao
    02-18-64
    03-26-64
    06-08-65
    07-01-66
    08-01-66
    08-15-66
    08-20-66
    10-12-66
    10-28-66
    11-08-66
    12-15-66
    05-04-67
    05-07-67
    05-12-67
    05-22-67
    05-29-67
    06-30-67
    07-07-67
    07-24-67
    07-26-67
    07-30-67
    08-04-67
    08-08-67
    08-10-67
    08-11-67*
    08-13-67
    08-22-67
    08-28-67
    09-02-67
    10-06-67
    10-12-67
    12-04-67
    01-01-68
    03-10-68
    03-25-68
    04-10-68
    04-20-68
    05-12-68
    06-02-68
    07-01-68
    08-01-68
    08-05-68
    08-15-68
    08-18-68
    08-21-68
    09-01-68
    09-07-68
    10-01-68
    01-01-69
    06-09-69
    08-01-69
    08-25-69
    10-01-69
    11-05-69
    04-01-70
    05-01-70
    07-01-70
    08-01-70
    09-03-70
    10-01-70
    01-01-71
    05-01-71
    05-07-71

08-01-71
08-27-71

21. Liu Shao-chi
    10-10-50
    05-29-51
    07-25-51
    08-10-51
    08-14-51
    08-30-51
    09-07-51
    09-20-51
    11-17-51
    03-25-53
    05-13-53
    07-03-53
    10-30-53
    09-21-54
    09-29-54
    10-15-54
    10-23-54
    11-18-54
    11-25-54
    01-28-55
    02-08-55
    03-11-55
    03-27-55
    05-11-55
    05-19-55
    08-10-55
    05-07-56
    05-15-56
    05-22-56
    09-23-56
    09-25-56
    10-09-56
    12-19-56
    03-05-57
    05-03-57
    11-14-57
    12-13-57
    02-14-58
    03-26-58
    05-06-58
    06-03-58
    06-10-58
    07-01-58
    07-26-58
    07-28-58
    08-12-58
    10-09-58
    11-04-58
    02-04-59
    04-29-59*
    05-15-59
    09-21-59
    09-23-59
    07-25-60
    09-14-60
    09-25-60
    11-07-60
    12-10-60
    12-22-60
    06-16-61
    07-01-61
    08-19-61
    09-13-61
    10-13-61
    02-14-62
    02-11-63
    04-12-63
    04-12-63*
    04-20-63

04-20-63	11-02-67	10-10-50	10-15-54
04-21-63	11-19-67	11-13-50	10-23-54
04-27-63*	12-07-67*	12-03-50	11-18-54
05-01-63*	01-01-68	12-26-50	12-25-54
05-07-63	01-07-68	12-31-50	01-08-55
05-10-63*	01-26-68	02-16-51*	02-23-55
05-18-63*	01-30-68*	06-25-51	03-29-55
05-23-63*	02-05-68	07-05-51	04-05-55
06-24-63	02-07-68	07-25-51	05-11-55
09-27-63	02-23-68*	08-16-51	06-09-55
09-15-63*	03-10-68	08-30-51*	06-12-55
09-29-63*	03-25-68	09-05-51	06-17-55
12-14-63	03-30-68	09-20-51	06-19-55
12-18-63	04-10-68	10-19-51	07-12-55
12-23-63	04-12-68	10-25-51	09-20-55
12-30-63	04-20-68	11-07-51	10-18-55
12-31-63	05-01-68	11-09-51	10-22-55
01-01-64	06-02-68	11-20-51	10-25-55
01-11-64	08-01-68	04-05-52	10-26-55
01-13-64	08-05-68	04-26-52	11-01-55
01-18-64	08-15-68	05-23-52*	11-08-55
01-23-64	08-18-68	07-01-52	11-17-55
01-29-64	08-28-68	10-01-52	12-08-55
02-01-64	09-01-68*	10-07-52	01-01-56
02-03-64	09-07-68	10-17-52	01-13-56
02-05-64	11-25-68*	10-19-52	01-29-56
02-06-64	01-01-69	11-05-52	02-07-56
02-20-64	02-21-69	11-18-52	03-04-56
02-26-64	03-22-69	11-26-52	03-28-56
03-03-64	05-04-69	01-06-53	06-15-56*
06-01-64	07-01-69	02-03-53	06-20-56
07-09-64	08-25-69	02-10-53	06-27-56
11-07-64	11-20-69	02-11-53	10-12-56
01-30-65	01-01-70	03-07-53	10-16-56
01-30-65	03-07-70	03-13-53	11-12-56*
03-02-65	03-29-70	03-28-53*	12-03-56
04-05-65*	04-01-70	05-01-53	12-09-56
07-30-65	05-01-70	05-05-53	12-22-56
03-27-66	07-09-70	06-20-53	01-12-57
03-27-66*	09-23-70	07-16-53	03-21-57
04-09-66	10-30-70	09-16-53	04-08-57
04-18-66		09-20-53	04-13-57*
04-20-66	22. Lo Jui-ching	10-18-53	04-22-57
04-21-66	07-31-67	11-07-53	04-23-57
04-21-66*	08-05-67	11-09-53	05-02-57
07-01-66	09-01-68	11-19-53	05-03-57
08-07-66		11-26-53	05-07-57
03-18-67	23. Lu Hsun	01-07-54	06-22-57*
04-08-67*	10-19-51*	01-21-54	07-23-57
04-15-67*	10-19-52*	01-22-54	07-24-57
04-21-67	08-02-58	02-07-54	07-25-57
04-24-67	05-04-63	02-17-54	07-28-57
05-04-67	03-10-64	02-18-54	08-01-57
05-07-67	08-17-66	02-24-54	08-10-57
05-30-67	10-19-66*	03-22-54	08-19-57
07-09-67*	07-28-67	04-13-54	08-24-57
07-24-67*	05-04-69	04-23-54	08-29-57
07-30-67		05-07-54	09-05-57
07-30-67	24. Lu Ting-yi	05-19-54	09-09-57
07-31-67	10-22-58	06-18-54	09-15-57
08-02-67*	08-15-60	06-26-54	09-25-57
08-05-67	05-28-67	07-01-54	10-11-57
08-08-67	05-29-67	07-06-54	11-03-57*
08-11-67	05-31-67	07-15-54	11-09-57
08-16-67	08-05-67	07-28-54	11-11-57
08-17-67	09-01-68	09-07-54	11-12-57
08-19-67		09-20-54	11-16-57
08-25-67	25. Mao Tse-tung	09-21-54	12-09-57
09-14-67	06-08-50	09-25-54	12-12-57
09-18-67	07-29-50	09-29-54	12-16-57
09-26-67	08-08-50	10-01-54	01-08-58
10-06-67	09-14-50	10-02-54	01-15-58
10-19-67	09-25-50	10-13-54	01-27-58

117

01-31-58
02-02-58
02-07-58
02-11-58
02-14-58
02-15-58
02-27-58
02-28-58
03-02-58
03-06-58
03-10-58
03-17-58
03-23-58
03-28-58
05-05-58
05-09-58
05-12-58
05-20-58
06-03-58
06-09-58
06-19-58*
06-23-58
07-01-58
07-26-58
07-28-58
07-30-58
08-02-58
08-04-58
08-08-58
08-13-58
09-10-58
09-11-58
09-13-58
09-14-58
09-18-58
09-24-58
09-30-58
09-30-58*
10-01-58
10-01-58
10-05-58*
10-12-58
10-13-58
10-18-58
10-19-58
10-23-58
10-24-58
11-07-58
11-10-58
11-12-58*
11-29-58*
12-21-58
12-28-58
01-01-59
01-16-59
02-05-59
02-14-59
02-21-59
03-20-59
04-18-59
04-29-59*
05-04-59*
07-11-59
07-17-59
07-23-59
08-06-59
08-28-59
08-29-59
09-13-59
09-20-59
09-23-59
10-01-59*
10-03-59*

11-01-59
11-09-59
11-10-59
12-08-59
12-27-59
01-01-60
01-07-60
01-08-60
01-20-60
01-23-60
01-28-60*
02-11-60
02-14-60
02-21-60
03-01-60
03-05-60
03-06-60*
03-07-60
03-08-60
03-14-60
03-16-60*
03-26-60
03-29-60
03-31-60
04-05-60*
04-07-60
04-12-60
04-19-60*
05-01-60
05-15-60*
05-16-60
05-16-60
05-20-60
05-23-60
05-26-60
05-27-60
05-28-60
06-01-60*
06-01-60
06-12-60
06-13-60
06-13-60
06-16-60
06-24-60
06-25-60
06-26-60
07-03-60
07-13-60
07-17-60
07-18-60
07-22-60
07-27-60
07-29-60
07-31-60
08-03-60
08-09-60*
08-12-60
08-15-60
08-18-60
08-21-60
08-27-60
09-16-60
09-25-60*
09-29-60
09-30-60*
10-01-60
10-19-60
10-22-60
10-23-60
11-03-60
11-07-60
11-10-60
11-18-60

11-20-60
11-23-60
11-24-60
11-30-60
12-03-60
12-04-60*
12-07-60
12-09-60
12-10-60
12-11-60
12-12-60
12-17-60
12-18-60
12-23-60
12-26-60
12-29-60
12-31-60
01-01-61
01-16-61
01-20-61
01-27-61
01-28-61
01-29-61*
01-30-61
02-02-61*
02-05-61
02-09-61
02-14-61
02-15-61
02-15-61
02-16-61
03-05-61*
03-09-61
03-11-61
04-02-61
04-03-61*
04-04-61
04-07-61*
05-04-61
06-04-61
07-01-61*
08-04-61
09-05-61
09-25-61
10-01-61
10-03-61
10-10-61
11-03-61
11-07-61
11-17-61
12-03-61
12-05-61
12-12-61
12-17-61
12-24-61
01-04-62
01-15-62
01-17-62
02-14-62
03-29-62
04-08-62
04-17-62
04-29-62
05-23-62*
06-02-62
07-07-62
10-01-62
10-22-62
10-28-62
11-07-62
11-09-62
11-15-62
11-26-62

12-22-62
01-09-63
01-11-63
01-25-63
02-07-63
02-11-63
03-24-63
03-25-63
03-27-63
04-06-63
05-01-63
05-04-63
05-08-63
06-05-63
06-19-63
06-22-63
07-07-63
07-21-63
07-23-63
07-25-63
08-06-63
08-08-63
08-13-63
08-29-63
09-02-63
09-20-63*
09-25-63
10-08-63*
10-20-63*
10-27-63
11-07-63
11-29-63
12-02-63
12-04-63
12-07-63
12-26-63
01-01-64
01-06-64
01-21-64
01-24-64
01-29-64
02-18-64
02-23-64
03-04-64
03-06-64
03-08-64
03-10-64
03-20-64
03-24-64*
03-26-64*
04-01-64
04-02-64*
04-04-64*
04-05-64*
04-11-64
04-14-64
04-24-64
04-30-64
05-04-64
05-08-64
05-15-64
05-26-64
05-27-64
05-30-64
06-04-64*
06-09-64
06-19-64*
06-24-64
07-08-64
07-12-64
08-01-64
08-03-64
08-05-64

08-08-64*	09-30-65	05-01-66*	01-25-67*
08-28-64	10-01-65*	05-04-66*	01-27-67*
08-29-64	10-09-65	05-08-66*	01-30-67
08-30-64	10-11-65	06-01-66*	02-01-67*
09-10-64*	10-16-65	06-01-66*	02-02-67*
10-01-64*	10-18-65	06-02-66*	02-10-67*
10-15-64	10-24-65	06-02-66*	02-11-67
10-24-64	10-28-65	06-03-66	02-17-67
11-07-64	11-01-65	06-04-66	03-01-67
11-17-64	11-05-65	06-08-66*	03-02-67*
12-01-64	11-05-65	06-08-66*	03-07-67
12-30-64	11-08-65*	06-16-66*	03-12-67*
01-01-65	11-13-65	06-18-66	03-13-67
01-05-65	11-28-65*	06-20-66*	03-18-67*
01-18-65	11-30-65	06-24-66*	04-02-67*
02-15-65	12-02-65*	60-25-66	04-08-67*
02-20-65	12-09-65	06-27-66	04-15-67
02-23-65	12-11-65*	06-27-66	04-21-67*
02-26-65	12-13-65*	06-29-66	04-24-67*
03-01-65*	12-16-65*	07-01-66*	04-26-67
03-04-65	12-18-65*	07-05-66	04-27-67
03-08-65	12-22-65	07-10-66	04-30-67*
03-11-65	12-23-65*	07-17-66	05-04-67*
03-14-65	12-27-65*	07-21-66	05-07-67*
03-28-65*	01-01-66*	07-23-66*	05-12-67*
04-02-65	01-02-66*	07-26-66*	05-14-67
04-04-65*	01-06-66*	07-28-66*	05-15-67
04-06-65	01-08-66*	07-29-66*	05-16-67
04-09-65*	01-14-66	08-01-66*	05-23-67*
04-10-65	01-16-66*	08-01-66*	05-23-67
04-11-65	01-18-66	08-08-66*	05-28-67*
04-20-65	01-19-66	08-08-66*	05-29-67
04-22-65*	01-21-66*	08-11-66*	05-29-67
04-26-65	01-24-66*	08-13-66*	05-31-67*
04-28-65	01-25-66*	08-15-66*	05-31-67
05-01-65	01-26-66	08-17-66*	06-01-67*
05-04-65*	01-27-66	08-20-66*	06-03-67
05-05-65*	01-29-66	08-23-66*	06-06-67
05-14-65	02-01-66	08-23-66	06-08-67
05-26-65	02-02-66	08-24-66*	06-11-67
05-30-65	02-05-66*	08-25-66*	06-14-67
06-01-65	02-06-66	08-26-66	06-15-67
06-02-65	02-07-66*	08-28-66*	06-18-67*
06-03-65*	02-09-66*	08-29-66*	06-18-67
06-04-65*	02-09-66	09-05-66*	06-21-67*
06-05-65	02-10-66	09-07-66*	06-22-67
06-08-65*	02-11-66*	09-08-66	06-28-67*
06-16-65	02-13-66*	09-11-66*	06-30-67
06-23-65	02-14-66*	09-15-66*	06-30-67*
07-02-65	02-16-66	09-19-66	07-05-67
07-03-65	02-20-66*	09-24-66*	07-05-67*
07-04-65	02-22-66	09-24-66	07-07-67*
07-06-65	02-27-66*	09-26-66*	07-09-67*
07-10-65	03-04-66*	10-01-66*	07-10-67
07-11-65*	03-11-66	10-10-66	07-16-67*
07-19-65	03-12-66	10-12-66*	07-21-67
07-22-65	03-16-66	10-19-66*	07-24-67
07-30-65	03-17-66	10-22-66*	07-26-67
08-07-65	03-27-66	10-22-66*	07-26-67
08-19-65	03-27-66	10-28-66*	07-28-67
08-21-65	03-31-66	11-08-66	07-29-67
08-31-65	04-01-66*	11-10-66	07-30-67
09-01-65	04-03-66*	11-10-66	07-30-67*
09-02-65	04-06-66*	11-25-66	07-31-67*
09-06-65*	04-06-66	12-07-66	08-02-67*
09-08-65	04-07-66	12-09-66*	08-04-67
09-10-65	04-12-66	12-15-66	08-05-67*
09-11-65	04-14-66	12-20-66	08-08-67*
09-19-65	04-15-66	12-24-66*	08-08-67*
09-21-65	04-21-66	12-26-66	08-10-67*
09-24-65*	04-22-66*	01-05-67*	08-11-67*
09-26-65*	04-22-66	01-19-67*	08-13-67
09-29-65	04-24-66	01-22-67*	08-16-67*

119

08-17-67*	11-29-68	08-19-71	02-02-57
08-19-67	12-14-68	08-27-71*	05-04-62
08-22-67	01-01-69*	09-09-71	05-23-67
08-25-67*	02-17-69*	09-18-71	05-28-67
08-26-67	02-21-69	10-28-71	05-29-67
08-28-67*	03-04-69	11-02-71	05-31-67
08-29-67*	03-22-69	11-08-71	08-05-67
09-02-67	04-17-69*	11-12-71	09-01-68
09-09-67	05-04-69*	11-20-71	
09-09-67*	06-09-69	12-01-71*	27. Peng Te-huai
09-10-67	07-01-69*	12-12-71	04-05-53
09-14-67*	08-01-69	01-01-72*	07-10-53
09-16-67	08-25-69*	03-09-72*	07-28-53
09-18-67*	11-05-69*	04-16-72*	12-05-53
09-22-67*	11-20-69	04-24-72	01-08-54
09-27-67	11-23-69	04-24-72*	05-12-55
09-27-67	11-28-69	05-23-72*	05-17-55
10-06-67*	11-29-69	05-25-72	07-18-55
10-12-67*	01-01-70*	06-10-72*	10-10-58
10-19-67*	02-03-70	06-25-72	10-11-58
10-20-67	03-07-70	07-06-72*	10-30-58
10-21-67*	03-29-70	08-01-72*	07-31-67
10-29-67	04-01-70*	09-01-72	08-05-67
11-02-67*	04-30-70	09-09-72	08-16-67*
11-19-67*	05-01-70*	09-30-72	05-03-68
11-26-67*	05-05-70	10-01-72*	09-01-68
11-28-67	05-23-70*	10-13-72	
11-29-67	06-09-70	11-18-72	28. Po Yi-po
12-01-67	06-25-70	01-01-73	09-09-59
12-04-67*	07-09-70	02-22-73	
12-07-67*	07-21-70	03-08-73	29. Soong Ching-ling
12-19-67	08-01-70	04-24-73	03-23-56
12-22-67*	08-20-70	07-11-73	04-11-56
01-01-68	08-06-70	08-07-73	04-29-59
01-07-68	09-02-70	09-11-73	06-01-59
01-30-68*	09-03-70	09-29-73*	03-03-64
02-02-68	09-14-70	10-01-73*	
02-03-68	09-23-70*	10-01-73	30. Sun Yat-sen
02-05-68*	10-12-70	01-01-74*	03-12-55*
02-07-68	10-15-70	02-02-74	11-12-56*
02-15-68	11-22-70	02-20-74*	09-22-59
02-23-68*	10-25-70	03-03-74	
03-10-68*	10-30-70*	03-08-74	31. Tan Chen-lin
03-19-68	11-08-70	03-15-74*	04-24-60
03-25-68	11-09-70	04-10-74	
03-30-68*	11-10-70	05-04-74*	32. Tao Chu
04-10-68*	11-20-70	06-18-74*	01-30-68
04-12-68*	11-21-70	07-01-74*	02-23-68*
04-20-68*	11-29-70	08-08-74	
05-01-68*	12-03-70	10-01-74*	33. Teng Hsiao-ping
05-03-68*	12-13-70	11-28-74*	10-09-56
05-12-68*	12-18-70	01-01-75*	11-28-56
05-17-68*	12-20-70	02-09-75*	10-21-57
05-27-68*	01-01-71*	02-28-75*	11-01-57
06-02-68*	01-06-71	03-11-75*	01-31-58
06-18-68*	01-11-71	03-21-75*	02-07-58
07-01-68*	01-23-71	03-23-75	07-21-63
08-01-68*	01-31-71*	04-18-75	07-01-66
08-05-68*	02-12-71	04-25-75	05-05-74
08-15-68*	02-14-71	05-20-75*	
08-18-68*	03-11-71	06-26-75*	34. Teng Ying-chao
08-21-68*	04-04-71	09-03-75*	06-01-59
08-28-68*	04-15-71	09-04-75*	
09-01-68*	04-25-71	09-09-75*	35. Teng To
09-07-68*	05-01-71	09-12-75*	09-01-68
09-12-68	05-05-71	10-01-75*	
09-18-68*	05-07-71*	10-19-75*	36. Tung Pi-wu
09-20-68	05-09-71	10-21-75*	04-29-59
09-25-68*	05-20-71*	10-25-75	06-01-59*
09-29-68	05-29-71	11-29-75	
10-01-68*	06-01-71		37. Wang Jen-chung
10-01-68*	07-11-71	26. Peng Chen	02-07-68
11-25-68*	08-01-71*	01-19-53	

38. Wang Ming
      07-07-67
      11-25-68
      07-01-69

39. Wu Han
      09-01-68

40. Wu Lung-hsi
      09-01-68

41. Yang Hsien-chien
      10-30-70

42. Yao Wen-yuan
      09-09-67*

G. Economy

1. General Economic Background
      03-17-49*
      07-29-49
      08-02-49
      02-06-50
      03-07-50
      03-10-50
      04-05-50
      08-17-50
      12-30-50
      02-11-51
      06-02-51
      07-29-51
      11-09-51
      11-20-51
      11-28-51
      01-01-52
      01-22-52
      04-05-52
      07-01-52
      10-01-52
      09-07-53
      09-13-55
      05-01-55
      01-12-56
      06-16-56*
      07-11-56
      08-26-56
      09-29-56
      10-31-56
      12-31-56
      06-26-57
      04-28-58

2. Economic Construction in the Early Years
      03-17-49*
      07-29-49
      02-06-50*
      03-07-50
      03-10-50
      03-22-50*
      04-05-50
      06-04-50*
      06-08-50
      06-11-50*
      06-17-50
      01-01-51
      01-04-51
      02-11-51
      02-13-51
      02-17-51
      03-16-51

04-05-51
04-10-51
05-26-51
06-04-51
06-16-51
07-05-51
07-11-51
07-30-51
08-05-51
08-14-51
08-20-51
09-20-51*
10-03-51
10-15-51
11-28-51
01-01-52
02-01-52
02-21-52
04-16-52
05-28-52
08-07-52
07-02-52
10-30-52
11-17-52
12-17-52
12-26-52
12-28-52
12-30-52
01-01-53
01-06-53
01-07-53
02-10-53
02-19-53
03-04-53
03-11-53
04-09-53
04-20-53
04-25-53
05-01-53
05-13-53
05-14-53
06-19-53
08-16-53
08-17-53
08-18-53
08-31-53
09-08-53
09-22-53
10-01-53
10-08-53
10-20-53
10-23-53
10-30-53*
11-05-53*
11-07-53
11-19-53
11-20-53
11-21-53
11-22-53
11-23-53
12-16-53*
12-24-53
12-25-53*
01-13-54
01-31-54*
02-17-54
03-10-54*
03-31-54
04-19-54
05-25-54
06-29-54
07-29-54
09-04-54

12-23-54
02-06-55

3. Economic Planning and the Five-Year Plans

   a. General Economic Planning
      06-16-51*
      12-17-52
      12-26-52
      02-12-53*
      02-25-53
      04-08-53*
      10-22-53
      11-19-53
      11-25-53
      12-29-53
      05-06-54*
      07-21-54
      08-22-54*
      09-14-54
      10-08-54
      10-27-54
      11-06-54*
      11-11-54*
      12-06-54
      12-20-54
      01-01-55
      01-27-55*
      04-16-55
      04-24-55
      05-21-55
      05-22-55*
      08-09-55
      09-04-55
      09-19-55
      09-26-55
      10-24-55*
      11-23-55
      11-25-55*
      12-22-55
      12-31-55
      01-06-56
      01-29-56*
      02-22-56
      02-29-56
      05-25-56
      06-15-56*
      06-20-56
      06-30-56
      09-15-56
      12-04-56*
      12-07-56
      12-19-56
      12-22-56*
      02-13-57
      02-17-57*
      03-31-57
      04-04-57
      04-11-57
      06-16-57
      07-21-57
      11-15-57
      12-12-57*
      01-06-58*
      01-31-58
      03-06-58
      08-06-58
      12-21-58
      01-01-59*
      01-09-59
      01-19-59*

01-30-59
01-31-59
02-24-59*
04-03-59
04-09-59*
04-15-59*
04-29-59
07-15-59*
07-17-59
07-24-59
08-16-59*
11-09-59
11-26-59
12-10-59*
12-21-59
12-25-59
02-11-60
02-27-60
03-12-60*
03-16-60*
03-31-60*
04-09-60
04-11-60*
05-01-60*
06-04-60
06-16-60
07-03-60*
09-07-60*
09-21-60*
10-07-60
01-14-61
01-23-61
01-27-61
04-28-61
08-04-61*
10-01-61*
12-05-61*
12-15-61*
01-01-62*
01-04-62*
01-12-62
04-08-62
06-06-62
06-15-62
10-22-62
11-09-62
11-12-62*
11-30-62*
12-02-62*
12-16-62
12-22-62
03-10-63
03-15-63
03-17-63
03-20-63
04-02-63*
04-08-63
05-01-63
07-07-63
10-27-63*
12-04-63*
12-26-63
01-01-64*
02-10-64*
05-01-64
06-16-64
10-15-64*
01-01-65
04-22-65
06-02-65*
07-06-65
07-30-65
12-04-65

122

02-21-69*

b. Balanced Economic
   Planning
   04-20-53
   04-23-53
   03-40-54*
   03-11-54
   06-18-54
   07-07-54
   08-13-54
   11-11-54*
   03-02-55
   03-22-55
   04-01-55
   05-05-55*
   05-06-55*
   05-14-55*
   06-19-55
   07-05-55
   07-29-55
   08-23-55
   12-22-55
   12-31-55
   01-01-56
   01-29-56
   02-27-56
   06-15-56*
   07-08-56
   07-09-56*
   09-15-56
   11-27-56*
   12-13-56*
   03-27-57*
   04-04-57
   06-16-57*
   07-24-57
   09-07-57
   11-18-57*
   11-21-57
   12-12-57
   01-06-58*
   02-12-58*
   02-28-58*
   05-12-58*
   06-03-58*
   07-01-58
   08-08-58
   09-05-58
   10-14-58
   12-25-58
   01-02-59
   01-20-59*
   02-23-59
   02-24-59
   03-14-59*
   04-09-59
   07-15-59*
   08-20-59*
   11-02-59
   11-22-59
   12-05-59*
   12-06-59
   12-10-59*
   01-11-60
   01-23-60*
   02-08-60*
   03-14-60
   03-27-60
   04-11-60
   04-13-60
   07-17-60*
   07-27-60*

09-21-60*
09-22-60
10-23-60*
01-01-61*
08-08-61
10-15-61
11-05-61
11-14-61
12-05-61
01-01-62
03-10-62*
05-03-62
11-03-62*
11-26-62
12-05-62*
01-25-63
01-30-63*
02-25-63
04-02-63*
10-16-63
01-28-64
02-16-64
06-23-64
07-17-64
10-27-64
05-12-65*
05-19-65*
06-16-65*
09-08-65*
01-02-66

c. First Five-Year Plan
   11-07-52
   12-31-52
   01-01-53
   01-15-53
   02-19-53
   09-06-53
   09-08-53
   09-16-53*
   09-22-53
   10-01-53
   10-06-53
   10-23-53
   10-30-53*
   11-05-53*
   11-17-53
   11-21-53
   11-22-53
   11-22-53
   11-27-53
   12-10-53
   12-25-53
   01-21-54
   01-28-54
   03-04-54
   03-16-54
   03-25-54
   04-15-54
   09-14-54*
   10-16-54*
   11-06-54*
   11-11-54*
   11-15-54
   01-01-55
   01-15-55
   01-27-55*
   03-14-55
   03-22-55
   04-05-55*
   04-07-55*
   04-27-55*
   05-05-55

05-14-55*
05-24-55
07-05-55*
07-08-55*
07-31-55*
08-09-55
08-23-55
08-31-55*
09-11-55
09-19-55
09-23-55*
09-26-55
10-01-55
10-24-55*
11-13-55
12-25-55*
01-01-56*
01-10-56
01-19-56
02-29-56
03-11-56
04-20-56
04-30-56
05-20-56
05-25-56*
06-15-56*
06-16-56
07-09-56
08-09-56
09-15-56
09-27-56
10-01-56*
12-04-56*
02-13-57
03-07-57
03-10-57
03-27-57
04-01-57
04-04-57
04-25-57
05-01-57
05-24-57
07-03-57
07-24-57
08-02-57
08-09-57
08-23-57
09-07-57
09-09-57
09-13-57
09-25-57
10-01-57*
10-10-57
11-02-57
11-14-57
12-09-57
12-12-57*
12-13-57
12-27-57
12-28-57
01-06-58*
01-21-58
01-23-58
02-02-58
02-12-58
04-11-58
04-24-58
05-12-58
06-06-58
09-01-58
01-06-59
02-20-59
02-21-59

02-23-59
02-24-59
04-15-59*
04-21-59
06-28-59
10-09-59
10-19-59
11-22-59
07-22-60
10-23-60
12-04-63

d. Second Five-Year Plan
   09-15-56
   09-25-56
   09-29-56*
   03-10-57
   04-01-57
   04-04-57
   05-09-57
   07-31-57
   08-23-57
   09-07-57*
   09-25-57*
   10-01-57
   10-10-57
   10-11-57*
   10-22-57
   10-25-57
   10-27-57*
   11-14-57
   11-16-57
   11-19-57
   11-24-57
   11-29-57
   12-02-57*
   12-13-57*
   12-28-57
   01-01-58
   01-21-58
   02-02-58*
   02-30-58*
   02-09-58*
   02-18-58*
   02-28-58*
   03-06-58*
   03-18-58
   04-11-58
   06-03-58*
   06-05-58
   06-06-58*
   08-28-58
   02-24-59
   05-04-59
   08-27-59*
   09-02-59
   09-03-59
   09-05-59
   09-20-59
   09-21-59
   09-23-59
   10-01-59*
   10-08-59*
   01-01-60
   01-23-60*
   03-08-60
   03-23-60
   03-31-60
   05-01-60*
   06-04-60
   01-01-61*
   01-01-62
   12-04-63

e. Third Five-Year Plan
  11-16-57
  02-07-63*
  03-17-63
  04-10-63
  04-13-63
  01-01-65
  01-05-65
  02-17-65
  02-22-65
  02-23-65
  10-16-65
  11-30-65
  12-22-65
  01-01-66*
  01-08-66
  01-26-66
  02-06-66
  02-09-66
  09-07-66
  09-15-66
  09-19-66
  10-01-70

f. Fourth Five-Year Plan
  01-01-71
  02-18-71
  06-20-71
  01-01-74
  04-10-74
  10-01-74
  01-01-75
  03-11-75

4. Socialist Transformation of the Economy

a. Private Enterprise
  06-04-50
  06-08-50*
  06-17-50*
  06-29-50
  01-17-51*
  12-13-51
  07-02-52
  08-07-52
  02-07-53
  10-06-53
  11-11-53*
  11-14-53*
  12-23-53
  12-25-53
  07-08-54
  09-06-54
  05-06-55*
  05-08-55
  05-22-55*
  08-13-55
  11-25-55
  01-03-56*
  01-11-56*
  01-17-56
  01-18-56
  01-22-56*
  02-11-56
  02-12-56
  02-22-56
  04-28-56*
  09-06-56
  11-30-56
  12-20-56

b. Part-State, Part-Private Enterprise
  06-08-50
  09-06-54*
  04-07-55
  05-06-55
  05-25-55*
  11-25-55*
  01-03-56*
  01-11-56*
  01-16-56
  01-18-56
  01-22-56*
  02-02-56
  02-11-56
  02-12-56
  02-22-56
  02-23-56
  03-17-56
  04-28-56
  06-30-56*
  07-08-56
  07-13-56*
  09-04-56*
  10-16-56
  10-17-56
  11-30-56*
  02-27-57*
  04-22-57*
  07-03-57
  08-13-57
  01-06-58

c. Socialist Transformation of Industry and Agriculture
  06-08-50*
  06-17-50*
  02-11-51
  02-13-51
  07-30-51*
  11-20-51
  02-07-52
  03-13-52*
  04-10-52
  10-30-52
  11-05-52
  12-28-52
  01-06-53
  01-29-53
  02-07-53
  10-14-53
  10-30-53
  11-05-53
  11-09-53
  11-11-53*
  11-14-53
  11-15-53
  11-16-53
  11-20-53
  11-25-53
  11-30-53
  12-03-53
  12-11-53
  12-12-53
  12-13-53*
  12-16-53
  12-20-53
  12-23-53
  12-25-53
  12-27-53
  12-30-53
  01-01-54*
  01-05-54
  01-07-54
  01-09-54
  01-13-54
  01-21-54
  01-25-54
  01-31-54
  02-11-54
  02-24-54
  03-01-54
  03-03-54
  03-05-54
  03-10-54*
  03-11-54*
  03-16-54
  03-31-54
  04-14-54
  04-17-54
  05-01-54
  05-17-54
  05-26-54
  06-16-54
  06-21-54
  06-22-54
  07-08-54
  09-06-54*
  09-14-54*
  09-21-54
  10-08-54
  10-09-54*
  11-11-54
  11-23-54
  11-24-54
  12-22-54
  01-01-55
  02-04-55
  03-14-55
  03-22-55
  03-30-55*
  04-07-55
  04-16-55
  04-22-55*
  05-06-55*
  05-14-55*
  05-25-55
  06-07-55*
  07-05-55
  07-08-55
  07-10-55
  08-10-55
  08-13-55
  09-07-55
  10-01-55
  10-24-55
  10-28-55
  11-22-55*
  11-25-55
  12-14-55*
  12-25-55*
  12-31-55
  01-01-56*
  01-03-56*
  01-11-56
  01-13-56
  01-16-56*
  01-17-56
  01-18-56
  01-19-56
  01-22-56*
  01-25-56
  01-29-56
  01-31-56*
  02-08-56
  02-11-56*
  02-12-56*
  02-22-56
  02-23-56
  02-29-56
  04-01-56
  04-08-56
  04-28-56*
  05-01-56*
  05-05-56
  05-25-56
  06-08-56
  06-15-56
  06-20-56
  06-30-56
  07-13-56
  09-06-56
  09-15-56
  10-17-56
  11-30-56
  12-08-56
  12-13-56
  12-16-56
  12-20-56
  01-01-57*
  04-22-57
  05-29-57*
  06-26-57
  07-03-57*
  08-13-57
  08-24-57
  01-06-58
  03-17-58
  06-05-58
  06-27-59
  03-01-60
  07-17-60*
  09-22-60
  12-17-61
  12-24-61
  04-02-64
  04-04-64
  02-23-65
  11-25-68

5. Industry

a. General Industrial Production
  02-11-51
  02-13-51
  01-01-52
  02-29-52*
  04-08-52
  04-16-52
  07-02-52
  07-13-52
  08-11-52
  12-28-52
  01-01-53
  02-12-53
  06-19-53
  06-23-53
  08-01-53*
  09-06-53
  09-08-53
  10-06-53
  11-17-53*
  11-20-53
  12-21-53
  12-29-53*
  01-28-54*
  03-03-54*

123

03-10-54
05-06-54
08-11-54
09-14-54
10-16-54
11-11-54
01-27-55
02-08-55*
03-22-55
04-07-55
04-16-55
05-01-55
06-09-55*
07-30-55*
08-20-55*
09-11-55*
09-19-55*
10-01-55
10-24-55
12-01-55
12-22-55*
12-25-55
01-01-56
01-06-56
01-10-56
01-19-56
01-22-56
01-25-56
01-29-56*
02-11-56*
02-12-56
02-23-56
02-29-56
03-13-56*
03-18-56
03-30-56*
04-08-56
04-10-56*
04-17-56*
04-20-56
04-30-56
05-01-56
05-03-56
05-05-56
05-11-56
05-15-56
05-23-56
05-25-56
06-05-56
06-21-56
06-30-56
07-08-56*
07-09-56
08-09-56
09-29-56
11-10-56
11-27-56
12-19-56
01-01-57
01-06-57
01-13-57
01-16-57
01-21-57
02-17-57*
03-10-57*
03-27-57*
03-31-57
04-01-57
04-04-57*
04-11-57
05-01-57*
05-21-57
06-04-57

06-16-57
07-03-57*
08-02-57*
08-08-57
08-09-57*
09-07-57
09-28-57
10-01-57
11-02-57
11-16-57
11-29-57
12-12-57
12-13-57*
01-01-58
01-06-58
01-31-58
02-09-58
02-18-58
02-28-58
03-06-58
03-24-58
03-29-58
04-27-58
05-01-58
05-29-58*
06-03-58*
06-10-58
06-10-58
06-14-58*
07-09-58*
07-24-58
08-03-58*
08-08-58*
08-27-58*
08-28-58*
09-01-58
09-05-58
09-14-58
09-15-58
09-27-58
10-01-58*
10-01-58
10-01-58*
10-04-58*
10-19-58
11-03-58*
11-09-58
11-17-58*
11-25-58
11-30-58
12-22-58*
12-28-58
01-01-59
01-02-59
01-05-59
01-06-59
01-30-59*
01-31-59
02-02-59*
02-06-59
02-11-59
02-12-59*
02-17-59
02-20-59
02-22-59
02-24-59
03-03-59*
03-08-59
03-13-59*
03-14-59
03-15-59
04-03-59
04-09-59*

04-10-59
04-18-59*
05-01-59
05-15-59
05-24-59*
06-17-59
06-28-59*
06-30-59*
07-04-59
07-06-59
07-17-59
07-24-59*
07-30-59
08-17-59
08-27-59
09-01-59*
09-11-59*
09-21-59
09-25-59
10-08-59*
10-10-59
10-16-59*
11-04-59*
11-12-59
11-22-59
11-26-59*
11-30-59
12-02-59
12-06-59
12-10-59*
12-21-59*
01-01-60
01-19-60
01-23-60*
01-26-60
02-04-60*
02-08-60*
02-27-60*
03-12-60
03-13-60
03-15-60
03-16-60
03-24-60
03-27-60*
03-29-60
04-11-60
04-13-60
05-01-60
05-07-60
06-04-60*
06-15-60*
06-15-60*
06-16-60*
06-25-60*
07-17-60*
07-18-60*
07-21-60*
07-25-60
07-26-60
07-29-60
08-16-60
08-18-60*
09-07-60*
09-12-60*
09-17-60*
10-01-60
10-06-60*
10-07-60*
10-18-60*
10-24-60*
12-03-60
12-04-60
12-17-60

01-01-61*
01-14-61
01-19-61*
01-30-61*
02-04-61*
02-11-61*
03-07-61
03-17-61
03-22-61*
03-29-61
06-04-61
06-08-61
08-08-61*
10-01-61
11-14-61*
11-16-61
11-17-61
11-25-61
12-05-61*
12-15-61
01-01-62*
01-12-62
03-10-62
04-17-62
05-29-62
10-01-62*
11-03-62
11-16-62
11-30-62*
12-05-62
12-16-62*
03-15-63*
03-24-63
04-02-63
04-08-63
05-01-63*
05-09-63
07-07-63
10-01-63*
12-02-63
12-04-63*
12-11-63
01-01-64*
02-09-64
03-18-64*
05-01-64
06-19-64
06-23-64*
10-01-64
12-15-64
01-23-65
02-23-65*
03-04-65
05-01-65
05-12-65*
06-02-65
06-04-65
06-16-65*
06-21-65*
07-06-65*
07-30-65*
09-08-65
09-24-65*
09-25-65
10-01-65
11-13-65
12-13-65*
12-22-65
01-24-66
01-26-66*
02-02-66*
02-16-66
03-25-66

04-03-66
05-01-66*
09-07-66
09-15-66
11-10-66*
12-26-66
06-14-67
01-01-68
02-21-69*
01-01-70
03-29-70*
05-07-71
01-01-74
04-10-74*
03-11-75*

b. Industrial Technology and Quality Control
01-17-53*
01-18-53*
01-25-53*
02-03-53*
02-12-53*
02-25-53*
04-02-53*
04-08-53*
05-15-53
06-23-53*
06-27-53*
07-18-53
08-01-53*
09-01-53
09-10-53
10-14-53*
10-17-53
11-15-53
11-17-53
11-18-53
12-01-53
12-17-53
12-18-53
01-14-54*
03-11-54
03-20-54
04-01-54
05-06-54
06-05-54*
07-21-54*
08-05-54
08-07-54*
08-28-54*
09-15-54
09-18-54*
10-05-54*
10-16-54
11-05-54
11-13-54
11-16-54
12-06-54*
12-08-54*
12-12-54*
01-01-55
01-03-55
01-12-55*
01-17-55*
02-08-55
03-02-55*
03-22-55*
03-28-55*
03-30-55*
04-16-55
04-16-55*
04-27-55

05-05-55
05-14-55
05-24-55*
05-29-55
06-09-55
06-29-55
07-01-55*
07-06-55*
07-28-55*
08-20-55
08-23-55*
08-31-55
09-07-55
09-10-55
09-11-55
09-19-55*
09-23-55
09-26-55
10-09-55
11-13-55
12-04-55
12-22-55
12-31-55
01-06-56*
01-10-56*
01-25-56*
02-15-56
02-26-56
03-11-56
03-13-56
03-16-56
03-18-56
03-19-56*
03-22-56*
03-30-56*
04-10-56
04-17-56
04-19-56*
04-20-56*
04-30-56
05-01-56
05-03-56
05-06-56*
05-07-56*
05-15-56*
05-20-56*
05-25-56*
06-15-56
06-20-56*
06-30-56*
07-09-56
07-15-56*
07-22-56*
07-26-56
07-31-56*
08-04-56*
08-09-56*
08-21-56
09-09-56*
10-25-56*
11-06-56
12-04-56*
12-05-56
12-07-56*
12-13-56
12-19-56*
01-06-57*
01-16-57*
02-07-57
02-13-57*
02-17-57
02-27-57
02-28-57*

03-10-57
03-13-57
03-14-57*
03-27-57*
04-01-57
04-04-57
04-11-57
04-28-57*
05-01-57*
05-22-57*
05-24-57*
06-04-57*
06-16-57*
07-31-57*
08-23-57*
09-13-57
09-23-57
10-15-57
11-02-57*
11-29-57*
12-27-57
01-06-58
01-17-58
01-21-58
02-02-58*
02-07-58*
02-15-58
03-22-58*
03-28-58
03-29-58*
03-31-58*
04-11-58*
06-02-58
06-03-58*
06-09-58
06-10-58
06-12-58
06-18-58
06-24-58*
07-09-58
07-10-58*
07-13-58*
07-15-58
07-22-58*
07-28-58*
08-06-58*
08-08-58
08-20-58*
08-22-58*
08-27-58
08-28-58*
08-29-58
09-01-58
09-05-58
09-12-58
09-16-58
09-17-58
09-19-58
09-20-58*
10-10-58*
10-12-58*
10-13-58*
10-15-58*
10-18-58*
10-23-58*
10-24-58
10-25-58*
10-26-58
11-03-58
11-04-58*
11-05-58*
11-08-58
11-16-58

11-24-58
11-30-58*
12-02-58*
12-05-58
12-06-58
12-07-58
12-20-58*
12-24-58
12-25-58
01-05-59*
01-06-59*
01-07-59
01-13-59*
01-18-59
01-22-59
01-31-59*
02-02-59
02-15-59*
02-20-59*
02-21-59
02-22-59
02-24-59
02-27-59*
02-28-59
03-02-59
03-10-59*
03-13-59*
03-15-59
03-17-59*
03-23-59*
03-29-59*
04-03-59*
04-04-59*
04-09-59
04-10-59*
04-16-59*
04-21-59*
05-01-59
05-11-59*
05-15-59*
05-19-59*
05-24-59*
05-25-59*
06-01-59
06-05-59
06-07-59*
06-09-59*
06-15-59*
06-26-59*
06-27-59
06-28-59*
07-06-59*
07-09-59*
07-17-59
07-26-59*
07-27-59*
08-01-59*
08-04-59*
08-09-59
08-16-59
08-17-59
08-22-59*
09-01-59
09-05-59
09-07-59
09-11-59
09-20-59*
10-08-59*
10-09-59*
10-12-59
10-14-59*
11-02-59*
11-04-59*

11-22-59*	09-26-60*	06-19-64*	12-13-56*
11-28-59	09-27-60	06-23-64*	01-06-57*
12-02-59	10-07-60*	07-16-64	04-04-57*
12-06-59*	10-10-60*	09-05-64*	04-09-57*
12-08-59	10-11-60*	01-23-65*	04-28-57
12-16-59*	10-11-60*	04-02-65	09-07-57*
12-20-59	10-14-60*	04-06-65*	10-25-57*
12-21-59	10-25-60	04-10-65*	12-19-57
12-25-59	10-27-60*	05-12-65*	01-06-58
12-27-59	10-29-60	06-02-65*	01-21-58*
01-02-60*	10-30-60*	06-08-65	06-03-58
01-06-60*	11-09-60	06-16-65	07-10-58
01-11-60*	11-11-60	06-21-65	07-15-58
01-19-60	11-12-60*	07-06-65*	07-17-58
01-26-60*	11-13-60	07-30-65*	08-08-58*
02-03-60*	11-18-60	09-08-65	08-20-58*
02-04-60*	12-03-60*	09-24-65*	08-22-58*
02-08-60	12-04-60	11-13-65*	08-27-58*
02-20-60*	12-15-60	11-30-65*	08-28-58
02-25-60*	12-28-60*	12-13-65	09-01-58*
02-27-60	01-14-61*	12-22-65*	09-05-58*
03-12-60	01-19-61*	01-06-66*	09-14-58*
03-12-60	02-07-61*	01-24-66	09-14-58*
03-15-60	02-11-61	02-10-66*	09-15-58*
03-16-60	02-20-61	03-25-66*	09-16-58*
03-24-60*	03-02-61*	05-01-66	09-17-58*
03-28-60*	03-13-61	02-21-69	09-20-58*
04-09-60*	03-22-61*	03-29-70	09-24-58*
04-11-60	03-28-61		10-01-58*
04-13-60	04-06-61*	c. Heavy Industry	10-01-58
04-14-60*	04-07-61	06-04-50*	10-04-58*
04-15-60	04-08-61*	07-29-51	10-09-58
04-17-60*	04-10-61	11-20-51	10-10-58*
05-01-60	04-14-61*	12-17-52	10-12-58*
05-03-60	04-20-61*	12-26-52	10-13-58*
05-07-60*	04-29-61*	04-07-53	10-15-58*
05-08-60*	05-28-61	05-01-53	10-17-58*
05-15-60*	06-04-61*	05-15-53	10-18-58*
05-16-60*	06-08-61*	06-23-53*	10-18-58*
05-23-60*	06-11-61	08-18-53*	10-19-58*
05-26-60*	08-04-61*	08-19-53*	10-20-58*
05-30-60*	08-08-61	10-18-53*	10-23-58*
06-04-60*	11-21-61	11-05-53	10-24-58*
06-08-60*	11-25-61*	11-17-53	10-26-58*
06-09-60*	12-05-61*	11-21-53	11-03-58*
06-15-60*	12-13-61*	11-22-53	11-05-58*
06-15-60	01-12-62	12-16-53	11-17-58*
06-19-60*	03-10-62	12-18-53	11-25-58*
06-23-60*	04-08-62*	12-27-53*	11-30-58*
06-25-60*	05-22-62	12-29-53	12-07-58*
07-03-60*	11-12-62	01-01-54	12-22-58*
07-04-60*	11-16-62*	01-28-54	12-24-58*
07-05-60	11-30-62*	03-03-54*	01-07-59*
07-08-60	12-05-62*	06-08-54	01-13-59*
07-11-60	12-16-62*	08-07-54	01-19-59*
07-18-60*	01-25-63*	08-13-54	01-20-59
07-21-60*	02-11-63	10-16-54	01-27-59
07-25-60*	03-15-63*	10-17-54	01-31-59*
07-29-60*	03-24-63*	12-06-54*	02-12-59*
08-06-60*	04-02-63	01-01-55	03-03-59*
08-07-60*	04-08-63*	01-17-55	03-10-59*
08-12-60	05-09-63*	02-17-55	03-17-59*
08-17-60	05-14-63	03-02-55	03-23-59*
08-18-60	09-02-63	03-22-55	03-29-59*
08-24-60*	12-02-63*	05-05-55*	04-03-59*
08-29-60*	12-04-63*	05-24-55	04-04-59*
08-31-60	12-11-63	07-08-55*	04-09-59
09-05-60*	01-01-64	08-23-55*	04-21-59*
09-08-60*	01-23-64	01-06-56	06-07-59*
09-13-60*	03-18-64	04-19-56*	07-04-59*
09-17-60*	04-14-64	05-23-56	07-09-59
09-19-60*	05-15-64	07-09-56*	08-01-59*
09-24-60*	05-29-64	12-07-56*	08-04-59*

09-01-59*
09-05-59*
09-11-59
09-27-59*
10-10-59*
10-12-59*
10-16-59*
11-02-59
11-05-59
11-22-59*
12-10-59
01-19-60*
02-04-60
02-08-60
02-27-60*
03-13-60
04-02-60*
05-01-60
05-03-60*
05-07-60*
05-08-60*
05-15-60*
06-15-60*
06-16-60*
07-19-60
07-21-60
08-07-60*
08-18-60*
08-29-60*
09-05-60*
09-22-60*
09-24-60*
10-06-60*
10-10-60
10-11-60*
10-22-60*
11-13-60*
12-04-60*
12-09-60*
12-17-60*
12-28-60*
01-09-61
01-14-61*
02-28-61
03-17-61
03-29-61*
06-11-61
07-22-61
11-14-61
10-22-62
02-07-63
02-20-63
03-10-63*
05-09-63*
06-23-64
04-06-65*
04-29-65
04-30-65
05-12-65*
06-16-65
11-13-65
11-30-65*
12-22-65*
01-24-66*
02-10-66*

d. Building Construction
03-28-55*
03-22-56*
04-20-56*
06-12-56
06-26-56*
08-04-56*

08-09-56*
10-11-56
11-27-56
01-04-57
01-06-57*
03-31-57*
08-09-57
01-07-58
02-02-58
03-29-58*
07-17-58*
11-16-58*
06-23-59
07-17-59
09-25-59*
10-10-59
01-17-60
03-27-60
07-03-60*
12-16-62

e. Light Industry
12-13-51
05-12-52
04-01-53
08-18-53*
08-19-53*
10-18-53*
11-05-53
12-16-53
12-18-53
12-23-53*
01-01-54
01-14-54
01-28-54
03-04-54
03-27-54
04-17-54
06-08-54
07-12-54
08-07-54
08-13-54
09-14-54*
10-16-54
11-19-54*
01-07-55*
01-17-55
02-17-55
10-04-55
12-02-55
03-16-56*
07-04-56*
07-09-56*
09-09-56*
01-04-57
04-02-57
04-20-57*
04-28-57
08-20-57*
09-26-57*
01-08-58*
04-11-58*
04-12-58*
08-29-58*
11-24-58*
12-20-58*
01-09-59*
01-18-59*
02-22-59*
02-23-59
03-14-59*
04-17-59*
05-23-59

05-25-59*
06-09-59*
06-30-59
07-24-59*
07-29-59*
10-14-59*
11-02-59
01-17-60*
02-20-60*
03-27-60*
03-28-60*
03-28-60*
05-30-60*
06-19-60*
07-04-60
07-24-60*
07-25-60*
09-26-60*
09-27-60*
10-16-60
11-09-60*
12-15-60*
01-16-61*
01-19-61
04-01-61
04-06-61*
04-08-61*
04-14-61*
04-20-61*
04-28-61*
05-07-61*
07-22-61
08-08-61*
11-21-61
12-13-61*
01-12-62*
03-15-62
12-05-62
02-20-63
04-25-63
10-14-63
10-16-63*
02-09-64
07-17-64*
09-05-64
05-04-65
06-16-65
03-25-66

f. Fuel and Power
08-05-51*
11-27-53*
12-18-53
03-03-54
06-14-54
10-17-54
07-20-55
05-09-56
05-23-56*
06-17-56*
09-05-56*
01-04-57
01-13-57*
01-27-57*
08-09-57
11-02-57*
05-15-58*
06-03-58
09-12-58*
10-13-58*
10-18-58*
10-25-58*
11-08-58*

12-02-58*
01-05-59*
01-06-59*
02-06-59*
02-15-59*
02-27-59*
04-03-59
04-09-59
05-11-59*
06-01-59
06-26-59*
06-28-59*
07-10-59*
07-27-59*
08-04-59*
08-08-59*
09-02-59*
09-11-59
10-16-59
01-19-60*
02-27-60
03-10-60*
03-12-60*
05-01-60
06-23-60*
07-05-60
07-08-60*
08-12-60
08-17-60*
09-05-60*
09-24-60*
10-11-60*
10-25-60*
10-30-60*
12-03-60
12-11-60*
12-28-60*
12-30-60*
12-31-60*
02-04-61
02-20-61*
02-22-61
03-02-61
05-16-61*
11-14-61
11-16-61
05-29-62
10-22-62
12-26-63*
01-01-64
09-07-65*
01-02-66*

g. Mining and Metallurgy
04-05-50
09-17-52
12-19-52*
06-12-53*
08-01-53*
08-18-53*
08-19-53*
09-01-53
10-18-53*
10-22-53*
11-17-53
11-27-53
12-18-53
01-01-54
01-28-54
03-03-54
06-08-54
06-14-54*
07-21-54*

127

08-07-54
08-13-54
01-17-55
02-17-55
04-16-55*
04-16-55*
09-11-55*
10-09-55*
05-20-56*
07-26-56*
01-13-57
01-27-57
02-07-57*
04-04-57
06-16-57
07-24-57
08-09-57*
09-07-57*
09-13-57*
11-02-57*
08-27-58
09-25-58*
12-15-58*
01-31-59*
02-06-59*
02-11-59*
04-09-59
06-17-59
07-10-59
09-01-59
09-11-59
10-12-59*
12-16-59
05-01-60
07-11-60*
08-06-60*
08-24-60*
10-06-60
10-10-60*
01-19-61
02-04-61*
03-07-61
03-29-61
03-31-61
04-07-61*
06-04-61
07-22-61
11-08-63
07-27-64

h. Local Industries
03-02-55*
11-13-55*
05-12-58*
05-29-58*
06-06-58*
06-10-58*
06-14-58
06-18-58*
06-21-58
07-10-58
08-08-58*
08-22-58
08-27-58*
08-28-58*
08-29-58*
09-01-58
09-25-58
09-27-58
10-04-58*
10-09-58
11-03-58*
11-17-58*

11-25-58*
01-04-59*
01-31-59
04-09-59
09-01-59
11-02-59
11-22-59*
11-30-59
01-19-60*
01-23-60
02-08-60*
05-01-60
05-07-60*
05-21-60*
06-22-60
07-04-60
07-19-60
07-23-60
07-26-60
08-07-60
09-27-60
10-29-60
10-29-60*
11-02-60*
11-09-60*
11-15-60*
12-28-60
01-14-61
07-17-64*
06-16-65
08-18-65*

i. Handicraft Industries
03-13-52
05-12-52
04-23-53*
09-20-53
12-21-53
01-01-54
03-10-54
04-14-54*
09-14-54
12-31-55*
01-13-56*
01-16-56
02-11-56
02-22-56
04-13-56*
05-10-56
12-20-56*
04-28-57
06-24-57*
07-29-57
08-26-57
09-26-57
11-21-57
12-27-57*
04-11-58*
07-10-58
06-30-59*
08-12-59
08-17-59*
07-04-60*
11-14-60
04-14-61*
05-07-61*
08-08-61
11-21-61
03-02-62*
03-15-62
05-20-62*
09-20-62
12-05-62*

04-25-63
10-27-63*
06-16-65

6. Agriculture

a. Agricultural Plans
and Policies
01-04-51*
06-07-51
03-26-53
04-11-53
05-17-53
05-26-54
07-04-54*
10-16-54
10-28-54*
01-01-55*
01-15-55
02-20-55
03-05-55
03-14-55
03-20-55
03-21-55
03-25-55
03-31-55*
04-01-55
05-10-55
05-27-55
07-04-55*
07-22-55
08-19-55
09-08-55*
09-09-55
09-25-55
09-27-55*
10-23-55*
11-11-55*
11-24-55
11-26-55
12-03-55*
12-13-55*
12-23-55*
03-04-56
03-09-56
03-12-56
04-02-56*
04-06-56*
05-06-56
05-26-56
06-02-56
06-10-56
06-20-56
07-10-56*
09-07-56*
09-13-56
12-13-56
01-14-57*
02-04-57*
02-21-57*
02-24-57*
03-22-57
04-08-57
04-21-57*
04-29-57
05-04-57*
05-20-57*
06-07-57*
07-09-57
07-24-57*
08-18-57*
09-07-57
09-21-57

09-25-57
10-10-57
10-11-57*
10-17-57
10-22-57
11-11-57
11-13-57*
12-04-57*
12-08-57
12-10-57*
01-06-58
02-03-58
02-28-58*
03-18-58
04-17-58
04-27-58
06-05-58*
06-06-58
06-06-58
07-01-58
08-14-58
09-19-58
10-14-58
11-09-58
12-21-58
12-25-58
01-02-59*
01-20-59
02-10-59
02-17-59
02-21-59
03-19-59*
05-16-59*
05-29-59
06-02-59
06-03-59
06-11-59
06-14-59
07-05-59
07-12-59
07-23-59*
08-03-59
08-20-59*
09-15-59*
09-17-59*
09-25-59
10-13-59
10-19-59*
11-05-59
12-04-59*
12-05-59*
12-08-59
12-22-59
01-14-60
02-05-60
02-10-60
03-10-60*
03-13-60
03-17-60*
04-01-60
04-03-60*
04-11-60*
04-12-60*
04-13-60*
04-21-60*
04-25-60
04-27-60*
05-05-60*
05-07-60*
05-11-60*
05-20-60*
07-19-60
07-31-60

08-25-60*
09-04-60
09-20-60
09-22-60*
10-17-60
10-23-60*
12-29-60
01-17-61*
01-23-61*
01-27-61
02-15-61
03-01-61*
03-19-61
03-24-61*
03-31-61
04-01-61*
04-02-61*
04-22-61*
04-28-61*
08-04-61*
08-25-61
08-29-61
09-08-61
10-25-61*
11-05-61
12-09-61*
01-01-62
02-16-62
03-10-62*
05-03-62*
09-08-62*
10-12-62
10-22-62*
11-02-62*
11-03-62*
11-26-62*
12-14-62
12-19-62*
02-12-63*
02-25-63*
03-07-63*
03-17-63*
04-25-63*
05-11-63
05-14-63
05-29-63
07-23-63
08-23-63*
08-27-63
10-14-63
10-16-63*
11-30-63
12-13-63
03-23-64
05-10-64
05-23-64*
06-09-64*
07-04-64*
07-05-64*
07-06-64*
08-05-64*
09-03-64*
09-21-64*
01-15-65
02-17-65*
02-20-65*
03-04-65
03-12-65*
03-14-65
03-28-65
04-17-65*
04-18-65*
04-23-65*

04-24-65*
07-10-65*
07-19-65
08-12-65*
08-31-65
01-27-66*
04-12-66
09-16-67*
03-22-69*
03-07-70*
04-16-72*
03-02-73
03-03-74

b. Agricultural Production
01-04-49
03-03-50
03-18-50
06-30-50
09-06-50
09-16-50
10-15-50
02-13-51
02-15-51*
03-02-51
03-16-51
03-17-51*
03-24-51*
03-28-51*
05-06-51*
06-01-51
07-05-51*
07-17-51
07-21-51
11-11-51
12-17-51*
01-01-52
02-27-52*
03-13-52
03-20-52*
04-02-52
05-28-52
06-08-52
08-11-52
09-04-52*
01-01-53
01-07-53*
02-27-53
04-01-53
04-11-53
05-17-53*
05-29-53*
06-06-53
06-10-53
06-26-53
07-23-53*
09-06-53
09-11-53*
09-12-53*
09-20-53
09-23-53*
10-06-53
10-20-53
11-05-53
11-09-53
11-15-53
11-16-53
11-18-53*
11-19-53
11-19-53
11-20-53
11-30-53
12-02-53*

12-03-53
12-11-53
12-17-53*
12-28-53*
01-05-54
01-06-54*
01-26-54
02-10-54*
02-20-54*
03-01-54
03-04-54
03-21-54
03-27-54*
03-28-54*
03-29-54*
04-18-54*
05-18-54
05-26-54
06-19-54
07-07-54
07-12-54*
07-26-54*
07-31-54
08-03-54
08-08-54*
09-14-54
09-17-54
09-20-54
10-06-54
10-16-54
10-17-54
10-28-54
11-11-54
11-17-54
12-19-54
01-01-55
01-07-55*
01-15-55*
01-23-55
02-28-55
03-09-55*
03-15-55
03-19-55*
03-20-55*
03-21-55
03-25-55*
03-31-55*
04-01-55
04-21-55
05-01-55
06-13-55*
07-04-55*
07-22-55*
07-23-55
08-03-55
08-19-55*
08-25-55
08-29-55
09-08-55
09-25-55
09-27-55
10-01-55
10-13-55*
10-15-55
10-16-55
10-22-55
10-24-55
11-13-55
11-26-55
12-03-55
12-11-55
12-23-55
01-01-56

01-14-56*
01-15-56*
01-23-56
01-24-56*
01-28-56*
03-04-56*
03-05-56
03-28-56*
04-02-56*
04-06-56*
05-01-56
05-06-56*
05-09-56*
05-16-56
05-17-56
05-23-56
05-24-56
04-15-56*
06-02-56
06-13-56
06-15-56
06-24-56*
07-02-56
07-09-56
07-10-56
07-27-56*
09-03-56
09-07-56
09-13-56
09-25-56*
09-29-56
10-03-56*
10-12-56
10-14-56
10-26-56*
10-27-56*
12-01-56
12-22-56
01-01-57
01-03-57
01-14-57
01-31-57
02-04-57*
02-10-57
02-11-57
02-18-57*
02-19-57
02-21-57*
02-24-57
03-01-57
03-02-57
03-11-57
03-18-57
03-23-57
03-24-57
03-31-57
04-01-57
04-02-57*
04-08-57
05-04-57*
05-04-57
05-08-57
05-09-57*
05-12-57
06-05-57
06-07-57
06-12-57*
07-03-57*
07-05-57
07-09-57*
07-11-57
07-22-57*
07-24-57*

129

08-02-57	06-20-58*	05-01-59	02-05-60*
08-05-57	07-05-58*	05-09-59	02-09-60*
08-08-57	07-09-58	05-10-59*	02-10-60
08-10-57	07-14-58	05-13-59	02-12-60*
08-12-57*	07-21-58*	05-16-59*	02-18-60*
08-15-57	07-23-58*	05-17-59*	02-21-60
08-20-57	07-24-58	05-29-59*	02-22-60*
08-22-57	07-25-58*	05-30-59*	02-23-60*
08-25-57*	07-26-58	05-31-59*	02-24-60*
08-26-57	07-28-58*	06-02-59	02-26-60*
08-30-57*	07-30-58	06-03-59	02-29-60
09-07-57	08-03-58*	06-03-59*	03-04-60*
09-08-57	08-03-58	06-10-59*	03-05-60*
09-20-57*	08-13-58*	06-11-59*	03-10-60*
09-22-57*	08-14-58*	06-14-59*	03-17-60*
09-26-57	08-18-58	06-16-59*	03-24-60
10-11-57*	08-21-58	06-22-59	03-29-60
10-17-57*	08-29-58*	06-29-59*	04-01-60*
10-27-57*	08-31-58*	07-05-59*	04-11-60
11-11-57*	09-03-58	07-12-59*	04-13-60
11-13-57*	09-04-58	07-15-59*	05-04-60*
11-16-57*	09-13-58*	07-18-59	05-05-60*
11-18-57*	09-13-58*	07-19-59	05-07-60
11-26-57*	09-23-58*	07-23-59*	05-09-60*
11-28-57	09-27-58	07-28-59*	05-10-60*
12-04-57*	09-27-58*	07-29-59	05-13-60
12-06-57	09-29-58	08-03-59*	05-14-60*
12-08-57*	09-30-58	08-07-59	05-14-60*
12-12-57	10-01-58*	08-08-59*	05-18-60*
12-19-57*	10-01-58*	08-12-59*	05-20-60*
12-19-57	10-04-58*	08-13-59*	05-24-60*
12-27-57	10-05-58	08-14-59*	05-29-60*
12-28-57*	10-09-58	08-14-59	06-15-60
01-01-58	10-11-58*	08-19-59	06-16-60
01-06-58	10-12-58*	08-20-59	06-17-60*
01-21-58*	10-19-58	08-21-59*	06-20-60*
01-29-58*	10-23-58	08-24-59*	06-21-60*
01-31-58	10-24-58*	08-29-59	06-27-60
02-04-58*	11-04-58	09-03-59	07-01-60
02-09-58	11-05-58*	09-07-59	07-02-60
02-15-58	11-13-58	09-08-59*	07-06-60
02-17-58*	11-21-58	09-11-59*	07-13-60*
02-28-58	11-22-58*	09-15-59*	07-17-60*
03-06-58	12-13-58*	09-17-59*	07-19-60*
03-10-58*	12-25-58*	09-22-59	07-20-60*
03-11-58	12-28-58*	09-25-59*	07-21-60
03-13-58	01-01-59	10-09-59*	07-22-60
03-22-58	01-02-59	10-11-59*	07-23-60
04-04-58	01-08-59*	10-13-59*	07-25-60*
04-07-58	01-12-59*	10-19-59*	07-26-60
04-09-58*	01-20-59	10-23-59*	07-27-60*
04-14-58*	01-21-59	10-25-59	07-28-60*
04-20-58	01-27-59	10-28-59	07-29-60
04-22-58*	01-30-59*	11-01-59	07-30-60*
04-23-58*	02-02-59	11-02-59	07-31-60*
04-27-58*	02-10-59*	11-05-59	08-01-60*
05-01-58	02-13-59*	11-10-59	08-04-60
05-06-58	02-17-59*	11-11-59	08-08-60*
05-13-58*	02-21-59*	11-16-59*	08-09-60*
05-14-58*	02-22-59	11-19-59*	08-10-60*
05-19-58	02-23-59*	11-22-59	08-13-60
05-21-58*	02-24-59	11-30-59*	08-14-60*
05-24-58	02-25-59*	12-04-59	08-18-60*
05-29-58*	03-09-59*	12-06-59	08-21-60*
06-04-58*	03-10-59*	12-08-59	08-23-60*
06-05-58*	03-13-59	12-15-59	08-25-60*
06-06-58*	03-16-59*	12-17-59	08-28-60*
06-10-58	03-19-59*	12-22-59*	09-04-60*
06-11-58*	03-21-59*	12-28-59	09-06-60*
06-12-58*	03-27-59*	01-01-60	09-09-60
06-14-58	04-01-59*	01-14-60	09-11-60*
06-14-58	04-04-59	01-23-60*	09-12-60
06-16-58	04-18-59*	01-26-60	09-20-60*

09-21-60*
09-22-60*
09-26-60*
09-29-60*
10-01-60
10-09-60*
10-13-60*
10-17-60*
10-19-60*
10-23-60*
10-27-60*
11-03-60
11-10-60
11-23-60*
12-18-60
01-01-61*
01-17-61
01-18-61*
01-20-61*
01-23-61*
01-26-61*
02-02-61
02-08-61
02-15-61*
02-17-61*
02-21-61
02-23-61*
02-23-61
02-24-61*
03-01-61*
03-08-61*
03-11-61
03-19-61
03-24-61*
03-31-61*
04-01-61
04-02-61
04-28-61
06-21-61
08-08-61*
08-23-61*
08-25-61*
09-15-61*
10-01-61
11-16-61
11-23-61
12-02-61*
12-12-61
12-27-61
01-01-62*
01-04-62*
01-18-62
01-24-62
02-16-62*
03-10-62*
03-15-62
04-06-62
04-10-62
04-17-62
04-29-62*
05-03-62*
05-12-62*
05-29-62
06-02-62
06-06-62*
06-08-62*
06-19-62*
06-27-62*
07-13-62
09-08-62*
09-20-62*
10-01-62*
10-12-62

10-23-62*
11-02-62*
11-03-62*
11-09-62*
11-16-62
11-26-62*
11-27-62*
11-30-62
12-02-62*
12-07-62*
12-14-62*
12-19-62*
12-22-62
01-30-63
02-12-63
02-17-63
02-20-63*
02-25-63*
03-07-63
03-10-63*
03-17-63
03-17-63*
03-29-63*
04-06-63*
04-23-63
04-25-63*
05-03-63
05-09-63
05-11-63*
05-14-63
05-19-63
05-29-63
06-10-63*
06-25-63*
07-13-63*
07-23-63
08-08-63*
08-23-63*
08-26-63
08-27-63*
08-29-63*
10-01-63*
10-14-63
10-16-63*
10-24-63*
11-16-63*
11-30-63
12-04-63
12-13-63
01-01-64*
01-19-64
01-23-64
01-30-64*
02-10-64
02-16-64
02-28-64
03-07-64*
03-11-64*
03-19-64*
03-23-64
04-19-64
05-01-64
05-04-64
05-10-64*
05-21-64*
05-23-64
05-26-64*
05-27-64*
06-09-64*
06-14-64
06-16-64*
06-23-64
07-04-64

07-05-64
07-06-64
07-27-64
08-05-64
08-06-64
08-14-64*
09-03-64
10-01-64
10-15-64
10-27-64*
11-16-64*
11-19-64
12-15-64
12-16-64
01-15-65*
02-17-65*
02-20-65*
02-22-65*
02-24-65*
02-27-65
03-04-65*
03-11-65
03-12-65*
03-28-65
04-23-65*
04-24-65*
04-28-65*
05-01-65
05-21-65
06-04-65
06-16-65*
06-23-65
07-02-65*
07-10-65
07-16-65
07-22-65*
08-14-65*
08-31-65*
09-15-65*
09-19-65
09-25-65
10-01-65
10-09-65
10-10-65*
10-16-65
11-01-65
11-05-65
12-16-65
12-18-65
12-23-65
12-26-65
01-16-66*
01-27-66
02-06-66
02-09-66*
02-16-66
02-23-66*
03-01-66
03-04-66
03-10-66
03-12-66
03-16-66*
04-12-66*
04-22-66*
05-01-66
05-08-66
09-07-66
09-15-66
09-19-66*
11-10-66
02-11-67*
05-31-67*
09-16-67

09-24-67*
01-01-68
02-21-69
03-22-69
01-01-70
03-07-70
02-18-71*
05-07-71
01-01-74
10-21-75*

c. Agricultural Sideline Production, Draft Animals, and Husbandry
03-14-55
03-19-55
05-27-55*
09-08-55
12-18-55*
02-25-56*
05-10-56*
05-17-56*
05-24-56*
07-03-56*
07-14-56*
08-19-56
09-07-56
09-13-56
09-14-56
01-15-57
02-10-57*
03-01-57*
03-15-57*
03-18-57
03-24-57
03-26-57
04-19-57*
05-09-57*
05-20-57*
06-02-57*
08-09-57
09-22-57
09-25-57*
09-26-57
10-11-57
10-28-57*
11-18-57*
11-30-57
12-04-57
12-16-57*
01-14-58*
03-13-58*
03-21-58
05-18-58
06-04-58*
07-21-58*
08-25-58*
10-23-58*
11-06-58*
11-10-58*
12-28-58*
01-02-59
01-20-59
01-27-59*
02-23-59*
05-20-59*
05-23-59
06-11-59
06-14-59
06-24-59*
07-11-59*
07-15-59
07-18-59

131

07-23-59
07-29-59
08-12-59
08-19-59
08-20-59
08-29-59
09-11-59
10-09-59
10-11-59*
11-05-59*
11-11-59*
11-16-59*
11-19-59*
12-17-59*
12-18-59*
12-23-59*
01-05-60*
01-09-60*
02-02-60*
02-07-60*
02-17-60*
02-18-60
02-25-60
02-28-60*
02-29-60*
03-07-60*
03-17-60*
03-28-60*
04-13-60
04-17-60*
04-26-60*
05-07-60
05-22-60*
06-22-60*
07-06-60*
07-09-60*
07-16-60*
07-19-60
07-20-60*
07-21-60*
07-31-60
07-31-60*
08-06-60*
08-07-60
08-10-60*
08-30-60*
08-31-60*
09-10-60*
09-19-60*
09-22-60
09-27-60*
09-29-60*
10-18-60*
10-27-60
10-29-60*
10-29-60*
11-06-60*
11-09-60*
11-14-60*
11-20-60
11-25-60
12-21-60
12-23-60*
12-29-60
01-08-61*
01-18-61
02-24-61*
02-26-61*
03-08-61
03-31-61
07-05-61*
08-04-61
08-23-61*

08-25-61
09-15-61
09-25-61*
10-11-61*
11-05-61*
11-10-61*
11-16-61
11-26-61*
12-02-61
01-22-62*
02-26-62*
04-29-62
05-03-62*
06-02-62*
06-10-62
07-13-62
09-20-62
10-22-62
11-02-62
11-26-62
12-07-62
01-30-63*
02-11-63
02-17-63*
02-25-63
03-17-63
03-29-63
05-14-63
05-19-63*
06-25-63*
07-18-63*
08-08-63
10-24-63*
11-14-63*
01-23-64
01-30-64
05-23-64
08-06-64
09-11-64
11-19-64
02-24-65*
02-27-65*
03-04-65
04-17-65*
04-18-65*
07-10-65*
07-19-65*
07-20-65*
07-22-65*
07-23-65
07-29-65*
08-14-65*
09-19-65*
09-25-65*
10-10-65*
10-24-65*
12-02-65
12-04-65*
01-29-66*
03-01-66*
03-10-66*
04-01-66
04-12-66*
03-22-69

d. Seasonal Planting and Harvest

1. Spring Planting
03-03-50
03-18-50*
05-10-50*
02-15-51*

03-02-51
03-17-51
03-24-51
02-27-52
03-20-52*
03-26-53
07-23-53
03-29-54*
04-26-54*
01-15-55*
03-05-55*
03-15-55*
03-19-55
04-21-55
05-10-55
02-15-56
03-04-56
03-05-56*
05-06-56
05-17-56
02-04-57*
02-16-57
03-03-57
03-18-57
03-20-57
04-19-57
03-25-58
04-17-58*
02-10-59*
03-19-59*
02-05-60*
02-10-60
02-18-60*
03-05-60
03-10-60*
03-17-60
03-17-60
03-19-60*
04-06-60*
04-21-60
04-25-60*
05-11-60*
01-17-61*
01-31-61*
02-06-61*
02-08-61
02-12-61
02-15-61*
03-01-61*
03-04-61
03-11-61
03-19-61
03-21-61*
03-25-61
03-31-61
04-28-61*
02-12-63
03-17-63*
04-23-63
05-03-63
03-19-64
02-22-65*
02-24-65
04-23-65*
04-15-66
02-11-67*
03-12-67*
03-13-67*
03-22-69*
03-07-70*
02-18-71
03-09-72*
03-02-73*

03-03-74*
02-28-75*

2. Summer Harvest and Planting
06-02-50*
05-06-51
07-17-51
05-28-52
07-04-54
06-06-55*
07-04-55
05-29-56*
05-29-56
06-06-56
06-10-56*
06-24-56*
06-06-57*
06-12-57
04-17-58
05-13-58*
05-21-58*
06-06-58
06-11-58
06-12-58
06-14-58
06-14-58*
06-16-58*
07-05-58
07-09-58
07-23-58*
07-28-58*
08-03-58
05-10-59*
05-13-59
05-16-59*
05-17-59*
05-29-59*
06-11-59*
07-12-59*
07-18-59
07-23-59*
04-01-60*
05-18-60*
05-25-60*
05-26-60*
06-05-60*
06-21-60
07-31-60*
05-30-63*
04-24-65*
06-03-65
05-31-67*

3. Autumn Harvest and Winter Sowing
09-16-50*
09-04-52*
09-12-53*
10-28-54*
08-19-55
09-09-55
09-17-55
09-25-55*
09-25-55*
11-26-55
08-19-56*
12-01-56
07-09-57
08-10-57
09-22-57*
02-01-58*
07-28-58*

	08-03-58	01-07-53	09-21-57	01-27-59*
	08-14-58*	03-26-53	09-25-57	02-10-59*
	08-31-58*	05-17-53	10-11-57	02-13-59*
	09-02-58	07-23-53*	10-22-57*	02-21-59*
	09-10-58	10-20-53*	10-25-57*	02-23-59*
	09-17-58*	01-06-54	10-27-57	02-25-59
	10-05-58*	03-27-54	11-16-57	03-09-59
	10-12-58*	03-29-54	11-18-57*	03-10-59*
	10-13-58*	04-26-54	11-24-57	03-13-59*
	11-06-58*	07-04-54	12-04-57	03-16-59*
	06-29-59*	08-08-54	12-06-57	03-19-59
	07-19-59*	09-17-54	12-10-57*	03-21-59*
	07-28-59*	10-17-54	12-19-57*	03-27-59
	08-07-59*	10-28-54	12-28-57	04-01-59*
	08-19-59*	01-06-55*	01-14-58	04-03-59
	09-08-59*	01-15-55	01-21-58*	04-04-59*
	09-17-59*	02-20-55*	01-29-58	04-08-59*
	10-09-59	03-15-55	02-15-58*	05-01-59
	10-12-59	03-31-55	02-17-58	05-09-59*
	10-17-59*	04-01-55	02-27-58	05-10-59
	10-23-59*	04-21-55*	03-25-58	05-16-59*
	10-28-59*	05-27-55*	04-04-58*	05-17-59
	11-30-59	06-06-55	04-09-58	05-19-59*
	07-20-60	06-13-55*	04-16-58*	05-20-59*
	07-31-60	08-14-55	04-17-58	05-24-59
	08-14-60*	08-19-55	04-21-58	05-31-59*
	08-21-60*	09-25-55	04-22-58*	06-02-59*
	08-25-60*	10-07-55*	04-27-58	06-03-59*
	08-26-60*	10-13-55*	05-06-58*	06-11-59*
	08-30-60	10-22-55	05-13-58	06-14-59
	09-01-60*	12-15-55*	05-14-58	06-16-59*
	09-03-60*	01-15-56	05-19-58*	06-22-59*
	09-04-60*	01-23-56	05-23-58*	06-24-59
	09-15-60*	01-24-56	05-24-58	06-29-59*
	09-18-60*	01-28-56*	06-04-58*	07-05-59*
	09-19-60*	02-14-56	06-06-58	07-12-59*
	09-20-60*	02-15-56*	06-12-58	07-18-59
	09-21-60	02-25-56	06-14-58	07-19-59*
	09-26-60*	04-02-56	06-16-58*	07-23-59*
	09-27-60	04-15-56*	06-18-58	07-28-59*
	09-27-60	05-06-56	06-23-58	08-03-59*
	10-05-60*	06-24-56*	07-01-58	08-07-59
	10-09-60	07-03-56	07-05-58*	08-08-59*
	10-16-60	07-10-56	07-10-58	08-12-59
	10-19-60*	09-03-56	07-22-58*	08-13-59*
	10-28-60*	09-25-56	07-25-58	08-14-59*
	01-06-61	10-03-56	07-26-58*	08-14-59
	08-25-61*	10-12-56*	07-28-58*	08-19-59*
	09-08-61*	10-26-56	08-14-58	08-21-59*
	09-25-61*	01-03-57*	08-21-58*	08-29-59
	10-15-61	01-04-57	08-31-58	09-03-59
	12-02-61	02-03-57	09-02-58*	09-08-59
	09-20-62*	02-04-57	09-12-58*	09-11-59
	11-02-62	02-16-57*	09-13-58*	09-15-59*
	11-27-62	02-18-57	09-13-58*	09-17-59
	08-23-63	02-21-57	09-17-58	10-11-59
	08-27-63	03-01-57	09-23-58	10-13-59*
	10-16-63*	03-03-57*	09-29-58	10-19-59*
	09-03-64*	03-11-57*	10-14-58	10-23-59*
	09-21-64	03-15-57*	10-18-58*	10-25-59*
	02-20-65	03-18-57*	10-19-58	10-28-59*
	09-25-65*	03-22-57	10-24-58	11-01-59
	09-07-66	03-24-57*	11-04-58*	11-02-59*
	09-19-66*	03-25-57*	11-05-58*	11-05-59*
	09-16-67*	04-01-57	11-06-58	11-10-59
	09-24-67*	04-02-57	11-21-58*	11-11-59
		04-08-57	11-22-58*	11-13-59
e. Agricultural Techniques,	04-29-57	11-26-58*	11-15-59*
Machinery, and Mech-	06-07-57*	12-13-58*	11-16-59*
anization	07-09-57*	12-25-58	11-19-59
	03-02-51*	07-19-57*	01-08-59*	11-28-59*
	03-24-52*	07-24-57*	01-20-59	12-04-59*
	09-04-52	09-07-57*	01-21-59*	12-05-59

133

12-08-59*	07-09-60*	02-21-61	06-10-63*
12-17-59*	07-16-60*	02-23-61	06-25-63
12-18-59	07-17-60*	02-23-61*	07-13-63*
12-22-59	07-19-60*	02-26-61*	07-17-63
12-23-59	07-21-60	02-28-61*	07-23-63*
12-30-59*	07-23-60*	03-01-61*	08-08-63
01-05-60*	07-24-60*	03-14-61*	08-23-63
01-09-60	07-25-60*	03-19-61*	08-26-63*
01-11-60	07-26-60*	03-21-61*	08-27-63
01-13-60*	07-29-60*	03-24-61*	09-20-63
01-14-60*	07-31-60*	04-11-61*	10-14-63
01-18-60*	07-31-60*	04-18-61*	10-16-63
01-26-60*	08-01-60*	04-22-61	11-26-63*
02-05-60*	08-04-60*	04-28-61	11-30-63
02-07-60*	08-05-60	06-11-61*	12-04-63
02-09-60*	08-06-60	07-05-61	12-13-63*
02-12-60*	08-07-60*	08-12-61*	01-01-64
02-16-60*	08-08-60*	08-23-61	01-06-64*
02-17-60*	08-10-60	08-25-61	01-19-64*
02-18-60	08-13-60*	09-08-61	01-24-64
02-22-60*	08-14-60	09-15-61	01-28-64*
02-23-60*	08-20-60*	10-25-61	01-30-64
02-25-60*	08-21-60*	11-03-61*	02-28-64
02-26-60*	08-23-60*	12-09-61*	03-07-64*
02-29-60	08-25-60	12-12-61	03-11-64*
03-02-60*	08-26-60*	12-27-61*	03-23-64*
03-04-60*	08-28-60*	01-18-62*	04-06-64*
03-06-60*	08-30-60*	01-20-62	04-19-64*
03-07-60*	09-03-60	01-22-62*	05-01-64
03-07-60*	09-04-60*	02-16-62*	05-10-64*
03-10-60*	09-06-60*	02-26-62*	05-23-64
03-10-60	09-09-60*	03-10-62*	05-26-64*
03-13-60*	09-10-60*	04-06-62*	05-27-64*
03-14-60	09-11-60	05-20-62*	06-09-64*
03-17-60	09-12-60*	06-02-62*	06-14-64*
03-17-60*	09-18-60*	06-08-62*	06-16-64*
06-01-60*	09-20-60	06-10-62*	06-23-64*
04-03-60	09-22-60*	07-13-62*	07-04-64*
04-06-60*	09-26-60*	09-08-62*	07-05-64*
04-12-60	09-27-60*	09-20-62*	07-06-64*
04-13-60*	09-29-60*	10-12-62*	07-12-64*
04-16-60*	10-05-60	10-22-62*	08-05-64*
04-17-60	10-13-60*	11-02-62	08-06-64
04-20-60*	10-17-60	11-03-62	08-14-64*
04-21-60	10-19-60	11-09-62*	09-03-64*
04-24-60	10-23-60	11-16-62*	10-15-64*
04-25-60*	10-28-60*	11-26-62	10-24-64*
04-26-60	10-28-60*	11-30-62	10-25-64*
04-27-60*	10-29-60	12-07-62*	10-27-64
05-04-60*	11-02-60*	12-14-62*	10-28-64
05-05-60	11-04-60*	12-16-62	11-16-64
05-07-60	11-06-60*	12-19-62*	11-19-64
05-09-60*	11-11-60*	12-22-62*	01-15-65*
05-10-60*	11-15-60*	01-25-63*	02-17-65*
05-11-60*	11-20-60	02-07-63	02-20-65*
05-13-60	11-22-60*	02-11-63*	02-24-65
05-14-60*	11-23-60*	02-17-63*	02-27-65*
05-14-60*	12-13-60	02-20-63	03-04-65*
05-18-60	12-18-60*	02-25-63	03-12-65*
05-20-60	12-20-60	03-07-63	03-28-65*
05-22-60	12-23-60*	03-10-63*	04-02-65
05-24-60*	01-06-61*	03-17-63	04-17-65*
05-25-60*	01-14-61	03-29-63	04-18-65
05-26-60*	01-17-61*	04-06-63*	04-23-65*
05-29-60*	01-18-61	04-23-63*	04-24-65
06-05-60*	01-19-61	04-25-63	04-29-65*
06-17-60*	01-23-61	05-03-63*	04-30-65*
06-20-60*	01-26-61*	05-09-63	05-21-65
06-22-60	01-31-61*	05-11-63*	06-03-65*
06-24-60*	02-04-61*	05-14-63*	07-02-65
06-27-60*	02-06-61*	05-19-63	07-10-65*
07-02-60*	02-09-61*	05-29-63*	07-19-65
07-05-60*	02-17-61*	06-02-63	07-22-65

08-12-65
08-18-65*
08-21-65*
08-31-65*
09-07-65*
09-15-65*
10-09-65
11-01-65
11-05-65
11-05-65*
12-23-65
01-16-66*
01-29-66
02-09-66
02-16-66
02-23-66*
03-10-66
04-12-66
04-22-66
05-08-66
09-24-67*
03-22-69
03-07-70
10-21-75

f. Agricultural Organization

1. Mutual Aid Teams
03-02-51
03-16-51
12-17-51
02-27-52
04-02-52
04-10-52*
09-04-52
05-01-53
09-02-53*
09-12-53
10-20-53
11-05-53
11-15-53
11-16-53
11-25-53
12-11-53
12-20-53
12-28-53
12-30-53
01-01-54
01-05-54
01-06-54
01-09-54*
01-16-54*
01-17-54
01-19-54*
01-26-54
01-29-54
02-01-54
03-10-54
03-27-54
03-29-54
05-01-54
05-26-54
07-07-54*
08-03-54
08-08-54
10-16-54
11-21-54
11-23-54
12-15-54*
01-24-55
02-04-55
10-22-55

10-25-55
10-30-55
04-14-56

2. Lower and Higher Agricultural Cooperatives
04-10-52*
04-15-52
06-08-52
09-04-52
03-26-53*
05-01-53
09-02-53
09-12-53
10-15-53
10-20-53
11-05-53
11-09-53
11-15-53
11-16-53
11-18-53
11-25-53
12-02-53*
12-06-53*
12-11-53
12-20-53
12-28-53
12-30-53
01-01-54
01-05-54
01-06-54
01-09-54*
01-16-54*
01-17-54
01-19-54*
01-26-54
01-29-54
02-01-54
03-10-54
03-21-54
03-27-54
03-29-54
05-01-54
05-18-54
05-26-54*
07-04-54*
07-07-54*
07-31-54*
08-03-54*
08-08-54
08-31-54*
09-01-54
09-12-54*
10-16-54
10-28-54*
11-21-54
11-23-54
12-04-54*
12-15-54*
01-01-55
01-06-55*
01-15-55
01-23-55
01-24-55
01-30-55*
02-04-55
02-19-55*
02-20-55
02-28-55*
03-05-55*
03-14-55*
03-15-55*
03-16-55

03-19-55
03-20-55
03-24-55
03-25-55
04-07-55
04-12-55
05-07-55*
05-27-55
06-13-55
06-27-55*
07-08-55*
09-08-55
09-17-55*
09-25-55*
09-25-55*
10-01-55
10-04-55
10-06-55
10-07-55*
10-15-55
10-22-55
10-25-55
10-28-55
10-29-55*
10-30-55
11-10-55
11-11-55
11-13-55*
11-17-55*
11-24-55
12-03-55*
12-07-55*
12-11-55*
12-13-55*
12-15-55
12-18-55
12-28-55*
12-29-55
01-13-56
01-16-56
01-27-56
01-28-56*
02-07-56
02-09-56*
02-10-56*
02-17-56
02-18-56
02-24-56
02-25-56
03-04-56*
03-09-56
03-12-56*
03-28-56
04-01-56
04-02-56
04-06-56*
05-10-56
05-13-56
05-17-56
05-24-56
05-29-56
05-29-56
06-06-56*
06-10-56*
06-13-56*
06-15-56
06-24-56
06-25-56*
06-27-56
07-02-56*
07-17-56
07-19-56
07-27-56*

07-29-56*
08-01-56
09-03-56
09-07-56
09-11-56
09-13-56*
09-14-56*
09-25-56*
10-10-56
10-12-56
10-22-56
10-27-56
11-22-56
11-24-56
11-28-56*
12-01-56*
01-14-57
01-31-57*
02-04-57
02-09-57*
02-10-57
02-16-57*
02-18-57
02-21-57
02-22-57*
02-24-57*
03-01-57*
03-02-57*
03-03-57
03-11-57*
03-17-57
03-18-57
03-20-57*
03-21-57
03-22-57*
03-23-57*
03-24-57
03-25-57*
03-26-57*
04-08-57
04-19-57*
04-21-57*
04-29-57*
05-04-57
05-14-57*
05-30-57
06-02-57*
06-06-57
07-05-57
07-09-57
07-19-57
08-07-57*
08-25-57*
08-28-57
09-09-57*
10-08-57*
10-11-57
10-27-57
11-16-57
11-24-57*
11-26-57
12-04-57*
12-06-57
12-07-57
12-16-57
12-22-57*
12-29-57
01-14-58
01-23-58*
02-04-58
02-16-58*
03-25-58
04-14-58

04-16-58*
05-19-58*
05-21-58
06-12-58
07-10-58
12-05-62

3. Communes
09-03-58*
09-04-58*
09-10-58*
09-17-58*
09-19-58
09-23-58*
09-26-58*
09-27-58
10-01-58*
10-01-58*
10-09-58*
10-11-58
10-13-58*
10-14-58
10-23-58
10-25-58*
11-05-58
11-06-58*
11-09-58
11-10-58*
11-21-58
11-22-58*
11-26-58*
12-04-58
12-07-58*
12-21-58*
12-23-58*
12-24-58*
12-25-58*
12-28-58
01-01-59
01-02-59*
01-05-59
01-08-59
01-09-59*
01-12-59
01-17-59*
01-18-59*
01-20-59*
01-21-59
01-22-59*
01-27-59
01-30-59
02-02-59
02-04-59
02-04-59
02-17-59*
02-23-59
03-08-59
03-09-59
03-13-59
03-14-59
03-25-59*
03-26-59*
04-04-59
04-13-59*
05-01-59
05-13-59*
05-17-59*
05-20-59
05-29-59*
05-30-59
06-03-59
06-09-59
06-10-59*

06-11-59
06-16-59
06-24-59
06-27-59
07-15-59
07-18-59
07-19-59
07-23-59
07-26-59*
07-29-59*
08-03-59
08-08-59*
08-13-59
08-18-59*
08-19-59
08-20-59
08-21-59
08-24-59
08-29-59*
09-03-59*
09-07-59
09-08-59*
09-11-59
09-15-59
09-20-59*
09-22-59*
09-26-59
10-09-59
10-12-59*
10-13-59
10-25-59
11-01-59
11-02-59
11-10-59
11-11-59*
11-13-59*
11-15-59
11-16-59
11-19-59*
11-22-59
11-30-59
12-04-59
12-05-59
12-06-59
12-08-59
12-15-59
12-17-59
12-22-59*
12-23-59*
12-28-59
12-30-59
01-01-60
01-04-60*
01-05-60*
01-06-60
01-08-60
01-09-60
01-13-60
01-14-60
01-18-60
01-23-60
02-02-60
02-07-60*
02-09-60*
02-10-60*
02-12-60
02-17-60*
02-18-60
02-21-60*
02-22-60
02-23-60*
02-24-60
02-26-60

02-28-60
02-29-60*
03-01-60
03-04-60
03-07-60*
03-10-60*
03-14-60*
03-16-60
03-17-60*
03-17-60
03-19-60*
03-21-60*
03-27-60
03-28-60
03-31-60
04-03-60*
04-06-60*
04-11-60
04-12-60*
04-13-60
04-15-60
04-19-60
04-20-60*
04-21-60*
04-25-60*
04-26-60
04-27-60*
05-05-60
05-06-60
05-07-60
05-10-60*
05-13-60*
05-18-60
05-21-60*
05-22-60
05-24-60
05-25-60*
05-26-60
06-01-60
06-05-60
06-20-60
06-21-60*
06-22-60*
06-24-60*
06-27-60*
07-01-60*
07-04-60
07-05-60*
07-09-60*
07-09-60
07-13-60*
07-16-60
07-17-60
07-21-60
07-21-60
07-22-60*
07-23-60*
07-24-60
07-25-60
07-26-60*
07-27-60
07-28-60
07-29-60*
07-31-60
08-01-60*
08-04-60
08-05-60*
08-06-60*
08-10-60
08-13-60
08-18-60
08-27-60
09-01-60

09-06-60
09-09-60*
09-10-60*
09-11-60*
09-15-60*
09-18-60*
09-19-60*
09-20-60
09-23-60*
09-26-60
09-27-60
09-27-60*
09-28-60
09-29-60
09-29-60*
10-09-60
10-13-60
10-16-60
10-17-60
10-19-60
10-23-60*
10-27-60
10-28-60*
10-29-60
10-29-60
11-03-60*
11-10-60
11-14-60*
11-15-60*
11-20-60*
11-23-60
11-25-60*
11-26-60
12-13-60*
12-14-60*
12-14-60*
12-18-60*
12-21-60*
12-23-60
12-29-60*
01-01-61
01-06-61*
01-08-61*
01-12-61*
01-20-61*
01-23-61
01-27-61*
01-31-61*
02-02-61
02-04-61*
02-05-61
02-15-61
02-24-61
02-26-61*
03-11-61
03-14-61*
03-19-61
03-25-61
03-26-61*
04-02-61*
04-11-61*
04-22-61*
06-21-61*
07-05-61
08-29-61
09-08-61*
09-21-61*
09-25-61*
09-28-61*
10-01-61*
10-11-61*
10-25-61*
11-03-61

137

11-05-61*
11-21-61
11-26-61
12-02-61
12-03-61*
12-12-61
12-27-61
01-01-62
01-04-62*
01-20-62
02-26-62
03-10-62*
04-10-62
04-29-62
05-12-62*
05-16-62*
05-20-62*
06-02-62
06-08-62
10-01-62
10-12-62
10-22-62*
10-23-62*
11-02-62
11-03-62
11-09-62*
11-27-62
12-02-62
01-11-63*
01-25-63*
01-30-63*
02-12-63
02-25-63
04-13-63
05-14-63
05-29-63*
05-30-63
06-02-63
07-04-63
07-17-63
10-01-63
10-14-63
10-16-63
10-24-63
11-14-63*
11-16-63
11-26-63
12-04-63
01-06-64
01-19-64
01-30-64
02-16-64
03-11-64
04-06-64*
05-30-64*
07-04-64
07-05-64
07-06-64
07-12-64
08-06-64
09-11-64
09-21-64
10-15-64
10-24-64
10-25-64*
10-28-64
12-15-64
02-15-65
02-17-65
02-20-65
04-11-65
04-17-65*
04-18-65*

05-05-65
05-21-65
06-04-65
06-05-65
06-08-65
06-23-65
07-02-65
07-11-65
07-16-65
07-22-65
07-23-65
07-29-65
08-14-65
08-18-65*
08-31-65
10-28-65*
11-01-65
12-02-65
12-04-65
02-11-67
11-20-69
07-09-70
09-23-70
10-21-75

4. State Farms and PLA-
   Run Farms
   04-01-55*
   08-14-55*
   09-21-57*
   03-18-58*
   11-16-59
   05-18-60
   02-15-61
   03-31-61
   09-15-61
   11-05-61
   11-16-61*
   05-03-62
   09-08-62
   01-30-63
   02-12-63
   01-19-64
   02-16-64
   03-23-64*
   08-06-64
   12-15-64
   12-16-64
   11-01-65
   04-01-66*

g. Rural Financial
   Relationships
   12-06-53
   03-28-54*
   08-03-54
   08-31-54*
   09-17-54
   11-23-54
   01-24-55
   02-19-55*
   03-09-55*
   03-14-55*
   05-06-55
   05-08-55
   06-26-55*
   08-03-55
   09-08-55*
   09-27-55
   11-11-55
   12-18-55
   03-04-56
   03-05-56

03-09-56
05-09-56
05-10-56
05-29-56*
06-02-56*
06-06-56*
06-10-56
07-02-56
07-29-56*
09-11-56*
10-14-56*
10-26-56*
11-22-56
11-24-56
12-01-56*
01-14-57
02-03-57
02-09-57*
02-22-57
03-20-57*
03-24-57
05-04-57
05-14-57*
06-06-57
06-18-57
08-05-57
08-10-57
08-15-57*
08-18-57*
08-30-57*
09-02-57
09-20-57*
09-26-57
10-11-57
12-06-57*
12-07-57*
12-15-57*
01-12-58*
05-12-58
05-21-58
06-05-58
06-06-58*
09-27-58
12-23-58*
04-13-59
05-13-59
05-20-59*
08-20-59
09-20-59
09-25-59*
10-17-59
12-05-59
12-15-59
12-17-59
12-20-59
12-23-59
01-08-60*
03-14-60
04-13-60
08-05-60*
09-21-60*
10-16-60*
11-20-60*
11-25-60*
11-30-60*
12-21-60*
12-29-60*
01-20-61*
02-15-61*
02-15-61
04-02-61*
07-05-61*
10-15-61*

11-05-61
01-01-62
03-10-62
04-10-62
04-29-62*
05-10-62*
05-16-62*
10-22-62
10-23-62*
12-02-62*
12-19-62
01-30-63*
04-23-63*
06-10-63
06-25-63
10-16-63
11-14-63*
11-26-63*
01-28-64*
03-11-64
05-26-64*
06-02-64
07-04-64
07-06-64*
09-11-64
09-21-64
10-27-64*
11-24-64*
12-06-64*
02-27-65
03-04-65
03-11-65
04-11-65*
04-17-65*
04-18-65*
06-23-65*
07-16-65
08-12-65
08-14-65

h. Water and Soil
   Conservation
   05-17-50*
   05-29-50*
   10-15-50*
   02-17-51*
   03-16-51*
   12-17-51
   03-20-52
   04-03-52*
   06-28-52
   07-20-52
   09-08-52
   12-27-52*
   01-18-53
   07-05-53*
   11-18-53*
   01-06-54
   08-02-54
   08-08-54
   10-06-54
   10-24-54*
   12-19-54*
   01-23-55
   07-20-55*
   02-17-56
   02-24-56*
   03-06-56*
   06-13-56*
   07-10-56
   09-03-56
   09-25-56
   01-03-57

02-03-57*	05-05-59*	03-05-61	i. Fishing
02-16-57	05-09-59*	03-31-61	10-10-56*
02-21-57	05-31-59	09-15-61*	02-23-59
03-24-57	06-01-59	11-16-61	03-13-59*
04-14-57*	06-03-59	11-23-61*	07-15-59
05-30-57	06-23-59*	12-09-61*	08-20-59
06-17-57	07-23-59	01-18-62*	10-09-59
07-05-57	07-28-59	01-20-62	03-02-60*
07-09-57	08-13-59	01-24-62*	04-13-60
07-19-57	08-14-59	03-29-62*	09-22-60
07-22-57*	08-14-59*	04-06-62*	10-27-60
07-24-57*	08-18-59*	04-10-62*	03-26-61*
09-07-57*	08-29-59	05-29-62	09-15-61*
09-08-57*	09-07-59*	06-06-62*	09-28-61*
09-25-57*	09-11-59	06-10-62*	11-05-61
10-11-57	10-10-59	07-13-62	11-16-61
10-17-57	10-19-59	09-20-62	02-25-63
10-22-57*	10-25-59*	10-12-62*	03-29-63*
10-27-57	11-01-59*	11-02-62	08-08-63
11-13-57	11-05-59	11-09-62	
11-15-57*	11-10-59	11-13-62*	j. Forestry
11-18-57*	11-12-59	11-26-62	05-17-50*
11-24-57	11-28-59*	02-11-63	02-15-51
12-04-57	12-08-59	02-12-63	03-27-51*
12-08-57	12-15-59*	02-25-63	08-17-51*
12-15-57*	12-20-59*	03-07-63*	03-06-52*
12-19-57*	12-25-59*	03-29-63	01-18-53*
01-12-58*	12-27-59*	03-31-63*	11-04-53*
01-14-58	12-30-59*	08-23-63	01-06-54
01-16-58*	01-13-60*	11-30-63*	02-05-56*
02-03-58	01-18-60*	12-13-63*	02-17-56*
02-26-58*	02-05-60	01-19-64	03-02-56*
02-27-58	02-07-60	01-24-64	09-03-56*
03-03-58*	02-09-60	01-30-64	12-05-56*
03-11-58*	02-10-60*	02-10-64	02-21-57
03-18-58*	02-12-60*	02-16-64	12-08-57
03-21-58*	02-16-60*	03-07-64	01-16-58
03-22-58	03-05-60	03-11-64*	01-23-58*
03-25-58*	03-14-60	03-23-64*	02-16-58*
04-04-58*	03-16-60	04-19-64*	04-08-58*
04-09-58	03-17-60*	05-23-64*	04-27-58
04-14-58	04-01-60	07-04-64*	09-25-58*
04-17-58	04-11-60	07-05-64*	02-23-59
04-20-58*	04-12-60	07-06-64*	03-09-59*
04-22-58*	04-24-60*	08-05-64*	06-27-59*
04-27-58	05-09-60*	08-06-64*	07-15-59
05-06-58	05-18-60	08-14-64*	08-09-59*
05-14-58	06-13-60*	10-28-64*	08-20-59
05-15-58*	06-17-60*	11-19-64*	10-09-59
05-24-58*	07-01-60	12-06-64*	11-13-59*
06-07-58*	07-02-60	12-15-64	11-22-59*
06-14-58	07-05-60*	12-16-64	12-17-59
06-16-58*	07-09-60*	01-15-65*	01-17-60*
06-20-58	07-19-60	02-15-65*	03-21-60*
07-02-58*	07-21-60	02-20-65	03-27-60*
07-21-58	07-24-60*	02-24-65	04-11-60
07-28-58	07-31-60	03-04-65	04-13-60
07-30-58*	08-08-60*	03-11-65	08-04-60*
08-18-58*	08-09-60	03-14-65*	09-04-60
08-31-58	08-18-60	04-11-65*	09-22-60
09-02-58*	08-21-60	08-05-65*	10-17-60*
09-13-58*	08-25-60	10-09-65*	10-27-60
09-17-58	09-12-60	10-16-65*	02-07-61*
09-23-58	09-28-60*	11-05-65*	02-23-61
10-14-58*	10-23-60	11-05-65	03-31-61*
10-24-58	11-22-60*	12-26-65*	11-05-61
11-22-58	12-13-60*	02-06-66	11-16-61
11-26-58*	12-14-60*	02-16-66	05-12-62
12-13-58*	12-20-60*	02-23-66*	05-29-62*
01-20-59	02-06-61*	03-12-66	06-19-62*
02-10-59	02-15-61	04-11-66	02-21-63*
02-13-59	02-21-61*	04-21-66*	02-25-63
02-25-59*	02-23-61*	04-22-66	03-31-63*

04-10-63*
04-25-63*
06-23-63*
08-08-63
05-23-64
08-06-64*
10-28-64
12-15-64*
12-16-64*
12-18-64*
02-15-65
02-24-65
03-11-65*
02-06-66*
03-12-66*
04-01-66
04-26-66*

7. Capital Construction
11-20-51
08-07-52
11-18-52*
12-17-52*
12-26-52*
12-28-52*
12-30-52*
01-01-53
01-17-53*
01-25-53*
02-12-53
04-02-53*
04-07-53
04-28-53*
05-01-53
08-01-53
08-18-53
09-06-53
09-08-53*
09-29-53*
10-01-53
10-06-53
10-14-53*
10-17-53*
10-22-53
10-30-53
11-05-53
11-22-53*
11-22-53*
11-27-53
12-01-53*
12-10-53*
12-13-53
12-16-53
12-18-53
12-23-53
12-25-53
12-27-53*
12-29-53
01-01-54
01-25-54*
02-25-54*
03-03-54
03-10-54
03-11-54
04-01-54*
04-15-54*
05-01-54
05-06-54
05-17-54*
06-18-54
08-05-54
08-07-54*
08-11-54*

08-12-54
08-13-54*
08-21-54
08-22-54
09-14-54
09-15-54*
10-02-54
10-05-54*
10-16-54
10-17-54
10-27-54
11-06-54*
11-11-54*
11-15-54*
12-23-54
01-01-55
01-12-55*
01-27-55*
02-07-55*
04-07-55
04-27-55*
05-05-55*
05-24-55*
06-19-55*
06-29-55*
07-01-55
07-06-55*
07-10-55
07-28-55*
08-09-55
09-11-55*
09-26-55*
10-24-55
11-23-55*
12-22-55
12-25-55
01-06-56*
03-19-56*
03-22-56*
04-09-56
04-20-56*
05-01-56
05-03-56
05-05-56
05-07-56
05-25-56
07-08-56
07-09-56
07-31-56*
08-04-56
08-09-56
09-01-56
11-27-56*
12-07-56
12-31-56
01-01-57
01-06-57*
02-13-57*
03-27-57
03-31-57*
04-09-57*
04-11-57*
05-01-57
05-08-57*
06-16-57*
07-03-57
07-24-57
07-31-57*
09-26-57
12-12-57
01-06-58
01-07-58
01-08-58

01-17-58
02-18-58
03-27-58
03-29-58
04-11-58
06-14-58
06-21-58*
07-15-58*
07-28-58
08-18-58
08-27-58
09-01-58
09-14-58
09-25-58
11-14-58*
11-16-58*
02-02-59
02-24-59*
02-28-59*
03-13-59
04-09-59
06-17-59
09-01-59
10-10-59*
10-13-59
11-01-59
11-12-59
11-22-59
12-06-59
12-10-59*
12-15-59
12-16-59
12-21-59
02-09-60
03-12-60*
03-15-60*
03-17-60
03-24-60
05-15-60
06-13-60
06-16-60
07-03-60*
08-07-60*
08-18-60
10-06-60
03-29-62
06-06-62*
04-10-63
08-23-63
11-30-63
12-04-63*
04-06-64
05-01-64
01-15-65*
02-24-65*
04-10-65*
04-22-65*
09-08-65*
11-30-65*
01-06-66
02-05-66
03-29-70*

8. Commerce

a. General Domestic Commerce
04-28-49*
07-29-49
08-02-49
06-06-50*
06-08-50
06-17-50

09-04-50*
12-16-50*
01-04-51*
04-01-51*
04-10-51*
06-01-51*
07-21-51*
09-14-51
11-28-51*
12-07-51
04-15-52
05-12-52*
05-28-52*
06-08-52*
07-02-52
12-31-52
04-30-53*
05-01-53
07-23-53*
09-06-53
10-06-53
10-07-53
11-05-53
12-21-53
03-04-54
04-11-54
09-20-54
09-25-54*
11-05-54
11-09-54*
05-06-55
05-08-55*
05-21-55
05-22-55*
07-08-55
08-13-55
12-14-55*
01-17-56
01-22-56
02-02-56
02-11-56
02-22-56
02-23-56
04-08-56
04-28-56*
05-01-56
05-25-56
06-08-56
09-04-56
09-08-56
10-16-56
11-22-56
01-29-57*
02-11-57*
02-19-57*
03-10-57
08-07-57*
08-12-57*
08-30-57
09-18-58
05-23-59*
06-14-59
07-17-59
09-20-59*
11-30-59
12-02-59
12-05-59
02-25-60
11-24-60*
04-14-61
07-16-65*
12-29-65*

1. State-Controlled Commerce
06-10-53*
09-20-53*
10-07-53*
10-15-53*
11-11-53
11-19-53*
11-19-53*
11-20-53*
11-23-53*
11-30-53*
12-02-53*
12-06-53*
12-17-53*
12-18-53
12-21-53*
12-28-53
01-01-54
01-05-54
01-06-54
01-14-54
02-10-54*
03-01-54*
03-10-54
03-27-54
03-28-54*
04-11-54*
04-14-54
04-18-54*
04-26-54*
05-01-54
05-18-54*
06-09-54*
06-19-54*
07-26-54*
09-14-54*
09-14-54
09-17-54*
09-20-54*
10-06-54*
10-09-54*
10-16-54
10-18-54*
11-09-54*
11-11-54
11-12-54*
11-17-54*
11-21-54
11-23-54
11-24-54*
12-07-54*
12-16-54*
01-01-55
02-04-55*
02-06-55*
03-09-55*
03-10-55*
03-15-55*
03-19-55
03-20-55*
03-21-55*
03-25-55
03-31-55
04-12-55
05-08-55*
05-10-55*
05-22-55*
05-27-55
06-07-55
06-18-55*
06-26-55*
07-07-55*

07-08-55
07-22-55*
07-24-55*
08-03-55
08-25-55*
08-27-55*
08-29-55*
09-04-55*
09-07-55*
09-08-55
09-09-55*
09-13-55*
10-04-55*
10-06-55*
10-07-55
10-08-55*
10-16-55*
11-10-55*
11-12-55*
11-22-55*
12-05-55*
12-14-55*
12-18-55
12-23-55
12-29-55*
02-25-56
03-09-56*
04-11-56
04-13-56*
04-14-56*
04-28-56*
05-10-56*
06-15-56
06-25-56*
06-30-56
07-06-56
07-09-56
07-13-56*
07-14-56
07-15-56
07-17-56*
07-19-56*
07-21-56*
09-11-56
09-14-56
09-15-56
10-10-56
10-14-56*
10-27-56
11-22-56
11-24-56*
12-08-56*
01-15-57*
01-29-57*
02-16-57*
02-27-57*
02-28-57*
03-25-57*
03-27-57
04-20-57
04-22-57
04-28-57
05-04-57
06-24-57
07-29-57*
08-05-57
08-15-57*
08-18-57*
08-20-57
08-25-57*
08-28-57
09-02-57
09-09-57*

09-13-57*
09-26-57*
10-20-57*
10-28-57*
11-10-57
11-16-57
11-18-57
11-27-57
12-19-57
12-22-57
01-10-58
02-14-58*
03-10-58
04-23-58*
05-18-58*
05-21-58*
07-30-58*
08-25-58*
09-19-58*
09-27-58*
10-23-58*
11-13-58*
11-26-58*
12-23-58
12-28-58
01-02-59
01-12-59*
01-15-59
02-24-59
03-26-59*
05-13-59*
05-23-59*
05-29-59*
05-30-59*
06-10-59*
07-06-59
07-13-59*
07-24-59
07-26-59*
08-08-59*
08-12-59*
08-20-59
08-24-59*
09-17-59
09-20-59*
09-25-59
10-12-59*
10-17-59*
10-28-59
11-12-59
11-16-59
12-01-59*
12-06-59
12-28-59*
02-22-60*
02-28-60*
03-02-60
03-28-60*
03-28-60
04-13-60
05-13-60*
05-16-60*
05-19-60*
07-23-60*
07-28-60*
08-31-60*
09-21-60*
09-29-60*
10-16-60*
10-18-60*
10-29-60*
11-03-60*
11-10-60*

11-14-60
11-24-60*
11-30-60*
12-03-60*
02-13-61*
02-26-61
03-21-61*
03-26-61*
05-05-61*
05-07-61*
05-20-61*
08-04-61
09-28-61
10-15-61*
11-05-61
11-14-61*
11-21-61*
12-12-61*
01-20-62*
03-02-62
03-15-62
04-22-62*
09-20-62*
10-23-62*
11-26-62
12-05-62
12-19-62
01-25-63
01-30-63
02-20-63
03-17-63
03-23-63*
06-25-63*
08-13-63*
10-14-63*
10-24-63*
10-27-63*
11-16-63*
01-23-64*
02-20-64*
05-26-64*
09-21-64*
11-24-64*
02-16-65*
04-18-65*
05-19-65*
06-04-65*
06-05-65*
06-16-65*
06-23-65*
07-16-65*
08-12-65*
09-25-65
09-26-65*
10-24-65*
12-29-65*
03-06-66*
09-19-66
07-03-74*

2. Rural Free Markets
04-10-52
11-19-53
03-01-54
06-09-54
02-04-55*
09-13-56
11-22-56*
01-29-57*
08-18-57*
09-09-57
12-22-57
06-04-65*

09-09-55
06-16-56*
02-12-58*
06-05-58
04-29-59
03-12-60
03-29-60
03-31-60
04-11-60*
04-29-62*
05-10-62
03-20-63
03-24-63*
01-01-64

e. Banking and Currency
04-28-49*
03-10-50*
03-22-50
06-06-50
06-11-50
02-11-51*
04-01-51
06-07-51
09-15-54*
02-21-55*
03-01-55*
07-11-55*
08-09-55
10-06-55*
08-16-59
03-29-60*
05-10-62*
04-23-53
01-28-64*
09-11-64

f. Credit Cooperatives and Loans
09-02-53*
11-30-53
12-06-53
12-28-53
02-10-54
09-12-54*
09-17-54
11-23-54*
04-12-55*
07-11-55*
10-06-55*
07-21-56
09-27-58
08-16-59
10-20-60
04-23-63*
01-28-64*
09-11-64*

g. Bonds
12-10-53*
01-31-54*
12-23-54*
10-06-55*
01-09-56*
12-31-56*
03-07-57*
11-14-57*
06-06-58*

h. Savings
12-14-53*
02-10-54
03-03-55*

07-11-55*
10-06-55*
02-12-56*
05-10-56
06-19-56*
03-04-57*
10-11-57
11-14-57*
02-02-58
06-04-59*
09-06-59*
09-20-59
04-29-62

i. Insurance
02-13-51*
01-10-53*
06-12-56*
03-04-57
11-21-57*
04-25-63

j. Statistical Work

1. Accounting System
06-04-51*
08-20-51*
11-05-52
12-29-52*
04-30-53
09-08-53
10-14-53
12-25-53
02-25-54
03-31-54*
04-24-54
05-17-54
06-04-54
06-18-54
08-03-54*
08-05-54
10-16-54
01-01-55
02-07-55*
03-21-55*
03-30-55
04-01-55
05-08-55
05-21-55
06-09-55
06-29-55
08-13-55
09-17-55
12-19-55
02-22-56*
03-09-56
06-15-56*
06-30-56
07-21-56
03-13-57
08-02-57*
09-13-57
10-10-57*
02-02-58
04-29-58*
08-13-58*
12-23-58*
03-15-59
07-17-59*
07-26-59
08-16-59*
08-19-59
09-11-59

10-17-59
03-10-60*
03-29-60*
04-11-60
08-05-60*
11-20-60
11-25-60
11-30-60*
12-21-60
12-29-60*
01-20-61*
11-05-61
12-24-61*
03-10-62
03-15-62*
05-10-62*
06-15-62*
12-22-62
01-09-63*
03-20-63*
03-23-63
04-10-63
07-07-63*
11-26-63
01-28-64
02-20-64
01-18-65*
06-08-65
09-26-65*
10-28-65*
04-01-66
06-14-67

2. Contract System
06-23-49
08-02-49*
06-04-50
03-28-54*
05-06-54
08-03-54
02-07-55
12-29-55
03-11-56
03-12-56
07-22-56*
05-21-58
07-15-58*
04-13-59*
05-23-59
03-12-60*
11-14-60
11-25-60
12-29-60*
04-10-61*
08-29-61
03-23-63
04-02-63

3. Work Reports
10-18-53*
11-09-55
12-19-55
02-22-56
03-13-57
08-02-57*
01-09-63

10. Management

a. General Management
06-23-49*
02-06-50*
06-03-50*

06-29-50
05-26-51*
12-13-51*
12-28-52*
01-06-53*
02-03-53*
02-25-53
04-02-53
04-08-53
04-30-53
05-15-53*
06-19-53*
06-23-53*
06-27-53*
07-18-53*
08-18-53
09-01-53*
09-08-53
09-10-53
10-01-53
10-06-53
10-07-53
11-15-53*
11-21-53
11-26-53*
12-17-53
12-18-53
12-24-53
12-25-53
12-29-53
01-01-54
01-14-54
01-28-54
02-24-54*
02-25-54
03-10-54
03-11-54
03-16-54
03-20-54*
04-15-54
04-18-54
05-06-54*
05-17-54
06-05-54*
07-26-54
08-03-54
08-05-54*
08-07-54*
08-13-54
08-21-54
08-28-54
09-06-54
09-15-54
09-18-54
10-16-54
10-27-54
11-06-54
11-13-54
11-19-54*
12-06-54*
12-08-54*
12-14-54
12-20-54*
01-03-55
01-12-55*
01-17-55
02-08-55
03-21-55
03-22-55
03-28-55
03-30-55*
04-01-55*
04-16-55

141

3. Primary Grain Markets
04-11-54*
05-18-54*
06-09-54*
11-12-54*
03-21-55
04-24-55*
05-10-55
07-07-55
10-23-55*
10-14-56*
11-24-56*

b. Foreign Trade
09-04-50*
04-21-51*
04-05-52
05-12-52
07-02-52
09-03-53
12-24-53
04-18-54
05-20-54
07-28-54
08-15-54
10-11-54
10-19-54
12-14-54
02-26-55
04-02-55*
04-04-55
04-15-55
04-29-55
06-02-55
06-02-55
07-09-55
08-26-55*
11-03-55
12-08-55
01-26-56
02-20-56
02-21-56
04-11-56
04-15-56
05-19-56
06-23-56*
07-05-56
07-28-56*
08-30-56
09-17-56*
10-06-56*
11-10-56*
11-29-56
12-27-56*
02-11-57
03-01-57
03-09-57
03-12-57
04-07-57
04-23-57
07-29-57
07-30-57
10-23-57
10-28-57
02-17-58*
03-06-58*
04-02-58
04-03-58*
04-08-58*
04-15-58*
05-11-58

05-16-58*
07-07-58
08-03-58
09-28-58*
12-24-58
01-17-59*
02-20-59*
03-19-59
04-30-59
08-24-59
09-05-59
09-20-59
03-11-60
03-25-60
09-08-60
11-17-60*
12-01-60*
01-11-61
02-01-61*
02-03-61*
08-22-61
10-04-62*
03-01-63
03-05-63
04-20-63
10-06-63*
10-27-63
11-23-63*
02-20-64
04-29-64
06-11-64*
06-19-64
06-25-64*
01-06-65
08-02-65
08-05-65
04-20-66
10-20-69
11-08-70

9. Finance

a. General Finance
03-07-50*
03-10-50
06-01-50
06-06-50
02-11-51
04-05-51*
04-06-51*
05-26-51
06-04-51
06-07-51*
07-21-51
07-30-51
11-20-51
11-23-51
12-07-51
01-12-52
02-21-52
02-19-53
10-01-53
10-06-53
11-05-53
12-18-53
04-24-54*
08-12-54
03-28-55
12-14-55
06-16-56*
03-17-57
03-27-57
04-11-57

04-22-57
06-06-57
11-18-57
01-12-58
01-17-58*
08-16-58*
09-01-59
09-11-59
05-16-60*
08-25-60
11-03-60*
01-27-61
12-24-61*
06-15-62*
10-22-62
01-09-63*
01-30-63
09-02-63
01-28-64*
07-17-64
11-24-64*
04-11-65*
12-29-65*

b. Tax

1. General Tax
03-10-50*
03-22-50*
12-22-50*
06-15-52
12-31-52*
09-06-53
10-06-53
10-29-53*
07-10-55*
07-21-56
10-10-56
04-01-57
09-09-57
06-10-58*
12-22-58

2. Agricultural Tax
01-04-49*
03-09-50*
03-22-50*
03-24-50
06-01-50*
09-06-50*
05-27-51*
06-23-51*
07-05-51
08-20-51
11-11-51
06-19-52*
08-31-53*
09-11-53*
01-06-54
02-10-54
10-06-54*
11-10-55*
10-14-56
12-31-56
04-01-57
06-06-57
09-20-57*
06-05-58*
01-20-62*

c. Prices
07-29-49*
03-22-50*

06-06-50*
06-08-50
06-11-50*
12-16-50
04-15-52*
04-01-53*
04-30-53
09-20-53
10-15-53
11-19-53*
11-23-53
11-30-53
03-01-54
03-27-54
03-28-54
04-18-54
05-17-54
05-18-54
09-14-54
12-23-54
09-20-54
10-09-54
11-17-54
11-24-54
02-06-55*
03-20-55*
05-31-55*
09-05-55
09-15-55
10-04-55
10-08-55*
11-10-55
12-15-55*
12-18-55*
12-29-55*
03-16-56
04-14-56
04-28-56
05-06-56
06-12-56
07-03-56
07-14-56*
07-15-56*
09-11-56*
10-03-56*
10-10-56
10-26-56
10-27-56
02-28-57*
03-01-57*
03-03-57*
04-01-57
05-04-57
05-20-57*
06-24-57*
07-19-57
06-10-59
03-29-60
11-21-61
03-15-63
06-25-63
02-27-65

d. Budget
03-07-50
03-22-50*
08-11-52*
02-19-53*
06-18-54*
02-07-55
05-14-55
07-10-55*
08-09-55*

04-16-55*	06-02-58	03-12-60*	06-11-61*
04-27-55	06-12-58	03-15-60*	06-21-61*
05-21-55*	07-13-58*	03-29-60	08-08-61
05-24-55*	07-15-58	04-01-60*	08-25-61
05-29-55	08-22-58	04-14-60	08-29-61*
06-07-55	09-20-58*	05-01-60	09-06-61*
06-21-55	10-09-58	05-22-60	09-15-61
07-06-55	10-10-58*	05-23-60*	10-15-61
07-17-55*	10-12-58	05-30-60*	11-05-61
07-23-55*	10-13-58	06-08-60*	11-22-61*
08-14-55*	10-23-58	06-21-60	12-05-61*
08-20-55	10-24-58	06-25-60*	12-24-61
08-31-55	10-25-58	07-08-60	01-24-62*
09-07-55	10-26-58	07-11-60*	03-02-62
09-10-55*	11-14-58*	07-18-60*	03-15-62*
09-19-55	11-24-58	07-21-60	04-08-62*
09-23-55*	11-29-58*	07-22-60*	04-10-62*
10-09-55	12-05-58*	07-25-60	04-29-62
12-04-55*	12-07-58	07-29-60*	05-03-62*
12-15-55*	12-24-58	07-31-60	05-10-62*
01-10-56	01-05-59	08-06-60	05-22-62*
01-11-56	01-07-59	08-12-60	06-15-62
01-25-56*	01-13-59	08-16-60*	07-13-62
02-08-56	01-20-59	08-18-60	09-20-62
02-11-56*	01-22-59*	08-31-60	10-23-62
02-12-56	01-31-59	09-05-60	11-02-62*
02-23-56	02-22-59*	09-13-60	11-03-62
02-26-56	02-23-59	09-19-60*	11-12-62*
03-11-56*	02-28-59*	10-07-60*	11-16-62
03-12-56*	03-02-59*	10-11-60	12-05-62
03-13-56*	03-10-59*	10-19-60	01-09-63*
03-18-56*	03-15-59*	10-24-60*	03-15-63
03-19-56	03-23-59*	10-25-60*	03-17-63
03-28-56	03-29-59*	11-13-60*	03-20-63*
04-06-56	04-03-59	11-14-60	03-23-63*
04-10-56*	04-04-59*	11-18-60	03-24-63
04-17-56	04-10-59*	11-20-60	04-02-63*
05-07-56	04-16-59*	11-25-60	04-08-63*
05-15-56	04-17-59*	11-30-60	04-10-63*
06-05-56	04-21-59*	12-03-60	04-23-63
06-05-56	05-11-59*	12-03-60*	05-01-63
06-30-56	05-15-59*	12-09-60*	05-03-63*
08-21-56*	05-17-59	12-10-60*	05-09-63*
09-06-56	05-19-59*	12-11-60*	05-11-63
09-09-56*	05-25-59	12-15-60*	05-14-63*
10-16-56	06-01-59	12-17-60	05-29-63
10-31-56*	06-05-59	12-21-60*	06-10-63
12-16-56*	06-07-59*	12-29-60*	07-07-63
02-07-57	06-09-59	01-04-61*	07-13-63*
02-27-57	06-15-59*	01-17-61	08-08-63
02-28-57	07-09-59*	01-18-61*	08-23-63*
03-14-57*	07-17-59*	01-19-61	08-26-63*
04-04-57*	07-24-59	01-20-61	08-27-63*
04-21-57*	07-29-59	01-30-61*	08-29-63
04-28-57	08-01-59*	02-05-61*	09-02-63*
05-22-57*	08-17-59*	02-08-61*	10-24-63
05-29-57	08-20-59*	02-15-61	11-14-63*
07-31-57	08-24-59	02-17-61	12-11-63
09-21-57*	09-05-59	02-24-61	12-13-63*
09-23-57	09-08-59*	03-02-61*	12-26-63
09-25-57	09-11-59	03-09-61	02-02-64
09-28-57	09-17-59	03-13-61*	02-20-64
10-08-57	10-10-59*	03-17-61*	03-18-64
11-02-57	10-11-59*	03-22-61*	03-19-64*
11-18-57*	10-12-59	03-24-61	03-20-64
11-29-57	11-09-59*	03-28-61	03-23-64
01-17-58	12-02-59	04-20-61*	04-02-64
02-07-58*	12-04-59	04-29-61*	04-04-64
03-01-58	12-06-59	05-05-61*	04-14-64
03-27-58	12-23-59	05-07-61	05-01-64
04-07-58	02-17-60	05-16-61	05-08-64
04-27-58	03-03-60	06-04-61*	05-10-64
05-07-58*	03-10-60	06-08-61	05-15-64

143

05-21-64
05-26-64
05-30-64*
06-14-64
06-23-64
07-04-64
07-16-64
08-05-64
09-22-64
11-19-64
11-24-64
02-20-65
02-22-65*
02-23-65
03-04-65
04-10-65
04-24-65*
05-12-65*
05-26-65*
06-02-65
06-08-65
06-16-65
06-21-65
07-02-65
07-06-65
07-30-65*
08-31-65
09-07-65*
09-08-65
09-24-65*
11-30-65
02-06-66*
04-01-66*
04-03-66*
11-10-66*
06-14-67
11-20-69

b. Soviet Responsibility System
05-29-57
11-18-57
02-17-59*
11-09-59
01-18-61
01-20-61
01-27-61
02-22-61*
05-07-61
06-08-61
06-11-61
08-29-61*
12-17-61*
03-15-63
03-20-63
04-08-63
05-14-63*
12-26-63

c. Labor Discipline
01-13-54*
02-25-54
06-05-54
06-06-54*
09-14-54
10-22-54*
11-03-54
11-18-54
12-13-54
01-01-55
04-01-55
03-12-56*
03-28-56

01-21-57*
05-13-57*
08-04-57*
09-22-57
09-23-57
11-02-57
11-02-57*
04-09-60*
11-10-66*
05-22-67
06-14-67

d. Triple Combination
10-23-58
10-26-58
11-05-58
11-08-58
12-05-58*
01-06-59
04-17-59*
11-09-59
08-29-60*
06-19-64
03-28-65
04-11-65
12-26-66*
09-18-67*
10-19-67*
01-01-68
08-28-68
02-21-69
11-20-69

11. Employment
07-28-50*
07-11-51*
08-04-52*
08-17-53*
04-19-54*
07-29-54*
01-25-55*
03-18-55*
05-06-55
07-17-55*
08-11-55
08-17-55*
12-11-55*
07-06-56
08-02-56*
04-08-57*
05-12-57
05-21-57*
07-11-57
07-15-57*
07-21-57*
07-23-57*
08-04-57*
08-08-57
08-22-57
08-26-57*
11-21-57*
12-19-57*
01-10-58
02-09-58*
04-30-58*
07-22-58*
10-09-58*
01-20-59
03-13-59*
05-17-59
06-11-59
06-14-59
06-29-59*

08-17-59
09-22-59
11-28-59
03-15-60
06-04-60*
07-27-60*
07-30-60
09-17-60*
10-17-60
03-17-61*
04-08-62*
05-22-62
06-27-63*
08-08-63*
07-17-64*
07-27-64*
02-24-65*

12. Working Conditions
09-17-52*
01-30-53*
07-18-53*
09-01-53*
01-17-54
01-17-55*
03-22-55*
05-05-56
05-07-56
05-16-56
06-05-56
06-12-56*
06-21-56*
09-01-56*
10-31-56*
01-16-57*
02-03-57
06-26-59*
06-25-60
12-09-60*
12-14-60*
03-09-61*
05-01-64
07-27-64

13. Wages

a. Workers' Wages
08-02-49*
02-06-50
09-15-55*
01-17-56
03-08-56
04-14-56
05-01-56
05-03-56*
05-11-56
07-06-56*
07-09-56
10-17-56*
01-15-57
02-11-57
02-12-57
03-10-57
04-01-57
04-28-57
05-21-57
08-02-57
11-21-57*
02-11-58*
03-15-58
03-02-62
10-27-63
07-17-64*

07-27-64
11-20-69

b. Peasants' Wages
03-16-51
01-19-54
06-05-54
06-19-54
08-03-54
08-31-54*
09-14-54
09-25-55
03-08-56
05-24-56
05-29-56*
05-29-56*
06-25-56*
06-27-56
08-01-56*
11-28-56
12-01-56
01-15-57
02-22-57*
03-23-57
04-01-57
04-19-57*
04-29-57
06-02-57
06-06-57*
07-19-57
09-08-57
11-21-57
12-06-57*
03-08-59
05-17-59
05-20-59
06-22-59
08-20-59
12-17-59
02-21-60*
03-14-60*
08-05-60
11-25-60
12-18-60*
12-29-60
01-12-61
04-02-61*
04-11-61*
07-05-61
08-12-61
08-25-61
08-29-61
11-05-61
01-30-63
06-25-63
10-16-63
10-24-63
11-16-63
04-06-64
09-21-64
04-17-65
04-18-65*
06-23-65
07-19-65
09-07-65
09-19-65*
10-10-65
04-01-66
03-22-69
11-20-69
03-07-70
07-09-70

14. Transportation and
    Communication

    a. General Transportation
       and Communication
       09-08-53
       09-22-53*
       11-17-53
       12-18-53
       03-04-54
       05-05-56
       05-25-56
       09-05-56*
       02-08-57
       06-03-58
       08-06-58
       02-20-59*
       03-13-59
       04-09-59
       05-24-59*
       11-12-59*
       03-14-60
       04-13-60
       08-18-60
       01-14-61
       02-20-63*
       02-02-64
       02-09-64
       05-19-65*
       08-12-65*
       02-02-66

    b. General Transportation
       04-05-50
       11-15-53*
       04-18-54
       05-11-54*
       06-19-54
       07-21-54*
       10-16-54
       10-17-54
       11-11-54
       12-25-54*
       07-01-55
       09-11-55
       02-02-56*
       07-07-56
       07-11-56
       12-13-56
       01-07-57*
       03-14-57*
       04-14-57
       02-09-58
       04-24-58*
       05-06-58
       06-12-58*
       07-13-58*
       09-18-58*
       09-27-58*
       12-28-58
       01-11-59*
       01-22-59*
       03-02-59*
       05-13-59
       05-29-59*
       06-14-59
       06-15-59*
       06-27-59
       08-12-59
       08-22-59*
       08-24-59
       09-26-59*
       10-16-59

       11-26-59
       12-02-59*
       12-06-59*
       12-21-59
       01-04-60*
       01-23-60
       02-03-60*
       02-25-60
       03-24-60*
       05-13-60
       05-16-60
       05-26-60*
       06-04-60
       06-16-60*
       08-31-60*
       09-11-60*
       10-19-60
       10-25-60*
       10-27-60*
       11-12-60*
       12-10-60*
       03-31-61
       11-16-61
       10-22-62
       02-11-63
       03-23-63
       04-10-63

    1. Railroads
       04-26-50
       11-05-52*
       12-31-52*
       02-25-53*
       02-06-54*
       05-08-54
       05-31-55*
       01-04-56*
       04-09-56
       09-01-56*
       01-13-57
       10-15-57*
       01-02-58*
       03-08-58*
       09-19-58*
       09-26-58*
       10-13-58
       11-04-58
       12-10-58*
       01-04-59*
       01-15-59*
       03-29-59
       07-10-59
       07-30-59*
       12-16-59*
       02-27-60
       03-15-60*
       04-14-60*
       05-01-60
       06-09-60*
       07-08-60*
       08-12-60*
       09-19-60*
       12-31-60*
       03-13-61*
       03-28-61*
       04-10-61*
       05-28-61
       07-16-64*
       01-18-65*

    2. Water Transportation
       12-04-55*
       07-30-58

       06-01-59*
       08-09-59*
       12-25-59*
       11-18-60*
       01-05-67

    3. Air Transportation
       05-15-55
       04-11-56*
       04-29-64*
       05-19-64*
       01-06-65*
       09-29-74*

    c. Postal and Tele-
       communications
       09-10-53*
       03-16-55*
       02-18-56*
       04-26-56
       08-15-56
       03-16-58*
       06-02-58*
       12-07-58*
       04-16-59*

15. Cities
    03-17-49
    05-16-50
    11-14-50*
    04-20-51
    04-15-52
    04-20-53*
    11-22-53*
    01-11-54
    01-17-54
    04-01-54
    05-11-54
    08-11-54*
    08-13-54*
    08-22-54*
    09-20-54
    11-14-54
    11-17-54
    11-24-54
    01-02-55*
    06-18-55*
    07-24-55*
    07-27-55*
    08-03-55
    08-04-55
    08-21-55
    08-25-55
    08-27-55*
    09-04-55
    09-13-55
    10-08-55
    10-23-55
    11-23-55*
    12-11-55
    12-14-55*
    04-28-56
    02-11-57
    05-09-57*
    05-20-57
    05-24-57*
    09-02-57*
    09-03-57
    10-28-57
    12-18-57
    12-19-57
    01-10-58
    01-29-58*

    04-30-58*
    07-21-58
    10-22-58
    05-13-59
    05-23-59
    05-30-59
    06-14-59*
    06-29-59
    07-06-59
    08-12-59*
    11-16-59*
    12-22-59*
    03-12-60*
    03-29-60*
    04-13-60
    05-07-60
    05-19-60*
    07-17-60*
    08-25-60
    10-27-60*
    01-18-61*
    04-29-61
    11-14-61
    12-12-61*
    06-25-63
    01-23-64
    07-27-64*
    05-05-65
    09-01-65
    03-31-66*

H. Education, Culture,
   and Health

   1. General Education, Cul-
      ture, and Health
      Concerns
      12-30-50
      10-30-51*
      11-20-51
      04-26-52
      08-11-52
      02-18-53
      03-25-54*
      08-12-54*
      11-14-54*
      11-28-54
      04-28-55
      05-04-55*
      06-23-55*
      07-08-55
      10-26-55
      01-01-56
      01-08-56
      01-12-56
      01-21-56
      02-06-56*
      02-27-56
      07-11-56
      07-23-56*
      08-26-56
      08-28-56
      09-10-56*
      09-29-56
      12-09-56
      12-17-56
      08-13-57*
      12-11-57
      02-10-58*
      03-17-58*
      04-13-58
      05-01-58
      05-20-58

06-01-58
06-09-58*
07-24-58
08-06-58
10-01-58*
10-01-58
10-04-58
11-01-58*
01-01-59
03-30-59
06-01-59*
09-01-59
09-19-59*
12-21-59
02-11-60
03-16-60
04-11-60
05-28-60
06-01-60*
06-12-60*
10-01-60
10-22-60
02-12-61*
02-23-61*
03-25-61*
06-26-61*
03-25-63
05-04-63
08-06-63
02-08-64*
06-06-64
02-26-65*
05-01-65
05-05-65
06-21-65
12-11-65
06-01-66
08-08-66
10-24-67*
11-26-67*
08-25-69
01-01-70
05-07-71

2. Education

a. Primary School
06-15-49*
05-31-50
07-28-50*
10-13-51*
06-01-52
03-17-53
08-27-53
12-03-53*
12-14-53*
04-19-54*
06-01-54
06-22-54
05-20-55
06-15-55*
09-05-55*
02-27-56*
03-26-56
06-01-56
08-13-56
10-05-56*
02-25-57
03-16-57
03-29-57
04-08-57
05-12-57
06-01-57*

07-11-57
08-08-57
08-26-57
11-11-57
02-10-58*
06-01-59
09-19-59
03-23-60
06-01-60*
08-03-60
03-27-63*
03-20-64
04-11-64
06-02-64*
05-30-65
03-07-67*
10-24-67*

b. Middle School
07-28-50*
04-05-51*
07-11-51
08-07-52*
01-22-53*
03-17-53
08-27-53
08-29-53*
09-25-53
02-02-54*
04-19-54*
05-20-55
06-15-55*
09-05-55*
02-27-56
03-26-56
05-12-56*
08-13-56
10-04-56
11-20-56
02-25-57
03-16-57
03-29-57
04-08-57
05-12-57
06-05-57
07-11-57
08-08-57
08-26-57
11-11-57
01-20-58*
02-10-58
04-21-58*
05-29-58*
06-01-59
06-11-59
09-19-59
12-21-59*
03-16-60*
03-23-60
04-05-60
08-03-60
03-27-63*
06-05-63*
03-20-64
04-11-64
05-30-65
03-31-66
06-18-66*
03-07-67*
10-24-67*

c. Higher Education
10-14-49*

06-04-50
08-03-50*
04-16-52
08-07-52*
09-24-52*
01-22-53*
08-16-53
08-17-53
08-29-53
09-25-53*
10-15-53*
12-22-53*
03-26-54
05-25-54*
07-29-54
02-20-55
03-18-55
05-15-55
06-30-55*
07-29-55
07-30-55*
09-06-55*
03-17-56*
05-12-56
08-02-56
10-04-56*
10-28-56
11-16-56
11-26-56*
12-03-56
12-04-56
12-17-56*
12-23-56*
02-25-57*
03-29-57
04-10-57
04-25-57*
05-27-57
07-15-57
07-21-57*
08-22-57*
01-17-58*
03-23-58
07-03-58*
07-11-58
04-03-59
06-11-59*
09-19-59
01-07-60*
04-05-60
05-17-60*
06-04-60*
08-03-60
10-15-60*
11-11-60
12-11-65
08-24-66
05-16-67
10-24-67*

d. Technical Education
04-08-52*
04-16-52*
09-24-52
08-16-53*
10-15-53
11-05-53
11-22-53
12-22-53
01-01-54
01-22-54
03-10-54
03-19-54

04-24-54*
05-15-54
05-25-54
06-30-54*
11-13-54*
01-03-55*
06-12-55*
06-23-55
07-30-55
02-27-56
03-17-56
08-02-56
10-25-56
10-29-56*
11-06-56
11-20-56*
12-04-56*
05-21-57*
06-07-57
02-10-58
04-21-58*
10-04-58*
04-03-59*
04-20-59*
06-27-59
08-17-59*
01-11-60
03-15-60
03-23-60
04-20-60*
08-03-60
09-08-60
10-22-60*
02-28-61*
06-27-61*
06-19-62
10-22-62
06-26-63
05-08-64*
03-28-65
04-02-65*
05-30-65
09-07-65*
12-11-65
03-07-67

e. Education of Workers and Peasants
06-04-50*
03-10-51
03-23-51
04-23-51
07-31-51
09-13-51
04-26-52
04-09-53*
08-29-53*
10-20-53
11-04-53
11-09-53
11-15-53
12-03-53
12-14-53
12-20-53
12-30-53
01-05-54
01-11-54
01-22-54*
02-02-54
02-20-54
03-10-54
04-24-54
05-25-54

11-21-54
06-23-55
06-30-55
12-06-55*
03-26-56*
04-01-56*
04-27-56*
10-29-56*
11-25-56*
02-05-57*
03-29-57
04-08-57
10-30-57
02-10-58*
03-07-58
05-29-58*
01-11-60
03-23-60*
05-11-60*
06-01-62
03-25-63*
06-01-63
06-19-63*
09-25-63*
10-08-63
01-03-64
01-06-64*
06-02-64*
09-06-65

f. Spare-Time Educational Activities for Workers, Peasants, and Cadres
06-04-50*
06-08-54
09-01-54*
11-13-54*
03-24-55*
04-03-55*
05-15-55*
05-20-55
06-12-55
06-23-55
07-15-55*
07-30-55
09-10-55
12-06-55
12-17-55*
01-18-56
01-21-56
02-06-56*
05-04-56*
05-11-56
05-15-56
12-03-56
01-28-57*
02-12-57
04-03-57
10-30-57*
11-19-57*
03-07-58
05-20-58*
05-27-58*
12-24-58*
12-29-58*
04-20-59*
06-17-59
11-10-59*
01-11-60*
02-09-60
03-03-60
03-16-60*
03-23-60*

04-05-60
05-28-60*
06-04-60*
06-13-60*
08-03-60*
09-08-60
03-29-61
06-11-61
06-27-61*
11-09-62
11-13-62
03-25-63
01-06-64*
01-26-64*
02-28-64
04-24-64
05-30-65
06-21-65*

g. Combination of Labor and Education
08-03-50*
06-30-54*
07-11-54*
11-28-54
05-20-55*
08-11-55
09-05-55*
09-20-55
08-06-56*
03-16-57*
03-29-57
04-08-57*
05-04-57
05-12-57*
06-01-57*
06-05-57*
07-11-57*
07-15-57*
07-21-57
08-08-57*
08-22-57*
08-26-57*
10-30-57
11-11-57*
12-09-57*
01-20-58*
01-31-58
02-10-58*
05-20-58
07-02-58*
07-11-58*
07-24-58*
09-25-58*
09-30-58*
10-04-58
12-29-58
04-03-59*
06-01-59*
07-11-59
09-01-59*
09-19-59*
12-21-59*
01-07-60
03-16-60*
04-05-60*
08-03-60
10-15-60*
03-27-63
06-01-63
06-05-63*
02-16-64*
02-28-64

03-20-64*
05-04-64*
03-28-65
04-22-65
05-05-65*
05-26-65*
05-30-65*
09-06-65*
12-09-65*
12-11-65*
12-23-65*
03-31-66*
05-04-66
09-07-66
09-19-66
07-09-67*
08-18-68
08-28-68
09-12-68*
02-17-69
05-04-69
03-07-70
07-09-70*
08-07-73*

h. Education Mobility
08-27-53
12-03-53*
04-19-54*
05-25-54
07-11-54*
07-29-54*
06-30-55
08-11-55*
03-17-56*
03-26-56
12-09-56
03-16-57
04-08-57*
05-12-57*
05-15-57
06-01-57
01-20-58*
04-21-58
07-11-58
09-30-58*
10-15-60*
06-05-63
04-11-64
05-05-65
05-26-65
06-18-66*
07-09-70

i. Teachers and Teacher Training
07-28-50
10-23-53*
06-30-54
06-23-55
07-29-55
07-30-55
12-06-55
02-12-56
08-12-56*
08-16-56
10-04-56
10-05-56*
10-28-56
11-20-56
11-26-56
12-17-56*
04-06-57

05-12-57
01-17-58
03-23-58
04-13-58
04-21-58
08-30-58*
12-29-58
03-30-59*
12-21-59*
03-16-60
05-11-60
08-03-60
01-28-61*
03-27-63
01-26-64
04-11-64*
05-04-64*
08-01-64
09-06-65*
08-24-66
09-15-66
03-07-67

3. Culture

a. Cultural Bureaucracy
07-08-51
11-16-52*
04-09-53
03-25-54*
05-23-54*
06-08-54*
07-15-54*
08-12-54*
04-03-55*
06-12-55
06-23-55*
07-13-55
07-27-55*
08-29-55
10-26-55
11-08-55
12-17-55
12-30-55
02-09-56
04-07-56*
04-23-56
05-18-56*
06-04-56*
08-28-56*
09-06-56*
09-08-56
10-02-56*
10-30-56
11-25-56
12-12-56
12-28-56*
01-05-57*
04-03-57*
04-27-57*
07-25-57
08-24-57
03-07-58*
03-28-58*
05-08-58*
05-20-58*
06-09-58*
08-02-58*
08-07-58*
09-16-58*
09-20-58
09-30-58*
10-07-58*

09-23-59*
03-27-60*
04-05-60*
05-15-60*
06-13-60
10-17-60
01-28-61
05-23-62
03-25-63*
04-01-64
05-12-64*
02-22-66*
02-27-66
06-02-66
05-28-67
05-23-70
05-23-72
09-04-75

b. Mass Media
02-04-49
10-21-49*
04-23-50*
04-23-50
06-06-50*
03-10-51*
03-23-51*
04-23-51*
07-13-51*
09-13-51
12-30-52*
02-03-53
04-20-54*
01-04-55
03-16-55*
07-27-55
12-30-55*
01-08-56*
04-26-56*
07-01-56*
07-04-56*
08-15-56*
12-12-56*
04-23-57
07-01-57*
08-14-57*
09-15-57
11-10-57
03-16-58*
03-19-58*
04-14-58
09-20-58*
11-01-58
05-11-60
09-08-60
09-30-60
03-25-63
06-26-63*
10-20-63
11-29-63*
02-05-64
02-28-64
05-12-64*
06-04-66
06-16-66*
06-20-66*
08-08-66*
08-24-66*
01-19-67*
04-08-67
04-24-67
05-23-67
05-28-67*

06-01-67*
08-05-67*
08-05-68*
09-01-68*

c. Language
06-04-50
06-06-51*
04-26-52*
04-09-53*
12-11-53*
06-24-54
09-01-54*
03-24-55*
10-26-55*
12-06-55*
12-11-55
02-03-56*
02-06-56
02-12-56*
04-01-56*
07-01-56
02-06-57*
11-19-57*
12-11-57*
04-19-58*
12-24-58*
11-10-59*
05-11-60*
08-03-60*
06-02-64

d. Literature and Art
01-24-51*
05-07-51*
05-20-51*
07-08-51*
10-19-51*
05-04-52*
05-23-52
10-19-52*
11-15-52
11-16-52*
10-08-53*
01-12-54*
05-23-54*
06-08-54
04-03-55*
05-03-55*
06-14-55*
07-13-55*
10-26-55
12-17-55*
01-08-56
02-09-56*
03-25-56*
04-07-56*
05-18-56*
06-04-56*
08-27-56*
10-02-56*
10-19-56*
10-30-56*
12-28-56*
12-30-56*
01-05-57
04-03-57*
04-10-57*
04-27-57*
07-25-57*
07-29-57*
08-31-57*
09-01-57*

11-12-57*
11-16-57
02-13-58
04-13-58
04-14-58*
04-26-58*
05-08-58*
08-02-58*
08-07-58*
08-30-58
09-16-58*
09-30-58*
10-07-58*
10-14-58
01-27-59
04-03-59
09-22-59
09-23-59*
04-05-60*
05-15-60*
06-13-60*
08-15-60*
05-23-62*
03-25-63
05-04-63
02-05-64*
03-10-64
04-01-64*
06-06-64*
08-01-64*
12-30-64*
04-20-65*
04-09-65*
02-22-66*
02-27-66*
06-01-66
06-02-66*
06-04-66
06-27-66
08-17-66
08-26-66*
10-19-66*
05-23-67*
05-28-67*
05-29-67*
05-31-67*
07-28-67
09-01-68*
05-04-69
05-23-70*
05-23-72*
09-04-75

e. History
09-22-49*
04-16-50
06-30-50
09-20-50
09-23-50
09-25-50
11-12-50
11-17-50
11-27-50
11-27-50
12-01-50
12-03-50
12-14-50
12-21-50*
12-30-50*
01-11-51*
02-16-51
04-23-51
05-20-51

09-18-51*
02-01-52
02-07-52
02-14-52
01-15-53
02-14-53
07-30-53
10-30-53
01-21-54
02-28-54
10-01-54
03-12-55*
03-29-55
04-09-55
04-23-55
04-21-56
04-23-56*
11-12-56
03-08-57
09-12-57
10-01-57
12-09-57
12-11-57*
03-05-58
07-21-58
07-30-58
03-31-59
04-18-59
05-04-59
08-21-59
09-12-59
09-22-59
10-01-59
01-24-60
01-24-60
01-27-60
02-01-60*
03-27-60*
04-08-60
06-26-60
07-06-60
09-30-60*
10-02-60
10-05-60
03-18-61*
10-01-61
10-10-61*
12-07-61
07-07-62*
05-04-63
11-23-63
06-25-64
09-24-64*
10-01-64
11-07-64
09-02-65*
11-07-65
06-03-66*
07-01-66*
07-07-67
07-31-67
03-19-68
11-25-68
05-04-69
08-01-69
07-11-71
04-24-72
08-01-72
09-30-72*
05-04-74
09-03-75
10-19-75*

f. Science
- 08-27-50*
- 08-07-52
- 09-15-52
- 12-19-52*
- 10-15-53
- 10-22-53
- 03-26-54*
- 10-20-54*
- 10-27-54
- 11-02-54*
- 02-20-55*
- 04-28-55
- 06-03-55*
- 09-05-55
- 09-06-55*
- 09-20-55
- 10-11-55*
- 12-02-55*
- 12-20-55*
- 01-29-56
- 01-31-56
- 03-21-56
- 04-03-56*
- 04-04-56
- 04-23-56
- 05-04-56*
- 05-20-56*
- 05-27-56*
- 05-28-56
- 06-04-56*
- 06-17-56
- 08-16-56
- 08-28-56*
- 09-09-56
- 09-10-56
- 11-06-56
- 11-16-56*
- 12-03-56*
- 12-17-56*
- 01-22-57
- 01-25-57*
- 03-19-57
- 04-08-57
- 04-10-57
- 06-07-57
- 07-21-57
- 07-29-57*
- 10-03-57
- 10-24-57*
- 11-10-57*
- 12-11-57
- 05-04-58
- 05-19-58
- 05-22-58*
- 06-03-58
- 06-18-58*
- 07-14-58*
- 09-19-58*
- 09-28-58*
- 11-01-58
- 11-13-58*
- 11-28-58*
- 12-06-58*
- 12-14-58*
- 01-06-59*
- 01-25-59*
- 03-21-59*
- 04-03-59
- 04-08-59*
- 11-04-59
- 01-07-60*
- 01-14-60
- 02-02-60
- 02-17-60
- 03-28-60
- 04-16-60
- 05-28-60
- 06-26-60
- 09-08-60*
- 10-28-60*
- 11-06-60*
- 02-12-61
- 02-23-61*
- 03-25-61*
- 04-18-61*
- 05-04-61
- 06-27-61*
- 11-25-61
- 10-12-62*
- 11-09-62
- 12-07-62*
- 12-14-62
- 12-22-62
- 02-11-63
- 02-17-63
- 03-27-63
- 03-29-63
- 04-06-63*
- 06-26-63*
- 07-23-63*
- 08-06-63*
- 09-20-63*
- 12-02-63
- 01-19-64*
- 01-24-64
- 03-07-64*
- 03-11-64
- 04-24-64*
- 05-10-64
- 05-21-64*
- 05-27-64*
- 05-29-64
- 06-09-64
- 06-16-64
- 08-21-64
- 09-01-64*
- 09-05-64*
- 10-22-64*
- 10-24-64*
- 10-25-64*
- 11-16-64*
- 01-23-65*
- 03-28-65
- 04-02-65*
- 04-06-65*
- 07-06-65
- 09-25-65
- 11-13-65*
- 11-28-65*
- 12-23-65*
- 01-06-66
- 01-20-66
- 01-24-66
- 01-26-66
- 02-10-66
- 04-03-66
- 04-22-66
- 05-04-66
- 05-08-66*
- 08-01-66
- 09-07-66
- 12-24-66*
- 05-01-70

g. Religion
- 05-28-51
- 10-17-58*

h. Holidays

1. New Year's
   - 01-01-51*
   - 01-01-52*
   - 01-01-53*
   - 01-01-54*
   - 01-01-55*
   - 01-01-57*
   - 01-01-58*
   - 01-01-59*
   - 01-01-60*
   - 01-28-60
   - 12-30-60
   - 01-01-61*
   - 01-16-61*
   - 01-01-64*
   - 01-01-65*
   - 01-01-68*
   - 01-01-69*
   - 01-01-70*
   - 01-01-71*
   - 01-01-72*
   - 01-01-73*
   - 01-01-74*
   - 01-01-75*

2. Spring Festival
   - 02-06-50*
   - 01-11-52
   - 01-11-54
   - 02-11-54
   - 01-24-55
   - 01-07-57*
   - 01-15-57*
   - 01-17-57
   - 01-27-57
   - 02-07-57*
   - 02-09-58*
   - 02-13-58*
   - 01-11-59*
   - 02-04-59
   - 02-15-61*
   - 02-15-61
   - 03-06-64
   - 02-02-68

3. February Seventh Incident
   - 02-07-53*
   - 02-07-54
   - 02-07-63*

4. International Women's Day
   - 03-08-52
   - 03-08-55
   - 03-08-56*
   - 03-08-57*
   - 03-08-58*
   - 03-08-60*
   - 03-08-61*
   - 03-08-63*
   - 03-08-64*
   - 03-08-65*
   - 03-08-66
   - 03-08-73*
   - 03-08-74*

5. International Labor Day
   - 05-01-52*
   - 05-01-53*
   - 05-01-54*
   - 05-01-55
   - 05-01-57
   - 05-01-58*
   - 05-01-59*
   - 05-01-60*
   - 05-01-61*
   - 05-01-62*
   - 05-01-63*
   - 05-01-64*
   - 05-01-65*
   - 05-01-66*
   - 04-30-67*
   - 05-01-68*
   - 05-01-70*
   - 05-01-71*

6. Youth Day
   - 05-03-50*
   - 05-04-53*
   - 05-04-54*
   - 05-04-55
   - 05-04-56
   - 05-04-57
   - 05-04-59*
   - 05-04-60*
   - 05-04-61*
   - 05-04-63*
   - 05-04-64*
   - 05-04-65*
   - 05-04-66*
   - 05-04-67*
   - 05-04-69*
   - 05-04-74*

7. International Children's Day
   - 05-31-50*
   - 06-01-51*
   - 06-01-52*
   - 06-01-53*
   - 06-01-54*
   - 06-01-55
   - 06-01-56
   - 06-01-58*
   - 06-01-60*
   - 06-01-61
   - 06-01-62*
   - 06-01-63*
   - 06-01-64*
   - 06-01-65*
   - 06-01-66*

8. Founding of the CCP
   - 07-01-50*
   - 07-01-52*
   - 07-01-54
   - 07-01-61*
   - 07-01-66*
   - 06-03-67*
   - 09-29-67
   - 07-01-68*
   - 07-01-69*
   - 07-01-70*
   - 07-01-74*

9. Army Day
   - 08-01-56
   - 08-01-62*

07-31-67*	06-24-54	08-31-56*	06-01-55*
08-01-68*	08-11-54	09-02-56*	02-10-56*
08-01-69*	10-20-54	10-07-56*	04-28-56
08-01-70*	11-02-54*	10-23-56*	05-01-56
08-01-71	11-30-55*	12-23-56	05-16-56
08-01-72*	12-02-55*	01-28-57*	06-05-56*
	12-20-55*	03-19-58*	06-05-56*

10. Victory in War of Resistance against Japan

	01-27-56	08-21-58*	06-26-56
	05-27-56*	09-11-58*	07-06-56
	05-28-56*	10-27-58*	07-21-56
09-03-53*	08-06-56	09-13-59*	08-01-56
09-03-55*	09-10-56	10-04-59*	08-05-56
09-02-65*	10-27-56*	05-28-60*	09-14-56*
09-03-70*	11-15-56*	06-26-60*	11-15-56*
09-03-75*	01-22-57*	04-04-61*	11-27-56
	03-19-57*	04-15-61*	02-08-57*

11. Founding of the PRC

	10-03-57*	08-20-62	02-09-57*
10-01-52*	10-24-57*	09-06-62*	03-04-57
10-01-53*	11-27-57	04-15-63*	03-10-57
10-01-54*	11-30-57*	06-01-63	03-17-57
10-01-55*	12-14-57*	06-27-63*	06-18-57
10-01-57*	12-23-57*	09-23-63*	08-02-57
09-29-58*	01-24-58*	09-27-63	09-03-57*
10-01-58*	02-13-58*	11-10-63*	11-21-57
04-29-59	02-27-58*	11-23-63*	11-27-57*
09-18-59	09-11-58*	04-11-64	12-18-57*
10-01-59	09-22-58*	10-11-64	02-11-58*
10-03-59	09-30-58*	04-20-65*	04-30-58*
10-01-60*	11-06-58*	04-26-65*	10-09-58
10-01-61*	01-17-59*	07-04-65*	10-22-58*
10-01-62*	01-25-59	09-11-65*	11-09-58
10-01-63*	02-04-59*	09-26-65*	12-28-58*
10-01-64	03-20-59*	09-29-65*	01-17-59
10-01-65*	07-25-59*	05-26-66*	02-04-59
10-01-66*	08-20-59*	09-05-66*	03-08-59*
10-01-68*	12-28-59*	11-25-66*	03-14-59
10-01-69*	03-26-60*	12-07-66*	05-13-59
10-01-70*	07-21-60*	11-02-71*	06-01-59
10-01-72*	11-04-60*	11-15-71*	06-23-59
10-01-73*	02-12-61*	05-09-72*	07-18-59*
10-01-74*	02-23-61*	06-10-72*	08-29-59
10-01-75*	03-25-61*	09-02-72*	09-22-59*
	06-26-61*	09-14-72*	12-05-59*

12. October Revolution

	07-22-61	08-25-73*	12-22-59
11-07-50	01-15-63*	09-07-73*	12-27-59*
11-07-51	08-06-63	09-17-74*	01-06-60*
11-07-52	01-24-64*	09-12-75*	02-21-60*
11-07-53	03-06-64*		03-03-60*
11-07-54*	04-05-64*	**c. Social Welfare**	04-15-60*
11-03-57*	04-24-64*	06-23-49	05-06-60*
11-04-57	02-26-65*	02-02-50	05-13-60
11-06-57*	09-01-65*	05-10-50	05-19-60*
11-25-57	11-05-65*	05-29-50	06-01-60*
11-07-58*	11-05-65*	05-31-50	06-15-60
11-07-59*	11-12-65*	06-29-50	06-21-60*
11-07-60*	11-28-65*	10-15-50	07-21-60*
11-07-61*	01-04-66	12-14-50*	08-18-60
11-07-62*	04-08-66*	04-27-51	09-23-60*
11-07-63*	08-08-74*	07-22-51*	10-17-60*
11-07-64*	04-25-75*	11-17-51	10-21-60*
11-07-65*	06-26-75*	01-11-52*	11-26-60*
		06-01-52	01-27-61

4. Health and Environment

b. Sports and Physical Fitness

		07-31-52	02-12-61*
		01-01-53	02-23-61
a. Public Health	10-22-49*	01-10-53*	03-25-61*
10-30-49*	11-25-51*	12-24-53	06-26-61*
04-05-51	02-09-54*	01-06-54	09-21-61*
05-17-51*	01-04-55	08-31-54	03-10-63
09-17-52*	10-02-55*	01-24-55*	12-16-65*
07-05-52*	10-10-55*	02-03-55	03-11-66
01-04-53*	07-23-56*	03-19-55	
02-28-53*	08-13-56*	04-25-55	**d. Population**
01-01-54	08-18-56*	04-30-55*	04-20-53*

01-17-54*
11-23-55
03-06-56
03-05-57*
12-19-57
01-10-58*
05-22-67

e. Weather, Natural Disasters, and Relief Work
05-10-50*
05-17-50
05-29-50*
09-16-50
10-15-50*
02-13-51
02-17-51
03-02-51
03-16-51
03-27-51
06-10-51*
07-17-51*
12-17-51
02-13-52*
02-27-52
03-06-52
03-20-52
04-03-52
07-20-52*
12-27-52*
05-17-53*
05-29-53*
06-06-53
07-05-53*
09-06-53
09-12-53
12-24-53
01-06-54*
03-24-54*
07-12-54*
08-02-54*
08-03-54
08-08-54*
09-14-54
10-06-54
10-16-54
10-24-54*
10-28-54
11-15-54
11-19-54
12-19-54*
01-01-55
01-15-55
02-03-55
03-19-55*
04-25-55
04-30-55
06-04-55*
07-20-55
08-19-55
12-30-55
01-15-56
02-05-56
02-17-56
02-24-56*
02-25-56
04-02-56
04-03-56*
05-28-56*
08-05-56*
08-19-56*
09-14-56*
10-12-56

01-22-57*
02-03-57
02-19-57
03-17-57*
04-02-57
05-30-57*
06-17-57*
06-18-57*
07-05-57*
07-09-57
07-22-57*
08-30-57
09-08-57*
09-09-57
09-20-57
10-17-57*
11-24-57*
11-26-57*
11-27-57*
03-11-58
03-21-58*
03-25-58*
04-22-58*
05-13-58
05-14-58
05-23-58*
06-16-58
07-28-58
08-14-58
08-18-58*
08-31-58
10-11-58*
10-14-58
11-21-58*
02-25-59
04-04-59*
06-03-59*
06-23-59*
07-18-59*
08-07-59*
08-13-59
08-14-59*
08-18-59*
08-21-59*
08-24-59
08-29-59
09-03-59
09-07-59*
10-11-59
11-01-59*
11-15-59*
12-05-59
12-28-59*
01-23-60
02-10-60*
03-14-60
04-24-60*
05-07-60
05-18-60
06-13-60*
07-01-60*
07-09-60*
08-08-60
08-09-60*
08-13-60
08-14-60*
08-18-60
08-23-60
08-25-60
09-03-60*
09-04-60
09-12-60
09-12-60*

09-28-60*
11-10-60
11-22-60
12-14-60*
12-29-60
01-01-61
01-08-61
01-23-61
02-06-61
02-21-61*
03-04-61*
03-24-61
04-01-61
11-23-61
12-02-61
12-12-61*
01-01-62
01-20-62
04-06-62*
05-29-62
06-08-62
07-13-62
09-20-62
10-12-62
10-23-62
11-02-62
12-14-62
03-07-63*
03-17-63
05-03-63*
05-11-63
06-23-63*
07-13-63*
10-16-63
10-21-63
11-16-63
01-06-64
01-19-64
01-30-64
03-06-64
03-11-64
04-19-64
07-04-64
07-05-64
07-06-64
08-05-64
08-06-64
09-03-64
02-20-65
03-11-65
04-23-65*
04-24-65
06-03-65*
12-26-65
01-01-66
02-07-66
02-13-66
03-11-66*
04-11-66
04-21-66
09-24-66*
09-26-66
03-02-73

I. Demographic, Class, and Occupational Groups

1. Women
03-08-50
04-16-50
05-31-50
09-29-51*

03-08-52
02-01-53
05-06-53
06-07-53*
01-29-54*
06-16-54
06-20-54
07-06-54
07-30-54*
07-31-54
09-15-54
11-01-54
03-08-55*
03-19-55
05-11-55
08-05-55*
03-08-56*
04-08-56*
04-24-56*
05-16-56
06-14-56*
08-02-56
09-10-56
01-12-57
03-08-57*
03-26-57*
06-13-57*
08-20-57
09-09-57*
12-16-57*
03-08-58*
06-08-58*
10-09-58
10-13-58*
10-25-58
11-10-58
12-04-58*
03-08-59*
03-14-59
09-23-59*
03-08-60*
04-15-60
05-06-60*
05-19-60
06-01-60
07-21-60
03-08-61*
03-25-61
06-26-61
03-08-63*
03-08-64*
03-08-65*
03-08-66*
10-22-66
03-08-73*
03-08-74*

2. Marriage and Family
03-08-50*
04-16-50*
09-29-51
03-08-52*
02-01-53*
05-06-53*
07-30-54
11-01-54
11-28-54*
03-08-55*
04-08-56
02-09-57
03-05-57*
03-08-57*
06-13-57

151

10-11-57
06-01-62*
03-08-63
01-03-64*
06-01-64*
07-27-64

3. Children and Youth
05-03-50*
05-31-50*
12-01-50*
12-14-50
06-01-51*
06-01-52*
02-01-53
05-04-53*
06-01-53*
06-18-53*
07-03-53*
11-11-53*
12-03-53
05-04-54*
06-01-54*
06-29-54*
07-30-54
08-09-54*
11-14-54*
11-28-54*
04-28-55
05-04-55*
06-01-55*
06-15-55
08-05-55*
08-21-55*
09-05-55
09-20-55*
09-29-55*
10-09-55
11-08-55*
01-12-56
01-21-56
02-23-56*
03-02-56*
03-05-56
03-07-56
03-08-56
05-04-56*
05-16-56
06-01-56*
08-13-56*
08-18-56*
10-07-56*
12-03-56*
12-09-56*
01-28-57*
03-08-57
03-16-57*
04-03-57*
05-04-57*
05-15-57
05-21-57
06-01-57*
08-11-57*
09-09-57
11-11-57
11-16-57
12-09-57*
12-16-57
01-20-58
01-23-58
01-31-58*
04-10-58*
05-04-58

06-01-58*
10-13-58
10-25-58
10-27-58
11-21-58*
01-17-59
02-10-59*
05-04-59*
06-01-59*
08-06-59*
08-28-59*
09-13-59*
09-22-59
04-15-60
05-06-60*
06-01-60*
07-21-60
10-22-60*
10-23-60*
01-28-61*
05-04-61*
06-01-61*
06-01-62*
03-08-63
03-27-63
05-04-63*
06-01-63*
01-03-64*
02-08-64
02-16-64*
02-28-64*
03-10-64
03-20-64*
05-04-64*
05-12-64
06-01-64*
07-08-64*
05-04-65*
06-01-65*
07-04-65
08-24-65*
12-09-65
12-23-65*
03-31-66*
05-04-66*
06-01-66*
08-28-66*
05-04-67
07-16-67*
02-22-73*
08-07-73*

4. Students
07-28-50
12-14-50*
04-25-51
07-11-51
07-20-51*
08-17-52
03-17-53
09-25-53*
07-11-54
11-14-54
05-20-55
06-15-55
06-30-55*
08-11-55*
12-11-55*
03-26-56*
05-12-56*
06-01-56*
06-09-56*
08-06-56*

10-04-56*
10-28-56*
11-20-56*
11-26-56
12-23-56*
03-29-57*
04-08-57*
04-24-57*
04-25-57*
05-12-57*
06-05-57*
07-11-57*
07-15-57*
07-21-57*
07-23-57
08-08-57*
08-22-57*
08-26-57*
10-30-57*
11-11-57*
12-09-57*
01-17-58
01-31-58
02-10-58
04-21-58
07-03-58*
07-11-58*
07-24-58*
09-04-58*
09-16-58*
09-25-58*
04-03-59*
06-11-59*
09-01-59*
12-21-59
02-11-60*
03-16-60
04-05-60
06-04-60*
05-04-61*
03-27-63
02-16-64
04-11-64*
05-04-64
07-04-65
09-06-65
12-09-65*
06-04-66
06-18-66
08-01-66
08-23-66*
08-23-66*
08-24-66
08-28-66
08-29-66*
09-07-66
09-11-66*
09-15-66
09-19-66
10-08-66
10-22-66*
11-10-66
01-22-67
01-27-67
02-01-67
03-07-67
03-18-67*
04-02-67*
04-21-67
05-22-67
05-31-67
07-09-67
08-28-67

09-22-67
10-06-67
10-12-67*
10-24-67
12-07-67
01-01-68
05-27-68
08-18-68*
09-12-68*
05-04-69

5. National Minorities
08-30-50*
09-30-50*
03-22-51*
05-28-51
06-14-51*
09-14-51*
08-13-52*
03-04-53
09-09-53*
10-10-53*
02-28-54*
04-17-54*
05-27-54
06-16-54
06-20-54
06-21-54
06-24-54*
07-03-54
09-15-54
12-25-54*
03-13-55*
09-30-55
02-03-56*
02-05-56
04-07-56
04-22-56*
09-08-56*
01-05-57*
01-23-57*
04-30-57*
08-24-57*
12-11-57
03-05-58*
04-19-58*
10-17-58
10-19-58*
10-26-58*
03-31-59
04-25-59
09-27-59
12-17-59
01-20-62
07-18-63*
12-30-64*
09-10-65
09-30-65
12-02-65
09-09-75*
10-01-75

6. Overseas Chinese
10-09-49*
07-26-54
03-03-55
04-23-55*
04-29-55*
09-14-55*
02-12-56
06-19-56
10-13-56*
05-21-57*

08-13-57*
07-03-58
08-25-58
12-12-59*
01-27-60*
03-18-60*
07-14-60*
12-24-60*
02-28-61*
12-10-62
03-05-63
04-28-63*
05-27-63*
08-28-63*
12-25-64*
03-30-66*
04-16-66
06-30-66*
10-08-66*
12-09-66*
04-27-67*
06-30-67
07-10-67*
09-10-67
10-29-67*

7. Workers
06-03-50*
06-04-50
06-17-50
06-29-50
08-17-50*
09-25-50*
12-01-50*
02-16-51
02-07-52*
02-16-52
04-08-52
05-01-52*
01-06-53*
01-10-53
02-07-53*
02-12-53*
05-01-53*
05-13-53*
05-15-53
07-08-53*
07-18-53
08-29-53
09-01-53
10-01-53
10-24-53
11-15-53
11-22-53
11-25-53*
12-12-53*
12-13-53*
12-24-53
01-01-54
01-11-54*
01-22-54
01-31-54
02-07-54*
02-08-54*
02-11-54*
03-12-54*
03-16-54
03-19-54
03-30-54
04-16-54*
04-19-54
05-01-54*
06-06-54*

06-08-54*
06-29-54*
08-11-54
08-28-54*
09-15-54
09-18-54
09-25-54
10-05-54
10-22-54*
11-06-54
11-15-54*
11-19-54*
12-08-54
12-12-54
12-13-54
12-20-54*
01-03-55*
02-17-55
03-04-55
04-07-55
04-22-55
05-01-55
07-08-55
07-17-55
07-23-55*
08-05-55
08-31-55
09-11-55
09-23-55
09-26-55
10-02-55*
10-08-55*
10-09-55
10-10-55*
11-22-55
12-01-55
12-15-55
12-17-55*
12-19-55
01-03-56
01-09-56
01-13-56
01-16-56
01-17-56
01-18-56
02-06-56
02-08-56
02-15-56*
02-23-56
03-08-56
03-11-56*
03-13-56*
03-16-56
03-17-56
03-19-56
03-30-56*
04-10-56
04-13-56
04-17-56*
04-20-56
04-27-56
04-30-56*
05-01-56
05-03-56
05-11-56*
05-15-56*
05-22-56
06-05-56*
06-05-56
06-08-56*
06-12-56
06-21-56*
06-26-56*

07-06-56
07-13-56
07-22-56
07-26-56*
08-21-56
09-04-56*
09-05-56
09-09-56
09-23-56
10-11-56*
10-17-56
10-29-56
10-31-56
11-06-56*
11-15-56
11-20-56
11-30-56
12-24-56*
12-31-56
01-06-57
01-21-57*
01-27-57*
02-05-57*
02-07-57*
02-08-57*
02-12-57
02-27-57
03-04-57
03-05-57
03-10-57*
04-01-57*
04-04-57
04-23-57
05-13-57*
05-21-57
05-24-57
05-29-57
06-10-57*
06-13-57
06-29-57
07-11-57
08-23-57
09-03-57
09-04-57*
09-18-57
09-23-57*
09-28-57
10-04-57
10-18-57
11-21-57
11-29-57
12-02-57*
12-09-57
12-13-57
12-18-57*
12-19-57
12-27-57
02-09-58*
02-11-58*
02-14-58*
03-07-58
03-08-58*
03-15-58*
03-24-58
03-27-58
03-28-58
03-31-58*
04-06-58*
04-20-58
05-01-58
05-07-58*
05-29-58
06-14-58

06-24-58
07-17-58*
07-28-58*
08-22-58
09-25-58*
10-12-58
10-22-58
10-23-58
11-08-58
11-14-58
11-16-58
12-05-58*
12-29-58*
01-05-59
01-09-59
02-02-59
02-06-59*
03-03-59
03-13-59
03-24-59*
03-29-59
04-10-59
04-17-59
04-20-59
05-01-59
05-11-59
05-15-59
05-19-59
06-04-59
06-17-59*
06-27-59
06-30-59
07-09-59
07-13-59*
07-27-59
07-29-59
08-17-59*
08-22-59
09-01-59
09-02-59*
09-05-59*
09-11-59
09-21-59*
09-25-59
09-27-59*
10-08-59
10-10-59
10-12-59
10-14-59
10-16-59
10-26-59*
11-04-59
11-09-59
11-12-59
11-26-59
11-28-59
12-01-59
12-21-59
12-27-59*
01-02-60*
01-04-60
01-11-60
01-23-60
02-03-60
02-04-60
02-25-60*
02-26-60*
03-03-60*
03-10-60*
03-13-60
03-15-60
03-24-60
03-29-60

153

04-07-60	10-08-63	09-25-68	03-25-55*
04-09-60*	10-20-63*	11-25-68	03-31-55*
04-11-60	11-08-63	02-17-69	04-12-55
04-17-60	12-02-63	02-21-69*	04-22-55
05-01-60	12-11-63	05-04-69	04-24-55
05-03-60	12-26-63	11-20-69	05-01-55
05-04-60	01-26-64*	03-29-70	05-07-55
05-08-60	02-02-64*	05-01-70	05-10-55
05-19-60	02-07-64	05-01-71	05-27-55*
06-04-60*	02-09-64	06-20-71	06-13-55
06-08-60	02-20-64	04-24-73*	06-26-55
06-13-60*	03-18-64	04-10-74	07-04-55*
06-13-60	04-04-64	07-03-74	07-07-55*
06-19-60	06-14-64		07-08-55
06-29-60	05-01-64	8. Peasants	07-11-55*
07-08-60*	05-29-64*	09-25-50*	07-22-55*
07-18-60	06-19-64	11-11-51	08-28-55
07-23-60	06-23-64	04-10-52	09-08-55
07-24-60	07-27-64	02-27-53*	09-13-55*
07-29-60*	09-22-64*	04-20-53*	09-23-55
07-29-60	09-24-64*	08-29-53	09-25-55*
08-03-60*	12-18-64	09-20-53	09-25-55
08-16-60*	01-18-65	09-23-53	09-27-55
09-07-60	01-23-65	10-01-53	10-04-55*
09-17-60*	02-23-65	11-09-53*	10-06-55*
09-24-60	02-26-65	11-15-53*	10-07-55
10-07-60	04-06-65	11-16-53*	10-13-55*
10-14-60	04-29-65	11-20-53*	10-16-55
10-17-60*	05-01-65*	11-25-53*	10-29-55
10-18-60*	05-26-65	11-30-53	11-02-55
10-30-60	06-21-65*	12-02-53	11-10-55
12-04-60	07-06-65*	12-03-53	11-12-55
12-07-60*	07-11-65	12-11-53*	11-13-55*
12-12-60*	07-30-65	12-12-53	11-17-55*
12-17-60	09-08-65	12-14-53	11-26-55
12-30-60*	09-24-65	12-17-53	12-03-55
01-04-61*	09-26-65	12-20-53*	12-05-55
01-09-61	01-08-66	12-24-53	12-06-55
01-16-61	01-16-66	12-28-53	12-18-55
01-30-61	01-30-66*	12-30-53*	12-28-55*
02-22-61	02-22-66*	01-01-54	12-29-55*
03-07-61	02-27-66	01-05-54*	01-01-56
03-09-61	04-03-66	01-11-54*	01-08-56
05-01-61	05-01-66	01-16-54	01-09-56
06-04-61*	06-04-66	01-17-54	01-14-56*
06-08-61	08-23-66	01-19-54	01-15-56
07-22-61	09-07-66	01-22-54	01-16-56
09-06-61*	09-11-66*	01-26-54*	01-23-56
10-10-61	09-15-66*	01-29-54*	01-24-56
11-14-61	09-26-66*	01-31-54	01-27-56*
11-25-61	10-22-66*	02-07-54	02-05-56
12-05-61	10-28-66	02-11-54*	02-07-56
12-17-61*	11-10-66	03-01-54	02-09-56
12-23-61*	12-26-66	03-12-54	02-10-56
03-02-62	01-19-67	03-21-54*	02-15-56
03-15-62	01-22-67*	04-28-54	02-17-56
04-08-62	01-26-67	05-01-54*	02-18-56
04-22-62	02-01-67	06-19-54	02-25-56
05-01-62*	02-02-67	07-07-54	03-05-56
11-12-62	02-10-67*	09-15-54	03-08-56
11-16-62	02-17-67	10-06-54	03-12-56*
12-05-62	05-04-67	11-12-54	03-26-56
12-14-62	06-18-67	11-17-54*	03-28-56
12-22-62*	07-05-67	11-21-54*	04-02-56
01-25-63*	09-22-67	11-23-54	04-14-56
02-07-63	10-06-67	12-07-54	05-01-56
02-11-63*	10-12-67	01-01-55*	05-05-56
03-15-63	05-01-68	01-30-55	05-06-56
04-10-63	05-27-68	02-03-55	05-09-56
05-01-63	08-18-68	03-09-55*	05-10-56
06-19-63*	08-28-68	03-14-55*	05-17-56
09-02-63	09-07-68	03-21-55	05-24-56
09-25-63	09-12-68	03-24-55*	05-29-56

05-29-56*	11-11-57	08-29-59	02-17-63
06-02-56	11-13-57	09-03-59	03-07-63
06-10-56*	11-14-57	09-11-59	03-25-63*
06-13-56	11-15-57	09-17-59	04-23-63
06-25-56	11-16-57*	09-22-59*	05-14-63
06-27-56	11-18-57	10-12-59	05-29-63
07-02-56*	11-19-57*	11-01-59	07-04-63
07-10-56	11-26-57*	11-10-59*	07-23-63
07-14-56	12-07-57*	11-11-59	07-29-63
07-17-56	12-09-57	11-15-59	08-26-63
07-19-56*	12-10-57	12-04-59	08-29-63
09-11-56	12-15-57	12-05-59	10-08-63
09-14-56	12-19-57*	12-28-59	10-16-63
09-25-56*	12-19-57	01-11-60	11-14-63
10-10-56	12-22-57*	01-14-60	11-16-63
10-12-56	12-28-57	01-18-60	12-07-63*
10-26-56	01-07-58	02-21-60	01-01-64
10-27-56*	01-14-58	02-26-60	01-06-64*
11-22-56*	02-16-58*	02-27-60	01-28-64
11-28-56	03-07-58	03-13-60	02-28-64
12-31-56	03-21-58	03-14-60*	03-07-64
01-29-57	03-22-58*	03-16-60	03-19-64
01-31-57	03-25-58	04-13-60	03-23-64
02-07-57	04-04-58	06-21-60*	04-06-64
02-09-57	04-08-58	06-27-60	04-24-64*
02-18-57*	04-12-58*	07-01-60	05-01-64
02-19-57	04-14-58	07-17-60	05-04-64
02-21-57	04-16-58	07-27-60	05-12-64*
02-22-57*	04-21-58	08-03-60*	05-21-64
02-24-57	04-23-58	08-05-60	05-26-64
03-01-57	05-01-58	08-20-60*	05-27-64
03-02-57*	05-09-58	09-19-60	06-02-64
03-03-57	05-15-58	09-23-60	06-14-64
03-05-57	05-19-58*	09-26-60	06-16-64*
03-11-57	05-21-58	10-17-60	07-05-64
03-15-57	05-22-58*	10-23-60*	07-06-64
03-20-57	06-05-58	11-04-60	07-12-64*
03-22-57*	06-14-58	02-12-61	07-17-64*
03-23-57*	06-18-58	02-24-61	07-27-64
03-24-57	06-20-58	03-19-61*	08-03-64
03-26-57*	07-01-58*	03-24-61	08-14-64
04-01-57*	07-21-58	03-31-61	08-28-64
04-08-57*	07-25-58*	04-01-61	09-11-64*
04-19-57	07-28-58	04-22-61	09-21-64
04-21-57	08-14-58*	06-21-61	10-24-64
04-29-57*	09-10-58*	07-05-61	10-25-64
05-08-57	09-13-58	08-08-61	10-27-64
05-09-57	09-23-58	08-12-61*	10-28-64
05-14-57	09-25-58*	08-25-61	11-16-64
05-24-57	09-27-58	09-21-61*	11-19-64
06-02-57*	09-29-58*	10-15-61	11-24-64
07-03-57	10-01-58	11-03-61*	12-06-64*
07-19-57*	10-09-58*	11-05-61	01-15-65
07-22-57	10-12-58	11-10-61	02-15-65
08-05-57*	10-24-58	11-21-61	02-17-65
08-07-57	10-25-58	12-03-61	02-22-65
08-10-57*	11-09-58*	12-09-61	02-24-65
08-12-57	11-10-58	12-12-61	02-26-65
08-15-57*	12-25-58	01-04-62	02-27-65
08-18-57	12-28-58	02-16-62	03-04-65
08-25-57	01-02-59	02-26-62	03-11-65
08-28-57	01-20-59	05-16-62	03-12-65
08-28-57*	02-02-59	06-02-62	03-28-65
09-02-57	03-10-59	07-13-62	04-11-65
09-08-57	03-25-59	09-20-62	04-17-65
09-20-57	04-04-59	11-09-62	04-23-65
09-22-57	05-01-59	11-27-62	04-28-65
09-25-57	05-13-59	12-02-62	04-30-65
10-06-57	05-16-59	12-07-62	05-05-65
10-11-57*	05-19-59	12-22-62*	06-05-65
10-20-57*	05-20-59	01-11-63	06-16-65
10-22-57	06-02-59*	01-25-63*	06-23-65
10-27-57*	07-12-59	02-11-63*	07-02-65

155

07-16-65
08-31-65
09-01-65*
09-07-65
09-19-65*
10-10-65
10-16-65
10-28-65
11-01-65
11-05-65
11-12-65
12-02-65
12-04-65
12-13-65*
12-16-65
12-22-65*
01-02-66
01-08-66
01-16-66
01-25-66*
01-26-66
01-27-66
02-10-66*
02-11-66
02-22-66
02-23-66
03-01-66
03-10-66
03-12-66
03-16-66
04-12-66
05-08-66*
06-04-66
08-01-66
08-23-66
09-07-66
09-11-66*
09-15-66*
09-19-66
09-24-66
11-10-66
02-11-67
03-12-67*
03-13-67*
04-21-67
05-04-67
05-31-67*
07-05-67
07-09-67
09-16-67
09-24-67
08-18-68
09-12-68
11-25-68
03-22-69
05-04-69
11-20-69
03-07-70
07-09-70*
03-23-70
03-18-71
03-03-74
06-26-75*

9. Worker-Peasant Alliance
03-17-49
06-30-50
09-20-50
10-01-53
11-09-53
11-25-53*
11-30-53
12-12-53

01-11-54*
02-07-54
02-11-54*
03-12-54
05-01-54
07-07-54
07-26-54
11-21-54
04-22-55
08-25-55
08-27-55
08-29-55
09-13-55
10-18-55
02-15-56
09-27-56
04-01-57*
06-11-57
07-23-57
09-02-57
11-13-57
02-11-58
07-01-58
08-06-58
08-12-58
09-25-59
11-02-59
11-16-59
03-13-60*
05-07-60
07-17-60
07-26-60*
08-10-60
09-30-60
03-18-61
08-08-61
12-12-61
11-26-62
12-02-62
12-05-62
01-25-63*
03-25-63
04-13-63
05-29-63
01-23-64
04-06-64
07-17-64
04-30-65
08-18-65
08-31-65
09-26-65
10-10-65
06-09-69
07-01-69
06-26-75

10. Scientists and
Technicians
08-17-50*
08-27-50*
04-16-52
06-14-52*
11-18-52
04-08-52
04-02-53
11-22-53
12-22-53
02-08-54
02-25-54
03-10-54
03-19-54*
03-26-54*
04-15-54

06-14-54
08-28-54*
10-05-54
10-23-54
10-27-54
11-28-54
12-12-54
12-13-54
01-03-55*
01-03-55*
01-25-55
02-20-55*
02-27-55*
03-18-55
03-22-55
04-07-55
06-03-55
07-30-55*
09-06-55
10-11-55
12-02-55*
12-15-55
12-20-55
01-27-56
01-29-56
01-31-56
02-08-56
02-23-56
03-16-56
03-17-56
03-19-56
03-30-56
04-03-56
04-10-56
04-19-56*
05-03-56
05-12-56
05-27-56
05-28-56
07-06-56
07-31-56
08-02-56*
08-12-56
08-28-56
09-10-56
10-16-56*
10-25-56
10-29-56
11-06-56*
11-16-56
11-20-56
12-03-56
12-04-56
01-24-57*
02-12-57*
04-14-57
09-28-57
10-03-57*
10-28-57
03-23-58*
04-06-58
06-03-58
06-18-58*
07-14-58*
09-22-58
12-06-58*
01-16-59
01-21-59
01-25-59
02-04-59
03-21-59
08-17-59*
12-28-59

01-11-60*
04-09-60*
04-13-60
04-20-60*
06-29-60
07-31-60
09-08-60*
09-22-60
11-11-60*
01-30-61
02-28-61
04-10-61
04-14-61
04-18-61
11-17-61*
11-25-61
12-23-61
12-24-61
06-15-62*
10-12-62
10-22-62
12-22-62
01-09-63*
02-11-63*
02-17-63
03-07-63
03-15-63
03-23-63
03-27-63
04-06-63
04-08-63*
05-14-63
06-26-63
07-23-63*
08-06-63
12-02-63*
12-04-63
12-11-63
01-06-64
01-26-64
02-28-64
03-07-64
03-23-64
04-05-64*
05-10-64
05-21-64
05-27-64
05-29-64*
06-19-64
08-21-64*
09-01-64
09-05-64*
09-22-64
10-24-64
10-25-64
11-16-64*
01-18-65
01-23-65
03-04-65
03-28-65*
04-10-65*
04-11-65
04-22-65*
04-29-65
04-30-65
05-05-65
06-21-65
07-06-65*
09-01-65*
09-07-65
09-15-65
09-24-65
12-13-65

12-22-65*
12-23-65
01-20-66*
01-24-66*
04-03-66
05-08-66
07-23-66*
08-01-66*
09-07-66
02-21-69

11. Intellectuals
07-28-50
08-27-50
02-16-51
09-24-52
12-22-53*
04-11-55
01-21-56
01-31-56
02-12-56*
03-17-56
03-21-56*
04-03-56
08-02-56
08-12-56*
08-16-56*
08-28-56
10-05-56*
10-19-56*
10-29-56
11-06-56
12-17-56
01-25-57*
04-06-57*
04-08-57
04-23-57
04-26-57
04-27-57
05-04-57
06-10-57
06-11-57
06-14-57*
06-29-57
07-01-57
07-11-57
07-16-57
07-18-57*
08-01-57
08-29-57
09-05-57
09-18-57*
10-06-57
10-28-57
11-11-57
11-12-57
11-16-57
02-10-58
02-13-58
03-06-58
03-23-58*
03-28-58
04-13-58*
05-29-58
07-24-58
08-30-58*
09-25-58
05-04-59
09-01-59
01-07-60*
02-11-60
09-25-60
11-17-61

03-27-63
02-16-64*
02-28-64*
03-20-64
05-04-64
05-12-64
08-01-64*
12-30-64
03-01-65
04-10-65
05-05-65*
12-09-65*
02-27-66
06-01-66
06-04-66
07-17-66
05-04-67*
07-09-67
09-01-68
09-12-68*
11-25-68
02-17-69
05-04-69*
08-25-69

12. Merchants, Commercial
Workers, and Peddlers
03-22-50
06-06-50*
06-08-50
06-11-50
06-17-50
12-22-50*
02-17-52*
02-21-52
04-10-52
06-15-52
07-02-52*
10-15-53
11-14-53
11-30-53
12-02-53
12-06-53
12-30-53
01-05-54
07-08-54*
09-17-54
09-20-54
09-25-54*
10-09-54
11-17-54
11-24-54
12-16-54
12-23-54
02-04-55*
03-10-55*
05-22-55
06-07-55
10-04-55
10-16-55
11-22-55*
12-14-55
01-01-56
01-03-56
01-09-56
01-11-56
01-16-56
01-17-56
02-11-56
02-12-56
02-23-56*
04-08-56
04-14-56*

05-10-56
07-13-56*
07-19-56*
07-21-56*
11-22-56
12-08-56
12-10-56*
12-20-56
12-24-56*
01-29-57
04-22-57*
06-11-57
07-03-57
07-16-57
08-07-57
12-29-57
03-01-60*
09-25-60
06-27-63
09-25-63*

13. Industrialists
12-22-50*
06-15-52
07-02-52*
11-14-53
07-08-54*
12-23-54
08-10-55
01-01-56
01-03-56
01-09-56
01-11-56
01-16-56
01-17-56
02-11-56
02-12-56
02-23-56*
04-08-56
04-22-57*
06-11-57
07-03-57
07-16-57
03-01-60*

14. Bourgeois Capitalists and
Petty Bourgeoisie
01-22-52
02-07-52*
02-16-52
02-21-52
02-29-52*
04-15-52
06-15-52
04-04-54
04-13-54*
05-27-54
11-14-54*
11-28-54
05-25-55*
08-10-55*
01-25-55
12-14-55
01-22-56
02-08-56*
02-12-56
06-08-56
09-04-56
10-16-56*
04-22-57
04-23-57
04-26-57
05-02-57

08-07-57
08-10-57
08-24-57
08-29-57
09-05-57
09-18-57
10-09-57*
10-21-57
03-17-58*
03-01-60*
09-30-60
05-08-63
08-03-64*
03-31-66*
04-14-66*
05-01-66
06-01-66*
06-01-66
06-02-66*
06-03-66*
06-04-66*
06-04-66
06-08-66
06-18-66
06-20-66
07-01-66
07-17-66*
07-28-66
08-08-66
08-13-66
08-28-66
08-29-66
09-05-66
09-15-66
12-26-66
01-19-67
01-22-67*
01-26-67
01-30-67
02-01-67
02-02-67
02-10-67
02-17-67
03-01-67
03-02-67*
03-07-67
03-12-67
03-18-67
04-02-67
04-08-67
04-15-67*
04-21-67*
04-24-67*
04-26-67*
05-04-67
05-07-67
05-16-67
05-29-67
05-31-67
06-01-67*
06-08-67
06-14-67
06-18-67
06-30-67
07-09-67
07-24-67
07-26-67*
07-28-67*
07-29-67
07-30-67*
07-30-67*
08-02-67*
08-05-67*

08-08-67*
08-11-67
08-13-67
08-16-67*
08-17-67*
08-19-67*
09-14-67
09-16-67
09-18-67
09-22-67
10-06-67
10-12-67
10-19-67
10-21-67
10-24-67
11-02-67*
11-19-67
12-04-67
12-07-67
01-01-68
06-02-68
09-01-68*
11-25-68
01-01-69
05-04-69
08-25-69

15. KMT Remnants and
    Reactionary Elements
    01-06-52
    01-12-52
    02-26-52*
    07-18-54
    07-03-55
    07-12-55
    07-16-55*
    07-25-55
    09-01-55
    02-12-56
    10-24-56
    09-18-57
    02-19-59
    03-11-59
    09-18-59
    02-10-61

16. Bad Classes
    06-30-50
    08-26-50*
    10-21-50*
    11-11-51
    02-16-52
    03-30-54
    04-04-54
    04-28-54*
    05-20-54
    05-21-54*
    06-12-54*
    06-20-54
    06-21-54
    07-18-54*
    08-01-54
    08-21-54*
    09-04-54*
    11-03-54
    11-10-54*
    11-23-54
    12-15-54*
    12-24-54*
    01-01-55
    01-08-55*
    01-17-55
    04-10-55*

04-14-55*
06-10-55*
07-03-55*
07-12-55*
07-16-55*
07-25-55*
08-22-55*
08-28-55*
09-01-55*
09-17-55
10-28-55*
11-28-55
12-10-55*
02-07-56*
03-01-56*
04-16-56*
04-25-56*
05-05-56
05-26-56*
07-02-56
07-12-56*
08-03-56*
10-22-56
10-24-56
04-08-57
05-02-57
05-17-57*
06-08-57
06-10-57
06-11-57*
06-12-57
06-14-57
06-22-57*
06-26-57
06-29-57*
07-01-57*
07-03-57
07-08-57*
07-10-57
07-15-57
07-16-57
07-28-57
07-18-57
08-02-57*
08-04-57
08-08-57
08-10-57*
08-14-57*
08-15-57
08-16-57*
08-19-57*
08-26-57
08-29-57*
09-01-57
09-02-57
09-05-57*
09-11-57*
09-15-57*
09-18-57*
09-23-57
10-03-57
10-08-57
10-09-57*
10-10-57
10-14-57*
10-23-57*
10-29-57*
11-01-57*
11-12-57*
11-13-57
12-07-57*
12-20-57*
12-22-57

12-27-57
12-29-57
01-01-58
01-15-58*
02-03-58
03-10-58*
05-05-58
05-08-58
06-19-58
08-02-58
08-12-58*
08-30-58
10-17-58*
09-01-59
09-18-59*
09-21-59
09-22-59
10-08-59
10-10-59
10-16-59
10-17-59
10-19-59
11-26-59
04-07-60*
08-15-60
06-19-63
08-28-64
08-30-64
02-01-65*
06-01-66
06-01-66
06-03-66
06-04-66
06-08-66
06-16-66*
06-24-66
07-01-66*
07-17-66*
12-26-66*
03-12-67
03-13-67
05-23-67
07-09-67
09-14-67
09-24-67
10-21-67
11-02-67
01-01-68
03-10-68
04-10-68
04-20-68
05-03-68
05-12-68
05-17-68
06-02-68
07-01-68
08-01-68
08-05-68
08-15-68
08-18-68
08-21-68*
08-28-68
09-01-68*
09-07-68
09-12-68
11-25-68
01-01-69
02-17-69
06-09-69
08-25-69
04-01-70
07-09-70

17. Counter-Revolutionary
    Revisionists
    03-02-67
    05-31-67
    06-08-67
    06-14-67
    08-05-67*
    08-16-67
    09-09-67*
    09-14-67
    09-16-67
    04-20-68*
    05-01-68*
    05-03-68
    05-12-68
    05-17-68*
    06-02-68
    07-01-68
    08-01-68
    08-05-68
    08-15-68
    08-21-68*
    08-28-68
    09-01-68*
    09-07-68
    10-01-68
    11-25-68
    01-01-69*
    08-25-69*
    10-01-69
    05-23-70
    10-01-70
    01-01-71
    01-31-71
    05-01-71
    05-07-71
    06-20-71
    03-09-72
    05-23-72
    10-01-72
    01-01-73
    02-22-73
    07-11-73
    01-01-74
    02-20-74
    03-15-74
    03-21-75
    06-26-75
    09-04-75*

J. Regions of China

1. General Geography
   10-10-53
   06-14-54
   06-16-54
   06-24-54
   10-24-54
   03-13-55
   07-20-55
   09-30-55*
   12-22-56*
   04-30-57
   06-26-57
   12-08-57*
   11-30-58*
   08-19-59
   09-12-59*
   09-12-59*
   12-15-59
   12-25-59
   01-29-60*
   01-29-60*

02-01-60*
03-25-60*
04-27-60
04-30-60
07-31-60*
08-03-60
08-04-60
09-28-60
10-02-60
10-20-60*
10-05-60*
10-05-60
01-05-61
01-10-61*
01-28-61*
03-24-61
05-03-61
10-13-61
10-14-61
11-16-61
12-07-61*
04-28-62
06-03-62
06-05-62*
06-27-62
07-09-62*
09-07-62*
09-22-62*
10-05-62*
10-10-62*
10-14-62*
10-27-62*
11-08-62*
11-20-62*
11-22-62*
12-10-62*
12-27-62*
12-29-62*
12-31-62
01-08-63*
01-19-63
01-21-63*
01-24-63*
01-28-63*
02-27-63
02-28-63
03-01-63*
03-04-63*
03-05-63*
04-03-63*
04-10-63
04-26-63
04-27-63
04-28-63
05-27-63*
07-28-63
08-23-63
08-26-63
08-27-63
10-13-63*
10-23-63
11-20-63*
11-21-63*
11-23-63*
02-10-64
02-20-64
02-26-64
03-03-64
04-19-64
05-10-64*
05-23-64*
06-09-64
07-27-64*

10-15-64
10-28-64*
10-30-64
03-02-65
03-09-65
03-14-65
03-28-65
05-19-65
08-02-65
09-11-65
09-18-65
10-09-65*
10-23-65
12-21-65
04-20-66
03-04-69*

2. North China

   a. General North China
01-04-49
04-28-49*
06-15-49*
06-23-49*
07-03-49*
10-14-49
10-27-49
10-30-49*
03-02-51
03-17-51
04-10-51
05-01-51
07-25-51
08-14-51
09-20-51
11-17-51
11-20-51
11-28-51
05-06-52
09-24-52
12-28-52
06-06-55
02-17-56
07-10-56*
08-19-56
02-06-57
07-24-57
08-15-57
05-24-58*
06-29-59
12-02-59
08-18-65
12-26-65*
09-25-68

   b. Hopei
12-19-51
03-25-53
05-18-54
06-12-54
12-19-54
04-15-55
04-06-56
10-22-57*
11-15-57
03-11-58*
04-29-58
07-30-58
08-18-58
10-07-58
06-16-60
06-19-60*
08-27-60

11-03-60
11-23-60*
02-09-61
03-04-61*
01-24-62
06-27-62*
07-04-63
09-20-63
10-16-63
12-07-63
06-02-64*
03-12-65
04-04-65
04-28-65
05-19-65*
07-03-65*
08-12-65
10-09-65
03-06-66
03-11-66*
09-24-66
02-05-68*
09-23-70

   c. Inner Mongolia
10-30-49*
04-01-51
08-13-52
02-28-54*
06-24-54
10-16-54
01-04-56
03-02-56
04-30-57*
06-27-59
09-27-59
01-20-62*
10-28-64
04-06-65
12-02-65*
01-29-66
03-01-66
03-10-66
04-12-66
11-02-67*

   d. Peking
02-04-49*
07-29-49
08-02-49*
10-22-49
11-21-49
05-16-50*
06-02-50*
08-22-50
11-14-50
12-16-50*
02-04-51*
03-11-51
03-26-51
04-03-51
04-04-51
08-10-51
12-13-51
03-12-52
01-22-53
03-28-55
01-11-56
01-13-56
01-16-56
03-21-56
04-26-56
05-21-57

09-21-57
09-23-57
09-28-57
10-06-57
11-12-57
02-07-58
02-14-58*
02-14-58
07-02-58
09-25-59*
01-06-60
03-15-60*
08-31-60*
12-17-60
02-20-61*
04-10-61
09-27-63
11-30-63
01-19-64
03-18-64
04-11-64
09-07-65
01-30-66*
03-20-66
03-25-66
04-15-66*
06-04-66
06-16-66
07-10-66
08-23-66*
08-24-66*
03-12-67
04-21-67*
05-22-67
06-01-67
07-26-67
08-10-67*
12-14-68
02-17-69
04-24-73

   e. Shansi
01-06-52
01-16-54
01-17-54
03-01-54
05-04-54
07-12-54
11-23-54
12-24-54
03-04-55
03-02-56
03-28-56
07-27-56
10-22-58
01-04-59
05-17-59
09-15-59
12-01-59*
05-11-60
06-23-60*
07-17-60
08-09-60
11-25-60
11-26-60*
01-12-61
01-31-61
10-11-61
11-03-61
06-02-63
08-17-63
09-20-63
11-26-63

02-10-64
05-15-64
06-14-64
07-04-64
07-06-64
07-12-64
10-28-64
03-12-65
05-21-65
07-10-65
11-12-65*
02-23-66
03-08-66
01-25-67*

f. Tientsin
07-29-49
04-04-51
04-06-51
04-09-51*
06-24-51
12-13-51
01-22-53
07-08-53
01-14-54
07-08-54
09-23-57
03-14-58
06-24-58
10-12-58*
07-27-59
05-19-60
10-24-60
04-06-61
11-22-61
01-12-62*
04-22-62*
09-05-64
11-28-65
12-07-67*

3. Northeast China

a. General Northeast China
10-30-49
02-11-51
03-14-51
03-17-51
04-01-51
06-16-51
11-09-51
11-20-51
11-23-51
03-08-52
06-28-52
09-24-52
11-26-52
01-24-53
02-24-53
04-14-53
07-28-53
12-24-53
01-17-55
03-06-56
08-19-56
02-06-57
01-21-58
02-21-58
08-08-58
08-20-58
12-02-59

b. Heilungkiang
05-08-54
06-04-54
01-06-57
03-11-57*
07-21-58
03-27-59
06-27-59
04-26-60*
04-06-64
07-29-65*
01-17-66
01-30-66*
03-08-66
08-26-66
02-02-67*
02-10-67*
03-04-69*

c. Kirin
11-05-52
12-31-52
10-13-54
01-15-55
10-25-57
01-30-61
03-02-61*
03-09-61*
11-16-64
03-10-68*

d. Liaoning
11-27-49
09-16-52
02-03-53
12-27-53
02-08-54
02-11-54
03-12-54
03-19-54
04-16-54*
05-15-53*
10-13-54
10-17-54
11-06-54
12-13-54
02-23-55
03-27-55
04-14-55
04-15-55
03-18-56
07-25-56
08-23-56
07-09-58
09-19-58*
03-10-60
05-15-60
07-26-60
08-12-60*
10-14-60*
01-09-61
03-28-61*
01-11-66*
10-22-66
05-12-68*

4. Northwest China

a. General Northwest China
08-30-50*
04-23-51
06-19-53

02-17-56
03-06-56
01-02-58*
01-16-58

b. Kansu
03-02-56
03-03-58*
07-29-65*
04-08-66*
01-26-68*

c. Ninghsia
10-17-58
10-26-58*
04-12-68*

d. Shensi
01-29-54
06-18-55
03-02-56
06-18-58
09-27-58
08-09-60
06-10-62
10-28-64
05-03-68*

e. Sinkiang
04-05-50
10-17-54
01-28-56
09-05-56*
03-29-62*
06-19-62*
09-07-62
12-29-62
03-01-63
04-03-63
09-30-65*
03-01-66
09-07-68*
10-01-75*

f. Tsinghai
12-25-54
04-26-60*
07-03-60
03-01-66
04-10-66*
08-13-67*

5. East China

a. General Coastal China
03-20-54*
04-14-55
06-06-55*
01-27-56
07-08-56*
07-09-56
08-19-56
10-03-56
05-30-57
05-27-60
06-30-63
09-15-65
09-25-68

b. Anhwei
05-20-54
07-17-56
01-12-58

03-10-58
05-09-58
07-30-58*
02-16-60*
03-15-60
08-07-60
09-01-60*
04-11-65*
12-27-65*
01-05-66*
04-11-66*
04-20-68*

c. Chekiang
03-23-54
04-14-54
01-30-55
03-11-55
12-13-55
01-28-56
07-16-56
02-03-57
12-29-57*
05-23-64
02-01-65
08-21-65*
04-22-66*

d. Fukien
01-21-55
04-08-55
01-20-56
08-13-57
06-23-59
06-27-59
05-27-60
09-09-60
06-05-63*
05-26-64
02-01-65
02-17-67*
08-21-68*

e. Kiangsi
12-06-51
10-19-58
11-16-61
06-16-64
07-11-65*
01-04-66*
04-26-66*
01-07-68*

f. Kiangsu
02-28-53*
12-11-53
11-23-54
03-19-55
02-04-58
03-19-58
03-27-58*
04-05-58*
04-20-58*
04-30-58
09-12-58
10-18-58
01-30-59
06-09-59*
07-24-60
08-06-60
11-14-60
01-22-62*
07-09-64

02-01-65
03-12-65*
06-16-66
03-25-68*

g. Shanghai
11-11-53
12-12-53
12-10-55
01-22-56
03-16-56
08-21-56
12-27-56
05-21-57
08-14-57
09-23-57
01-08-58
08-28-58
10-19-58
06-28-59
11-16-59
03-29-60
06-30-60*
09-13-60*
12-04-60*
01-18-61
04-06-61
04-18-61*
11-22-61*
11-25-61
05-08-63*
10-20-63
04-11-64
04-14-64
01-13-66*
02-08-66*
02-26-66*
02-28-66
03-16-66*
04-07-66*
01-19-67*
01-25-67
04-15-67
06-08-67*
08-26-67*
09-18-67
02-22-73
04-24-73

h. Shantung
07-26-53*
12-03-53
04-14-54
04-06-56
08-29-56
07-22-57
01-07-60
02-24-60*
10-10-60*
10-25-61*
03-12-65
03-14-65*
10-10-65
10-16-65
01-30-67*
03-02-67

6. Central-South China

a. General Central-South
   China
06-06-55*
01-27-56

10-03-56
05-30-57
08-15-57
11-15-57
07-28-59
02-17-61
05-10-64
09-15-65
01-16-66
09-25-68

b. Canton
10-16-49*
11-10-56
11-08-66

c. Honan
03-09-50
03-24-50
12-19-51
01-06-54
03-01-54
09-11-54
12-19-54
06-17-55
03-02-56
05-06-56
04-14-57
07-22-57
11-15-57
01-20-58
03-21-58
05-18-58
06-07-58*
09-04-58*
09-17-58*
09-26-58*
10-04-58
10-09-58
10-17-58*
10-18-58*

d. Hunan
03-07-51
06-04-54
11-17-54
12-13-54
12-18-57
10-18-58*
08-06-60
03-01-65
04-10-68*

e. Hupei
02-26-52
04-23-53
02-06-54
05-17-54
07-18-54
12-19-54
01-28-55
07-17-56
04-09-57*
10-15-57
01-12-58*
01-29-58*
08-13-58
12-15-59
03-05-60
08-21-60
03-05-61*
05-21-65*
07-26-67

07-28-67*
07-29-67*
07-30-67*
07-30-67*
08-02-67*
08-04-67*
08-17-67
02-07-68*

f. Kwangsi
11-15-53
02-07-56
05-06-56
02-03-57
06-18-57
03-05-58*
08-02-58
10-18-58
10-20-58*
06-23-59
06-27-60*
06-04-64*
07-17-64*
07-23-65*
02-05-66
02-23-66
08-28-68*
07-03-74*

g. Kwangtung
04-14-54
08-01-54
01-21-55
09-27-55
02-03-57
07-05-57
08-13-57
02-04-58
08-02-58
09-19-58*
06-23-59
06-15-60
08-17-60*
01-12-61
02-05-61
11-05-61
12-12-61
02-26-62*
06-30-63
01-30-64
07-09-64
02-01-65
03-11-65*
04-12-65
07-13-65
08-07-65
02-06-66
02-23-68*

7. Southwest China

a. General Southwest
   China
03-06-56
10-03-56
01-02-58*

b. Kweichow
06-03-51
01-20-58
02-10-58
09-16-58*
09-16-60*

02-02-61
02-01-67*
03-01-67

c. Szechuan
02-29-52
03-23-54
03-14-55
09-01-56
10-11-56
07-04-59*
11-16-59
01-08-60*
05-07-60
05-13-60
07-29-60
09-17-60
09-24-60
11-18-60*
02-22-61*
03-17-61
07-27-64
09-22-64
04-17-65
04-18-65*
05-04-65
05-26-65*
07-20-65*
06-02-68*

d. Tibet
11-17-50*
05-28-51*
04-30-54*
06-26-54
12-25-54*
03-13-55*
04-22-56*
09-24-56
09-26-56
03-31-59*
04-12-59
04-25-59*
04-29-59*
05-01-59
05-04-59
09-12-59
09-16-59
10-24-59*
01-01-60
08-13-60
10-19-60
02-25-61
12-22-61
06-03-62*
09-22-62*
11-08-62
01-19-63
04-03-63
01-10-65
09-10-65*
09-30-65*
12-21-65*
12-27-65
09-07-68*
01-31-72
09-09-75*

e. Yunnan
08-09-60
04-29-65
04-30-65*
08-15-68*

K. **Military**

1. General Defense
    10-16-49*
    11-30-49*
    01-05-50
    04-21-50*
    12-01-50*
    12-06-50
    01-01-52
    07-01-52
    08-11-52
    06-18-54
    11-01-54*
    11-25-54
    12-25-54
    01-04-55*
    01-21-55
    01-24-55
    02-15-55
    02-23-55*
    03-29-55*
    04-19-55
    07-31-55
    08-01-55
    03-07-56*
    08-29-56
    09-08-56
    09-29-56
    01-17-57
    03-12-57*
    06-13-57
    08-02-58*
    09-09-58
    09-12-58*
    09-21-58
    09-28-58
    09-30-58
    10-10-58*
    10-11-58*
    10-21-58
    03-31-59
    04-25-59
    09-12-59
    09-16-59
    01-21-60
    04-19-60
    05-27-60
    02-15-61*
    07-09-62*
    08-01-62
    09-07-62*
    09-22-62*
    10-10-62
    10-14-62*
    10-27-62*
    12-30-62
    01-28-63
    03-05-63
    04-03-63*
    05-27-63
    06-08-63
    06-22-63
    06-30-63*
    10-13-63*
    11-21-63
    07-09-64*
    09-10-64
    10-22-64*
    03-29-65

    04-05-65
    04-12-65*
    06-27-65*
    09-21-65*
    09-30-65
    05-13-66
    01-05-67*
    08-28-67
    02-23-68
    03-10-68
    08-21-68
    03-04-69*
    08-01-69*
    01-01-70
    08-01-70*
    09-03-70
    08-01-71*
    08-01-72*

2. Nuclear Weapons
    05-15-50*
    11-12-50
    11-17-50*
    10-07-51*
    08-14-53
    12-26-53*
    01-04-54
    06-02-54
    07-05-54*
    10-04-54*
    01-10-55
    01-19-55*
    01-20-55
    01-22-55*
    02-12-55
    02-13-55*
    02-14-55
    02-25-55*
    03-07-55
    03-17-55*
    03-26-55
    03-29-55
    04-06-55
    04-08-55*
    04-13-55
    04-26-55
    05-02-55*
    05-17-55
    06-05-55
    06-20-55
    06-25-55
    07-02-55
    07-14-55
    07-18-55
    08-06-55*
    08-08-55*
    09-03-55
    09-21-55*
    10-03-55*
    10-19-55
    10-27-55
    11-14-55
    12-09-55
    01-20-56
    03-03-56
    03-20-56*
    03-29-56*
    04-04-56*
    04-12-56*
    04-29-56
    05-21-56
    06-17-56
    06-22-56*

    08-07-56*
    08-13-56*
    09-16-56*
    11-13-56
    11-19-56*
    04-05-57*
    05-03-57
    05-10-57*
    05-15-57*
    06-06-57*
    06-10-57
    06-19-57
    08-06-57*
    08-16-57
    08-17-57
    08-18-57*
    09-10-57*
    09-14-57*
    09-17-57
    09-24-57*
    10-05-57
    10-12-57
    10-16-57*
    10-18-57
    11-09-57
    12-14-57*
    12-21-57
    12-30-57*
    01-11-58*
    01-19-58
    02-06-58
    02-08-58
    02-14-58
    02-15-58
    03-10-58
    03-11-58
    03-12-58
    03-15-58
    03-20-58
    03-20-58
    04-01-58*
    04-07-58*
    04-09-58
    05-11-58
    05-17-58
    05-28-58
    06-22-58
    06-25-58
    07-07-58
    07-07-58
    07-25-58
    08-03-58
    08-08-58
    08-16-58*
    08-22-58*
    09-01-58*
    09-21-58
    09-22-58
    11-07-58
    11-12-58
    12-09-58
    07-22-59
    08-05-59
    09-29-59
    11-07-59
    01-27-59
    01-01-60
    01-16-60*
    01-20-60
    01-21-60
    02-06-60
    05-13-60*
    05-16-60

    05-20-60
    05-28-60
    06-07-60*
    06-25-60
    07-07-60*
    07-28-60
    08-11-60*
    08-13-60*
    09-08-60
    10-20-60
    10-25-60
    12-07-60
    12-12-60
    01-01-61
    06-01-61
    06-09-61
    08-17-61*
    09-01-61*
    09-18-61
    10-03-61
    10-19-61
    12-01-61
    01-01-62
    01-15-62
    01-19-62
    04-03-62*
    04-27-62
    04-28-62*
    06-21-62*
    08-09-62*
    09-15-62
    11-05-62
    11-15-62
    11-29-62
    03-08-63
    07-19-63*
    08-02-63*
    08-03-63*
    08-10-63*
    08-30-63*
    10-19-63*
    11-09-63
    12-30-63
    01-18-64
    01-23-64
    01-29-64
    02-05-64
    03-04-64
    06-25-64
    08-06-64*
    10-22-64*
    11-22-64*
    12-31-64*
    01-01-65
    02-01-65
    02-14-65
    03-09-65
    08-11-65*
    12-24-65
    12-27-65
    01-30-66*
    02-20-66
    08-25-66
    06-22-67*
    05-01-70

3. People's Liberation Arm

    a. Air Force
        03-29-55*
        08-01-57
        06-30-63*
        03-06-64

07-09-64*	06-08-65*	05-01-68	07-03-51*
02-01-65	07-04-65	05-03-68	07-29-51
04-05-65	07-13-65	06-02-68	08-08-51
08-22-67*	07-30-65	08-01-68*	08-11-51*
09-09-67*	09-21-65*	08-15-68	08-16-51
08-21-68	09-24-65	08-18-68	08-18-51
	09-26-65	08-21-68	08-26-51*
b. Army	11-30-65	08-28-68	09-12-51*
09-25-50*	01-08-66	09-07-68	09-20-51
11-17-50*	01-16-66	09-25-68	09-23-51
02-17-54*	01-18-66*	10-01-68	09-30-51
07-24-54*	02-02-66	11-25-68	10-20-51
01-04-55	02-09-66	12-14-68	10-25-51
01-21-55*	02-22-66	01-01-69	11-07-51
01-24-55*	04-22-66	02-17-69	11-09-51
01-25-55	05-13-66	03-04-69*	11-10-51
02-16-55	06-08-66*	08-01-69*	11-12-51
03-29-55*	07-01-66	10-01-69	11-14-51*
04-19-55	07-28-66*	08-01-70*	11-20-51
08-01-55	08-01-66*	04-24-72	11-27-51*
09-28-55*	08-28-66*	09-29-73	12-25-51*
04-22-56	09-15-66*	09-09-75	12-26-51*
12-31-56	09-19-66	10-01-75	01-01-52
08-01-57*	09-24-66*	10-19-75*	01-07-52*
11-28-57*	10-12-66		01-19-52*
09-09-58	10-22-66	4. Conscription	02-14-52
09-28-58	11-08-66*	11-01-54*	02-20-52
09-30-58	11-18-66*	01-04-55	02-20-52*
10-11-58	01-25-67*	02-15-55*	02-23-52
03-31-59*	02-02-67	04-19-55*	02-26-52*
04-25-59*	02-10-67*	07-05-55	03-01-52*
05-17-59	02-17-67	08-01-55*	03-08-52*
04-19-60	03-02-67	01-17-57	03-19-52*
05-28-60*	03-12-67		04-07-52*
02-15-61*	04-21-67	5. Military Training	04-29-52*
08-01-62*	05-04-67	03-29-55	05-06-52*
10-14-62	05-07-67*	03-07-56*	05-09-52*
10-27-62	05-12-67*	08-01-57	05-14-52
12-30-62	05-16-67*	02-18-64*	05-16-52*
01-28-63	05-22-67	11-17-64	06-22-52*
05-08-63*	05-29-67	06-08-65	06-25-52*
06-01-63	05-31-67	09-15-66	06-28-52*
09-25-63	07-26-67*	05-16-67*	06-29-52*
10-08-63*	07-29-67*	08-11-67	07-01-52
10-13-63	07-30-67	08-28-67	07-09-52
11-11-63	07-30-67		07-11-52*
11-21-63	07-31-67*	6. Korean War	07-15-52*
01-01-64	08-02-67	06-27-50*	07-27-52*
02-01-64*	08-04-67*	11-12-50*	07-28-52
02-02-64*	08-08-67	11-17-50	08-11-52
02-18-64*	08-11-67*	11-20-50*	08-12-52*
02-20-64	08-13-67	11-25-50*	08-15-52*
02-23-64*	08-17-67	12-02-50*	09-15-52
02-24-64	08-22-67	12-03-50	10-02-52
03-06-64*	08-28-67*	12-07-50*	10-09-52*
03-07-64	09-02-67*	12-13-50	10-13-52
03-08-64	09-09-67	12-17-50	10-17-52
03-10-64*	09-09-67*	12-21-50	10-18-52*
03-18-64	09-16-67	12-27-50	10-25-52*
03-24-64	10-12-67	01-05-51*	11-06-52*
03-26-64*	11-02-67	01-15-51	11-11-52
04-02-64	12-04-67	01-24-51	11-29-52*
04-04-64*	12-07-67	01-26-51	12-09-52*
04-05-64*	01-01-68*	02-03-51*	12-14-52
09-10-64*	01-07-68	02-19-51	12-16-52*
11-17-64	01-30-68	03-17-51	12-18-52*
01-01-65	02-05-68	03-29-51*	12-23-52*
02-01-65	02-07-68	05-30-51*	12-23-52
02-15-65	02-23-68	06-02-51*	12-25-52
02-26-65	03-10-68	06-15-51	12-27-52
03-01-65	03-30-68	06-22-51	01-01-53
03-29-65	04-12-68	06-22-51*	01-01-53
04-09-65	04-20-68	06-25-51*	01-24-53*

163

02-02-53*	10-25-58	12-07-53	07-31-52*
02-08-53*	12-24-59	01-14-54	01-11-52*
02-10-53	04-29-60*	02-17-54	04-26-52
02-24-53*	06-25-60*	03-15-54	01-01-53*
03-01-53*	10-25-60*	06-25-54	12-24-53*
03-12-53*	06-25-61*	07-27-54	02-01-54*
04-05-53*	07-10-61	09-09-54*	02-17-54
04-12-53*	06-25-62*	09-22-54*	07-24-54
04-14-53	06-06-63	10-25-54	01-04-55
04-29-53	06-25-64*	11-01-54	01-24-55*
05-16-53*	06-25-65*	10-12-55*	01-25-55*
05-31-53*	08-03-65	06-28-57	02-15-55
06-09-53*	10-25-65*	02-08-58	04-25-55*
06-21-53*	04-06-66	02-20-58*	04-30-55
06-23-53	06-25-66*	02-21-58*	08-17-55*
06-25-53*	06-24-70	02-22-58	10-15-55*
07-10-53*	06-25-70*	03-13-58	02-10-56*
07-21-53*	07-27-70	05-05-58	02-12-56
07-28-53*	10-25-70*	06-25-58	03-07-56
08-12-53*		08-03-58	08-01-56*
08-15-53*	7. Chinese People's	10-25-58*	08-23-56
08-25-53*	Volunteers	11-22-58	11-18-56*
09-03-53	11-12-50*	10-29-59	01-17-57*
09-13-53*	11-17-50	12-24-59	08-01-57
09-14-53*	11-20-50*	04-29-60	02-19-58*
09-24-53*	11-25-50*	10-25-60*	02-04-59*
09-27-53	12-02-50*	07-10-61	04-25-59
10-05-53*	12-03-50	06-25-62	05-28-59*
10-05-53*	12-07-50*	06-06-63	01-28-60*
10-09-53*	12-13-50	10-25-65*	02-15-61
10-13-53*	12-17-50	04-06-66	09-24-66*
10-25-53*	12-21-50	08-25-66	05-16-67*
10-27-53*	12-27-50	06-25-70	08-28-67*
10-31-53*	01-15-51	10-25-70*	05-17-68
11-03-53*	05-30-51	07-27-71	08-01-69*
11-12-53*	06-02-51	06-25-72	01-01-70
11-13-53*	06-25-51	07-27-73	08-01-70
11-18-53	07-03-51	06-25-74	
11-24-53	07-20-51	06-25-75	L. International
11-28-53*	08-11-51	10-25-75*	Relations
12-01-53	08-26-51		
12-01-53*	09-12-51	8. Militia	1. General International
12-05-53*	09-23-51*	04-28-54	Relations
12-07-53*	09-30-51	10-01-58	10-08-49*
12-08-53	10-20-51	04-19-60*	10-17-49
12-15-53*	10-25-51	11-17-64*	04-05-50
12-26-53*	11-09-51	09-21-65*	07-31-55
01-08-54*	11-10-51	09-29-73*	09-03-55
01-10-54*	11-14-51		10-01-55
01-20-54*	11-20-51	9. Army Propaganda	06-28-56*
01-27-54*	11-27-51	Activities	07-18-56*
01-30-54*	12-25-51	07-08-51	08-26-56*
02-22-54	01-01-52	02-26-52*	09-27-56
03-08-54	01-19-52	01-01-55	09-29-56
03-15-54	02-17-52*	08-01-57	10-01-56*
04-03-54*	02-20-52	02-01-64*	10-06-56
04-21-54	02-23-52	11-17-64	10-15-56
05-12-54	02-26-52	03-01-65*	10-21-56
06-18-54*	04-29-52	11-08-65*	04-12-57
06-25-54	06-25-52	08-01-69*	06-28-57*
06-27-54	07-11-52	01-01-70	07-17-57
07-09-54	08-15-52	06-24-70	01-01-62
07-10-54*	10-09-52	08-01-70	04-03-62
07-16-54	10-25-52*	05-07-71*	04-18-62
07-26-54	11-29-52	06-20-71	03-09-63*
07-27-54*	12-25-52	01-01-74	04-21-66
09-09-54*	01-01-53	01-01-75	08-15-66
09-22-54*	02-08-53		
10-25-54*	09-27-53	10. Civil-Military	2. International Law
03-06-55*	10-05-53	Relations	12-24-53
10-12-55*	10-05-53	02-02-50*	04-21-54
06-28-57	10-25-53*	12-14-50*	05-20-54
09-22-58	12-05-53	07-22-51*	07-16-54

165

07-26-54	07-24-62	04-04-55	10-07-59
07-28-54	10-06-62*	04-18-55*	11-07-59*
08-20-54	10-10-62*	04-22-55	01-01-60
08-26-54	10-14-62*	04-23-55	02-02-60
08-29-54	10-27-62*	04-26-55	02-14-60
10-11-54	01-28-63	08-24-55	03-06-60
10-21-54	02-08-63	09-21-55	04-11-60*
12-05-54	06-04-63	12-21-55	04-17-60*
01-29-55	06-08-63	12-27-55	04-18-60*
01-31-55	06-16-63*	01-02-56*	04-27-60
02-01-55	09-12-63	01-05-56	04-30-60
02-05-55	10-13-63	01-26-56	05-20-60
02-09-55	10-19-63	02-13-56	06-30-60*
02-16-55	10-23-63	02-19-56	07-06-60*
02-18-55	10-25-63*	02-21-56*	07-12-60
03-01-55	11-21-63	03-23-56	07-16-60*
03-03-55	11-22-63	04-16-56	07-29-60
03-07-55	01-01-64	04-18-56	08-17-60
03-26-55	01-29-64	04-24-56	08-22-60
04-08-55	04-09-64	05-19-56	09-02-60
04-08-55	04-11-64*	06-01-56	10-01-60
04-12-55	04-16-64*	06-09-56*	10-05-60
04-13-55	05-12-64	06-14-56	10-18-60
05-15-55	07-05-64*	06-18-56	10-28-60
06-28-55	07-20-64*	06-23-56	11-28-60*
10-20-55	10-14-64	07-30-56*	12-07-60*
02-04-56	02-09-65	08-17-56	12-12-60*
03-10-56	02-10-65	08-20-56	12-15-60
03-20-56	03-25-65*	08-24-56	12-17-60
04-07-56	04-07-65*	09-17-56	12-20-60*
07-01-56*	04-12-65*	09-21-56	12-22-60
07-24-56	04-15-65*	11-03-56*	01-10-61
08-11-56	04-16-65	11-05-56	01-22-61
08-14-56	04-21-65*	11-19-56	04-04-61
11-08-56	04-21-65*	11-21-56	04-27-61
09-23-57*	05-14-65	11-23-56	05-04-61
04-03-58*	05-25-65*	01-18-57	08-14-61*
04-15-58*	09-11-65	01-30-57	09-19-61*
04-17-58	03-04-69	02-01-57	09-09-61*
05-17-58	11-08-70	03-30-57	12-01-61*
08-05-58	11-20-70*	04-07-57	12-02-61*
09-07-58*		04-12-57	04-01-62
09-12-58*	3. Struggle against Imperi-	04-20-57	05-01-62
09-15-58*	alism and Colonialism	04-24-57*	08-18-62
09-22-58*	01-19-50	08-03-57	10-20-62*
09-28-58*	09-20-50	08-31-57	11-15-62*
10-10-58*	09-23-50	09-17-57	02-04-63*
10-11-58*	09-24-50	10-04-57	02-13-63*
12-12-58	12-03-50	10-28-57	03-04-63
12-14-58	12-07-50	11-06-57	03-06-63
09-16-59	12-13-50	11-25-57*	04-18-63*
01-15-60	12-17-50	12-26-57*	04-20-63
05-27-60*	12-21-50	01-04-58*	04-21-63
08-13-60	01-01-51	03-14-58	04-26-63
08-28-60	01-08-51	04-24-58*	05-23-63
12-22-60	02-21-51*	04-25-58*	07-05-63*
02-24-60	05-28-51	06-08-58*	09-23-63
04-12-61	06-01-51	09-04-58	09-29-63
04-26-61	06-24-51	09-16-58	11-10-63
04-27-61	07-20-51	09-30-58	11-23-63
05-18-61	11-12-51	10-14-58	12-14-63*
05-19-61	11-20-51	11-12-58*	12-23-63*
05-24-61	12-13-51	01-01-59*	12-30-63*
07-14-61	05-01-52	01-24-59	01-01-64
07-20-61	02-21-53*	01-28-59	01-13-64
11-30-61	12-30-53	03-18-59*	01-18-64*
12-30-61*	04-04-54	04-15-59*	01-21-64*
06-07-62	04-13-54	04-25-59*	01-23-64
06-21-62	04-28-54	05-01-59	01-29-64*
06-23-62	05-27-54	08-06-59	02-01-64
06-25-62	10-01-54	08-29-59	03-02-64
07-12-62	02-21-55*	09-12-59	04-10-64
07-19-62*	03-12-55	09-21-59*	04-15-64*

04-18-64*
05-16-64
05-20-64*
06-11-64
06-15-64
06-19-64
06-25-64
07-23-64*
08-21-64
09-01-64*
09-29-64*
10-03-64
10-14-64*
10-24-64*
10-30-64
11-06-64
11-15-64
01-01-65
04-18-65*
05-20-65
06-26-65
06-29-65*
09-26-65
11-22-65
05-26-66*
06-27-66
07-23-66
08-01-66
08-19-66
09-08-66
06-18-67
07-05-67
10-20-67
02-03-68
05-27-68*
06-18-68
08-02-70*
08-06-70
09-14-70*
02-12-71
08-19-71
10-06-71
11-02-71
11-15-71
11-16-71
12-12-71*
12-16-71
12-27-71
01-14-72
02-17-72
04-02-72
04-17-72
05-14-72
05-25-72*
06-25-72*
06-30-72
09-02-72
09-14-72
09-28-72
10-16-72
11-08-72
11-15-72
11-25-72
11-30-72
12-09-72
01-10-73
01-26-73*
03-25-73
04-19-73*
05-25-73*
06-20-73
07-27-73
08-25-73*
09-13-73*
09-16-73
09-29-73
10-01-73
11-06-73*
12-08-73*
02-21-74*
02-25-74*
03-22-74
03-24-74*
04-09-74
04-30-74*
05-05-74
05-06-74*
05-11-74*
05-17-74*
05-28-74
06-20-74
06-23-74
06-30-74*
07-22-74*
08-17-74
08-23-74
09-02-74*
09-08-74*
09-17-74*
10-04-74*
11-05-74
11-10-74*
12-16-74*
12-19-74*
01-07-75*
01-09-75*
01-22-75
02-20-75*
02-27-75
03-12-75
04-01-75
04-18-75
05-20-75
06-07-75
06-11-75
06-27-75
06-30-75
08-03-75*
10-06-75
11-07-75
11-11-75
11-14-75
11-16-75
11-20-75
12-21-75

4. International Conferences
   and Organizations

   a. International
      Conferences

      1. Second World Peace
         Conference
         11-17-50*
         11-25-50*
         12-27-50*

      2. Five-Power Peace
         Conference
         03-23-51
         08-10-51
         05-14-52*
         06-04-52*
         07-28-52
         09-21-52
         10-02-52*
         10-13-52*
         10-25-52
         11-06-52
         10-09-53*
         11-18-53*
         01-10-54
         01-27-54
         01-30-54
         02-14-54
         02-22-54*
         02-23-54*
         03-08-54*
         04-21-54*
         05-12-54*
         05-20-54
         06-18-54*

      3. International Economic
         Conference
         04-05-52*

      4. Congress of Peoples
         for Peace
         12-14-52*
         12-23-52*

      5. Stockholm Conferences
         06-27-54*
         07-25-58*
         08-16-58

      6. Geneva Conferences
         07-10-54
         07-22-54*
         07-26-54
         07-27-54
         07-27-54
         08-20-54
         04-12-55*
         06-20-55
         06-22-55
         06-24-55
         06-25-55
         06-28-55
         07-09-55*
         07-18-55*
         07-21-55
         07-26-55*
         08-06-55*
         08-07-55*
         08-08-55*
         08-15-55
         08-16-55
         09-02-55
         09-03-55
         09-18-55*
         09-21-55
         09-24-55
         10-03-55
         10-14-55*
         10-27-55*
         10-31-55*
         11-03-55
         11-06-55
         11-14-55*
         11-19-55*
         01-02-56
         02-13-56
         02-14-56
         03-24-56
         04-29-56
         07-18-56
07-24-56
08-08-56
11-23-56
07-20-57
02-22-58
03-09-58
07-11-58*
07-24-58
09-01-58
02-19-59*
03-11-59*
04-07-59*
07-17-59
07-20-59*
07-24-59
09-17-59*
10-07-59
05-16-60*
05-20-60*
05-22-60
06-07-60
06-13-60
07-07-60*
07-13-60*
07-17-60*
07-20-60*
12-25-60
01-15-61
02-10-61*
02-25-61
04-27-61*
05-18-61*
05-19-61
05-24-61*
05-26-61
06-14-61
06-17-61
06-23-61
07-20-61
08-09-61
09-01-61
11-30-61
12-21-61*
01-03-62
01-19-62
02-25-62
04-03-62*
04-28-62
06-07-62
06-25-62
07-12-62*
07-19-62*
07-24-62*
08-20-62
10-06-62
03-06-63
03-11-63
04-05-63
04-17-63
04-27-63
05-01-63
05-07-63
05-16-63
06-04-63
06-16-63*
07-19-63
11-22-63
04-09-64
04-22-64
05-01-64
05-13-64
05-29-64
06-15-64

07-05-64
07-20-64*
08-29-64
10-06-64
11-03-64
11-22-64
11-25-64
01-14-65
03-29-65
04-15-65*
05-03-65
05-07-55
07-20-65*
02-02-66
07-05-66
07-24-66
09-27-67
07-20-71*

7. *Soviet-European Conference*
08-10-54*
11-30-54*
12-04-54*

8. *London Nine-Power Conference*
10-07-54
10-10-54

9. *Asian-African Conferences*
01-05-55*
02-21-55
04-04-55*
04-13-55*
04-13-55*
04-17-55
04-18-55*
04-22-55
04-23-55*
04-26-55*
05-26-55
05-30-55*
06-02-55
06-25-55
07-05-55
08-24-55
08-26-55
09-21-55
09-24-55
10-20-55
11-06-55
01-02-56
02-13-56
02-14-56
02-21-56
03-23-56
04-11-56*
04-18-56*
05-19-56
06-01-56*
06-09-56*
06-28-56*
07-05-56
07-18-56
08-20-56
10-18-56
11-05-56
01-24-57
02-07-57
04-18-57*
04-24-57

08-13-57
09-10-57
07-19-57
12-26-57*
12-30-57
01-04-58
04-24-58
07-24-58
10-14-58*
12-02-58
02-10-59*
03-20-59
04-18-59*
09-23-59
01-24-60
02-02-60*
04-11-60*
04-17-60*
04-18-60*
01-26-61*
04-04-61
04-16-61*
06-13-61
06-16-61
04-18-62*
12-31-62
01-02-63*
01-08-63*
01-28-63
02-04-63*
02-13-63*
02-27-63
02-28-63
03-01-63
03-04-63
04-04-63
04-12-63
04-15-63
04-17-63
04-18-63*
04-21-63
04-26-63
05-03-63*
12-14-63
12-18-63
12-23-63*
12-30-63
01-18-64
02-01-64
02-04-64
02-05-64
02-20-64
02-26-64
03-03-64
04-10-64*
04-18-64*
05-20-64
10-06-64
11-05-64
11-13-64
01-30-65
02-17-65
02-25-65
03-02-65
03-09-65
04-18-65*
05-20-65*
06-03-65
06-10-65
06-20-65*
06-29-65*
07-18-65
07-27-65

07-29-65
09-11-65
09-27-65
10-23-65*
10-29-65*
11-04-65*
01-18-66*
04-26-66*
06-27-66*
07-10-66*
06-18-67*

10. *Bangkok Conference*
03-01-55*
03-07-55

11. *Moscow Congresses of Communists and Workers*
03-26-55*
05-09-55
03-29-56
11-25-57*
05-05-58
05-26-58*
05-29-58
06-04-58
06-20-58
11-19-58
02-06-60*
01-22-61*
02-01-61
03-08-61
12-01-61*
11-15-62*
11-28-62
01-27-63*
03-08-63

12. *Warsaw Pact Conferences*
05-12-55*
05-17-55*
11-03-56
03-30-57
09-28-58
09-30-58

13. *Helsinki Conference*
07-02-55*

14. *World Congress of Mothers*
07-14-55*

15. *Inter-Parliamentary Union Conference*
08-30-55*

16. *Asian Countries Conference*
04-06-55*

17. *Colombo Conferences*
03-23-56
06-10-57*
06-19-57*
12-10-62*
12-31-62
01-28-63*
03-05-63*
04-03-63
04-21-63
04-27-63

05-01-63
05-27-63
10-13-63*

18. *London Disarmament Conferences*
04-12-56
08-10-56
08-14-56
08-17-56
08-25-56*
09-21-56
08-06-57*
08-17-57*
07-31-58*

19. *Japan Disarmament Conferences*
08-13-56*
08-18-57*
08-22-58*
08-05-59*
08-11-60*
08-17-61*
08-09-62*
08-10-63*
08-06-64*
08-11-65*

20. *World Youth Festivals*
08-11-57*
08-06-59*

21. *Conferences of Independent African States and African Heads of State*
04-25-58*
09-02-60*
01-03-61*
05-28-63*
12-30-63
06-20-74*

22. *Baghdad Pact Conference*
07-31-58*

23. *Accra Conference*
12-15-58*

24. *Wellington Conference*
04-12-59*

25. *East-West Ministers Conference*
05-16-59

26. *Bucharest Conference*
06-29-60*

27. *OAS Conferences*
09-01-60*
07-29-64*
01-23-71*

28. *Latin America-Mexico Conference*
03-13-61*

29. *All-African People's Conference*
04-02-61*

30. Conferences of Non-
    Aligned Nations
    09-09-61*
    09-13-61
    04-12-63
    10-14-64*
    11-15-64
    09-14-70*
    09-13-73*

31. Niteroi Congress
    04-04-63*

32. Addis Ababa Conferences
    02-01-64
    05-25-73*

33. Japan Peace Conference
    03-04-64*

34. Pyongyang Economic
    Conference
    06-25-64*

35. African Summit
    Conferences
    07-23-64*
    08-03-75*

36. Peking Science
    Conferences
    08-21-64*
    09-01-64*
    07-23-66*
    08-01-66*

37. Arab Summit
    Conference
    09-14-64*

38. Indochina People's
    Conference
    02-15-65*
    02-25-65*
    03-12-65*

39. Honolulu Conference
    07-30-65
    02-12-66*
    02-15-66

40. Geneva Indochina
    Conferences
    04-30-70*
    07-20-71*
    04-25-72*
    07-20-72
    04-24-74

41. Paris Vietnam Peace
    Talks
    07-04-71*
    01-28-73
    03-01-73
    03-03-73*
    04-03-73

42. Asian Ping-Pong
    Founding Conference
    05-09-72*
    09-02-72
    09-14-72*

b. International Red Cross
    03-19-52
    06-29-52
    08-11-52*
    08-12-52
    09-14-55
    11-02-57*
    11-09-57

c. International Federation
    of Democratic Youth
    09-24-50*
    08-09-54*

d. International Scientific
    Commission Investi-
    gating Germ Warfare
    09-15-52*

e. International Union of
    Students
    04-25-51*
    09-04-58*
    09-16-58*

f. International Women's
    Organizations
    10-13-49*
    06-25-52
    06-07-53*
    04-24-56*
    06-14-56*
    06-08-58*

g. NATO
    12-21-57*

h. SEATO
    12-14-54
    03-10-58*
    03-12-58
    03-15-58*
    06-05-60*
    04-28-64*

i. United Nations
    11-27-49*
    01-05-50
    06-29-50
    07-24-50
    08-07-50*
    08-15-50
    08-28-50
    08-28-50*
    09-01-50
    09-19-50*
    09-23-50*
    09-25-50
    09-27-50*
    10-09-50*
    11-20-50
    11-27-50
    12-03-50*
    12-13-50
    12-14-50
    12-17-50*
    12-23-50*
    12-27-50*
    12-27-50
    02-08-51
    02-19-51
    02-28-51*
    03-04-51*

04-27-51
06-25-51
07-03-51
08-11-51
08-16-51
09-12-51
11-14-51
11-27-51
12-26-51
01-07-52
02-04-52
02-20-52
02-23-52
03-08-52
03-19-52
06-22-52
06-29-52
10-13-52
10-18-52
11-06-52
11-29-52
12-16-52
12-23-52
02-24-53
03-12-53*
04-05-53
04-12-53*
04-14-53
04-29-53
06-25-53
07-28-53
08-14-53
08-25-53*
08-28-53
09-14-53
09-27-53
10-09-53
10-31-53
11-12-53
12-05-53
12-07-53*
12-08-53
12-15-53
01-27-54
08-29-54
10-04-54
10-11-54
10-21-54*
10-29-54
12-05-54
01-29-55
01-31-55*
02-01-55*
02-05-55*
02-18-55
02-25-55*
03-17-55*
06-20-55*
06-25-55
06-28-55*
07-14-55
07-26-55*
08-05-55
08-12-55
09-21-55*
09-24-55*
10-12-55
10-27-55
11-14-55
11-18-55*
11-21-55*
12-09-55
12-27-55

12-30-55
03-03-56
06-03-56
06-22-56
11-05-56
11-08-56
11-13-56*
11-13-56
11-14-56*
12-06-56
01-12-57
01-15-57*
05-21-57
09-06-57
09-14-57*
09-16-57*
09-24-57
09-24-57*
09-27-57*
10-05-57
10-16-57
12-17-57
01-04-58
02-22-58
04-01-58
07-01-58
07-17-58
07-21-58
07-22-58
07-23-58*
07-25-58
07-27-58
08-07-58
08-08-58
08-10-58*
08-16-58*
08-17-58*
08-19-58*
08-21-58*
08-23-58*
11-22-58
02-05-59
02-19-59
07-11-59
09-21-59
10-24-59*
10-29-59
12-24-59
01-16-60
04-29-60
06-07-60
06-10-60
07-20-60
07-29-60*
08-22-60*
09-15-60
09-28-60
09-29-60
10-12-60*
10-19-60*
11-12-60
11-25-60*
12-09-60*
12-11-60
12-12-60
01-03-61
01-15-61
01-26-61
02-16-61
02-18-61*
02-25-61
03-03-61*
03-09-61*

03-16-61*
04-02-61
04-15-61
05-26-61
06-24-61
06-30-61*
07-11-61*
07-14-61*
09-09-61
09-13-61
09-22-61*
10-03-61
10-19-61
12-02-61
12-12-61
12-20-61
12-22-61*
12-30-61*
01-15-62
01-17-62
02-14-62
06-25-62
07-02-62
08-18-62
11-05-62
11-18-62
11-29-62
12-23-62
12-24-62*
01-19-63
02-04-63
04-15-63
04-21-63
04-21-63
05-01-63
05-07-63
08-30-63
09-29-63*
10-19-63
10-25-63*
12-01-63
12-18-63*
12-18-63*
01-01-64
01-18-64
01-29-64
01-29-64
02-01-64
02-04-64
02-26-64
03-02-64
04-15-64
05-06-64
05-16-64
06-24-64
06-25-64
07-01-64
08-08-64*
08-15-64
08-29-64
11-22-64
11-25-64
12-04-64*
01-06-65*
01-10-65*
01-17-65
01-23-65*
01-30-65
02-10-65
02-25-65*
03-09-65
04-12-65*
04-28-65

05-18-65*
05-20-65
05-20-65
06-26-65*
08-02-65
08-03-65
08-07-65*
09-14-65*
09-18-65
09-27-65
09-28-65
09-30-65*
10-05-65
10-23-65
10-25-65
10-29-65
11-18-65
11-19-65*
12-01-65*
12-19-65
12-21-65*
12-25-65*
12-27-65*
01-18-66
02-02-66*
09-24-66*
10-10-66*
12-02-66*
05-29-67*
06-06-67
06-11-67*
06-22-67
09-27-67*
09-27-67
11-10-70
12-03-70
12-18-70
01-07-71
02-12-71
06-01-71
10-06-71
10-28-71*
12-27-71*
01-01-72
01-31-72
02-03-72*
02-17-72
05-14-72
08-02-72*
08-28-72*
09-09-72
10-01-72
04-11-73
07-27-73
10-26-73
11-09-73
11-24-73*
02-25-74
04-09-74*
05-05-74*
09-09-75
10-25-75

j. World Federation of
   Scientific Workers
   04-04-56*
   09-27-63*

k. World Federation of
   Trade Unions
   10-13-49*
   05-01-52
   06-04-52

06-25-52
10-04-57*
10-18-57*
06-10-60*
06-02-61

1. World Peace Council
   10-02-49*
   05-15-50*
   08-14-50
   11-17-50
   02-28-51*
   03-04-51*
   04-12-51*
   11-12-51*
   02-23-52
   04-07-52
   05-06-52
   07-09-52*
   07-28-52*
   06-23-53*
   12-01-53
   12-01-53*
   06-02-54*
   11-27-54*
   01-22-55
   02-13-55
   06-22-55*
   04-12-56*
   08-07-56
   04-05-57*
   06-19-57*
   08-16-58
   05-16-59*
   07-16-60*

M. Africa

1. North Africa

   a. General North Africa
      04-04-55
      04-13-55
      04-18-55
      04-26-55
      12-26-57
      01-04-58
      12-01-58
      12-15-58*
      01-28-59
      04-05-59
      01-21-60
      04-30-60
      08-28-60
      12-07-60
      12-17-60
      12-20-60*
      05-01-61
      06-02-61*
      02-04-63*
      02-13-63*
      04-15-63*
      05-28-63
      11-10-63
      11-23-63
      12-01-63*
      01-13-64*
      02-06-64*
      03-03-64
      04-10-64
      04-15-64*
      04-18-64
      07-23-64*

09-14-64*
03-21-65
04-18-65*
11-04-65
04-15-66*

b. Algeria
   11-13-56
   11-14-56
   03-30-58*
   05-23-58*
   08-19-58
   09-23-58*
   12-01-58*
   12-01-58*
   12-03-58
   12-21-58*
   02-19-59
   04-05-59
   03-12-60
   04-30-60*
   05-20-60*
   09-14-60
   09-29-60*
   10-06-60*
   11-01-60*
   12-12-60
   12-14-60*
   01-03-61*
   01-26-61*
   03-16-61
   04-02-61*
   05-08-61
   06-30-61
   08-19-61
   09-09-61
   09-13-61
   11-01-61*
   12-02-61*
   03-20-62*
   04-15-62*
   04-18-62
   07-05-62*
   09-31-62*
   11-01-62*
   02-27-63
   04-15-63
   05-01-63
   05-28-63
   07-05-63*
   09-29-63*
   12-01-63
   12-14-63
   12-30-63*
   11-01-64*
   06-29-65*
   10-29-65
   04-07-65
   08-02-72
   02-25-74*

c. Mali
   06-20-60*
   10-18-60*
   10-28-60*
   01-01-61
   01-23-64*
   09-29-64*
   11-05-64*
   12-18-65
   06-20-73*

169

d. Mauritania
   07-27-65*
   10-20-67*

e. Morocco
   02-14-52
   12-23-52
   11-02-58*
   12-14-63
   01-01-64*

f. Niger
   06-07-60*
   07-22-74*

g. Sudan
   01-05-56*
   12-02-58*
   02-01-64*
   05-16-64*
   05-20-64*
   08-06-70*

h. Tunisia
   02-14-52
   12-23-52
   09-09-61
   01-13-64*
   04-01-75*

i. United Arab Republic
   10-31-51*
   02-14-52
   06-02-55*
   08-26-55*
   10-14-55
   02-20-56
   05-19-56*
   06-18-56*
   07-05-56
   07-30-56*
   08-10-56*
   08-11-56*
   08-14-56*
   08-17-56*
   08-24-56
   08-25-56
   09-12-56*
   09-21-56*
   10-18-56
   11-01-56*
   11-02-56*
   11-03-56*
   11-05-56*
   11-07-56
   11-07-56*
   11-08-56*
   11-09-56*
   11-13-56*
   11-13-56*
   11-14-56
   11-17-56*
   11-23-56
   12-02-56
   12-06-56
   12-06-56*
   12-09-56*
   12-25-56*
   01-01-57*
   01-08-57
   04-24-57
   06-18-57*
   07-26-57*

08-17-57*
09-04-57
10-22-57
12-31-57
02-23-58
02-24-58*
05-17-58*
05-20-58
07-17-58
07-21-58*
07-22-58
07-29-58
08-08-58
08-10-58
09-07-58
12-01-58
02-10-59
03-20-59*
03-03-61
04-21-63*
04-26-63*
12-14-63
12-23-63*
04-07-65
12-18-65
05-29-67*
06-06-67
06-11-67
06-15-67
06-05-72*
10-15-73*
10-26-73*

2. Sub-Saharan Africa

   a. General Sub-Saharan Africa
      01-05-55*
      04-04-55
      04-13-55
      04-18-55
      04-22-55
      04-26-55
      04-18-56
      04-18-57
      04-24-57
      12-26-57
      01-01-58
      01-04-58
      04-25-58*
      12-15-58*
      01-24-59
      01-28-59
      04-15-59*
      01-21-60
      02-02-60*
      04-30-60
      07-20-60
      08-28-60
      09-10-60
      11-25-60
      11-28-60*
      12-07-60
      12-20-60*
      04-02-61*
      04-15-61*
      04-16-61*
      05-01-61
      06-02-61*
      12-02-61*
      12-12-61
      04-15-62*
      12-09-62

02-04-63*
02-13-63*
04-15-63*
05-28-63*
07-05-63
10-25-63
11-10-63
11-23-63
12-01-63*
12-14-63*
01-21-64
02-06-64*
03-03-64
04-10-64
04-15-64*
04-18-64
07-23-64*
09-14-64*
10-14-64
04-18-65*
11-04-65
12-18-65
04-15-66*
11-28-67
09-14-70
05-25-72*
05-25-73*
08-25-73
09-07-73
04-09-74
05-05-74
06-20-74*
08-03-75*

b. Central Africa

   1. Angola
      05-09-61*
      06-24-61*
      06-30-61
      09-09-61
      09-13-61
      04-15-62
      05-28-63
      08-11-63
      02-04-64*
      01-22-75*
      11-14-75*

   2. Cameroon
      02-19-59*
      04-04-71*
      03-25-73*

   3. Chad
      08-17-60*
      11-30-72*

   4. Central African Republic
      08-17-60*
      10-03-64*
      04-15-66

   5. Gabon
      08-17-60*
      04-30-74*
      10-04-74*
      06-27-75*

   6. People's Republic of the Congo
      08-17-60*

02-24-64*
08-15-64*
09-28-64*
10-04-64*
12-18-65
08-29-66*
09-27-67*
07-27-73*
02-27-75*

7. Sao Tome and Principe
   07-18-75*
   12-21-75*

8. Zaire
   01-24-59*
   11-25-59*
   06-30-60*
   07-12-60*
   07-20-60*
   07-29-60*
   07-30-60*
   08-22-60*
   09-02-60*
   07-14-60
   09-15-60*
   09-28-60
   09-29-60
   10-19-60
   11-25-60*
   12-09-60*
   12-12-60
   01-03-61*
   01-15-61*
   01-22-61*
   01-26-61*
   02-16-61*
   02-18-61*
   02-22-61*
   02-25-61
   03-03-61*
   03-16-61*
   04-02-61*
   04-15-61
   05-08-61*
   06-30-61*
   08-19-61*
   09-09-61
   09-13-61
   12-02-61*
   01-17-62*
   04-15-62
   04-18-62
   12-23-62
   04-15-63
   05-28-63
   12-01-63
   05-06-64*
   06-24-64*
   08-15-64*
   11-01-64
   11-28-64*
   12-01-64*
   12-03-64
   12-05-64*
   01-17-65*
   01-10-65
   02-02-65
   02-10-65
   02-17-65
   02-25-65*
   02-25-65

07-12-65
07-18-65
10-29-65
11-29-65
12-18-65
12-21-65
12-27-65
02-20-66
02-20-66
02-23-66
04-15-66
11-28-67*
07-21-70*
01-10-73*
12-16-74*

9. *Zambia*
   10-24-64*
   11-06-64*
   11-15-64
   12-18-65
   08-19-66*
   06-21-67*
   02-21-74*

c. East Africa

1. *Burundi*
   07-02-62*
   12-24-63*
   04-28-64*
   08-02-64*
   02-02-65*

2. *Comoro Islands*
   11-20-75*

3. *Ethiopia*
   02-03-64*
   12-03-70*
   10-06-71*

4. *Kenya*
   12-23-52
   12-12-63*
   12-15-63*

5. *Malagasy Republic*
   06-26-60*
   11-08-72*

6. *Malawi*
   07-06-64*

7. *Mauritius*
   04-17-72*
   09-17-74*

8. *Mozambique*
   05-28-63
   09-14-74*
   02-20-75*
   06-25-75*

9. *Rwanda*
   01-15-61
   07-02-62*
   11-16-71*

10. *Somalia*
    06-26-60*
    07-01-60*
    12-17-60*

01-01-61
08-04-63*
08-11-63*
02-05-64*
02-06-64
07-21-65*
07-29-65*
09-08-66*
05-14-72*

11. *Tanganyika*
    12-09-61*
    12-12-61*
    12-09-62*
    06-11-64*
    06-19-64*
    02-17-65*

12. *Tanzania*
    12-05-64
    02-17-65*
    02-25-65*
    02-25-65
    06-03-65
    06-10-65*
    11-22-65*
    12-18-65
    02-20-66*
    06-18-68*
    03-24-74*

13. *Uganda*
    07-05-59*
    10-09-62*
    10-20-62*
    07-12-65*
    07-18-65*

14. *Zanzibar*
    12-10-63*
    12-13-63*
    06-11-64*
    06-19-64*

d. South Africa

1. *Botswana*
   01-09-75*

2. *Rhodesia*
   04-15-63
   11-09-65*
   11-14-65*
   12-18-65*
   12-27-65
   02-23-66
   04-15-66
   08-19-66
   10-20-67

3. *South Africa*
   08-11-63
   07-21-65
   11-14-65
   12-18-65
   04-15-66

e. West Africa

1. *Dahomey*
   08-07-60*
   11-15-64*
   04-15-66

2. *Gambia*
   02-18-65*
   12-19-74*
   06-11-75*

3. *Ghana*
   03-06-57*
   07-01-60*
   07-06-60*
   01-01-61
   08-14-61*
   08-19-61*
   08-22-61*
   09-09-61
   08-18-62*
   01-24-63*
   01-18-64*
   05-20-65*
   12-18-65
   02-23-66*
   04-15-66

4. *Guinea*
   10-09-58*
   10-05-59*
   09-10-60*
   09-14-60*
   09-15-60
   01-01-61
   09-09-61
   09-13-61*
   05-28-63
   01-29-64*
   09-13-65*
   12-18-65
   10-22-70*
   02-09-72*
   01-26-73*
   10-01-73*
   03-22-74*
   09-06-74*

5. *Ivory Coast*
   08-07-60*

6. *Liberia*
   03-03-61

7. *Nigeria*
   10-01-60*
   02-12-71*
   09-08-74*

8. *Senegal*
   12-12-71*
   05-06-74*

9. *Sierra Leone*
   04-27-61*
   11-06-73*

10. *Togo*
    04-28-60*
    09-28-72*
    09-02-74*

11. *Upper Volta*
    08-07-60*
    04-15-66
    09-16-73*

N. **North America**

1. *Canada*
   10-18-52
   11-21-55
   11-09-56
   06-23-61
   06-07-62
   05-16-63
   05-11-65
   09-27-67
   05-27-68
   10-15-70*
   10-10-73*

2. *The Caribbean*

   a. General Caribbean
      05-01-61
      07-26-61*
      02-27-63*
      01-21-64
      01-01-65
      08-25-73
      09-07-73
      04-09-74
      05-05-74

   b. Cuba
      08-05-58
      01-04-59*
      01-23-59*
      07-14-59
      03-02-60*
      03-20-60
      07-17-60*
      08-28-60
      09-29-60*
      10-06-60
      10-12-60
      10-19-60
      11-17-60*
      11-19-60*
      12-01-60*
      12-12-60
      12-26-60*
      01-01-61
      01-01-61*
      03-13-61*
      04-17-61*
      04-21-61*
      04-19-61*
      05-08-61*
      06-01-61
      06-30-61
      09-09-61
      09-22-61*
      10-03-61*
      01-02-62*
      01-15-62
      02-10-62*
      04-18-62
      07-26-62*
      10-24-62*
      10-28-62*
      10-31-62*
      11-01-62
      11-05-62*
      11-15-62
      11-18-62*
      11-29-62*
      12-25-62
      01-02-63*

171

02-27-63*
03-08-63
04-04-63*
04-17-63*
07-26-63*
10-21-63*
10-25-63
01-01-64*
04-17-64*
04-30-64
05-05-64*
07-26-64*
07-29-64*
10-14-64
01-01-65*
02-10-65
04-20-65*
07-24-65
01-01-66*

c. Dominica
04-24-66*

d. Dominican Republic
04-30-64
05-03-65*
05-11-65*
05-14-65*
05-18-65*
07-18-65
11-29-65
12-21-65
12-27-65
01-01-66
01-18-66
02-20-66
02-20-66

e. Haiti
08-05-58*

f. Jamaica
11-25-72*

3. Central America

a. General Central America
09-11-58
01-21-60
03-20-60
08-28-60
11-17-60
12-07-60
12-26-60*
07-26-61
07-26-62
01-02-63
11-10-63
11-23-63
01-21-64
04-17-64*
04-20-65
05-11-65
09-14-70
11-20-70*
08-25-73
09-07-73
04-09-74
05-05-74

b. Guatemala
07-02-54

11-19-60
04-19-61

c. Mexico
03-20-60
03-13-61
05-11-65
02-17-72*
04-19-73*

d. Nicaragua
11-19-60*
04-30-64

e. Panama
01-12-64*
01-20-64*

4. United States

a. Domestic U.S.
10-17-49*
10-24-49*
08-11-52
11-11-52*
01-29-53
06-02-53*
06-21-53*
10-25-53
06-22-54
08-30-54*
10-04-54
02-21-55
12-30-57*
01-19-58*
05-01-58
05-16-58
07-22-58
09-27-58
11-07-58
11-16-58
01-01-59
01-04-59
02-05-59
01-21-60
02-08-60
07-07-60*
11-19-60
01-01-61
05-01-61
06-01-61*
09-05-61
01-15-62*
01-19-62*
04-03-62*
03-08-63*
05-01-63
08-12-63*
08-08-64*
05-14-65
08-03-65
08-19-65*
10-18-65*
11-29-65*
01-19-66*
08-08-66*
05-27-68
04-17-69*
06-25-70
05-20-71

b. General International U.S.
10-02-49
04-22-50
05-15-50
11-17-50
11-25-50*
12-27-50*
08-10-51
10-07-51
11-07-51
11-12-51
04-05-52
07-28-52
10-01-52
10-17-52
12-23-52
03-28-53
11-18-53
12-09-53*
12-26-53
01-04-54
02-14-54
02-17-54
02-22-54
02-23-54
03-08-54*
06-02-54
07-02-54
07-05-54
07-26-54*
07-27-54
10-04-54*
11-07-54
01-01-55
01-10-55*
01-19-55
01-20-55
01-22-55*
02-13-55*
02-25-55
03-17-55
04-04-55
04-06-55
04-22-55
04-26-55
05-02-55*
05-12-55
05-17-55
06-20-55*
06-22-55
06-28-55
07-02-55
07-14-55
08-06-55
08-07-55
08-08-55
08-30-55
09-03-55
09-21-55
09-22-55
10-03-55
10-14-55*
10-27-55*
10-31-55
11-03-55
11-14-55*
11-19-55
11-21-55*
12-09-55
12-30-55
01-02-56
02-01-56

02-14-56
02-19-56
02-21-56
03-20-56*
04-12-56
04-18-56
06-17-56
06-28-56
07-12-56
07-18-56*
08-07-56*
08-13-56*
09-12-56
09-16-56
10-21-56*
11-13-56
11-19-56
12-06-56
12-25-56
01-24-57*
02-02-57
02-14-57
03-28-57
04-05-57
04-15-57
04-18-57
04-24-57
05-15-57*
06-10-57
06-18-57
06-19-57
06-28-57
08-03-57
08-06-57
08-11-57
08-17-57
08-18-57
09-06-57*
09-14-57
09-24-57
09-27-57
10-05-57
10-07-57
10-12-57
10-13-57*
10-16-57*
11-02-57*
11-06-57
11-09-57*
11-09-57
11-25-57*
12-14-57*
12-17-57
12-21-57
12-30-57*
12-31-57
01-01-58
01-04-58*
01-11-58*
01-19-58*
03-11-58*
04-01-58*
04-07-58*
04-24-58*
05-05-58
05-16-58
05-17-58
05-23-58
05-28-58
06-04-58
06-08-58
06-22-58
07-23-58

07-29-58*
07-30-58*
08-05-58*
08-16-58*
08-16-58
08-23-58*
09-01-58*
09-30-58
10-01-58*
10-01-58
10-04-58
11-12-58*
11-19-58*
12-21-58
01-01-59
01-28-59
02-05-59*
02-10-59
03-18-59*
03-31-59
04-02-59*
06-03-59*
06-22-59
07-11-59
07-14-59
08-05-59*
08-05-59*
09-15-59
09-15-59*
09-21-59*
10-03-59
10-12-59*
10-24-59*
11-07-59*
11-25-59
11-27-59*
01-01-60
01-16-60*
01-20-60
01-21-60*
01-22-60*
02-06-60
02-11-60
02-14-60*
04-04-60*
04-17-60
04-18-60*
04-19-60
05-09-60*
05-15-60*
05-16-60*
05-20-60*
05-27-60*
05-28-60*
06-01-60
06-02-60
06-07-60*
06-10-60*
06-29-60
07-01-60*
07-07-60*
07-16-60
07-28-60
08-11-60*
08-13-60*
08-16-60
08-28-60
09-28-60
09-29-60*
10-01-60
10-02-60
10-05-60
10-06-60*

10-19-60*
10-28-60*
11-07-60
11-21-60
12-07-60
12-12-60
12-20-60
01-01-61*
01-22-61
04-13-61
05-01-61
05-08-61*
06-01-61*
07-01-61
07-12-61
07-16-61*
08-17-61*
09-01-61
09-09-61*
09-13-61
09-22-61*
10-01-61
10-10-61
11-08-61
12-01-61*
01-01-62*
01-15-62*
01-19-62*
01-22-62*
04-03-62*
04-18-62*
04-28-62*
06-21-62*
08-01-62
08-09-62*
09-17-62
11-01-62
11-15-62*
12-10-62
12-31-62
01-27-63
02-04-63*
02-13-63
02-27-63*
03-08-63*
03-08-63
03-09-63
04-12-63
04-18-63
05-03-63
05-18-63
06-24-63*
07-13-63
07-19-63*
08-02-63*
08-03-63*
08-10-63
08-11-63
08-30-63*
09-23-63*
09-27-63
10-01-63
10-19-63*
11-10-63
11-23-63
12-18-63*
12-18-63*
01-01-64
01-11-64
01-21-64*
08-06-64
10-01-64
10-11-64*

10-14-64*
10-22-64*
11-05-64
11-07-64
11-22-64*
11-29-64
12-04-64*
01-01-65
01-06-65*
01-10-65*
01-23-65
01-30-65*
02-14-65*
02-25-65*
04-01-65
04-18-65*
05-14-65*
05-16-65*
05-20-65
06-01-65
06-03-65*
06-26-65*
07-18-65
07-29-65
09-02-65*
09-11-65
09-13-65
09-14-65
09-30-65
11-04-65*
11-19-65*
12-01-65
12-21-65*
12-27-65*
01-01-66
01-18-66*
01-18-66
01-30-66
02-20-66
02-23-66
03-27-66*
03-30-66*
04-26-66*
04-28-66
05-01-66
05-15-66
06-25-66
06-27-66*
06-29-66
06-30-66
07-10-66
07-23-66
08-25-66*
08-29-66
09-05-66*
10-01-66
10-08-66
10-19-66
11-10-66
11-29-66
12-07-66
04-30-67
05-14-67
06-18-67
06-22-67*
07-07-67
09-26-67
09-27-67*
10-20-67
10-29-67
11-29-67
01-01-68
05-01-68

09-20-68
09-29-68
10-01-68
11-29-68
03-04-69
04-17-69
06-09-69
08-01-69
08-25-69
10-01-69
11-23-69
11-29-69
01-01-70
07-21-70
08-01-70
09-14-70*
10-01-70
11-29-70
01-01-71
05-01-71
05-20-71*
11-29-71
12-27-71
01-01-72
10-01-72*
01-01-73
09-13-73
10-15-73
10-26-73*
11-29-73
01-01-74
02-25-74
04-09-74*
05-05-74*
10-18-74
11-10-74
01-07-75
01-22-75
05-09-75
08-03-75
10-29-75

c. U.S. and Asia

1. *General U.S. and Asia*
03-18-50
09-18-50*
12-06-50
12-13-50
12-21-50*
12-27-50
03-23-51
02-04-52*
05-14-52
07-07-52*
10-13-52
12-14-52
02-21-53*
09-03-53
03-15-54
06-26-54
07-09-54*
07-24-54
08-15-54
10-01-54
10-19-54
11-01-54
12-02-54
01-04-55
01-05-55
03-29-55
04-04-55*
04-18-55*

173

04-23-55	08-01-71	3. *U.S. and Korea*	08-11-52
07-05-55	09-03-75*	06-27-50*	08-12-52*
08-01-55	11-11-75	06-29-50*	08-15-52*
10-12-55*		07-24-50*	09-15-52
10-20-55*	2. *U.S. and Japan*	08-05-50	10-02-52
11-06-55	01-17-50*	08-07-50	10-09-52*
12-27-55	02-06-50	08-15-50*	10-18-52*
03-24-56	02-16-50	08-28-50*	10-25-52
10-07-56	06-09-50*	08-28-50*	11-06-52
06-23-57*	08-05-50	09-01-50*	11-11-52
06-25-57*	09-03-50*	09-19-50*	11-29-52
03-10-58*	09-18-50*	09-23-50*	12-09-52*
04-17-58	11-27-50*	09-25-50*	12-16-52*
12-04-58	01-28-51	09-27-50*	12-18-52*
12-09-58	04-22-51*	10-09-50*	12-23-52*
12-12-58	05-26-51	11-12-50*	12-23-52
04-18-59	06-15-51	11-17-50	12-25-52
06-25-59	08-16-51*	11-20-50*	12-27-52
07-17-59*	08-29-51	11-25-50*	01-24-53*
01-15-60*	09-10-51*	12-02-50*	02-02-53*
02-01-60	09-12-51*	12-07-50*	02-10-53
03-25-60	09-18-51*	12-13-50*	02-24-53*
04-11-60	09-23-51	12-14-50*	03-01-53*
06-13-60*	05-07-52*	12-17-50*	03-12-53
06-17-60*	09-03-52*	12-21-50*	04-05-53*
06-21-60*	09-21-52	12-23-50	04-12-53*
06-25-60*	10-30-53	12-27-50*	04-14-53
08-03-60	03-13-54	12-27-50*	04-29-53*
10-25-60*	12-30-54*	12-28-50	05-16-53*
02-28-61	02-26-55	01-26-51*	05-31-53*
04-16-61*	04-02-55	02-03-51*	06-09-53*
02-14-62	10-19-55	02-14-51	06-21-53*
04-27-62*	11-20-55	02-19-51	06-23-53
05-04-62*	10-06-56*	03-29-51	06-25-53
06-25-62*	05-23-57	06-02-51	07-10-53*
07-07-62*	07-30-57*	06-22-51*	07-21-53*
09-06-62	05-11-58	06-25-51	07-28-53*
10-04-62	07-07-58*	07-03-51*	08-12-53*
09-15-63*	11-20-58*	07-29-51	08-14-53*
10-13-63	03-06-59*	08-11-51*	08-15-53
11-21-63	03-07-59*	08-26-51*	08-25-53*
03-27-64*	03-19-59	10-20-51*	09-13-53*
12-03-64	04-16-59*	10-25-51	09-14-53*
12-31-64*	04-28-59*	11-09-51	09-24-53*
01-28-65	08-05-59*	11-10-51	10-05-53*
02-01-65*	09-23-59*	11-14-51*	10-05-53*
02-23-65*	10-22-59*	11-27-51*	10-09-53*
03-09-65*	12-03-59*	12-25-51*	10-13-53*
04-07-65*	01-24-60*	12-26-51*	10-25-53*
06-19-65*	02-01-60	01-01-52	10-27-53*
06-25-65*	03-06-60	01-07-52	10-31-53*
07-11-65	05-10-60*	02-14-52	11-03-53*
08-07-65	05-12-60*	02-20-52*	11-12-53*
08-11-65	05-14-60*	02-20-52*	11-13-53
11-08-65*	05-16-60*	02-23-52*	11-24-53
11-15-65*	05-22-60*	02-26-52*	11-28-53*
11-16-65*	05-29-60*	03-01-52*	12-01-53
11-18-65*	06-03-60*	03-08-52*	12-01-53*
12-24-65*	06-05-60*	03-19-52*	12-05-53*
12-25-65*	06-05-60	04-07-52*	12-07-53*
02-20-66*	06-20-60*	04-29-52*	12-08-53
03-29-66*	06-24-60*	05-01-52	12-15-53*
07-11-66*	10-20-60*	05-06-52*	12-26-53*
11-25-66	06-09-61*	05-09-52*	01-08-54*
06-30-67	06-16-61*	05-16-52*	01-10-54*
06-30-67	06-23-61*	06-22-52*	01-20-54*
07-10-67	09-18-61*	06-25-52*	01-27-54*
06-23-70*	12-28-62*	06-29-52*	01-30-54*
06-24-70*	03-04-64*	07-09-52	04-03-54*
06-25-70*	08-24-65	07-11-52*	04-21-54*
07-27-70*	11-28-69*	07-15-52*	05-12-54*
12-18-70*	09-03-70*	07-15-52	06-18-54*
06-25-71	09-18-71*	07-27-52*	06-25-54

175

07-10-54*
07-27-54
09-09-54
09-22-54
10-25-54
03-06-55*
04-13-55
08-12-55
08-15-55
08-18-55
11-18-55
12-24-55
06-03-56*
01-15-57*
06-01-57*
06-28-57
07-27-57*
02-06-58*
02-08-58*
02-20-58*
02-21-58*
02-22-58*
03-13-58*
07-27-58
08-03-58
09-28-58
10-25-58
11-22-58*
06-25-59*
07-17-59
10-29-59*
12-24-59*
04-25-60*
04-29-60*
08-15-60*
11-12-60*
12-11-60*
03-09-61*
05-21-61*
06-25-61*
07-10-61
09-20-61
12-12-61*
06-16-62*
06-23-62*
07-02-62
07-11-62*
10-24-62*
12-24-62*
12-28-62*
02-08-63*
06-06-63*
07-11-63
07-27-63*
09-09-63
09-29-63*
06-05-64*
06-25-64*
02-28-65*
04-17-65*
04-20-65*
06-25-65*
09-08-65*
10-25-65*
04-19-66*
06-25-66*
10-25-70*
04-15-71*
07-11-71*
07-27-71*
09-09-71*
01-29-72*
04-24-72*

06-25-72*
07-09-72*
08-02-72*
09-09-72*
04-11-73*
06-25-73*
07-27-73*
09-09-73*
11-24-73*
06-25-74*
07-04-74*
09-09-74*
04-18-75*
06-25-75*
09-09-75*
10-10-75
10-25-75*

4. *U.S. and P.R.C.*
03-18-50*
04-21-50
08-28-50*
09-18-50*
09-19-50*
09-23-50*
09-25-50*
09-27-50*
10-09-50
11-07-50
11-12-50*
11-17-50
11-20-50*
11-25-50*
11-27-50*
12-01-50
12-02-50*
12-03-50*
12-07-50*
12-13-50*
12-14-50*
12-21-50*
12-26-50
12-27-50*
12-27-50*
12-28-50
12-30-50*
03-21-51*
04-06-51
04-24-51
04-26-51*
04-27-51*
08-18-51*
09-05-51*
12-13-51
06-28-52*
07-16-53
07-28-54*
08-01-54*
09-13-54*
10-11-54
11-25-54
01-08-55
04-08-55*
04-10-55
04-13-55
04-17-55*
04-18-55
09-12-55*
09-24-55*
03-10-56*
04-25-56
07-12-56
08-29-56*

11-10-56
05-10-57*
06-13-57*
09-15-57
07-03-58*
08-16-58*
08-28-58
05-12-60*
05-27-60
09-08-60*
09-30-60
10-12-60*
02-15-61
12-22-61*
08-20-62*
09-15-62*
10-01-62
12-30-62*
06-30-63*
10-25-63*
11-11-63*
11-20-63
01-29-64*
02-20-64
07-01-64*
07-06-64*
07-09-64*
07-15-64*
08-02-64*
04-05-65
04-12-65*
06-27-65
10-01-65
11-15-65*
04-06-66*
04-21-66
05-13-66*
12-02-66*
01-05-67*
07-10-67
09-09-67*
09-10-67
05-01-70
10-15-70
11-08-70
12-03-70
04-04-71
07-27-71*
10-28-71*

5. *U.S. and Taiwan*
01-05-50*
06-29-50*
08-05-50*
08-28-50*
08-28-50*
09-01-50*
09-18-50*
09-19-50*
09-25-50*
09-27-50*
01-23-52
12-24-53*
07-16-54*
07-23-54*
08-20-54
08-26-54*
08-29-54*
09-05-54
10-11-54
10-21-54*
11-20-54*
11-27-54

12-05-54*
12-10-54*
12-28-54*
12-29-54*
01-21-55
01-29-55*
01-31-55
02-01-55
02-05-55*
02-09-55*
02-12-55*
02-16-55
02-18-55*
02-21-55*
02-23-55
03-07-55
04-13-55
04-29-55
06-05-55
10-20-55*
01-20-56*
02-04-56
10-23-56
05-25-57*
05-28-57*
06-01-57*
07-30-57
04-03-58
04-15-58
08-02-58
09-07-58*
09-09-58*
09-11-58*
09-12-58*
09-15-58*
09-21-58*
09-22-58*
09-28-58*
09-30-58*
10-10-58*
10-11-58*
10-21-58*
10-30-58*
07-14-61*
12-22-61
12-30-61*
10-09-62
06-08-63
06-22-63*
11-05-63*
05-12-64*
07-01-64*
06-27-65*
06-27-66*
05-29-71
06-25-71*
07-11-71

6. *U.S. and South Asia*
08-28-53
10-31-54
04-04-55
03-07-59*
12-07-61*
12-20-61*
06-05-62
11-08-62
12-23-62*
07-28-63*
08-22-63*
07-19-65*
09-18-65*

7. U.S. and Southeast
   Asia

11-30-49*	05-18-61*	09-24-64*	01-14-66*
05-19-50	05-18-61*	09-27-64*	01-19-66*
06-29-50	05-19-61*	10-06-64*	01-24-66*
08-19-50	05-24-61*	11-03-64*	01-30-66*
09-02-50	05-26-61*	11-25-64*	02-01-66*
07-24-51	06-10-61*	12-20-64*	02-02-66*
09-02-53	06-14-61*	12-22-64	02-12-66*
12-19-53	06-17-61*	01-02-65*	02-15-66*
05-09-54	06-23-61*	01-06-65*	03-17-66*
07-14-54	07-20-61*	01-14-65*	03-25-66*
07-22-54	08-09-61*	02-09-65*	03-27-66*
09-13-54	10-19-61*	02-10-65*	04-16-66
03-01-55*	11-30-61*	02-12-65*	05-01-66*
03-03-55*	12-19-61*	02-15-65*	07-05-66*
03-13-55	12-21-61*	02-19-65*	07-18-66*
04-04-55	12-21-61	02-25-65*	07-24-66*
04-12-55	01-03-62*	03-01-65*	08-01-66
04-13-55	02-25-62*	03-04-65*	08-07-66
06-24-55*	05-19-62*	03-12-65*	08-08-66
06-25-55	06-07-62*	03-17-65*	09-24-66*
07-09-55*	06-14-62*	03-22-65*	10-10-66*
07-21-55	06-22-62*	03-25-65*	12-15-66*
08-16-55	06-25-62*	03-25-65*	12-20-66*
09-02-55	07-12-62*	03-29-65*	03-19-67*
09-18-55	07-19-62*	04-01-65*	04-27-67
03-03-56	07-24-62*	04-05-65*	05-23-67*
04-07-56	08-19-62	04-07-65	06-08-67*
06-23-56	10-06-62*	04-12-65*	07-21-67*
07-24-56*	10-13-62*	04-12-65*	08-08-67
11-23-56	12-20-62*	04-13-65*	08-22-67*
05-21-57	04-05-63*	04-15-65*	08-29-67*
07-20-57*	04-17-63*	04-16-65*	09-21-67*
08-29-57	04-27-63	04-21-65*	09-27-67*
02-15-58*	05-01-63	04-22-65*	12-19-67*
03-09-58*	05-02-63	04-24-65*	02-02-68*
03-12-58*	05-10-63*	04-28-65*	02-15-68*
03-14-58*	05-16-63*	05-01-65*	03-19-68*
03-15-58	06-04-63*	05-03-65*	08-28-68
05-03-58*	06-16-63*	05-04-65*	02-03-70*
05-17-58*	07-19-63*	05-07-65*	04-30-70*
08-20-58*	09-12-63*	05-20-65*	05-05-70*
08-24-58*	11-04-63*	05-20-65*	06-09-70
01-21-59	11-15-63*	06-05-65*	09-02-70*
02-19-59	11-22-63*	06-11-65*	10-12-70*
03-10-59	12-20-63*	06-20-65*	11-09-70*
03-11-59*	03-04-64*	07-05-65*	11-21-70*
04-07-59*	03-27-64*	07-12-65*	11-22-70*
04-12-59*	04-04-64*	07-13-65*	12-13-70*
05-20-59*	04-09-64*	07-20-65*	12-20-70*
07-20-59	04-22-64*	07-24-65	01-06-71*
09-17-59	04-28-64*	07-30-65*	02-14-71*
06-05-60*	05-01-64*	08-03-65*	03-11-71*
07-13-60*	05-07-64*	08-07-65*	03-23-71*
07-14-60	05-13-64*	09-02-65*	03-28-71*
07-17-60*	05-18-64*	09-21-65	04-25-71*
07-20-60*	05-28-64*	09-27-65	05-05-71*
09-02-60*	05-29-64*	09-28-65*	05-20-71
09-12-60	06-15-64*	10-05-65*	06-06-71*
11-21-60	06-27-64*	10-18-65*	07-04-71*
12-16-60*	07-01-64*	10-23-65	07-20-71*
12-22-60	07-05-64*	10-29-65	08-31-71*
12-25-60*	07-09-64*	11-05-65*	09-02-71*
01-10-61	07-20-64*	11-08-65*	10-12-71*
01-15-61	08-06-64*	11-09-65*	11-09-71*
02-10-61*	08-07-64*	11-18-65	11-20-71*
02-25-61*	08-08-64*	11-19-65	11-28-71*
03-12-61*	08-09-64*	11-29-65*	02-04-72*
04-12-61*	08-15-64	12-09-65*	03-23-72*
04-22-61*	08-27-64*	12-14-65*	04-18-72*
04-26-61*	08-29-64*	12-19-65*	04-25-72*
04-27-61*	09-09-64*	12-19-65*	06-06-72*
	09-09-64*	12-24-65*	06-25-72
	09-20-64*	01-04-66*	07-20-72*

177

07-28-72*
08-04-72*
08-13-72*
09-01-72*
11-01-72*
11-09-72*
12-24-72
12-27-72*
01-28-73*
02-23-73*
03-01-73*
03-03-73*
03-23-73*
04-03-73*
04-11-73*
04-25-73*
06-04-73*
06-06-73*
06-17-73*
07-05-73
09-02-73*
10-12-73*
11-09-73*
11-18-73*
01-27-74*
03-23-74*
04-01-74*
04-07-74*
04-24-74*
06-06-74*
09-02-74*
10-12-74
02-03-75*
03-23-75*
04-18-75*
04-25-75*
05-01-75*
05-20-75*
06-06-75*
08-15-75*
09-02-75
09-22-75*
10-12-75
12-06-75*

d. U.S. and Australia
and New Zealand
10-22-49*

e. U.S. and Europe
10-26-49
11-01-49
02-16-50
11-30-52
07-03-53
04-09-54
05-20-54*
07-28-54
09-15-54
10-07-54
10-10-54
10-29-54
11-16-54
11-30-54
12-04-54
03-26-55*
04-09-55
04-18-55
05-09-55*
05-16-55
05-17-55
06-11-55
12-24-55

12-26-55
01-07-56
07-20-56
11-04-56
11-21-56
12-15-56*
08-16-57*
09-16-57*
09-24-57
06-20-58
07-07-58*
11-30-58
03-05-59
03-14-59
03-20-59
05-16-59
07-09-59
10-07-59*
01-09-60
06-28-61*
08-10-61*
03-25-65
04-09-65*
04-19-75

f. U.S. and Latin America
01-04-59*
01-23-59*
03-02-60*
03-20-60*
07-17-60*
09-01-60*
09-29-60
11-17-60*
11-19-60*
12-01-60*
12-26-60
01-01-61*
03-13-61*
04-17-61*
04-19-61*
04-21-61*
06-30-61*
07-26-61*
08-13-61
09-22-61
10-03-61*
01-02-62*
02-10-62*
07-26-62*
10-24-62*
10-28-62*
10-31-62*
11-05-62*
11-18-62*
11-29-62*
12-25-62
01-02-63*
04-04-63*
04-17-63*
07-26-63*
10-21-63*
01-01-64*
01-12-64*
01-20-64*
04-11-64
04-16-64*
04-17-64*
04-30-64*
05-05-64*
07-26-64*
07-29-64*
12-25-64*

01-01-65*
04-20-65*
04-21-65*
05-03-65*
05-11-65*
05-18-65*
01-01-66
04-24-66*
05-15-66
11-20-70*
01-07-71*
01-23-71*
01-04-71

g. U.S. and Middle East
and North Africa
10-31-51
03-03-56*
06-18-56
08-10-56
08-11-56
08-14-56*
08-17-56
08-25-56
09-21-56
10-20-56
11-02-56
11-07-56*
11-07-56
11-08-56
11-09-56
11-13-56
11-17-56
12-02-56
12-25-56
01-01-57
01-08-57*
01-12-57*
01-20-57
02-20-57*
05-01-57*
07-26-57
08-14-57
08-17-57*
09-04-57*
09-10-57*
09-14-57
09-15-57*
10-04-57
10-18-57*
10-22-57*
10-28-57
11-04-57
02-24-58
03-30-58
05-20-58*
05-30-58*
07-01-58*
07-16-58
07-17-58*
07-18-58*
07-20-58*
07-21-58*
07-21-58
07-22-58*
07-23-58*
07-25-58*
07-25-58*
07-25-58*
07-26-58*
07-27-58*
07-31-58*
08-03-58*

08-04-58*
08-07-58*
08-08-58*
08-10-58*
08-17-58*
08-19-58*
08-20-58
08-21-58*
08-23-58*
08-26-58*
10-28-58*
12-01-58
03-07-59*
03-20-59*
03-26-59*
04-05-59
07-18-59
05-04-60*
05-20-60*
09-14-60
09-15-60*
09-29-60
11-01-60
01-03-61*
01-26-61*
07-04-61
07-11-61
03-17-64*
06-01-64
09-14-64
03-21-65*
03-27-66*
05-29-67*
06-06-67*
06-11-67*
06-15-67*
08-02-70
08-06-70
05-03-71*
06-05-72*

h. U.S. and Sub-Saharan
Africa
09-23-58
12-15-58
04-15-59
02-02-60
07-06-60*
07-12-60*
07-20-60*
07-29-60*
07-30-60
08-22-60
09-02-60*
11-25-60*
11-28-60*
12-09-60*
01-03-61*
01-15-61*
01-22-61*
02-16-61*
02-18-61*
02-22-61*
03-03-61*
03-16-61*
04-02-61
04-15-61*
04-16-61*
05-09-61
06-02-61
06-24-61
06-30-61*
12-02-61

01-17-62*
03-20-62
04-15-62*
07-02-62
04-15-63*
05-28-63
08-04-63
12-01-63
12-10-63
02-04-64
04-15-64
05-06-64*
06-24-64*
07-23-64
08-02-64*
08-15-64*
09-28-64
10-04-64*
11-01-64
11-28-64*
12-01-64*
12-05-64*
01-17-65*
02-02-65*
02-17-65
02-25-65*
07-12-65
12-18-65
04-15-66*
05-26-66
09-27-67
11-28-67*
12-21-75

   i. U.S. and U.S.S.R.
      09-27-50
      12-27-50*
      01-16-53
      09-23-57*
      09-27-57
      09-29-59*
      05-13-60*
      10-19-60*

O. Asia

  1. General Asia
     09-18-50
     03-23-51*
     04-22-51
     09-10-51
     09-18-51
     02-14-52
     05-14-52
     06-04-52
     07-28-52
     09-03-53
     06-02-54
     06-26-54
     07-02-54*
     07-09-54*
     07-26-54
     08-20-54
     10-19-54
     10-31-54
     12-02-54
     12-05-54
     12-10-54
     01-01-55
     01-05-55*
     01-10-55
     01-29-55
     02-09-55

02-12-55
02-21-55
04-06-55
04-13-55
04-13-55
04-18-55
04-22-55
04-26-55
10-14-55
10-20-55
12-21-55
01-26-56
02-13-56
02-21-56
04-18-56
06-01-56
11-10-56
04-18-57
04-24-57
12-26-57
01-01-58
01-04-58
09-11-58
09-15-58
01-28-59
04-15-59
01-01-60
01-15-60
01-21-60
04-30-60
08-03-60
08-11-60
08-13-60*
08-28-60
09-08-60
12-12-60
12-15-60
12-20-60*
04-16-61*
05-01-61
05-03-61
02-04-63*
02-13-63*
10-25-63
11-09-63
11-10-63
11-11-63
11-23-63
01-21-64
03-03-64
04-10-64
04-18-64
04-18-65*
04-20-65
11-04-65
09-14-70
08-25-73
09-07-73
04-09-74
05-05-74
09-17-74*

  2. Central Asia--People's
     Republic of Mongolia
     10-17-49*
     10-05-52*
     11-26-54*
     12-27-55*
     12-30-55*
     03-01-56*
     07-11-56*
     08-30-56*
     05-18-57*

01-04-58
12-24-58*
07-11-59*
04-08-60*
06-01-60*
07-11-61*
12-25-62*
12-27-62*

  3. East Asia

   a. Democratic People's
     Republic of Korea
     06-27-50*
     07-24-50*
     08-07-50*
     08-15-50*
     09-01-50
     09-19-50
     11-12-50*
     11-17-50
     11-20-50*
     11-25-50
     12-02-50*
     12-06-50*
     12-07-50*
     12-13-50*
     12-17-50*
     12-21-50*
     12-23-50*
     08-15-53*
     09-13-53
     09-27-53*
     10-05-53*
     10-09-53*
     11-13-53*
     11-24-53*
     12-08-53*
     03-05-54*
     06-25-54*
     06-27-54
     07-26-54
     10-25-54*
     03-06-55*
     08-12-55
     08-15-55*
     08-18-55*
     10-12-55*
     11-18-55*
     11-21-55
     12-24-55*
     06-03-56
     01-15-57*
     06-01-57*
     06-23-57*
     06-25-57
     06-28-57*
     07-27-57
     02-06-58*
     02-08-58*
     02-14-58
     02-20-58*
     02-21-58*
     02-22-58*
     03-13-58*
     05-05-58*
     07-27-58
     08-03-58*
     09-28-58*
     10-25-58
     11-22-58*
     12-04-58*
     12-09-58*

06-25-59*
07-17-59*
10-29-59
12-24-59*
04-25-60
06-25-60
08-15-60*
10-25-60
11-12-60*
12-11-60*
03-09-61*
05-21-61
06-25-61*
07-10-61*
07-12-61*
07-16-61*
09-20-61*
12-12-61*
05-04-62*
06-16-62*
06-23-62*
06-25-62*
07-02-62
10-24-62*
07-11-62*
12-24-62*
12-28-62*
01-27-63
02-08-63*
06-06-63*
06-24-63*
07-11-63*
07-27-63*
08-29-63*
09-09-63*
09-15-63*
09-29-63*
09-29-63*
11-23-63*
12-18-63
06-25-64
06-25-64*
10-11-64*
02-23-65
04-17-65*
05-25-65*
06-19-65*
06-25-65
10-23-65
10-25-65*
11-08-65
11-18-65*
11-19-65
12-01-65*
12-24-65
12-25-65
03-29-66
06-25-66*
06-27-66
07-11-66*
06-24-70*
06-25-70*
07-27-70
10-25-70
04-15-71*
08-25-71*
07-11-71*
07-27-71*
09-09-71*
01-29-72*
04-24-72*
06-25-72*
07-09-72*

         08-02-72*   10-30-53*   06-03-60*   06-27-66
         09-09-72*   03-13-54*   06-05-60*   07-11-66
         04-11-73*   03-15-54*   06-13-60   07-24-66
         06-25-73*   07-23-54   06-17-60*   07-07-67
         07-27-73*   07-27-54   06-20-60*   09-10-67*
         09-09-73*   08-15-54   06-21-60*   09-27-67
         11-24-73*   12-10-54   06-24-60*   11-28-69*
         06-25-74*   12-30-54*   06-25-60   06-23-70*
         07-04-74*   01-22-55   08-11-60*   06-24-70
         09-09-74*   02-26-55*   08-13-60*   06-25-70
         04-18-75*   03-29-55   08-15-60   04-15-71*
         06-25-75*   04-02-55*   10-20-60*   06-25-71*
         09-09-75*   08-06-55*   12-07-60   07-11-71*
         10-10-75*   09-14-55*   12-12-60   07-27-71*
         10-25-75*   10-19-55*   06-09-61*   09-09-71*
                                11-20-55*   06-16-61*   09-18-71*
b. Hong Kong   12-02-55*   06-23-61*   10-28-71
         03-14-55*   03-20-56   06-23-61   06-25-72
         04-13-55   07-01-56   08-17-61   09-30-72*
         04-17-55   08-07-56*   09-18-61*   10-01-72
         05-15-55*   08-13-56*   12-30-61*   09-29-74*
         05-28-55   10-06-56*   01-22-62*   09-03-75*
         04-11-56   10-21-56*   04-18-62   10-10-75*
         10-07-56   12-14-56   04-27-62
         10-24-56*   12-27-56*   06-23-62   d. Taiwan (China)
         08-28-58*   04-23-57*   06-25-62   01-05-50*
         08-31-58*   05-23-57*   07-07-62*   03-18-50
         03-08-63*   06-25-57   08-09-62*   04-21-50*
         06-03-67*   07-30-57*   09-06-62   06-29-50
         07-05-67*   08-06-57   09-15-62   08-05-50*
                                08-18-57*   10-24-62   08-28-50
c. Japan   09-23-57   10-28-62*   08-28-50*
         11-30-49   03-06-58*   12-30-62   09-25-50
         01-17-50   04-03-58*   02-08-63   11-12-50
         02-06-50*   04-15-58*   08-10-63   11-20-50
         02-16-50*   04-17-58*   10-05-63*   11-27-50
         09-03-50*   05-11-58*   10-06-63*   11-27-50
         09-18-50   05-16-58*   03-04-64*   12-03-50
         11-27-50*   07-07-58*   03-27-64   12-13-50
         12-21-50   07-23-58*   05-12-64   12-17-50
         01-11-51*   08-08-58   06-05-64   12-21-50
         01-28-51*   08-22-58   06-25-64   12-23-50
         02-14-51*   09-22-58   08-06-64   02-08-51*
         04-22-51*   11-20-58*   12-03-64*   02-28-51*
         05-26-51*   03-06-59*   12-04-64   05-04-51
         06-15-51*   03-07-59*   02-14-65   05-26-51
         06-22-51   03-19-59*   02-23-65*   05-28-51
         08-11-51   04-12-59   02-25-65   06-15-51
         08-16-51*   04-16-59*   02-28-65*   06-22-51
         08-29-51   04-28-59*   04-07-65   06-25-51
         09-10-51   08-05-59*   05-25-65*   08-16-51
         09-18-51   09-23-59*   06-19-65*   08-29-51
         09-23-51   10-22-59*   06-25-65*   01-23-52*
         11-07-51   11-27-59*   06-25-65   02-04-52*
         11-12-51   12-03-59*   06-27-65   05-07-52
         01-23-52   01-15-60*   08-11-65*   07-07-52
         02-14-52   01-20-60   08-24-65*   09-16-52
         02-23-52   01-21-60*   09-02-65*   04-29-53
         05-01-52   01-24-60*   09-08-65   10-05-53
         05-07-52*   02-01-60   10-25-65   10-30-53
         05-14-52   02-06-60   11-08-65*   11-28-53
         06-29-52   04-04-60*   11-15-65*   12-24-53*
         07-07-52*   04-18-60   11-16-65*   01-08-54
         07-09-52   04-19-60   11-18-65*   02-14-54
         07-15-52   04-29-60   11-19-65   02-17-54
         07-28-52   05-04-60   12-01-65   05-20-54*
         09-03-52*   05-10-60*   12-24-65*   07-09-54*
         09-16-52   05-12-60*   01-14-66   07-16-54*
         09-21-52*   05-14-60   02-20-66   07-23-54*
         10-01-52   05-16-60*   03-17-66   07-24-54
         10-02-52   05-22-60*   03-29-66*   07-26-54*
         10-13-52   05-28-60   04-19-66   08-01-54*
         09-03-53   05-29-60*   06-25-66   08-15-54

179

08-20-54*	07-03-58	05-07-63	11-04-71
08-26-54*	07-25-58*	05-27-63	11-12-71
08-29-54*	07-27-58	06-08-63	11-16-71
09-05-54*	08-02-58*	06-22-63*	12-12-71
09-13-54*	08-16-58	06-30-63*	01-14-72
09-29-54	08-21-58*	08-30-63	02-20-72
10-01-54	08-31-58*	10-19-63	02-27-72
10-06-54	09-07-58*	10-25-63*	04-17-72
10-11-54*	09-09-58*	11-04-63	06-07-72
10-21-54*	09-15-58*	11-05-63*	06-25-72*
11-01-54	09-21-58*	11-09-63	09-28-72
11-20-54*	09-22-58*	11-11-63*	09-30-72*
11-27-54	09-28-58*	12-18-63	10-16-72
12-05-54*	09-30-58*	01-18-64	11-08-72
12-10-54*	09-30-58	01-29-64*	11-18-72
12-28-54*	10-01-58	02-20-64	11-30-72
12-29-54	10-10-58*	02-26-64	12-24-72
12-30-54	10-11-58*	04-16-64	03-12-73*
01-01-55	10-21-58*	04-28-64*	06-25-73
01-01-55*	10-30-58*	05-12-64*	08-25-73
01-04-55	11-19-58	05-18-64	09-16-73
01-21-55*	12-12-58*	06-24-64	03-22-74
01-29-55*	01-01-59	07-01-64*	04-30-74
01-31-55*	04-16-59	07-06-64*	05-28-74
02-01-55*	10-24-59	07-09-64*	06-25-74
02-05-55*	01-01-60	07-15-64*	06-30-74
02-09-55*	01-21-60	10-03-64	07-22-74
02-12-55*	04-11-60	10-06-64	08-17-74
02-16-55*	04-19-60	12-04-64*	10-18-74
02-18-55*	05-04-60	02-01-65*	01-09-75
02-21-55	05-13-60	03-28-65	06-25-75
02-26-55	05-20-60	04-21-65*	11-16-75
03-07-55*	05-27-60*	04-28-65	
03-29-55	06-13-60	06-26-65	e. Republic of Korea
04-04-55	06-21-60*	06-27-65*	09-13-53
04-06-55	06-25-60	07-27-65	10-09-53
04-08-55	08-03-60	08-07-65*	11-24-53*
04-13-55*	08-13-60	09-02-65	12-08-53*
04-13-55	09-08-60*	11-16-65	03-05-54*
04-17-55*	10-06-60	11-18-65	06-25-54*
04-26-55	10-12-60	11-19-65*	06-27-54
05-28-55	10-20-60	12-19-65	07-23-54
06-28-55	10-25-60	01-18-66	07-26-54
09-24-55	02-15-61	04-06-66	08-15-54
10-14-55	05-18-61*	06-27-66*	10-25-54*
10-20-55	06-17-61	06-30-66	03-06-55*
01-20-56	06-23-61	07-11-66	03-29-55
01-26-56	07-14-61*	12-02-66*	08-12-55*
01-31-56	09-09-61	09-09-67	08-15-55
02-04-56*	09-22-61	09-10-67*	08-18-55*
04-11-56	10-03-61	10-29-67	10-12-55
04-25-56	12-12-61	08-21-68	11-18-55*
07-12-56	12-22-61*	01-01-69	06-03-56*
09-02-56	12-30-61*	07-31-69	06-25-57
10-07-56	01-15-62	11-28-69	07-27-57*
10-13-56	02-14-62	01-01-70	02-06-58*
10-23-56	04-27-62	06-24-70	02-08-58
04-23-57	05-04-62	06-25-70	02-20-58
05-10-57*	06-25-62*	08-01-70	03-13-58*
05-25-57*	07-02-62	09-03-70	07-27-58
05-28-57*	07-07-62	10-15-70	09-28-58
06-13-57	07-11-62	11-08-70	06-25-59*
06-23-57	08-01-62	12-03-70	10-29-59*
06-25-57	08-20-62*	12-18-70	04-25-60*
07-30-57	09-06-62	02-12-71	04-29-60*
08-01-57	09-15-62*	04-04-71	05-04-60
09-15-57	10-04-62	06-25-71	05-28-60
09-23-57	10-09-62	07-11-71	05-13-60
11-02-57	12-30-62*	08-01-71	06-21-60*
11-09-57*	01-02-63	08-19-71	06-25-60*
04-03-58	02-08-63	09-18-71	10-25-60
04-15-58*	03-08-63	10-28-71	11-12-60*
05-17-58	04-12-63	10-28-71	12-11-60*

03-09-61*
05-21-61*
06-25-61*
07-10-61
07-12-61
09-20-61
12-12-61*
04-27-62
06-16-62*
06-23-62*
06-25-62*
07-02-62
07-11-62*
10-24-62
12-24-62*
12-28-62*
12-30-62
02-08-63*
06-06-63
07-27-63*
09-09-63
09-15-63
09-29-63*
11-05-63
12-18-63*
03-04-64
03-27-64*
06-05-64*
06-25-64*
01-10-65
01-14-65*
02-09-65
02-23-65*
02-25-65
02-25-65
02-28-65*
04-07-65*
04-17-65*
04-20-65*
05-25-65*
06-19-65*
06-25-65*
06-25-65*
07-11-65
07-13-65
08-03-65
09-08-65*
10-25-65
11-04-65
11-08-65*
11-15-65*
11-16-65
11-18-65*
12-01-65*
12-24-65*
12-25-65*
02-20-66
03-29-66
04-19-66*
06-25-66*
07-11-66
08-25-66
04-15-71*
07-11-71*
07-27-71*
09-09-71*
09-18-71
01-29-72*
04-24-72*
06-25-72
07-09-72*
09-09-72*
04-11-73*

06-25-73*
07-27-73*
09-09-73*
11-24-73
06-25-74
07-04-74*
09-09-74*
06-25-75
09-09-75*
10-10-75*
10-25-75

4. South Asia

   a. Afghanistan
      12-21-55*
      01-02-56
      01-24-57*
      10-23-57*
      10-28-57*
      09-05-59*
      08-28-60*
      12-13-60*
      01-01-61
      03-04-63
      11-20-63*
      11-23-63*
      10-30-64*
      11-13-64*
      03-26-65*
      04-05-65*
      08-26-65*
      03-27-66*
      04-09-66*
      04-21-66*

   b. Bangladesh
      08-28-72*
      05-11-74*
      10-08-75*

   c. India
      07-24-50
      09-23-50
      11-17-50*
      08-29-51*
      02-14-52
      05-01-52
      07-28-52
      12-23-52
      06-25-53
      07-21-53
      08-28-53*
      09-14-53
      10-05-53
      10-09-53
      10-13-53
      11-03-53
      11-28-53
      12-09-53
      04-21-54
      04-30-54*
      06-26-54*
      07-02-54
      10-19-54*
      10-31-54*
      12-02-54
      01-05-55
      01-22-55
      02-09-55
      02-18-55
      04-04-55*
      04-12-55*

04-13-55
04-17-55
04-18-55
04-22-55
06-14-55*
06-28-55*
08-24-55*
12-17-55*
01-02-56
01-26-56*
02-20-56
03-24-56*
04-11-56
08-10-56*
08-17-56
09-24-56
10-08-56
12-11-56*
01-30-57
09-14-57
09-17-57*
09-19-57*
11-09-57
02-15-58
09-07-58
03-31-59
04-29-59
05-20-59
09-12-59*
09-16-59*
04-27-60*
03-03-61
12-07-61*
12-20-61*
06-03-62*
06-05-62*
06-07-62
07-09-62*
09-06-62
09-07-62*
09-22-62*
10-10-62*
10-14-62*
10-27-62*
11-08-62*
11-20-62*
11-22-62*
12-10-62*
12-15-62
12-23-62*
12-27-62*
12-29-62
12-31-62*
01-08-63*
01-24-63*
01-28-63*
03-05-63*
03-09-63*
01-02-63
02-27-63*
02-28-63
04-03-63*
04-21-63
04-26-63
04-27-63
04-28-63*
05-03-63
05-07-63
05-16-63
05-27-63*
06-08-63*
07-28-63*
08-22-63*

08-28-63*
10-13-63*
11-21-63*
01-18-64
02-20-64
02-26-64
03-02-64*
03-03-64
10-14-64
07-19-65
08-07-65
09-10-65
09-11-65*
09-14-65*
09-18-65*
09-30-65
09-30-65
10-23-65
11-04-65
12-21-65
12-27-65
03-27-66
04-18-66*
07-18-66
07-24-66
10-10-66
06-28-67*
07-05-67*
12-27-71*
01-31-72*
02-03-72*
08-28-72*
05-11-74*

   d. Nepal
      09-24-56*
      09-26-56*
      10-08-56*
      01-30-57*
      03-11-60*
      03-25-60*
      04-30-60*
      01-01-61
      09-29-61*
      10-13-61*
      04-28-62*
      10-05-62*
      10-27-62*
      11-20-62
      12-27-62
      01-19-63*
      01-21-63
      07-28-63
      10-23-63*
      04-05-65*
      04-28-65*
      03-27-66
      11-15-72*
      12-08-73*

   e. Pakistan
      08-28-53*
      09-14-53
      12-09-53*
      03-23-56*
      10-18-56*
      10-24-56*
      12-26-56*
      03-07-59*
      06-05-62*
      12-29-62*
      03-01-63*
      03-04-63*

07-28-63
02-26-64*
03-03-64*
04-28-64
04-29-64*
01-06-65
03-02-65*
03-09-65*
03-28-65*
04-05-65*
04-07-65
06-03-65*
07-19-65*
09-11-65*
09-14-65*
09-18-65*
10-23-65
11-19-65
12-27-65
03-27-66*
04-18-66*
04-21-66*
08-07-66*
11-10-70*
12-27-71*
01-31-72*
08-28-72*
05-11-74*
10-08-75*

f. Republic of Maldives
10-16-72*

g. Sri Lanka
09-17-56*
02-17-57*
03-03-61
10-04-62*
12-10-62
12-31-62*
01-08-63*
01-28-63
03-02-64*
03-03-64*
09-21-64*
06-25-72*

5. Southeast Asia

a. General Southeast Asia
08-16-51
07-28-52
09-13-54*
03-24-56
12-11-56
07-30-57
10-28-57
11-27-59
12-22-60
02-10-61
02-28-61
12-30-61*
09-15-62
08-06-64
10-14-64
06-23-70
02-14-71*
03-11-71
03-28-71*
04-25-71*
06-06-71*
07-20-71*
10-12-71*

04-25-72*
07-20-72*
04-03-73*
04-25-73*
04-24-74*
05-20-75*
12-06-75*

b. Burma
08-29-51
02-14-52
05-01-52
09-14-53
12-09-53
07-02-54
12-02-54
12-14-54
01-05-55
02-18-55
06-28-55
11-06-55*
01-02-56
02-20-56
04-11-56*
11-11-56*
12-21-56*
07-17-57*
07-17-57*
12-04-57*
02-19-59
03-18-59
01-24-60*
01-29-60*
02-01-60*
03-25-60
04-30-60*
10-02-60*
10-05-60*
01-10-61*
01-28-61*
10-14-61*
10-27-62
11-20-62
12-27-62
04-12-63*
04-20-63*
04-27-63*
05-23-63
02-20-64*
03-03-64*
01-28-65*
04-07-65
07-24-65*
08-02-65*
03-27-66
04-20-66*
04-21-66*
06-30-67*
07-10-67*
11-11-75*

c. Cambodia
07-14-54
07-22-54
03-01-55
03-13-55*
04-12-55*
06-24-55*
02-13-56*
02-20-56*
04-07-56*
06-23-56*
07-24-56

08-08-56
11-29-56*
07-20-57
07-24-58*
08-15-58*
08-20-58
08-25-58*
03-11-59
07-20-59
05-10-60*
12-15-60*
12-22-60*
01-01-61
01-15-61
02-25-61
03-12-61
05-03-61*
12-19-61*
10-06-62
02-12-63*
02-28-63*
05-01-63*
05-07-63*
05-23-63
10-19-63*
10-25-63
11-09-63*
11-22-63*
03-27-64
04-09-64
04-28-64
05-13-64
05-19-64*
06-15-64
07-20-64*
08-07-64
09-27-64*
10-06-64*
11-03-64*
12-20-64
01-06-65
01-14-65
02-01-65
02-10-65
02-15-65
02-23-65
02-25-65
02-25-65
03-12-65
05-03-65*
05-04-65*
05-20-65*
06-20-65
07-19-65
07-20-65
07-30-65
09-28-65*
10-05-65*
11-19-65
12-14-65
12-19-65*
12-24-65*
01-04-66*
01-18-66
01-19-66
02-20-66
02-23-66
03-17-66
03-27-66
11-25-66
12-07-66
04-30-70*
05-05-70*

06-09-70
06-25-70
07-27-70
10-12-70
10-22-70
11-09-70*
12-13-70
12-18-70*
03-23-71*
05-05-71*
11-09-71*
03-23-72*
07-28-72*
11-09-72*
03-23-73*
04-11-73*
07-05-73*
11-09-73*
03-23-74*
04-01-74*
03-23-75*
04-18-75*
04-25-75*
08-15-75*

d. Democratic People's Republic of Vietnam
05-19-50*
08-19-50*
09-02-50*
09-25-50*
03-27-51*
06-25-51
07-24-51*
05-14-52
12-14-52
12-23-52
09-02-53*
12-01-53
12-19-53*
02-14-54
02-22-54
03-08-54
04-03-54*
04-21-54*
05-09-54*
05-12-54
06-02-54
07-09-54
07-14-54*
07-22-54*
07-26-54
03-01-55
04-04-55
04-12-55*
06-08-55*
06-25-55*
07-09-55*
07-21-55*
08-16-55*
09-02-55
09-18-55*
03-03-56*
07-07-56*
07-24-56*
07-28-56*
11-23-56*
07-20-57
08-29-57*
02-15-58*
03-09-58*
12-04-58*
01-21-59

02-20-59*
03-10-59*
03-11-59
05-20-59
07-17-59*
07-20-59*
09-17-59
05-15-60*
07-13-60*
07-17-60*
07-20-60*
09-02-60*
09-12-60*
01-15-61
02-01-61*
04-12-61
06-10-61*
06-17-61*
07-20-61*
10-19-61
11-30-61
02-25-62
06-07-62*
06-22-62*
07-19-62*
07-24-62
10-06-62
10-13-62*
05-10-63*
05-16-63
05-18-63*
05-23-63
09-12-63
03-04-64
05-07-64*
05-19-64
06-27-64*
07-09-64*
07-15-64*
07-20-64*
08-06-64*
08-07-64*
08-08-64
08-09-64*
08-15-64
08-29-64
09-09-64*
09-20-64*
09-24-64*
11-25-64
12-22-64*
02-09-65*
02-10-65*
02-12-65*
02-14-65*
02-15-65
02-19-65*
03-01-65
03-04-65*
03-09-65
03-12-65
03-17-65*
03-22-65*
03-25-65
03-29-65*
04-05-65*
04-07-65
04-12-65*
04-12-65*
04-13-65*
04-15-65*
04-16-65*
04-21-65*

04-22-65*
04-24-65*
04-28-65*
05-01-65*
05-03-65
05-07-65
05-20-65*
06-01-65
06-03-65
06-05-65
07-05-65*
07-11-65*
07-12-65*
07-13-65*
07-20-65*
07-24-65
08-03-65
08-07-65
09-02-65
09-02-65*
09-08-65
11-05-65
11-08-65*
11-19-65
11-29-65
12-14-65*
12-19-65
12-27-65
01-14-66*
01-18-66
01-24-66*
01-30-66*
02-01-66*
02-02-66*
02-12-66
02-23-66
03-25-66
03-27-66
03-29-66
05-01-66*
05-13-66
07-05-66*
07-18-66*
07-24-66*
08-07-66
08-08-66
08-25-66
09-24-66*
10-10-66*
12-15-66*
12-20-66*
03-19-67*
05-23-67
06-08-67*
06-22-67*
07-21-67*
08-29-67
09-21-67
09-27-67*
09-27-67*
12-19-67
02-02-68
03-19-68*
02-03-70*
04-30-70*
06-09-70
06-25-70
07-27-70
09-02-70*
10-12-70
11-21-70*
11-22-70*
12-13-70*

12-18-70
12-20-70
02-14-71*
03-11-71*
07-04-71
07-20-71
08-31-71
09-02-71*
11-20-71*
11-28-71*
02-04-72*
04-18-72*
04-25-72*
06-06-72*
07-20-72*
08-04-72*
08-13-72*
09-01-72*
11-01-72*
12-27-72*
01-28-73*
03-01-73*
03-03-73
04-03-73*
04-25-73*
06-04-73*
06-06-73*
06-17-73*
09-02-73*
11-18-73*
01-27-74*
04-24-74*
06-06-74*
09-02-74*
02-03-75*
04-25-75*
05-01-75*
06-06-75*
09-02-75*
09-22-75*
12-06-75

e. Indonesia
02-14-52
12-14-52
12-23-52
09-14-53
04-13-55
14-22-55
04-23-55
04-29-55*
05-26-55*
05-28-55*
05-30-55*
06-02-55*
04-11-56
06-01-56
09-13-56*
09-30-56*
10-15-56*
05-06-57
08-13-57
12-17-57*
01-01-58*
03-10-58
03-12-58*
03-14-58*
03-15-58*
05-17-58*
06-20-58
03-10-59*
03-18-59
12-12-59*

01-27-60
03-18-60*
07-14-60*
12-24-60*
04-04-61*
06-13-61*
06-13-61
06-16-61*
09-09-61
12-21-61*
04-01-62*
04-18-62
08-19-62*
08-20-62
09-06-62
01-02-63*
01-08-63*
04-12-63*
04-18-63
04-21-63*
05-01-63
05-02-63*
05-03-63
05-23-63
06-27-63
07-28-63
09-23-63*
09-27-63*
11-10-63*
11-23-63*
03-27-64
04-10-64
04-18-64
05-28-64*
09-09-64*
10-11-64*
10-14-64
01-06-65*
01-06-65*
01-23-65*
01-10-65
01-30-65*
02-25-65
04-18-65
06-20-65
07-19-65
09-27-65*
10-29-65
03-30-66*
04-16-66*
04-26-66
04-27-66*
06-30-66*
10-08-66*
12-09-66
04-27-67*
10-29-67*
08-01-70

f. Laos
07-14-54
07-22-54
03-01-55
03-03-55*
07-24-56
08-08-56*
08-20-56*
08-26-56*
01-02-57*
07-20-57
05-03-58*
02-19-59*
03-11-59*

183

05-20-59*
07-20-59
09-17-59*
11-21-60*
12-12-60
12-16-60*
01-10-61*
01-15-61*
01-26-61*
02-10-61*
02-25-61*
03-12-61*
04-22-61*
04-26-61*
04-27-61*
05-08-61*
05-18-61*
05-18-61*
05-19-61*
05-24-61*
05-26-61*
06-01-61
06-14-61*
06-17-61
06-23-61*
08-09-61*
09-09-61
10-19-61
12-21-61*
01-03-62*
01-19-62
04-18-62
04-27-62
05-04-62
05-19-62*
06-07-62
06-14-62*
06-25-62
06-25-62*
07-12-62*
07-24-62*
08-20-62
10-06-62
03-06-63*
03-11-63*
04-05-63*
04-17-63*
04-27-63
05-01-63
05-07-63
05-16-63*
06-04-63*
06-16-63*
07-28-63
03-27-64
04-04-64*
04-09-64*
04-22-64*
04-28-64
05-01-64*
05-13-64*
05-29-64*
06-15-64*
06-27-64
07-05-64*
07-20-64*
08-06-64
11-03-64
12-20-64
01-02-65*
01-10-65
01-14-65
02-01-65

02-09-65
02-10-65
02-15-65
02-23-65
02-25-65
02-25-65
03-12-65
05-03-65
07-20-65
07-30-65*
09-28-65
10-05-65
11-09-65*
12-14-65
12-19-65
12-24-65
01-04-66
01-19-66
03-17-66
03-27-66
04-06-66
10-10-66
04-30-70*
05-05-70
06-09-70
06-25-70
07-27-70
10-12-70*
11-09-70
12-13-70
01-06-71*
08-31-71*
02-23-73*
03-01-73*
09-16-73*
10-12-73*
04-07-74*
10-12-74*
10-12-75*

g. Malaya
10-09-49*
08-31-52*
12-23-52
10-24-59
02-25-61
03-12-61*

h. Malaysia
03-27-64*
05-28-64*
09-09-64*
01-06-65*
01-10-65
01-23-65
01-30-65
10-29-65
11-04-65
04-27-67
10-29-67
05-28-74*

i. Philippines
05-07-52
07-23-54
03-29-55
05-17-58
11-27-59
05-04-60
06-13-60
06-21-60*
03-12-61
05-18-61

06-23-61
04-27-62
06-07-75*

j. Republic of Vietnam
11-30-49
06-25-51
05-14-52
12-14-52
12-23-52
09-02-53*
12-01-53
12-19-53*
02-14-54
02-22-54
03-08-54
04-03-54*
04-21-54*
06-02-54
07-14-54*
07-22-54*
07-26-54
03-01-55
04-04-55
06-08-55
07-09-55
07-21-55*
08-16-55*
09-02-55
09-18-55*
11-06-55
03-03-56
07-24-56*
05-21-57*
06-23-57
07-20-57*
08-29-57
02-15-58
03-09-58*
08-15-58
08-20-58
01-21-59*
03-11-59*
07-17-59*
07-20-59*
11-27-59
05-04-60
09-12-60
12-25-60*
02-25-61*
03-12-61
04-12-61*
05-24-61
05-26-61
06-10-61
06-17-61
07-20-61*
08-09-61
10-19-61*
11-30-61*
01-15-62
02-25-62*
04-18-62
04-27-62
05-04-62
05-19-62*
06-07-62*
06-22-62*
06-25-62
07-19-62*
07-24-62
10-06-62*
10-13-62*

12-20-62*
05-01-63
05-10-63*
05-18-63
07-19-63*
07-28-63
08-11-63
09-12-63*
11-04-63*
11-05-63
11-15-63*
11-22-63
12-20-63*
03-04-64*
03-27-64
04-09-64
04-28-64*
05-07-64
05-13-64
05-18-64*
06-15-64
06-24-64
07-05-64
07-09-64
07-20-64*
08-27-64*
08-29-64*
09-09-64*
09-20-64*
09-24-64*
11-03-64
11-25-64*
12-20-64*
12-22-64
01-02-65*
01-06-65*
01-14-65*
02-01-65
02-09-65
02-10-65*
02-12-65*
02-14-65
02-15-65
02-19-65*
02-25-65
02-25-65
03-01-65*
03-04-65
03-09-65
03-17-65
03-22-65*
03-25-65*
03-25-65*
03-29-65*
04-12-65*
04-12-65*
04-13-65*
04-15-65*
04-16-65*
04-21-65*
04-22-65*
04-24-65*
04-28-65*
05-01-65*
05-03-65*
05-07-65*
05-14-65*
05-20-65
06-03-65
06-05-65*
06-11-65*
06-20-65*
07-05-65

07-11-65
07-13-65
07-18-65
07-20-65*
07-24-65
07-30-65*
08-03-65*
08-07-65*
08-07-65
08-11-65
09-02-65
09-21-65
09-28-65
10-05-65
10-23-65
10-29-65
11-04-65
11-05-65*
11-08-65*
11-09-65
11-18-65
11-19-65*
11-29-65*
12-09-65*
12-14-65*
12-19-65
12-19-65*
12-24-65
12-27-65
01-04-66
01-14-66*
01-18-66*
01-19-66*
01-24-66*
01-30-66*
02-01-66
02-02-66*
02-12-66*
02-15-66*
02-20-66
02-20-66
02-23-66
03-17-66*
03-25-66*
03-27-66*
03-27-66*
03-29-66
04-06-66
04-19-66
04-26-66
05-01-66
05-01-66
06-25-66
06-27-66
06-29-66
07-05-66*
07-10-66
07-11-66
07-18-66*
07-24-66*
08-07-66
08-08-66
08-25-66
09-24-66*
10-10-66*
12-20-66*
03-19-67*
05-23-67*
06-08-67*
06-22-67*
07-21-67*
08-29-67*
09-21-67*

09-27-67*
09-27-67*
10-20-67
12-19-67*
02-02-68*
02-15-68*
03-19-68*
04-30-70
05-05-70
06-09-70
06-25-70
07-27-70
09-02-70
10-12-70
11-09-70
12-13-70*
12-20-70*
07-04-71*
09-02-71*
11-20-71*
11-28-71*
02-04-72*
04-18-72*
06-06-72*
08-04-72*
08-13-72*
09-01-72*
11-01-72*
02-27-72*
01-28-73*
03-01-73*
03-03-73*
06-04-73*
06-06-73*
06-17-73
09-02-73*
11-18-73*
01-27-74*
06-06-74*
09-02-74*
02-03-75
04-25-75*
05-01-75*
06-06-75*
09-02-75

k. Singapore
08-20-58*
08-24-58*

l. Thailand
07-23-54
03-01-55
03-29-55
03-15-58
03-11-59
07-20-59
08-03-60*
08-28-60
09-28-60*
12-16-60
12-25-60*
01-01-61
01-05-61*
02-25-61
03-12-61
05-08-61
05-18-61
05-24-61
05-26-61
06-23-61
08-09-61
12-19-61*

04-27-62
05-19-62*
06-07-62
06-25-62
07-12-62
07-24-62
04-27-63
05-16-63
11-22-63
05-13-64
05-18-64
06-15-64
07-30-65
11-19-65
12-19-65
12-24-65
01-04-66
01-19-66
02-20-66
03-17-66
08-31-71*
06-30-75*

P. Australia and
   New Zealand
10-09-49*
10-22-49*
03-23-51*
05-07-52
05-14-52
06-04-52
07-28-52
01-31-55
02-05-55
05-28-64
07-13-65
03-17-66
12-24-72*
10-31-73*
11-07-75*
11-16-75*

Q. Europe

1. Eastern Europe

a. General Eastern Europe
03-26-55
05-02-55
05-17-55
10-05-55
10-31-55
02-01-56
02-28-56
05-30-56*
06-14-56
09-17-56
11-03-56*
11-13-56
11-14-56
12-15-56*
02-02-57
04-04-57
01-11-58
01-13-59
01-21-60
05-08-61
09-20-68
03-04-69
11-29-70

b. Albania
11-29-54*

11-30-54
11-21-55
04-20-57*
05-10-57*
01-17-59
06-03-59*
11-29-59*
06-02-60*
01-11-61*
02-03-61*
02-22-61*
11-08-61*
11-28-62*
12-15-62
01-27-63
02-27-63*
07-10-63*
10-19-63
10-25-63
12-31-63*
01-11-64*
02-06-64
11-29-64*
02-25-65
04-01-65*
04-07-65
04-28-66*
05-01-66
05-15-66*
06-25-66*
06-29-66*
11-10-66*
11-29-66*
05-14-67*
09-26-67*
11-29-67*
09-20-68*
09-29-68*
11-29-68*
11-23-69*
11-29-69*
11-29-70*
01-11-71*
11-08-71*
11-29-71*
11-28-72*
11-29-73*
11-29-74*
11-29-75*

c. Bulgaria
12-13-51
09-09-54*
11-30-54
11-21-55
02-23-57*
09-14-57*
10-12-57*
09-22-58*
11-29-58*
09-09-59*

d. Czechoslovakia
12-13-51*
11-30-52*
03-16-53*
01-20-54
11-30-54
01-19-55
04-15-55*
05-09-55*
03-03-56
05-14-56*

185

02-01-57*
03-09-57*
03-28-57*
09-27-57*
11-23-57*
12-30-57
05-16-59
05-09-60*
07-28-60
03-27-62*
12-15-62*
09-20-68

e. German Democratic Republic
10-13-49*
10-26-49*
07-03-53*
08-28-53*
11-10-53
12-01-53
02-23-54
04-09-54*
07-27-54*
07-28-54*
08-10-54
09-15-54
10-07-54*
10-10-54*
10-29-54*
11-16-54*
11-27-54
11-30-54
12-04-54
01-19-55
01-20-55*
05-09-55*
05-17-55
10-27-55
10-31-55*
12-08-55*
12-24-55*
12-26-55*
12-30-55*
04-21-56*
07-20-56*
08-22-56*
12-25-56*
03-28-57
08-16-57
12-30-57
11-20-58*
12-14-58
01-13-59*
01-22-59*
01-23-59*
01-28-59*
03-14-59*
03-20-59*
04-30-59*
05-16-59*
06-22-59*
10-07-59*
01-09-60*
01-20-60*
02-06-60
09-09-60*
12-25-60*
06-28-61*
08-10-61*
01-27-63*
08-30-63
10-07-64*

04-09-65*
06-29-66

f. Hungary
12-13-51
11-30-54
04-04-55*
11-25-55
11-03-56*
11-04-56*
11-05-56*
11-07-56
11-13-56
11-14-56*
11-21-56
11-23-56
12-06-56
12-15-56
01-01-57
01-09-57
01-19-57*
03-30-57*
04-04-57*
06-22-57
09-06-57*
09-16-57*
09-24-57*
09-27-57*
10-05-57*
10-12-57
02-23-58
05-05-58
05-28-58
06-19-58
06-20-58*
04-29-59*
05-07-59*
12-07-59*
04-04-60*
10-19-60

g. Poland
11-27-49*
08-11-52
04-14-53*
09-27-53*
12-24-53*
01-20-54
05-20-54*
07-22-54*
07-28-54
11-30-54
01-19-55
04-28-55
03-15-56*
07-12-56*
11-04-56
11-21-56*
01-18-57*
01-24-57*
04-07-57*
04-12-57*
12-30-57
03-20-58*
04-08-58*
03-21-59*
05-16-59
05-20-59
07-22-59*
07-24-59*
07-28-60*
09-28-61*
07-24-62

05-16-63
06-04-63
06-16-63
10-25-63

h. Rumania
08-23-54*
11-30-54
01-19-55
11-21-55
05-08-56*
12-06-56*
04-30-57*
01-10-58*
04-02-58*
04-09-58*
04-28-58*
05-28-58
08-23-59*
08-23-64*
03-21-65*
04-07-65
08-05-65*
11-19-65
06-17-66*
06-09-70*
06-01-71*
08-23-74*

i. Yugoslavia
08-27-49*
12-03-50
12-13-51
01-16-53
04-04-54
06-05-55*
08-29-55*
11-29-55*
06-22-56*
08-17-56
02-23-57
09-12-57*
09-16-57*
05-05-58
06-04-58*
06-20-58
11-19-58
02-05-59
03-18-59*
02-06-60
11-21-60
01-11-61
01-22-61*
02-03-61
02-22-61
03-18-61
09-09-61*
11-08-61
12-01-61
01-01-62
09-17-62*
11-15-62*
11-18-62
11-28-62
12-23-62
01-08-63
01-27-63*
02-13-63
02-27-63
03-08-63
03-09-63
05-18-63
12-31-63

01-11-64*
10-14-64
11-29-64
01-10-65
08-07-65
06-25-66
10-10-66
11-10-66
09-27-67
11-29-67
10-06-75*

2. Scandinavia

a. Denmark
10-18-74*

b. Finland
09-22-55*
10-12-60

c. Iceland
12-16-71*

d. Norway
08-21-58
12-21-65

e. Sweden
07-23-58

3. Southern Europe

a. Cyprus
08-16-60*
01-10-65
01-14-72*
05-17-74*

b. Greece
11-01-49*
02-23-57
10-22-57
06-03-59
07-09-59*
08-16-60
06-07-72*

c. Italy
08-09-54
05-29-58*
06-03-59
07-01-60*
03-16-61
02-03-64
01-14-66
11-08-70*

d. Malta
02-27-72*
04-02-72*
01-07-75*

e. Portugal
08-24-55*
02-21-56
07-30-60
05-09-61
06-24-61*
09-13-61
12-09-61
12-20-61*
04-15-62

05-28-63
08-11-63
02-04-64
12-05-64
02-17-65
12-18-65
01-18-66
04-15-66
01-26-73*
10-01-73*
06-20-74
07-22-74
09-06-74*
09-14-74*
01-22-75*
02-20-75
06-25-75
07-18-75
11-14-75*
12-21-75*

f. San Marino
05-09-71*

g. Spain
11-14-56
12-26-60
06-28-61
03-12-73*

4. Western Europe

a. General Western Europe
04-05-52
11-18-53
02-23-54
06-02-54
07-26-54
07-27-54
07-28-54
08-10-54
09-15-54
10-10-54
10-29-54
11-16-54*
03-26-55
04-08-55
05-09-55
05-16-55
07-18-55
10-14-55
10-31-55
11-19-55
12-08-55
11-10-56
10-04-57
12-21-57*
12-30-57
01-11-58
01-13-59
04-02-59*
05-01-61
10-07-64
05-27-68
09-20-68

b. Austria
04-18-55*
05-16-55*
05-29-71*

c. Belgium
01-24-59*

11-25-59*
06-30-60*
07-12-60*
07-20-60*
07-29-60*
07-30-60*
08-22-60*
09-02-60
09-15-60
11-25-60
01-15-61*
01-22-61*
02-16-61*
02-18-61*
02-22-61*
03-03-61*
03-16-61*
06-30-61
07-13-61
01-17-62
07-02-62
05-06-64
06-24-64
11-28-64
12-01-64
12-03-64
12-05-64*
01-10-65
01-17-65*
02-02-65*
10-28-71*
04-19-75*

d. Federal Republic of Germany
11-12-51
05-01-52
07-09-52
07-28-52
07-03-53
08-28-53*
11-18-53
12-01-53
02-23-54
07-27-54*
07-28-54
08-10-54
09-15-54*
10-07-54*
10-10-54*
10-29-54*
11-16-54*
11-27-54
11-30-54
12-04-54
01-10-55
01-20-55*
03-26-55
04-09-55*
07-18-55
09-16-55*
09-23-55*
11-19-55
12-08-55
06-22-56
07-20-56*
08-22-56*
11-21-56
08-16-57
06-22-58
07-07-58*
11-30-58*
12-14-58*

01-13-59*
01-22-59
01-28-59
03-05-59*
03-14-59*
03-20-59*
04-30-59
05-16-59*
06-22-59*
07-24-59
10-07-59
01-09-60*
01-16-60
01-20-60
02-06-60
04-04-60*
04-19-60
05-16-60
05-20-60
07-07-60
07-28-60*
12-07-60
12-12-60
12-25-60
03-16-61
03-18-61
06-23-61
06-28-61*
08-10-61*
09-01-61
12-09-61
01-19-62
12-23-62
08-30-63*
10-07-64
02-14-65
03-25-65*
04-09-65*
05-16-65*
01-14-66
03-25-66
10-13-72*
05-09-75*
10-29-75*

e. France
05-19-50*
08-19-50
09-02-50*
12-07-50
04-12-51*
07-24-51
11-12-51
05-01-52
05-14-52
12-23-52
08-14-53
09-02-53
10-09-53
11-18-53
12-01-53
12-19-53
02-22-54
02-23-54
03-08-54
04-03-54
04-21-54
05-09-54
07-14-54
07-22-54
07-27-54
09-15-54
10-07-54

10-29-54
11-30-54
12-04-54
01-10-55
02-18-55
03-26-55
06-08-55
09-02-55
10-27-55
10-31-55*
01-07-56*
02-21-56
03-03-56
04-12-56
05-21-56*
06-28-56
07-18-56
08-10-56
08-11-56
08-14-56
08-17-56
08-25-56
09-12-56
09-21-56
11-01-56*
11-02-56*
11-03-56*
11-05-56
11-07-56*
11-07-56*
11-08-56*
11-09-56*
11-13-56*
11-13-56
11-14-56
11-17-56*
12-02-56
12-06-56
12-06-56*
12-09-56
12-25-56
01-01-57
01-08-57
01-12-57
02-20-57
06-18-57
06-19-57
09-10-57
09-24-57
10-22-57
03-15-58
03-30-58*
04-01-58
05-23-58*
05-30-58*
06-22-58
07-21-58
07-30-58
08-03-58
08-08-58
08-16-58
09-23-58*
10-09-58
11-30-58
12-01-58
12-03-58*
12-14-58
12-15-58
02-19-59
03-23-59*
04-05-59
01-16-60
02-02-60

03-12-60*	i. United Kingdom	09-12-56	08-19-58
04-28-60*	10-09-50	09-21-56	08-20-58*
04-30-60*	11-17-50	10-24-56	08-21-58*
05-16-60	11-17-50	11-01-56*	08-22-58
05-20-60	11-20-50	11-02-56*	08-23-58*
05-20-60*	11-25-50	11-03-56*	08-24-58*
06-20-60*	12-03-50	11-05-56	08-26-58
06-26-60*	12-07-50	11-07-56*	08-28-58*
08-07-60*	12-13-50*	11-07-56*	08-31-58*
08-17-60*	02-19-51	11-08-56*	09-01-58*
09-10-60	08-16-51*	11-09-56*	09-11-58
09-29-60*	05-29-51	11-11-56	09-23-58
10-06-60	09-10-51	11-13-56*	10-28-58
11-01-60*	10-31-51	11-13-56	11-07-58
12-14-60*	11-12-51	11-14-56	11-19-58
01-03-61*	11-14-51	11-17-56*	11-30-58
01-26-61	11-27-51	12-02-56	12-01-58
02-10-61	05-01-52	12-06-56	12-12-58*
03-12-61	05-14-52	12-06-56*	12-14-58
03-16-61	08-11-52	12-09-56	12-15-58
03-18-61*	08-11-52	12-25-56	01-05-59
06-14-61	12-23-52	01-01-57	02-19-59
06-23-61	01-16-53	01-08-57	03-05-59*
06-28-61	03-28-53	01-10-57*	03-20-59
08-10-61	07-21-53	01-12-57	03-26-59
08-19-61	08-14-53	02-20-57	04-29-59
09-09-61	10-09-53	03-06-57*	07-05-59*
09-13-61	11-18-53	03-28-57	07-14-59
11-01-61*	12-24-53	04-05-57	07-18-59*
12-02-61	02-22-54	05-03-57*	09-12-59*
03-20-62*	02-23-54	05-15-57	09-17-59
04-15-62	03-08-54	06-13-57	10-01-59
07-05-62*	04-03-54	06-18-57	01-16-60
02-13-63	04-21-54	06-19-57	02-01-60
02-27-63	07-23-54	08-14-57*	05-16-60
05-01-63	07-27-54	08-31-57*	05-20-60
05-10-63	07-28-54	09-10-57	06-26-60*
05-28-63	08-15-54*	09-23-57	07-01-60*
07-19-63	10-29-54	09-24-57	07-01-60
01-21-64	10-31-54	10-22-57	07-07-60
01-29-64*	11-30-54	12-21-57	07-30-60
03-04-64	12-04-54	12-30-57	08-16-60*
04-28-64	12-05-54	12-31-57	10-01-60*
05-07-64	12-28-54	02-24-58	10-02-60
05-18-64	01-10-55	03-11-58	12-25-60
12-20-64	01-31-55	04-01-58	02-10-61
07-20-65	02-18-55	04-07-58*	03-12-61
08-03-65	02-25-55	06-20-58	03-16-61
07-24-66	03-06-55*	06-22-58	06-28-61
03-19-67	03-06-55	07-01-58*	07-04-61*
05-27-68*	03-26-55	07-16-58	07-11-61*
09-02-70	05-15-55	07-18-58*	08-10-61
09-01-72	06-08-55	07-20-58*	09-01-61
09-11-73*	10-27-55	07-21-58	09-13-61
02-03-75	10-31-55	07-21-58	12-09-61
	10-31-55*	07-22-58*	10-09-62
f. Ireland	12-09-55	07-23-58*	12-09-62
10-24-59	01-05-56	07-25-58*	12-23-62
	02-21-56	07-25-58*	12-29-62
g. Luxembourg	03-03-56	07-25-58	05-01-63
11-18-72*	04-11-56	07-26-58*	07-19-63
	04-12-56	07-27-58*	07-28-63
h. The Netherlands	04-29-56*	07-29-58	08-03-63
04-23-55	06-18-56	07-30-58*	08-22-63
12-17-57*	06-28-56	07-31-58*	08-30-63
01-01-58*	07-18-56	08-03-58*	12-12-63
12-21-61	08-07-56*	08-04-58*	01-21-64
08-19-62*	08-10-56	08-07-58*	03-27-64
04-12-63	08-11-56	08-08-58*	05-12-64
05-02-63	08-13-56	08-10-58*	05-28-64
12-21-65	08-14-56	08-16-58	05-29-64
	08-17-56	08-16-58	06-11-64
	08-25-56	08-17-58	06-15-64

189

07-05-64
07-06-64
09-09-64*
09-14-64
12-03-64
12-05-64
01-06-65
01-10-65
01-23-65
01-30-65*
02-18-65
05-03-65
07-20-65
11-09-65*
11-14-65
12-18-65*
12-21-65
12-27-65
02-20-66
02-23-66
05-26-66*
07-18-66
07-24-66
08-19-66
10-10-66
05-23-67
05-29-67
06-03-67*
06-06-67
06-11-67
06-15-67
07-05-67*
09-27-67
12-01-67*

R. South America

1. General South America
08-05-58
09-11-58
01-23-59
01-28-59
01-21-60
03-20-60
08-28-60
11-17-60
12-07-60
12-20-60*
12-26-60*
03-13-61
03-13-61
06-30-61*
07-26-61
01-02-62
02-10-62
07-26-62
01-02-63
04-04-63*
04-17-63*
11-10-63
11-23-63
04-17-64*
04-30-64*
01-01-65
04-20-65
05-11-65
09-14-70
11-20-70*
08-25-73
09-07-73
04-09-74
05-05-74

2. Argentina
02-20-72*

3. Brazil
02-21-56
08-13-61*
04-11-64*
04-16-64*
04-30-64*
12-25-64*
04-21-65*
08-17-74*

4. Chile
01-07-71*

5. Guyana
05-26-66*
06-30-72*
03-12-75*

6. Peru
11-04-71*

7. Trinidad and Tobago
06-23-74*
11-05-74*

8. Venezuela
08-05-58*
06-30-74*

S. The Middle East

1. General Middle East
12-09-53
07-26-54
02-21-56
03-03-56*
04-18-56
04-29-56
06-01-56
11-10-56
01-08-57*
01-12-57*
02-20-57*
04-18-57
04-24-57
07-26-57
09-11-57*
09-24-57
10-12-57
10-13-57
10-18-57*
10-28-57
12-26-57
01-01-58
01-04-58
09-11-58
09-15-58
09-23-58
01-01-59
04-05-59
01-21-60
04-30-60
08-28-60
12-07-60
12-20-60*
05-01-61
04-15-62*
11-10-63
11-23-63
12-14-63*

03-03-64
03-17-64*
09-14-64*
03-21-65
04-18-65*
05-16-65*
05-29-67*
06-06-67*
06-11-67*
06-15-67*
06-18-67
06-22-67*
10-20-67
06-25-70
08-01-70
08-06-70
09-14-70
08-25-73
09-07-73
04-09-74
05-05-74
06-20-74

2. Iran
10-31-51*
02-14-52
03-07-59*
03-26-59
08-19-71*
09-17-74

3. Iraq
12-02-56
07-21-57
07-16-58*
07-17-58
07-21-58*
07-22-58*
07-26-58
07-29-58
07-31-58*
08-03-58*
08-04-58*
08-05-58*
08-07-58
08-08-58
08-10-58
08-26-58*
09-30-58*
11-07-58
11-19-58
12-01-58
02-10-59
03-18-59
03-20-59*
03-26-59*
07-14-59*
07-04-61
07-11-61

4. Israel
11-01-56
11-05-56
11-08-56
11-13-56*
11-13-56
12-02-56
12-06-56
12-09-56
12-25-56
01-01-57
08-17-57
09-15-57

10-22-57
03-17-64*
01-10-65
03-21-65*
05-16-65*
10-29-65
01-18-66
05-15-66
05-29-67
06-06-67*
06-11-67*
06-15-67
10-20-67
02-03-68
08-02-70
08-06-70
09-14-70
05-03-71*
06-05-72
10-15-73*
10-26-73*

5. Jordan
12-02-56
05-01-57*
09-10-57*
07-18-58*
07-20-58*
07-21-58
07-22-58
07-23-58*
07-26-58*
07-27-58*
07-31-58
08-04-58
08-07-58*
08-08-58*
08-10-58*
08-17-58*
08-19-58
08-20-58
08-21-58
08-23-58
11-07-58
03-20-59
06-11-67
05-03-71*
06-05-72*

6. Kuwait
07-04-61*
07-11-61*

7. Lebanon
09-10-57*
05-20-58*
05-30-58*
06-20-58
07-01-58*
07-16-58
07-17-58*
07-18-58*
07-20-58*
07-21-58*
07-21-58
07-22-58
07-23-58*
07-26-58*
07-27-58*
08-04-58
08-05-58*
08-07-58*
08-08-58*

08-10-58*
08-17-58*
08-19-58*
08-20-58
08-21-58
08-23-58
08-26-58
11-07-58
03-20-59
11-12-71*

8. Oman
08-14-53*
09-10-57*
07-18-59*
06-15-64

9. Palestine
03-17-64*
03-21-65*
05-15-66*
02-03-68
05-03-71*
06-05-72*
10-15-73*
10-26-73*

10. People's Democratic Republic of Yemen
06-11-64
06-15-64
12-01-67*
02-03-68*
08-02-70*
11-10-74*

11. Saudi Arabia
07-22-58
02-25-65

12. Syria
07-05-56*
06-24-56
12-02-56*
08-17-57*
09-04-57*
09-10-57*
09-15-57*
09-24-57
10-18-57*
10-22-57*
02-23-58
02-24-58*
05-20-58
07-31-58
03-20-59
06-06-67
06-11-67
06-05-72*
10-15-73*
10-26-73*

13. Turkey
12-09-53
02-23-57
09-04-57
09-15-57
10-18-57
10-22-57*
07-31-58
08-08-58
05-04-60*
05-28-60

06-13-60
06-25-60
03-07-59*
03-26-59
08-16-60
08-22-63

14. Yemen Arabic Republic
08-24-56*
01-10-57*
12-31-57*
01-13-58*
06-01-64*
06-11-64*
06-15-64*

T. U.S.S.R.

1. Domestic U.S.S.R.
04-05-50
11-07-50*
02-11-51
02-13-51
04-23-51
04-23-51*
05-17-51
11-09-51
12-07-51
12-17-51
04-05-52
05-01-52
09-24-52
10-01-52
10-07-52*
10-17-52*
10-19-52
01-16-53*
07-12-53*
07-30-53*
08-16-53
12-27-53*
05-27-54
06-22-54
04-22-55
05-05-55
12-30-55
02-14-56
02-19-56*
02-28-56*
03-17-56
06-14-56
10-04-56
02-15-57*
04-08-57
05-26-57*
08-11-57
09-29-57
11-04-57*
11-06-57*
11-27-57
02-02-58
02-14-58*
02-23-58*
03-20-58*
04-02-58*
05-16-58*
10-04-58*
11-07-58*
11-16-58*
11-19-58*
01-01-59
01-04-59*
02-05-59*

02-14-59*
07-03-59*
09-15-59*
10-12-59*
11-07-59*
01-22-60*
05-09-60
11-07-60*
12-10-60
12-12-60
02-14-61
03-18-61
11-07-61
08-16-62*
11-07-62*
08-03-63*
11-07-63*
08-03-64
11-07-64*
11-07-65
11-18-65
04-06-66
04-14-66
06-01-66
06-04-66
06-24-66
07-01-66
02-06-67
05-23-67
05-29-67
08-05-67
08-08-67*
09-18-68

2. U.S.S.R. Leaders

a. Stalin
10-06-49
10-11-49*
10-21-49*
12-18-49*
12-21-49*
02-16-50*
03-24-50
04-22-50*
10-10-50
10-14-50
11-07-50*
12-26-50
02-19-51*
10-07-51*
11-07-51
01-05-52
04-10-52
05-01-52
06-14-52
07-01-52
09-01-52
10-07-52
10-17-52
10-30-52*
11-07-52
11-26-52
12-14-52
12-27-62*
12-29-52
02-18-53
02-21-53
03-06-53*
03-07-53*
03-11-53*
03-13-53
03-14-53

03-28-53*
04-25-53
04-28-53
05-05-53
06-20-53
06-23-53
07-30-53
10-01-53
10-15-53
11-02-53
11-07-53
11-16-53
11-23-53
11-25-53
12-25-53
01-04-54
01-07-54
01-13-54
01-21-54
01-29-54
02-07-54
02-24-54
02-28-54
03-01-54
03-03-54
03-05-54*
03-10-54
03-11-54
03-19-54
03-28-54
04-19-54
04-23-54
05-01-54
06-05-54
07-15-54
08-01-54
08-07-54
11-03-54
12-13-54
01-30-55
02-04-55
03-18-55
03-30-55
11-07-55
03-18-61
02-14-65
04-22-66
07-01-66
05-09-75*
09-03-75

b. Khruschov
10-13-57*
12-30-57
06-22-58*
07-25-58*
07-30-58
08-04-58
08-08-58
09-11-58
09-22-58
11-07-58
11-16-58
02-05-59
02-14-59
03-20-59
06-22-59
09-15-59*
09-29-59*
01-16-60
05-20-60
05-28-60
10-12-60

10-19-60
12-10-60
03-03-61
06-01-61
06-28-61*
01-27-63*
08-03-63
08-22-63
08-30-63
08-06-64
09-24-64
11-07-64
11-29-64
12-03-64
01-01-65
02-25-65
05-14-65
08-11-65
09-02-65
09-18-65
09-30-65
10-01-65
11-18-65
12-27-65
01-01-66
01-13-66
04-22-66
04-28-66
05-15-66
07-01-66
01-01-70

c. Brezhnev and Kosygin
12-10-60
09-26-67
01-01-70

3. General International
   U.S.S.R.
10-02-49
05-15-50
09-23-50
10-07-51
08-11-52
10-05-52
11-18-53*
12-01-53
12-26-53
01-04-54*
07-05-54*
07-22-54*
08-23-54
09-09-54
10-04-54*
11-26-54*
01-05-55
01-10-55*
02-13-55
02-25-55
03-26-55*
04-18-55*
05-02-55*
05-09-55
05-16-55
05-17-55
06-20-55
06-28-55*
07-18-55
08-07-55*
08-08-55*
09-21-55
09-22-55*
10-03-55

10-05-55*
10-14-55*
10-27-55*
10-31-55*
11-03-55
11-07-55*
11-14-55*
11-19-55
11-21-55*
02-01-56*
03-29-56*
04-12-56
04-24-56
05-30-56*
06-17-56
07-11-56*
08-07-56
08-13-56
09-13-56*
09-16-56
10-21-56*
11-03-56*
11-07-56*
11-12-56
11-13-56
11-19-56*
01-24-57
02-15-57*
04-05-57
05-15-57*
05-18-57
05-26-57*
06-06-57*
08-18-57
09-14-57
09-23-57*
09-24-57*
10-05-57
10-07-57*
10-13-57*
10-16-57*
11-04-57*
11-06-57*
11-09-57*
11-15-57
12-14-57*
12-21-57
12-30-57*
01-01-58
01-11-58*
01-19-58*
02-14-58*
03-11-58*
04-01-58*
04-02-58
04-07-58*
05-16-58*
05-17-58
05-26-58
05-28-58
06-04-58
06-08-58
06-22-58*
07-17-58
07-22-58
07-25-58
07-29-58*
08-04-58
08-08-58*
08-16-58
09-01-58*
10-04-58*
11-07-58

11-19-58*
01-28-59
04-02-59
06-03-59*
06-22-59*
07-24-59*
08-05-59*
08-05-59
08-23-59
09-21-59*
10-07-59*
10-22-59
11-07-59
12-07-59*
01-09-60
01-16-60*
01-21-60
04-04-60
04-08-60
05-09-60*
05-09-60*
05-12-60
05-14-60
05-15-60*
05-16-60*
05-20-60*
06-01-60
06-02-60
06-07-60*
06-10-60
06-29-60
07-07-60*
07-16-60
09-02-60
09-29-60
10-01-60
10-12-60
10-19-60
11-21-60*
12-12-60
12-20-60
01-01-61*
01-22-61
02-16-61
04-13-61*
05-01-61
06-01-61*
07-12-61
09-01-61*
09-22-61
11-07-61
04-03-62
04-28-62
06-21-62
08-16-62*
09-17-62
07-19-63
07-26-63*
08-02-63*
08-03-63*
10-19-63*
12-18-63
05-05-64
02-25-65
05-20-65
10-23-65
11-04-65
11-18-65*
12-27-65*
01-18-66*
01-19-66
01-30-66*
02-20-66

03-29-66
04-28-66
05-01-66
06-27-66
06-29-66
07-10-66
07-11-66
07-18-66
07-24-66
09-24-66
10-10-66
10-19-66
11-10-66
11-29-66
12-15-66
12-20-66
04-27-67
04-30-67
05-14-67*
05-23-67
06-22-67*
07-07-67
08-29-67
09-10-67
09-26-67
09-27-67*
09-27-67
10-29-67
01-01-68
05-01-68
11-29-68
04-17-69
06-09-69
08-01-69
08-25-69
11-23-69
11-29-69
01-01-70
11-29-70
01-01-71
05-01-71
05-20-71
11-29-71
12-27-71
01-01-72
01-31-72*
02-03-72
05-25-72
06-05-72*
08-28-72*
10-01-72*
11-28-72*
05-25-73
09-13-73
10-15-73
10-26-73*
11-29-73
01-01-74
02-25-74
04-09-74*
05-05-74*
05-06-74
09-14-74
10-18-74
11-10-74
11-29-74*
12-16-74
01-07-75
01-22-75
04-25-75
05-01-75
05-09-75*
05-20-75

191

4. U.S.S.R. and Asia

a. U.S.S.R. and Japan
08-03-75*
10-06-75
10-29-75
11-29-75

a. U.S.S.R. and Japan
02-06-50*
02-16-50
11-27-50*
08-29-51
09-10-51
12-30-54*
12-02-55*
12-14-56*
09-03-75

b. U.S.S.R. and Korea
07-24-50*
08-07-50
08-15-50
09-01-50
09-19-50
10-09-50*
12-06-50
05-26-51
06-15-51*
06-25-51
07-03-51
08-10-51*
10-20-51*
11-12-51
01-07-52*
02-20-52*
06-22-52*
06-29-52
11-06-52*
11-29-52*
04-05-53
04-12-53
04-29-53
04-31-53*
06-23-53
06-25-53
07-28-53
08-12-53
08-25-53
09-14-53
09-27-53*
10-09-53
10-31-53
02-22-54
02-23-54
03-08-54*
04-03-54
04-21-54
05-12-54
06-18-54
10-25-54
01-29-55
11-19-55*
01-02-56
04-05-57
02-06-58
02-22-58*
05-05-58
07-17-59
12-11-60

c. U.S.S.R. and P.R.C.

1. U.S.S.R. and P.R.C.:
   Culture
10-14-49
02-16-50*
03-18-50*
04-05-50
10-15-51*
05-04-52
11-15-52*
01-22-53
08-27-53
10-15-53
10-23-53
02-14-54
04-24-54
05-15-54
06-30-54
10-02-54*
10-13-54
12-26-54
04-28-55*
06-17-56*
08-31-56*
10-24-57
11-03-57*
04-24-58
10-04-58
02-14-60
02-14-65*

2. U.S.S.R. and P.R.C.:
   Economics
02-16-50*
03-18-50*
04-05-50*
04-26-50*
04-05-52
09-01-52
09-16-52
11-05-52
11-07-52
11-18-52
12-31-52
01-17-53
01-29-53
01-31-53
02-10-53
03-28-53*
04-23-53
04-25-53
04-28-53
06-19-53
09-16-53*
10-22-53
10-30-53
11-07-53
11-16-53
12-16-53
12-25-53
01-01-54
01-21-54
02-14-54*
03-03-54
03-19-54
05-08-54
06-05-54
08-18-54
10-01-54
10-02-54*
10-13-54*
10-17-54*

10-23-54*
10-27-54*
11-07-54*
11-26-54
12-26-54*
01-01-55
02-21-55
04-16-55
04-27-55
06-23-55
07-30-55
11-07-55*
01-04-56
02-14-56
04-09-56*
06-17-56*
12-04-56
01-20-57
02-14-57
04-04-57
04-09-57
04-15-57
06-07-57
09-29-57
10-12-57
10-15-57
10-31-57*
11-03-57*
02-14-58*
04-24-58*
06-21-58
09-14-58*
02-14-59*
09-27-59*
10-03-59
11-07-59
01-01-60
02-14-60
05-03-60*
12-10-60
02-14-61*
05-29-64

3. U.S.S.R. and P.R.C.:
   Politics
10-06-49*
10-08-49*
10-11-49*
10-21-49*
11-27-49*
12-18-49*
12-21-49*
02-16-50*
03-18-50*
04-05-50*
04-22-50*
07-24-50
09-01-50
09-19-50
09-23-50
11-07-50*
11-12-50
11-17-50
12-03-50*
12-17-50
12-21-50
12-27-50
02-14-51*
02-23-51*
04-22-51
07-20-51
09-18-51*
10-15-51*

11-07-51*
01-23-52
02-04-52*
02-14-52*
05-07-52
09-01-52*
09-03-52
09-16-52*
11-07-52*
12-31-52
01-23-53
02-14-53*
02-23-53*
03-06-53*
05-01-53
11-07-53
02-14-54*
03-22-54
03-30-54
07-24-54
08-18-54
10-13-54*
11-07-54
12-29-54*
01-19-55*
02-14-55
02-23-55*
03-12-55
11-07-55*
06-21-56*
01-20-57*
02-02-57
02-14-57*
03-28-57
04-15-57*
04-16-57*
05-06-57*
09-29-57*
10-31-57*
11-03-57*
11-06-57
12-13-57
02-12-58
02-23-58
04-24-58
08-04-58*
09-28-58*
01-04-59
01-05-59
01-19-59
04-15-59
04-21-59
04-29-59
10-01-59
10-03-59*
10-04-59
10-24-59
01-24-60*
02-14-60*
03-31-60
11-07-60
11-21-60*
12-07-60
12-10-60*
01-22-61*
02-14-61*
07-01-61
10-01-61
10-10-61
11-07-61
11-08-61
12-01-61
12-22-61

02-14-62*
09-17-62*
10-01-62
12-12-62*
12-31-62
01-27-63*
02-13-63
02-27-63*
07-10-63*
07-13-63*
08-03-63*
08-22-63
11-07-63*
12-04-63
12-31-63
01-11-64*
09-24-64*
09-24-64
02-14-65*
11-07-65
05-15-66*
06-27-66*
07-23-66
10-01-66
11-10-66
12-02-66
01-27-67*
02-01-67*
02-06-67*
07-10-67
09-09-67
11-29-67
09-20-68
10-01-68
11-29-68
03-04-69*
10-01-69
05-01-70
08-01-70
10-01-70
01-01-71
09-18-71
11-08-71*
12-27-71
01-01-73
09-29-73
05-09-75
10-01-75*

4. *U.S.S.R. and P.R.C.: Soviet Advisors*
02-16-50*
04-26-50*
12-31-51
01-25-53
05-15-53
09-16-53
09-29-53
10-14-53
10-17-53
11-22-53
12-27-53
01-25-54
02-06-54
02-14-54
10-23-54*
10-27-54*
12-26-54*
02-23-55
06-12-55
12-02-55
01-04-56
02-14-56

04-30-56
07-31-56
04-14-57
10-15-57
02-14-61
12-04-63

d. U.S.S.R. and Taiwan
09-01-50
02-01-55
02-05-55
02-12-55
02-18-55*
03-07-55

e. U.S.S.R. and South Asia
06-25-55*
06-28-55
11-20-55*
12-21-55*
01-26-56
09-17-56
08-22-63*
09-18-65*

f. U.S.S.R. and Southeast Asia
11-06-55*
11-20-55
12-09-55*
05-20-59
09-17-59
03-06-60*
12-25-60*
05-18-61
05-24-61
06-14-61
07-24-62
07-21-67
02-03-70
04-18-75
11-11-75

5. U.S.S.R. and Europe

a. U.S.S.R. and General Europe
05-09-55
05-12-55
07-18-56
07-22-59
06-28-61
02-27-63
06-25-66
09-20-68*
09-29-68

b. U.S.S.R. and Albania
04-20-57*
02-22-61
01-27-63

c. U.S.S.R. and Austria
04-18-55*
05-16-55

d. U.S.S.R. and Belgium
04-19-75*

e. U.S.S.R. and Bulgaria
02-23-57*

f. U.S.S.R. and Czechoslovakia
02-01-57*

g. U.S.S.R. and Federal Republic of Germany and German Democratic Republic
10-13-49*
10-26-49
08-28-53*
07-27-54*
08-10-54*
09-15-54
10-07-54
10-10-54
10-29-54
11-16-54*
11-30-54
01-20-55*
04-09-55
06-11-55*
09-18-55*
07-23-55*
12-08-55
07-20-56*
08-16-57*
11-30-58
12-14-58
01-13-59*
03-05-59
03-14-59
03-20-59*
08-10-61*

h. U.S.S.R. and France
05-21-56*

i. U.S.S.R. and Greece
11-01-49

j. U.S.S.R. and Hungary
11-05-56*
11-14-56
12-06-56*
01-09-57
01-19-57*
03-30-57*
04-04-57*
09-16-57*
04-04-60*

k. U.S.S.R. and Poland
11-21-56*
01-18-57*

l. U.S.S.R. and Rumania
12-06-56*

m. U.S.S.R. and United Kingdom
04-29-56*
05-03-57*

n. U.S.S.R. and Yugoslavia
08-27-49
06-05-55*
08-29-55
11-29-55
06-22-56*
01-27-63

6. U.S.S.R. and Latin America and the Caribbean
09-01-60
11-05-62*
11-18-62
11-20-70

7. U.S.S.R. and the Middle East and North Africa
10-31-51
11-07-55
03-03-56
06-17-56
08-11-56*
09-21-56
10-20-56*
11-07-56
11-09-56*
11-13-56
11-14-56
11-17-56
05-01-57
09-10-57
10-18-57
10-22-57
05-17-58*
07-20-58
08-07-58*
08-10-58
10-28-58
05-15-66
05-29-67
06-06-67
06-11-67
06-15-67

8. U.S.S.R. and Sub-Saharan Africa
12-09-60
01-15-61
02-18-61
03-03-61
04-15-66
11-28-67
11-14-75*
12-21-75*

9. U.S.S.R. and U.S.
09-23-50
09-27-50
12-27-52
03-16-53
08-14-53*
12-09-53
10-21-54
09-11-58*
09-10-59*
09-15-59*
09-29-59*
05-13-60*
05-28-60
01-21-64
09-24-64
05-14-65
05-18-65
06-26-65*
09-02-65
11-18-65*
01-30-66*
06-25-66
07-05-66
09-21-67

193

U. **International Communist Parties**

1. Communist Bloc
   - 01-19-50*
   - 12-13-51
   - 04-05-52
   - 05-01-52
   - 05-04-52
   - 02-21-53
   - 12-19-53*
   - 11-29-54
   - 01-01-55
   - 01-19-55
   - 02-12-55
   - 05-12-55
   - 12-08-55
   - 03-15-56
   - 03-29-56
   - 04-18-56
   - 04-21-56
   - 01-09-57*
   - 01-20-57
   - 02-01-57
   - 02-02-57*
   - 03-09-57
   - 04-07-57
   - 04-15-57
   - 04-20-57
   - 09-14-57
   - 11-09-57
   - 11-25-57
   - 01-01-58*
   - 04-09-58
   - 05-01-58
   - 05-26-58*
   - 05-28-58*
   - 06-04-58
   - 07-07-58*
   - 07-29-58*
   - 08-03-58
   - 09-22-58
   - 09-28-58
   - 10-01-58*
   - 11-19-58
   - 01-01-59*
   - 01-28-59*
   - 03-21-59
   - 11-07-59
   - 01-01-60
   - 01-21-60*
   - 02-06-60
   - 05-01-60
   - 10-19-60
   - 11-07-60
   - 11-17-60
   - 11-21-60
   - 12-07-60*
   - 12-12-60*
   - 12-25-60
   - 05-01-61
   - 07-16-61
   - 11-08-61
   - 12-01-61*
   - 01-27-63*
   - 02-27-63*
   - 05-01-63
   - 06-24-63
   - 09-09-63
   - 01-11-64
   - 11-07-64
   - 11-10-66*

2. Communist Parties Out of Power

   a. General Communist Parties Out of Power
      - 11-25-57
      - 11-19-58
      - 12-01-61*

   b. French Communist Party
      - 09-02-53
      - 12-19-53
      - 01-07-56*
      - 11-14-56
      - 05-23-58*
      - 05-30-58
      - 08-16-58*
      - 12-03-58*
      - 03-23-59*
      - 03-20-62
      - 02-27-63*

   c. Indian Communist Party
      - 12-07-61
      - 03-09-63*
      - 07-05-67*

   d. Italian Communist Party
      - 11-04-56
      - 05-29-58*
      - 12-31-62*

   e. Japanese Communist Party
      - 01-17-50*
      - 06-09-50*
      - 09-03-50*
      - 07-15-52*
      - 04-23-57
      - 04-03-58
      - 05-11-58
      - 03-06-59*
      - 04-16-59*
      - 04-28-59*
      - 10-22-59*
      - 12-03-59*
      - 01-15-60
      - 05-16-60
      - 05-29-60
      - 06-03-60
      - 06-05-60
      - 06-20-60
      - 06-24-60
      - 08-11-60
      - 10-20-60
      - 06-09-61
      - 06-16-61*
      - 06-23-61*
      - 08-09-62
      - 12-03-64*
      - 02-23-65
      - 09-18-68*

   f. Mongolian Communist Party
      - 10-17-49

   g. United States Communist Party
      - 10-24-49
      - 08-30-54*
      - 09-05-61*
      - 01-15-62*
      - 03-08-63*
      - 08-08-67

   h. Vietnamese Communist Party
      - 03-03-56